IRANIAN-SAUDI RIVALRY SINCE 1979

IRANIAN-SAUDI RIVALRY SINCE 1979

In the Words of Kings and Clerics

Talal Mohammad

I.B. TAURIS

LONDON • NEW YORK • OXFORD • NEW DELHI • SYDNEY

I.B. TAURIS
Bloomsbury Publishing Plc
50 Bedford Square, London, WC1B 3DP, UK
1385 Broadway, New York, NY 10018, USA
29 Earlsfort Terrace, Dublin 2, Ireland

BLOOMSBURY, I.B. TAURIS and the I.B. Tauris logo are trademarks
of Bloomsbury Publishing Plc

First published in Great Britain 2023
This paperback edition published 2024

Series design by Adriana Brioso
Cover images © [left] Khamenei.ir (CC-BY-4.0); [right] Bandar Algaloud/Saudi
Kingdom Council/Anadolu Agency/Getty Images

A catalogue record for this book is available from the British Library.

A catalog record for this book is available from the Library of Congress.

ISBN: HB: 978-0-7556-3472-9
        PB: 978-0-7556-3476-7
        ePDF: 978-0-7556-3473-6
        eBook: 978-0-7556-3474-3

Typeset by RefineCatch Limited, Bungay, Suffolk

To find out more about our authors and books visit www.bloomsbury.com
and sign up for our newsletters.

'Remember that the citizens of the state are of two categories. They are either your brethren in religion or your brethren in kind'

— *Imam Ali ibn Abi Taleb*

To my mother, thank you for everything.

CONTENTS

PREFACE

The journey to writing this book began ten years ago as I left a meeting at St Antony's College at the University of Oxford with many questions on my mind, contemplating the direction my doctoral project was taking after defending my initial PhD proposal in September 2013. What began as an attempt to study Shi'i–Wahhabi strife and regional Iranian–Saudi confrontation ended with a project that focused on Iranian–Saudi Othering. Sitting in a crowded train after defending my initial proposal, I pondered upon the queries raised by the assessors and their suggestions to re-think issues around the nature and origin of Iranian–Saudi rivalry. As I travelled between Oxford and Cambridge later that afternoon, thoughts on the nature of enmity, rivalry, and the relations between Iran and Saudi Arabia rushed through my mind. Aware that many studies in the past few years have focused on the international relations, security, and political dimensions of Iranian–Saudi relations, a very few had utilized discourse, language, politics, and power simultaneously to define their relations, enmity, and sectarian strife outside the traditional lenses of security and foreign relations. While researching sectarian rivalry, Shi'i–Sunni strife, and Arab–Persian rivalry, an interest developed to understand if these were the natural by-product of rivalry or a tool used in international relations. Therefore, answering these questions required a strong understanding and knowledge of the language, history, culture, and the politics of the governmental, tribal, and religious levels.

I had initially trained as a geneticist at the universities of Sheffield and Cambridge. I completed a PhD on the genetic anthropology and genealogy of Bedouin tribes and the Sayyids, descendants of the Prophet Mohammad. This not only gave me an understanding of the science of genetics but also of the anthropological and cultural components that make up those distinct groups. This led me to conduct fieldwork and research the interaction between the Bedouin tribes and Sayyids – many of whom were clerics, predominantly from Iran and Iraq at a time when Saddam had just fallen and the region had witnessed a watershed shift. This provided me with the groundwork and understanding to undertake the research project that later led to this book.

In the year 2019, I joined St Anthony's College at the University of Oxford as an academic visitor to carry out research and revise my DPhil dissertation into a book. I was very grateful that Professor Eugene Rogan had suggested and advised me to strengthen the novel concept that I had worked on in examining Iranian–Saudi relations and to apply it to the period from the Arab Spring (2010–11) to the present moment (at that time). Furthermore, I was also very grateful to the book proposal reviewers at Bloomsbury's I.B. Tauris imprint for their suggestions that contributed to the book taking its current form.

However, this book would have never seen the light of day had it not been for the supervision and guidance of my supervisors, Professor Edmund Herzig and the late Professor Rosemary Hollis. Their guidance was incredibly helpful, particularly at the DPhil stage when they invested a lot of their invaluable time and effort in ensuring I overcome many obstacles. Indeed, I encountered many challenges as I drafted chapters of my dissertation, and researched and analysed thousands of editorials, sermons, and political speeches spanning a four-decade period across three languages and multiple states.

As I wrote this book I thought about my audience and who would gain what from my modest addition to the vast pool of literature on Iranian–Saudi relations. My aim is for every person who is interested in the affairs of the Middle East in general, and Saudi–Iranian relations in particular, to be able to understand these relations without the complexity and limitations of language or jargon. Although this book falls under the scholarly non-fiction, educational genre, I have attempted to write it with a wide audience in mind. This audience ranges from those with a deep interest in current affairs through to students who aim to specialize in this field to think tanks and experts as well as private and governmental decision-makers and stakeholders in the international community. In keeping my audience in mind, I began my book with an introduction to the theme and questions I aim to raise in the monograph and a brief discussion situating my book amid the many exciting and fascinating studies that have been published by experts and colleagues in the field. For the same reason, in hindsight I have done my utmost to consider the sensitivity of some of the topics for particular audiences, including geographical names such as Persian or Arabian Gulf for example, or Israel and Zionist/Zionism labels. Another highly sensitive issue is the decision to place which country's name before the other. I resolved this issue by opting for alphabetical order, i.e. Iranian–Saudi, in the title. However, throughout the text, I have changed the order at times (Saudi–Iranian and Iranian–Saudi) and also used the capitals of both states (Riyadh and Tehran) to refer to their relationship. Ultimately, this book aims to take the reader on a journey of over four decades of 'Iranian–Saudi Rivalry Since 1979, in the Words of Kings and Clerics'.

ACKNOWLEDGEMENTS

I would like to thank all those that gave me direction and encouragement since the project began as a doctoral dissertation a decade ago. I am thankful to my supervisor at Oxford University, Prof. Edmund Herzig, for his invaluable advice, guidance, and patience since the early days of this project. I had just shifted career paths and I was still feeling my way into social sciences. It is very saddening that I cannot share the joy and personally thank my late supervisor, Prof. Rosemary Hollis. Rosie had mentored me from my early days as a postgraduate student at City (University of London) in 2010 up to her passing in June 2020. She was not just a driving force and source of support and encouragement, but also an invaluable source of knowledge and experience. She is truly missed!

I am grateful to Prof. Eugene Rogan at the Middle East Centre (MEC) at St Antony's, for his continuous support, particularly during the pandemic. Prof. Rogan's suggestions were the spark that gave the book its current form. I would also like to show my appreciation to Prof. Michael Willis the current director of the MEC for hosting me for another academic year. My time at St Antony's, given the restrictions and limitations of the COVID-19 period, was invaluable.

This book would not have seen the light had it not been for the support, encouragement, and motivation of my family and friends. I would like to thank Nishant for reading through the chapters of the manuscript as I was revising the earlier parts of my dissertation. I am also thankful for his assistance with suggestions and editing the latter chapters that make up the second half of the book. I am also thankful to my copy-editor, Andrew Hodges, for reading through my work as well as giving his invaluable suggestions and support. A heartfelt gratitude goes out to my writing coach, Nicole Janz. Thank you for making the writing process a lot more manageable. The team at Bloomsbury's I.B. Tauris deserve a lot of thanks, particularly Sophie Rudland for his patience and support. I am lucky to have a very supportive family. My siblings have been a source of continuous support. A special mention goes to my uncle, Ebrahim Roushanaei, who has always supported me and lifted my spirits when I was down. This project would not have seen the light without help in the field. I am eternally thankful to Omid and Erfan for their efforts.

Three people stand out in my journey. Hussain Al-Ghareeb for his ongoing support, aid and encouragement. Sayyid Hassan Bahr Al-Uloom for continuously cheering on and boosting morale, especially when it got really tough and bleak. There were times where I doubted taking on such an endeavour, and there are those that are put on one's path to listen, guide, aid, and keep matters in perspective. Thank you Sayyid Nizar Zalzaleh for being there every day throughout this journey. To an old friend, Mohammad Mustafa, thank you for helping pave the way for the start of this journey.

I gratefully acknowledge the funding received towards my doctorate from the Al-Bahar family. Thanks to Talal Al-Bahar and the late Jassim Al-Bahar, I was able to continue my research in two of the world's most prestigious academic institutions and greatest sources of knowledge.

And finally to my mother, who has been by my side in every step of my academic career. I thank you for supporting, encouraging, and living with me through every single minute of it. Without you, I would not have had the courage to embark on my journey of knowledge. I owe it all to you! Thank you for being a great role model!

NOTE ON TRANSLATION AND TRANSLITERATION

Where possible, I have used the translation and transliteration style of the *International Journal of Middle Eastern Studies (IJMES).*[2] Definitions for Arabic and Persian terms have been provided with reference to the *Oxford Dictionary of Islam (Esposito, 2003)* and *Dictionary of Islam (Hughes and Hughes, 1995)*. Any translated material within the text was translated by the author unless otherwise noted.

ABBREVIATIONS

AWACS	Airborne Warning and Control System
CDLR	Committee for the Defense of Legitimate Rights
EU	European Union
GCC	Gulf Cooperation Council
FPA	Foreign Policy Analysis
IRGC	Iranian Revolutionary Guard Corps
IRP	Islamic Republic Party
MEK/MKO	Mojahedin-e-Khalq Organization
OIC	Organisation of Islamic Cooperation
OPEC	Organization of the Petroleum Exporting Countries
PLO	Palestinian Liberation Organisation
SANG	Saudi Arabian National Guard
UIA	United Iraqi Alliance
UK	United Kingdom
UN	United Nations
US	United States
USSR	Union of Soviet Socialist Republics
WMD	Weapons of Mass Destruction

Chapter 1

INTRODUCTION: RIVALRY, OTHERING, AND THE NECESSARY ENEMY

Saudi Arabia and Iran have been rivals seeking regional dominance for decades. This rivalry has led the region into chaos, manifesting itself in conflicts across the Middle East. More recently, the animosity between these two oil-rich states has sharpened. The relatively recent wars in Syria and Yemen along with competition in Lebanon and Iraq since the fall of Saddam are prime examples. The relationship between the two states was not always marred with enmity. Iranian–Saudi relations under the Shah were cordial. This was cemented through the United States' Twin Pillars policy at the height of the Cold War. This regional security policy promoted Tehran and Riyadh as local guardians of US regional interests, particularly in the Persian Gulf[1]. Both countries also shared good diplomatic ties, as demonstrated by the high-level visits between Riyadh and Tehran's monarchies. The Shah of Iran's visit to Riyadh in January 1978 would be his last. Months later, Iran would undergo a revolution, one that would take many by surprise.

To chants of 'Long Live Khomeini' ('*Durūd bar Khomeini*'), millions of Iranians flooded the streets of Tehran on 1 February 1979 to mark the return of Ayatollah Khomeini, their messiah, or the 'Imam' as many have come to know him. That afternoon sealed the fate of two and a half millennia of monarchical rule in Iran and marked a turning point in the history of the twentieth century. This revolution resulted in the Islamic Republic of Iran becoming a dominant concern in world politics for more than four decades, particularly in the Middle East, and in the Arab and Islamic worlds. The Khomeini-led revolution did not only topple the

---

1. I recognize that there is an ongoing dispute between Iran and Arab states on the use of the term Persian Gulf and Arabian Gulf. In this book I do not seek to define the term nor argue its origins. However, this book employs the definition set by the United Nations Working Paper No. 61 after the 2006 meeting of the United Nations Group of Experts on Geographical Names that the term 'Persian Gulf' is the standard geographical designation in its official documents. I would like to emphasize that the designations employed and the presentation of the material in this book do not imply the expression of any opinion whatsoever on my part concerning the legal status of any country, territory, city or area or of its authorities, or concerning the delimitation of its frontiers or boundaries.

monarchical system in Iran, it also upended the regional order and set the stage for decades of confrontation, tension, and rivalry with Saudi Arabia.

The impact of the Islamic Revolution unnerved the United States and its allies. Ayatollah Khomeini's 'Neither East nor West' policy along with the 'export of the revolution' rattled the cages of both the Western and regional states alike. Iran's renouncing of cooperation with the United States signalled an end to America's Twin Pillars policy. Regionally, for the Arab countries, predominantly Saudi Arabia and the Arab states of the Persian Gulf, exporting the revolution was seen as a threat to both their monarchical rule and as an act that encouraged the Shi'i minorities to demand their rights. It was this sense of threat that sowed the seeds of rivalry between the Kingdom of Saudi Arabia and the Islamic Republic of Iran; the implications of this rivalry would be witnessed across global, regional, and domestic political transformations spanning more than four decades.

This book focuses on Othering in five periods encompassing key watershed episodes that occurred during successive Iranian presidencies: Bani-Sadr and Khamenei: From the Revolution up to the death of Ayatollah Khomeini; Rafsanjani: 'Active Neutrality' and the road to détente 1989–1997; Khatami: initiation of the 'Dialogue of Civilizations' and convening of the Organization of the Islamic Conference Summit meeting in Iran 1997–1999; Ahmadinejad (2005–2013): the bombing of the al-Askari Shrine in Samarra, Iraq, and the consequent sectarian war, the Israeli wars with Hezbollah and Hamas in 2006 and 2009 respectively, and the formative period of the Arab Spring; Rouhani (2013–2021): the Iran nuclear deal, the wars in Syria, the Saudi–Houthi war in Yemen and the subsequent attacks on Aramco, Trump's 'Maximum Pressure', and the assassination of Qassem Soleimani.

This book deals with a series of political transformations and their relationship with discursive changes that Iran and Saudi Arabia have undergone in terms of defining their 'Self' and 'Other'. More specifically, the book examines Iran's transformation from a US and Western ally to a revolutionary vanguard state. It considers how this new revolutionary state reshaped the local and regional agenda of its reactionary Other, Saudi Arabia. In so doing, it explores Self and Other representations in the context of Saudi–Iranian confrontation and Shi'i–Wahhabi strife. To understand how these images have been constructed, we need to grasp the respective states' elites' conception of themselves and their state. This conception emerged over time, and so the book takes a diachronic approach, covering Iranian–Saudi relations from 1979 to 2020. The analysis focuses on watershed episodes, which took place during six Iranian presidential terms, the tenure of two Supreme Leaders, and the reign of four Saudi kings.

Since the 1979 Islamic Revolution in Iran, the relationship between Iran and Saudi Arabia has undergone a number of shifts, ranging from: intense hostility during the Iran-Iraq War when Saudi Arabia supported Saddam Hussein; a reduction in tension during President Rafsanjani's reign, which was a period of economic rebuilding; rapprochement as a result of President Khatami's 'Dialogue of Civilizations'; the resumption of intense rivalry and tensions during the Ahmadinejad period, which witnessed a return to revolutionary rhetoric in Iran, and coincided with heightened Sunni–Shi'i tensions in post-Saddam Iraq; and attempts of détente and rapprochement under the Rouhani presidency, which coincided with the turbulent events of the Arab Spring throughout the region; the rise of Mohammad bin Salman; and the election of Donald Trump to the White House.

The book sets out to answer questions that emanate from the two states' competing claims to lie at the heart of the Islamic world and the issue of how they are both vying for regional leadership. Both states make assertions rooted in their historical and religious imagery. For instance, Saudi Arabia's claim is rooted in Arab superiority and Islamic purity. It views itself as the cradle of Islam, the place of revelation of the Holy Quran to the Prophet Mohammad, and as home to the two most holy shrines of Islam – Mecca, and Medina. In contrast, Iran's claim is based on a heritage of cultural prestige and science highlighted by a Persian civilization that spans thousands of years. Furthermore, since the revolution in 1979, Iran has also made claims based on leadership of the Islamic world and on a fight for the plight of the 'oppressed'. Yet how can the phenomenon of Othering be understood in the Iranian–Saudi discourse, and how does it relate to political rivalry and religious conflict? Are the discourses primarily political or religious in character? How closely interrelated or independent of one another are the political, religious, and media discourses? How do the discourses of Othering function in practice? Crucially, how did these discourses of Othering change during the aforementioned periods and watershed episodes? And finally, what does this tell us about the responsiveness of Iranian–Saudi discourses to changes in bilateral relations?

This brings us to the central contentions I make in this book. First, it is the first study to analyse primary Saudi and Iranian discourse simultaneously in the original language and within this paradigm. This book is also the first work to examine Iranian and Saudi political, religious, and media discourse mutually, across a four-decade period. As I will elaborate more in the next section, many studies have been published on Iranian–Saudi relations. However, none at the time of writing have studied Iranian–Saudi rivalry through mutual Othering, while also covering this extensive time frame. Although previous studies such as Ram (1994) have offered an in-depth analysis of Iranian religious discourse, exemplified by the Friday sermons, the study does not focus on Saudi Arabia. Also, previous discourse analysis studies of Iranian and Saudi editorials, such as those of Mirzaee and Gharibeh (2015), or Khosravinik (2015), which discuss the discourses of the (national) Self and Other, do not analyse Iranian or Saudi newspapers extensively, or they focus on Saudi–Iranian representations of the Other across a broad chronological time frame or through the analysis of multiple events (Khosravinik 2015; Mirzaee and Gharibeh 2015). This study will therefore apply for the first time the concept of Othering and the representation of the Other to both halves of the Iranian–Saudi relationship since the 1979 revolution. Second, this book will relate the Iranian and Saudi discourses of Othering to the changing pattern of events and relations, to questions of power, and to acts carried out by the states towards one another across the various historical episodes. Finally, it will analyse how Iran and Saudi Arabia frame each other across three discourse genres, in media editorials, sermons, and decision-makers' speeches.

The book employs a diachronic methodology wherein each chapter focuses on a chronology. The chapters identify important epochs and events in the timeline of Iranian–Saudi relations, thus allowing for an understanding of how the discourses and discursive representations of Self and Other shifted over time. The book begins with a chapter on the historical and political background to the study. The theoretical framework of Othering through the works of Foucault, Said, and Herrmann and Fischerkeller's concept of the 'necessary enemy', are also briefly discussed.

The book is divided into five parts. Part I discusses Iranian–Saudi relations in its post-revolutionary formative stages. Its chapters discuss the revolution, the Iran–Iraq War, and the formation of Iranian and Saudi discourses of Self and Other. The period under examination will illuminate certain episodes from the early post-revolutionary period up to the death of Ayatollah Khomeini in 1989. Chapters 2 and 3 investigate the formation of the Iranian and Saudi Self and their Other, and mutual Othering during the foundational period of the Islamic Revolution of Iran, including the Bani-Sadr and Khamenei presidencies. This part analyses Iranian and Saudi identities during the Islamic Revolution, the US hostage crisis, the siege of Mecca, and the Qatif protests of 1979. The period also covers the death of Khaled al-Saud and the succession of Fahd as head of the Al Saud dynasty, including the rise of a new crown prince, Abdullah Al Saud. Furthermore, this part also discusses the hajj and its centrality to Iranian–Saudi relations, rivalry, and the definition of the Self and Other.

Part II examines the post-Khomeini era of Iranian–Saudi relations. Chapters 4 and 5 look at Iran under the leadership of its second Supreme Leader, Ayatollah Khamenei, and the emergence of a post-war political system. These chapters also discuss a shift in Iran's foreign policy to 'active neutrality', as well as the initial seeds of Saudi–Iranian détente during the Iraqi invasion of Kuwait in 1990 and its liberation in 1991. Chapter 6 deals with Khatami's 'Dialogue of Civilizations' and how Iranian–Saudi détente during the Rafsanjani administration gained momentum and paved the way for rapprochement. This chapter also focuses on the Iranian–Saudi shift from détente to rapprochement, the Tehran Organization of the Islamic Conference (OIC) Summit, and the road leading to a security pact between the two states. This part also sheds light on the rise of the Taliban, the visits to Saudi Arabia by Rafsanjani and Khatami in 1998 and 1999 respectively, GCC security, and OPEC.

Part III reviews Iranian–Saudi relations after the fall of Saddam in 2003, with individual chapters reviewing relations between the two states as rapprochement gradually ended with the advent of the Ahmadinejad presidency. Chapter 7 examines the Iranian Self and its Other through the election of Ahmadinejad and the return to Iran's revolutionary rhetoric of the 1980s. This chapter also sheds light on the impact of Iran's nuclear programme on the representation of the Iranian Self and its Other. Saudi representations of the Self and Other are also discussed by investigating the impact of terrorism and Al-Qaeda on the construction of the image of the Saudi Self and its Other. Chapter 8 and 9 examine how the shrine bombings in Iraq, the Hezbollah–Israel 34-Day War, and the

Gaza War of 2009 respectively, shaped Iranian–Saudi rivalry and respective representations.

Part IV reviews Iranian–Saudi rivalry and Othering since the events of the Arab Spring in 2011 and the battle for regional hegemony. Chapter 10 covers the 2009 elections in Iran and the later Green Movement protests, including their impact on Iran's image. The chapter also examines the Saudi Shi'i protests in Medina in the same year, while also investigating the events of the Arab Spring in Tunisia, Egypt, and Bahrain, and how they shaped Iranian–Saudi relations and mutual representations. Chapter 11 is dedicated to the war in Syria and how the rivalry intensified and shaped the discourse of enmity and rivalry between the two states. Chapter 12 focuses on Iran becoming a nuclear state under Rouhani and its impact on relations with Riyadh. The chapter also illuminates Iranian attempts to rekindle the détente of the 1990s. The rise of ISIS and its impact on regional rivalry, sectarianism, and domestic security is studied in terms of how it relates to Iranian–Saudi imagery and framing.

Part V includes Chapters 13 to 15. These discuss relations under a young crown prince, Mohammad bin Salman, and the election of a populist president in the US, Donald Trump. Chapter 13 discusses the war in Yemen, the execution of Nimr al-Nimr and the severing of Saudi diplomatic relations with Iran. This chapter examines how the election of Trump upended the Obama-era Iran policy and reshaped Iranian–Saudi rivalry. Chapters 14 and 15 look at relations in three years of the Trump presidency, focusing on Trump's 'Maximum Pressure' on Iran, the turbulence in the Persian Gulf through the Tanker Wars, the attacks on Saudi oil facilities, and the assassination of Qassem Soleimani in 2020. Chapter 16, the conclusion, answers the questions set out above by bringing together a summary of the main findings presented in this book. Finally, the epilogue will discuss the events in the first year since the election of Biden to the White House, particularly in the period following talks between Iran and Saudi Arabia.

Anthology of the Relevant Literature on Saudi–Iranian Relations

The arguments in this book draw on the constructivist paradigm, and to understand how this book contributes to the wider literature on Iranian–Saudi relations, the book will first consider the relevant literature on this topic. An extensive study published by Keynoush (2016), which focuses on the historical evolution of the balance of power in Iranian–Saudi relations in general and their rivalry in particular, poses a central question: 'Is the rivalry between Saudi Arabia and Iran a cause of regional instability, or is it a *consequence* of that instability?' Keynoush (2016) argues that the core of Iranian–Saudi rivalry is due to regional foreign interventions, first and foremost by the US, that give rise to instability in the Persian Gulf. This, according to Keynoush, is the main reason for the agitation present in the Iranian–Saudi balance of power. The author further argues that unlike other studies that imply that Iranian–Saudi rivalry is based on hegemonic ambitions and realist views, what may illuminate the nature of their relationship is the fact that 'the two states compete for influence based on narrowly defined ideological and/or nationalistic world views' (Keynoush 2016: 2). Therefore, Keynoush argues that by applying a historical methodology, namely a neorealist theoretical framework, focusing on the balance of power, and exploring both the contentions and common interests of Iran and Saudi Arabia, a better understanding of their rivalry may be achieved.

Constructivist approaches to studying Iranian–Saudi relations have also considered the sectarian and ideological differences that emerged after the Iranian Revolution of 1979 (Keddie and Matthee 2002; Mabon 2013; Wehrey et al. 2009; Wehrey 2013, 2018). Keddie and Matthee (2002) and Mabon (2013) contend that ideological and religious differences form the cornerstone of Iranian–Saudi rivalry. Furthermore, studies of this nature gained prominence because of two episodes: the 1979 revolution and the fall of Saddam in 2003. The result of both watershed events saw the creation of a Shi'i theocracy in Iran and later a Shi'i revival in Iraq. Vali Nasr (2007) argues that the Iranian Revolution did not attain its desired effect since neighbouring states did not revolt against their regimes. As a result, 'Tehran began spreading money and organizational help to create Shi'a militants and revolutionary groups that would call for Islamic revolutions' (Nasr 2007: 143). The Saudi response to their new rivals was twofold: a strategic backing of Saddam for eight years; and a Saudi propaganda machine that 'underscored Khomeini's Shi'a identity on the one hand and the divide between Shi'ism and Sunnism on the Other'. This metamorphosed the conflict between the two states into an ideological one (Nasr 2007: 156). AlToraifi (2012) proposes that this religious-ideological approach and the underlying cause of their rivalry pivot on two main hypotheses. One assumption is the fact that the Iranian Revolution gave rise to a rivalry over world Islamic leadership, exemplified by the hajj demonstrations. The second was the fall of Saddam and the subsequent rise of the Shi'a in the region, which generated a domestic challenge to the Saudi state and therefore transformed the rivalry into a cold war of sorts between the two states.

Mabon's (2013) study adopts a theoretical framework based on Hinnebusch's modified realism and constructivism, which Mabon refers to as 'the Incongruence Dilemma'. This refers to the use of a combination of classical realist positions while applying constructivism to highlight the importance of identity (Mabon 2013: 18). Mabon discusses Iranian–Saudi rivalry by considering the implications and importance of identity on state security, that is to say that the 'incongruence of identity' in a given country can lead to internal security ramifications. The author argues that the adopted framework is applied on three levels: to political structure and state formation, which shapes the norms and identities of a particular regime; to the role of agency and identity groups in the form of religion and nationalism, which in turns impacts on the internal security dilemma and then affects the territorial sovereignty of the state and how it responds to threats; and an approach that 'explains how internal security dilemmas manifest themselves at the external level' (Mabon 2013: 36), when mainly driven by soft power. This allows external actors to undermine legitimacy and stability, thus affecting regional security (Mabon 2013).

The author discusses Iranian–Saudi relations by detailing the conflict between the two states and highlighting the ideological and geopolitical rivalry that includes 'Arab–Persian tensions', sectarian differences, and the different incidents that reflected their rivalry after the 1979 Iranian Revolution. Mabon underlines the doctrinal and ideological differences between the two states and their sects. Regional security is also discussed, including Bahrain, the UAE islands, proxy groups in the Levant and Iraq, and the effect of this rivalry on the Arab street. Also, Mabon (2013) argues for the importance of historical and religious narratives in the state formation of Saudi Arabia and Iran. The argument therefore focuses on the significance of religion as a tool of legitimacy that regimes use 'to resolve internal security dilemmas and to demonstrate external legitimacy and vitality'. This in turn gives rise to 'a soft power security dilemma guiding the [Iranian–Saudi] rivalry' (Mabon 2013: 106). Further discussions are focused on the role of religion in Iran and Saudi Arabia and the tensions between the internal identity groups such as the Shi'a and Wahhabis in Saudi Arabia, and the Sunni sect in Iran (Mabon 2013: 111–12). Therefore, the study highlights state suspicion towards its minorities, and Saudi attitudes towards the Shi'a and their suspected links and loyalty to Iran, thus demonstrating 'how the ideological [and internal] sphere feeds into the geopolitical sphere' (Mabon 2013: 139).

The publication, however, has limitations and shortcomings. First, the study is based on secondary sources, predominantly not in the original language (Arabic or Persian). Second, the book does not discuss the dynamics of the incidents that shape the rivalry in great depth, especially since Iranian–Saudi relations are complex, with a rivalry based on an interwoven web of ideological and geopolitical competitions. Finally, where the theoretical framework does adequately discuss Saudi–Iranian rivalry, it unfortunately does not take into account any periods of détente and rapprochement in the 1990s. While Mabon's incongruence dilemma may explain the ideological rivalry between Iran and Saudi Arabia, it can also be argued that Rafsanjani and Khatami's pragmatism and the sectarian tools used by both states are due to geopolitical 'games' and not ideological issues that govern Iranian–Saudi relations.

While this book focuses on Iranian–Saudi relations, these states' relationship with the US is also an important piece of the puzzle. Beeman's (2005) study was one of the first to engage with perceptions of Iran and the construction of the Iranian Other. Beeman (2005) utilizes images and constructions of the 'Mad Mullah and Great Satan' to highlight the mutual Othering of Iran and the US. The study discusses the political rhetoric in Iranian–US relations and its relationship to the context of Iranian National Character.[2] That is to say, an interpretation of systems of regularized and patterned communication, both linguistic and non-linguistic, may exist within societies. With this in mind, Beeman's study uses

---

2. For a discussion on the concept of the Iranian national character, see Beeman, William O. 1976. 'What is (Iranian) national character? A sociolinguistic approach', *Iranian Studies*, 9: 22–48.

linguistic anthropology to study the 'official pronouncements between governments of Iran and the United States and their representatives ... regarding the Other nation' (Beeman 2005: 5). Through an analysis of 'symbolic communication ... between officials who lay claim to representing the policies of their nations', the author discusses the 'cultural underpinnings of the long-standing feud between the United States and Iran' (Beeman 2005: vi–vii). The analysis of 'mutual demonization' constitutes the bulk of this work with a central argument that the conflict between Iran and the US is based primarily on a postmodern cultural conflict rather than fundamental differences between the two states. This leads each country to construct an image of the Other to sustain the image of that country's enemy, in this case the 'Mad Mullah' and the 'Great Satan'. Beeman (2005) discusses the role of the Iranian media in constructing the US as its Other in a historical manner, that is, by analysing and detailing the evolution of the Iranian newspaper discourse in the periods before and after the revolution. In contrast to this study, I do not dissect and analyse the discourses in the newspaper headlines, articles, and editorials; instead, I focus on the general tone. This is equally true for the discourse of the ulama. To give an example, Beeman (2005: 66) draws on Khomeini's writings to argue that the Other, in this case Western powers, are 'opposed to Islam' and that the ulama are 'facing this force'. However, Beeman does not quote or discuss other clerical discourses, such as Friday prayer sermons, to support such an argument. Islamic tropes such as Imam Hussein and Yazid were used to describe the construction of the Self and the Other, and the struggle for virtue against corruption. Nevertheless, Beeman does not employ primary sources, such as ulama sermons, to discuss these representations and constructions, or to contextualize the specific discourse of Khomeini. In contrast, this book analyses a range of sermons, editorials, and speeches to detail the narratives and tropes of martyrdom that define the Iranian Self and its Other.

Since the 'Arab Spring', a few studies have surfaced dealing with representations of the Self and the Other, with regard to Iran and Saudi Arabia. These studies have focused on two main aspects, Shi'a–Sunni sectarianism (Ghobadzadeh and Akbarzadeh 2015) and US and Arab views of the Iranian Other (de Buitrago 2015; de Buitrago 2016). Ghobadzadeh and Akbarzadeh discuss the roots of the current sectarian conflicts in the Middle East through the concept of 'Othering theology'. These authors argue that sectarianism and religious Othering in the Middle East is 'rooted in a solid theological articulation proposed by classic Islamic political theology'. By examining texts from leading theologians, Ghobadzadeh and Akbarzadeh (2015: 692) contextualize the politico-historical narrative and theological polemics, thus exploring how Othering is used 'to justify violence against the Shi'a sect in the Muslim world'. The study concluded that Shi'i Othering has become part of the politico-religious discourse and has diffused into all strata of society, therefore allowing Othering rhetoric to expand beyond theology to become an intricate part of how people view the Shi'i Other. In the Saudi context, the study suggests that 'Othering discourse has become deeply entrenched in Saudi Arabia's educational curriculum, which denigrates all except those who subscribe to Wahhabism' (Ghobadzadeh and Akbarzadeh 2015: 700). Although the research examines Othering discourse towards the Shi'a, the authors also acknowledge the fact that their study is incomplete as they do not analyse the Othering discourse in revolutionary Iran, and how this Iranian discourse depicted the Sunni governments in the region.

Perceptions of Iran and constructions of the Iranian Other are the focus of two main studies, the first by de Buitrago on US and Arab 'Othering' of Iran (2015); and the second on 'constructions of the USA Self vis-à-vis the Iranian Other' (2016). De Buitrago (2015) discusses Self–Other constructions by the Arab States, mainly by Saudi Arabia, the UAE, and Syria; alongside those of the US towards Iran, through analysing the discourse of decision-makers. The study discusses the main narratives and perceptions of threat conveyed by the aforementioned states and their construction of the Self and the Iranian Other, mainly through 'contemporary and recent relations' rather than historical ones (de Buitrago 2015: 86). In the specific case of Saudi Arabia, de Buitrago only dedicates a short section (de Buitrago 2015: 94–97) to discussing the Self and the Iranian Other mainly through the analysis of UN General Assembly speeches. The study briefly highlights the construction of the Saudi Arabian Self as 'fostering regional stability, dialogue and cooperation' (de Buitrago 2015: 95), while painting an image of a corrupt and aggressive Iranian Other that gives good reason for imperative foreign intervention in the region (2015: 97). The Iranian nuclear programme and its possible weapons of mass destruction are considered as threats, as is hegemony in the GCC (e.g. among the UAE islands) and intervention in Syria as part of the Arab Spring (2015: 96).

By examining the role of emotions in US discourse on Iran, de Buitrago (2016: 155) engages with 'the constructions of the USA Self vis-à-vis the Iranian Other, to articulations of threat and processes of Othering'. The study examines the role of emotions in US policy towards Iran. It considers the revolution of 1979, the hostage crisis, and the US security and policy discourse that has constructed the Iranian 'Other as a threat, trauma and mistrust' (de Buitrago 2016: 158). Significantly, the book chapter discusses the use of metaphors like the 'axis of evil' in the Bush era, which led to the creation of 'a discourse–policy trap' (de Buitrago 2016: 158–59), thus making a clear distinction between US allies and enemies. Furthermore, the study focuses on the US decision makers' narrative vis-à-vis Iran and how that constructs the Iranian leadership as a threat to American national, global, and regional interests and stability. De Buitrago argues that constructing Iran as a 'negative' and 'evil' Other 'dichotomously contrasts to the construction of a good US Self' (2016: 157). Both studies by de Buitrago (2015, 2016) examine the construction of an Iranian Other by analysing US and Arab decision makers' discourse on Iran. However, the studies do not consider the public and media discourse, nor do they analyse the construction of the Iranian Self, and therefore, the Iranian Othering of Arab States or the US, particularly Saudi Arabia.

Theoretical Underpinnings

This book examines the mutual representation of the 'Other' through the macro-lens of constructivism from a multidimensional approach. This approach considers the concept of 'Othering' and its dichotomies, the image of enmity between rivals, how discursive formations are framed and spun within narratives, and how 'regimes of truths' are disseminated. Three main theories in the study of Othering have been deployed in this book: Foucault's depiction of power-knowledge relations, Said's concept of Othering and dichotomies in his work on Orientalism, and Herrmann and Fischerkeller's image theory based on the image of the enemy.

Foucault, the Power-knowledge Nexus, and Discourse Analysis

The clash between Saudi Arabia and Iran is understood here as one based on constructed 'regimes of truth' and discursive formations that can be labelled nationalisms, imperialisms, or religious fundamentalisms. This book will assume that such discourses are systemic, and that they have the capacity to articulate, produce, and make things happen:

> Each society has its regime of truth, its 'general polities' of truth – that is, the types of discourse it accepts and makes function as true; the mechanisms and instances that enable one to distinguish true and false statements; the means by which each is sanctioned; the techniques and procedures accorded value in the acquisition of truth; the status of those who are charged with saying what counts as true.
>
> (Foucault 2002b: 131)

This 'truth' that Foucault refers to here flows throughout all layers of society as he understands it to be 'a system of ordered procedures for the production, regulation, distribution and circulation of statements', i.e. discourse (Foucault 2002b: 132). On Foucault's view, discourse produces knowledge that is observed as the truth, which in turn affects social practices such as political decision-making. This knowledge becomes 'true' because of how power operates within society, especially since this truth is bound up in systems of power. This is accomplished in two ways: first, systems of power produce and sustain the truth; and second, they are also bound 'to effects of power which it induces and which extend it [truth]' (Foucault 2002b: 132). This book deals with a 'social regime of truth' interpreted in this context as a 'state-propaganda-produced regime of truth' as applied to Saudi–Iranian Othering.

In this setting, exclusionary governing discourses include sectarianism and Pan-Arabism, as well as binary constellations and dichotomies such as 'infidel versus Muslim', 'Arab versus *ajam*', 'civilized versus barbarian', all of which operate to create juxtapositions, sometimes in isolation. I draw here on Foucault's notion that without a particular discourse about a subject (or issue) no knowledge could exist. For example, without narratives spun by Islamic radicals or the neo-colonial discourses of the far right in the West, the clash between Islam and the West in the form of racism or Islamic fundamentalism would not exist. The cultural artefacts that have given rise to 'us' and 'them' make up a construction that is disseminated and is manifest through discourses such as media, books, political speech, and dialogue.

Foucault argues that there is no model or concise method for conducting discourse analysis (Foucault et al. 1991: 73–86; Foucault 2002b). However, this book employs Willig's (2008) six stages of Foucauldian discourse analysis within this power–knowledge and genealogical paradigm (Willig 2008). This allows me to study Saudi–Iranian representations of the Other across a forty-two-year period through the watershed episodes selected. In addition, Foucauldian discourse analysis is a suitable technique since it 'can be carried out wherever there is meaning' (Parker and Bolton 1999: 1). For such an analysis, the text and discourse selection is extremely important. I will select texts that highlight a language that represents Othering within each watershed episode. For example, editorials from both Saudi Arabia and Iran will be selected from the first three years of the Iran–Iraq War (1980–1982) as a certain historical moment, and the selected texts will be used to identify the different discursive formations in the mutual representation of the Other.

The aim here is to identify 'objects' and how they are referred to in the discourse. Given that the discourse is defined as a set of meanings that contain objects, it makes the discourse used a representational practice that gives rise to an 'object of reality' when using words such as nouns in reference to the object (Parker 1992: 8–9). What do these objects refer to and how are they described? Finding answers to these questions will be especially important, bearing in mind that the discourse of Othering is an object in itself, and it can be described in terms of stereotypes or racism, such as portraying the Shi'a as heretics and fire-worshippers, or Saudis as lizard-eating desert barbarians.

I suggested earlier that the chosen discourses are state propaganda rather than a regime of truth constructed by society. However, state discourses have been disseminated into Saudi and Iranian societies through political, religious, and media discourses, thereby becoming part of citizens' discursive realities. More specifically, these discursive constructions give rise to 'certain ways-of-seeing the world and certain ways-of-being in the world. Discourses offer *subject positions*, which, when taken up, have implications for subjectivity and experience' (Willig and Stainton-Rogers 2007: 172, *emphasis in original*). By analysing subject positions, we can begin to grasp which actors generate the discourse of Othering, for what purpose and for which target audience; and from there, of how the representation of the Other affirms the identity and character of the Self in Saudi and Iranian discourse. Finally, this book applies Foucault's concept of intertextuality (Foucault 2002a: 25–26) through an analysis of multiple texts and discourses. This permits the analysis of a range of texts across a historical time frame to identify any overlap in the discourses, since Foucauldian discourse analysis deals with texts at a macro-level. Here, the representation of the Other is studied over the watershed episodes, with any overlapping and reoccurrences highlighted.

Said and Orientalism

Foucault's approach to discourse analysis also influenced Edward Said's idea of Orientalism (1978). One stark contribution was Said's rejection of the notion that the humanities were free of bias and generated pure knowledge, as held in traditional liberal understandings. By borrowing Foucault's notion of the relationship between power and knowledge, Said views the production of knowledge as deeply rooted in the operations and applications of power through constellations of institutionalized scholars and artists who are governed by the dominant ideology and the political requirements of the society that they belong to. Although such constellations may exist in Iran and Saudi Arabia, this view may not be totally applicable to the Iranian–Saudi constructivist mechanism that is the focus of this research, because the Iran–Saudi power conditions are not unequal: one cannot speak of a dominant and weak side, or of a powerful and powerless side. They both may be regarded as 'rough equals' or equal antagonists that are competing for domination of the region in a Middle East 'Cold War'. However, Said's Orientalism is applicable to Saudi–Iranian relations in that they 'cannot seriously be studied without their force, or more precisely their configuration, of power also being studied' (Said 1978: 5).

Besides Orientalism, this book also employs Said's interpretation of Foucauldian knowledge construction, where power is observed as an impersonal force operating through multiple sites and channels, thereby constructing a 'pastoral regime' that controls its subjects by reforming and subduing them so that they become objects of power within the social system. This understanding of Foucault lay at the heart of Said's thought on the control of knowledge and the linking of all forms of a 'will to knowledge' and modes of cultural representations of the Other in the exercise of power (Moore-Gilbert 1997: 36). A second key adaptation of Foucault by Said is the idea that discourse 'constructs' the objects of its knowledge, as discourse 'produces reality, it produces domains of objects and rituals of truth' (Foucault 2012: 10; Said 1978). Said therefore argues that a 'regime of truth' i.e. the disciplinary power inscribed in Orientalism, transforms the 'real' East into a 'discursive' Orient or, as Moore-Gilbert (1997: 37) argues, it 'substitutes one for the other'; hence constructing and representing an image of the Other. This book investigates the similar process through which Saudi and Iranian 'regimes of truth' seek to transform the Other (Iran, Saudi Arabia) into the discursive Other (Iran and Saudi Arabia as sources of threat and danger to national and regional stability and to the 'approved' political, religious, and social order).

One such argument of the representation of the Other discussed by Said is the European ideology that depicted Europeans as superior in comparison to the Orient, arguing that this superior identity is rooted in their ideology and maintained through the discourse. This is accomplished by constructing the Other as different from the Self, which can be both negatively represented and – in some instances – positively represented while maintaining the view that everything about the Self is positive. This binary representation and the dichotomies of the Self and Other, us and them, and inferior and superior is adopted here to investigate dichotomies used in Iranian–Saudi discourses, such as *rāfidī* and *nasibī*, *ajam* and Arab. Similarly, just as Said observed that the relationship between the Orient and Occident is based on binary oppositions, this notion will also be adopted and adapted to investigate the 'regimes of truth' in different Iranian and Saudi discourses that demonstrate the discursive practice of Othering.

Binary Representation and Othering   According to Said, Othering employs binary representations or dichotomies between the Self, in his case Western identity, and the Other, i.e. an Oriental identity. This book views dichotomies as Othering techniques employed between Saudi Arabia and Iran. These techniques include Saudi Othering, which consists of Arab superiority and is based on Mecca being viewed as the cradle of Islam. It ascribes a sense of primacy, purity, and uncorrupted nature to Arabs, who are contrasted with a Persian Other that is viewed as inferior, corrupted by historical heresy as they were converted from Zoroastrianism to Islam by the Arabs. On the other hand, Iranian representations of a Saudi Other would include a superiority grounded in Persian civilization that spans thousands of years as opposed to Arab cultural inferiority and a desert lifestyle. Finally, religious Othering as a technique will also be investigated, wherein the Saudi representation of the Self would be as a Wahhabi puritan in opposition to an Iranian Shi'i infidel; and conversely the Iranian Self, which would represent Shi'i martyrdom versus Yazidi tyranny and Godlessness encompassed in a Saudi Other.

This book also makes a slight departure from Foucault and Said, whose concepts share two main characteristics. First, both are interested mainly in discourses that are present throughout a society and in which numerous actors participate in the discourse construction. Second, Said discusses to a greater extent discourses of Othering in the context of unequal power relations in which a more powerful dominant group (e.g. a White majority, the Occident, etc.) distinguishes itself as superior to a weaker subordinate or subaltern group (e.g. the Orient, the Black minority, etc.). The case of Iran and Saudi Arabia is different. The power relations are not unequal and one cannot speak of a dominant and weak side, or of a powerful and powerless side. Both may be regarded as 'rough equals' or equal antagonists that are competing for the domination of the region in a Middle East 'cold war'. These differences necessitate the use of other approaches and concepts in addition to those of Foucault and Said.

Image Theory, the Other and the 'Necessary Enemy'   I employ the image theory developed by Herrmann and Fischerkeller (1995) in their work on the Cold War (and the Iran–Iraq war), and the notion of the 'necessary enemy', found in their work and in that of Stein (1985) and Herrmann (1985). Image theory proposes that humans have innate cognitive limitations and are thus constantly sorting, analysing, and interpreting the information they intend to process. Through this process, developing images of humans – such as an image of an enemy or a friend – becomes both a common occurrence and a 'necessary' one. The development of the image of the Other according to this includes three main variables of distinguishing the Other as: 1) a threat or an opportunity; 2) culturally similar or inferior; and 3) more, less, or similarly powerful (Herrmann 1985; Herrmann and Fischerkeller 1995; Schaffer 2011: 135). Consequently, these three variables form 'ideal types of images' of the Other, for instance, of an enemy that is either threatening with a similar culture and that is an equal in power; or an ally that is inferior in culture with less power and that is an opportunity to be taken advantage of.

The most researched images include those of the enemy, ally, barbarian, and imperialist (Alexander, Brewer, and Herrmann 1999). Herrmann and Fischerkeller (1995) understand mirror imaging as occurring only when the Other is compatible in terms of goals, equality in power, trustworthiness, cooperativeness, and cultural equality. Furthermore, the representations of both the 'barbarian' and the 'imperialist' arise from a negative interdependence wherein both groups compete and the failure of one results in the achievement of the Other's goals and ambitions (Herrmann and Fischerkeller 1995; Trifiletti et al. 2012).

During the Cold War, the propaganda mechanism revolved around the constructed image of the enemy, i.e. the US, which became a dominant and characteristic theme within the stereotypical representation and identity construction of the Other as an enemy. This representation was based on a 'binary paradigm' that included opposing but also complementary policies known as 'the symbiosis of American anti-communism and Soviet anti-capitalism' (Stein 1985). This binary can be compared with the Saudi pro-Sunni and Iranian pro-Shi'i labels. This cultivated an 'imaginary war' in which both sides complementarily designed specific internal cultures and reaction systems, in addition to their developing on the cultural, ideological, psychological, and imaginary levels through the image of the Other as a 'necessary enemy, whose political outcomes contributed to internal aims and priorities' (Kaldor 1990).

According to Finlay et al. (1967: 7), people have always needed an enemy or scapegoat and if one is not present, then the Other as an enemy and scapegoat will be created. This is the 'necessary enemy' (Finlay, Holsti, and Fagen 1967: 7), where its role is more fixed than those taking up the role (Murray and Meyers 1999) – in other words, regardless of who is the enemy, an enemy has to always be present. 'Necessary enemies' serve two main purposes: a psychological one where the need for an enemy arises from the need for targets for externalizing frustration, fears and hostilities; and a political purpose where leaders create enemies to mobilize their audiences around common aims (Murray and Meyers 1999). Through propaganda discourses, these two purposes shape an image of the enemy that operates as a mirror image wherein 'each side attributes the same virtues to itself and the same vices to the enemy. We are trustworthy, peace-loving, honourable and humanitarian; they are treacherous, warlike and cruel' (Stein 1985: 254).

This book examines whether this concept of a necessary enemy can be found in the Iran–Saudi context, whether regionally or internationally for both political and psychological purposes and through propaganda discourses and constructions of the enemy. It also investigates how the image of the Other as an enemy was constructed through recurrent simplified, familiar, and predictable symbols of stereotyping and the construction of the image of the enemy, such as the export of the revolution in Iran's case or the demise of 'real Islam' in the case of Saudi Arabia. This pattern, most notably observed in US–Soviet Othering, becomes continually refined through propaganda discourse, stereotyping, or 'ritualized rhetoric' (Herrmann 1985) that entails fixed expressions, exaggeration, or the distortion of truth (up to the point of lying) (Witkowska 2008).

In constructing the necessary enemy, there are specific images that have extremely powerful historical, cultural, and religious connotations and resonances such as Karbala, Yazid and Hussein, the Prophet Mohammad, and the infidels of Mecca. An essential feature of such images is that their significance and power as metaphors and analogies is recognized by their respective audiences. In turn, these images can be mobilized by each respective side, around which a set of discourses can orbit or rotate; discourses that are more specific to the prevailing local, regional, or international context, but which draw on the images' power as metaphors or analogies. The Karbala narrative and the martyrdom of Hussein, for example, was employed in different situations by the Iranian revolutionary leadership. It facilitated additional elite discourses on the oppressed versus the oppressor, the struggle for justice, and the need for revolutionary and religious perseverance.

In addition, political and religious actors mobilize these images within their discourses and narratives, which change according to both the context and the dominant political agenda. These images have a power of resonance, which sticks in the mind of the audience. They are easily mobilized and deployed, especially because they naturally relate to notions such as good versus evil, Shi'a versus Sunni etc. Furthermore, these images also allow us the opportunity to gain insight into the construction of the self-image that each country's elite possesses, thereby revealing something of these elites' religious, cultural, and ideological basis. When the Saudi ruler drew on imagery from the Prophet Mohammad's companion Umar for instance, the ruler facilitated a discourse emphasizing prestige and encompassing his fairness, chivalry, and piety. In the Iranian discourse, for example, the use of Imam Ali's images allows the construction of an elite discourse in which the Iranian revolutionary regime reminds the population of Imam Ali's chivalry, leadership, knowledge, wisdom, and resistance to oppression and worldly desires, thus further propagating such an image. The images themselves are therefore not necessarily innately political in character or nature. Instead, they are mobilized in chosen moments to allow the construction and communication of additional and related elite discourses in a variety of contexts and in order to meet a range of strategic needs and purposes. Chapters 2–15 will therefore identify the images specific to each respective time frame and highlight the principal discourses associated with them in those specific contexts.

Text and Discourse Selection

This book investigates the epistemology of Othering and otherness by analysing three main spheres or discourses, namely the political, religious, and media spheres. The chosen respective domains considered are as follows: speeches by the political elite in Iran and Saudi Arabia, the Friday prayer sermons delivered in both Saudi Arabia and Iran, and newspaper editorials from four main newspapers representative of each country. Let us look at each of these in more detail:

Political Speeches I selected speeches on political themes by members of the political elite in Iran and Saudi Arabia. Political speeches are viewed here as

ideological constructs that satisfy the elite's political objectives and that also serve
to link language with political actions that either come before or after the political
speech (al-Rasheed 1996). Discourse analysis of political speech is most successful
when it covers both linguistic and political behaviours. This can be achieved on a
macro-level by investigating the 'communicative situation', i.e. the status of the
elite, time (episode), and location (audience) of the speech coupled with a text
function to determine which linguistic structures and techniques a speaker utilizes
to transmit a particular construction by the elite. This macro-level analysis
investigates aspects of power, dominance, and groupings (for example Shi'a/
Wahhabi, Arab/Ajam, conservative/reformist), which are used here to study
representations of the Other. Moreover, these speeches are also employed by
members of the political establishment to reinforce their position, the position
of the state, or the political institution they belong to. They achieve this by using
political discourse to affirm the position of authority and status of the Self and to
undermine the Other.

Four main criteria must be met when choosing appropriate discourses for
analysis: subject, period, audience, and speaker (who must be a member of the
elite). In this context, both domestic (local/national) and international publics
should be considered. Such speeches capture how the elite in Iran and Saudi Arabia
refer to the Other in one particular moment when speaking to a crowd of Iranians
or Saudis, for example, on the religious occasions of the al-Adha, Ramadan
festivals, and Muharram; national celebrations such as the National Day in Saudi
Arabia and the Anniversary of the Revolution in Iran. Speeches addressed to
international audiences, e.g. by elites at the UN General Assembly and the
Organization of the Islamic Conference (OIC) are also investigated. These reflect
the identity of the state, elite membership or status, and the representation of the
Other on an international level.

I chose members that belonged to the centres of power, i.e. formal actors who
represent the elite in the respective states. These included the Supreme Leader
(Iran), the king of Saudi Arabia, the foreign ministers of both states, the president
of Iran, the crown prince and minister of defence in Saudi Arabia, and the speakers
of the Majles and the Shura Council (*Majlis Ashūrā*) in Iran and Saudi Arabia
respectively. It is important to consider that language as part of political discourse
is concerned with who has the permission to say what and to whom – which is
intertwined with power and social status (Wareing 2004: 9). How an elite member
– such as the crown prince or Majles speaker – uses the language depends on how
they perceive themselves and what identity they want to convey, e.g. the group they
belong to, or their state; and to whom the speech is addressed and where. In short,
invaluable inferences can be made about political elites from the way they talk
(Meyerhoff 2006).

Friday Prayer Sermons   Understanding the background and importance of the
Friday prayer sermons (*khutbah*) is key to understanding their inclusion here. The
role of the *ulama* and their relationship with the state should also be examined.
The *khutbah* or sermon in Islam is a speech given by a religious scholar. It has a

static position in Islamic ritual, i.e. it is a compulsory event that all Muslims have to attend as part of Friday prayers. It precedes the prayer and consists of two segments. A 'warning sermon' or the 'sermon of exhortation' takes place first. This is a longer *khutbah* followed by a shorter, descriptive *khutbah* known as a 'qualifying sermon'. Besides serving a religious function, the *khutbah* has always served an important political function since the days of the Prophet Mohammad (Ram 1994: 19). This importance still applies to the contemporary nation state. While the *khutbah* is a significant part of the ritualistic and religious framework of Islam, here I analyse the Friday sermons' political and socio-political dimensions.

The (socio-)political significance of the *khutbah* began with the establishment of the first mosque in 620 CE when Mohammad controlled the religious and political community of Islam (Ram 1994; Fathi 1984: 89) giving it a political nature, adherence to which at that time showed allegiance to the newly formed *ummah* (Ram 1994: 9). This procedure continued throughout the tenure of the four caliphs as they created a pulpit (*minbar*) emphasizing their roles as spokespersons for the community, or they employed governors or generals to do so on their behalf. These representatives consequently issued orders, pronounced policy decisions, or expressed the view of the Caliph on certain issues (Pedersen 2012).

The Islamic Republic of Iran attached a political significance to the Friday sermon in four main respects. The first is the ability to propagate political messages to the audience. Second, the Friday Prayer Council established guidelines for all the Friday sermon leaders to adhere to. Third, the Tehran sermon is broadcast nationally on television and radio and published the next day in the newspapers (*Kayhan* and *Ettela'at*). Fourth, the sermon creates a bond and relationship between the clergy and the nation by raising awareness. Its contents serve as role models and examples to the public (Kamrava and Hassan-Yari 2004).

As in Saudi Arabia, internal and external factors also influenced the Iranian Friday sermons. In the first eight years after the revolution, Iran faced a long war against Iraq. With that war in mind, the sermon preacher was most often a member of the Islamic Republic Party (IRP) who was charged as being a representative of Khomeini (Ram 1994: 29). As a result, the bulk of the war saw the Tehran sermon presided over by either Khamenei in his capacity as president or Rafsanjani as Majles speaker. Moreover, the pulpit was used as a forum to establish Iran's identity as a righteous, pious state that shows bravery. It also identified itself with major Islamic themes such as Hussein's Karbala or the wars the Prophet Mohammad undertook in the early days of his Islamic mission. To be exact, Iran aimed to portray an image of the Self as the oppressed Mohammad or Hussein, against the Other of the infidels of Quraish or Yazid. However, the main pillar of Iran's revolutionary ideology in the 1980s was the export of the revolution. For example, in 1980 Khamenei's sermon spoke of the export of the revolution not with the sword, but by elucidating the message because Iran has no offensive weapons; it prefers not to use them also because technology is used by 'other states' in the East and West against other countries (sermon on 29 Feburary 1980 in Ram 1994: 180).

Newspapers Newspaper editorials act as the mouthpiece of a particular newspaper and reflect its ideology. Lagonikos (2005) observes that editorials have become known as the mouthpiece because people use them to follow up on the main arguments when discussing political, religious, and national issues within a state. Furthermore, since the media sphere contains an overwhelming amount of information, people turn to expert opinions to sieve this information for them. Both these reasons have allowed newspapers to shape the socio-political environment through the eyes of an ideological group that shares similar beliefs and values that are defined in the newspapers they read (Lagonikos 2005; Reah 2002). It is through these editorials that the shared beliefs and values are argued in an effective and persuasive manner to defend positions against the Other. News is commented on and discussed in a multidimensional fashion, providing recommendations, warnings, or predictions by employing various strategies. These include the use of rhetoric, stereotypes, and polarized vocabulary to describe the Other, whether they be states or other actors. These strategies propagate a positive image of 'us' and a negative image of 'them' (van Dijk 2005: 17–33). This opens the door to elaborating on the conditions and reasons behind my selection of particular Saudi and Iranian newspapers.

To cover the views representative of Iran and Saudi Arabia in newspaper editorials, I used four main conditions to guide my selection of newspapers. The first two conditions included a high reader base and archives that cover all the episodes from 1979 to 2020. The third condition is the coverage of international events in their editorials. The fourth condition is the representation of the main official views within Iran and Saudi Arabia. It is important to note that when investigating the role of the press in Saudi Arabia and Iran, it is apparent that Saudi Arabia has no kind of reformist-led press. However, while the Iranian press includes a reformist press, these newspapers have been subject to frequent temporary and permanent bans. Although this makes an analysis of the comparison between Iranian newspapers difficult and asymmetrical, it is not an impossible task and can offer insight into the Iranian discourse of Othering on both sides of the Iranian political spectrum.

The collected data is focused on seven Iranian and four Saudi newspapers that cover a range of political orientations and target audiences during every one of the watershed episodes. The Iranian newspapers are divided into two groups: conservative newspapers that include *Kayhan, Jomhouri Eslami, Ettela'at* and *Resalat*; and reformist newspapers that include *Salam, Aftab-e Yazd, and Etemaad*.[3] The Saudi newspapers are *Asharq Al-Awsat, al-Riyadh, al-Hayat, and al-Madina*.[4] This approach permits the investigation of how the Other is represented not only

---

3. Circulation of the Iranian newspapers: *Kayhan*: 100,000, *Ettela'at*: 90,000, *Resalat*: 50,000 *Salam*: 100,000 *Aftab-e Yazd*: 100,000 *Etemaad*: 100,000 (Mahtafar et al., 2009; IMP & Monroe, 2012).

4. Circulation of the Saudi newspapers: *Asharq Al-Awsat*: 237,000, *al-Riyadh*: 150,000, *al-Hayat*: 100,000, *al-Madina*: 60,000 (WAN-IFRA, 2008).

between the Saudi and Iranian contexts but also in an intra-Iranian milieu exemplified by the aforementioned newspapers. Editorials rather than articles were chosen for analysis because they reflect a wider range of ideological positions (at least in the case of Iran), and they set out deliberately to form opinions, whereas articles are often more concerned with conveying information. The selection was restricted to textual content, ignoring photographs, pictures, and their accompanying captions. Editorials are not normally illustrated and dealing with images is beyond the scope of this study.

There are differences between the Saudi and Iranian newspapers in terms of style, content, and level of criticism. The Saudi editorials are short and brief, particularly *al-Madina* and *al-Riyadh*, and they tend to be very confrontational and explicit with their use of vocabulary when referring to states or actors towards which the state may have an animosity. On the other hand, the Iranian editorials are comprehensive, sometimes longer than a single column and continuing on the newspaper's second page. As for the style, Iranian newspapers are mainly implicit when referring to Arab and Muslim states and actors, but explicit when criticizing the West. On the national level, as discussed earlier, Iranian newspapers are very critical regarding the administrations of various presidents as opposed to Saudi newspapers that include very limited and brief criticism. Iranian newspapers have been known to thoroughly criticize members within different branches of the establishment, such as the president, ministers, and different branches of the armed forces. However, Saudi newspapers have been known to tread very carefully when criticizing religious or sensitive branches of the country (for example the police, intelligence, the army) – especially those held by members of the monarchy. This may result in a decrease in variation that may be a cause for some concern, since it may limit the usefulness of the sources in exploring the different mainstream views within the Saudi system. However, this may also reflect the mainstream views' lack of diversity within the Saudi system. Overall, although there are differences between the Iranian and Saudi newspapers, they are still viable sources to act as datasets to explore the epistemology of Saudi–Iranian rivalry and Othering. Through the macro-lens of constructivism and the aforementioned theories of Othering, the remaining chapters will discuss how rivalry and mutual Othering were shaped and reshaped between Iran and Saudi Arabia over more than four decades.

Part 1

Chapter 2

REVOLUTION, WAR, AND THE FORMATION OF IRANIAN DISCOURSES OF SELF AND OTHER

Introduction

The end of the 1970s saw great changes in the Middle East. These included the first peace agreement between a major Arab state, Egypt, and Israel; the revolutionary creation of the first Shi'i theocracy led by a jurist; and the ousting of a 2,500-year-old monarchical system in Iran. This resulted in a new regime that would endure eight years of an 'imposed war' that sent tremors throughout the Middle East for years to follow. Amid these historical shifts, this chapter discusses Iranian representations of the (Saudi) Other between 1979 and 1983 in order to analyse the different discursive strategies employed by Iran in a period of tension and war. In turn, the next chapter considers Saudi representations of the (Iranian) Other. These chapters identify discursive shifts that resulted from domestic, regional, and international events. More broadly, they set the scene for the analysis in the later chapters.

Crucially, this period laid the foundations for later events, particularly in terms of Iran's transformation from being a US and Western ally in the region to being a revolutionary vanguard state. This new revolutionary state in turn reshaped the local and regional agenda of its reactionary Other, namely Saudi Arabia. As a result, in the formative years after the revolution a set of Self and Othering discourses and tropes emerged, reflecting the political and ideological pressures both states were experiencing. During the early years of the defence and survival of the revolutionary state, innovative and powerful politico-religious languages developed, which would reappear during later periods in line with changing regional and international contexts.

Three main arguments emerge from the material here presented. First, religion – or more precisely sect – was not an area of contention between both states at the beginning of the post-revolutionary period. This was especially the case since the overall narrative between both states in the post-revolutionary period up to the start of the war was one of acceptance and mutual respect. The issue of sectarianism was employed as a tool and discursive strategy for two main reasons. On the Iranian side it was framed in terms of Saudi assistance to Saddam and the growing Saudi fear of Iranian calls to export the revolution. Events such as the hajj incidents, weapons procurement, and the Fahd peace plan (for the Arab–Israeli conflict) were all tools utilized by these states.

Second, the shift in narrative and in representations of the Other was directly proportional to the events that took place in both states. Although Saudi Arabia reacted to Iran's actions because of its realpolitik, thus protecting its Arab and Islamic identity both internationally and regionally, Iran's representation of the Saudi Other was a form of 'organized aggressiveness'. That is to say, Iran's demonizing construction of the Saudi state, clerics, and its monarchy disregarded foreign-policy considerations, thus signifying the naivety of the newly founded revolutionary state. The Iranian representation of the Saudi Other had an internal agenda based on two main motives: the sustainability of clerical consolidation, mainly by the Islamic Republic Party (IRP) members; and the *levée en masse* of youth to the war front to further consolidate power and to win the war, aided and abetted by demonizing the enemy, the Other.

Third, the success of the Iranian revolution not only influenced Iranian identity, but also Saudi identity. The siege of the Mecca and the Qatif (Muharram) uprisings in November and December 1979 respectively affirmed a strong Saudi sense of Self. Various events, particularly the siege and Shi'i uprisings, allowed the monarchy to reaffirm the image of the Imam of the Ummah, the development of the state and the Saudi kingdom's prestige as the cradle of Islam. Also, the US embassy hostage crisis (undertaken by Iranian students), the subsequent failures of rescue attempts, and the clerical consolidation of the different organs of state power, alongside the regaining of territory and advances in the war, allowed the Iranians to emphasize their identity and therefore shape their view and construction of the Saudi Other. I contend that these discourses of divinity and prestige that relate to the 'hidden hand of God' not only deemed their revolution holy and successful, but also viewed it as exporting God's will, since the newly formed Islamic Republic was not only holy, but also divine in that it was an extension of Imam Ali's Caliphate and government in waiting for the twelfth Imam, the Mahdi. The republic was considered holy as it applies God's laws on earth, and divine as it fulfils the Islamic prophecies of the Mahdi coming to prepare to spread 'peace on earth' after an age of 'tyranny and evil'.

Khomeini's revolution in 1979 led to a similar transformation in Iran that had ramifications on Saudi Arabia. In Iran, the revolution reshaped the state from a monarchy into a secular-Islamic structure, and Iran finally witnessed the full clerical consolidation of control over the state. Meanwhile, in Saudi Arabia the ramifications of the Iranian revolution saw Shi'i uprisings in the Eastern Province and – albeit as an indirect result – the siege of Mecca. Ironically, it can be argued that both states shared this moment of transformation as they both experienced ideological, religious, and military dangers. As a result, the two states underwent clerical consolidation of their respective governments and societies: in Iran, the intention was to instil a revolutionary interpretation of a modern Islamic state, while in Saudi Arabia a more reactionary approach shored up its religious and ideological position.

In the years following the Khomeini-led revolution in Iran and the siege of Mecca by Juhayman al-Otaibi, identities and images of both Iran and Saudi Arabia evolved. The next two sections will discuss how this occurred. More generally, the contention that the discourses are political in nature and character underpins the arguments made. The discourses relate to ongoing political events, such as domestic political rivalry in Iran and the consolidation of the clergy, the siege of Mecca and the Qatif uprising and Saudi Arabia, and the Iran–Iraq war. Shifts from positive to negative Self–Other constructions linked to events in both states. The state contexts are multi-layered: different actors have drawn on either the Khomeini or Fahd narrative, allowing different newspapers, the *ulama* and political elites to utilize certain discourses for internal and external consumption. For instance, Islamic imagery such as *fitna*, or Persian expansionism, were employed to mobilize discourses on sectarianism, sedition, expansion, and hegemony.

Defining the Self and the Other in the Islamic Republic of Iran

The 'Den of Spies' and Operation Eagle Claw

Over the 444 days of the hostage crisis (4 November 1979–20 January 1981), the newly created Islamic government used the episode to shape its image and identity both domestically and internationally, demonstrating how divine intervention and Islamic steadfastness had resulted in the underdog defeating the arrogant US. The latter's seizure of the US embassy, which Khomeini termed a 'den of spies', by the students of the Line of the Imam (*Khat-i Imām*), set a precedent in breaking international laws and norms. Khomeini's response and his representation of the Iranian Self highlighted an image of fearlessness, strength and asceticism, and martyrdom, as expressed in the following passage:

> We do not fear anything. We do not fear the weapons that are in the possession of the illogical, because we do not want to be very attached to this world ... Our nation has been drastically transformed: young people come to me and ask me to ask God for their martyrdom. The same thing happens for some mothers who ask me to ask God for their only child's martyrdom ... Could one ever defeat a vigilant nation?
>
> (Khomeini 1979b)

Khomeini's slogans, particularly 'America can do no wrong [to us]!' were repeated by the newspapers, clerics, and especially IRP members such as Beheshti, Khamenei, Rafsanjani, and Raja'i[1] in their sermons and speeches. This narrative of

---

1. Ayatollah Mohammad Beheshti (1928–1981) A prominent cleric that played a key role in revolution and establishing the Islamic Republic in 1979. Founded the Iranian Republic Party (IRP) and was a Majles Member. He was assassinated in the bombing of the IRP headquarters in 1981. Ali Khamenei (b. 1939) was elected Supreme Leader (*valiy-i*

defiance and resistance against an 'arrogant oppressor' was a platform on which to create an image of the Iranian Self that was based on Islamic supremacy, intertwined in the discourse of a victorious oppressor with 'revolutionary spirit' ('*rūḥ hā-yi inqilābī*', i.e. the spirit of revolution). This spirit had pulled Iran from the 'swamps' (*lajanzār*) thereby sending 'shivers into the White House, fear into the Kremlin', and forcing Britain into a 'spiral' (*usturlāba*). Moreover, it established a dichotomy between the good Iranian Self versus an evil Other: 'Like those that followed Moses and destroyed the Pharaoh, so will they destroy the oppressor, namely the US' (Khamenei 1980e).

Operation Eagle Claw, which Carter launched on 24 April 1980, was one of the principal episodes related to the US hostage crisis, which was used to paint the post-revolutionary Iran with the brush of divinity and – according to Khomeini – draw an analogy with the Islamic conquests where God's 'invisible hand was at work' (Khomeini 1980d). The discourses propagated in newspaper editorials and sermons followed Khomeini's Islamic parallel. They discursively constructed the Iranian Self as at the centre of Islam, namely Mecca, with Carter as the infidel Himyarite king, Abraha, with his elephants (helicopters) attempting to destroy the *Ka'ba*, that is, Iran.[2] Khomeini's 'invisible hand', the sandstorm in the Tabas desert, was equated with the *Abābīl* birds that destroyed his helicopters and resulted in his demise (*Ettela'at* 1980; *Jomhouri Eslami* 1980e). In turn, Khomeini recited: 'Have you not considered [O Muhammad], how your Lord dealt with the companions of the *elephant*?' (Khomeini 1980e; *Ettela'at* 1980; *Jomhouri Eslami* 1980e; Rafsanjani 1981a).

The different Iranian discourse genres mobilized the failure of Operation Eagle Claw to highlight different aspects. The images employed strengthen the construction of the Self and the Other; the discourse used is primarily political and is intended to ease the mobilization, and bolster and embolden the Self–Other discourse. Here, they used Islamic and historical references such as Abraha, the

faqih) of Iran since the death of Khomeini in 1989 and was a key revolutionary leader representing Khomeini in his years of exile. Served as the head of the IRGC, he was elected as president in 1981 after the dismissal of Bani Sadr and was reelected in 1985. Khamenei was also a founding member of the IRP. Also a cleric, Akbar Hashemi Bahramani Rafsanjani (1934–2017) was one of Khomeini's revolutionary leaders and helped establish the IRP, served on the Revolutionary Council, and was elected Majles speaker in 1980 for two terms. Rafsanjani played a key role in Iran's foreign policy and was elected president in 1988 paving the way for post-war Iran. Mohammad Raja'i (1933–1981) was a Revolutionary and key politician, IRP member and served as second prime minister (1980) and later president in 1981. Killed in MKO/MEK terrorist attack on IRP headquarters in 1981.

   2. This relates to an attack by Abraha, a Christian king of Yemen marching to Mecca with a large army of elephants. The narrative relays that the war elephants were intended to be used to demolish the Ka'aba. However, God sent birds (Ababil) with stones of fire that destroyed the army.

Ahl al-bayt narrative and Imam Ali function to borrow from the images' associated power, allowing them to be mobilized and communicated to the audience, stressing dichotomies such as the oppressed versus the oppressor in the process. The frame was one of Iran as a nation and state resisting an aggressor, while the country was blessed with divine protection, thus making it God's chosen nation and government. Most importantly, Iran's leadership of the Islamic world was emphasized by drawing parallels with Mecca and an attack on the cradle of Islam. The representation of the Iranian Self was constructed discursively as a message to the Mohammad of the contemporary era, namely Khomeini, while an attack on Iran was juxtaposed to an attack on Mecca by a powerful aggressor, the present-day Abraha, that is the US. The implication of divine intervention served a specific purpose; an image that Iran was not just a contemporary Islamic government, while Khomeini reaffirmed his notion of Iran as exemplifying the continuation of prophetic governance and true Islamic revival. Consequently, Iranian discourse emphasized the Self in the position of Islamic leadership, in turn challenging Saudi Arabia's decades-old position as the pre-eminent leader of the Islamic world.

Moreover, the crisis was utilized even when its repercussions would result in serious consequences for Iran, such as sanctions and an oil embargo. The Iranian discourse prepared and mobilized its masses for a possible economic downturn by once again drawing parallels between the Ahl al-bayt (Family of the House of the Prophet Mohammad) and notions of jihad, independence and self-sacrifice. Imam Ali was one such figure juxtaposed with Iranian society, and the discourses of Iranians concentrated on the definition of jihad in Imam Ali's context. Ali Khamenei, then a member of the Majles and a Friday prayer Imam, held that the latter's jihad was 'one of the gates of paradise', and thus the Iranian jihad against US sanctions must take the form of self-reliance alongside Muslim unity against the enemies of Islam (Khamenei 1980f). To raise morale, Khamenei asserted that Iranians should not be like 'rabbits eaten while they are asleep', quoting Imam Ali's saying that 'By God, I shall not be eaten like a (weak) animal in my sleep' (Khamenei 1980d). This juxtaposition with the Ahl al-bayt defines the Iranian Self as the contemporary Imam Ali engaged in a struggle against the Other – the modern-day enemy of true and pious Islam.

This clerical discourse underlined the reaction of the newly founded revolutionary state to sanctions based on a relationship between the *mustaz'afin* (oppressed) and *mustakbirin* (oppressors), whereas in Iran the oppressed were 'true Muslims' and always victorious. Khamenei represented this Islamic victory as one that could only be accomplished through 'Islamic conviction', making it a glorified duty 'to sever all relations with aggressive powers' (Khamenei 1980h). Thus, the Iranian Self was represented as an oppressed 'true Muslim', fighting oppression by cutting relations with the US, thereby enforcing self-dependence because if Islamic countries were truly abiding by Islam, they would cease their dependence on 'world devouring' powers (Khamenei 1980h). The discourse of Iran fighting oppression and resisting sanctions imposed by an aggressor was employed to enhance the country's position relative to regional states such as Saudi Arabia. This stress on the narrative of the Islamic duty to fight the aggressor thus highlighted the Self as a true believer, recalling Ali and his strength and piety, and the Other – be it Saudi Arabia or other Arab states – as less Islamic, collaborating with and being subservient to the enemies of Islam.

Islamic Consolidation and Constitution: the Creation of an Absolute Islamic State Identity

The compelling metamorphosis of the Iranian state into an entirely Islamic one was extended by the Iranian constitution and the creation of the Assembly of Experts with an overwhelming IRP and clerical majority. This created an Islamic constitution with the valī-yi faqīh as its cornerstone and representative of the infallibles, the Ahl al-bayt. Furthermore, the establishment of an Iran based on an Islamic identity involved constitutional revisions, such as the mandatory article that deems it imperative for the Iranian president to be male and Shi'a while retaining an article on Islamic *fiqh* in the Sunni regions. The significance of this is twofold. First, Iran's identity was therefore not only Islamic but also based on a Shi'i-led state, i.e. a transnational Shi'i leadership. Second, the Iranian leadership also attempted to reflect a sense of fairness and equality towards the Sunni sect by allowing them to practise Islam according to their own jurisprudence. These revisions (March 1979) marked a move away from Khomeini's silence over the absence of the valī-yi faqīh rule, 'or the power which was given to the people's voice and vote as the basis of the new Islamic Republic, or the absence of the role of Islamic jurists as the guardians of the people' (Adib-Moghaddam 2014: 100) to a full implementation of the *valī-yi faqīh*. While one group argued for civil and state sovereignty within the constitution, the clerical group contended that the constitution should be an Islamic one with clear power ascribed to clerics and the *valī-yi faqīh* (*Ettela'at* 1979a).

The election of the Assembly of Experts for Constitution (*Majlis-i Khubrigān-i Qanūn-i 'asāsī*) in June 1979 accurately reflected the Islamic image of the newly founded post-revolutionary state. Numerous sermons by Khomeini, his protégés and the clerics allied with him, helped them to gain an overwhelming majority within the assembly, 79 per cent of whom were allied with the clergy (*Jomhouri Eslami* 1979a; *Ettela'at* 1979b). This substantial majority embedded the notion of an Islamic identity through the preparation of an Islamic constitution that saw the clergy and the valī-yi faqīh assume power positions with Islam at the heart and soul of the government.

Following the adoption of the new constitution the official identity of Iran was now Islamic of the Shi'i sect and with a Shi'i leadership. Not only was the religion and sect of the state officially 'Islamic Twelver Shi'ism', both the president and prime minister had to be 'practising' Shi'a. They were overseen by a *faqīh*, the central authority of the state, with clerics exercising clear dominance over the institutions of the state given that the legal system now adhered to Islamic – and specifically Shi'i Twelver – jurisprudence. An institution, the Guardian Council of the Constitution, was created to veto any law or legal article that did not adhere to Islamic principles, and they also oversaw the legislative branch, i.e. the Majles.

Accordingly, an Islamic revolutionary state with a clearly defined Shi'i identity and an exclusively Shi'i clerical and political leadership constructed an image of an Iranian challenge to the Saudi Other, particularly since the Self was constructed as anti-monarchical and that an export of the revolution was crucial in order to purify and Islamize the region. This construction of the Self during this period therefore led to an inherent definition of the Other. Given this, it can be argued that the construction of the Iranian Self naturally resulted in the construction of the Saudi Other, rather than Iranian animosity towards Saudi Arabia being the trigger for a distinctive definition of the Iranian Self.

Rivalry, the Majles, Imposed War, and Full Islamic Governance

The establishment of a 'jurist-accommodating' constitution with an approval rate of 99.5 per cent (Nohlen, Grotz, and Hartmann 2001: 72) did not mark the end of Iranian political rivalries and the shaping of the identity and image of the Islamic state. Khomeini and his protégés, especially the members of the IRP, had fulfilled their goal of enshrining Islamic law and jurisprudence within the system, thereby assuming a firm grip on the system's organs. By virtue of a 'miracle of fulfilling the goal of an Islamic revolution in less than a year' (*Jomhouri Eslami* 1980d), the left-leaning Bani-Sadr won the presidential elections, receiving over 75 per cent of the votes cast, sparking a strong rivalry with the IRP led by Beheshti.

It was clear that while the IRP respected and understood the warm relationship between Khomeini and Bani-Sadr, the IRP also emphasized the notion that they were guardians of the faith, thus upholding the tenets of Islam. The IRP chairman also attempted to meld together the image of the party with that of the state, in other words one of divinity, piety, and servitude to Islam. One instance that typifies this notion was the IRP's affirmation of 'the Imam's dictum that a cleric should not stand in presidential elections'. Therefore, by once again drawing parallels with Imam Ali's views on governance and the Caliphate, Beheshti stated that the 'presidency, state posts and positions are not worth a mosquito's wing (to us) [since] the party to us does not equate to God' (Beheshti 1980; *Jomhouri Eslami* 1980k), echoing closely the 'goat's sneeze' (*'aftat 'anz*) proverb by Imam Ali.

The IRP's emphasis on Iran's Islamic Self as a revolutionary Islamic (Shi'i) identity (*'huwiyat-i Islāmī-yi inqilābī'*) was also evident in domestic political rivalry through the relentless discourses criticizing Bani-Sadr, as evidenced by the speeches, sermons, and editorials featured in newspapers allied with the IRP. The editorials in *Jomhouri Eslami* echoed the clerical narrative that the president should adhere to the governance of the Prophet Mohammad and Imam Ali. The new revolutionary Iran's president should eradicate anti- or counter-revolutionaries and maintain the international dimension of the revolution by aiding the *mustaz'afin* against the *mustakbir* in line with the identity and image of the 'red line of Alavi Shi'ism' (*'khat-i surkh-i tashayu'-i 'alawī'*) (*Jomhouri Eslami* 1980f). The emphasis on the path of red Alavi Shi'ism reflects an image of the state's Shi'i identity. Consequently, when combining this identity with Khomeini's discourse of exporting the revolution and allegations of supporting uprisings in predominantly

Shi'a regions, this mirrors an aggressive and threatening image of the Iranian Self in relation to the Other, namely the regional Arab states.

Since the IRP controlled most of the major organs of the state and gradually consolidated power in its different branches, including the legislature (the Majles), the legal realm (the courts) and among the clerics (the Guardian Council), they felt confident enough to nominate a clerical IRP candidate, Rafsanjani, for the position of Majles speaker. Moreover, their majority also allowed them to shape the image of the cabinet as representative of the Iranian Self. These candidates were defined as 'saviours of the oppressed' and the 'fruits of the martyrs of the revolution' in relation to their revolutionary history and service to the people (*Jomhouri Eslami* 1980j). The editorial discourses in *Jomhouri Eslami* (1980j), *Kayhan* (1980) and *Ettela'at* (1980), adopted a line focusing on the Islamic identity of the Iranian state, which reflected the fact that all three newspapers were either under the control of an Islamic party or run by a cleric. The editorial advice was also offered that Islamic parliamentarians should 'visit the martyrs of the revolution' at Behesht-i Zahra cemetery once a week, and visit the '*mustaz'afīn*' in the deprived areas of the state (*Jomhouri Eslami* 1980j), thereby cultivating a cabinet that would reflect an image of resistance and Islamic sacrifice. Khomeini reinforced this image by arguing that 'even if the whole world was against us, we should do as the prophets did; like Moses opposing the Pharaoh, we should stand and defend Islam' (Khomeini 1980d). Consequently, Iran's identity was juxtaposed and aligned with that of the prophets. Friday prayer sermons also stressed the Islamic identity of the state, which was deemed to have a 'divine mandate' (Khamenei 1980b). Khamenei propagated Khomeini's narrative of prophetic imagery by assigning a divine and sacred duty to the clergy in protecting the state, arguing that 'God only knows how much responsibility and effort the clergy has accepted and applied from the beginning of this divine revolution ... We asked for nothing in return ... and one can see that when gazing at the infallible face of the Imam (Khomeini)' (Khamenei 1980b). The Majles, its members, and the cabinet would be pious *Maktabī* (one who follows Islam in its totality, see Hiro 2013: 162), of a modest background, understanding of the nature of poverty and hunger and therefore representative of pure Mohammedan Islam ('*Islām-i Nāb-i Muḥamadī*') and serving as the protector and preserver of the Quran and Islamic jurisprudence. This led to a leftist president (Bani-Sadr) with a cabinet controlled by the IRP.

Milani (1994: 176) argues that the rivalry between the IRP and Bani-Sadr was based on the difference in their 'socioeconomic, educational, and ideological backgrounds' that in turn made them 'bitter rivals, not partners' (Milani 1994). However, while class and background clearly may have influenced the relationship between Bani-Sadr and his IRP counterpart, Raja'i was only an IRP tool who allowed Beheshti (a cleric) and the IRP central committee (mostly clerics) in taking control of the executive branch of the state. In addition, the IRP worked as an Islamic collective, meeting and taking group decisions before placing them before the Majles and voting for them. Editorials in the IRP-owned *Jomhouri Eslami* (1980l) criticized Bani-Sadr's character, deeming him arrogant. The editorial characterized him as a man of 'show', equating him with the secular

Mosadegh, 'a dweller of palaces ... belittling the oppressed and modest figures' such as the Raja'i, thus defining the elected secular president as having a weak and distorted personality with classist tendencies (*Jomhouri Eslami* 1980l). Clerical voices criticizing Bani-Sadr came from senior figures in the religious hierarchy; Rafsanjani underlined his secular tendencies and class (Rafsanjani 1981f). These accusations also became common currency in IRP publications. Bani-Sadr was accused of working against the wishes of the Rahbar and the Islamic constitution by intending to appoint *munāfiqīn* (hypocrites), Western and Eastern accommodating 'liberals' and 'Marxists' instead of Muslims who could establish 'unity amongst the people of Iran' (*Jomhouri Eslami* 1980l, 1980h).

Accordingly, what occurred was an internal Othering as both groups demonized each other, a trend that was developed by the clerical axis in order to Other their enemy, whether internally or externally. Such manoeuvres were clearly aimed at cornering Bani-Sadr and parading him as a secular figure working against the Islamic character of the revolution (Raja'i 1980). He was being 'Othered' since insulting clerics and the Majles was also an insult to the constitution, which places the jurist at the top of its pyramid. Consequently, allusions were made that Bani-Sadr was insulting Khomeini himself. This resulted in calls for his impeachment, Bani-Sadr's resulting flight and exile from Iran in 1980, and the rise of the IRP to the presidency and total clerical control over Iran's branches of power, thus underlining that the clerical axis was developing a tendency to Other its enemy.

IRP Consolidation, Assassinations, and the Iranian Self

The '*Haft-iTīr* bombing (7 *Tir* or 28 June) resulted in the deaths of over seventy members of the IRP, including Beheshti, twenty-seven Majles members, and four cabinet ministers. This was followed weeks later by a second bomb that targeted the Supreme Defence Council, assassinating the newly elected president Muhammad Ali Raja'i (Bani-Sadr's replacement), and his new prime minister, Muhammad Javad Bahonar (a former education minister). Within a short space of time, the newly formed Islamic Republic suffered a series of disconcerting blows, with the clerical apparatus losing its main cadres and protégés. However, the path was arguably now clear for clerics to take matters into their own hands, consolidate power, build on the ruins of the assassinations and work towards fulfilling the grand goal – a fully Islamic state. This would be a state with a Supreme Jurist at its helm, a clerical establishment overseeing the legislative and executive branches, with Islamic networks and foundations managing society. The identity of the state was now Islamic, a continuation of the government of the Prophet and Imam Ali and preparation for the Mahdi (Khomeini 1981d), built on the blood of martyrs either during the revolution or in the early post-revolutionary phase of creating an Islamic state. Symbolism was crucial in consolidating power and reaffirming the identity of the state. Key dates in the Islamic calendar came to symbolize different occasions such as Imam Ali's birthday, which became Father's Day; the birthday of the Prophet's daughter (Fatema) became Mother's Day and an Iranian 'Women's Day'. In addition, key dates in the Iranian calendar were celebrated to remind people of the journey undertaken by Khomeini from exile to revolution, with the assassinations of notable revolutionaries such as Motahari, Taleqani and later the 'Martyrs of Haft-i Tīr' and Bahonar and Raja'i.

The assassination of key Iranian figures – especially clerics and IRP members, i.e. the 'Martyrs of Haft-i Tīr' – were juxtaposed with Islamic (and especially Shi'i) events. Iranian Friday sermons, newspapers, and speeches utilized the Karbala narrative, martyrdom, and zeal for Imam Hussein to highlight these assassinations, and to attract and motivate the masses to continue the struggle against an internal and external enemy. The number of martyrs was rounded up to seventy-two, and thus became 'Beheshti and the seventy-two companions (martyrs)', which echoed 'Imam Hussein and the seventy-two martyrs' (Rafsanjani 1981a, 1982a; Mousavi 1983). The number was used by Rafsanjani in an approximate and ambiguous manner where the words used were '*haftād wa chand*' i.e. 'seventy something' and 'more than seventy-two persons . . . that is seventy-four persons because two joined them later' in reference to the assassination of Bahonar and Raja'i. Furthermore, the editorials also repeated the trope of martyrdom. This imagery and symbolism was repeated when the atrocity was contrasted with the discourse of divinity and prophetic personas. They described the 'enemies of righteousness, and the paths of prophecy, Imam's and jurists at the end of time', who thought that by assassinating 'men with characteristics of divinity, they can (also) end humanity' (Khomeini 1981e; *Jomhouri Eslami* 1981h). The resilience of the Iranian nation was highlighted by the continuation of its struggle, since the death of Beheshti would not end Iran's path just as the 'the throwing of Ibrahim in the fire by Nimrod, or Cane had killed Abel' or the 'martyrdom of Ali as he prayed on the *miḥrāb* (pulpit), Imam Hassan's poisoning or Imam Hussein and his seventy-two companions' (*Jomhouri Eslami* 1981h) had failed to prevent the rise of the true Islamic Mohammedan path. The message highlighted here was that 'Iran is full of Beheshtis' and the internal struggle to rid the state of 'liberals, imperialists and Marxists', who aimed to destabilize an Islamic Iran would continue while the externally imposed war of 'Islam versus infidelity', the export of the revolution and the creation of the 'real Islam' would also rage on (*Jomhouri Eslami* 1981h; Ram 1994: 90).

The juxtaposition of the IRP assassinations with the Karbala narrative and the discourse of martyrdom served more than one purpose. First, it mobilized the Karbala narrative to project an image of holy and prophetic legitimacy to an Iranian domestic audience. In addition, the discourse of true Islam and the elimination of secular groups may have served as a raison d'être to project an image of defiance in relation to Western and Eastern powers and borrow a prestige based on resisting the Yazids of the era – namely the US and the Soviet Union – in order to inspire support among the regional masses. As a result, the image of the Iranian Self as embodying a state on an inevitable righteous historical path was created, inevitably defining a Saudi Other as the opposite, the Nimrod, Cane, and Yazid of the contemporary epoch. This supports the argument that although the above discourses stress the true Islam and the religion's strength and resilience, the historical images of Nimrod and the Karbala paradigm were intended to mobilize the masses, while the associated discourses enhance the images by comparing the states, leaderships, and events with the historical images employed, thereby serving both states' political agendas.

The Definition of Iran's Other

The crucible of the Iranian revolution and the formation of an Islamic state led to the manufacturing of a discourse that concentrated on a well-defined image of the Self and the Other. The Iranian Self, since the victory of the revolution, was defined by certain significant clerical actors – principally Khomeini as a defender of Islam and the saviour of the oppressed from the oppressors – and an extension of a prophetic heritage and line. That is to say, the newly formed Islamic Republic was a continuation of the fourth Caliphate of Imam Ali, and a state in waiting for the coming of the Mahdi. Moreover, the Iranian Self began with a clear definition of its Other through Khomeini's slogan 'neither East nor West'. This in turn helped to identify Iran's external enemies, chiefly the United States (including its supposed Zionist[3] and imperialistic leadership alongside its support for Israel), and the Soviet Union.

The formation of a new system of governance and constitution alongside the democratic process that the state was undergoing also gave rise to political rivalries that can be defined as an internal Other, or an internal enemy. To the clerically led IRP, the internal enemy and Other was obvious, namely all those who opposed a theocracy led by a jurist and a government overseen by a cleric. The internal Other was one of three, either a monarchist or secular American, Western, imperialist, and Zionist-backed group, or a communist of the Tudeh party supported by the Soviet Union. Moreover, it can also be argued that Iran had a 'supra-Other', namely the US and the labels attached to it such as imperialist and Zionist, that helped to create an 'inner Other' as discussed above, from which an outer-Other was derived. That is to say, there was an 'inner enemy' that emerged after the revolution and dominated Iranian discourse until clerical consolidation in June 1981 and an 'outer enemy' that was accused of aiding the internal enemy at first, but that then gradually began to have a share in Iranian discourse since the beginning of the imposed war, a trope that later dominated Iranian discourse after the IRP consolidated their control over the major organs of state power.

Crucially, while Iran 'Othered' Saudi Arabia, Iran was not affected by Saudi domestic events or incidents. The siege of Mecca or the Qatif demonstrations did not have a direct effect on discourse production in Iran. This can be attributed to

---

3. It is imperative to stress that throughout this book I do not seek to define the term Zionist and/or Zionism from my own personal perspective. The terms are employed to demonstrate how the discourse in Saudi Arabia and Iran is constructed and how their discourse constructors utilize such terms to define the Self and the Other. The mention of the terms such as and relating to Zionist, Zionism, or Israel is not an attempt to discuss the State of Israel, Judaism, the Jewish populace and beliefs, or the Jewish State.

the Iranian domestic political environment and status quo, which was dominated mainly by internal rivalries and the construction of an Islamic state. However, Saudi domestic incidents and events were utilized by Iran in propagating a regional or Saudi Other and the resultant discourse production. Nevertheless, the Iranian revolution, the imposed war, and Iranian discourse in general affected Saudi Arabia and influenced the discourse the latter directed towards Iran. Furthermore, it is worth highlighting that as the discourse genres constructed and promulgated the discourse on Saudi Arabia, they employed historical and religious metaphors and imagery. The discourses related to these images shifted in line with political events occurring in both states. The images – denigrative and pejorative as they may be – were utilized to embolden the elite narrative while allowing the more contemporary and political discourse to be associated with the images used, especially since the latter can be readily mobilized and employed in a variety of settings.

The newspaper editorials on the first day of the Iran–Iraq war framed the invasion as a war between the US and Iran (*Jomhouri Eslami* 1980a), with Iraq represented by Khomeini as a tool, a 'tail of the US' (Khomeini 1980a). The speeches by Khomeini as well as the Friday sermons by Khamenei and Rafsanjani were two-tiered. The first tier emphasized the narrative of a war between imperialism and Zionism on the one hand, with the US and its 'tails' at its helm, versus Islam and its revolution. The narrative was that the Islamic revolution should be maintained, and thus any internal enemies should be caught and handed over to the authorities, while any attempts to divide the Iranian nation should be averted. As a result, the war defined Iran's enemies in terms of an internal Other that collaborated with the US and Zionism to spread dissent within the Iranian nation, and an external enemy – namely Iraq and its associates – who were aiming to destroy Iran from the outside and thus hinder its Islamic revolution. Finally, Khomeini's discourse incorporated his views on the war and its relation to imperialism, Zionism, and hegemony. The second tier drew on the war directly. During the Iran–Iraq war, Khomeini's narrative constructed and represented the Saudi 'Other'. This discourse witnessed a shift from cordial Islamic relations and unity to implicit allusions and references, and it shifted to explicit references and denigration of the Saudi state, its clerics, and monarchy as the war progressed and relations worsened.

Rivalry Begins: Constructing Saudi Arabia as Iran's Other

The formation of the Saudi Other was gradual. Examining the different discourses by different members of the elite allows us to examine how they represented and constructed the Saudi Other, particularly since the Iranian regime during this phase was a 'top down' – or pyramid-like – hierarchical discourse-generating structure where the top set the state's direction and narrative, which were to be implemented at all lower levels. Therefore, while Khomeini 'set the stage' for Iran's foreign policy, his position was based on his Islamic leadership. This may suggest that he took on a more reserved and less confrontational discourse in relation to the Saudi Other. The focus in the discourse of the elite (namely the main state discourse manufacturers: the Supreme Leader, president, and parliamentary speaker) in Khomeini's pronouncements was on regional states that were assisting Saddam, such as Gulf sheikhdoms (*shaykh nishīnhā-yi Khalīj*), Jordan and Egypt (Khomeini 1980a, 1980b, 1981a, 1981b, 1984) with an implicit referral to the Saudi Other. While Khomeini's continual call for an export of the revolution (examples include: Khomeini 1979a; *Jomhouri Eslami* 1979b) was emphasized in Iran's immediate post-revolutionary discourse, his rhetoric towards Saudi Arabia and its monarchy was nevertheless one of brotherly peace and Islamic unity, especially in the immediate aftermath of the revolution and the first month of the Iran–Iraq war. This was exemplified by his telegrams and letters to the Saudi monarchy, Khaled, and Fahd, thanking them for their messages after leaving hospital (Khomeini 1980g, 1980f). However, while Khomeini's discourse was built on 'brotherly relations', it also propagated a tone of advice or custodianship of the Islamic world, hoping for an end to colonialism, especially in terms of relations with the United States:

My greatest pleasure would be when all the Eastern and Western colonial powers, especially the hegemonic America, end their domination of Muslims and holy Islam so they may live in brotherly love, independence and regain their lost glory.

Telegram to King Khaled 17/03/1980

It is hoped that all Muslims of the world learn from the superior teachings of Islam, end their dependence on the imperialist powers of the world, especially hegemonic America, and regain their independence.

Telegram to Fahd 17/03/1980

On the other hand, the shift in narrative and the explicit representation of the Saudi Other began with the advent of the imposed war on Iran. Through his position as Friday prayer Imam, Khamenei defined Iran's external threats and enemies as all those who aided Iraq. Less than two weeks into the war, Khamenei characterized the role of Saudi Arabia and its monarchy as a 'corrupt royal family with all their [Islamic] claims cheering [Saddam] on . . .' while he also did not shy away from asking rhetorically 'We have to distinguish who we are exactly at war with?' (Khamenei 1980a). It is therefore apparent that the first figure to explicitly represent the Saudi Other as an enemy and morally corrupt was Khamenei. Initially, this discourse was only maintained by Khamenei, who was an IRP member, the editor-in-chief of the *Jomhouri Eslami* newspaper that was owned and operated by the IRP. This marked the beginning of Saudi denigration and explicit representations of the Other, and it was carried out by a cleric who was a discourse promulgator and a close confidant of Khomeini.

Iranian editorials, mainly in *Jomhouri Eslami*, frequently criticized and attacked Saudi Arabia, publishing additional editorials that concentrated mainly on corruption in the Arab leadership in general and in Gulf monarchies in particular. The difference between these articles and the front- or last-page editorials was that they reflected the tabloid nature of the articles, especially since many were translations from leftist newspapers. The extended articles in *Jomhouri Eslami* focused on three main tropes: the debauchery and corruption of monarchs such as those in Saudi Arabia, Arab aid to Saddam during the war, and Arab and Saudi subservience to Israel and Zionism. Moreover, these articles emphasized criticism of the Saudi monarchy and connected the latter with different domestic, regional, and international events (*Jomhouri Eslami* 1980c, 1980b). This included Saudi aid for Iraq in its border skirmishes and hostilities with Iran, oil-production quotas and OPEC pricing, and earlier events such as the siege of Mecca and the Ashura uprising in Qatif, which were blamed on the monarchy and the National Guard. Except for *Jomhouri Eslami* (1979a, 1980i), an outspoken response, mainly from editorials on the incidents in Mecca and Qatif, came after a silence lasting approximately ten months. The editorials had gone as far as framing the siege as an act of Islamic heroism with Juhayman al-Otaibi represented as a 'martyr' (*shahīd*) (*Jomhouri Eslami* 1981p, 1981c). Also, the editorials depicted the incident as a response to social and economic discrimination in Saudi Arabia (*Jomhouri Eslami* 1981c). The delay in discussing this incident could have been because the Iranian newspapers, *Ettela'at* and *Kayhan* in particular, were focused more on domestic post-revolutionary political dynamics. As the dust settled, the criticism and propaganda directed at Saudi Arabia was intended as retaliation regarding the latter's military aid to Iraq. The IRP-owned *Jomhouri Eslami* were clearly the main newspaper who made extensive use of the incident.

It was not until the OIC conference in January 1981 that the representation of Saudi Arabia in all three Iranian discourse genres (media, political, and religious) was explicit. *Ettela'at*'s editorials explicitly mentioned Saudi Arabia, its leadership, and clerics at the advent of the Taif Islamic Conference. While *Ettela'at*'s main editorial (1981a) usually made brief mention of Saudi Arabia, normally in the context of discussing the GCC states, its additional editorial, *Tafsīr-i Siyāsī-yi Rūz*, engaged with the topic of Saudi Arabia, especially during the period of Saudi weapons procurement and US support for the establishment of the GCC from February 1981 onwards. *Ettela'at* attempted to answer the question 'Why does Saudi Arabia want all these weapons?' and thus framed Saudi Arabia in terms of the main trope of subservience to the West, replacing the Shah as the West's ally while 'aiding the benefits of the West' by procuring weapons from the US, France, and West Germany (*Ettela'at* 1981b). The Iranian newspapers and their editorial discourse underscores that these newspapers were highly organized propaganda machines with a multifaceted agenda aimed at 'educating' and directing Iranian society through different, purposely written editorials that focused on internal dynamics, religion, Iran's revolutionary foreign policy, and the 'imposed war'. Furthermore, the newspapers reflect their closeness to the political dynamics of the state.

This coincided with certain shifts in stance and context as the state moved towards a holistic Islamic government. In the early days of post-revolution Iran, the *Ettela'at* editorials focused mainly on the internal dynamics of the state. They covered Khomeini's speeches defining the identity of the Iranian state and the main events that were affecting the nation. However, as the war began, the coverage became more diverse, ranging from war to state identity, and covering speeches. In addition, as the state underwent clerical consolidation, so their control over newspapers such as *Ettela'at* was extended. *Ettela'at's* editorials became more aligned with the IRP-controlled *Jomhouri Eslami*, especially in their rhetoric and representation of the Iranian Other. *Kayhan*, which previously discussed Iranian dynamics in a rational non-rhetorical and neutral tone, also shifted with the departure of Bani-Sadr and the IRP's strengthened position. The paper's editorial strategy in representing the Iranian Other, namely Saudi Arabia, shifted it from being a 'centrist' newspaper to a radical leaning one, reflecting the clerical consolidation that was gathering pace. By October 1981 the editorials of all three newspapers were somewhat homogenous. They projected fixed notions of Saudi Arabia, the export of the revolution, and retaliation for Saudi assistance to Saddam, which shaped a polarized editorial representation of the Saudi Other (*Jomhouri Eslami* 1981o; *Kayhan* 1981).

Iran's path towards clerical consolidation also witnessed Rafsanjani's election as the Majles speaker in July 1980. Rafsanjani was very explicit in his narrativizing of Saudi Arabia and the GCC. In Rafsanjani's discourse, whether domestically or in the international arena, Saudi Arabia was framed in a way like that of Khomeini and Khamenei. This explicit representation was now a 'common currency', mainly reflecting Saudi Arabia's subservience to the US and Israel, and support for Iraq. Nevertheless, Rafsanjani's representation of Saudi Arabia evolved into an aggressive criticism of the morality of the Saudi and Arab Gulf rulers as corrupt debauchers who looted the wealth of the Muslim nations:

> while reactionary states associated with imperialism like Kuwait, Jordan, Saudi Arabia and Egypt do nothing but drink their nation's blood and plunder people's wealth, and [have] a long history of [plundering] oil and bread ... but, instead there is a long record of brothels, houses of debauchery and dancing ...
>
> (Rafsanjani 1981e)

This narrative was the first of its kind in Iranian discourse and one that would resonate with future tropes of immorality and licentiousness, especially in editorials. Iranian representations of Saudi Arabia gained prominence in the discourse after Bani-Sadr's exile and the election of Khamenei as president (October 1981) and the appointment of Rafsanjani as Friday prayer Imam (July 1981), as well as his role as Majles speaker. Discourse manufacture and dissemination was now in the care of two main clerics, Khamenei and Rafsanjani, both of whom were manufacturing discourse as members of the political elite. They were both close confidants of Khomeini who regularly advised them, and they both personally disseminated their discourse to the masses through Friday prayer sermons or to newspapers they controlled, predominantly *Jomhouri Eslami*. Furthermore, after the 7 Tir bombings and the later assassination of the IRP elite, including Beheshti and Bahonar, there was a vacuum in the main senior clerical cadres and among Khomeini's close confidants. This gave Khamenei and Rafsanjani a favourable environment in which to advise Khomeini on foreign-policy issues, mainly in relation to the war and regional relations.

Recovering territory and military victories in the war with Iraq were also possibly a turning point in Iranian discourse. The beginning of Iraqi withdrawal from Iran and the recapture of Iranian cities between March and May 1982 signalled a more polarized and confidant discourse towards the Other. The editorial discourse towards the war shifted from a defensive position where Iran was at war with Zionism and imperialism, to a discussion of the revolutionary state's victories (*Jomhouri Eslami* 1982c), Iran's leadership of the Persian Gulf as a 'father and protector from the greed of Great Satan' (*Jomhouri Eslami* 1982b), and advice offered to the GCC states to 'sever ties with Iraq and align with Iran' (Moussavi 1982). The latter was a discourse also propagated and manufactured by Khamenei wherein his argument was that Iran was a protector and custodian of the region while no one had 'the right to interfere in Persian Gulf affairs' (Khamenei 1983).

Khamenei's injury, and later his election as president, increased his duties and therefore paved the way for other temporary Friday prayer imams to give sermons, predominantly Rafsanjani (Algar 2011). Moreover, while other appointed imams were distinguished scholars such as Ayatollah Ardabili, the Chief Justice, or Ayatollah Emami-Kashani, they were arguably discourse propagators and not producers. As a result, the Iranian rhetorical discourse towards Saudi Arabia was amplified rather than diversified. As Iran made gains on the war front, the narrative of a superior Self and a weak or inferior Saudi Other gained prominence from the pulpit and in the newspapers. Saudi Arabia and the Gulf states were represented as weak and in fear of being 'defeated by Iran' and afraid 'of its masters' (*Jomhouri Eslami* 1982h; Emami-Kashani 1982). Iranian editorials also began to respond to denigrating narratives from Saudi editorials (*Jomhouri Eslami* 1982e). Metaphors such as *majūs* and *wathaniya* (Zoroastrian Pagans) that had featured in Saudi editorials (*al-Madina* 1982a; *al-Riyadh* 1982a) were employed in their Iranian equivalents and were regurgitated to the Iranian masses in an attempt to highlight the historic hatred the Arabs, as represented by Saudi Arabia, had for Iran, therefore underlying the historic Arab–Ajam cleavage.

Conclusion

This chapter has focused on defining the Iranian Self and Other since 1979, in the early post-revolutionary period. Iran's Othering of Saudi Arabia was naive and evidenced an inexperienced, newly founded state that did not factor in foreign-policy ramifications. Religion and sect were not particular areas of contention in this epoch. Nevertheless, a sectarian narrative was used as a tool and discursive strategy in Iranian discourse. Moreover, Iran's Othering of Saudi Arabia was directly proportional to events that took place in both states. That is to say, the analysis showed that the Iranian Revolution affected Iranian identity and allowed for Iran to construct its Other. The US hostage crisis, clerical consolidation and advances in the war permitted the Iranians to highlight the identity of a divine revolution that blossomed into an extension of Imam Ali's caliphate and government in waiting for the Mahdi.

From the previous examination of Iranian discourses between 1979 and 1983, it can be observed that these discourses were political in nature and their religious characters were based on tools and devices aimed at emboldening the Iranian representation of the Self and the Other. The religious polemics that Iran developed were tools of denigration and negative construction and representation of the Other, although they simultaneously acted as discursive strategies of positive Self-construction by using self-glorification techniques. These included the religiously orientated juxtaposition of the Self with Ahlulbayt in Iranian discourses. Furthermore, the examination of the Iranian discourse genres reveals a shift. The Iranian discourse on Saudi Arabia moved towards a negative representation, mainly after the advent of the Iran–Iraq War, a pattern of representation that gained momentum after clerical consolidation via the IRP.

Moreover, an interesting issue is that different discourse genres reveal a relationship between the discourse within Iran towards Saudi Arabia. These include the broad themes of the relationship that Khomeini pursued in defining the Other. These themes and narratives were then developed in elite discourses and were finally disseminated to the different layers of society through the production of state propaganda in the form of religious sermons or editorials in Saudi Arabia and Iran respectively. In Iran, the upper-level elite set the broad tone of inter-state relations and constructions of the Other. This was represented by Khomeini. Overall, Khomeini's discourse implicitly represented the Saudi Other. However, it was more explicit and blunter in nature in comparison with other genres, particularly in the Friday sermons, as well as the editorials and political speeches aimed at the domestic audience.

Additionally, the analysis of the discourses of Othering show that they functioned in two distinct ways, i.e. mainly through attributes of the Self and highlighting attributes of the Other, via 'building blocks' or 'interpretative repertoires' (Wetherell and Potter 1988: 171). The analysis of this timeframe witnessed three main 'supra-themes' that were regularly highlighted in the discourse of the Other by Iran. These include subservience to imperialism and Zionism, deception and a hidden agenda, and domestic and social inequality. In each of these themes, different techniques and repertoires were employed – these included the metaphors, stereotypes, and predication strategies that discursively constructed the Saudi Other. The examination of Iranian and Saudi discourse has shown that the Iranian representation of the Saudi Other predominated, with a larger number of tropes, themes, and discursive techniques overall. The Iranian discourse targeted different aspects of the Saudi Other, ranging from subservience to the West to sectarianism.

The Iranian representation of the Other began weeks after the start of the imposed war with the mention of two main supra-themes questioning the morality of the monarchy and accusing them of Zionist subservience. The tropes focused on the corruption of the Al Saud, their moral and Islamic credentials, and the plundering of people's wealth, which was then spent on debauchery and pleasures. Furthermore, subservience to Zionism and the US was represented mainly by comparing the monarchy to the Shah's regime and their submission to the US and Israel. Additionally, Iran questioned Saudi Arabia's moral and Islamic credentials. Also, Iranian discourses employed discursive strategies of representing the Other that drew on historical and Islamic tropes. The Iranian discourse employed the Prophetic narrative and Prophet Mohammad's quest to spread Islam when representing the Saudi Other. The Saudi monarchy – and especially Fahd – were identified with the infidels and Iran with the Prophet and his companions. Iran identified itself with Islam and the Ahlulbayt, and particularly with being a continuation of Imam Ali's caliphate amid associations with Karbala, martyrdom, and Imam Hussein's zeal.

As Iran was defining its new Self amid the post-revolutionary domestic turbulence and a bloody war with Iraq, Saudi Arabia was also defining the image of its Self and its Other. The Iranian revolution and Khomeini's calling for its export would resonate across the Persian Gulf to Saudi Arabia. The events of the Shi'i uprising in Qatif along with the siege of Mecca sent shivers down the kingdom's spine. It is these fears that also prompted the different Saudi discourse genres to conceptualize, construct and frame a plethora of discursive constructions highlighting the image of the kingdom and its monarchy and define its Other, Iran.

Chapter 3

SIEGE, PROTESTS, AND THE HAJJ:
SAUDI ARABIA FROM KHALID TO FAHD

Introduction

Religion and royalty have been historically closely interwoven in the Saudi kingdom. This form of 'theo-monarchical' rule has been put to the test on more than one occasion: both internally during the 1979 Siege of Mecca and externally after the fall of the Shah and the establishing of the Islamic Republic in Iran.[1] This chapter will discuss Saudi identity on both the domestic and international front, including shifts in the nature of the clergy and the position of the monarchy, the effect of the Siege of Mecca on Saudi self-image and monarchical identity, and, finally, changes in the Saudi discourse following the 1979 Iranian Revolution.

The chapter will consider Saudi (state) identity. It will consider the political weakness of King Khaled, due to his ill health, up until his death in 1982 that allowed Fahd, the crown prince, to act as the de facto ruler, hence facilitating the rise of the Sudairis. The consequences that followed the siege of Mecca will also be discussed, illustrating later changes in the Saudi image. In addition, the image of the Al Saud as the imams of the Ummah will also be examined as well as assessing the effect that this had on the internal and external image and identity of Saudi Arabia. Finally, the external image of the Saudi state – especially with regard to the Middle East, the Islamic World and the West – will be contextualized.

In addition, the Iran–Iraq War and the momentum that it created will also be discussed in relation to the Saudi Self and Other. The heavy losses on both sides in the Iran–Iraq War would usher in maritime dangers, resulting in the Tanker War, which began in 1984. This pushed Iranian–Saudi Othering to new heights. Furthermore, the issue of the hajj and its relationship to the image of the Saudi Self and Other will also be discussed in this chapter. I argue that both Iran and Saudi Arabia adopted tropes and repertoires that highlighted their competition for leadership of and legitimacy within the Islamic world.

---

1. Saudi Arabia did not submit to the different ideologies – including Nasserism and Baathism – that championed the Arab cause; nor did it manufacture its own ideology.

Khalid and Fahd

According to Niblock (2006: 47), Saudi Arabia's period of main development and economic transformation lasted from roughly 1962 to 1979, during which the monarchy and leadership consolidated their position. This change was characterized by steadier tribal and religious relations, stable oil revenue (especially during the late 1960s and early 1970s), extensive economic and social development, and the legal and institutional reform that Faisal had established during his tenure as crown prince and king. Furthermore, the Al Saud's relationship with the Bedouin tribes of Najd and the merchant families of Hejaz were also key, reflected in exceptional subsidies from the government given mainly to the tribes. However, religion was the primary basis of the legitimacy the monarchy used to buttress their leadership. This was employed both domestically and externally as the basis from which they developed and sustained their image and foreign policy. Although the ascension of Khalid did not alter the dynamics of the Saudi state, two main elements changed: the ulama's background and the rise of a faction of the monarchy, the 'Sudairi Seven'.[2] In addition, on the economic front, Faisal paved the way for the kingdom's transformation via the introduction of five-year development plans, the second of which ran from 1975 to 1980. These plans allowed the state to further depend on oil revenues.

The Siege of Mecca

Between 1975 and 1982, Saudi Arabia was ruled by King Khalid, with Fahd as crown prince and de facto ruler until he assumed the throne in 1982, ruling until 2005. Khalid was ill-equipped to run a state mainly due to lack of interest, illness, his lack of sophistication compared with Faisal or Fahd, and because he was 'homeschooled' in the palace (Cordesman 2003: 17). Consequently, in his capacity as crown prince, Fahd, who studied at the Princes' School and served under his brother Faisal in the Ministry of Foreign Affairs, acted as both caretaker and main decision-maker in the kingdom, thereby continuing Faisal's plans to develop Saudi Arabia's economy and maintain its influence in regional and international political arenas. The image and identity that lay behind the al Saud political leadership – particularly their constituting the 'Imam' of the Ummah – was called into question during the 1979 Siege of Mecca. The siege of the Masjid al-Harām occurred in November and December 1979, carried out by Juhayman al-Otaiabi and the (Saudi) Ikhwan with the aim of overthrowing the Saudi monarchy. Accusing the monarchy and especially Fahd (Cordesman 2003: 173) of 'spreading corruption' (*'intishhār*

---

2. They are the seven sons of King Abdulaziz al-Saud from his wife Hussa bint Ahmad Al Sudairi. The Sudairi Seven include King Fahd along with princes Sultan, Abdel-Rahman, Nayef, Turki, Salman and Ahmed, who are full brothers. They all held positions of significance, except for Abdel-Rahman and Turki.

al-fasād), Juhayman al-Otaiabi called on the people to rise up against the Saudi state and to cut all ties with the West, its governments and specifically Christians (*al-Nasārā*), and to eliminate all sources of social corruption and deviation (from the Islamic path), while insisting on the application of strict Sharia (al-Hazimi 2011). The latter demand appealed to the clergy's legitimacy; however, it would be the monarchy that ended up on high alert and bore the brunt of the ulama's anxiety.

The immediate press release from Ministry of the Interior described Juhayman, his group, and Mohammad al-Qahtani ('the Mahdi') as 'a coterie that has gone astray from the Islamic religion' ('*zumrah khārija ʿalā-l-dīn al-ʾIslāmī*'), 'an aggressive group' ('*fiʾatun bāghiya*'), or 'Kharijites' (*khawārij*). This was a measure to distance the state-sponsored religion and clergy from the group. Press editorial echoed this, mentioning a similar 'internal Othering' that aimed to segregate 'true from false Islam'. They were represented as an 'apostate group, the enemies of Islam' (*al-Riyadh* 1979d), and as the 'filth of Satan' (*al-Riyadh* 1979b; *Asharq Al-Awsat* 1979c) that aimed to 'undermine the great edifice from the inside after trying to destroy it from the outside'. Their actions were compared to the Arabs' contemporary enemy, Israel, thus legitimizing the use of force and sheltering the Saudi elite from any public criticism in case of deaths due to the actions of the state within the Grand Mosque. The use of force was justified by representing the militant group as having 'committed a "heinous crime", which Islamic history has still not yet witnessed', with the exception of the 'Israeli crime that aspired to burn down the al-Aqsa mosque, rather unsuccessfully, a few years ago' (*al-Riyadh* 1979c; *Asharq Al-Awsat* 1979c).

Another aim was to withdraw any source of legitimacy in the militants' cultivation of the identity and image of jihad and martyrdom. The monarchical narrative would uphold their legitimacy and image as Imams of the Ummah serving Islam and its clerics. Khalid made it clear that his orders to 'liberate' the Grand Mosque only came after the total approval of the ulama. A fatwā signed by over thirty clerics, the most notable of which was Abdulaziz bin Baz, Juhayman's former mentor, allowed the Saudi government to 'arrest and fight the group'. One interesting issue is the differences in how the militants were represented. Whereas the state had constructed them as 'straying' from Islam (or as Nayef finally labelled them, a 'corrupt junta that dissented from the Islamic religion' ('*al-tughmah al-fāsida al-khārija ʿan-l-dīn ul-ʾIslamī*') (al-Saud 1979d), the ulama were more reserved in their representation of Juhayman and his followers, labelling them as a 'group' (*al-jamāʿa*) (*Assakina* 2010). Also, the monarchy endeavoured to stop the incident from taking on an international dimension by quickly denying any link between Iran and the incident. More specifically, they prevented the incident from being described as a consequence of the Iranian Revolution, since that might affect the image of the monarchy and the state. Nayef, the minister of the interior, was clear that 'there was no relation between the US and this incident . . . there was no proof of any link between this group and Iran or any other nationality' (*Assakina* 2010), especially since Khomeini had accused '"US imperialism and international Zionism" of conspiring with the group to carry out the siege' (Khomeini 1979c).

What later ensued was a quick revamping of the Saudi image that worked in three distinct ways: internally through speeches and policies that were recast as conservative, externally through media interviews and appearances, and internally via newspaper editorials that highlighted the role of the monarchy and the state. On the domestic level, the monarchy reiterated and reaffirmed its position within society. First, the role of the monarchy was characterized as being guardians and servants of the holy shrines. In their words, this was 'the most munificent and cherished [task that] we are honoured with', expressing the monarch's gratitude to 'our dear nation for its spirit of steadfastness and understanding', while reminding the people of the position of the king as the imam of the ummah and to support and be at the service of 'the one vested with authority' ('*walī al-'amr*') in times of 'joy and sorrow' ('*fī -l-sarā'ī wal-darā*') (al-Saud 1979a; *Asharq Al-Awsat* 1979b). Additionally, the identity of the monarchy was juxtaposed with that of the Prophet and his followers, who were 'martyred for the sake of the banner of monotheism (*tawhīd*) to remain elevated and supreme for eternity'. Hence, the monarchs' position as the imams was legitimized, and they were represented as 'willing to sacrifice their blood and become martyrs to uphold the word of righteousness and eliminate falsehood, never intimated by swords, conspiracies or wars' (*al-Riyadh* 1979c). At the same time, in his capacity as minister of the interior, Nayef reiterated the same narrative of the monarchy being at the service of Islam, the holy shrines, and the king and crown prince. He emphasized that he as well as the other royal family members, such as the 'Sultan, and Fawaz bin Abdulaziz were at the scene to remedy the situation ... Prince Sultan personally took charge, and we were all striving to implement the instructions of the king and crown prince' (al-Saud 1979c).

Shifting towards a more conservative state, Fahd gave the Islamists, i.e. the ulama of Najd, the power to enforce a stricter Islamic regimen on the education system and on social practices as a whole, a development that caused the modernization ethos that Faisal had envisioned to freeze. The Al Saud had consolidated their stronghold, legitimacy and image by reinforcing a radical and conservative Islamic education system. This was achieved by standardizing the Islamic curricula in schools, which resulted in Saudi society's indoctrination and Wahhabisation from the bottom up. Also, gender segregation was established in higher education and an enlarged budget was made available to the religious institutions. These in turn gave rise to committees of virtue, similar to those set up in Iran after the revolution, known as the *Hay'at al-'amr Bil-ma'rūf wa al-Nahī 'an al-Munkar* that gave the 'police of public virtue' (*Mutawa'īn*), control over civil liberties and freedoms such as limited mobility for women unless accompanied by a *mahram*, i.e. an unmarriageable kin. Overall, these steps ensured that the monarchy had a legitimate monopoly over the state and that the partnership between the Wahhabi ulama and the Al Saud continued. As such, the monarchy made sure that in any future crisis, such as a 'deviation from the path', the Wahhabi ulama would innately protect and legitimize the state's rulers in social and religious spheres, while also strengthening the clerical presence throughout the state (Shahi 2013: 109–10; Trofimov 2008).

Externally, the principal monarchical figures such as Fahd and the foreign minister, Saud al-Faisal, gave interviews to local and international media over a one-year period with the aim of restoring the image of both the monarchy and the state, underlining their respective stability, legitimacy, and strength. The royals, once again, raced to polish up the image, identity, and legitimacy of the House of Saud. Fahd's representation of the Saudi state reflected an image of alertness and security with claims that they had been aware of the existence of 'this group and its level and competence' for six years. On the other hand, Fahd constructed an image of Saudi society as one of naivety combined with religious zeal (*al-Riyadh* 1980b).

The militant group, Fahd opined, only targeted 'simple people with a weak understanding of the Islamic faith', and the kingdom was therefore filled with 'naive people while religious fervour and piety is deeper [in Saudi Arabia] than in any other country'. The monarchy's identity was constructed as clever, worldly, and vigilant with a responsibility to 'shepherd', rule over and guide a naive and religiously humble 'flock'. The image Fahd wanted to cultivate in the international community was of a strong state unshaken by an 'ordinary naive individual that one cannot comprehend or understand if he was spoken to … with no further dimensions and depth to the incident' (*al-Riyadh* 1980b).

The state identity was defined as religious and pious with a populace that was in the service of, and revolved around, the monarchy. The legitimacy of the ulama and their strength was also highlighted as an 'independent [group] that we have no authority over', and this group was instrumental in ending the incident by 'issuing a fatwa'. Fahd and Saud al-Faisal also highlighted the winners and losers after the siege of the Grand Mosque, emphasizing how it served a certain enemy of the Arab world and of Islam in general, in relation to the Western and non-Islamic world. While downplaying the situation, they also saw it as an 'occurrence [that] is one of the most gruesome of incidents; it has been taken advantage of in the worst ways' by the West. Fahd stated that the US and Europe used and exaggerated the situation because 'they do not want to see a safe, developed, and stable Saudi Arabia… sustaining its aid to the Arab countries and especially the Palestinian people'. Like the newly Islamic Iran, the al Saud saw the US, and 'Western imperialism' as the demons that 'want[s] "us" [Saudi Arabia] to fall and suffer setbacks', because the fall of Saudi Arabia 'benefits Israel [and] the global Zionist movement and those who adhere to it' (*al-Riyadh* 1980b). This was all based around the intention to 'divide the Arab and Islamic ummah' (*Asharq Al-Awsat* 1980a).

The Iranian Revolution and Saudi Identity

While the Siege of Mecca had an immense impact on Saudi state identity, as did the Iranian Revolution in 1979, the war imposed on Iran by Saddam was its ultimate challenge since the interaction of the revolution with the war radicalized the challenges facing Saudi security. As Wilson and Graham (1994: 104) argued, an Islamic Iran not only threatened Saudi Arabia's regional status, but also its very existence. The consequences that followed the revolution led the kingdom to pursue measures that attempted to consolidate its position as a regional leader while also balancing the power of both Iran and Iraq. Saudi Arabia would employ religion, oil, and regional alliances to give itself the legitimacy and image it required to uphold its existence (Nevo 1998: 34; Wilson and Graham 1994: 104).

Although some commentators have observed that the Islamic Revolution in Iran was received with caution in Saudi Arabia (Niblock 2004: 80; Safran 1985: 357; Keynoush 2016: 105), the initial signals were of positive optimism. The overtures from the Saudi state were loud and clear. The king congratulated Khomeini after the March 1979 referendum and the creation of the Islamic Republic of Iran. The message was one of 'positive repercussions in the Kingdom of Saudi Arabia', and even though Wahhabism views the Shi'i sect as heretical, the official communiqué recognized Iran as a nation 'that abides by the Islamic Sharia through doctrine, approach and application' with Khomeini at the 'forefront of those who aspire to the victory of Islam and Muslims everywhere' (al-Saud 1979b). This was followed shortly after by Prince Abdullah praising Iran in the Saudi press and extending an olive branch based on potential collaboration: 'The new regime in Iran has removed all the obstacles and restrictions in the face of cooperation . . . since Islam governs our relationship', and a future collaboration would have an 'Islamic dynamism'. Iran was given not only Islamic legitimacy as a flagbearer but the Saudi position also demonstrated 'relief that the Islamic Republic of Iran has chosen the path of peace rather than of heavy militarization' as the basis of their new-found relationship (*Gulf News Agency* 1979).

Moreover, although Saudi Arabia had now lost a regional competitor, with Iran previously referred to as the 'policeman of the Gulf',[3] the rivalry was more a security concern than an ideological conflict. Until the revolution, Saudi Arabia had been at the helm of the Islamic world, as it had no ideological competitor. With Khomeini's call for an export of the revolution and the rhetoric that followed, this honeymoon period ended quickly. Iran now posed a threat to the Saudi state. This threat, as Niblock (2004: 79) demonstrates clearly, came in two forms: external security and 'ideological legitimacy with domestic stability'. Nothing exemplifies this dual threat more than the situation in the Eastern Province, where the local Shi'a had suffered years of discrimination. The domestic challenge for the Saudi state was due to the Iranian Revolution motivating the Shi'a and inspiring them to demonstrate, with the most notable protest being the Qatif Uprising during Ashura in December 1979, days after the Siege of Mecca.

Shi'i Instability: The Eastern Province

At the same time as the Siege of Mecca, in Saudi Arabia's Eastern Province, the Shi'a had also been affected by Khomeini's Islamic Revolution. While many observed that it was 'Khomeini's incessant call for uprisings in the name of (Shiite)

---

3. In the late 1960s and 1970s, many viewed the *Shah* as acting as the '*policeman*' of *the Persian Gulf*, in return obtaining overwhelming US support (Rosemary Said Zahlan, 2016: 144).

Islam' (Quandt 1981: 96) that led to two uprisings in the space of a few months, these disturbances were not new to the region given its history of social and religious discrimination since the creation of the Saudi state (Helms 1981: 92–94, 95–102). However, what was different this time was the rise in morale due to the nearby presence of a Shi'a state. The state reaction was harsh and relatively swift. It included the deployment of 20,000 members of the National Guard, which saw the deaths of tens and the injury of hundreds of Shi'i protestors, possibly the harshest response since the uprising of 1958 (Jones 2010: 201–2).

The rebellion came to be known as the Muharram Uprising, (*'intifāḍat Muharam*) by the Shi'i population and clergy, and it was referred to as the 'Qatif Uprising' (*'intifāḍat al-Qaṭīf*) by the secular, communist, and Nasserite-leaning groups in the Eastern Province. The uprising was a wave that allowed all those that wanted to end any form of discrimination to ride it. As al-Rasheed (1998: 122–25) argues, the protests were largely made up of ARAMCO employees and students from the University of Minerals and Technology in Dhahran (al-Rasheed 1998: 122–25). These groups threatened the al Saud since they had an influence on the economic lifeline of the state, i.e. oil, and they could penetrate and permeate local society with their speeches and narratives. This argument supports Niblock's (2004: 80) view that the 'threat was intensified by the revolution's ability to reach inside the Saudi domestic environment and affect the attitudes of Saudi citizens'.

The animosity that Khomeini and the Iranian Revolution felt towards the US had now crossed the border into Saudi Arabia. The Shi'a workforce in the ARAMCO refinery had allegedly 'chased' US employees away from a sensitive refinery according to a US consulate cable. This cable also mentioned that the Saudi Shi'a employees had been expressing 'anti-Americanism' as a result of Khomeini's broadcasts and in reaction to the Shah's presence in the US. Indeed, there is evidence that this anti-Americanism was spreading to other regions such as Qatif and Saihat (Lindstrom 1979b, 1979a). On 10 Muharram, a date that marks the commemoration of Ashura, the martyrdom of the revered Shi'i Imam, and grandson of the Prophet Mohammad, Imam Hussein, a plethora of grievances were aired. The demonstrations were anti-al Saud and not anti-Sunni. The Shi'a were protesting against the al Saud's social and religious discrimination, invoking anti-Americanism in their calls to stop selling oil to the US, and acknowledging Khomeini's call for an Islamic Revolution in their slogans 'Neither Sunni, nor Shi'i, an Islamic Revolution' ('*lā suniyya lā shī'iyya ... thawra thawra islāmiyya*') and 'death to al Saud' ('*al-mawt li-āl Su'ūd*') (Matthiesen 2010: 106).

With the Iranian Revolution casting doubt on the legitimacy of the al Saud – including their relationship with the US – and the transformation of their Shi'a nationals from Arab Shi'a into oppressed Shi'a Saudis, the latter now echoed Khomeini's animosity towards the arrogant, *istikbār* powers. As such, the grip of the al Saud over the kingdom and their leadership prestige was questioned further. Not only did Juhayman's Wahhabi Ikhwan group question the al Saud and its relationship with the infidel America in Mecca, the Shi'a in the Eastern Province also questioned this relationship with the US. However, while the Iranians were cleared of any involvement in the Mecca siege, the signs of their involvement as a part of their export of the revolution ('*sudūr-i inqilāb*') foreign policy was clearly present in the slogans used and the posters of Khomeini on display during the protests. As Khomeini declared his vision that 'we must at any expense export our revolution to all the Islamic countries and entire world' (Khomeini 1980c), al Saud understood this as an ideological struggle with Iran, one that questioned its legitimacy and image and that had national and international implications. Two main concerns arose for the monarchy: their leadership status from an Islamic and regional standpoint, and their status as a trusted partner to the US after the fall of the Shah. Also, this period's early stages offer evidence that it was a regime that had acted implicitly, versus one that showed explicit animosity represented by Khomeini's export of the revolution. Moreover, while the Saudi Shi'a may have been affected by Khomeini's call and their morale may have risen, there was no explicit sectarian dimension or animosity towards Saudi Arabia. Nevertheless, it can be argued that the Saudi state feared that Khomeini's calls would lead to the Shi'a revolting against a Sunni state in a Shi'a-majority region of the kingdom. Consequently, the al Saud had to prove their image, presence, and legitimacy as strong rulers domestically, including steering the main regional power in the Gulf, acting as an Islamic leader controlling the capital of the Islamic world, and safeguarding pilgrims under its 'protection and service', while also acting as a trusted international partner to the US.

Consolidating Saudi Arabia's Islamic and Arab Credentials

Before the al Saud consolidated Saudi Arabia's identity and image, and reinforced the legitimacy of their leadership, they first collaborated with their strongest ally, the US. As Trofimov (2008) explains, initially the CIA provided intelligence to Fahd on the possible Shi'a sabotaging of the major Ras Tanura refinery. Second, the monarchy, represented by Bandar bin Sultan, assured the US that the Shi'i uprisings would be suppressed if the US were to provide the Saudi monarchy with intelligence and disregard any human-rights abuses (Trofimov 2008: 199). What followed later was a clear strategy by the al Saud to revamp their image and legitimacy. First, the minister of the interior, Nayef bin Abdulaziz, trivialized the uprising as an act of 'temporary enthusiasm [in a] sentimental congregation' that would end immediately. In addition, Nayef's speech at the University of Oil and Minerals in the Eastern Province offered a narrative that legitimized the state, the monarchy, and the norm of Islam as the state's guide and compass. He affirmed that Saudi Arabia's security is guaranteed because 'everyone applies Islam in every matter and adheres to the ways of the pious predecessors' (*al-Salaf*), which in itself is like holding on to this 'precious gem', and keeping the peace is like the 'successors' (*Khalaf*). The kingdom's identity was defined as making up part of 'one Arab Muslim nation', with the prestige 'of being a nation honoured by God who chose his Prophet from them, and bestowed upon it and its language the Quran' (al-Saud 1980b). The Saudi leadership was therefore attempting to define the Saudi Self and affirm its regional role to both regional and global audiences. Nayef's narrative was clear: Saudi Arabia was a 'blessed' Arab nation and Islamic leader in general; one that had a specific Sunni 'Salafi' identity.

The monarchy also played down any regional ramifications that might have affected Saudi Arabia. Domestically, this was described as a normal occurrence, especially at a time when all 'the world is living in a state of turmoil and how one hears and notices what occurs every day in other countries', in a clear allusion to the revolution in Iran (al-Saud 1980b). A similar argument was made by Fahd to bolster the stable image of Saudi Arabia while downplaying the revolution in Iran as an event that symbolizes 'rocks thrown into lakes causing ripples that reach all its shores', and thus the Iranian Revolution is 'bound to leave direct or indirect ramifications'. Additionally, the identity of Islam and respect of other nations was underlined in the 'respect of the Iranian people from the early days' – this was an attempt to show the position of an important regional power that other states would not challenge. Fahd stated with cautious positivity that the Saudi state's approach is to maintain the 'best of relations with the new regime in Iran', even though there were 'abusive statements', and the Iranian ministers and officials were quick to condemn these (abusive) statements as they 'do not represent the official state narrative and that of the Imam' (*al-Riyadh* 1980b).

However, the main bid to reassert the monarchy's Islamic credentials was based on the commitment to at least partially democratize the ruling system. Less than two months after the incidents at Mecca and Qatif, Fahd announced his plans to establish a Consultative Assembly (al-Saud 1980a), yet it would be another twelve years before a Consultative Assembly would be established in Saudi Arabia.

Ultimately, the epicentre of al Saud identity and their restoration of Islamic credentials was the financial expenditure on infrastructure and support for religious activities. By early 1980, the state had allocated funding for major infrastructure projects, three of which were in the Eastern Province and concentrated on deprived and underdeveloped villages that were witnessing the main uprisings. These projects arrived after visits from the king and members of the royal family over the six months immediately after the protests (*al-Nadwa* 1982). However, the bulk of the funding went to the clergy. Along with the appointment of Najdi ulama such as al-Sheikh and Bin Baz, the ulama now had the funding to strengthen their presence in addition to attracting foreign students from other countries to spread the Wahhabi doctrine (Niblock 2004: 80).

The press also played a role in defining the role of clerics and the state. The argument centred on the role of the 'imam' as a 'revivalist that rose to see the country living in a state of neo-ignorance *jāhiliyah*' (*al-Riyadh* 1979e). Abdulwahab was exemplified as a 'man of political and military leadership with a duty that allowed him to look forward, and through his teachings achieve unity of the Arabian Peninsula under the banner of Islam' and that 'for the first time ... gave birth to an Arabian Islamic state' (*al-Riyadh* 1979e). The clerics' position was legitimized through their continuation of Abdulwahab's role, and their support for the leaders of al Saud. The local editorials legitimized the role of the ulama by defining their contribution to the formation of a strong union in the Arabian Peninsula. They were highlighted as the supporters and partners of the al Saud given their 'responsibility in consolidating this state, building and expanding its borders to create the primordial nucleus for the first Arab union, the sanctuary and rescuer that the Islamic masses had been looking for' (*al-Riyadh* 1979e). In terms of the role of the 'ulama as being silent on Westernization and supportive of the collaboration of the al Saud with the "Christians and the West"', as Juhayman had alleged, the editorials refuted this claim by demonstrating that the clerics and religion were the precursors of development. In other words, the 'cohesion between the two leaderships is enough to guarantee that religion and its clerics were never a reason for being backwards or an obstacle against development' (*al-Riyadh* 1979e), with the Holy Mosque being the model for social development. The ulama were now partners alongside the leadership, holding a clear social role that would 'protect the honour and unity of Muslims' as well as being entrusted with the state's property that would be used for future development, since 'religion supports the construction of life in a way permissible to God' (*al-Riyadh* 1979e). The efforts at securing a partnership now meant that – like Iran – the Saudi state was also experiencing a shift towards clerical consolidation. The hierarchy already matched that of post-revolutionary Iran. A king and crown prince set the broad contours of the discourse, with elite ministers who propagated and tweaked the narrative depending on the context.

Propaganda, the US, and Zionism: Keeping Up Appearances

Saudi editorials accused the 'enemies of Arabs and Islam' of implementing a campaign initiated by 'foreign news sources' that were intended to discredit the state. Western media commentaries were described as seeking to 'weaken the people's morale'; they were therefore accused of attempting to diminish the state's legitimacy through 'poisonous channels that serve their states' military and political goals', thereby giving rise to 'disputes between religious and ethnic minorities' (*al-Riyadh* 1979a). Other daily editorials, such as those featured in *Asharq Al-Awsat*, sought to 'reply to the spreading of rumours and propaganda' by quoting and referencing Nayef, the minister of the interior. However, the government intentionally asked Saudi media outlets to allow Western news agencies to continue writing because they have 'no basis and we have the truth and facts', and that 'later the lies and propaganda will blow up in their face' (*Asharq Al-Awsat* 1979a). Consequently, and using the pretext of the threat of Western media campaigns as a delegitimizing and destabilizing force in the kingdom in particular and the Gulf in general, the monarchy moved to control the media in the Gulf by centralizing and unifying the regional media. Under the guise of a conference, a meeting of Arab Gulf Ministers of Information was set up within a month of the Mecca siege.

Saudi concerns over their image were focused chiefly on Western critics. This was mainly because the image of Saudi Arabia as a stable regional and Islamic leader came into question. In this instance, the Saudi representation of the Other focused primarily on the West rather than Iran, especially since Iran was not the main attacker at this stage. However, the Saudi discourse towards the West arguably served two main purposes. First, it can be described as an attempt by the Saudi state to refute allegations made by the Saudi Shi'a and Juhayman, regarding subservience to the US. In addition, it can be seen as a Saudi strategy of mimicking the Iranian anti-imperialistic discourse against the US, thus preventing any future regional political isolation among the masses.

The results of the press conference, as observed through the statements of the Saudi minister of information, portrayed the turbulent recent events as an issue affecting the whole Gulf region (*al-Riyadh* 1979). That is to say, any sedition in Saudi Arabia would spread to all the Gulf states, and the potential fall of the al Saud would be followed by the collapse of all the other Arab Gulf monarchies. As a result, the kingdom decided to take charge and employ the news agencies to 'repel the propaganda and deception campaigns from the hostile media apparatuses that particularly of late targeted and undermined the countries of the region through careful monitoring of the regional media agencies'. This, as the Saudi media described, would also ensure that the Gulf media agencies would serve 'the development and urban development issues between the people of the region' (*Asharq Al-Awsat* 1979c; *al-Riyadh* 1979d, 1979b). Saudi Arabia now had a firm grip on the information that its nationals – and more importantly the entire Gulf region population – consumed, easing its task of restoring its leadership in both the domestic and regional arena.

Moreover, in its endeavour to consolidate its identity as a legitimate monarchy, as the imam of the ummah, and as an Islamic and Arab leader, Saudi Arabia – and Fahd in particular – was attempting to achieve a rather delicate balance. Echoing Khomeini's anti-US and anti-Israeli rhetoric, Fahd fomented a state narrative that attempted to complement the Iranian discourse of 'Zionist evil', the 'Great Satan', and 'communist infidels', while refuting Iranian allegations of Saudi subservience to the US. Fahd also endeavoured to allay the negative discourse of the Ikhwan in Mecca and the Shi'a in Qatif, while simultaneously avoiding direct confrontation with Iranian rhetoric, in the hope of calming relations with the neo-revolutionary state.

First, like Khomeini, Fahd found an enemy in the 'Zionist state'. He blamed the latter for a propaganda campaign aimed at 'corrupting our image in the minds of the Arab and international public opinion'. This also gave the monarchy a further excuse to extend its control and regulate the media. A similar move to that of the IRP and Khomeini, the Saudis now accused the media of spreading fabrications and propaganda against the Saudi regime to tarnish its image on the domestic and international arena. The Saudi aim was to 'help all those who seek the truth, for Saudi has nothing to hide', especially since they were now 'convinced that we have to change our understanding'. Fahd's new contention was to 'unveil the truth' and face the challenges they bring 'no matter how bitter' in order to 'ease' the task of journalism in its 'quest for the truth instead of neglecting it' (al-Saud 1979d). Fahd's statements may have been an attempt to alleviate international criticism of Saudi Arabia as a closed state with no freedoms. However, more importantly, Fahd's main aim may possibly have been to fill the media vacuum that Khomeini and Iran filled with their anti-Israeli and pro-Palestinian narrative of the oppressed and oppressor.

One central 'truth' was that of the plight of the Palestinian people, and the propaganda attempts to 'discredit the Saudi political stance in relation to Arab and Palestinian affairs' (al-Saud 1979d). Without mentioning or alluding to Iranian rhetoric, the Saudi narrative accused a particular 'group' of seeking to 'tarnish the image of every Arab leader or state' who had a positive role in Arab affairs (al-Saud 1979d). However, while suggesting that Fahd may have been attempting to dispel Khomeini's anti-Arab narrative by mimicking his stance against 'Global Zionism', Fahd also identified Saudi Arabia as victim of a defamation campaign that could only be cleared through 'entering the media arena', thereby highlighting the role of the kingdom and its domestic and international politics. As he continued, 'However, when we fall subject to rumours and inventions and mistakes we did not commit, we shall not stay silent, we shall defend'. Saudi Arabia was clearly signalling its shift from a passive to an active player in the regulation of state, regional, and international media (al-Saud 1979d). Moreover, Fahd's narrative was a mirror image of the Iranian discourse, aiming to represent the Saudi state, much like Iran, as a victim of hegemonic propaganda. Like Iran, Fahd's narrative of disclosing the truth aimed to propagate a narrative of resistance to the enemies of Saudi Arabia, defined by the Zionist state, which were also represented by Fahd as the enemies of Islam. Consequently, the Saudi discourse was primarily aimed at matching if not complementing the Iranian discourse towards Israel and the enemies of Islam, signalling an air of regional and Islamic rivalry and competition in their discourse.

Saudi Arabia's leadership role in the Islamic and Arab worlds was highlighted further by their once again echoing a Khomeini-like narrative of 'Neither East nor West', albeit in a rather less antagonistic fashion. It can be argued that Saudi Arabia's discourse reflected the efficacy of Khomeini's rhetorical statements. The Saudi image of Islamic leadership was possibly also at risk of being overshadowed by Khomeini's hard line. Consequently, the representation of the Saudi Self as a mirror image of the Iranian Other, i.e., as opposed to US hegemony, or for instance the Soviet invasion of Afghanistan, was crucial in preserving Saudi legitimacy and their image of Islamic and Arab leadership.

Iran did not attack the legitimacy of al Saud or Saudi Arabia during this period (March 1979 to June 1981) and the former's rhetoric was focused on the US and Zionism, the oppressed and the oppressor. Iranian discourse also engaged with the 'US hostage crisis', and domestic rivalries such as the Bani-Sadr and MKO[4] rivalry with the IRP, the former being represented as an internal enemy serving the interests of an outer enemy, namely the US, imperialism and Zionism. Saudi Arabia's rhetoric, however, was focused more on the Soviet invasion of Afghanistan, the Yemen war and Arab–Israeli affairs. While the Saudi monarchy criticized Israel and its stance towards the Arabs, Fahd's rhetoric on Islam's enemies and Israel's supposed attempts to undermine Saudi Arabia was first observed in his speeches after the siege of the Grand Mosque in Mecca.

4. The Mojahedin Khalq Organization, a militant oppositional group designated by Iran as a terrorist organisation and described by the UN as being "involved in terrorist activities". See Crane, Keith; Lal, Rollie (2008). *Iran's Political, Demographic, and Economic Vulnerabilities*. Rand Publishing.

Soviet advancements in Afghanistan were acknowledged as a threat by Saudi Arabia, especially as the Democratic Republic of Yemen had established close ties to the Soviet Union and had signed the Aden Treaty Tripartite Alliance, known as the Aden Pact[5] (Malik 1990: 246). Fahd's narrative, which was set out from the perspective of an 'Arab leader', approved of 'an Arab regime benefiting from the aid supplied by a superpower'. However, and mimicking Khomeini's dismay, there was a need to consolidate an identity of self-reliance and independence such that 'one should not give commitments (to superpowers) since they are not in favour of their [i.e. the Saudi] regime or their neighbours'. The notion of colonialism and its impact on Arab states and the Orient was emphasized, resonating with revolutionary Iran's discourse on the fight against post-colonialism and 'not allowing it the opportunity to return' (al-Saud 1979d, 1980a). The narrative of the self-reliance and independence of Arab states propagated included an emphasis on education, development, and knowledge. Like the Iranian discourse of educational independence and the development of an Islamic nation with Iran at its forefront, Fahd's narrative echoed a similar message. However, it was one based on an Arab identity, unity and self-reliance, similar to an argument made by Saddam Hussein in his speeches (Esposito and Voll 1996: 56–58). Fahd argued that '(we) as Arabs have scientists and specialists whether in Arab countries or abroad and we could benefit from their expertise' (al-Saud 1979d). Addressing a similar narrative to Saddam, Saudi Arabia conveyed a multifaceted definition of the Saudi Self. First, it defined its Arab Self, where it sought to project an image as the unifier of Arabs. Second, an image of independence from superpowers was highlighted like Khomeini's 'neither East nor West' policy. Finally – and again like Khomeini – Fahd sought to highlight the Saudi Self as being at the forefront of Islam and the fight against 'global Zionism'.

Defining Saudi Arabia's Other

Somewhat similar to Khomeini, the king and crown prince of Saudi Arabia set the parameters of the relationship between Saudi Arabia and other states. Unlike the Iranian elite, it is possible to split the Saudi higher orders into two layers, namely the king and crown prince in one layer, and the leading ministers in the other,[6] as all the positions under the crown prince complemented each other. Therefore, both layers' discourse production is similar if not at times identical to one another.

5. Libya, South Yemen and Ethiopia formed the Aden Treaty Tripartite Alliance in 1981; it included a joint defence commitment (Military Balance 1986). For a more extensive discussion on Soviet-Yemen relations see Malik (1990).

6. The leading ministers include the two deputy prime ministers: first deputy prime minister and minister of interior, second deputy prime minister and minister of defence, and the minister of foreign affairs.

Although he was the king of Saudi Arabia, Khalid was in power until 1982, and so the main tasks related to governing the state were handed over to the crown prince, Fahd. Like Iran, Saudi Arabia also applied a 'top-down' pyramid-like hierarchy of governance that also reflected its discourse construction. While the king and crown prince sketched out that main direction of the state and its identity, the main ministers 'filled in' and 'coloured' the sketch. The king and crown prince took a more implicit tone in their discourse, leaving the ministers to take an explicit narrative. Moreover, discourse production in Saudi Arabia was based on three main approaches: first, setting out and sketching the main foreign-policy guidelines of the state; second, highlighting a Saudi identity as an Islamic and Arab leader; and, finally, placing an emphasis on taking a benign and neutral stance towards intra- and inter-Arab and Islamic affairs, combined with a staunch position on Western affairs towards the Islamic and Arab world, predominantly as concerns Arab–Israeli affairs.

At the start of Iran's post-revolutionary period, the Saudi public narrative and tone towards Iran was positive in overall terms, with narratives based on themes of Islamic brotherhood, neighbourliness, and potential future cooperation. This position was reflected by Fahd in his speeches, press conferences and interviews. One such position was framed around Fahd's 'respect for Khomeini's convictions ... we will not change our perspective on him' (Lawzi 1980). However, private telegrams and memos arguably presented a different image. Fahd's position was that 'what is happening in Iran is dangerous for Islam and Muslims; it is a chauvinistic revolution that threatens the region ... what is happening in Iran is not Islamic ...'. Furthermore, his stance on the Shah's rule was that, 'We support every regime that exhibits legitimacy in its country, and this legitimacy applies to the Shah's regime' (al-Kawaz 2014: 23–24).

Similarly, with the advent of the war, the Saudi monarch and crown prince also observed highly distinct public and private positions. The public narrative was that the 'Iran–Iraq war should end immediately', and that it is a 'great loss for both the region and the Islamic Ummah'. The second was that the Saudi position was not a personalized one against Iran, but 'part of a collective Arab standpoint'. However, in private calls and memos released by the royal court, for example in September 1981 in telephone calls to Saddam, the king maintained that 'We are with you in the past and present, and we are with you in your just war to retrieve your stolen land and right to enforce your legal and total sovereignty over [the territory]' (*al-Ahram* 1980; *al-Jazira* 1980).

The Saudi editorials printed between 1979 and 1983 reflected three main themes. The first included coverage and analysis of national and international accomplishments, visits and speeches by the royal elite, including the king, crown prince and ministers of the interior, defence, and foreign affairs. Second, the editorials covered regional Arab and Islamic affairs, including the Palestinian and Israeli issues, the Lebanese civil war, the Afghan–Soviet war, and Saudi Arabia's stance on these questions. Finally, the newspapers covered Iran, and from more than one angle. The topics covered mainly included the Iran–Iraq war, the hajj, the export of the revolution and Iranian expansionist aspirations in the Persian Gulf.

In the discussion of the images used to construct Iran as the Saudi Other, it is important to highlight that the images were used to demonize the newly formed Islamic Republic. In other words, the employment of dehumanizing strategies, denigrating nicknames, and the victimization of the people by the Iranian state was a discourse grounded in using easily mobilized images to sway Saudi and Arab audiences.

The format of Saudi editorials in the period between 1979 and 1983 followed a broadly similar pattern in all three newspapers, all of which – except for *Asharq Al-Awsat* – published one daily editorial that concentrated on a single theme, while the difference was in the given article's length. In addition, except for *al-Riyadh*, the newspaper editorials were short, unless the editorial covered an event or topic related to the king or crown prince. Furthermore, the difference between the newspapers was their individual target audience and the explicit or implicit tone used to discuss a theme, especially with regards to Iran.

Asharq Al-Awsat and *al-Riyadh*'s editorials discussed Iran from the onset of the war (*al-Riyadh* 1980a; *Asharq Al-Awsat* 1980b). *Asharq Al-Awsat*'s discourse and therefore its representation of Iran was less rhetorical and polarized than that of *al-Riyadh* and *al-Madina*, mainly because of its international focus. Nevertheless, the *Asharq Al-Awsat* articles led to a shift in Saudi representations of Iran. Although the articles were to some extent skewed in favour of Iraq, the overall message at the beginning of the war anticipated 'peace between two Islamic neighbours'. However, as Iran made battlefront gains, the depiction of the Iranian Other shifted to a polarized discourse. This intensified from March 1982, coinciding with the liberation of Khoramshahr and the beginning of the Iraqi retreat (*Asharq Al-Awsat* 1982). The *al-Madina* and *al-Riyadh* editorials on the other hand were aimed at a more locally orientated audience. Covering the events from the beginning of the war, *al-Madina* reacted to both the Iranian advances and governmental press releases relating to the military front and Rafsanjani and Khamenei's rhetoric towards Saudi Arabia and its monarchy. On the other hand, *al-Riyadh* discussed Iran in its editorials from November 1981, after Iran began to make significant gains on the battlefront, such as retaking the city of Abadan.

The Saudi editorial discourse witnessed two main strategies, or 'supra-strategies' when representing the Iranian state. These included delegitimizing and dehumanizing (supra) strategies. Each would encompass different techniques to identify the Iranian Other or the Saudi Self within the discourse. The editorials attempted mainly to delegitimize the Iranian Other by criticizing the Iranian state and revolution. That is to say, the first approach taken by the Saudis was divide the people from the state by arguing for the victimization of the former by the latter, a similar strategy to that undertaken in Iranian discourse (Khamenei 1981b). The second and more significant approach was the employment of descriptive nominations and referential strategies, i.e. denigrating 'nicknames' such as the 'Government of the Signs (of God)' (*Hukūmat al-'āyāt*) (*al-Riyadh* 1981b), which belittles the status of the *'Āyatu 'Alāh'* (the sign of Allah) to a nickname 'the signs' (*al-'āyāt*). The newspapers *al-Madina* and *al-Riyadh* also aimed to highlight the illegitimacy of the Iranian regime and its revolution. The Saudi discourse focused on the Iranian Revolution as 'fake' with 'fake slogans', in other words developing a narrative aimed at denigrating Khomeini. Saudi editorials framed Khomeini as inept in terms of his Islamic scholarship and the Iranians as a naive nation deceived by 'Khomeini's brand of Islam', which did not adhere to the principles and teachings of the Sunnah and also used 'narrow-minded slogans'. Therefore, Saudi editorials resonated with a discourse based on weak Iranian governance and the victimization of the 'Iranian Muslim nation' (*al-Riyadh* 1981b; *al-Madina* 1982b). The Saudi editorials also called on the Saudi and Arab reader to inculcate a distinction between the state and the people, for as one editorial argued, 'the Iranian people are not Khomeini or the Revolutionary Guard. Iran is a nation of 35 million Muslim males and females' (*al-Madina* 1982). They took the strategy of highlighting the falsehood of Khomeini's Islamic narrative, while simultaneously showing the Islamic nature of the people and their victimization under the tyranny of a 'fake Islam'. The Saudi discourse, therefore, aimed to communicate a clear message; the Saudi Self identifies with the Iranian nation, but not with its non-Islamic leadership.

The delegitimization strategies employed by the Saudi editorial discourse also reacted to Iranian rhetoric directed at Saudi Arabia, such as supposed Saudi collaboration and subservience to imperialism and Zionism. This was particularly visible in a novel editorial in *al-Madina* (*al-Madina* 1981e), which was aimed specifically at fending off Khomeini's harsh criticism (Khomeini 1981h) and Rafsanjani's Friday prayer sermon (Rafsanjani 1981c). It also responded to the Iranian clerical discourse aimed at Fahd's peace plan for Arab relations with Israel. The Iranian Other was clearly defined. The clergy were summed up as 'foul examples of frivolity and stupidity ... following the path of Satan, the path of insults, on a blessed Friday'. Their manners were defined as un-Islamic and 'polluting people's ears and desecrating a great Halal Muslim festival' (*al-Madina* 1981e). Furthermore, the un-Islamic nature of the Saudi Other also defined Khomeini as an enemy to Islam and Saudi Arabia, especially since:

> the Supreme Leader and his followers apply barbaric manners that are as distant to Islam as could be ... but more than that ... it is the manner in which the ruling regime in Iran treat our Muslim brethren around Iran that does not relate to Islam or to the tenets of brotherhood, or national dignity.

On the other hand, the Saudi Self was simultaneously defined through a strategy that rhetorically asked 'Why does the Iranian regime resent the Kingdom of Saudi Arabia? And the king of Saudi Arabia? And the Saudi Peace Plan?' By employing a question-and-answer strategy, the Saudi Self was defined by describing the Saudi Other. The Saudi discourse defined Iranian resentfulness in one phrase, 'spiteful or malevolent' (*ḥāqidūn*) and asked 'Why are they spiteful?' The answers highlighted Saudi international prestige and Islamic leadership and relations since 'no one listens to or respects them (Iran) [but] all the Islamic world ... respects and appreciates Saudi Arabia and its rational voice'. The Saudi prerogative and motivation behind the Peace Plan was therefore defined as an 'Islamic goal ... to attain dignity for the Palestinian people ... in a logical and rational manner', whereas an un-Islamic Iran aspired to hinder Fahd's plan out of spitefulness and hypocrisy 'especially since their war efforts could have been spent on liberating Palestine rather than insulting Saudi Arabia and its initiatives' (*al-Madina* 1981e). Therefore, the discourse represents a narrative of Iranian hypocrisy symbolized by Khomeini's 'fake slogans' of Palestinian support, anger, and frustration at Saudi Arabia's prestige of Islamic and Arab leadership. These narratives of hypocrisy and contestation over the Arab and Islamic leadership continued as both countries took their rivalry to the hajj, with attempts at mutual Othering.

Contesting Legitimacy and Leadership: Iran and Saudi Arabia and the Hajj

The hajj season was also utilized by Iran to export its revolution and extend its 'public relations' work to include other pilgrims from around the globe. The demonstrations of 1981 were the first occasion witnessing a direct confrontation between Iranian pilgrims and Saudi security forces. The confrontations may have been linked to developments in the Iran–Iraq war, especially after Saudi support for Iraq increased, mainly as a response to fears of Khomeini's increased emphasis on exporting the revolution (Marschall 2003: 50). The demonstrations began at the Prophet's Mosque in Medina with conflicting reports emerging about the incident. The Iranian narrative linked the demonstrations to an act of retaliation against the arrest of two Iranians for embracing and reading supplications at the shrine, which the Saudis denied through a response issued by Nayef, the minister of the interior, who attributed the incident to an attack on Saudi police (al-Saud 1981e).

The Saudi press compared the Iranian pilgrims to 'saboteurs and criminals', equivalent to those that 'King Abdulaziz put an end to in an era of looting and chaos that ended with his reign' (*al-Madina* 1981d). The Saudi editorials refuted the Iranian narrative, stating that it falsely propagated claims in order to stir up a media war between Islamic states (*Asharq Al-Awsat* 1981a). However, the Saudi line, as an immediate reaction to the incident, sought to differentiate between the Iranian people and Khomeini. This was an attempt to represent the Iranian people as religiously naive, oppressed, and misled by Khomeini. The Saudi discourse showed sympathy and offered compromise to Iranians, yet it was harshly critical of the regime and of the 'divine demagogue-like figure' in a reference to Khomeini. The Saudi discourse directed blame at Khomeini for 'encouraging his people to disturb the peace at God's holiest sites by praising him as they do prophets and messengers', labelling the Iranian state as 'Khawarij', i.e. as an Islamic sect who were not spreading Islam but were rather 'exporting chaos and political crises outside its borders' (*Asharq Al-Awsat* 1981d). This was invoked while quoting Nayef's statements that 'the hajj season is a season of worship which cannot be exploited for any acts of religious, political and ideological calling' (al-Saud 1981e; *al-Riyadh* 1981e).

The demonstrations continued in Mecca, where more pilgrims were arrested. An exchange of letters between Khalid and Khomeini followed, with the former expressing his dismay at the Iranian pilgrims' demonstrations as constituting actions 'that are incompatible with the status of the Iranian people' (al-Saud 1981c). The reply from Khomeini was a clear denial of any un-Islamic intentions, but he did emphasize that both holy sites at Mecca and Medina were political Islamic centres. Khomeini's remarks clearly affirmed the notions of 'liberation from infidels' (*barā 'at az mushrikīn*) and the 'unity of Muslim society' (*wahdat-i Muslimīn*), which he argued were upheld as the Islamic duties of the hajj in Mecca and Medina respectively. Khomeini's reply also took aim at the role of Saudi Arabia in the Middle East and its acquisition of US weaponry, principally the Airborne Warning And Control System (AWACS). Khomeini charged that the role of every Muslim was to demonstrate against 'the enemies of Islam, US and Israel and Imperialism', underlining that the 'US has put the AWACS at the Saudi's disposal to serve its interests and those of Israel' (Khomeini 1981e).

The Saudi position on the AWACS and on weapons deals in general was reflected in and depicted as a manifestation of the struggle and competition between Arabs and Zionism. It was not, as the Iranians had proclaimed, at the service of Israel, Iraq, or under US control. Painting the US's hesitance in selling the AWACS to Saudi Arabia as a Zionist conspiracy, the Saudi media promulgated the narrative of a war against Islam and the Arabs in the US Congress. This sounded similar to Khomeini's pronouncements and the Iranian editorial discursive trope of a Zionist conspiracy. Their discourse asserted that the deal's potential failure would be reflected in the US's weakness vis-à-vis Israel and the latter's lobbying influence in Washington. In contrast, the eventual approval by US Congress of the sale was understood as a win for all Arabs, and thereby as an affirmation of the discourse of Arab leadership. The approval was constructed as the US 'keeping a promise and pledge made to the kingdom', and therefore, preserving a friendship with the Saudis that equalled a 'friendship with the Arabs' (*al-Madina* 1980). Thus, the Saudi discourse was also a response to Iranian claims and its narrative of subservience to the US and Israel; the Saudi discourse interpreted Saudi Arabia not as a servant of the US but as a regional leader.

However, a more direct response ensued after the hajj of 1981, equating Iran to Israel and accusing Iran of collaborating against Saudi Arabia. Prince Sultan, the defence minister, attacked Iran harshly, labelling it a 'bloodthirsty nation that supported the Jewish regime in its rabid attacks against Saudi Arabia in the name of Islam' (*al-Madina* 1981g). Sultan's argument started a wave of criticisms and accusations of 'Iranian hypocrisy under the guise of supporting the *mustaz 'afin*' (*Asharq Al-Awsat* 1981b), i.e. the Palestinians. This was accompanied by jealousy because of the 'amazing results that Saudi diplomacy and politics delivered with the AWACS purchase and the international praise it received' (*al-Madina* 1981a). Consequently, the Saudi reaction resulted from the Iranian state and clerical narratives, coupled with Khomeini's calls to export the revolution. This led in turn to the hajj demonstrations that challenged Saudi legitimacy. On the Iranian side, its anti-Saudi narrative was based on Saudi Arabia's support for Saddam Hussein, the Saudi lowering of the price of oil, and Iran's claim to leadership of the Islamic world.

Three months into the war, Arab support and aid to Iraq became obvious. Although this aid was heavily criticized and discussed in the Iranian political and clerical discourse, the Iranian editorials (*Jomhouri Eslami* 1980b; *Ettela'at* 1981b) – especially *Jomhouri Eslami* – initially focused on the details of US weapons sales to Saudi Arabia and its aid to Iraq. Saudi collaboration with Iraq against Iran was represented by the loan and later procurement of four AWACS planes. The editorial emphasized the role of Saudi Arabia as a vanguard of Saddam's interests in the war against Iran and the Iranian revolution through sharing sensitive information collected by US AWACS planes in the Persian Gulf region. The editorials framed Saudi Arabia in three ways. These frames focused on subservience to US imperialism and its hegemonic aspirations, aid to Saddam in his war against Iran, and a takeover of the Shah's role in procuring weapons from Western states out of fear that the Saudi monarchy might fall just as the Shah had, through a populist revolution (*Jomhouri Eslami* 1980b; *Ettela'at* 1981b).

One of the very rare occasions in which Khomeini referred explicitly to the Saudi leadership was during the hajj incident of 1981. In a letter responding to King Khalid (Khomeini 1981e), Khomeini articulated three main referential constructions. First, he depicted the Saudi government as corrupt, asserting the illegitimacy of the Saudi ulama, and indicating that the king was weak by dint of his being unaware of domestic affairs. Second, Khomeini explicitly referenced Saudi officials as agents of deceit who were hiding facts from the king. Finally, Khomeini conceded that Saudi Arabia was at the centre of the Islamic world and cooperation was therefore a necessity. Khomeini's response was not published in the Saudi media, and therefore, the exact form of retaliation to the letter cannot be evaluated. However, it can be argued that the letter's repercussions were an extension of Saudi representation of the Iranians as saboteurs and Kharijites on the one hand, and chaos-causing troublemakers intent on disrupting the spiritual journey of other pilgrims on the other.

Khomeini cast doubt on the honesty and professionalism of Saudi officials and the ulama. In turn, his characterization of the Saudi monarch was of a figure who had appointed corrupt officials and who might be deceived into believing that the Iranian Self was corrupt and the slogans chanted by the Iranian pilgrims were 'distorted' *(tahrīf shudih)*. Khomeini also impugned the legitimacy of the Saudi ulama, by questioning their Islamic teachings and knowledge of the Prophetic traditions. According to Khomeini, the Iranian slogans against Israel and the US conformed to the teachings of Islam, and the hajj was a political occasion that ensured the lifting of the Muslim people's oppression, as well as being an occasion to denounce the looters of their wealth. Therefore, the actions by the Saudi state and the ulama were constructed by Khomeini as contradicting and acting against the path of 'all the prophets, especially the Prophet Mohammad', questioning the knowledge and legitimacy of Mohammad's teachings (*Jomhouri Eslami* 1981l).

Khomeini's second explicit construction was of the Saudi officials as agents of deception and suppressors of facts, with Khalid's strength as a ruler also called into question. Khomeini asked the Saudi monarch explicitly if he knew of the 'atrocities occurring in the two holy mosques', in a statement that grounded notions of naivety, ignorance, and assault on Muslims in a place of divine sanctity that was 'next to the Prophet's grave'. The Other was constructed as a naive king who had 'demonstrated matters to you in a wrong and misguided manner'. Consequently, the Iranian Self was constructed by Khomeini as the exact opposite of the Saudi Other, constructing the Self as a liberator of the Islamic states from superpower subservience, thereby 'bringing the Muslims of the world under the flag of unity, totally committed to progressive Islamic laws … reintroducing the glory of Muslims in early Islam' (*Jomhouri Eslami* 1981l). Moreover, Khomeini's narrative also implicitly represented the Saudi Other as being influenced by a corrupt clergy that sought – and had achieved – control over the Saudi leadership, as represented by the king. This highlights another implicit narrative, that of Khomeini questioning the al Saud's suitability and the leadership of Mecca and the two holy mosques.

The implicit narratives and framing would not last long. The Iran–Iraq war would gain momentum, with heavy losses on both sides, but especially for Iran. The war would usher in maritime dangers, mainly in the Persian Gulf region, resulting in the Tanker Wars beginning in 1984. This would push Iranian–Saudi Othering to new heights. The hajj issue would arise again in 1987, with hundreds of Iranian lives being lost on this occasion, amid an exchange of accusations on both sides, a severing of diplomatic ties, and a three-year Iranian boycott of the hajj.

Chaos in Mecca: the 1987 Hajj and the Severing of Ties

Torn by a long war with Iraq, an incident in Mecca on 31 July 1987 resulted in the death of 275 Iranian pilgrims, with scores more injured. The audience sought an explanation for what had occurred, as images showed bullet-riddled bodies being broadcast on Iranian screens. The next day, protests on the streets of Tehran led to an attack on the Saudi and Kuwaiti embassies. Conflicting reports came from both sides, Iranian and Saudi, as to the reason behind the attacks. Furthermore, different scholars have suggested different reasons for the protests. Alnahas (2007) argues that Riyadh blamed Tehran for the outbreak of clashes as the Iranians attempted to seize the Grand Mosque and challenge al Saud's leadership of the Islamic world by declaring Khomeini the leader of the Muslim world. However, Kramer (2009), on the other hand, argued that there was a direct relationship between the Iranian protests and the US presence in the Persian Gulf to escort Kuwaiti tankers.

On 3 July 1987, Khomeini's former hajj representative, Khoiniha, gave a speech discussing Kuwait's decision to invite foreign navies to escort its tankers. In his speech the cleric argued that in this hajj season, 'a mere march or demonstration will not suffice' and that the Rahbar's representative should be allowed to 'conduct a referendum among the pilgrims over the emir of Kuwait's decision', asking that 'the Saudi government neither oppose this, nor send its guards to the Great Mosque. Let us see what happens' (Mousavi-Khoeiniha 1987). Nevertheless, Khomeini's instructions in his annual hajj statement two days before the pilgrimage ran contrary to Khoiniha's speech. The pilgrims were instructed to 'avoid clashes, insults, and disputes', and a stark warning was issued to those intent on disrupting the ritual and 'who might embark on spontaneous moves' (Khomeini 1987a).

However, on 31 July, tensions ran high as the Iranian pilgrims – as per their annual ritual – chanted slogans denouncing the US, Israel, and arrogance, such as 'Death to America, Death to Israel, Death to Arrogance (*Istikbār*)'. The clashes resulted in both a human cost and strained relations leading to a further low point, producing discourses in both Saudi Arabia and Iran that asserted Islamic legitimacy, leadership, power, and influence.

The Blame Game

In a first response from the Saudi Cabinet of Ministers headed by King Fahd, a statement was read by the minister of information, Ali al-Sha'ir, as a strategized response to the incidents (*SPA 1987*). First, it framed the incident as a cause of Iranian disrespect for the sanctity of the Holy Mosque, Saudi regulations, and Sharia law. The incident itself was represented as a criminal act because the clashes were blamed on the 'mob acts of some Iranian pilgrims' that 'contradict the teachings of the noble religion', Islam (*SPA 1987*). Second, the Saudi discourse attempted to counter the Iranian narrative of the events, going as far as vilifying the Iranian pilgrims. In their statement, the Saudi cabinet described the Iranian description of the events as fabricated, arguing that the demonstrators were responsible for harming the innocent, and representing the Iranian demonstrators as deviant Muslims who were apprehended in their efforts to disturb and storm the Holy Mosque (*SPA 1987*).

Third, the Saudi discourse emphasized the image of the Saudi Self (primarily the monarchy) as a responsible Islamic leader and 'honoured by God with serving the two holy mosques ... devoted with all its material and human resources to serving the pilgrims' (*SPA 1987*). In essence, given the number of deaths and casualties, especially those associated with a major Islamic country such as Iran, Riyadh was now worried about the image of the Self and its monarch as the Custodian of the Two Holy Mosques and as leader of the Islamic world. Consequently, the statement emphasized that the king is 'dedicated to providing the pilgrims' satisfaction, security, and safety', in an explicit affirmation of Saudi Arabia's image of generosity and service to its Muslim guests (*SPA 1987*). The image of the Saudi Self came also at the expense of its Other, Iran. Given the number of Iranian pilgrims dead and injured in the clashes, the Saudi discourse aimed to represent their relationship with Tehran as one based on tolerance, Islamic kinship, eliminating any image of enmity towards Tehran. The cabinet's statement explicitly stressed that Riyadh had 'spared no means of attempting amicable understanding or Islamic cooperation' with Tehran (*SPA 1987*). However, the Saudi discourse also represented Riyadh's tolerance as a source of its strength which 'in many cases was due to confidence in God and ourselves and above all the safety of two million hajj pilgrims' (*SPA 1987*). Therefore, while highlighting a Saudi image of the Self as a responsible, tolerant, generous, and hospitable Islamic leader, Iran was inherently constructed in the Saudi discourse as lawless and disrespectful of Saudi and Islamic laws, and as having endangered the lives of Islamic pilgrims for the sake of advancing its 'revolutionary agenda' (*SPA 1987*).

It is exactly this statement that led the Speaker of the Majles, Akbar Hashemi Rafsanjani, to lead protests in Tehran and to give a fiery sermon that not only demonized Saudi Arabia and its monarchy but also highlighted Iran's position as a revolutionary power on the international stage as the most notable Iranian response (Rafsanjani 1987).

Rafsanjani's speech was strategized to first define Iran's role in the incident, distancing it from any Saudi allegations of domestic interference, malevolence, and disruption of the hajj. In essence, it was an explicit counter-narrative that pushed back against the Saudi official statement released immediately after the incident. While Rafsanjani's speech was elaborate in how it discussed and countered the Saudi statement against the Iranian pilgrims, the speech primarily attempted to answer one main question that was lingering in the minds of many Iranians protesting on the streets of Tehran: 'Why were the Iranian pilgrims targeted in the Mecca?' (Rafsanjani 1987)

Initially, the official Iranian discourse, articulated by Rafsanjani, framed the incident as a revenge and face-saving measure by the 'oppressed powers' and their 'perpetrators' in response to a series of 'humiliations' suffered by the US in the Persian Gulf (Rafsanjani 1987). These 'humiliations', as Rafsanjani argued to his audience, included America's 'disgraceful defeat . . . in the Persian Gulf' in the 'saga of the USS frigate Stark' (Rafsanjani 1987) that was struck by Iraqi jets on 18 May 1987 as they escorted Kuwaiti oil tankers (Leonard 2013: 866). Branded by Tehran as 'the most disgraceful event in US military history' (Rafsanjani 1987), Rafsanjani opined that it was these 'humiliations that forced the United States to create a tragic incident in the world' – the Mecca incident (Rafsanjani 1987). Consequently, the official Iranian discourse constructed the incident as part of Iran's war with 'arrogance' (*istkbār*), where the Iranian pilgrims were victims in that war, as America was its 'plotter' and Saudi Arabia its 'perpetrator' (Rafsanjani 1987). That is to say, at the macro-level the speech was strategically designed to discursively construct the incident as a criminal act planned by the US and carried out by Riyadh in subservience to Washington.

In an attempt to refute Riyadh's allegations that the Iranian pilgrims had called for the ousting of al Saud, Rafsanjani emphasized that the 'slogans were not aimed at the [Saudi] leaders' and at 'the very people who have called themselves the Custodian of the Two Holy Mosques', as claimed by the Saudis (Rafsanjani 1987). The Majles speaker argued that the 'slogans were Death to America . . . Israel . . . and arrogance'. This 'arrogance', according to Rafsanjani, was that represented by the 'warmongers of the region', in a veiled reference to Saddam and his regional supporters (Rafsanjani 1987). Furthermore, the official Iranian discourse articulated by Rafsanjani attempted to define the incident's cause and motive. Framing the incident as a plot led by the US and Israel in retribution towards Iran, Rafsanjani defined the incident as a 'crime' and 'calamity' that is 'unique in the history of humanity' (Rafsanjani 1987).

Rafsanjani's official Iranian discourse highlighted a collaborative network of planners and conspirators to the incident. That is to say, there was collaboration and teamwork involved on the part of the planners (the United States) and the conspirators (Saudi Arabia). This thus defined al Saud's role to Iran's domestic and international audience. According to Rafsanjani, the 'crime' had 'plotters' and 'perpetrators'. The former was defined as 'Western arrogance, especially the United States', and the latter as 'the vile rulers of al Saud – at the head of the list of criminals and vile tyrants of history' (Rafsanjani 1987). This division of labour also brought in a narrative of Western subservience. According to Rafsanjani, Iran 'has no doubt that the incident would take place without the orders and special demand of the superpower' because of the relationship between the US and Saudi Arabia. It is this relationship that Rafsanjani defined as a 'master ordering a servant', thus framing Riyadh and the al Saud as 'slaves' who were 'forced to carry out this crime' that they 'cannot exonerate [themselves from] as agent and executioner' (Rafsanjani 1987).

Drawing on historical parallels, Rafsanjani aimed to construct the incident as an act of Saudi genocide with the al Saud as its perpetrators. This was accomplished by utilizing themes and historical incidents that were familiar domestically, regionally, and internationally. To the international community, an implicit referral to genocide was made by positioning the al Saud alongside historically renowned 'major criminals' such as 'Hitler, the Mongols, and the criminals who are today's world leaders . . . in Vietnam and places' (Rafsanjani 1987). Rafsanjani's speech also aimed to determine Iran's role in the incident by defining the Self in opposition to its Other, Saudi Arabia. Regionally, comparisons were made in clashes between Israel and Palestine. Rafsanjani argued that the Mecca 'incident most comparable with this crime would be the atrocities of Dayr Yasin in Palestine' where 'terrorist Israeli rulers' had 'separated out the women' and 'opened fire on the men' (Rafsanjani 1987). Therefore, the official Iranian discourse attempted to represent the al Saud as 'Israeli terrorists' and the Iranian pilgrims as 'innocent Palestinians'. Thus, the Iranian Self was represented as a victim of 'Saudi rulers who hypocritically called themselves the Custodian of the Two Holy Mosques', and who attacked the Iranians for 'chanting slogans for the liberation of Israel' (Rafsanjani 1987).

On the domestic front, the official Iranian discourse framed the incident's gravity to the public by drawing on two main narratives: the clashes during the Pahlavi era and the utilization of the Ahl-al-bayt narrative. By drawing parallels with the Shah, Rafsanjani's speech brought in themes of monarchical tyranny and hypocrisy to the narrative. The Majles speaker differentiated between the 'incident on the bloody Black Friday of 8 September 1978 . . . carried out by the Pahlavi dynasty, the friends of Fahd' (Rafsanjani 1987), thus explicitly framing Fahd as a tyrannical despot who murders innocent Iranians. However, the difference, according to Rafsanjani, was that the Iranians were protesting the Shah's court, while in Mecca, the Iranians were 'guests of the Saudi court' and 'guests of God' (Rafsanjani 1987). Rafsanjani cast doubt on the Saudi narrative of being a generous state, and Muslims were guests of the kingdom and of God. In constructing the al Saud as hypocrites, the Iranian discourse aimed to counter the Saudi discourse of hospitality and generosity as superficial.

To the Iranian domestic audience, the attacks on Iranian pilgrims led them to be represented as martyrs in the service of their religion and the Shi'a sect, labelling al Saud as an 'evil clique' in charge of 'Wahhabi executioners' who had set a precedent 'in their short history' (Rafsanjani 1987). The audience were reminded that the deaths of Iranians in Mecca were synonymous with the 'record of great massacres . . . in Mecca and Medina . . . in Khaybar, in Ahsa, and in the eastern part of Saudi Arabia', all of which were anti-Shi'i in nature (Rafsanjani 1987). Furthermore, historical parallels were drawn with Wahhabi attacks and the destruction of the Shi'i shrines 'in Karbala and Najaf' where 'they destroyed educational institutions, set fire to libraries, destroyed Islamic buildings . . . and very precious houses from the times of the Prophets and Caliphs' (Rafsanjani 1987). Therefore, while the Iranian discourse emphasized the Iranian Self as a martyr in the path of true Mohammedan Islam and the fight against tyranny and oppression, it also questioned Saudi Arabia's Islamicness, legitimacy, and leadership. Rafsanjani's discourse interpreted the Saudi monarchy as Wahhabi supporters who had a longstanding enmity with Shi'ism. They were interpreted as ignorant of Islam and as having destroyed its heritage and culture, in subservience to the Western hegemony defined by the US and Israel.

With narratives polarizing further, Khomeini – in line with Rafsanjani's narrative – issued a statement to the pilgrims, in which he ascribed the incident to the Saudi monarchy and employed themes of treachery, cowardice, and US subservience on the part of the Saudi monarchy. In Khomeini's opinion, the al Saud were 'vile and ungodly', and their leadership in the Islamic world consisted of 'daggers which have always pierced the hearts of the Muslims from the back' (Khomeini 1987b). The clashes in Mecca and the Iranians' deaths gave rise to referential nominations that represented the al Saud as 'blind', 'inept', and 'spineless', with 'ugly faces' that serve as 'US puppets' (Khomeini 1987b). Saudi Arabia was characterized as a 'blot of shame' placed by the US in the Islamic world. According to the Iranian leadership, the remedy was to 'hold the US responsible for the crimes in Mecca' and deal with America 'at an opportune time' (Khomeini 1987b) . For Saudi Arabia the warning was far more explicit: 'The blood of the martyrs must be avenged by uprooting the Saudi rulers in the region' (Khomeini 1987b). According to Rafsanjani, this 'true revenge' was twofold: wrest 'the colossal and precious wealth belonging to the Islamic world which lies under the soil of the Arabian Peninsula from the control of criminals, the agents of colonialism', and 'divest the control of the holy shrines and the Holy Mosque from the contaminated existence of the Wahhabis' (Rafsanjani 1987). The latter comment particularly raised the ire of the al Saud and pushed the discourse and narrative to not only include control over Mecca but also leadership of the Islamic world. It thus gave rise to campaigns seeking to influence opinion within the Arab and Islamic world.

The Fight Over Mecca

As the weeks passed by, the claims made by both Riyadh and Tehran picked up speed and the narratives leaned towards sedition, terrorism, Islamic identity, and legitimacy. On 25 August 1987, the minister of interior, Nayef bin Abdulaziz, held a press conference with the Arab media to discuss the findings of an investigation into the Mecca incident. In his description of the events and the Iranian pilgrims' objectives from the demonstrations, the minister adopted an implicit sectarian narrative that accused Tehran of 'sedition' *(fitna)* and terrorism in suggesting that Iran's intentions were to spark sedition in Arabia and that the rulers of Tehran were terrorists with plans to spoil the pilgrimage (al-Saud 1987b).

Questioning the Islamic identity of Iran, Nayef affirmed that there were historical roots for Iranian hatred of Saudi Arabia and Iran has sinister intentions towards the Islamic world (al-Saud 1987b). He also outlined sectarian motives that are reflected in Iran's hatred for Sunni Islam. Nayef argued that Iran's grievance was that they wished to 'erect a monument to Ali ibn Abi Talib', the fourth Caliph, revered by the Shi'a as an infallible member of the Ahl-al-Bayt (al-Saud 1987b). The minister argued that Riyadh's rejection was based on the grounds that there was no such order from God or his Prophet and that Iranians wanted to erect an idol to worship, which is antithetical to Islamic practice (al-Saud 1987b). Therefore, the Saudi official discourse had represented Iran as a sectarian terrorist state that has targeted not only Saudi Arabia, but also the entire Islamic world. By constructing Iran as a non-Islamic Other, the Saudi Self naturally aimed to position itself as the symbol of true Islam, as Sunni – identifying with the majority of Muslim world, as protectors of the two holy shrines, and as a defender of the Arab-Islamic world. It is this discourse and narrative that would be utilized in an international campaign in both states to influence Muslim opinion abroad.

In a series of tit-for-tat moves, both Iran and Saudi Arabia held conferences in a bid to sway Muslim public opinion abroad. Opening an Islamic conference convened through the Muslim World League in October 1987, the Saudi king's speech targeted Tehran and condemned Iranians for the clashes and the incident in Mecca. Encoding a discourse of Iranian sedition, terrorism, and the destruction of the Islamic world, Fahd – like his brother Nayef – argued that the Iranian government was 'accustomed to terrorism', while the kingdom has been protecting the hajj pilgrims by 'quelling seditions' by Iranian pilgrims (al-Saud 1987a). Holding another Islamic conference a few weeks later, titled the International Congress on Safeguarding the Sanctity and Security of the Great Mosque, Iran countered Saudi narratives. Speeches by Rafsanjani and Ayatollah Montazeri – then Khomeini's designated successor – targeted al Saud's legitimacy as Islamic leaders and their fitness to administer Mecca and Medina, with Rafsanjani calling for the 'liberation of Mecca' from al Saud and establishing an 'Islamic International Consortium' to govern Mecca and Medina.

Montazeri drew historic and cultural parallels to characterize the al Saud amid the Mecca incident in terms of a contrast between the al Saud and the Umayyad caliphate (Montazeri 1987). Drawing on the Ahl-al-Bayt trope, Montazeri characterized the Mecca incident and the Iranian–Saudi rivalry as a modern-day battle over the legitimacy and leadership of the Islamic world. In this context, Iran symbolized the Ahl-al-Bayt, and Fahd was a modern-day 'Muawiyya', the first Umayyad Caliph who fought Imam Ali over Islamic leadership. Montazeri argued that the Mecca incident 'violated the sanctity and immunity of the house of God' just as 'the attack of Muawwiya's forces who plundered the jewels of the Muslim women' (Montazeri 1987). Furthermore, Montazeri criticized the Saudi monarchy as a 'bunch of English agents from Najd', and as invaders of the Islamic Holy lands. As for the Saudi ulama, Montazeri argued that they are the 'enemies of Islam and the colonialists succeeded in influencing the thoughts and attitudes of Muslims and the ulama ... and preachers' (Montazeri 1987) . These 'enemies' were defined as the US and Zionism, while the al Saud were their 'agents placed in charge of the destiny of Islam and Muslims', and their ulama were 'evil court mullahs'. The 'only path to salvation', according to Iran's second most powerful cleric, was 'for Muslims to recognize their real enemy and its lackey agents and strengthen ... Islamic movements' in the Islamic world (Montazeri 1987) .

Montazeri's rebuke of the al Saud was compounded by using the 'Israeli occupation of Palestine' trope (Montazeri 1987). In an implicit comparison with the Palestine–Israel affair, the Saudi monarchy was represented as an illegitimate occupier of Islamic Holy land, placed in power by the US and Israel. The Saudi discourse questioned Iran's Islamic identity, denouncing the rulers in Tehran for sedition and terrorism, while the Iranian narratives and discourse aimed to cast doubt on al Saud's Islamic credentials and leadership. This discourse aimed to challenge the legitimacy of the Saudi monarchy to govern and administer the hajj and the Islamic sites in Mecca and Medina (Montazeri 1987) . It would be this exact discourse that would lead Saudi Arabia to make strict changes to the hajj quotas the year after. This would also lead to Iran's boycott of the hajj.

A Watershed Moment: Severing of Ties and the 'Poisonous Chalice'

The tit-for-tat Islamic conferences continued into the summer of 1988. In using these conferences to impose changes on the annual hajj pilgrimage, Riyadh pushed to ban demonstrations with slogans like 'Liberation from the infidels' and 'Against global arrogance'. Furthermore, the Saudis decided to reduce the number of pilgrims. In a new move that was endorsed in a Saudi-lobbied meeting at the Organization of the Islamic Conference (OIC) (Ziadé 1988), Riyadh suggested a quota system wherein the number of pilgrims would be proportional to the population of the country, at 1,000 pilgrims per million. In Iran's case its 150,000 pilgrim quota was reduced to 45,000. In his OIC speech in Amman, Saud al-Faisal, the Saudi foreign minister, clarified that the limitation on the numbers of pilgrims was due to 'great projects to improve the hajj facilities', emphasizing 'equal opportunities for all Muslims', and distancing the revisions from any security aspect or from the Mecca incident (al-Saud 1987c). Iran's reaction to being blamed as guilty was to brand the OIC resolution a consequence of Riyadh's bribery and corruption. The Iranian representative, Sheikh Mohammad Ali Taskhiri, pulled out of the meeting, opining that 'reactionary resolutions' were attained through 'Saudi money' (Taskhiri 1987).

Kramer (2009:176) argued that Riyadh was fully aware that Khomeini would not accept any reduction in the number of Iranian pilgrims and that this would lead to an Iranian boycott of the hajj (Kramer 2009). In March 1988 Khomeini warned that 'it is impossible for the pilgrims to attend hajj rituals and not demonstrate against world arrogance' (Khomeini 1988b). Iran's Supreme Leader argued that 'disowning infidels' is one the tenets and 'political duties of the hajj, and without it our pilgrimage will not be a hajj' (Khomeini 1988b). Iranian editorials framed the Saudi measures as a move to appease Israel and the US, which silences any voice that supported Palestine and the 'oppressed'. On 28 April 1988, Saudi Arabia severed diplomatic ties with Iran, thus making it impossible for Iranian pilgrims to apply for hajj visas. Iran's response came through a fatwa by Khomeini stating that the hajj is to be boycotted (Marschall 2003). Iranian editorials framed the severing of diplomatic relations as Western subservience, employing religious tropes questioning the legitimacy of the al Saud and their leadership of the Islamic world. In their editorial, the newspaper *Kayhan* used tropes of hypocrisy, Wahhabism, and anti-Islamic sentiments towards the Muslim world *(Kayhan 1988)*. The editorials argued that 'the al Saud has finally taken off its mask' and has 'shown its true anti-Islamic face' *(Kayhan 1988)*. According to Iranian editorial discourse, the Saudi decision to sever ties with Tehran was due to a 'growing fear by the US of the Islamic movements in the region' *(Kayhan 1988)*. *Kayhan* opined that it was now the 'obligation of the Muslim world to wipe out ... the corrupt and anti-Islam Wahhabi elements' from Mecca *(Kayhan 1988)*. Therefore, the Iranian editorial discourse defined the Saudi actions a consequence of US orders, made out of fear of an Iranian-led Islamic movement.

As the first anniversary of the 1987 Mecca incident was approaching, Saudi Arabia defended its stance, i.e. the new hajj regulations and its severing of ties with Tehran. Saudi official discourse began framing the reasons behind the cut in ties as a security measure. The minister of the interior, Nayef, argued that the kingdom cannot place trust in mere anticipation of Iran's rulers respecting Islamic sanctities, and therefore the measures taken by the kingdom were to 'prevent any attitude that would disturb security' (al-Saud 198b). The crown prince, Abdullah bin Abdulaziz, repeated a similar discourse on security. In an interview, the prince argued that Riyadh was committed to 'the prevention of any attempts to disturb the hajj atmosphere through demagogic demonstrations or provocative slogans', defining the Iranian-led hajj demonstrations as an 'undermining of security' (al-Saud 1988a). However, the Saudi official discourse had also begun to discuss a ceasefire between Iran and Iraq. This included the intertwining of the discourse on the hajj with Iran's reluctance to accept UN Resolution 598. The Saudi discourse portrayed the ceasefire as utilizing tropes of Iranian hegemony, expansion, and ambitions of a revival of a Persian Empire. Prince Abdullah bin Abdulaziz opined that the 'war will not end until the Tehran regime responds to the aspirations of the fraternal Iranian people' (al-Saud 1988a). In alluding to Khomeini's 'export of the revolution', Abdullah contended that Tehran should realize that 'revolutions cannot be exported, imported', arguing that 'Islam is the only bond between Islamic nations and not hegemony or expansion' (al-Saud 1988a). The crown prince was implicitly asserting that it was time for Iran to return to 'pure Islam' and 'respect thy neighbour' and abolish the notions of 'Persian expansion and hegemony' (al-Saud 1988a).

On 20 July 1988, in a sermon marking the first anniversary of the 1987 hajj incident, Khomeini responded to Saudi Arabia (Khomeini 1988a). He elaborated on the hajj incident, the boycott, and most importantly accepted Resolution 598, thus agreeing to a ceasefire with Iraq. It was in his last hajj sermon that Khomeini expressed his views of Saudi Arabia, its rulers, leadership, and ulama. Employing tropes of Wahhabism, the Ahl-al-Bayt, and narratives of hypocrisy, Khomeini defined the Mecca incident as a massacre that could not be forgiven (Khomeini 1988a). The al Saud were depicted as leaders of the centres of Wahhabism, sedition, and espionage. Drawing parallels to the Karbala narrative and Imam Hussain versus Yazid, Khomeini represented al Saud's reaction to the hajj demonstrations of 1987 as a 'sword of blasphemy and division, which had been hidden in the hypocritical cloak of Yazid's followers and descendants of the Umayyad dynasty [i.e. Al Saud]. God's curse be upon them; they had to come out again from the same cloak of Abu Sufyan's heirs to destroy and kill [the Muslims]' (Khomeini 1988a).

Once again, the Iranian pilgrims were positioned alongside Imam Hussein and his followers in Karbala, in contrast to the modern-day Yazid and the Umayyads, Fahd, the al Saud, and the Saudi ulama. To Khomeini, the Mecca incident was a battle between the oppressed and the oppressor – Islam versus Global Arrogance – just like Iran's war with Iraq. The world according to Khomeini was 'thirsty for . . . the pure Islam of Mohammad' (Khomeini 1988a). The Ayatollah opined that he 'has bared his chest to all the arrows of misfortune . . . in front of . . . the enemy . . . and all lovers of martyrdom' (Khomeini 1988a). However, Khomeini said he was 'unhappy because I have survived and have drunk the poisoned chalice of accepting the resolution [598] and feel ashamed in front of the greatness and sacrifices of this great nation' (Khomeini 1988a). The UN process related to the war began immediately after Khomeini's acceptance of the ceasefire.

Less than a year later, on 3 June 1989, Khomeini passed away, leaving behind him a will that had explicitly mentioned Saudi Arabia and its monarch:

> Even if it were possible to forgive Saddam Hussein, it would never be possible to forgive Saudi Arabia.
>
> (Ismael and Ismael 1994: 194)

> And in this age when the age of oppression of the Islamic world by the United States and the Soviet Union and their allies . . . including the al Saud, these traitors to the great sanctuary of God – the curse of God and the angels and the Messenger against them – should be reminded and cursed.
>
> (Khomeini 1989)

Iran mourned its revolutionary leader. As millions turned out to mark his passing, a new Supreme Leader was elected, Ali Khamenei. The Majles speaker was elected as president. Iran would begin to seek détente and rapprochement with the international community and its neighbours in a bid to rebuild its economy after a devastating eight-year war. In the first few months in his position as president in 1989, Rafsanjani explicitly argued that Iran needs to 'stop making enemies' (Rafsanjani and Ramazani 1990), thus signalling an about-turn on Iran's foreign policy. One of the countries that Iran would later approach was Saudi Arabia, leaving behind Khomeini's comments and his last will and testament.

Conclusion

Like Iran, for Saudi Arabia the discursive construction of the Self and the Other displayed four main characteristics. First, religion and sect were not areas of contention. However, sect was employed as a tool and discursive strategy in Saudi discourse, particularly in relation to fears of Iranian export of the revolution. Second, as with Iranian Othering, the Saudi discourse construction was directly proportional to the domestic events that took place. Third, the Saudi discourse construction was reactive. It could be argued that the Saudi reaction to Iranian rhetoric was to preserve its image of Islamic and regional leadership. Finally, the analysis showed that the Iranian revolution affected the Saudi identity and allowed for Riyadh to construct its Other. For instance, the siege of the Grand Mosque in Mecca and the Qatif Shi'i demonstrations led the Saudi leadership to re-emphasize its image of the Imamate and leadership of the Islamic world.

An analysis of Saudi discourses between 1979 and 1983 reveals that these discourses were clearly political in nature and their religious characters were based on tools and devices strategized to bolster the Saudi representation of the Self and Other. In another similarity with Iran, Saudi religious discourse was a tool used to denigrate and negatively construct representations of the Other. Moreover, in addition to Othering, religious discourse simultaneously employed discursive strategies for creating positive constructions of the Self using self-glorification techniques. Whereas Iran used the Shi'i trope of Ahlulbayt, Saudi Arabia in contrast drew on Abdulwahab or the Prophet Mohammad's companions. Another characteristic of Saudi representations of its Iranian Other was the shift in representation. Saudi Arabia's negative representation of the Iranian Other gradually gained pace in response to Iranian calls for an export of the revolution, particularly after Iran's battlefield successes.

Another interesting aspect is that the different Saudi discourse genres reveal a relationship between the discourse within the Kingdom and towards Iran. These include the broad themes of the relationship set by the Saudi king and crown prince towards the Other. These themes and narratives were then deployed in elite discourses and were finally disseminated to the different layers of society through the production of state propaganda in the form of religious sermons or editorials. That is to say, the upper-level elite set the broad tone of inter-state relations and representations of the Other. In Saudi Arabia, this was represented by the king and crown prince. Overall, the discourse by Khalid as king and Fahd as crown prince propagated an Islamic brotherly community and unity. In a mirror image of Iran, Saudi editorials and the ministerial domestic discourse – especially, the Ministry of the Interior – was explicit and connected with incidents that arose between the two states. These negative discourses and representations became visible, especially in the Hajj incidents of 1981 and 1987, allegations of bombing the Kuwaiti refineries, and the alleged attempt of an Iranian supported coup d'état in Bahrain.

The analysis of different epochs witnessed three main 'supra-themes' and 'supra-strategies' that were regularly highlighted in the discourse of the Other by both states. These included expansionism through hegemony and sedition; a deception and hidden agenda; and strategies of victimization and de-legitimization. In each of the aforementioned themes, different techniques and repertoires were employed such as metaphors, stereotypes and predication strategies that discursively construct the Iranian Other. In contrast to the Iranian construction of the Saudi Other, Saudi discourse was basic, lacked detail and 'artistic imagination' in their representation, and tended to mainly focus on the moral and Islamic credentials of the Iranian government. While Iran first constructed the Saudi Other as immoral and un-Islamic, Saudi discourse represented Iran after the clerical consolidation by the IRP, by questioning Khomeini's persona as a demagogue, misleading his people, and brandishing fake Islamic slogans. Iranian battlefield victories, especially, their advancement into Iraq, resulted in the mixing of religious and political repertoires focused on Iran in Saudi discourse, and typically followed the line that the Khomeini-led state was attempting to resurrect the Persian Empire and was also pursuing a programme of Shi'i expansion.

The Saudi discourse utilized the trope of sedition to highlight the Saudi Self and respond to Tehran's construction of Riyadh's image in Iranian discourse. The Iranian utilization of the Fahd peace proposal was key in highlighting the Saudi Other as subservient to Zionism, with its AWACs weapons procurement used by the Iranians to illustrate Saudi subservience and spying on behalf of the US. Mirroring this trope, the Saudi discourse utilized religious repertoires of *fitna* as a result of the Hajj incident, thus implicating the Iranian Other as a source of sedition and dividing the Islamic *ummah*. The Saudi discourses also utilized discursive strategies of representing the Other by employing historical and Islamic tropes. Discourses from revolutionary Iran and Khomeini juxtaposed the Iranian Self as the Prophet Mohammad and Imam Hussain of our time, and Saudi Arabia and Fahd as the infidels, Umayyads, and the Muawiyyah and Yazid of our time, infamous for their enmity to 'real Islam'. Saudi representation of Iran also took into account historical events. Saudi utilization of a revival of the Persian Empire by Khomeini and an export of the revolution juxtaposed Iran with hegemonic ambitions, and identified itself with the Islam of the predecessors, during the caliphate, framing a revolutionary Iran as pagan empire of our time, seeking revenge for an Islamic conquest fourteen centuries ago.

These discourses of the Self and Other in Iran and Saudi Arabia would not always remain negative and denigrative. Not long after drinking from 'the poisoned chalice', the war between Iran and Iraq ended, Khomeini died, and a new regional war would begin. In this war, Iran would seize the opportunity and recalibrate its relations with their 'Umayyads', al-Saud, and discreetly aid its Gulf neighbours against their once ally, Saddam.

Part 2

Chapter 4

CALM AFTER THE STORM:
SAUDI-IRANIAN DÉTENTE

Introduction: Iran and Saudi Arabia After the First Gulf War

The death of Ayatollah Khomeini marked the end of an era that would leave a major impression in Iranian history and shape its domestic and foreign politics. As millions came out grieving the death, the clerics in Iran met as the Assembly of Experts and voted in a new Supreme Leader (*Valy-i Faqih*), then Hojat al-Islam Ali Khamenei. His election paved the way for presidential elections, which saw Rafsanjani emerge as president with a landslide victory of 95 per cent. Rafsanjani lobbied for amendments in the existing constitution, which were successfully passed in a referendum (Ehteshami 2002: 34). Of a total of forty-two amendments, the articles pertaining to the qualification of the Supreme Leader changed, permitting an ulama of lower rank to hold the position of Supreme Spiritual Leader (*Valy-i Faqih*). Since Khamenei was not one of the highest-ranking clerics in Twelver Shi'ism i.e., a *Marj-i Taqlid*, these changes validated his election. Other amendments were geared towards strengthening the decision-making apparatus in post-war Iran and Rafsanjani's grip on Iranian foreign policy, including articles that established the creation of the Supreme National Security Council (SNSC) under the president's leadership.

The immediate post-Khomeini period witnessed a cabinet led by a pragmatic president with reconstruction and economic reform – after a tumultuous eight-year war – as its main aim, which caused a further shift in the image of the Rafsanjani cabinet. The 1989 cabinet was composed of twenty-two ministers and included only four clerics, which was an asymmetric representation in comparison with the Followers of Imam Khomeini's Line (*Khat-i Imam*). The latter dominated the Majles, which was comprised of 122 ulama with a total of 270 members (Hiro 2001: 25). Voted in before Khomeini's death in April 1988, this Majles enjoyed a majority from the radical association, the Society of Combatant Clerics (*Majma-i Ruhaniyat-i Mobraz-i Tehran*). This party was formed after the dissolution of the Islamic Republic Party (IRP); it was led by its newly elected speaker, Mehdi Karrubi, and it included militant radicals, such as Ali Akbar Mohtashemi and Muhammad Musavi Khoeiniha (Hiro 2003: 26).

Although Khomeini was dead and the war was over, it was this radical-led parliament that a pragmatic Rafsanjani had to deal with in both domestic and foreign policy matters, especially as Iran sought to normalize its relations with its neighbours. However, Rafsanjani's position was bolstered by an ally, the newly elected Supreme Leader, Ali Khamenei. Behrooz (1991) and Milani (1993) argued that in 1989 Iranian foreign policy showed signs of centralization due to a pragmatic Rafsanjani coupling with a 'mid-ranking' cleric, Khamenei, as the new Supreme Leader (*Valy-i Faqih*) (Milani 1993; Behrooz 1991). Rafsanjani's eight-year presidency witnessed a host of drastic shifts, wherein Iran mainly moved away from its ultra-radical stance to a détente-leaning foreign policy. This policy was aimed at ending Iran's international isolation, especially with its neighbours, and at giving the state an opportunity to rebuild its impoverished economy with the advent of the low oil prices of the 1990s. However, for Rafsanjani, this proved to be a challenge.

Iranian–US relations were equally strained. Iran adopted a position of 'active neutrality'[1] during Saddam's invasion of Kuwait and the later war that liberated Kuwait. The US under George HW Bush's tenure declared that 'goodwill begets goodwill' (Gheissari 2009: 355), authorizing US energy companies to import Iranian oil and releasing $250 million to Iran for an undelivered shipment of weapons procured during the Shah's time. More importantly, the US did not block a much-needed World Bank loan to rebuild the Iranian economy and went so far as to announce that Iran would play a role in regional security (Gheissari 2009). The thaw in US–Iranian relations was short-lived. The end of the 1990–1991 Gulf War saw the US presence in the Persian Gulf increase, which coincided with the collapse of the Soviet Union. In addition, the US adopted a policy of 'dual containment' towards Iraq and Iran in 1993, labelling them 'rogue states' with the US Congress passing a bill on 'covert action against Iran' to establish regime change in 1995 (Herzig 2004; Hiro 2001).

This chapter discusses Iranian–Saudi relations after the death of Ayatollah Khomeini and the election of his successor, Ayatollah Ali Khamenei. Furthermore, this chapter focuses on two main events. First, the Hajj incident of 1989, where although Iran had boycotted the pilgrimage, the incident was nevertheless an area of contention in Iran as they moved to shed led on Riyadh's management and oversight of the holy shrines. Second, Saddam's invasion of Kuwait, Iran's 'active neutrality', and the recalibration of Tehran's relations with the international community, the region, and particularly Saudi Arabia are also discussed. This chapter highlights how both domestic and external forces played a decisive role in initiating Saudi–Iranian détente under the Rafsanjani presidency, taking into account the domestic split between the *Khat-i Imam* dominated Majles along with the ulama versus the pragmatic Rafsanjani, and the position of the new Supreme

---

1. Rafsanjani's 'active neutrality' is defined as Iran standing on the sidelines while maximizing its benefits. For a detailed discussion please see Milani (1992)

Leader as a balance between these two competing forces. Furthermore, the regional build-up of US forces in Saudi Arabia, Saddam's ceasefire and offerings to Tehran, along with Saudi–Iranian Othering are also discussed.

There are four main arguments that run through this chapter. First, the Iranian establishment was split over détente with Saudi Arabia and the West, particularly the US. Second, I argue that Rafsanjani's pragmatism and neutrality was central to Iranian–Saudi representations of the Other in the official discourse. This represented a maturing of the Iranian regime compared with the aggressive rhetoric of the Khomeini-led period. Furthermore, I argue that Othering and discursive constructions in both states began to metamorphose under Rafsanjani's tenure, particularly in the official discourse . These resulted in narratives of Islamic unity and economic collaboration upon the liberation of Kuwait. On a final note, I argue that Saudi–Iranian Othering in this period was directly related to the emerging split in the identity of the Iranian leadership and how this in turn was perceived by Saudi Arabia. As Rafsanjani continued to lead a pragmatic foreign policy, Saudi discursive constructions of the Iranian Other also changed, leading to narratives emphasizing geopolitical significance and fraternal Islamic relations.

Iranian Representations

Foreign policy after the death of Khomeini was characterized by an Iranian willingness to open up to the region and re-establish relations with the international community. With regards to Saudi Arabia, Tehran's intent to restart relations with the kingdom began in the period immediately after the Ayatollah Khomeini's acceptance of the ceasefire with Iraq in July 1988 (Karsh, 2009). Saudi Arabia had also demonstrated signs of a willingness to establish détente with Iran. Al-Sultan (2016) argues that King Fahd had ordered the Saudi Arabian media to cease its criticism of Iran (Al-Sultan and Saeid 2016). Fahd argued that 'problems with Iran . . . cannot continue' and he asked the Saudi media outlets to 'take the initiative' in the hope that 'we get the same in return' (al-Saud 1988). This was reciprocated by Ayatollah Khomeini as a return of a gesture of good faith. The Iranian press was asked to cease its criticism of Saudi Arabia. Revealed later in his memoirs (2012), Rafsanjani opined that 'the Imam [i.e. Ayatollah Khomeini] said that in response to King Fahd's step to prohibit Arab media from anti-Iran propaganda, we shall also stop anti-Saudi Arabian propaganda' (Rafsanjani 2012: 68). However, the desire for the Rafsanjani-led pragmatists to mend relations with Riyadh was not easy sailing.

By the end of 1988, there were official voices in Iran that explicitly called for the normalization of relations with Saudi Arabia. In a Majles session, Rafsanjani, then still acting as speaker, argued that 'in the not-too-distant future relations will normalize with Saudi Arabia'. Rafsanjani called for both countries to 'resolve issues concerning our relations' (Rafsanjani 1988). The death of Ayatollah Khomeini did not necessarily impede the normalization of relations with Riyadh. However, it was the events in Saudi Arabia that hindered such détente from taking place. The hajj of 1989 witnessed bombings in Mecca. Iran boycotted the hajj for the second year due to the 1987 incident and objections to Riyadh's pilgrim quotas and their not agreeing to Iranian-led annual hajj demonstrations. Absent from the hajj, Iran was quick to distant itself while framing Saudi Arabia for the incident. Rafsanjani argued that the 'Saudis themselves did it' to alleviate the 'pressure from the true Muslims of the world' and for 'depriving Iran from participating in the hajj' (Rafsanjani 1989). The aftermath included the arrest of Shi'i citizens from the Arab states of the Persian Gulf. Of those, sixteen Shi'i Kuwaitis confessed on Saudi television and were later executed (Murden 1995). The confessions stated that the explosives were supplied by the Iranian embassy in Kuwait, an allegation immediately denied by Tehran. This led the Iranian discourse to once again return to its pre-ceasefire rhetoric and propaganda.

The official Iranian discourse framed the bombings as a conspiracy planned and executed by the US and carried out by Saudi Arabia. As for the executions, the Iranian foreign-ministry statement labelled the confessions as 'false allegations disseminated by the Saudi government'. The executions were framed as carried out on 'Kuwaiti Muslims' in an explicit distancing from the Saudi sectarian label of the alleged perpetrators as Shi'a. Once again, the Saudi government's legitimacy and leadership was questioned. Iranian discourse emphasized the 'anti-Islamic nature' of the Saudi rulers. Iranian media discourse utilized tropes of 'Saudi barbarism'. *Kayhan* (1989) and *Jomhouri Eslami* (1989) argued that the 'torture' and the 'bloodshed' at the 'hand of Saudi rulers during the hajj' should be 'held accountable by the Islamic world' *(Kayhan* 1989; *Jomhouri Eslami* 1989). Khamenei's sermon echoed the tropes of Saudi barbarism. In response to the executions, Khamenei branded the beheadings a 'plague ... and a crime at the hands of the rulers of Saudi Arabia'. Furthermore, by employing a discourse of victimization and discrimination, Khamenei defined the executed men as 'dear martyrs' that were 'killed for the crime of supporting the Islamic Republic and their love for the Imam [Khomeini]' (Khamenei 1989).

The official response from Riyadh, however, was far from the rhetoric employed during the Iran–Iraq war. In a speech, King Fahd responded to the Iranian statements. The monarch explicitly opined that Riyadh had 'not accused Iran ... with the bombings' (al-Saud 1989). The Saudi leadership understood that Iran was beginning a new era. It had a new Supreme Leader, and a newly elected pragmatic president. While Rafsanjani sought to mend relations and begin a new chapter in Iran's foreign policy, Khamenei aimed to establish his image as the new leader of the Islamic Ummah in general, and the Shi'a, in particular. The low oil prices in the post-Gulf War period aggravated the powers in the region, especially Iran and Iraq. Both sought to rebuild their economies and pay their debts. Iraq, especially, owed the Arab states of the Persian Gulf – Kuwait and Saudi Arabia in particular – billions of dollars in debt. Both countries were demanding Iraq pay its debts, which, along with low oil revenue, led to the regional order upending. This shift in the regional order was a result of Saddam's decision to invade Kuwait in August 1990. This invasion shifted the global and regional balance of power, pushing Iran and its neighbours, particularly Saudi Arabia, towards détente and rapprochement.

Iraq's 1990 Invasion of Kuwait: The Road to Détente

After an eight-year war with Iran, Iraq invaded Kuwait on 2 August 1990 and remained there for a period of seven months. Following its expulsion in February 1991 by the US and coalition forces, Iraq was 'relegated to a pre-industrial age' (Boutros-Ghali and United Nations 1996: 186–188). In addition, this invasion started an era of a US presence throughout the Persian Gulf, thus putting Iran in a dilemma as both of Iran's main adversaries were on the verge of war. Iran, under Rafsanjani's presidency, took an 'actively neutral' stance throughout the seven months. This strategy of active neutrality was permitted by the Khamenei-Rafsanjani alliance. It was also this alliance and strategy that allowed Iran to adhere to two main fundamental objectives: the strength and survival of Iran as an Islamic Republic. Furthermore, Iran's 'active neutrality' also included secondary objectives: mending regional relations, working on the diplomatic and economic reconstruction of a war-torn Iran, and maintaining the image of the Islamic Republic as regional power and leader of the Islamic world (Amineh 2007: 158–159; Mohammad 2011: 17–18). Iranian discourse aimed to construct, represent, and highlight the latter objective in particular.

The invasion of Kuwait brought about opportunities for Iran. As the US was invited by Riyadh to station its forces in the kingdom, Baghdad moved to ease the pressure with Iran and propose a ceasefire. Seeking concessions with Iran, Saddam contacted his Iranian counterpart, accepting the 1975 Algerian Accord as well as Iran's conditions for a full and final peace treaty between the two states. This was hailed in Iran as a 'divine victory' and as a capitulation by Saddam in meeting Iran's demands. It would also become the main narrative that Iranian domestic discourse would use to convince its people of its active-neutrality strategy and mitigate any disappointment or upset by the Iranian masses with the re-establishment of relations with Iraq and the GCC, particularly Saudi Arabia and Kuwait. It is also this discourse of divine victory that became the foundation on which Iran defined its Self as it represented the Other in the coming months. This foundation became the source of the tropes and repertoires Iranian discourse would employ in its discourse genres.

Manifesting the Iranian Self: Condemnation, Resentment, and Islamic Legitimacy   Iran's response came immediately after Iraq had invaded Kuwait. On 2 August the Iranian foreign ministry issued a statement condemning the attack and calling on Iraq to withdraw from Kuwait. In the same statement, Iranian officials implicitly expressed their concerns with foreign troops entering the region as a result of Saddam's aggression (Foreign Ministry 1990b, 1990a). The supra-discourse across all genres entailed a condemnation of Saddam's invasion and strong opposition to the presence of US troops in the region, especially in 'holy lands'. Khamenei opined that 'Iran's stance was decisive' and it 'ran contrary to other governments', i.e. Saudi Arabia and the GCC states. Ayatollah Khamenei stressed that 'we condemn aggression be it from Iraq or the US'. The 'presence of American forces in Saudi Arabia' was framed by Iran's new Supreme Leader as a service 'in the interest of Zionism and arrogance, to the detriment of Islam, Muslims, and against the Islamic Revolution' (Khamenei 1990a). This narrative was echoed by Rafsanjani. Speaking at a Friday prayer sermon in Tehran, the Iranian president promulgated Ayatollah Khamenei's discourse of condemnation of Kuwait's invasion *(Rafsanjani 1990)*. Utilizing Islamic tropes, Rafsanjani argued that Iran 'adopted its stance based on our Islamic and Koranic inspirations'. Highlighting the Iranian Self as adhering to 'true Mohammedan Islam', Rafsanjani exploited the Kuwaiti crisis to represent Iran's Islamic leadership and legitimacy (Rafsanjani 1990). The president argued that 'Islamic teachings have been the basis of our decisions', and as such 'aggression against Kuwait cannot be acceptable to us at any time' (Rafsanjani 1990).

Divine Retribution and Intervention   Iran's domestic discourse represented the invasion of Kuwait as an act of divine retribution. This was evident in the editorials and Friday prayer sermons. Kuwait and Saudi Arabia's fate was framed as a karmic response to their support for Iraq during the eight-year imposed war on Iran. *Jomhouri Eslami* situated the 'present fate of the al-Sabah and al-Saud regimes' in their 'support for Iraq in its aggression against Iran' *(Jomhouri Eslami 1990)*. However, it was the Friday sermons that delved deep into this discourse. Framed in the Islamic concept of *Adālat* (Arabic: *Adālah*), i.e. divine justice, the Iranian ulama framed Kuwait's invasion and Saddam's threats to Saudi Arabia as God's revenge or wrath for the suffering that Iran had undergone. In one of the first Friday sermons following the invasion of Kuwait, Ayatollah Mousavi-Ardabili reminded the audience of the 'great deal of agony' that the 'Imam, our leader, our elder statesman' had endured, in reference to the late Ayatollah Khomeini, as 'he drank from the chalice of poison' and passed away 'before witnessing a day such as today', that is, Saddam's invasion of Kuwait (Mousavi Ardabili 1990b). The Friday Imam reminded the audience that Iran had once warned the Arab states of the Persian Gulf, especially Kuwait, that Saddam may attack them one day (Mousavi Ardabili 1990b).

The divine-retribution framing was also present in later sermons. Saudi Arabia as Iran's Other was represented as a humiliated and weak state because it had gone against Iran. Iranian religious discourse argued that the countries colluded in facilitating a war on Iran. In other words, Saudi Arabia, Iraq, and the US had been ashamed and disgraced in their own sense and in front of the world, in contrast to Iran's divine victory. Ayatollah Emami-Kashani argued in his sermon that 'the only party which rose from the midst of the clouds was the sun of the Islamic Republic and the sun of Islam' (Emami-Kashani 1990). This victory was framed as one that was born out of a war between *Haq* and *Bātil*, i.e. Truth versus Falsehood. Employing Islamic tropes from the Quran, Iran's image was constructed as the bearer of the flag of truth 'which has its roots in God'. This was achieved through 'people's unity, martyrdom, devotion, imprisonment, tears, prayers, and self-sacrifice' versus Saddam and his supporters, which included Saudi Arabia (Emami-Kashani 1990). This 'divine war' was about to continue as Iranian discourse discussed US involvement against Saddam.

US Conspiracy, Hegemony, and Oil The invasion of Kuwait led Saudi Arabia to request military assistance from Washington. The issue was first taken to the UN Security Council (UNSC). After a formal condemnation from the UN and a call for Iraq to withdraw its troops from Kuwait, the UNSC passed Resolution 661 on 6 August 1990, imposing an embargo on Iraq (including sanctions), which gave Saudi Arabia a legal standing to request military assistance from the US. On the same day, King Fahd made an official request to George HW Bush inviting US forces to Saudi Arabia to support Saudi Arabia. Washington immediately dispatched 40,000 troops. In retaliation, on 8 August 1990 Saddam annexed Kuwait, labelling it 'Iraq's nineteenth province' (Hiro 2001: 30). There is no doubt that the move raised Iran's fears. Iran had suffered losses at the hands of the US during the eight-year war. These included US support for Saddam, their involvement in the 'Tanker Wars (1984–1988), and the downing of an Iran Air flight by a missile fired from the US carrier USS Vincennes on 3 July 1988 (Simons 2016: 314; El-Shazly 2016). It is, therefore, not surprising that Iran would react with some hostility towards US military presence in Saudi Arabia. The Iranian discourse framed the US military presence in the Persian Gulf as part of its hegemony and expansion. This brought in tropes of a US–Iraq conspiracy to invade Kuwait and Saudi Arabia, gaining hegemony over oil and energy supplies, and control of OPEC. These representations had one goal in mind, asserting that the US was in the region to confront Iran.

Iranian discourse, especially the media and religious discourse, argued that Saudi Arabia's invitation was part of Washington's 'long-wished ambitions' to have a 'lasting presence in Saudi Arabia and the whole region'. According to *Jomhouri Eslami*, this presence needed a pretext, therefore, the US was 'presently working to create psychological ground to justify the [US] military build-up', using the 'Iraqi seizure of Kuwait … as an excuse for the dispatch of … military forces to the region' (*Jomhouri Eslami* 1990). Similarly, *Kayhan* (16 August 1990) compounded this narrative by bringing in tropes of a 'game' for oil and energy hegemony. Iranian editorial discourse argued that 'the real issue is not the sovereignty of the al-Sabah or the al-Saud but the continued ability of Washington to dictate oil pricing policy in the Middle East' and that the 'two [families] have been committed proxies in this game' (*Kayhan* 1990).

While the domestic discourse, represented mainly by the editorials and the religious sermons, framed US regional presence and the invasion in the context of a conspiracy, the official Iranian discourse, represented by the Foreign Ministry and the SNSC, maintained Rafsanjani's strategy of 'active neutrality'. Iran's chief diplomat, Velayati, and the Secretary General of the SNSC, Hassan Rouhani, made neutral and balanced comments towards Saudi Arabia and the US regional presence. In an interview on Iranian television, Velayati was explicitly asked if the invasion had a 'purely American nature' and if the 'US was behind this incident?' The foreign minister emphasized that while 'the US … is exploiting this situation as a pretext … it is unlikely … that this was a predesigned scenario' (Velayati 1990a). In response to the same question, Rouhani, a cleric and politician, argued that while Saddam 'may have reached a collaboration with some Arab leaders', it was 'unlikely that Saddam had such a collaboration ... with the US, the Soviet Union' (Rouhani 1990).

Iranian discourse was beginning to witness a split in its representation of the Other. The media and religious genre maintained the post-revolutionary rhetoric that represented Saudi Arabia and the US in a negative light, while the official position adopted a neutral tone towards Iran's adversaries. Simply put, the Iranian discourse was strategized and the domestic populace was fed with harsh representations of the US and the Arab states of the Persian Gulf, particularly Saudi Arabia, while the discourse aimed at the international community was moderate and defined Iran as a country that had shifted from its post-revolutionary wartime posture. The Iranian domestic discourse promulgators took into account the fact that a year had elapsed since Khomeini's death, and the memory of the war and its humanitarian and material losses were still fresh in the mind of the people. Therefore, if the domestic discourse were to show a rapid shift in its tone and narratives towards the West and the Gulf states, then that may have created turbulence within the Islamic Republic. As the events of the Kuwait invasion unfolded, so did the strategies of Iranian discourse construction, its repertoires, and narratives.

Occupying the Holy Lands: Treason, Debauchery, and Conspiracy   The invitation of non-Muslim troops onto Saudi soil had appeared to worry the Saudi monarchy. The presence of the US military on soil that is referred to as the 'land of the two holy mosques' (*bilād al-haramayn*) would be incompatible with al-Saud's label of protectors of the holy lands, and more specifically the title of Custodian of the Two Holy Mosques bestowed upon King Fahd in 1986 in replacement of the title 'Your Majesty' (*Sahib al-Jalālah*) (Shahi 2013: 84). This Islamic title, denoting the status of the Caliph of Islam constructed an image of the Saudi monarch as the leader of the Islamic world, symbolizing legitimacy and leadership. Hosting a non-Muslim army on Islamic soil to fight another Islamic country would jeopardize the position of the kingdom as the cradle of Islam and its ideational centre, and the monarch as its leader and protector in the eyes of the Islamic world.

King Fahd sought a religious edict, a *fatwa*, from the Supreme Council of Ulama. On August 13 1990, three days after Bush informed Congress of his decision to deploy troops to Saudi Arabia, Sheikh Abdulaziz bin Baz, the chairman of the Supreme Council of Ulama, issued the fatwa supporting the deployment of troops on Saudi soil. The fatwa legitimized King Fahd's decision, giving the monarch 'all possible means' to protect the kingdom by 'bringing together forces equipped with instruments capable of frightening and terrorizing the one [Saddam] who wanted to commit an aggression against this country' *(SPA 1990)*. The king was represented as 'the man in charge of the affairs of Muslims' and was therefore granted permission and 'should seek the assistance of one who has the ability to attain the intended aim', i.e. the US, as dictated by the 'Quran and the Prophet's Sunna' *(SPA 1990)*. The justification was that the king had to 'be ready and take precautions before it is too late' *(SPA 1990)*. Iranian discourse, the media and religious discourse in particular, capitalized on Riyadh's decision to deploy foreign troops to the kingdom.

The monarch's decision to host US troops on Saudi soil was met with harsh rhetoric, from the Iranian press and religious discourse, that aimed to discursively construct images of Iran's Other, Saudi Arabia, as weak and subservient to the US. The country was portrayed as committing treason and conspiring against Islam, with tropes such as debauchery in the service of the 'infidel occupier' used. On the day the fatwa was released, Iranian editorials began projecting an image of a weak and subservient kingdom as the al-Saud sought aid from 'those who themselves have been the root cause of insecurity in the region' (*Jomhouri Eslami* 1990). The 'establishing of security' by the US military would bear a 'heavy cost on the region's nations to safeguard the throne of the corrupt al-Saud regime' through the 'payment of petrodollars belonging to the people' (*Jomhouri Eslami* 1990; *IRNA* 1990). King Fahd's invitation of the US military was framed as US domination over Saudi Arabia (*Jomhouri Eslami* 1990). *Jomhouri Eslami* argued that 'Saudi Arabia would be turned into the fifty-second state of America' as the 'US has annexed Saudi Arabia to its realm' (*Jomhouri Eslami* 1990). The editorial implicitly referred to the annexation of the 'holy cities of Mecca and Medina', and the al-Saud had now become a 'terrible disgrace ... and an insult to Islam and Muslims' (*Jomhouri Eslami* 1990). By representing al-Saud as weak and subservient to the US, the Iranian editorials suggested that the Saudi monarch is afraid of losing his throne and has jeopardized the Islamic holy cities of Mecca and Medina; it was the latter claim that cast a dark shadow on al-Saud's legitimacy and leadership of the Islamic world and on the rightfulness of the Saudi ulama.

Iranian discourse criticized the Saudi ulama and the fatwa, allowing the US to deploy troops on the kingdom's soil, drawing on tropes of treason and debauchery. *Jomhouri Eslami* lashed out against what they termed the '[royal] court ulama'[2] (*Jomhouri Eslami* 1990), a derogatory reference to clerics in the service of royals and their courts. The newspaper editorial referred to the bin Baz as a 'court mufti' who had issued a fatwa that justified 'such treason' that led to the 'justification of the US expedition to Saudi Arabia' by the 'throne of the root of corruption' in a pejorative reference to the al-Saud (*Jomhouri Eslami* 1990). This would also be the same newspaper that would set off the discourse of debauchery and the tropes of prostitution and alcohol in the service of the 'US occupier' (*Jomhouri Eslami* 1990), which would be promulgated by the religious discourse in the Friday sermons of Tehran.

Jomhouri Eslami called on the ulama of the Islamic world to rise against the agreement forged by 'Cairo and Riyadh to dispatch 10,000 Egyptian women to Saudi Arabia to American forces'. The Iranian press discourse framed the Saudi monarchy and ulama as panderers in the service of the US military. As for the rumour of dispatching Egyptian women to American forces, that could be attributed to rhetoric against President Mubarak of Egypt, as Cairo supported Iraq during the war. Iranian domestic discourse represented Riyadh as committing treason to Islam

---

2. *'Ulama al-Salātīn' or 'Ulama al-Balāt'* (Court Ulama).

and the holy cities of Mecca and Medina, by providing pleasure to the Americans. The Iranian press discourse argued that 'the custodians of the holy places … Saudi rulers, have justified their treason against Islam in the context of security' *(Jomhouri Eslami* 1990), thus, 'desecrating the sanctity of the holy shrines in Mecca and Medina' *(Jomhouri Eslami* 1990). The Iranian press discourse constructed an image of disparity between 'true Mohammedan Islam' *(Islam-i Nāb-i Mohammadī)* and Saudi Islam, where the former represented 'true Islam' and the latter, debauchery and treason. This representation would also be extracted from the press discourse and employed in the religious discourse of the Friday imams.

From the pulpit in Tehran, Ayatollah Mousavi-Ardabili utilized the trope of debauchery, treason, and pandering in the service of the US. Much like the editorials, the Friday Imam charged that 'Americans are busy engaged in debauchery' with 'half-naked dancers imported to Saudi Arabia' (Mousavi Ardabili 1990a). Ayatollah Mousavi-Ardabili represented Fahd as desecrating the holy shrines. The cleric argued that these troops were 'living close to the shrine of the Prophet and the House of God', i.e. Medina and Mecca, respectively (Mousavi Ardabili 1990a). Iranian religious discourse also targeted Iraq's supporters during the war. Like the editorials that mentioned 10,000 Egyptian prostitutes, the alcoholic drinks were imported from Saddam's main ally – Jordan (Mousavi Ardabili 1990a). Iranian clerical discourse aimed to show the Iranian domestic audience that these countries and rulers were still enemies in the eyes of the Islamic Republic and that Khomeini-era views and opinions on Saddam, and his then supporters, King Fahd of Saudi Arabia, Hussein of Jordan, and Hassan and Morocco, were still viewed negatively. According to Iranian domestic discourse, this service included the importing of alcohol from Jordan and prostitutes from Egypt to serve non-Muslim troops 'living close to the Prophet's shrine and House of God', the Kaaba (Mousavi Ardabili 1990a). Iranian discourse targeted and criticized the legitimacy and leadership of the al-Saud and the title of Custodian of the Two Holy Mosques.

Jihad vs Active Neutrality   By September 1990, the US military build-up was gaining traction. The US had received a financial commitment from King Fahd while the US secretary of state, James Baker, was on a visit to Saudi Arabia. The Iranian government, headed by Rafsanjani, engaged in its 'active neutrality'. One sign of this neutrality was the resumption of diplomatic ties between Tehran and Baghdad on 10 September 1990 (Lea 2001: 60). Iraq, through its foreign minister, Tariq Aziz, had allegedly offered Iran a war reparations package valued at $25 billion if Tehran would establish economic ties that would alleviate the UN-imposed sanctions against Baghdad (Kamrava 2011: 200). In keeping with its active neutrality policy, the Iranian president rejected the proposal. This was to show its neighbours that it would not negate their trust, and to show the international community that Iran adhered to international law and UN rules. Similarly, the official Iranian discourse condemned military action against Iraq. This condemnation of war gave rise to two main features of Iranian discourse. First, that Iranian discourse was divided into three layers: the government discourse that portrayed Iran's wishes to return to the fold of the international community and repair its regional image; second, a domestic discourse represented by the press, parliament, and the ulama; and third, Khamenei, who constructed a discourse that merged both neutrality and rhetoric. The second feature was that the domestic discourse had begun to show a split and the narrative towards Iran's Other was not uniform. These features were exemplified as signs of a military operation against Iraq were becoming apparent.

On 12 September 1990, the newly elected Supreme Leader, Ayatollah Khamenei, elaborated on the Islamic Republic's position regarding the regional events. The discourse was strategized in that it included a combination of positions that considered Iran's 'active neutrality', the domestic populace after an eight-year war, and his position as the Valy-i Faqih and the leader of the Islamic world. Ayatollah Khamenei defined Iran's position from the military build-up towards Iraq as an American invasion, representing the US as aggressors (Khamenei 1990b). In the context of active neutrality, the Supreme Leader argued that Iran 'has been announcing for years that we are ready to sit down with the countries of the region and help each other secure the Persian Gulf' (Khamenei 1990b). To the domestic populace he sought to remind the Iranian people that the Islamic Republic is still in a war against the oppression. To the domestic audience, Iran's position on Kuwait emanated from its Islamic responsibility and teaching, that is fighting global arrogance, (*istikābr-i jahānī*). This arrogance was represented by the US and Saddam. Khamenei argued that the US got involved in the Kuwait invasion and the region because of their 'hatred and hatred for Islam and the Islamic Republic and the Islamic Revolution' (Khamenei 1990b). To the Iranian people, Iraq was still an enemy, and the US 'strengthened and supported Iraq as much as possible'. Khamenei sought to remind the Iranian people and the Islamic world that the US stood for 'global arrogance', 'aggression', and 'greed' and that America wanted to 'invade the Persian Gulf region'. The Supreme Leader argued that this 'invasion' must be met with 'jihad for the sake of God' (*'Jihād fī Sabīl Allah'*) and 'whoever is killed is a martyr' (Khamenei 1990b).

By employing the discourse on jihad and martyrdom, Ayatollah Khamenei was not literally inviting the Iranians or the Islamic world to participate in a holy war against the US. Instead, he was emphasizing the image of Khomeini's Islamic Republic, one that stands for fighting the US. The message to the Iranian masses and the Islamic world was that he shall continue the path and principles of the revolution set by the founder of the Islamic Republic, Ayatollah Khomeini. Through his discourse, Ayatollah Khamenei sought to inform the international community, principally Iran's neighbours, that Iran was open to mending its relations with the Arab and Islamic world, including the GCC states. To the domestic audience the newly elected Supreme Leader was assuring the Iranian masses, which had just come out of a harsh eight-year war, that Iran's position in relation to the US, Saddam, and those regional countries that had supported him had not changed. However, the discourse on jihad would be utilized by other actors in Iran and would demonstrate a new plurality of voices among Iranian discourse constructors.

Iran's parliament condemned the US military presence in the Persian Gulf. However, there were voices that began to call for a collaboration with Iraq against the US. Majles members of the ultra-conservative Combatant Clergy Association and *Khat-i Imam* members, such as the former minister of the interior, Ali Akbar Mohtashemi, and Sadiq Khalkhali, the Majles foreign-affairs committee chairman, called for a military alliance with Iraq against America and Israel (Khalkhali 1990). Echoing Ayatollah Khamenei's calls for jihad, Mohtashemi argued that 'from this moment we must begin to organize the jihad and struggle against America' (Mohtashemi 1990). Indeed, the Tehran parliamentarian took advantage of the occasion of Holy Defence Week to call on Iranians to denounce the aggression of the US and its allies and to 'take part in the jihad called forth by the Supreme Leader of the revolution [i.e. Ayatollah Khamenei]' (Mohtashemi 1991a). These calls for jihad continued as the war began between the US-led forces and Saddam in January1991. Mohtashemi maintained that the Iranian government join a jihad against the US and Israel (Mohtashemi 1991b). Mohtashemi's calls for jihad caused a split in the Iranian domestic discourse, particularly among the ulama (Mohtashemi 1991a). The chairman of the experts, Ayatollah Ali Meshkini, rebuked Mohtashemi. He argued, 'Do not connect this war with Islam . . . it is a war between dictators' (Meshkini 1991). The domestic discourse on the Iraqi invasion of Kuwait and the presence of US troops in the region had shown plurality. Members of the *Khat-i Imam* clerics were calling for a jihad, while others viewed the war as one between dictators, Saddam, al-Saud, and the al-Sabah, thus not equating to an Islamic jihad. Meanwhile, the government official discourse, mainly the president and the foreign minister, maintained a discourse of neutrality and distanced themselves from Khamenei's calls for jihad.

Reaping the Fruits of Neutrality

In a visit to the US as part of the UN General Assembly meetings, Velayati implicitly agreed to a US temporary presence because he mentioned that Iran opposed the permanent presence of foreign troops in the region, repeating Iran's objection to the 'prolongation' of the troops' presence and not to their presence per se. As for a war with Iraq, Velayati argued that 'if sanctions fail there is no solution but a military one'. Velayati hinted at the possibility of relations with the US, acknowledging US proposals to improve relations but arguing that the US has not 'changed its main policy towards Iran' (Velayati 1990c; Christian Science Monitor and Houk 1990). As part of his UN trip, Velayati hosted the GCC representatives and began discussing a normalization of relations (Abidi and Singh 1991). This was a continuation of his August tour of the GCC where he carried Rafsanjani's message to Oman, UAE, and Qatar. Through Rafsanjani's strategy of active neutrality, Iran was on route to détente with Saudi Arabia.

On 16 January 1991 the US president, George Bush, announced the start of a military attack on Iraq, Operation Desert Storm. By then, Iranian and Saudi Arabian officials had met on a few occasions. In addition to the threat of Saddam, the issue of the hajj was the door to Iranian–Saudi détente. In a meeting at the UN on 30 September 1990, both countries' foreign ministers agreed that the issue of the hajj was of high importance. In his meeting with Saud al-Faisal, Velayati called for 'regional cooperation' on matters of 'regional security'. As for the pilgrimage, Velayati said he 'hope[d] that the existing obstacles will be removed from the path of the hajj as soon as possible' (Velayati 1990b). Riyadh's response was a clear affirmation of their decision to turn a new leaf with Tehran. Saud al-Faisal agreed on regional cooperation in matters of security. As for the hajj, the kingdom was 'very eager to see the Muslim people of Iran travel to Saudi Arabia', emphasizing that the government would 'ensure that the Iranian Muslims can perform their hajj rituals in the manner they desire' (al-Saud 1990). Saudi Arabia had implicitly signalled its intention to reverse its decision to put limits on the number of Iranian pilgrims as well as its annual hajj demonstration. Iran was legitimized in Saudi official discourse. On 3 October 1990, the Saudi foreign minister announced that they were 'prepared to open talks with Iran on restoring normal diplomatic relations' (*Asharq Al-Awsat* 1990). Tehran had begun to reap the fruits of Rafsanjani's seeds of active neutrality.

On 26 February 1991, Kuwait was freed from Saddam's occupation. Iran had kept its promises and remained neutral throughout the invasion and military operations. The Saudi official discourse had ignored the rhetoric and narratives spun by the Iranian domestic discourse over the seven months. The kingdom's state discourse towards Iran had now thawed. This began with a reversal of Riyadh's position towards the Iran–Iraq war. King Fahd argued that 'we were aware that Iraq's victory over Iran was almost impossible' (al-Saud 1991b). Iran's geographical and political status was also redefined. The Islamic Republic of Iran was now defined as a 'neighbouring country' rather than as a threat (al-Saud 1991b). Saudi official discourse through the monarch now described relations with Iran as pertaining to a country with whom the kingdom shared many ties amid regional proximity to the Gulf countries. The discourse was framed around unity. Fahd argued that the 'one Gulf brings us [the GCC states including Iran] together' (al-Saud 1991b). Through the discourse of unity, King Fahd explicitly called for a 'coexistence with Iran that must be formulated' (al-Saud 1991a). The Saudi monarch highlighted the strategic importance of Iran, arguing that the 'GCC states never took positions antagonistic to Iran' (al-Saud 1991a). King Fahd now wanted 'good and peaceful relations with Iran' (al-Saud 1991a). The kingdom and its GCC allies were now ready to 'seriously review relations between the [Persian] Gulf states and Iran' (al-Saud 1991a).

On 26 March 1991, as the Iranians were celebrating their new year (*Norouz*), Tehran and Riyadh resumed diplomatic relations (Fürtig 2002: 55). The Iranians ended their boycott of the hajj. In a meeting between the Iranian and Saudi hajj officials on 4 April 1991, Riyadh agreed to an accepted quota of 110, 000 Iranian pilgrims and the holding of their annual demonstrations during the pilgrimage (*SPA* 1990). Three weeks later, the Iranian foreign minister visited Saudi Arabia. The visit was the fruit of five rounds of meetings between the two foreign ministers. Saudi Arabia and Iran had officially entered détente. In their meeting in Riyadh, discussions focused on 'maintaining close, strategic cooperation on ensuring regional security' (Velayati 1991). The discourse of the elite from both countries now focused on cooperation at the bilateral and regional level. Saudi Arabia reciprocated the visit.

On 6 June 1991 the Saudi foreign minister led a delegation to Tehran. In a meeting with Rafsanjani, Saud al-Faisal represented Iran as a 'great and dear country' (al-Saud 1991c). The Saudi official discourse now framed relations with Iran in the context of fraternity. The 'people of Saudi Arabia are very happy about the positive developments between the two countries', opined the Saudi foreign minister (al-Saud 1991c). Riyadh's representation of Iran shifted towards 'cooperation ... in the political and economic fields'. Saudi official discourse constructed Riyadh's relations with Iran in terms of unity and the sharing of interests, which would have 'significant effects on the Islamic Ummah' (al-Saud 1991c). Rafsanjani's strategy had become a success. Iran had shifted its foreign policy from antagonism to cooperation. Adopting a discourse of Islamic unity and tropes of Islamic brotherhood and cooperation, Rafsanjani argued that there were 'vast existing grounds for the expansion of cooperation ... this is necessary for the realization of common interests based on Islamic beliefs and preservation of the interests of both countries and the region' *(Rafsanjani 1991)*. This unity and cooperation would become evident throughout Rafsanjani's presidency, as the president moved to cement ties with Riyadh and sustain détente between both states.

Conclusion

The late 1980s were marked by mutual intent in both Saudi Arabia and Iran towards détente. In Iran, this was commonplace among the upper-level elite, starting with Ayatollah Khomeini immediately after the ceasefire with Iraq. Furthermore, an olive branch by Fahd weeks after the ceasefire led to a positive Iranian reaction from the Supreme Leader. However, while both states had such initial intent to normalize relations, the events within Saudi Arabia, such as the Mecca bombings of 1989, hindered any normalization, with Iran exploiting the bombings to vindicate its image after the 1987 hajj incident. The Iranian discourse framed the 1989 hajj bombings as an act of conspiracy planned by the United States and carried out by Saudi Arabia. The incident also brought in tropes of Saudi subservience to the US and sectarianism, and Iranian Islamic and Shi'i leadership. The promulgation of this trope in Iranian discourse aimed to highlight the Saudi Other as a sectarian state that targets the Shi'a, while clarifying the new position of Khamenei as Supreme Leader and his image of Shi'i and Islamic leadership. This was compounded by use of the narrative of the Kuwaiti Shi'a implicated in the bombings and executed as a result of 'torture and forced confessions'.

In response, Saudi Arabia played down Iranian rhetoric towards Saudi Arabia, with Fahd distancing Tehran from the bombings. King Fahd's toning down of the Iranian discourse and animosity could be attributed to the low oil prices, and to attempts to balance regional power amid changing Iraqi–GCC dynamics, given that the billions in debt that Saddam owed to the GCC was being demanded by

Saudi Arabia and Kuwait. Furthermore, Fahd's position was an attempt to maintain calm and domestic balance, particularly in the Shi'i-dense Eastern province. Domestically, Iran evidenced a split in discourse construction on Saudi Arabia. While Rafsanjani aimed to mend the relations and begin a new chapter in Iran's post-war foreign policy, Khamenei aspired to establish his image as a Valy-i Faqih and as new leader of the Islamic Ummah in general and of the Shi'a in particular. In other words, both Iran and Saudi Arabia had mutual concerns. They endeavoured to maintain domestic and economic stability. This was particularly the case as Tehran sought to rebuild its economy and infrastructure after a devastating war, and Riyadh tried to regain its debts from Saddam amid dwindling oil prices. On the foreign policy front, both countries sought to recalibrate their regional relations, particularly in relation to a shift in regional politics after the end of the Iran–Iraq War.

The 1990 Iraqi invasion of Kuwait brought about opportunities for Iran, especially as both Iraq and the GCC states vied for Tehran's support. Rafsanjani's pragmatism in his role as president allowed Iran to exploit the regional animosity by implementing a policy of 'active neutrality'. This stance was permitted through an alliance between Khamenei and Rafsanjani allowing Iran to maintain its strength and survival. In addition, Iran's active neutrality allowed it to mend its regional relations, undergo economic reconstruction, and highlight its image as a regional power and leader of the Islamic world.

Immediately after Saddam's invasion of Kuwait, Iran condemned the attack, calling on Baghdad to withdraw its forces from Kuwait. Although Iran retained its position of active neutrality, the implications of this position on the Iranian discourses of the Self and Other were significant, as the analysis has shown. When the invasion began, Iran seized the opportunity to bolster and shore up its image of the Iranian Self. This was accomplished through a supra-discourse across all genres condemning Saddam's invasion and opposing foreign troops in the region, particularly in the Holy Lands. This condemnation resulted in two main discourses, the first being that the Iraqi invasion was in the interest of 'Zionism' and to the detriment of Islam and the Islamic Revolution, while the second highlighted the image of the Iranian Self as representative of true Mohammedan Islam and its leadership and legitimacy of the Islamic world.

The domestic discourse, particularly in the editorials and Friday prayer sermons, framed the invasion as an act of divine intervention and retribution, whereby the Gulf countries, particularly Kuwait and Saudi Arabia, had aided Saddam against Iran during the war. The trope of 'divine justice' (*adalat*) was employed. This discourse on the invasion was also exploited to highlight Iran's triumph against Saddam's aggression as a 'divine victory' and to formulate an image of Saudi military inferiority and weakness. The Iranian discourse also framed the invasion through tropes of a joint US–Iraq collaboration and conspiracy to invade Kuwait and Saudi Arabia, seeking to dominate the Persian Gulf's oil and energy supplies and gain control of OPEC. These representations had one goal in mind, asserting that the US had planned this invasion of Kuwait to establish its presence in the region with Iran in mind.

The Iranian domestic discourses framed the US arrival and presence in Saudi Arabia as an occupation of Mecca and Medina, and treason by the Al Saud and their ulama. These discourses of the Other were bolstered by utilizing tropes of treason, debauchery, and the ulama as being servants of the royal courts. The invasion of Kuwait brought about Iraqi overtures that included a comprehensive rapprochement through an economic package with Baghdad aiming to bypass UN-led sanctions through Iran. However, Iran's active neutrality prompted Tehran to reject this Iraqi overture, highlighting the Iranian Self as a trustworthy neighbour and a responsible international actor that respects the rule of law set by the UN resolutions. With the advent of war, a split emerged in the Iranian discourse. One group, represented by Rafsanjani, advocated active neutrality. A second group, represented by some members of the Majles along with the some ulama, called for a joint jihad with Iraq against the US. Ayatollah Khamenei, on the other hand, took a balanced position and constructed a discourse that merged both neutrality and negative rhetoric.

Iran's active neutrality in its foreign-policy discourse had shown signs of maturity in that they had implicitly agreed to a temporary US regional presence contrary to the Iranian domestic course. Furthermore, Iran exploited the regional events to rebuild its relationship with its neighbours and recalibrate its foreign policy by highlighting discourses of regional cooperation and regional security. All this occurred while Saudi Arabia began to highlight Iran's regional role, its Islamic identity, and invited Iran to participate in the hajj, thus ending the 1987 Iranian boycott and reversing Riyadh's ban on Tehran's hajj activities. Saudi Arabian discourse, particularly that of Fahd, underwent a complete reversal of Iran as its Other. The Saudi elite discourse now represented Iran fraternally, highlighting Iran's image of military superiority against Iraq, and calling for coexistence with Iran, highlighting its importance and peaceful relations with Tehran. The kingdom had now also called for a serious review of the GCC's relations with Iran. Tehran's relations with Saudi Arabia in the aftermath of Kuwait's liberation were showing signs of a thaw. The exchanges in visits between the foreign ministers of both states and Iran's return to the Hajj with all the conditions and restrictions imposed by Riyadh removed were clearly fruits reaped from Rafsanjani's pragmatism and 'active neutrality'. Months later, the Iranian president would begin to forge a relationship with Saudi Arabia's Crown Prince Abdullah bin Abdulaziz. This relationship would be key to furthering Iranian–Saudi détente, and this would extend to a total rapprochement under the auspices of the next Iranian president, Mohammad Khatami.

Chapter 5

BUILDING BRIDGES: FROM DÉTENTE TO RAPPROCHEMENT

Introduction

The 1990s were marked by an end to two major regional wars in the Middle East, resulting in weak economies coupled with low oil prices. Iran emerged from an enemy-imposed eight-year war with Iraq with heavy losses both to its economy and its international relations. In addition, the landslide victory of Khatami in 1997 provided a launch pad for Iran to alleviate its domestic pressures and end its era of international and regional isolation. Khatami's agenda attempted to reform not only the state but also Iran's international image through more press freedom (Shahidi 2007:48). The task was a tumultuous one. Khatami inherited a troubled Iranian foreign policy, including the Salman Rushdie fatwa and the Mykonos bombings in Germany. At the same time, in the Persian Gulf region the dispute over the UAE islands was a distraction, as the Islamic Republic was still seeking to export the revolution.

Furthermore, Hunter (2010: 185) argued that relations between the Arab states and Iran were 'uneven', i.e. the relations were good and neutral with some, such as Kuwait and Oman, but tense or negative with others, such as Bahrain and the UAE (Hunter 2010). In addition, the sectarian turbulence in Bahrain led to accusations of Iranian involvement and meddling in Bahrain's domestic affairs. In June 1993, Bahraini authorities accused the Iranian Revolutionary Guards Corps (IRGC) of setting up the group *Hizbollah-i Bahrain* with the intention of carrying out terrorist activities, leading Bahrain to recall its ambassador from Iran (Hiro 2001: 217). The dispute over the islands with the UAE led to a shift in position from the Emiratis; they demanded that any Iranian détente with the GCC be linked to settling the issue of the islands. The UAE took the case to the UN in April and August 1992 in order to protest against two incidents in which Iran expelled foreign workers employed by the UAE on charges of espionage, requesting that they have Iranian working visas.

Like Iran, Saudi Arabia also ended a war with Iraq after the invasion of Kuwait, which posed a grave threat to the GCC states. Consequently, both states had internal issues to confront. Domestically, Iranians suffered the effects of a weak economy and an infrastructure in need of immediate reconstruction along with an increasingly disgruntled youth. Saudi Arabia's participation in the liberation of Kuwait witnessed the construction of bases housing foreign troops on Saudi soil.

The presence of the US military shifted the character of the US–Saudi relationship from between equal partners to a relationship that allowed the US to utilize Saudi territory and resources, thereby gaining an upper hand in political and strategic developments in the Persian Gulf region (Niblock 2006). Furthermore, Saudi Arabia carried the financial burden of maintaining the US presence on Saudi soil and a large portion of financing the 1991 Gulf War, contributing US$60 billion (Niblock 2006).

Niblock (2006: 153) argued that the US presence and high expenditure allowed for 'radical Islamists to mobilize domestic and international Islamic opinion against' the kingdom (Niblock 2006). Saudi links with the US had a negative effect on the monarchy's legitimacy and credibility in Sunni Islamic circles. The 1990s gave rise to radical Islamism, mainly bin Laden and the Saudi awakening (*Sahwa*) of the ulama. The former had heavy repercussions in terms of Saudi domestic stability and on the kingdom's relations with the US. Furthermore, Bergen (2001: 87–90) argues that bin Laden sought to create an international Islamic army that would fight against US military involvement in the Islamic world, such as in Somalia. In turn, the creation of Al-Qaeda saw the rise of international terrorism in the 1990s, epitomized by the bombing of the World Trade Centre in 1993 and the bombing of a US installation in Riyadh in November 1995, possibly in retaliation for the execution of the Sunni opposition activist Abdallah al-Hudhaif in August 1995, followed by the Khobar bombings in June 1996 when nineteen US service members were killed. Niblock (2006: 154) contends that it is not clear that bin Laden had direct links to these attacks; however, his ideological mindset and speeches may have encouraged the attacks.

On the domestic front, the Sahwa imams also gained momentum and popularity as they criticized the Saudi government's increasing alliance with the West. These, along with low oil prices, also led to a rise in discontent and the formation of an internal opposition, principally marked by the Sahwa ulama. These opposition voices included young aspiring imams such as Sefr Al-Hawalli and Salman Al-Ouda, along with an exile-based opposition that led to the establishment of the Committee for the Defense of Legitimate Rights (*CDLR*) in addition to the later emergence of Osama bin Laden as an opposition figure.

The Saudi leadership witnessed the rise of the pan-Arab and Islamic Crown Prince Abdullah as de facto ruler of Saudi Arabia following Fahd's debilitating stroke in November 1995. Furthermore, the 1990s proved to be a troublesome period for the Saudi state. In addition to the financial instability that eclipsed the Saudi economy after the Gulf War in 1991, the Islamist opposition steered the country towards a cycle of violence. From a foreign-affairs perspective, Clinton's election in 1993 and the Netanyahu government in Israel complicated the Saudi role as an Arab and Islamic leader. Clinton opted to relegate Saudi Arabia from its role as a regional ally in the Arab peace process to a secondary power consulted when needed. Israel's settlement expansion and derailing of the peace process also strained relations with Saudi Arabia, particularly since Fahd had championed the process of Arab peace since the Fahd Peace Plan of 1981, leading up to the Oslo and Madrid accords.

Now let us move to consider Iranian–Saudi representations of the Self and the Other during Rafsanjani's détente in the late 1990s. At this time, the economies were depressed, mainly due to low oil prices, which resulted in a security threat emanating from Iraq, terrorism, and more importantly the threat of the Taliban to Iran. This was accompanied by a discursive shift away from negative themes and rhetoric of treachery and 'Zionist subservience', to language leaning towards confidence building and trust and cooperation, in addition to underlining the geopolitical, cultural, and historical prestige of both states. Images such as the 'ominous triangle' gave rise to discourses of a collaboration between the US, Pakistan, and the Taliban. This bolstered the Iranian narrative towards the US and its allies, without jeopardizing any attempts at a rapprochement with Saudi Arabia. Similarly, images such as of Persian culture and prestige, and Saudi Arabia housing the cradle of Islam, were utilized by both states to strengthen their discourses on regional and Islamic cooperation and leadership. Clearly, differences in religious and political stances and opinions did not inhibit a positive image construction and discourse of the Other.

This chapter highlights how both domestic and external forces played a decisive role in the Saudi–Iranian détente and rapprochement as well as in Saudi–Iranian Othering. There are four main arguments that run through this chapter. First, the Iranian establishment was united over rapprochement with Saudi Arabia but divided on Western détente. Second, I argue that neutrality was central to Iranian–Saudi representations of the Other. This represented a maturing of the Iranian regime compared with the aggressive rhetoric of the 1980s. Furthermore, I argue that Othering and discursive constructions in both states evolved between Rafsanjani's tenure and Khatami's presidency. These resulted in narratives of Islamic unity, economic collaboration and, later, security cooperation. On a final note, I argue that Saudi–Iranian Othering in this period was directly related to the identity of the Iranian leadership and how this in turn was perceived by Saudi Arabia. As Khatami ascended the presidency, Saudi discursive constructions of the Iranian Other also changed, leading to narratives emphasizing geopolitical significance as well as historical and cultural prestige.

The 1997 OIC Summit and the Iranian Self's 'Split Personality'

Iranian foreign policy in the 1997–1999 period was in many ways an extension of Rafsanjani's foreign policy of détente in the aftermath of the Iran–Iraq war. Khatami's presidency, from August 1997 to August 2005, attempted to create the conditions for rapprochement and to break Iran's isolation by mending its relations on both the global and Middle East levels. The Iranian discourse and narrative was neutral overall – if not positive – towards external states, except for Pakistan and Turkey. It was Pakistan's support for the Taliban and Turkey's strategic alliance with Israel that gave rise to the Iranian Othering of both states, especially in its editorials. With regards to the Arab states of the Middle East, there was a clear split in Iranian discourse. While Iranian elite discourse was overall neutral towards the

Arab states, its editorials were critical, especially with regards to Saudi recognition of the Taliban, the Iranian–UAE dispute over the three islands, and Israeli plans to announce Jerusalem as its capital. In the case of Saudi Arabia, Iranian alterity was illustrated mainly in the press, and it was isolated to incidents related mainly to the Taliban and US presence in the Persian Gulf. As part of his 'dialogue among civilisations', Khatami's mandate was to establish a mechanism that would melt the ice-cold relations between Iran and the international community that had prevailed since 1979. Khatami suggested that the Iranian government could employ this dialogue 'to avoid any action or behaviour causing tensions', thereby presenting a rebranded image of Iran, namely a peaceful Iranian Self, but also one that would resist 'any power wishing to exercise dominance over us' while supporting any oppressed states or people, including 'Palestinians oppressed by Israel' (Khatami 1997a, 1997f, 1998b).

The OIC was a forum utilized by Iran to showcase its new peaceful image and build bridges as promoted by détente and rapprochement. Khatami's discourse at the OIC summit demonstrated how inter-religious dialogue, formulated in his premise of a dialogue among civilizations, could be employed to consolidate Iran's image and position in the Islamic world and international affairs. However, and in contrast to Khatami's speech, Khamenei demonstrated a rather different approach and image of Iran, one that reaffirmed Iran's revolutionary principles adopted since the revolution and maintained throughout an eight-year war. This difference in image representation, I argue, reflects a form of 'split personality' in the discourse of the 'rebranded' Iranian Self. Khatami's reformist and pragmatist approach was intended to improve relations with the West, whereas the radical approach of Khamenei highlighted the Iranian revolutionary narrative proclaimed since 1979.

Pragmatic and radical aspects of the Iranian discourse were reflected in the opening speeches of the OIC summit. Pragmatically, Khatami – in discussing the relations between the Islamic Ummah, the West, and Iran – attempted to highlight a 'deep-rooted understanding' of Western culture, by going beyond 'superficialities to reach its superficial basis and the fundamentals of its value' (Khatami 1997d). Khamenei's fiery speech highlighted the radical aspects, wherein he decried the Western Other as 'a camp of arrogance', employing 'political, military, scientific, and military capabilities ... to interfere in the affairs of other nations and governments, plunder their wealth, oppress nations, and stigmatize cultures and traditions' (Khamenei 1997a).

In contrast to Khatami's pragmatism about the role of the OIC in creating a new and just world order, Khamenei's radical positioning against the Western Other contrasted with rapprochement and détente and Khatami's pragmatism on the same stage. In conceptualizing the Western Other, Khamenei's speech focused on defending Iran's right to its Islamic government after the Islamic Revolution and with representing Islam in Iran as a holistic image of Islam. In defining Western efforts to muddy the Iranian image by attacking the revolutionary government, Khamenei defended and conceptualized the Iranian Self as an antithetical ideal to Western propaganda against it. For Khamenei, the US was still the 'Great Satan', and the West was still under a Zionist influence (Khamenei

1997a). In adopting such contrasting approaches, Khatami and Khamenei can be understood as opening up to different audiences; Khatami's pragmatic approach showed an Iran open to all yet willing to commit to 'perseverance in the face of difficulties' (Khatami 1997d). In short, Khatami looked 'both ways' in contrast to Khamenei, who was addressing the Islamic world. Notwithstanding these differences, Khamenei continued Khomeini's neither East nor West policy, to end regional and international isolation imposed by both the West and its immediate neighbours in light of the 1979 revolution.

The Iranian editorial discourse represented Iran as the leaders of the Islamic world, constructing the image of Iran as 'flagbearer of Islam'. The editorials further defined Iran's position at the OIC as a country defending Islamic unity and brotherhood, whereas Khamenei was portrayed as the 'reviver of Islamic unity', defining Iran's role in rapprochement towards Saudi Arabia. However, a split was apparent in the editorial discourse. One of the sides in the editorial discourse persisted on defining the Iranian Self as the true leader of the Islamic world, defined by 'Islamic government' (*Kayhan* 1997c). This was done while retaining Khatami's 'Western civilization' discourse as an imperative for developing unity. Based on this true 'Islamic' identity of the Iranian government and the OIC nations returning to the origins of Islam ('asālathā-yi Islāmī), the discourse of Iran solving the problem of the Islamic world was emphasized as well (*Resalat* 1997c).

The significance of this representation is twofold. First it highlighted Iran's internal divisions regarding the definition of détente and the Other. For Khatami, détente could be achieved internationally, whereas Khamenei's view of détente was framed on an Islamic and regional level. The Other defined by Khamenei was a continuation of the revolutionary 1980s narrative, but to Khatami, the Other was based on successful dialogue and confidence building. Second, the overall narrative and notion of détente and rapprochement on the regional and Islamic level attempt to project an image of a mature post-war Iran. Although the 1980s rhetoric of Islamic leadership and Western denigration still existed, the relinquishing of the polarizing criticism of the GCC and Arab states reflected a desire to break Iran's isolation and achieve its domestic goals of economic and infrastructure reconstruction.

Afghanistan, the Taliban, and the 'Ominous Triangle'

The Rafsanjani and Khatami eras were marked by significant developments in Afghanistan. By 1992, the Soviet-backed People's Democratic Party (PDP) had been ousted and a civil war erupted that saw Pakistani, Saudi-Arabian as well as Iranian involvement. By 1995, the different factional supporters were clear: Iran supported the Northern Alliance that included the Hazaras, Ismaili Shi'a, Tajiks, and Uzbeks; while Pakistan and Saudi Arabia supported the Pakistan-trained Taliban who took control of Kabul in 1996. Keynoush (2016: 146) argues that 'even tensions in Afghanistan failed to disrupt the Saudi-Iranian rapprochement', while the first three years of the Khatami presidency coincided with several major incidents in Afghanistan that directly affected Iran: the Taliban attack and capture of Mazar-i Sharif and the accompanying execution of nine Iranian diplomats, and the fall of Kabul to the Taliban. Furthermore, while the discourse discussed Iran's Other in relation to the Taliban, images such as the *Musalas-i shūm* or 'Ominous Triangle' were employed to highlight and embolden the sectarian narrative that Iran propagated towards the Taliban and the US, without infringing on their attempts at détente with Saudi Arabia.

Arguably, two reasons underpinned the official silence regarding Saudi and Pakistani support for the Taliban. First, Iran's focus was on breaking its regional isolation and achieving rapprochement with both its neighbours, chiefly Saudi Arabia. Second, and as Clawson (1998) contends, the rise of the Taliban could 'stir unrest among the two million Afghans in Iran' while also being a contributing factor to Sunni–Shi'i tensions in eastern Iran where the Sunnis made up a third of the population (Clawson 1998: 77). However, the overall Iranian editorial press discourse was much more vocal and agitated. At the start of the Khatami presidency, the official recognition of the Taliban by Saudi Arabia, the UAE and Pakistan generated a mixed response.

On the day Mazar-i Sharif fell, the Pakistani government was quick to announce that it would recognize the Taliban government, thereby ending their isolation (Burns 1997). UAE and Saudi Arabia quickly followed. The reaction of Iranian officials was neutral: they said that responding to the events was an internal matter. Newspaper headlines focused mainly on Khatami's inauguration with editorials commenting and criticizing American, Saudi, and Pakistani involvement in Afghanistan. As will be discussed below, the newspapers clearly took over the role of criticism from the state, which was not ready to risk a much-needed détente with the leading GCC state. Therefore, the main pillars of the state, that is the government, ulama, and Supreme Leader, adopted a mainly silent or neutral stance towards Saudi Arabia and the UAE, reflecting a state developing a more mature diplomatic agenda compared with the immediate post-revolutionary period, while allocating certain tasks to different organs of the state. Like Saudi Arabia in the 1980s, elite voices were mainly neutral and the role of criticism was devolved to what could be defined as independent non-state actors, in this case newspaper editorials.

On the eve of the official election results, Rafsanjani made it clear that 'it has always been our policy not to interfere in the internal affairs of other states, however, we believe the path of war as a way of solving Afghanistan's problems to be an erroneous one' (Rafsanjani 1997c). Rafsanjani's neutral reaction to the fall of Mazar-i Sharif to the Taliban and the exile of General Dostum stressed that Iran's policy had always been 'to be on good terms with all states that are recognized by the UN, while until now, the previous government of Afghanistan has been formally recognized by the UN and we are waiting for the future'. While Rafsanjani stopped short of recognizing the Taliban government, he did not denigrate or condemn the rise of the Taliban or its sponsoring states (Rafsanjani 1997c). Similarly, the spokesman for the Ministry of Foreign Affairs echoed Rafsanjani's narrative of Afghan self-determination, adding that 'external interference will not solve Afghanistan's problems and those who believe that through their interference they can overcome the Afghan people's will are repeating a historic mistake' while promoting dialogue between the 'different ethnicities is the best solution to solving Afghanistan's problems' (Iranian Foreign Ministry 1997). Like Rafsanjani's neutrality, the response stopped short of naming Pakistan and Saudi Arabia for their support of the Taliban. The Friday prayer sermons also followed this official line. According to the clergy, the events taking place in Afghanistan were a 'domestic matter' and 'unclear', shifting from the rhetoric of the previous decade and adopting a conciliatory tone by advising jihadi groups 'to set aside their differences and commit to dialogue' (Yazdi 1997).

On the other hand, the editorial discourse gave rise to two main themes: A sectarian narrative that viewed the Shi'a of Afghanistan as in danger because of the Taliban's rise (*Resalat* 1997a; *Jomhouri Eslami* 1997b), and a narrative that identified a conspiracy and collaboration between 'America, Saudi Arabia, and Pakistan, which are clearly tilting the international balance in support of the terrorist Taliban' (*Jomhouri Eslami* 1997b). It is this aid and conspiracy that the Iranian editorials referred to as 'Musalas-i shūm', that is, the 'ominous triangle' (*Jomhouri Eslami* 1997g; *Kayhan* 1997e). This allegory served to embolden the discourse on the Iranian Other, demonizing Pakistan and the Wahhabi ideology, yet it stopped short of directly targeting the Saudi state. As earlier suggested, regardless of the religious ideology and views on the Other, if the political agendas were served – in this case attempts at détente and rapprochement – then a more implicit, neutral or positive discourse can be constructed to serve those agendas. During this period the agenda of Iran was to break out of its international isolation, strengthen its economy, and sustain regional security amid an increasing US regional presence, an Iraqi threat, and the Taliban on its borders.

The execution of the Iranian diplomats was followed by an immediate response from the Iranian state by the president and later the Supreme Leader, with the Friday sermons propagating Khamenei's narrative. He defined the atrocity as one fomented by 'global arrogance' and executed by the state of Pakistan who had utilized the Taliban as a tool of US hegemonic expansion. This, according to Khamenei, underlined that Pakistani control over Afghanistan gave the US full control over transnational oil pipelines in the service of US energy companies (Khamenei 1998). Khatami's response sought to maintain a dialogue and good neighbourly relations. He condemned the Taliban and criticized Pakistan slightly, but stopped short of implicating the Pakistani state in the takeover of Mazar-i Sharif or the execution of the Iranian diplomats (Khatami 1998a). However, the state's criticism of Pakistan was shouldered by the foreign ministry, chiefly by Kamal Kharrazi, who was more explicit in his condemnation of Pakistani support for the Taliban, holding Pakistan accountable for the Taliban's successes and the 'barbaric hostilities' in Mazar-i Sharif (Kharrazi 1998). The Iranian elite's construction of the Other was directed at Iran's historic enemy, the US, rather than at regional states that officially recognized the Taliban government. Elite discourse on Saudi Arabia was silent, thereby underlining Iran's political calculation as it put the long-term goals of détente and rapprochement ahead of vociferous reaction.

This signified a shift in position, with Saudi Arabia no longer featuring on Iran's list of enemies.

A polarized but strategic and calculated response was palpable in clerical and editorial discourses. In line with the government, there was no mention of Saudi Arabia in the Friday sermons, where the imams leading these prayers are seen as representatives of the Supreme Spiritual Leader, the valy-i faqih, and so mentioning Saudi Arabia would be construed as an official response. The imams, however, shaped the potency of rhetoric and narrative towards Iran's Other. Even among them, those imams who held cabinet positions used a balanced tone in critiquing Pakistan. However, clerics such as Jannat and Emami-Kashani employed an abrasive narrative towards Pakistan, alluding to Saudi Arabia and the Wahhabi ideology responsible for the Taliban's 'barbarism'. In the editorials, a similar approach was noticeable, holding Pakistan responsible as an executor of America's regional agendas, along with Saudis, terming the trio the 'ominous triangle'. By naming the US as a perpetrator in a geopolitical sense on the eastern front of Iran, the Saudis were held responsible for funding and expanding the Wahhabi ideology.

The positionality and ideological predilections of the editorials, along with their reader bases, defined the editorial orientation. This was especially true in the case of *Jomhouri Eslami*, a leading newspaper and critic of the Iranian state who blamed state complacency and weakness. Perhaps in hindsight, such a critique was directed at the right-wing opposition to Khatami, which believed that Khatami's dialogue and diplomacy had ventured far enough to jeopardize Iranian borders. Criticizing the Ministry of Foreign Affairs for its silence on recent changes, the editorial blamed the Iranian ministry for entrusting the 'ominous triangle' with the life of the Iranian diplomats in Pakistan (*Jomhouri Eslami* 1998c). Critiquing the diplomatic overture in Khatami's policy – and going as far as to name it the 'negligence' of the political apparatus – the criticism in the editorial referred back to the Other i.e. to the ominous triangle of the US, Saudi Arabia, and Pakistan. A major shared trope in Iranian discourse towards Saudi Arabia and the 'ominous triangle' utilized a narrative of a murderous and savage Taliban, which was a direct consequence of Wahhabism. Therefore, the editorials discursively constructed Saudi Arabia as a country that adopted a specific ideology while spreading Wahhabi-inspired barbarism. The potency of this representation was first witnessed in *Resalat* (1998b), which defined the Taliban as reflecting a version of Islam characterized by US 'terror and savagery', funded by Saudi Arabia, and executed by Pakistan.

As for the ideological and financial aspects, the editorial suggested that Saudi support for the Taliban goes beyond simple political considerations and strategic mechanics, and the Islam of the Taliban has affinities with Saudi Wahhabism. Drawing a parallel with the Serbian massacres, the editorials juxtaposed the Taliban's massacre of Hazara Shi'a in Mazar-i-Sharif with 'the era of Karadžić and Mladić' (*Jomhouri Eslami* 1998c). While a rare occurrence, the narrative blamed Saudi Arabia directly for the atrocities and terror against the Shi'i Muslims, and the Saudis were discursively constructed as anti-Shi'a and as sectarians fracturing the unity of the Islamic world. Moreover, characterizing the rise of Taliban and its advances as a conspiracy against Iran and Islam (*Kayhan* 1998b; *Resalat* 1998b, 1998c), the narrative raised was like the 1980s Iran–Iraq war, where Saddam's imposed war against Iran was represented as a conspiracy against the revolution and 'true' representation of global Islam (*islām-i-jahānī*). The rise of the Taliban, in this perspective, was seen as an attempt to undermine 'real Mohammedan Islam' with alternative Islam along the Iranian borders (Resalat 1998c). Such narratives were used to promulgate the idea that Saudi Arabia – through its partnership with the US – is trying to fund and stop the rise of 'real Islam' and hinder 'the spread of revolution' (*Kayhan* 1998d) by besieging Iran from all directions (*Kayhan* 1998c). However, all these references were implicit, and they show the cautious approaches adopted by the editorials to not contradict the political elites and their approaches to rapprochement with Saudi Arabia. By showing the leanings of the Taliban's extremism towards Saudi ideology implicitly, the editorials did not intend to hinder rapprochement but rather sought to produce a positive representation of the Iranian Self.

The editorials reconstructed the Saudi Other in Khamenei's (Khamenei 1998) sermon and emphasized geopolitical rhetoric, echoing the narratives of greed and energy hegemony and victimization of the people of Afghanistan and Pakistan, and asserting the Saudi link with the Taliban and the role of latter in producing a transnational security threat (*Jomhouri Eslami* 1998f, *Kayhan* 1998a, *Resalat* 1998a). Regurgitating the argument that Saudi funding was intended to restrict the continuation of the 'true Islam and political Islam', the editorials discursively constructed the Saudi as an Other in terms of funding US interests in Central Asia and creating a route from Afghanistan through Pakistan, towards the Persian Gulf where the US has established bases. Moreover, the geopolitical assessment was also employed to discuss the case of the Persian Gulf, US aggression, and a narrative of the Arabs' historical animosity towards Persians and Iran amid the current geopolitical challenges and Iraq War of the 1980s.

The silence and neutrality of the Iranian elite alongside the active role of the editorials convey the state's calculated political priorities compared with the defensiveness and counter-reaction of the 1980s. Building on the speeches and statements of the elite and the ulama's sermons, the Iranian press discourse took on the explicit role of constructing Iran's Other. In an era of détente and rapprochement, Iranian editorials may have attributed Taliban atrocities and funding to Saudi Arabia, but they avoided the previous pattern of systematic denigration, which can be attributed to the holistic vision of regional rapprochement, especially with Saudi Arabia and the GCC states, in an attempt to alleviate Iran's isolation and economic woes.

Saudi Representations

Amid Saudi Arabia's economic downturn and the rise of the Sahwa movement, Crown Prince Abdullah became the de facto ruler following Fahd's debilitating stroke in November 1995. In this context, the representation of the Saudi Self and the Other was defined by US foreign policy towards the Middle East, the withering of Saudi finances, and the personal characteristics of Abdullah as a Pan-Arabist, conforming to his tribal background and Islamist-leaning persona. There was also an interesting shift in the representation of the Saudi Self, especially the 'low profile', and at times the silence, of the editorials when discussing the kingdom's domestic affairs.

Saudi Arabia's internal and external Others can be said to be intertwined, in the sense that the domestic opposition, mainly composed of Islamists, spun narratives revolving around wealth and expenditure at the one end and subservience to Western powers at the other end. As the regional events of the 1990s combined with the domestic circumstances of the Saudi state, the external Other can be defined as the US and Israel. I also argue that Saudi Arabia's relations with the US under the Clinton presidency, including US foreign policy, the deterioration of the 'Arab Peace Process' under the Netanyahu government, and Saudi financial difficulties, played a role in the representation of the Saudi Self and its external Other. With regards to Iran, I suggest that Saudi fears of any implication of Iran in the Khobar bombings led to the latter being discounted as a Saudi Other. This was mainly due to Saudi fears of a military attack against Iran, which would have led to a regional war with detrimental domestic, economic, and geopolitical repercussions.

The Khobar Bombings: Clerical Opposition, Economic Downturn, and Social Instability

With Saddam's invasion of Kuwait and Operation Desert Storm in 1991, Saudi Arabia's financial resources were seriously depleted, after a $60 billion expenditure and the defence contracts it committed to before and after the war (Bronson 2006: 206). Furthermore, the presence of US bases gave rise to opposition within the clerical establishment, represented by young clerics known as the 'Sahwa', and led by Safer al-Hawali and Salman al-Auda who, as Bronson (2006: 207) argues, operated 'on the fringe of the official establishment'. As with Juhayman in 1979, the young clerics again questioned the legitimacy of the state. This time, questions revolved around the dependence of the state on foreign troops to defend the holy lands, especially given the mammoth arms expenditure of these years.

The Khobar bombings in June 1996 and the state's reactions best demonstrate the representation of the Saudi Self and its internal Other. Unlike the siege of Mecca in 1979 that witnessed continual press conferences on the part of the minister of the interior, Nayef, or Fahd's interviews with the international media, the Saudi reaction to the Khobar bombings was a cautious one. In this author's opinion, the response to the attacks was tactful, with different discourse genres dealing with an incident in a coherent and structured manner so as not to give the opposition a sense of victory or project an image of a weak state. To downplay the attacks, the state took decisive steps to disseminate information and calculate its responses. These included short statements by the Saudi elite – i.e. by Fahd and Abdullah – in the days following the bombings. However, issues of terrorism and responses to the narratives spun by the Islamic opposition were later highlighted in speeches such as at the Shura Council, Hajj, and international conferences including the GCC summits. Furthermore, there was a general silence from Nayef and the ministry of the interior so as not to lay blame on the wrong group or derail the investigations. The response from the foreign ministry was initially at ambassadorial level rather than ministerial, constituting another move to downplay the value of the attack and to deflect attention away from those responsible. As for the press, short editorials spanning two days were released, published two days after the bombings, which was also a clear sign that the press was also under security orders. The ulama also took three days to condemn the bombings. The clerical response, when it came, took three forms: Friday sermons condemning the attack, a statement released by the Board of Senior Ulama, and a religious edict by Sheikh bin Baz.

The royal response came in the form of replies to foreign leaders' (primarily from the Arab Gulf states and the US) expressions of solidarity. Crown Prince Abdullah was the first to release a statement via a solidarity call with the Sheikh of Bahrain, restricting press statements to 'condemnation of the bombing' and declaring that 'such terrorist acts will not diminish or get the better of the [kingdom's] security and stability' (al-Saud 1996a). Fahd echoed a similar message, while also clearly labelling the bombing as a terrorist act that not only Islam, but also 'all monotheistic religions condemn and do not recognize as an appropriate manner in dealing with matters, no matter the reasons or justifications' (al-Saud 1996c). This was a clear reaffirmation of the general stance of Saudi Arabia's moderate Islam.

In turn, a supra-narrative of 'moderate Islam' was projected through Saudi Arabia's ambassador to the UK, Ghazi Algosaibi (Saudi Foreign Ministry 1996). This externally directed narrative attempted to use four main messages to frame the kingdom. The first was that Saudi Arabia was on a path of moderate Islam and the Khobar bombings would not 'change its moderate course'. The second was that the general Saudi public was moderate and 'outraged', signifying that the Saudi populace rejected such an ideology and 'such wanton acts of mayhem'. The third was that terrorism was not isolated to Islam and Saudi Arabia; it was a 'worldwide epidemic … and Saudi Arabia is no exception'. The final message was of a friendly Saudi Arabia that bore no animosity to the West or its allies. The ambassador's statement argued that the US was an ally and friend, representing US personnel as 'guests … engaged in helping the Saudi armed forces [to] defend the country' (Saudi Foreign Ministry 1996). Therefore, the narrative was clear, discursively representing Saudi Arabia as Islamically moderate and safe, accepting of foreigners and non-Muslims, and a victim of global terrorism.

The editorial response to the Khobar bombings shifted from the total silence observed by *al-Madina*, to an echo of the state narrative in *Asharq Al-Awsat* and *al-Riyadh*, with *al-Hayat* commenting on the lack of information disseminated by the Saudi state. The editorials, mainly *Asharq Al-Awsat* and *al-Riyadh*, echoed the state narrative through three main tropes. First, the incident in Khobar – terrorism – was a foreign phenomenon imported to Saudi Arabia, and the 'Khobar perpetrators may have been professionally trained in Arab and Islamic capitals' (*Asharq Al-Awsat* 1996; *al-Riyadh* 1997o). *Asharq Al-Awsat* highlighted the 'culture and principles of Saudi Arabia' that would not condone such an act, thereby stressing the notion of moderation within Saudi's Islamic culture (*Asharq Al-Awsat* 1996). The notion of moderation in Saudi Islamic culture was intertwined with the state's supposed leniency and toleration. *Al-Riyadh* argued that 'Saudi Arabia is not a country that is based on parties and divisions', and no matter the 'difference of opinion, no party will ever resort to violence and revenge', hinting at the Islamic opposition in Saudi Arabia since 1991, which included opposition to the state 'that has always respected these practices and nurtured them' (*al-Riyadh* 1997o). On a similar note, *al-Hayat* emphasized the 'trust the people have in the security services' in apprehending the perpetrators as they had in the past, referring to other incidents in Saudi Arabia such as the Riyadh bombings in November 1995 (*al-Hayat* 1996). The second trope observed in the editorials was the representation of Saudi stability, strength, and longevity. The editorials suggested that 'Saudi Arabia's domestic and foreign policies ... are the result of years of experience and productive work, while it will not be an easy task to eradicate' these efforts (*Asharq Al-Awsat* 1996). The third trope put Saudi at war with international terrorism. Propagated mainly in *al-Riyadh*, whose editorials were aimed at a more domestic audience, the narrative attempted to highlight the strength of the Saudi state by downplaying the attack and any Saudi negligence, principally by equating Saudi with other states: 'Other Arab cities with high security standards as good as the kingdom's, as well as large countries that possess technologies and capabilities more than all the third world combined ... have fallen victim to terrorism'. Therefore, to the domestic audience, the message was clear: Saudi Arabia was dealing with a criminal while blaming foreign powers and organizations, and was therefore in an international war against terrorism (*al-Riyadh* 1997o).

In the aftermath of the Khobar bombings, the Saudi state was attacked by the Islamist opposition – mainly by bin Laden – as deceiving the 'ordinary man ... suffering from taxes and bad services' in a country that was the largest oil producer in the world. This critique held that the attacks were justified and legitimate, and it underlined the fact that Saudi society was at one with the Sahwa speeches in the mosques, the latter emphasizing that Saudi Arabia had 'become an American colony ... and what happened [in Riyadh and Khobar] in two bombings ... is evidence of the anger of Saudi people against America ... their real enemy is America' (Fisk 1996). It is therefore clear that the internal Other for the Saudi state was the religious opposition, that is the Sahwa and bin Laden. However, it is noteworthy that the state did little to define the internal Other in the Saudi discourse, especially considering the Khobar bombings. Instead, the elite discourse, especially that of Fahd and Abdullah, underlined the economic recovery, the drive towards democracy through the Shura Council, and solidarity with the Palestinians, all of which were founded on Islamic and Arab principles, thus highlighting their legitimacy without mentioning the internal Other.

When juxtaposing the events in Saudi Arabia, its economic downturn, and the narrative of clerical opposition within mainstream Saudi discourse, it is evident that the state attempted to legitimize its role in representing the Saudi Self. The speeches were aimed at legitimizing the al-Sauds and indirectly fending off the opposition's narrative through three main messages. First, a representation of Islamic service was promulgated, cementing the al-Saud's Islamic credentials and their servitude to Islam by affirming the kingdom's Islamic identity. In a speech to the Shura Council Fahd stated that the council was:

> adopted according to a fixed Islamic approach that was bestowed in Allah's holy book and his Prophet's Sunna . . . Our country, thanks to Allah, is at the zenith of its strength. Firstly, [Saudi Arabia] is solid in its Islamic doctrine, and in the many gifts and abundant natural resources that Allah has bestowed on it. From these gifts, God has granted us success in expanding the holy sites and mosques . . . and this is our duty.
>
> (al-Saud 1997g)

Second, the opposition's accusations of lavish spending, along with a dwindling economy dependent on the US, was countered with a representation of Saudi Arabia as a country rooted in development values and perseverance, with its citizens as the state's utmost priority. Arguing that 'the region has gone through [a lot] in the past few years from serious incidents that have exhausted our economy and development', Fahd promulgated an image of a self-sufficient manufacturing state with an economy that was 'much stronger that others may envisage', with factories and capabilities that 'evolve day by day . . . manufacturing has advanced, and our factories are in the thousands, manufacturing different necessary products and accessories'. Indirectly responding to bin Laden's criticism of the negligent nature of the state towards the 'suffering ordinary man', Fahd reinforced the image of the responsibility of the al-Saud towards their people with the state working 'with resoluteness and determination to achieve all that guarantees citizens' happiness and prosperity' (al-Saud 1997g).

Third, during the 1997 Hajj season, Fahd defined Saudi Arabia's support for a 'comprehensive and fair peace that alleviates the oppressed and returns invaded Arab lands to their owners in Palestine and Syria and Lebanon', condemning the 'building of settlements [and] any action in the Holy City that goes against its status quo and the rights of its legitimate people' (al-Saud 1997e). Fahd's aim was clear; the role of Saudi Islamic and Arab leadership was emphasized as a state that cared for the plight of Arabs, their lands, and religious sites. Therefore, Fahd implicitly countered the opposition's representation of a weak and subservient Saudi state.

Saudi Editorials and the Saudi Other

It is intriguing that all Saudi newspapers promulgated a narrative of US subservience towards Israel, as well as of US treachery towards the Arab and

Islamic world following its two vetoes in the UNSC.[1] On the other hand, *al-Madina* and *al-Riyadh*, although different in their political alignments, since the former was Islamist and the latter Pan-Arab, also represented US treachery during a fake peace process, where all Israel wanted to achieve was to take Arab lands under cover of US protection via the peace process. Similarly, both newspapers also highlighted Saudi Arabia's role in the comprehensive peace process. Saudi Arabia was constructed as the designer and initiator of peace, keeping Jerusalem and Islamic rights at the forefront of its mission, possibly in a bid to appease their domestic audience after the derailment of the peace process.

As argued earlier, the use of images and discourse construction can shift with changes in political agendas as well as in the political environment. Saudi discourse, such as the editorials, constructed an image of a war of Israel against Islam with the US aiding the former, highlighting tropes of US–Israeli treachery, Arab weakness, and the leadership role of Saudi Arabia in the Arab and Islamic world. Images were readily available and mobilized to enhance the image of the Saudi Self to both domestic and external audiences. These included the use of images of a biased US stance towards Israel in the Arab Peace Process and the Oslo treaty as 'acquiescence contracts', Saudi Arabia as the protector of the Arab and Islamic world, the kingdom's support and sacrifice to the Arab world in general and the Palestinians in particular, and the image of a powerful Saudi monarchy that extensively travelled the world in aid and support of the Palestinians.

Like the Iranian discourse, the Saudi discourses framed the US as an ally and subservient to Israel and Zionism. Arguing that the draft resolutions were unanimously supported by all the international community, including the European members – namely the UK, France, Sweden, and Portugal – Saudi editorials discursively constructed the US as heavily swayed and pressured by Israel, labelling it 'a puzzling position ... an excuse that does not convince anyone' with the US a 'biased mediator' neglecting its role as an intermediary (*Asharq Al-Awsat* 1997c). Even before the veto, the Pan-Arab *al-Riyadh* and Islamist-leaning *al-Madina* editorials constructed an image of Israeli–US collaboration as 'a judge and criminal sharing a bed, thinking and articulating a verdict in an identical fashion that benefits their goals and liking' (*al-Riyadh* 1997a), going as far as describing the Israel position towards the peace agreements as 'acquiescence contracts' (*'uqūd 'ith 'ān*) (*al-Madina* 1997c), metaphorically constructing Israel as the sole actor ordering around all other parties, including the US and the Arabs. According to *al-Madina* (1997c) 'Benyamin Netanyahu attempted to...convert the Arab–Israeli negotiations into a system that produces Arab acquiescence to Israeli will in the Middle East'.

1. On 7 March 1997 the US vetoed the Resolution (S/1997/165) calling on Israel to refrain from any settlement activity at the Jabal Abu Ghneim area of East Jerusalem. A second resolution (S/1997/241) was vetoed by the US once again on 21 March 1997 calling on Israel to immediately cease construction of the Jabal Abu Ghneim settlement, as well as all other Israeli settlement activities in the occupied territories.

The second trope constructed US support for Israel as a war against Islam and the Arab world. Pan-Arab leaning newspapers, such as *Asharq Al-Awsat* and *al-Riyadh* also advanced the argument that the US and Israel were in a state of war with the Muslim and Arab worlds. Following the second US veto on 22 March 1997, *Asharq Al-Awsat* opined that the construction of settlements by the Netanyahu government was purposely done to 'defy the nationalist and religious emotions of the Arabs and Muslims', framing Israel as an instigator of violence by building the settlement in Eastern Jerusalem while covered by US vetoes. Therefore, the US was implicitly represented as a collaborator in a war against Muslims and Arabs. Moreover, the conspiracy promoted by the Saudi editorial also characterized the Israeli–US agenda as a bid to 'complete the hegemony over Jerusalem and isolate it completely', before the prospects of further peace negotiations (*Asharq Al-Awsat* 1997g).

Furthermore, Israeli–US treachery was also a main trope argued by Islamist editorials, while echoing a more polarized narrative branding the peace process as a form of deception and a 'red herring'. In a further attempt to implicitly construct the US as a 'treacherous collaborator', *al-Madina* argued that the Oslo and Madrid accords, which were sponsored by the US, were a diversion. The editorials argued that consecutive Israeli administrations planned for a complete takeover of Jerusalem by delaying any discussions over the Holy City to 'expand Israeli control over Jerusalem at the expense of the West Bank' (*al-Madina* 1997a). *Al-Madina* also observed that 'what differentiates [the Israeli Labour Party] is the age and experience' of its leaders involved, where both have similar hegemonic ambitions, since they demand that 'all of Jerusalem be the eternal capital of Israel ... both want to keep the lands in the West Bank, Gaza, and Golan'. According to *al-Madina*, Israel's 'strategic aim', supported by a US veto, was 'total hegemony over the Middle East region ... the aim is one, only the tactics differ' (*al-Madina* 1997a). The newspaper further argued that although the 'US asserts it is against building settlements in the occupied Arab lands ... claiming that it does not help the peace process', the main purpose behind such a slogan was to appease the Arabs 'every time the Israelis attempted to confiscate Arab lands or build new settlements on them' (*al-Madina* 1997a), at a time when the Palestinians have only 'received less than 3 per cent of their occupied lands ... since the Oslo accords' (*al-Madina* 1997e).

The Saudi editorials did not limit their criticism to Israel and the US; they also targeted the Palestinians in particular, and Arabs in general. By using a trope of Arab weakness, the editorials built up a discursive image of Saudi strength. The Arab states were weak entities that accepted 'pre-planned US decisions' during their Washington visits, because 'matters have already been settled and agreed with Israel' (*al-Riyadh* 1997i). Arab weakness was also constructed as an aspect of Palestinian naivety where they 'lacked knowledge of their [Israeli] counterparts' during the peace talks, therefore prompting them to rely on Arab and foreign specialists who made them subject to exploitation by the US and Israel (*al-Riyadh* 1997i).

Saudi editorials also used the Islamic summit in Pakistan (23–24 March 1997) to highlight Saudi Arabia's part in the Arab peace process. Fahd's initial spearheading of the peace process during the Reagan and Bush administrations was under threat as Jerusalem was subject to the building of settlements. The aforementioned, in addition to an Islamic opposition that branded Saudi Arabia as weak and subservient to the US, gave Saudi Arabia even more reason to highlight its position as a leader of the Islamic and Arab world, in addition to underlining the 'sacrifices' made by the kingdom for the Arab world. Aimed at a domestic audience, both *al-Riyadh* and *al-Madina* published exclusive editorials covering Saudi Arabia's role.

These articles relayed three main messages. First, the Saudi commitment towards a comprehensive and just Arab peace process, one that preceded the Madrid and Oslo conferences, namely the 1982 Fahd Peace Plan. Second, the sacrifices Saudi Arabia had made under Fahd and his battle to garner support for the Palestinian cause in the international arena. The editorials constructed the Saudi endeavours and negotiations in relation to Jerusalem as the 'essence of the struggle' for a just peace, affirming the message that 'this comes from the fact that Saudi Arabia is a model of an Islamic state in a modern era ... with Jerusalem stemming from its Islamic conscience and beliefs that are held dearly by the Custodian of the Two Holy Mosques' (*al-Madina* 1997d). Third, they underlined the role Saudi Arabia played in the international arena, with the editorials covering the visits of the Emirs and Prince Sultan bin Abdulaziz on his tour of Europe and the US. *Al-Riyadh*, for example, attempted to represent the Saudi role as one that covered more than arms procurement and business contracts. The editorial asserted that 'Prince Sultan managed to convey with full clarity the steady position of the kingdom regarding the peace process on his political tour to the US, France, and Britain'. Furthermore, *al-Riyadh* promoted the prestige of Saudi leadership and its role in the Islamic and Arab world by stressing the Sultan's 'defence of the Palestinian cause and the importance of maintaining Jerusalem's Islamic identity ... and the kingdom's lack of support for Israel's settlement expansions' (*al-Riyadh* 1997c).

By constructing Israel as Saudi Arabia's Other and projecting that through Pan-Arab and Pan-Islamic voices, the Saudi Self was reaffirmed as an Islamic and Arab leader, contrary to the opposition's criticisms of the state. The discursive constructions highlighting Saudi Arabia's leadership and its Arab and Islamic roles could be said to be aimed mainly at a domestic audience at a time when opposition voices such as bin Laden and the CDLR were rising amid a series of terrorist bombings. Therefore, Saudi domestic stability and its sustainability as a leader in the international arena were behind these constructions and definitions of the Self and Other in this period.

Iran, the Khobar Bombings, and US–Saudi Relations

The tensions between Saudi Arabia and the US during the Clinton era increased due to the predicaments and pressures of the Arab–Israeli Peace process, and US deployment and strikes against Iraq e.g. during Operation Desert Fox (1998) (Potter and Sick 2002: 265). In addition, the Khobar bombings (1996) and the limited cooperation with the US investigators in the investigation contributed to the tensions and led to speculation (Benjamin and Simon 2002; Alsultan and Saeid 2016: 98–100). One of the supposed reasons was the Saudi fears of Iranian involvement and the escalation of tensions between Iran and the US, which would jeopardize Saudi domestic stability through Iran-backed Shi'i groups and attacks on oil fields. In turn, this would increase economic woes for Saudis. Another reason for not cooperating was the possible challenges to the Saudi–US security alliance and arms sales.

The newspaper and editorial coverage and the official response to the investigations and bombings was extremely limited in order to contain any damage to the Saudi image and to limit the possibility of information leaks during the investigation. Freeh (2007) argues that initial Saudi-led investigations found that an unknown Iranian-affiliated Shi'i group, *Hizbollāh al-Hijāz* (Hezbollah in the Hijaz), were responsible for the bombings. This took the Saudi leadership by surprise since the government had mended its relations with the Shi'a by pardoning Shi'a leaders and delcaring an amnesty that saw many return from exile, as well as providing the Shi'a with jobs in both the government and private sectors (Bradley 2015: 82–83; Alsultan and Saeid 2016: 98–100; Freeh 2007).

While the investigation findings were not shared with their US counterparts, the US aggravation led to the release of a unilateral statement by the US defence secretary, suggesting a possible connection with Iran and pressurizing the Saudis to release their findings to the US (*NPR* 1996).

The threat of ending US involvement in the investigation on the grounds of a lack of cooperation, and a leaked article in *The Guardian* (1996) suggesting the arrest of forty suspects, provoked a Saudi response. The Saudi response clearly intended to not disclose any information to the US over fears of damaging rapprochement with Iran, while denying Iranian involvement. Nayef, the minister of the interior, questioned the reliability of the claims and the US intelligence and suggested that they are looking for the 'whole truth … not half-truths or the accusations of others' (al-Saud 1996d).

Prince Sultan's 'balancing act' during this period included a trip to the US and Europe, assuring complete transparency in the investigations and a continuation of the regional détente and rapprochement with Iran, alleviating tensions with the US. It also sustained détente at times of low oil prices and an economic slowdown, and it managed to exert leverage over Iran while appeasing the US to allow for modernization and regional supremacy through an arms deal.

Even with the suspects' arrests, the Saudi authorities maintained their silence both officially and in media discourses. Despite the efforts made by the Canadian and the US authorities in establishing links of apprehended suspects with Iran, the official Saudi reaction did not change, with the response being 'we do not acquit or accuse anyone (al-Saud 1997i; *Asharq Al-Awsat* 1997e). A similar silence from Iran ensued. Both states were experiencing a heavy economic downturn and domestic opposition; war was not an option for either Saudi Arabia or Iran, and so both states did not respond. Addressing the domestic audience, *al-Riyadh* employed three main strategies that targeted the Saudi audience: defending the narrative from Nayef and the state (*al-Riyadh* 1997m, 1997b), representing the kingdom as resilient and independent (*al-Riyadh* 1997n), and promoting a nuanced narrative echoing the kingdom's 'balancing act'. Refraining from naming Iran, the editorials criticized Iran implicitly and defended Nayef for not jumping to conclusions and not naming a person or a country until the investigations were complete (*al-Riyadh* 1997b). Simultaneously, the editorials criticized the US for blaming other countries and not taking its own responsibilities seriously (*al-Riyadh* 1997m, 1997b). Supporting the state's stance by highlighting its 'independence' from a country with great leverage, the editorials lauded the state for having its principle of justice based on 'trust and ethics' (*al-Riyadh* 1997b).

Much like the Saudi state narrative and Nayef's claim, *al-Riyadh* also balanced between the US and Iran. Suggesting that Saudi Arabia has declined to become part of any conspiracy or naming names to produce instability, the Saudi approach has been to avoid bloodshed (1997b). In other words, *al-Riyadh* asserted a Saudi image of independence, maturity, and leadership capable of maintaining peace and stability domestically, repair any damages to image done by the bombing, while avoiding tensions internationally with Iran or the US. The Saudi stance towards Iran with regards to the Khobar bombings, exemplified by Nayef, supports the Introduction's central contention that the differences in religious and political stances and opinions may not inhibit the construction of a neutral or positive construction of the Other. In this instance, the Saudi construction of Iran is demonstrated by silence coupled with a reluctance to blame Iran.

Iranian–Saudi Othering

The efforts of Rafsanjani since the OIC meeting in Senegal in 1991 managed to improve relations between the GCC states and Iran. Building on the encounter between Rafsanjani and Abdullah in Dakar, Rafsanjani argued in a much more recent interview (2011) that 'it was contrary to Abdullah's expectations that the president of Iran in that current [political] climate would behave in that manner ... and that allowed for some of the ice in our relations to break' (*Iran Diplomacy* 2011), which in turn paved the way for Iran to host the OIC summit in Tehran in 1997. However, according to Rafsanjani, Saudi Arabia had been assessing Iran's foreign policy and intentions for nearly six years (*Iran Diplomacy* 2011), before the confidential meetings held in 1996 improved relations (Mousavian and Shahidsaless 2014: 245–46).

Confidence Building Before the OIC Tehran Summit

The election of Khatami in May 1997 transformed good faith gestures and confidence-building measures from ice-breaking détente to warm rapprochement. As we will see, this led to a shift in Iranian–Saudi relations during Rafsanjani's tenure to a discourse of cooperation. The efforts led by Rafsanjani in the post-Iran–Iraq war period gave rise to improved relations, marked by a series of speeches calling for renewed relations, confidence-building measures, and regional cooperation. The first significant indication of this improvement in relations was during Khatami's tenure and was exemplified by the visit of his foreign minister, Kamal Kharrazi to Saudi Arabia (the way having been paved by Ali Akbar Velayati's visit in March 1997);[2] this was the first visit by an Iranian foreign minister in four years (Cordesman 2003a: 45). The famous encounter between Rafsanjani and Abdullah bin Abdulaziz in Islamabad two weeks later gave a further indication of the upturn in relations. Both states' narratives focused mainly on confidence building, with Iran arguing for a strengthening of trust and expansion of cooperation between the two states (Velayati 1997a).

Although Saudi discourse was mainly silent and implicit in comparison with Iran's explicit discourse, Saudi Arabia constructed a representation of neighbourly and fraternal relations with Iran. Khatami's election further emboldened a positive Saudi representation of Iran, drawing on Iran's historic, cultural, and geopolitical significance. The Iranian construction of Saudi Arabia employed the narratives of Islamic brotherhood and joint leadership, admitting Saudi Arabia's leading role and Mecca as being the 'cradle of Islam'. Consequently, and as discussed below, differences in religious and political opinions did not inhibit the construction of a positive image of each other, given that this construction served both states' political agendas.

Velayati's Historic Visit to Saudi Arabia   With a diplomatic mandate that spanned ten countries including all the GCC states, Velayati's historic visit communicated two main messages. First, trust and confidence building were imperative for détente and rapprochement between Saudi Arabia and Iran. Second, regional security was the responsibility of regional states and not external powers such as the US. Therefore, Iran's roadmap to accomplishing these messages was based in fulfilling two main objectives – the invitation of King Fahd to the OIC summit in Tehran and the establishment of a cooperation committee to overcome any mistrust, therein beginning a new chapter of cooperation on the Arab and Islamic fronts.

The Iranian domestic reaction towards Velayati's overture was positive. The state media narrative represented the visit as 'highly significant ... and likely to ease tension' (Islamic Republic News Agency 1997a). The editorials were silent overall, dedicating their columns to domestic affairs such as Khamenei's speeches to the IRGC (*Kayhan* 1997b) and the first anniversary of the death of Khomeini's son Ahmad (*Jomhouri Eslami* 1997f). The state response was reflected mainly in the foreign minister's interviews and statements, projecting a shift from the rhetoric of the 1980s to a discursive construction of peaceful cooperation with its neighbour, Saudi Arabia. On his visit to Riyadh, Velayati emphasized 'expansion of cooperation and the creation of mutual trust', such as respecting international

---

2. President Rafsanjani's long-serving foreign minister became a foreign policy adviser to the Supreme Leader after standing down from his ministerial position.

norms and treaties. Velayati framed Saudi Arabia as a leader with whom Iran could share Islamic and regional leadership – the latter by respecting borders and regional security. On Israel, for instance, Saudi cooperation was a 'determining factor in preserving stability and security in the region and in resolving the problems of the Islamic world' (*Velayati* 1997b). On the matter of GCC security, Iran was represented as respectful of territorial boundaries, where 'doors were open with the UAE for bilateral talks . . . to resolve misunderstandings' on the issue of the Islands, for example, while 'close cooperation strengthens the maintaining of security in the region' in relation to regional threats (*Velayati* 1997b).

Abdullah's statement and response to the Iranian foreign minister's visit was published by Iranian state media and not disseminated by the Saudi press. The statement released by the IRNA depicted Iranian–Saudi relations as fraternal, quoting Abdullah as announcing that Iran's 'brothers in Saudi Arabia wish Iranians prosperity' in addition to 'strengthening the friendly relations and historical amity' of both states (*IRNA* 1997a). In a response, Saudi Arabia stopped short of confirming the Iranian narrative. In an interview with *Asharq Al-Awsat*, Prince Sultan framed Iran both as a 'Muslim neighbouring country', yet as one that was viewed with caution and suspicion since it had to take 'practical steps to strengthen its relations' in the Persian Gulf and base these relations on 'not interfering in the internal affairs of other countries' (al-Saud 1997j). Furthermore, the Prince Sultan's avoidance of any confirmation of Velayati's comments that both states had 'begun a new chapter' in their relations (*IRNA* 1997a) went alongside Saudi acceptance of any state that wished to have 'good relations . . . love and harmony' with the kingdom (*Saudi Press Agency* 1997b).

Although the Saudi state was silent, its overall aspirations were reflected in a single editorial published in the domestically focused *al-Riyadh* (1997f). The article focused on the 'kingdom and Iran and the drafting of a distant future', highlighting a new chapter in cooperation between both states. Echoing Abdullah's statements in the Iranian state media, *al-Riyadh*'s editorial highlighted the fraternal Islamic nature of relations with Iran, and the sharing of 'one of the most dangerous waterways . . . dangerous sources of wealth . . . and common factors that allow for security interests' (*al-Riyadh* 1997f). Furthermore, the notion of a 'common Islamic belief' aimed to diminish any sectarian influence on the turbulent relationship, instead shifting the argument to a common security threat in the 'current national and international circumstances' in 'one of the most dangerous and volatile hotspots', i.e. the Persian Gulf (*al-Riyadh* 1997f). Contrary to Prince Sultan's cautious statements in the media, the *al-Riyadh* article depicted both states as threatened by similar 'internal or external forces that are too narrow minded to see the horizon', framing Iran as 'brothers sharing the same future, and friends that share extraordinary interests' (*al-Riyadh* 1997f). *Al-Riyadh* established a pragmatic narrative. It represented Iran as a 'great culture', highlighting the 'brotherly visit' as a chance to 'build a new platform of trust and an environment of tolerance', basing any future dialogue and cooperation on the 'ethics of Islam and the chivalry of men' (*al-Riyadh* 1997f). There were two possible main reasons for this positive representation of Iran in *al-Riyadh*. First, the influence that the Emir of Riyadh, Salman bin Abdulaziz al-Saud, has on the newspaper, which naturally supports the vision of the state and monarchy. Second, the political position of the editor, Yousef al-Kuwailit, who argues for united Islamic and Arab cooperation.

Iranian enthusiasm and the mostly cautious Saudi response could have three explanations. First, Iranian foreign policy objectives, outlined in Khatami's first UN speech, demonstrated a clear intention to work cooperatively on the international and regional level in order to resolve past differences, and establish 'security, development and prosperity in the third world' (Khatami 1998b). Second, the Iranians were in difficult circumstances economically and diplomatically, facing years of regional isolation and high unemployment levels amid an economic downturn and low oil prices. Second, the mixed Saudi response, between a welcoming Abdullah and a cautious Sultan, could either mean that there were conflicting views and opinions in the Saudi royal family, or a cautious balancing between potential détente with Iran and maintaining Saudi relations with the US.

The Rafsanjani–Abdullah Meeting in Islamabad Although the Rafsanjani–Abdullah encounter during the extraordinary OIC summit in Islamabad (23–24 March 1997)is thought to have begun a rapprochement in relations, it was covered much less than the Velayati visit that preceded the summit. Mousavian (2015) and al-Sultan (2016: 110) argue that the overture by Rafsanjani had such a positive effect that Abdullah's reactions moved rapidly. Over two decades later, Rafsanjani (*Iran Diplomacy* 2011) opined that the change in Iranian–Saudi relations occurred during the extraordinary OIC summit in Islamabad, which coincided with Pakistan's National Day. According to Rafsanjani, Abdullah responded so positively towards Iran during the summit that he ordered that a previous statement by Saud al-Faisal be disregarded and that the Saudi crown prince, Abdullah, would be heading a delegation to the OIC summit in Tehran (9–11 December 1997). However, the encounter was not covered by any Saudi or Iranian editorial. There could be two reasons for this. First, both leaders requested that their overtures be kept quiet until concrete developments could be made, a view held by Moussavian and Shahidsaless (2014: 246–47). The second reason is that during that period, the editorial discourse around foreign affairs in both states focused mainly on Israeli settlement building and how the Netanyahu government was impeding the Arab peace process.

The state narrative was reflected mainly in Rafsanjani's press conference held immediately after the summit, which focused on the general aspects of bilateral relations while not revealing any details, thus representing Saudi Arabia as a positive counterpart engaged in fruitful dialogue. It can be argued that Rafsanjani's reservation in discussing his private discussions with Abdullah confirms Moussavian's argument that both statesmen decided to keep certain discussions informal in a bid to negotiate a 'grand agreement' (Mousavian and Shahidsaless 2014: 246–47). In response to new developments between Tehran and Riyadh,

Rafsanjani argued that relations between Iran and Saudi Arabia were 'expanding', highlighting that there was 'full understanding between the two countries ... and all areas of interest (to both states) were discussed in the meeting with the Saudi crown prince', (Rafsanjani 1997b) thereby stressing discussions that 'to a certain extent, cleared the ambiguities regarding our relations with the southern Persian Gulf States, allowing us to become closer' (Rafsanjani 1997b, 1997a). Furthermore, Rafsanjani represented the 'good relations' between 'two Islamic neighbours' as being problematic for certain 'forces', implicitly alluding to the US, the latter aiming to 'ruin the mutual understanding and expansion (of ties) through disinformation', underlying that the only way to move forward was to 'remove any misunderstandings' via the 'exchange of high-ranking officials' (*IRNA* 1997c).

The Saudi response to the Rafsanjani–Abdullah encounter was similarly taciturn, with little reference made in the Saudi press, and an overall silence from Saudi state officials. The state press branded the event as a 'closed meeting', and echoed Rafsanjani's previous statements of 'discussing the relations between the two states ... reviewing the main issues in the Islamic arena' (*SPA* 1997). The Saudi reticence was so complete that the Saudi media quoted the Iranian News Agency press releases rather than a statement from the Saudi authorities or their official news agency as their source for the announcement of Abdullah attending the OIC summit in Tehran (*Asharq Al-Awsat* 1997b). Furthermore, Saudi reporting of the status of the relations with Iran was narrated through interviews with Iranian officials rather than Saudi ones. An interview with the Iranian ambassador to Riyadh days after the summit framed the Iranian position as 'a serious political orientation' towards rapprochement with Saudi Arabia, as both states were 'the largest Muslim neighbours in the region'. The Iranian shift now framed the relationship as they 'need each other in different areas of cooperation, consultation in diverse arenas and mutual coordination', further promulgating the Iranian state discourse of 'preservation of regional security and cooperation' (*Asharq Al-Awsat* 1997e). The reactions of both states were a near mirror image. In Iran – except for Rafsanjani and his foreign minister Velayati – the Iranian leadership was cloaked in silence. No reactions were made by Khamenei, the clergy or the editorials, an echo of the silent Saudi leadership, clergy, and editorial voices.

The Saudi silence and use of Iranian discourse to project rapprochement and the representation of the Other may have been due to two main reasons. First, by using Iranian discourse to highlight the process and the rapprochement between both states, the Saudi silence could communicate that it was Iran that desired improved relations and Saudi Arabia was acceding to this request from a position of power, that is to say, Saudi silence offered the opportunity to construct the Saudi Self as forgiving, thus abiding by Islamic principles of forgiveness and charity. Hence, the image communicated to the Saudi audience is that the Saudi monarch was forgiving years of Iranian threats and trespasses from a position of Islamic leadership and strength. Second, Saudi silence and the employment of Iranian discourse implicitly constructed an image of the weakness of Saudi Arabia's Other, namely Iran, which was placed in the role of having to petition Saudi Arabia. When the Saudi public consumed the Iranian narrative highlighted in Saudi discourse, it imbibed a projection of Saudi prestige, and of Iranian deference towards Saudi Arabia, which was implicitly constructed as a retreat from its previous position of revolutionary zeal and threatening power.

Conclusion

Khatami's period as president began with him rebranding Iran, creating an image of a peaceful Iranian Self. The OIC was the medium used to showcase Iran's new peaceful orientation and build bridges amid détente and rapprochement, not only regionally but also with Saudi Arabia through inter-religious dialogues and Khatami's premise of a 'dialogue of civilizations.' However, Khatami's plan did not sail smoothly, as was visible at the Tehran OIC conference. While Khatami aimed to reach out to the Islamic and international world, in general, Khamenei demonstrated a different approach, emphasizing Iran's revolutionary principles. This was the beginning of a 'split personality' in the discourses of the Iranian Self. This 'split' in the Iranian Self can be defined as the directions in which Khamenei and Khatami orientated their discourse. While Khatami looked 'both ways' i.e. both to the East and West, Khamenei directed his discourse towards the Islamic world, marking out a continuity with Iran's revolutionary principles.

The highlight of the Iranian period of détente and rapprochement was that although the post-revolutionary rhetoric – deeply rooted in the 1980s – was still present in the Iranian discourse, it was aimed at the West and not at the regional level, i.e. at Saudi Arabia and the GCC. One of the major areas of contention between Iran and Saudi Arabia in the 1990s was that of the Taliban. However, although Saudi Arabia supported the Taliban, the official Iranian discourse refrained from negatively representing Saudi Arabia as its Other. In the case of Afghanistan, images such as the Ominous Triangle were employed by both the official discourse and the press and ulama to construct the image of Iran's Other. With the press and the ulama, Saudi Arabia was mentioned as part of the Ominous Triangle, while the official discourse subscribed to silent Othering. This silent Othering had two main goals. The first was to break Iran's regional isolation and achieve rapprochement with its neighbours, principally Saudi Arabia. The second goal was not to stir domestic unrest since Iran housed over two million Afghans during that period.

The official Iranian discourse maintained an image of neutrality in a marked shift from the 1980s. In the case of Afghanistan, as the Taliban rose to power, Iran's official narrative was one of Afghan self-determination, where even the clergy followed the official line, claiming that the domestic problems of Afghanistan were an internal matter. Iran was rebranding from being an 'exporter of the revolution' to a country that does not interfere in its neighbours' affairs. The most notable example of Iran's silent Othering and shift in its position towards representing Saudi Arabia can be observed in the case of the execution of the Iranian diplomats in Mazar-i-Sharif in 1998. The Iranian elite's construction of the Other was directed at the US rather than the regional states that had recognized the Taliban government, such as Saudi Arabia. This exemplified Iran's strategy of keeping silent on Saudi Arabia in order to put the long-term goals of détente and rapprochement ahead of any nefarious discourse of its Saudi Other. When Saudi Arabia was mentioned by the domestic discourse, it was alluded to through the Wahhabi trope, blaming this ideology and the Saudi propagation of Wahhabism for the Taliban's atrocities against the Iranian diplomats. The Iranian editorials shouldered the Othering of Saudi Arabia in the case of the diplomats by reconstructing and building on Khamenei's discourse towards the incident. Furthermore, the vocal editorials in combination with the neutrality of the official Iranian discourse projected an image of Iranian pragmatism and political priorities, which marked a shift from the rhetorical stance and counter-reaction of the post-revolutionary 1980s.

Saudi Arabia was going through a period of domestic instability marked by the rise of the Sahwa movement in opposition to the presence of US forces on Saudi soil. Furthermore, Saudi Arabia was also undergoing a shift in its leadership as the crown prince was not at the helm as de facto ruler. In addition to the domestic instability, the pan-Arab, tribal, and Islamist-leaning identity of the crown prince all allowed for a shift in the representation of the Saudi Self and its Other. Saudi Arabia's internal and external Others were intertwined. The Islamists' domestic opposition spun narratives revolving around wasted wealth and subservience to Western powers. Therefore, Saudi Arabia's domestic Other was mimicking the 1980s Iranian tropes. Furthermore, the US–Saudi relationship was also deteriorating, particularly since Clinton sidelined Riyadh in the Arab Peace Process that Fahd had already initiated in 1981. Consequently, the external Other had changed now to Israel and – to a certain extent – the United States. Finally, as with Iran, Saudi Arabia also endeavoured to achieve rapprochement with Iran.

The crisis of the Khobar bombings in 1996 dismissed any implication of Iran in the incident. This was due to three main factors. First, if Iran had been implicated then there might have been a military attack against Iran by the US that would have led to a regional war, which Riyadh feared. Second, due to the presence of Saddam as a shared, regional threat with Iran, Saudi Arabia attempted to achieve a balance of power in the region by coalescing Iran and pursuing a positive and friendly relationship. Third, both countries' economies were in depression, particularly with very low oil prices. Hence, rapprochement between Iran and Saudi Arabia was imperative to achieve cooperation within OPEC and raise the oil prices. Shared regional and domestic threats were the impetus behind Saudi Arabia's rapprochement and the shift in the representation of the Self and the Other in both countries.

The Iranian overtures towards Saudi Arabia were bearing fruit. Rafsanjani's détente paved the way to rapprochement with Riyadh. As Khatami settled into his presidential seat, themes like Islamic unity would gradually metamorphose into 'regional cooperation', putting to one side any domestic or regional events that could have affected both countries' relationship. This would be signified by the historic hosting of the OIC in Tehran with a high-level Saudi presence.

Chapter 6

THE KHATAMI PRESIDENCY AND THE OIC: FROM CONFIDENCE BUILDING TO ISLAMIC UNITY AND COOPERATION

Introduction

Confidence-building measures initiated during Rafsanjani's tenure came to fruition at the end of his presidency, peaking with the election of Khatami in May 1997. This possibly gave the Saudi leadership assurance that the road towards rapprochement initiated by Rafsanjani would be sustained and developed under Khatami's leadership. The rapid improvement in relations between Saudi Arabia and Iran was perhaps informed by a trust in Rafsanjani that stemmed not only from his consistent attempts at confidence-building measures, but also from him being an experienced and reliable statesman whose protégé had been elected president, very much against the odds, further illustrating Rafsanjani's political acumen. Furthermore, Khatami's persona and his message to the world, later exemplified by his calls for a dialogue of civilizations, rang loud and clear early during his political campaign, then as president-elect and from his first day in office. The results were immediate.

The Saudi King Fahd's recognition of the elections was framed in his representation of Iran as a 'brotherly country' and he gave the telegram he sent a personalized tint in congratulating Khatami on behalf of 'myself [the king] personally in the trust placed in you by the Iranian nation'. Furthermore, the Saudi overture was explicit, representing Iran not only as a country with whom it endeavoured to 'strengthen good relations', but a king's recognition of Iran as a possible partner in 'the service of our Islamic cause' (al-Saud 1997h). Khatami's electoral victory had aligned Saudi Arabia with Iran's narrative, with Islamic unity leading to regional cooperation. Saudi Arabia's positive narrative was reciprocated by Khatami, who stressed the 'expansion and development of all aspects of relations with the Arab and Islamic countries' and expressing Iran's ambitions for 'cooperation in regional and international security, which is highly important to us'.

The period between Khatami acting as president-elect to his swearing in demonstrated a preparation for transfer of duties with a sustained agenda of positive Iranian–Saudi relations. However, what was noticeable in the Iranian discourse towards Saudi Arabia was a shift from confidence building to cooperation and unity on matters of Islamic leadership and regional security respectively. The shift within Saudi discourse on the other hand was gradual and two-tiered. Overall, Fahd and Abdullah promulgated a very positive representation of Iran. In the period leading from elections to inauguration, princes such as Sultan and the editorials framed Iran in a positive light. However, they also conveyed a confidence-building narrative calling on Iran to match its shift in foreign policy with actions. These constructions and narratives are evident in the details that follow.

Khatami's Election and a Shift from Détente to Rapprochement

The telegrams exchanged over Khatami's election and the later press editorials ushered in a period characterized mainly by a shift from improved Iranian relations with the GCC in general and Saudi Arabia in particular, to regional security and economic cooperation, shaped by the US presence in the Persian Gulf and Saudi Arabia's relationship with the US, and its influence on OPEC respectively. Furthermore, Saudi editorials promulgated a 'trust but verify' narrative: *Asharq Al-Awsat*, for example, explicitly stated that 'when it comes to matters of international politics, actions are always more important than statements' (*Asharq Al-Awsat* 1997d) in response to Khatami's calls for closer regional relations. In an interview with the Iranian newspaper *Jomhouri Eslami*, Rafsanjani cast similar doubt on the sustainability of Arab rapprochement. The Iranian argument for a delay in rapprochement was attributed to external influence and colonialism, implying that although the Arab states of the Persian Gulf desired rapprochement, they were still under colonial rule and limited in their choices. Rafsanjani's argument framed the rapprochement as unfavourable to the US and Britain, as it would make these Islamic countries strong, a situation in which pressure or other factors 'aid in the destruction of negotiations with our Arab brothers ... They [Arabs] view that it is in their best interest and is imperative that we become friends and cooperate' (Rafsanjani 1997d). The GCC that Rafsanjani was sketching was one administered by 'colonialists that have bridgeheads *(sarpulhā)* where their colonies were once rooted ... weighing heavily on the extent to which they [colonialists] would allow these relations to be sustained and successful. It is questionable and doubtful...' (Rafsanjani 1997d).

However, the Saudi rulers' narrative lacked any doubt. Saudi Arabia sent the minister of state, Abdulaziz Khoweiter, to convey that the kingdom would send 'the highest-level delegation to the OIC summit' in Tehran (IRNA 1997b). Khoweiter was quoted in the Iranian press as saying that the main purpose of the visit was to 'expand relations between two Muslim countries', a clear sign that the Saudi narrative was beginning to shift towards cooperation (IRNA 1997b). Rafsanjani argued that the visit conveyed messages of support for Iran's OIC summit, framing the summit as 'important for the Islamic world' and therefore amplifying Iran's important position in the region and Islamic world. The need for Saudi–Iranian collaboration on Islamic matters was posed in terms of Saudi 'worries regarding the situation in the Middle East and the conference in Qatar'[1]; the kingdom wished 'to talk a little bit more with Iran and cooperate and consult' (Rafsanjani 1997d). Rafsanjani represented the visit as reflecting the Saudi need for Iran, signalling Iran's geopolitical significance and weight, as well as progress in rapprochement with Saudi Arabia.

Of as much symbolic as economic significance, cooperation began directly after the Rafsanjani–Abdullah encounter in Islamabad. This was marked by the resumption of direct flights between Tehran and Riyadh. Major trade agreements were also signed days after the Khoweiter visit. The difference in the event's reporting was evident, with Tehran elaborating and Saudi Arabia using a more neutral tone. The Saudi press hailed the trade agreements but discussed them in general terms, highlighting the nature of the economic cooperation as including different sectors such as agriculture, transportation, food, and beverages (*SPA* 1997a). The Iranian state discourse, on the other hand, discussed details. It bolstered the role of semi-state institutions, framing the Iranian–Saudi cooperation as edging on full normalization. The Iranian state media and an interview with the Iranian ambassador to Saudi Arabia discussed the cooperation as being a collaboration between the Foundation for the Deprived and War Disabled (*Bunyād-i Mustazafān wa Jānbāzān*) and the Imam Reza Foundation (*Āstān-i Quds-i Razavī*), while through 'negotiations with three main Saudi trade centres a joint venture was established under the name al-Fā'izīn' (The Winners)' (*Asharq Al-Awsat* 1997e; *Jomhouri Eslami* 1997c). The Iranian discourse aimed to construct a stronger image of a new dawn in Iranian ties with the kingdom, possibly counteracting the Saudi 'actions should speak louder than words' theme promulgated by the Saudi editorials (*Asharq Al-Awsat* 1997d, 1997j, 1997f; *al-Riyadh* 1997d; *al-Madina* 1997b) and royals such as Prince Sultan (al-Saud 1997k).

Furthermore, there were two sides to the 'double narrative' promulgated by Sultan and the editorials. The first praised Iran's history and geopolitical importance. The second demanded that Iran prove itself to the region in general and the kingdom in particular via actions and intentions that backed up official statements. Sultan's speech towards Iran mentioned four conditions for full rapprochement with the GCC and Saudi Arabia, namely 'mutual respect ... trust between both parties ... and clarity in Iran's intentions and discussing differences' (al-Saud 1997k). These conditions were directly promulgated in Saudi editorials, which also added that responsibility lay with Khatami since the president 'has an unprecedented chance to return Iran to the position it rightly deserves in the international community ... he has to understand that good intentions beget good intentions ... good intentions have to be accompanied with direct and positive actions'. Similarly,

---

1. In November 1997 Qatar hosted the MENA economic summit and invited Israel as a participant. Saudi Arabia and a number of other Arab countries including Egypt withdrew from the conference. Saudi Arabia cited its grievance at Israel's treatment of Palestinians and the Arab Peace Process as its excuse for its withdrawal. See Cordesman, A (2003: 74)

other editorials focused on Khatami, linking him with the formulation of a new Iranian foreign policy and Iran's global position and image, omitting any mention of Khamenei, the clergy, or even Rafsanjani. Possibly because Khamenei, and to a lesser extent Rafsanjani – especially since 1989 – shared a turbulent history with the Arab states, especially with Saudi Arabia and GCC.

The Saudi discourse identified Khatami with a new Iran, recognizing its historical and geopolitical position. The frame shifted from a mere regional neighbour to 'a neighbouring country ... that has its weight in the Asian geographical region' (*al-Riyadh* 1997d), and a 'country with such a culture and history ... a plurality ... overlapping with other regions and peoples with different dimensions and antiquities, making Iran a centre of historical attraction' (*al-Riyadh* 1997j). The representation of Iran as a Saudi Other also shifted to include the recognition of Iran's Shi'i sect as Islamic kin, thereby underlining Islamic unity. Iran was presented as a country 'with an Islamic identity and foundation', making it of 'great importance to neighbouring states ... who share mutual interests and goals with Iran'. The narrative was clear; while Iran had to prove its intentions, the Saudi editorials explicitly articulated the view that the 'Arabs and Iranians are in the same boat' and any developments in Iran 'would reflect on many countries, especially those linked with Iran in many sensitive areas', a reference to Saudi Arabia and the GCC states (*al-Riyadh* 1997j). Khatami was ubiquitous in mentions of a new era in relations, with the potential to be a 'regional power that can play a leading role in the region ... [a country] where civilization and culture is a power that allows it to have an effective presence in the Islamic world' (*Asharq Al-Awsat* 1997f).

As *Asharq Al-Awsat* clearly stated, Iran's 'only viable exit is to take notice of the benefits it could reap from sowing the seeds of good neighbourliness and trust in the Arab world where it could find an ally and friend at a time when friends and allies are rare' (*Asharq Al-Awsat* 1997f). Consequently, the Saudi discourse discursively constructed the image of Iran as a Saudi Other through its positive framing of Khatami. That is to say, Khamenei and Rafsanjani's Iran was viewed with an air of mistrust and suspicion, while Khatami's Iran was accepted as a model for peace and historical and cultural prestige. The Saudi discourse went as far as to implicitly define Shi'ism through Khatami. Khatami's representation of Shi'ism was acceptable, in contrast to that of the other pillars of the Iranian state.

Iranian–Saudi Relations, Islamic Unity, and the OIC Tehran Summit

The Saudi narrative of Iranian significance and geopolitical value echoed throughout the GCC. Jamil al-Hujailan, who was both a Saudi official and the secretary-general of the GCC, promulgated the narrative of Iranian prestige, highlighting Iran as a 'big and strong neighbour ... a major factor in regional stability' (Hujailan 1997b, 1997a). The newly appointed foreign minister, Kamal Kharrazi, began a rapprochement tour conveying Khatami's foreign policy towards the region in general and Saudi Arabia in particular. Kharrazi's discourse mirrored

Saudi discursive constructions of Saudi geopolitical significance, while representing the Iranian Self through Khatami's priorities of 'expansion of relations with neighbours and regional countries' (Kharrazi 1997) through 'Islamic unity, understanding, and friendship'. This extolling of Saudi Arabia's regional importance paved the way for a discussion of 'economic cooperation with Saudi Arabia ... that [will] lead to economic prosperity, preserving the interests of the region and the Islamic world' (Kharrazi 1997). Since Iran's economy and inflation were a cause for concern after a lengthy war and low oil prices, such an Iranian discursive construction of Saudi Arabia was arguably being utilized to alleviate economic pressures. The Saudi response was welcoming, supporting Iran's narrative of cooperation and Islamic solidarity. However, it stopped short of explicitly announcing the nature of the cooperation. Saud al-Faisal, the Saudi foreign minister, explicitly highlighted that any cooperation with Iran would have a 'positive impact on the region' (al-Faisal 1997), supporting the monarch and crown prince's rapprochement with Iran, and dispelling previous doubts by Saudi ministers and editorials regarding Iranian statements, citing a 'new chapter' in their relations with the kingdom.

Conservative and hard-line Iranian editorials were generally silent on the Kharrazi GCC tour. However, an editorial published by *Jomhouri Eslami* criticized the GCC and Saudi demands for 'good intentions' and actions (*husn-i niyat*) (*Jomhouri Eslami* 1997e). The editorial argued that 'one-sided good intentions without reciprocation can hurt the regional position of the Islamic Republic', implicitly constructing an image of regional and Saudi treachery. The editorial supported this framing by reminding the audience that it was the 'GCC that amassed the largest funding for Baghdad's war machine over the eight-year war ... reaching $80 billion ... the ramifications are still experienced to this day' (*Jomhouri Eslami* 1997e). The Iranian editorial narrative constructed the GCC as 'not showing any good intentions towards the Islamic Republic after the war', requesting that Iran 'experience political vigilance and tactfulness' in their new foreign policy (*Jomhouri Eslami* 1997e). Therefore, it could be said that while the state discourse constructed a narrative of unity and cooperation, the press editorials, i.e. the messages they disseminated vis-à-vis mirror-image messages in the Saudi press, cast doubts on future relations and the intentions of the Other.

Saudi–Iranian Mutual Representations at the OIC

In the mid-1990s, while still president, Rafsanjani[2] played a crucial role in hosting the OIC meeting in Iran (Tehran, December 1997), which was crucial in many

---

2. Rafsanjani's tenure as president ended on 3 August 1997. Between 1983 and 2017 Rafsanjani was a member of the Assembly of Experts and was elected as its Chairman in 2007–2011. In addition, Rafsanjani was the Chairman of Expediency Discernment (1989–2017).

ways for Iran–Saudi relations. First, Iran's approach towards King Abdullah was congenial, as al-Sultan (2016) and Keynoush (2016) have argued. Second, there was an emphasis on the discourse of Islamic unity, present in the declaration of Islamic Unity Week, representing an effort to exert greater control over resources (especially over oil) and create an Islamic economy to avoid conflicts while respecting the sectarian interpretations and symbols. This summit was also crucial in terms of changing and increasingly positive representations of counterparts. Khamenei represented Saudi Arabia in a fraternal light, suggesting the misunderstandings were produced by enemies. He proposed a Saudi–Iran cooperation not just on bilateral and regional matters but also on the matters pertaining to Islamic ummah and suggesting Iran's willingness to expand relations with Saudis in various fields. Former president Rafsanjani's speech echoed this narrative of friendship and cooperation, painting a positive picture of Saudi Arabia since the Islamic revolution.

In line with Khamenei and Rafsanjani's representation, Khatami's discourse represented Saudi Arabia in a fashion that matched both the Dialogue among Civilizations policy and general rapprochement. Khatami suggested a recipe for cooperation: 'The secret to the success of the Islamic world lies in two fundamental criteria, thought and opinion on the one hand, and understanding and solidarity on the other' (Khatami 1997e). Consequently, the Iranian discourse produced on Saudi Arabia represented the Other in a positive light alongside showing a unity among the leadership regarding rapprochement. King Abdullah showed a positive approach and promulgated a discourse of Saudi Arabia's victimhood against extremist forces, an approach that mirrored Khamenei's 'Islamic Unity'. While evoking such discourses, King Abdullah emphasized unity within Islamic sects against extremism and represented Iran as an Other that was a friend who promoted a valid school of Islamic thought.

Abdullah's statements and requests for cooperation and unity were manoeuvres that served several purposes. First, they were intended to rescue the dwindling economies of both states. Second, there was the issue of 'keeping Iraq in check' (Cordesman 2003: 45) due to fears of a hegemonic Saddam. Third, this was an attempt at mediating between Iran and the US to deter any American attack on Iran that could spill over to the GCC and Saudi Arabia in particular. Abdullah's statements clearly constructed how the Saudi Self characterized its Other, with Saudi Arabia as the Self, the 'brother to the Iranian nation and leadership ... and friends to the US, a great and friendly country' (al-Saud 1997a). These statements attempted to balance Iran and the US, which can be supported by Cordesman's (2003: 46) observation that Abdullah 'was careful to qualify his remarks [which] aimed to deter any US attack on Iran if the latter was implicated in the Khobar bombings'.

The editorial discourses in both Iran and Saudi Arabia covered the OIC Summit in Tehran and presented an amicable discourse in line with the leaders of their respective countries. However, the Iranian editorials did not make any specific mention of Saudi Arabia but rather referred to the Islamic world in general. In contrast, the Saudi discourses mentioned and praised the Iranian leadership. This difference was partly rooted in a general mood wherein the Iranian people had strong feelings against Saudi Arabia and the GCC states for their support of Saddam during the eight-year war, and the Iranian establishment risked a backlash. However, the Iranian and Saudi editorials also differed in their focus on the OIC in another way. The Iranian editorials attributed the success of the OIC to Khamenei and his role, while the Saudi editorials saw Khatami as the moderate and attributed success to him, in contrast. Both editorials took this selective strategy due to their vested perspectives in demonstrating the success of the OIC meeting and of Iran's foreign policy.

Both the Iranian and Saudi editorial discourses, however, focused on the idea of Islamic unity and brotherhood and anticipated the outcomes in their own contexts. The Iranian editorial discourses viewed the OIC Summit in Tehran and Islamic unity and brotherhood as being Iran's achievements. Reporting on Iran as a flagbearer of Islamic unity and brotherhood, the editorials credited Iran with following the revolutionary spirit of Islamic revolution, representing *Islam-i-nab* (pure Islam), and modelling the Iranian approach to the Islamic world as that of forgiveness and fraternalization. In contrast, the Saudi editorials, while questioning the success and outcomes of the OIC summits, acknowledged Iran's behaviour as that of a responsible actor and highlighted the role Abdullah offered to mediate between an 'Iranian brother' and 'American friend', balanced against its own foreign-policy approaches. By the end of the summit, however, the Saudi editorials had changed their positions on both the success of the OIC and on Iran, and they labelled the OIC Tehran Summit's outcome and Iran's role as a positive one for regional stability. By the end of the summit, the Saudi editorials reported on Iran as a nation that had matured, a part of the Persian Gulf security network, and a country that had raised its voice against extremism and terrorism, and had emerged as a major regional and international player.

After the OIC Summit: Elite Visits and Mutual Cooperation

The period after the OIC summit witnessed a range of bridge-building visits that led to regular ministerial exchanges between the two states. However, two primary visits from Iran, and two from Saudi Arabia allowed for enhanced cooperation on the one hand and the cementing of relationships on the other. Rafsanjani's historic visit to Saudi Arabia in February 1998 witnessed negotiations with different pillars of the Saudi state, focusing on economic cooperation and security, especially at a time when oil prices were at their lowest and there was an increased US military build-up in the region in preparation for an attack on Saddam. Furthermore, Rafsanjani's visit was ushered in with the signing of an agreement in May 1998 in Tehran, which the Saudi foreign minister, Saud al-Faisal, attended. On the parliamentary level, the speakers of the Saudi Shura Council and the Iranian Majles exchanged visits in November 1998 and October 1999 respectively. However, the second set of historic visits were in May 1999 by the Saudi defence minister, Sultan bin Abdul Aziz, followed shortly by Khatami. These exchanges were followed by further agreements on energy production, the expansion of investment, cultural and sports relations, and the establishment of military ties through the exchange of military attachés. How, then, did the Saudi and Iranian discourses of each other evolve amid this shift to a focus on cooperation and the expansion of relations?

Rafsanjani's Landmark Visit to Saudi Arabia, OPEC, and Economic Agreements   The Iranian visit aimed to build bridges with every dimension of the Saudi establishment. One such area of vital interest and necessity to both states was the matter of OPEC and the low and steadily falling oil prices that affected the economies of both states. Iran's Majles held the Khatami government accountable for not being able to stabilize oil prices. This resulted in further pressure on Khatami's government, his economic agenda, and in essence on the reconstruction path paved by Rafsanjani since 1989. The Majles gave Iran's oil minister an ultimatum: either increase oil prices or 'consider a withdrawal from OPEC' (Zanganeh 1998). Iran was more negatively affected by low oil prices than Saudi Arabia, especially due to its difficulties in raising production to fulfil its OPEC quota. Iran was therefore in greater need of Saudi cooperation than vice versa. Furthermore, due to 'current circumstances in the region' (IRNA 1998a), the meetings were also of benefit to Saudi Arabia. In addition to oil prices, Saudi interests in Iran also included a balance of power to deter any Iranian collaboration with Iraq, especially as the US was threatening to strike Iraq on the one hand, while the Saudis did not wish to risk isolation or diminished power if the Iranian–US détente was achieved thanks to Khatami's moderate government and foreign policy of détente and rapprochement.

The Iranian and Saudi discourses also represented the visit, i.e. the expansion of ties and cooperation, differently. The various news outlets in each country also differed from one another in their narratives and constructions of the details of the visit. Whereas Iranian discourse went to great lengths to describe all the details, the Saudi narrative maintained a general line, releasing sporadic details. One such example is how the visit was framed. To prepare for Rafsanjani's visit, the Iranian state narrative framed the visit as 'serving a turning point in relations' between the two states (IRNA 1998a). At Rafsanjani's meeting with the Saudi monarch and crown prince, Iran's attempt at rapprochement followed its previous mantra that 'improved relations that would benefit the Islamic world', blaming any previous hostilities as a Western conspiracy as 'enemies have long aimed at constantly setting Iran against Saudi Arabia'. Rafsanjani's remarks further alluded to two additional lines of cooperation that Iran desired, namely regarding security and oil. The former was implicitly alluded to by attributing Middle Eastern crises such as the Iran–Iraq war, the invasion of Kuwait, and the existence of foreign military bases, to severed ties between the two states, with the latter achievable by 'cooperation in OPEC ... leading to more efficient use' of oil revenue, signalling increased leverage in the international oil market and joint leadership of the Islamic world (Rafsanjani 1998b).

Iranian state media cited Saudi sources that highlighted Fahd's welcoming of Rafsanjani. The Iranian media repeated the Saudi narrative, positively echoing the air of solidarity at Rafsanjani's request. Iranian state media framed the relationship between the two states by citing Saudi sources. Fahd, for example, was quoted as instructing the oil ministry to cooperate with Iran (al-Saud 1998) to portray a Saudi desire to strengthen relations with Iran. The difference in the construction of the relationship between Iran and Saudi Arabia is also evident in Rafsanjani's interviews with the newspapers. In an interview with the liberal leaning Saudi Newspaper *Okaz*, Rafsanjani discursively constructed the Other as an equal in terms of fate, economic gains, and mutual benefits. Saudi Arabia as an Other was an equal to the Self, where if one sows, both reap. This is exemplified in Rafsanjani's argument that Iran could act as a 'bridge with Central Asia . . . for exporting Saudi products', in addition to a common 'market for industrial and non-industrial goods' (*Okaz* 1998).

The desire for an expansion of relations with Saudi Arabia was also exemplified in Rafsanjani's speech at the Saudi Shura Council. Elaborating on Iran's historical identity and prestige and juxtaposing it to the role of Saudi Arabia in Islam, Rafsanjani's speech framed Iran and Saudi Arabia as equals. By employing a historical and Islamic narrative, Rafsanjani highlighted the historical prestige of the Iranian Self as a 'powerful country with an ancient civilization'. Saudi Arabia as Iran's Other was represented as an equal, referring to it as a 'source of divine gifts, birthplace of the Prophet, and the land of divine revelation and the Quran'. This construction went as far as explicitly representing Saudi Islamic prestige and source of divinity as eternal, one that would 'continue until the day of resurrection' (Rafsanjani 1998b). This speech to the Saudi Shura Council arguably aimed to propagate the image of a revolutionary Iran entering a new phase, communicating the wishes of Khatami and the Islamic Republic to the Saudi elite, and admitting that the kingdom was a powerful state and that Iran needed its cooperation.

Rafsanjani also sought to build bridges with the clerical establishment, meeting with Abdulaziz ibn Baz, the Grand Mufti of Saudi Arabia. However, no details of their discussions were published in either Saudi or Iranian discourses. Furthermore, the Saudi clergy's overall silence eclipsed the historic visit, except for a single incident that explicitly criticized Iran, Shi'ism and Western conspiracies against Islam and Saudi Arabia. The sectarian narrative by Sheikh Ali ibn Abdurrahman al-Huthaify, imam of the Great Mosque of Medina (Prophet's Mosque), was the first sign of an explicit denigration of Iran since the two states had sought rapprochement. It is this author's opinion that, like Iran, there was a 'split personality' in the Saudi establishment, one that was also directed towards US and Western imperialism. However, what differed was that although the Saudi religious establishment was silent, al-Huthaify's vociferous opinion epitomized Iran as Saudi Arabia's Other. As I discuss below, the response from Iran was a complete volte-face compared with the norms of the 1980s. This could be interpreted as a sign of maturity on the part of the Iranian clerical establishment, which was now capable of a composed neutrality and silence, which included positive opinions of Saudi Arabia and its ulama.

While the sermon denigrated and insulted Iran and the Shi'i sect, it also criticized the efforts of the Saudi state in general and the crown prince, Abdullah, in particular. Employing sectarian and historical tropes, the Iranians and Shi'a were characterized as 'followers of Ibn Saba,[3] the Jew, and of Abu Lu'lu-ah, the *majūsī* [Zoroastrian or fire-worshipper]' (Huthayfi 1998). In a set of rhetorical questions asking 'How can there be reconciliation between the Sunnis and the *rāfiḍah* (Shi'a)?' the cleric propagated a sectarian Wahhabi narrative intertwining Shi'i beliefs with Khomeini's role as valī-yi faqīh, accusing the Shi'a of 'swearing and abusing the three Caliphs', and creating a narrative of heresy, and claiming the Shi'a 'believe Khomeini, the imam of deviation, to be infallible ... and [to be] the deputy of their [Shi'i] concocted Mahdi' (Huthayfi 1998). To al-Huthaify, Shi'ism was a heresy, while Iran and its government were therefore leading a world heresy antagonistic to Islam.

Furthermore, in criticizing calls for Islamic unity, al-Huthaify explicitly shunned the thought, claiming that 'we [the Sunnis] will not draw closer to them by a length of a breath', going so far as to label them as constituting 'greater harm to Islam then even Jews and Christians'. It is here where the 'split personality' between the monarchy and a member of the religious establishment is evident. In addition, the sermon also censured the US and Western powers as aligned with the Shi'a, while 'enemies of Islam have united in their false beliefs to fight against Islam'. Depicting Saudi Arabia as the 'only representative, model Islamic government', the senior cleric claimed on live television that the US and world powers were the sworn enemies of the Kingdom of Saudi Arabia, the greatest centre of Islam. Recalling a sermon from Tehran, the Saudi cleric mirrored Iranian clerical discourse in preaching that 'America and Britain are ... threatening the kingdom's survival and safety ... their blatant enmity, evil intentions, destructive intentions in Saudi Arabia have now become clear, are now common knowledge' (Huthayfi 1998).

The Saudi discourse did not comment on or criticize the actions of the cleric. However, the Iranian media reported that the crown prince, Abdullah, had apologized to Rafsanjani and dismissed al-Huthaify from the position he had held since 1979 (*al-Madina* 1998; *Jomhouri Eslami* 1998b). Both al-Sultan and Saeed (2016: 102) argue that the dismissal of Huthaify was made to appease Rafsanjani. However, it is important to mention that the sermon did not only criticize Iran and Shi'ism, it also called into question the overtures of the Saudi state and its moves to establish rapprochement. The rise in fundamentalism preached by bin Laden and the al-Sahwa clerics against the monarchy and the US in terms of a foreign presence in the kingdom was also an issue that the sermon might have exacerbated. Iranian silence could also be viewed in light of the severe challenges facing Tehran at that time, especially regarding OPEC oil prices, a rise in US military presence

---

3. Abdullah ibn Saba' was a Jewish convert to Islam of Yemenite origin. Ibn Saba's origins and political role are controversial and contested in early sources. The general view is that he is attributed the extremist ideas of Ali's divinity and divine appointment known as *ghuluw*, advocating that Ali's relationship to Mohammad was as close as Aron's relationship to Moses. Also, he propagated the belief that Ali was not dead and would be resurrected to bring righteousness and justice on earth (Oxford Dictionary of Islam).

in the region, and the need for Saudi cooperation in resuming relations with other regional states, especially the GCC.

As discussed previously, the Iranian clerical response to the Huthaify incident marked a complete shift from Iran's Khomeini-era polarizing rhetoric. Iran's construction of Saudi Arabia no longer emphasized its 'Otherness', but rather used tropes of Islamic unity and promoted the state narrative. Two Friday sermons in Iran exhibited a positive response to the incident in Saudi Arabia. Saudi Arabia as an Other was constructed as Iran's 'neighbours across the Persian Gulf', explicitly calling for rapprochement and efforts 'to overcome their differences'. Even the ultra-conservative Ayatollah Ahmad Jannati argued for 'stronger ties between the region's two economic and political powers' (Jannati 1998a). Like Saudi Arabia, the Iranian positive representation of its Other perhaps reflected an attempt to change the image it projected to regional and Islamic states.

The Iranian ulama also took on a softer narrative in response to the Saudi Friday prayer incident. Following the state line, the cleric praised the trip as 'good ... except for the incident at the Friday prayers', putting the incident down to 'differences with Saudi Arabia in the past that cannot remain', whereas a state that was once constructed as an enemy of the revolution, were now 'Muslim brothers' and the two states needed to rise from 'slumber and unite' (Jannati 1998a). The second sermon, led by Emami-Kashani, a conservative cleric who has often stood in opposition to reform, represented the Saudi ulama in a positive light, interpreting the incident as an isolated one by a deviant cleric who did not represent the mainstream Saudi clerical institution. Emami-Kashani observed that the 'Saudi ulama have said that we should unite as brothers, especially since the Islamic world is increasingly awake and aware day by day', explicitly referring to Huthaify's denigration of the Shi'a and Iran as an action by 'ignorant and hired people' while the Islamic world as well as the Saudi ulama's position in the Islamic world would 'achieve more homogeneity ... due to the lashes suffered ... at the hands of global arrogance' (Emami-Kashani 1998).

The shift in Iran's narrative towards Saudi Arabia was, I believe, due to a holistic line adopted by all the pillars of the state. Iran, with Khamenei at the helm, the executive and legislative branches, as well as the clerical establishment, were in total synchrony, understanding that rapprochement and constructive bridge-building with Saudi Arabia could lead to a very much needed positive outcome.

The Sultan and Khatami Visits: Iranian Requests for Security and Defence Cooperation The visit by Sheikh Mohammed bin Jubair, the head of the Saudi Shura Council, in November 1998 to Iran for the Inter-Parliamentary Union received a different treatment in both Iranian and Saudi editorials. The Iranian editorials reported on the speeches made in detail, while the Saudi editorials gave brief reports. The Iranian media attempted to frame the emphasis of the Iran–Saudi ties as based on historical ties and prestige. Yet, the Saudi media's response was cool and cautious, grounded in a domestic Wahhabi discourse that branded the Shi'a as heretics. In balancing the internal discourses with the more liberal and fraternizing speeches made during bin Jubair's visit, the Saudi media represented the Saudi monarchy's approach as seeking a critical balance of relations with Iran, while not sharing all information with its own public. In a similar course of events after the visit by the Saudi defence minister, Sultan bin Abdulaziz, to Tehran in May 1999, the Iranian and Saudi media differed in their reporting. The Iranian sources described the details and statements of officials while the Saudi media did not. The Saudi media represented this visit as based on Iran's own desire for rapprochement, while the Iranian media and the Iranian vice-president, i.e. the counterpart of the Saudi defence minister, defined this visit as bilateral and as geared towards mutually improving relations.

The Saudi defence minister's meetings with Rafsanjani, Khatami, and Khamenei led the Iranian authority figures to produce a multi-layered discourse. While Rafsanjani and Khamenei emphasized the necessity of a security pact and a common threat to both countries, Khatami focused on the prestige of Saudi Arabia in his discourse. Such a layered approach shows the different relationship that each pillar of Iranian politics had with Saudi Arabia. Rafsanjani and Khatami took a more explicit approach, emphasizing 'energy and economy' and 'culture and prestige', respectively, in contrast to Khamenei, who only made an implicit call for a pact. Each of these major Iranian actors, however, shared a similarity in emphasizing Islamic unity and brotherhood and bilateral ties and their necessity between Iran and Saudi Arabia. Rafsanjani emphasized an agreement with Saudi Arabia at OPEC to save plummeting oil prices and employed a discourse emphasizing a mutual Other of Iran and Saudi Arabia in the Gulf – the United States of America. However, the Saudi response to the Iranian approach and discourses was a cautious one. In signing memorandums on collaboration, the Saudi defence minister responded to the mutual Othering of America by suggesting that 'America . . . is a friend to everyone' and 'no problems exist between Iran, Saudi Arabia, and the US' (al-Saud 1999b).

Amid these numerous discourses, the Saudi position emerged clearly: trust and time were major factors, the US was a friend, and there were no regional threats with an American presence. The Saudi stance clarified that Iran and Saudi Arabia needed to build mutual trust to sign sensitive agreements. Such a stance confirmed Ali Shamkhani's statements, wherein the Saudi defence minister suggested to him that the presence of the US on Saudi soil was a part of the UN agreement and not a product of its military alliance (Shamkhani 1999). A defence pact with Iran, therefore, will take time to build trust based on the current trajectory of rapprochement. Saudi Arabia's stance indicated to its allies the progress of rapprochement with its new-found friend, Iran. However, its transition to a strategic relationship was not within sight yet. Following Prince Sultan's visit to Iran, Khatami visited Saudi Arabia in May 1999 for a ten-day tour. Becoming the first Iranian head of state to visit Saudi Arabia since 1979, Khatami's visit was considered auspicious since he was greeted by an ailing Fahd at the airport (Kazemi 2000, 134–35). In his meetings and discussions with Fahd, Abdullah, and Saud al-Faisal, Khatami continued to promulgate a pro-pact discourse, emphasizing the need for a security arrangement and a collaboration in 'the spirit of mutual respect and interests (Khatami 1999d)'.

The Saudis responded with gestures and highlighted the Iranian positions, alluding that all the final hurdles had been removed. Decorating Khatami with the Chain of Badr of the Order of King Abdulaziz – the highest Saudi award bestowed on Muslim leaders – Fahd accepted Khatami's arguments and suggested that the 'door [was] now open to both countries' (al-Saud, 1999c). Defining the relationship between Saudi and Iran in personal terms, Khatami represented Iran, while Saudi Arabia was represented by the al-Saud family. Even the most sceptical elements of the Saudi government voiced their opinions in line with Fahd – including the Saudi foreign minister, who responded to the questions on security cooperation by suggesting that enough trust has been built to address such a sensitive issue.

Just over a year later, on 19 April 2001, Saudi Arabia and Iran signed a security agreement in Tehran. Amid a visit to Iran, the Saudi Interior Minister Prince Nayef bin Abdulaziz signed the historic pact with his counterpart Abdolvahed Mussavi-Lari. The relationship between both states had undergone a noticeable shift. Nayef represented Iran's security as 'akin to Saudi Arabia's security and vice versa' and that 'both countries are serious in cementing relations and coordinating efforts on various Islamic issues' (Al-Maeena 2001).

Conclusion

Domestic and external forces were the main factors behind Saudi–Iranian détente and rapprochement. These included Iran's vulnerable economy, domestic turbulence, regional security threats such as Saddam, and an increased US military presence. This represented a significant shift from the 1980s, where the export of the revolution and competition over Islamic and regional leadership were the main forces influencing Saudi–Iranian relations. There are several conclusions that can be drawn from this period. First, the Iranian establishment was divided in terms of Western rapprochement, especially with the US, but united in its stance towards the region in general and Saudi Arabia in particular. This gave rise to a 'split personality', defined by Khamenei's views of détente versus Khatami's dialogue of civilizations, or a revolutionary image versus a diplomatic one. Second, Iranian–Saudi representations of the Other were shrouded in neutrality and silence. An Iranian shift in the representation of the Other signified a move away from the early revolutionary upheaval of the Islamic Republic to the confidence-building stances of the Rafsanjani–Khatami era.

Conversely, Saudi Arabia's tactful representation of the Iranian Other was a consequence of domestic and external threats, such as a rise in terrorism, a weak economy, and a belligerent Iraq. Third, Iranian–Saudi Othering evolved as the states' relations shifted from détente during the Rafsanjani presidency to rapprochement during the Khatami tenure. This allowed for narratives and Othering to shift from confidence building and trust to cooperation and finally partnership. These were exemplified by respect for territorial integrity, economic cooperation, and the signing of a security pact in 2001. Finally, Saudi–Iranian representations of the Other directly related to the identity of the respective leaderships. Saudi Arabia's representation of Iran shifted with Khatami's electoral victory, and the Saudi construction of the Islamic Republic was shaped by its opinion of Khatami. In other words, the representation of Iranian geopolitical, historical, and cultural prestige was reflected in the positive narratives that the Saudi discourse developed around the person of Khatami.

Furthermore, Iranian–Saudi representations of the Self and the Other also mainly revolved around discursive acts of confidence building, Islamic unity, and inter-state cooperation. In addition, the most noticeable aspect of this period was the 'silent Othering' that overshadowed the discourse of both states. While both states arguably exhibited very sophisticated discourses that drew on well-honed antagonistic rhetoric and languages, both states deliberately chose not to mobilize them in negative constructions of the Other. This 'silent Othering' was also a forced strategy on the part of the two states' intent regarding rapprochement, thereby alleviating their respective economic woes, balancing regional threats from a common enemy, i.e. Saddam, and averting a regional war. However, as will be witnessed in the coming chapters, as the threat of Saddam ended, a new arena of competition would emerge between the two states and this rapprochement would therefore begin to regress. This regression would be catalysed by the election of a new president to Iran, Mahmoud Ahmadinejad.

Part 3

Chapter 7

AHMADINEJAD'S VICTORY AND ABDULLAH'S THRONE: THE BEGINNING OF THE END FOR RAPPROCHEMENT

Introduction

The 2000s witnessed major shifts on both international and regional levels. In the US, the World Trade Centre attacks by Al-Qaeda in 2001 led to the international war on terror. This led to the US invasion of Afghanistan and the fall of the Taliban government. In the Middle East, the US invasion of Iraq and the fall of Saddam Hussein in 2003 affected the Middle East's political and regional landscape. Iranian-backed groups entered the Iraqi government, and for the first time a Twelver Shi'a-led government in the Arab Middle East came into existence. Furthermore, Iranian supported groups in Lebanon and Palestine, along with Syria, gave Iran a central and dynamic role in the region. This posed a challenge to the Arab states in general and Saudi Arabia in particular.

The attacks on the World Trade Centre in New York in September 2001 was planned and executed by Al-Qaeda to inflict as much damage on the US as possible. This damage was aimed at demoralizing the American public, thereby pressuring the US administration to end their military presence in Saudi Arabia, abandon sanctions against Iraq, withdraw support from Saudi Arabia and other Arab regimes such as Egypt, and stop US support for Israel (Fishel 2002). Out of the 19 hijackers that carried out the attacks, 15 were of Saudi nationality. In addition, the relationship between the US and Saudi Arabia shifted. American policies towards Saudi Arabia were affected by the perception that Saudi Arabia bore some responsibility, albeit indirectly, for the attacks while US public opinion perceived Saudi Arabia in a negative light. The attacks resulted in the invasion of Afghanistan, the displacing of the Taliban, and the search for bin Laden and Al-Qaeda. Saudi Arabia non-participation in Afghanistan (and later in Iraq in 2003), was a clear sign of the change in US–Saudi relations (Niblock 2006: 164).

US hostility towards Iraq altered its policy to a military position towards Iraq. Saudi Arabia, however, maintained its policy of conservative and defensive containment as a means of conventional deterrence. Furthermore, Saudi Arabia did not confirm US accusations against Iraq sponsoring Al-Qaeda and concealment of a secret WMD programme (Zeino-Mahmalat 2012). The diverging perceptions of an Iraqi threat after 9/11 led to a straining of US–Saudi relations. Saudi Arabia did not consider Iraq a direct threat, therefore it aimed to maintain the pre-war balance of power in the Persian Gulf between Saudi Arabia, Iran, and Iraq (Zeino-Mahmalat 2012). Saudi Arabia feared that regime change in Iraq would disturb the balance of power, as Iran and Iraq counterbalanced each other. Therefore, US-led regime change would destabilize the Middle East as a whole, and give rise to innumerable security threats (Zeino-Mahmalat 2012).

The period following the World Trade Centre bombings were difficult for Saudi Arabia. The kingdom had suffered from a wave of terrorist attacks since the mid-1990s. However, since the fall of Saddam in 2003, attacks had increased proportionally, including the targeting Saudi governmental and diplomatic compounds such as the US consulate in 2004 and 2006 respectively. US criticism of Saudi Arabia grew, with calls for more democracy as President Bush launched his grand plan for reform in the Middle East. Saudi-led initiatives such as the conference on terrorism in February 2005, democratic reform through municipality elections, calls for more female participation in the political process, and suggestions for women to be allowed to drive were all part of a campaign to revamp Saudi Arabia's international image.

The post-September 2001 context also had an effect on Iranian foreign policy. The Iranian government underwent foreign policy adjustments with a view to maximize its gains regionally and internationally. Khatami's tenure witnessed a more flexible approach to the US and strengthened relations with the EU and Russia. Regionally, Iran established détente with the Arab world and the Persian Gulf in particular. The Iranian government sought to improve its role and image in the international community while Khatami's 'Dialogue of Civilizations' ensured that Iran would be well on its way in its attempting to break out of international isolation.

The move towards a more flexible foreign policy in relation to the US was due to a more aggressive American presence, and Iran's complete encirclement by 2003. US bases were compared to a 'security belt' that included Kuwait, Turkey, Afghanistan, Azerbaijan, Uzbekistan and, by 2003, Iraq (Afrasiabi and Maleki 2003). As a result, Iran's foreign policy took a position of 'active neutrality', that had started with the invasion of Kuwait in 1990, and continued during the war in Afghanistan, and the US invasion of Iraq. Consequently, Iran had a greater regional role, attempting to demonstrate an image of a responsible regional partner while deflecting the US label of the country acting as a 'rogue state' since the revolution in 1979.

The events of 9/11 shaped Iranian–US discussions on Afghanistan. Iran had maintained during the 1990s that the Taliban were a regional menace and the attacks on the World Trade Centre naturally convinced the US of the Iranian view of the Taliban (Afrasiabi and Maleki 2003). Discussions could be described as fruitful with Iran agreeing to rescue any US army personnel, and apprehend fleeing Al-Qaeda fighters attempting to escape Afghanistan by crossing Iranian borders. In addition, Afrasiabi and Maleki (2003) argues that the Iranian role was more prominent in inter-Afghani factional talks. The US asked Iran to intervene and unite certain Afghani factions in an attempt to avert another civil war and bloodbath, while putting the pro-Iranian Northern Alliance in control of Kabul.

The US invasion of Iraq led to the overthrow of Saddam and the Baath party, thereby eliminating Iran's most immediate threat. Furthermore, the rise of Shi'i political parties in Iraq – many of whom were in exile in Iran – led to a rise in Iran's regional prominence. The dismay in the Middle East was explicit, with Jordan's King Abdullah labelling the Iranian influence in the Middle East as constituting a 'Shi'a Crescent'. This period coincided with Iranian–EU nuclear talks that were strained, resulting in the EU troika of Britain, German, and France to declare that Iran was enriching and producing nuclear fuel covertly in violation of the Nuclear Proliferation Treaty (NPT). Although Iran agreed in November 2003 to suspend uranium enrichment while negotiations continued, the threat of US and Israeli military strikes loomed in the background.

In 2004, Iranian progress in constructing a heavy-water nuclear reactor in Arak led to the suspension of nuclear talks with the EU troika, due to the risk of possible production of plutonium that could be used in nuclear weapons. Furthermore, the *Majles* elections in February 2004 gave rise to a majority 'principlist' ultra-hard-line faction in parliament. Khamenei's support of the principlists, the constant criticism of the reformist factions with regards to the nuclear negotiations, and the rise of the IRGC's influence on state policies, led to a hardline shift in Iran's foreign policy. In addition, the election of Ahmadinejad, a candidate supported by the IRGC and ultra-conservatives, moved Iranian foreign policy away from détente and rapprochement towards confrontation and post-revolutionary rhetoric (Keynoush 2016).

The election of Mahmoud Ahmadinejad signalled a change from the Khatami era of rapprochement with Saudi Arabia to a gradual rivalry. Ahmadinejad's promises of a return to revolutionary ideological dynamism enhanced Iran's regional role in the Middle East. Strengthened relations with Bashar al-Assad of Syria, Hezbollah in Lebanon and Hamas in Palestine indicated Iran's regional ambitions. In addition, the Israeli–Hezbollah war in 2006 and the Gaza War of 2008–09 underscored Iran's dynamic role in the Middle East and the effect it had on Saudi regional and Islamic leadership. The Iranian nuclear programme, and Iranian rhetoric towards Israel and the Holocaust, further agitated the region and gave rise to a populist narrative that appealed to the Arab street.

In this chapter, I build on the contentions I made in the Introduction with regards to the relationship between state dynamics and how the discourse relates to political events. That is to say, the War on Terror, the fall of Saddam, and to some extent the state of the two respective economies and the rise in oil prices had an effect on the change in the discourse and the relationship between both states in general. That, coupled with the rise of the principlists and the IRGC, shifted the discourse away from rapprochement to the use of negative discourse constructions and images. Consequently, the Khatami period demonstrated the contention I made earlier, namely that differences such as sectarian and religious views did not inhibit a more positive discourse (and image) developing, given that the political circumstances were moving in a positive direction. In this chapter, I argue that the political circumstances were not moving in the right direction for both states, especially with the increasing Iranian presence in Arab affairs such as Iraq, Lebanon, and Palestine. Consequently, in this chapter I demonstrate that the construction of the image of the Other allowed for the mobilization of images that have a diverse use, including certain religious and historical comparisons such as the narratives and metaphors discussing the Prophet Mohammad and the Karbala paradigm. These images which have an innate multiplicity resonate in all Arab and Islamic cultures, thereby facilitating a wider target audience on both a domestic and external level. Therefore, the political and religious actors in both states mobilize the images to satisfy different political agendas. Images with Islamic metaphors such as Saudi Arabia being the 'cradle of Islam', verses and scriptures shedding light on the importance of the Hajj, and the utilization of comparisons to the Prophet's companions, allowed for discourses of Saudi legitimacy, significance, and Islamic and Arab leadership. Iranian use of the image of the 'Ominous Triangle', Karbala, Imam Hussain, were employed to construct a discourse of Arab meandering, targeting democracy and the Shi'a in Iraq. The targeting of the Askari shrine and the Islamic image of attacking infallibles as with Yazid, gave rise to a discourse of Saudi collaboration with US–Zionism against Islam. Furthermore, as Iran became more strident, and Saudi Arabia sought to tackle its international image, relations between the two countries began to gradually sour after a period of neutral and positive elite representations in the Rafsanjani and Khatami period. To convey these shifts, this chapter will analyse 'snapshots' of the period stretching from Ahmadinejad's victory in 2005 and Abdullah's ascension to the throne that same year, up to the bombings in Iraq in February 2006.

Ahmadinejad's Victory, Islamic Leadership, and Cooperation

The initial Saudi representation of Iran under Ahmadinejad was positive, as witnessed in the telegrams congratulating the new Iranian president, which 'looked forward to strengthening the existing relations [with a] brotherly Iran' (al-Saud 2005g, 2005h). The positive discourse of cooperation and fraternal relations was reciprocated in the first instance by Ahmadinejad as part of his victory press conference, praising the Persian Gulf Arab states as 'brothers' in pursuit of 'trust and cooperation [and the] expansion of ties with regional countries' (Ahmadinejad 2005c; Asefi 2005) It was not long, however, before relations and mutual representations took a turn for the worse.

A visit by the Syrian president, Bashar al-Assad, two days after the formal inauguration of the Iranian president, was an alarming sign for Saudi officials, especially since Saudi Arabia had attempted to sway Syria away from Iran for several years (Wehrey et al. 2009). While emphasizing the long collaboration and strengthening of relations between the two states, Ahmadinejad's populist rhetoric constructed this as a 'new beginning' and a battle 'to defend the Islamic Ummah' in a bid to 'play an effective role in the region and the world of Islam [thereby] protecting the region and the world of Islam from possible invasions' (Ahmadinejad

2005h). In addition to relations with Syria, Iran's expansion in the Middle East – highlighted by its role in Iraq through its alliance with Shi'i factions, and its support for Hezbollah and Hamas – was tilting the balance of power in its favour. While these were not entirely new, Iran's scope for involvement in Iraq expanded significantly in the years after 2003, while its support for Hezbollah and Hamas was boosted following Ahmadinejad's election. On the Iranian side, international pressure regarding its nuclear programme, the presence of US bases on its doorstep, and a turbulent Iraq embroiled in sectarian violence that could spill across its borders, formed the grounds to continue the rapprochement with Saudi Arabia. Consequently, and as will be discussed below, Iranian relations with Saudi Arabia were two-pronged: Ahmadinejad and his cabinet represented one strand, while Rafsanjani in his capacity as the chairman of the Expediency Council represented the other strand.

Iraq witnessed significant events in 2005. These included Iraqi parliamentary elections, the drafting of Iraq's constitution, and increased sectarian violence. In January, the United Iraqi Alliance (UIA), the Iraqi Shi'i party, won a majority of seats in the interim parliament. As a result, the Shi'a had control over the drafting of the constitution. Felter and Fishman (2008) argue that Iranian-supported UIA members played an instrumental role in drafting the new Iraqi constitution, which was boycotted by the Sunni parties. Saudi–Iranian cooperation was therefore imperative, especially given the threat of sectarian violence reaching Iraq's neighbours, i.e. the Arab Gulf states such as Saudi Arabia and Bahrain and, to a lesser extent, Kuwait (Felter and Fishman 2008). This, amalgamated with Ahmadinejad's populist revolutionary rhetoric, may have led the Iranians to accept a Saudi invitation to Rafsanjani in September 2005, a move aimed at ensuring a continuation of rapprochement and détente.

Rafsanjani's visit demonstrated a clear Iranian intent to expand their relations with Saudi Arabia. Over a course of approximately a week, Rafsanjani's speeches, sermons, and press interviews reflected four main discourses leading to a positive representation of each state. The first was a discourse of cooperation and sharing of the leadership of the Middle East and Islamic world. The second was a discourse on Islamic unity, coexistence, and anti-sectarianism, which was constructed as both countries' objective. Third, a discourse of cooperation was emphasized regarding Arab–Israeli affairs. The fourth was a discourse on the Saudi and Iranian right to develop nuclear energy as advocated by both leaderships.

The discourse on cooperation and shared regional leadership was reflected in Rafsanjani's characterization of Saudi Arabia's 'valuable role in the issues of the Islamic world', a discursive construction of shared values, historical relations and cooperation whereby if both states 'unite and take on a joint position they can ... solve the problems of the region' (Rafsanjani 2005c). Furthermore, implicitly dismissing Iranian domination of Iraq, Saudi Arabia was depicted as a country that could 'cooperate on the fate and future of Iraq [by involving] regional countries, including Jordan and Turkey'. Consequently, Rafsanjani's discourse attempted to represent Saudi Arabia as a regional leader that could 'play a useful and constructive role' as opposed to the media reports that framed the Saudis as abetting the terrorist violence in Iraq since 2003 (Rafsanjani 2005c). The Iranian narrative of Saudi leadership and collaboration went so far as to represent the monarch as a leader with 'characteristics that can guide the two countries'. This reference to leadership implicitly framed the king's status with the Valī-yi Faqīh, the only position in Iran that could guide the country and the Ummah. In an interview with the Saudi newspaper *Okaz*, Rafsanjani attributed to the Saudi king the characteristics of 'moderation', 'unity of the Islamic world', and 'rationality' (Rafsanjani 2005b), qualities that would normally be attributed to the valī-yi faqīh, i.e. to Khomeini and Khamenei.

Sectarianism was represented discursively as an infidel conspiracy that 'causes division among the Muslims in the world'. The solution and remedy proposed by Rafsanjani was Iranian–Saudi Sunni–Shi'i 'collaboration and cooperation ... to stand against this great conspiracy'. In addition, the Iranian Self and the Saudi Other were constructed as peaceful with 'problems ... resolved through holding discussions and conducting research', rather than through violence. Turning a blind eye to any Saudi role in the sectarian violence in Iraq and Afghanistan, the issue of sectarianism was characterized as a 'real problem in the Islamic world', emphasizing that 'killing Shi'as and attacking mosques' (Rafsanjani 2005d) is not part of Islam. The sectarian narrative was also intertwined with the discourse on Israel and Zionism. Relating the plight of 'Palestinians that has lasted ... fifty years' to sectarian strife, the Arab–Israeli issue caused 'irreparable harm to the Islamic world' (Rafsanjani 2005d). Rafsanjani therefore attempted to represent a shared role with Saudi Arabia in relation to regional and Islamic matters, sustaining the path of détente and rapprochement since 1996.

Iranian discussion of Saudi human rights and treatment of the Shi'a did not go unnoticed. Highlighting the difference in the eight years since he had last visited the kingdom, Rafsanjani characterized the status of the Saudi Shi'a as improving. He referred explicitly to the possibility of 'holding religious programmes and celebrations', which was a clear indication of 'peaceful coexistence' between the two sects. Amid sectarian violence in Iraq, a rise in Wahhabi anti-Shi'i rhetoric, and US calls for democracy in the Middle East, Rafsanjani's representation of a monarch who implemented human rights and who was making the 'situation of the Shi'a...better, day by day' painted a positive picture at odds with the negative discourse on Saudi human rights and sectarianism, while representing Iran too as desiring coexistence and mutual respect, including acceptance of Sunni communities. Furthermore, Rafsanjani's position was represented as expressing a 'shared belief by King Abdullah ... [that] coexistence ... would be strengthened day by day ... with no reason for discrimination between the two strata' (Rafsanjani 2005e).

On matters relating to the recognition and establishment of relations with Israel, Rafsanjani depicted Saudi Arabia as taking a similar position to Iran, that is to say, the Saudi Other positively reflected the Iranian Self in its stance towards Israel. Previous speeches by Al-Qaeda (bin Laden 2004) had accused the Saudi monarchy of collusion with Israel against the Palestinians in particular and the Islamic world as a whole. Similarly, Iranian conservative narratives also implicitly accused Saudi Arabia of the same allegations. Consequently, Rafsanjani's narrative was a positive representation of Saudi Arabia, framing Abdullah as both holding 'positions ... similar to ... Iran', and expressing a comparable tone towards any country that formally recognized Israel. According to Rafsanjani, the Saudi king 'was furious about the fact that some countries ... establish ties with Israel', and he 'rebuked' those leaders that did recognize Israel. Therefore, like the Iranian leadership, Abdullah was represented as taking a moral stance towards the Islamic world, alluding to his support for the oppressed against a 'Zionist oppressor' (Rafsanjani 2005e).

Although Rafsanjani's visit was in response to an invitation by King Abdullah, there was no extensive coverage of the visit by the Saudi press, except for a speech by Abdullah and an interview with the *Okaz* newspaper. Abdullah's discourse on Iran reflected three crucial issues. First, that Iran was equal to the Saudi-Arabian Self, having a 'special Islamic and political status [that is] very important for us' (al-Saud 2005f). Second, Iranian–Saudi relations were framed as 'strategic' while it was a 'responsibility' of a monarch to 'work with Iran [thereby] strengthening cooperation and strategic relations'. Implicitly referring to US–Iranian enmity, and amid US threats against Iran, Saudi Arabia framed the relations as 'important and necessary [while] noting not to allow any disruptions or weakening of these relations' (al-Saud 2005f). The Saudi discourse of cooperation, sustained rapprochement, and support was explicit in terms of its positive comments on Iran's nuclear dossier. Arguing against the West's approach to Iran's nuclear programme, it echoed the Iranian mantra of regional nuclear rights. Abdullah opined that 'peaceful nuclear power is the right of all countries, including the Islamic countries' (al-Saud 2005f), an argument made in the Iranian discourse of a Western conspiracy to deny Islamic countries the right to develop nuclear energy.

However, the Saudi elite representation of Iran during this period was not always so positive. One example of this was a think-tank session held in New York after the UN General Assembly sessions. Responding to questions on a 'peaceful resolution' and 'troop withdrawal' from Iraq (al-Saud 2005l), Saud al-Faisal did not hesitate to interweave a discourse on sectarianism, Arab losses, and Iranian expansionism. The Saudi discourse conflicted with the Iranian narrative of democracy and an inclusive constitution. Saud al-Faisal's criticism of Iran was possibly due to frustration at Iranian expansion in the Middle East. Saudi criticism of Iran was two-tiered, implicit where it criticized Iraqi practices and the domestic situation, and explicit in denigrating Iran's direct role in Iraq. The democratic processes of elections and constitution drafting were criticized and argued as 'not ... going to solve the problem of Iraq', relating Iraq's troubles to a country 'jarred apart', with Sunnis 'a separate entity from the Shi'a', while stressing their joint identity as Arabs (al-Saud 2005l).

Although Rafsanjani and Abdullah aspired to reduce the level of sectarian tension through a discourse of unity and cooperation, Saudi discourse in the international arena focused on civil war and regional expansionism. Iraq's burdens were related to sectarian and ethnic fragmentation that had led to conflict and civil war as well as deeper Iranian involvement. Saudi worries concerning Iranian expansionism were framed as part of a discourse of hegemony. Iranian control of a 'pacified' southern Iraq was due to the establishment of 'police forces ... armed groups and militias'. Saud al-Faisal also depicted Iran as employing corrupt methods, installing rogue elements, 'paying money, installing their own people ... establishing police forces ... and reinforcing their presence' (al-Saud 2005l). Consequently, the Saudi discourse implicitly described the Self as fearful of a pro-Iran Shi'i presence on its doorstep, yet it explicitly defined the Iranian Other by highlighting the nature of the governmental administration in southern Iraq, that is to say, Iraqi corruption, sectarianism, and chaos were all due to the Iranian influence that employed 'their own people'. Moreover, the establishment of a 'corrupt' Shi'i presence was also portrayed as due to 'protection by British and American forces in the area', implicitly alluding to Western naivety or collusion with Iran. However, in al-Faisal's criticism of Iran and the Western powers in Iraq, the most striking confession that emphasized Saudi fears was the belief that Iraq was being offered to Iran.

> [T]o us it seems out of this world that you do this. We fought a war together to keep Iran from occupying Iraq after Iraq was driven out of Kuwait. Now we are handing the whole country over to Iran without reason.
>
> (al-Saud 2005l)

The Iranian response was calm and measured, reflecting a discourse of surprise, cooperation, and friendship. Initially, there was no response from the elite, ulama, or editorials. However, Keynoush (2016) argues that the Iranian foreign minister, Mottaki, cancelled a trip to Riyadh to signal his opposition to his counterpart's statements. In their daily briefing, the spokesperson for the foreign ministry, Hamid Asefi, responded to Saud al-Faisal's remarks (Asefi 2005). Although Iran had been chastised for interference in Iraq and for sowing discord, Saudi Arabia was represented positively and characterized as a 'friend' (Asefi 2005). The response was also two-tiered. First, there was a particular representation of the image of Saudi Arabia. Second, al-Faisal's claims were refuted through a definition of the Iranian Self. In the former, al-Faisal's statements were deemed 'unrealistic', 'surprising and unreasonable', and unexpected from 'friends in the region' (Asefi 2005). The criticisms were depicted as un-Islamic, and therefore open to exploitation by the 'enemies of Islam', thereby generating an implicit image of Saudi naivety. By promulgating a non-sectarian discourse, Iran assured Saudi Arabia that it respected 'the unity of Iraqi groups and tribes' while desiring the 'establishment of peace and stability' (Asefi 2005). Accordingly, Iranian discourse sought to identify the Iranian Self with Saudi Arabia. It aimed to assure Saudi Arabia that Iran had no expansionist and hegemonic ambitions; it shared the Saudi view on Iraqi unity, and it rejected foreign interference in Iraq. Therefore, while al-Faisal's discourse was in tune with the monarch's – especially during the Rafsanjani visit – the Iranian representation of Saudi Arabia was in line with the ruling elite.

Israel and the Holocaust: Iranian and Saudi Implicit Representations of Each Other

It was not long after the inauguration that Ahmadinejad discussed his foreign policy outlook with the international community. In a speech at the UN General Assembly in September 2005, the Iranian president promulgated a discourse of equality, justice, respect and peace among members of the international community (Ahmadinejad 2005g). In the case of Palestine and peace in the Middle East, he argued that 'durable peace . . . through justice' and the 'establishment of a democratic Palestinian state with Jerusalem as its capital' would be the only solution to the Arab–Israeli crisis (Ahmadinejad 2005g). A hostile discourse towards Israel would later be communicated to a domestic audience. In a speech at the World without Zionism conference, Ahmadinejad's populist discourse emphasized the obliteration of Israel, with the country being 'wiped from the pages of history' (*az safha-yi tārīkh mahv shavad*).[1] The speech also defined the position of the new Iranian administration in terms of the Israeli–Arab peace process. The president argued that 'anyone who recognizes Israel will burn in the fire of the Islamic Ummah' (Ahmadinejad 2005j), an implicit referral to Arab states such as Egypt, Jordan, and Saudi Arabia, which was the whole purpose of the speech. Furthermore, the president constructed a discourse identifying Arab naivety. He referred to the acceptance of a 'Zionist regime' as being due to pressure from other 'dominating regimes'. This reflected a 'misunderstanding' of the situation, or 'selfishness' in terms of an attempt to achieve regional ambitions. This discourse on Arab naivety allowed for an implicit representation of Saudi Arabia as 'one of the foremost countries [that] made a mistake a few years ago [in] formalizing the existence of an illegitimate Zionist regime' (Ahmadinejad 2005j).

The peak of Ahmadinejad's populist discourse on Israel was the extraordinary OIC meeting in Mecca in December 2005. Organized by the Saudi king, the conference was his first international debut after his ascension to the throne in August 2005. Molavi (2005: 1) argues that this was a 'chance for him to shine on a world stage'. The conference was intended to discuss Islamic extremism, and it was an ambitious plan to introduce an image of an Islamic renaissance (Molavi 2006). However, Ahmadinejad's stance on the authenticity of the Holocaust and the Israeli–Palestinian conflict eclipsed and overshadowed the aims of the conference and implicitly criticized Saudi Arabia's leadership of the Islamic world. In his formal speech at the conference, Ahmadinejad argued that the main obstacle of the Islamic world was the 'usurious regime in Occupied Palestine', stressing that it was not 'logical and rational [to] recognize this fake government'. Therefore, Saudi Arabia's aims for a holistic Arab–Israeli peace initiative were implausible, while any country formalizing its relationship with 'oppression, arrogance, and domination . . . is a disappointment to humanity'. This led to Ahmadinejad's argument further defining the position of 'some Islamic countries' as being

1. The translation was adapted from Naji (2008: 140).

'threatened by great powers' (Ahmadinejad 2005f), implicitly representing Saudi Arabia as a weak state. Consequently, the president's discourse constructed an image of Saudi subservience to the West and Zionism.

However, the main comment that stole the limelight from the king's goals and moment was Ahmadinejad's remarks on Holocaust denial and his calling on Western countries to give the Jews in Israel land in Europe. In a press conference with Saudi news agencies, Ahmadinejad's populist discourse on Holocaust denial and confrontation with the West – alongside championing Palestinian rights – illuminated Saudi Arabia's role and its position in the Islamic and Arab world. This implicit discursive construction of the Iranian Islamic leadership came at a time when bin Laden's speeches advocated a similar argument, alleging that Saudi Arabia was complicit in 'Western crimes' and subservient to Western powers and Israel, to the detriment of Islam and the Palestinian people. Ahmadinejad's statements represented a clear shift in discourse from the softening position held by the Khatami government, which had allowed Saudi Arabia to lead the Arab–Israeli peace process with no overt Iranian opposition. Consequently, a return to a Khomeini-era revolutionary discourse proved to be a dilemma in the Saudi representation of Iran:

> Although we do not accept this claim (the Holocaust), if we assume that it is true, our question to the Europeans is whether the murder of the innocent Jews by Hitler is the reason for the support of the occupiers of Jerusalem? ... If the Europeans are right they should offer part of their territory, from Germany, Austria, or elsewhere, so that the Jews can install their state there.
>
> (Ahmadinejad 2005d)

The Saudi response consisted of tactical silence, which reflected their quietist diplomacy. An illustration of this was Turki al-Faisal's speech at Washington's Middle East Institute:

> As far as the condemnation of Iran's statements on Israel, we prefer to deal directly with the Iranians and tell them face to face what we think of their statements rather than making a public issue of it and gaining some cookies, if you like, from those who might want to disperse that to other countries.
>
> (al-Saud 2005)

Saudi Arabia's discourse did not discuss Ahmadinejad's statements on Israel, his refutation of the Holocaust, and his moving the Israeli state to Europe. Instead, the discourse focused on terrorism, Islamic unity and cooperation, and a dialogue of civilizations, an adoption of the language promulgated by Khatami during his presidency. Saudi Arabia's religious discourse promulgated the monarch's narrative of a peaceful Islam and acceptance of the Other, highlighting 'Arab and Islamic civilisation' and what actually constituted this civilization (bin Humaid 2005). The Islamic world was defined as 'suffering from weakness, disintegration and the spirit of defeat ... waste and loss ... a gloomy image', implicitly referring to the rise in terrorism in the kingdom and the turmoil in Iraq. Resonating with Abdullah's OIC speech, the 'sedition, injustices, and abuses' had to be reviewed, representing a new image of Islam (bin Humaid 2005). This image and representation of Islam was defined in implicit opposition to Ahmadinejad's depiction of the scientific dimension of Islam as based on nuclear rights. In turn, the Saudi ulama represented Islam as a 'civilisation built on religion, namely principles and values, not just materialism, inventions and discoveries' (bin Humaid 2005). A 'balance in thinking' between the 'spiritual and material' was defined as the main tenet of an Islamic civilization (bin Humaid 2005). This clearly exemplifies one implicit response to the Iranian discourse on scientific prestige and the scientific advancements made during the Islamic empire, which gave Western civilization its contemporary scientific status. It also exemplifies the narrative of the West seeking to create a nuclear apartheid and keep the Islamic world in the dark ages. (Ahmadinejad 2005g; Jannati 2005).

Furthermore, the Saudi editorial discourse focused on the main theme of the OIC, terrorism. The newspaper *al-Riyadh*, for example, argued that the OIC summit was at a crossroads, defining the image of Islam as one that had 'internal contradictions' more intense than their 'clash with the outside world', i.e. the West (*al-Riyadh* 2005). The Saudi discourse painted an image of an Islam that was ailing from within. Contrary to the Iranian discourse that related the cause of regional problems to the West and 'Zionism', Saudi discourse argued that the problems in the Islamic world were due to internal 'disputes' that gave rise to three afflictions: 'political Islam', sectarianism and terrorism. They were implicitly referring chiefly to Iran, and then secondly to Iraq and Iranian dominance there, and third, to terrorism in Saudi Arabia and Iraq. The Saudi editorial discourse further promoted the monarch's discourse on a 'dialogue with all other forces and in harmony with civilizations' (al-Saud 2005e; *al-Riyadh* 2005b, 2005a).

The Askari Shrine Bombings, Sectarian Violence, and Iranian–Saudi Othering in 2006

The Iraqi elections in 2005 saw the dominance of the Shi'a in Iraq, especially since the Sunnis initially boycotted the elections. The elections were a clear illustration of voters' ethnic and sectarian attitudes (Henderson 2007: 38). This isolation and social fragmentation played a role in the Sunni insurgency. The latter represented an amalgamation of jihadist and Baathist elements that targeted the Shi'a, in turn causing a retaliation that led to a vicious cycle of violence. The most significant of these episodes was the attack on the Askari Shrine in Samarra on 22 February 2006. Henderson (2007: 38) argues that these attacks were significant in that both Saudi Arabia and Iran saw Iraq as a major element of their respective spheres of influence, and therefore both were 'not prepared to concede to the other'.

Iranian and Saudi official responses propagated a discourse of cooperation, tolerance, and Islamic unity with their respective Friday sermons arguing that sedition and external conspiracies were the main cause of the bombings and sectarian violence. The elite discourse discussed a narrative of a 'spillover effect' amid calls for unity and the combatting of terrorism. Iranian editorials pushed a discourse of Western and 'Zionist' conspiracies, on occasion alluding to terrorism and sectarian conflict as the work of Wahhabism. The Saudi press, on the other hand, discussed the weakness of politicians and the role of government while calling for dialogue between all Iraqi groups. The Askari shrine bombings and the upsurge of sectarian violence that ensued led to a regression in mutual Iranian–Saudi representations, which shifted from positive representations to neutrality and implicit negative constructions of the Other. Furthermore, through the constructions of different discourse genres, the representation of the Other utilized historical, sectarian, and pejorative tropes. In the case of Iran, a return to the Ominous Triangle trope was predominant in the press discourse. Historico-religious images of the Prophet Mohammad, Karbala, and Imam Hussein were promulgated by the political and religious elite to construct the Other. At the same time, sectarian tropes constructed Iran as meandering in Arab affairs and emboldened by the depiction of an outcast Sunni and Arab minority through representations of foreign occupation and Iranian meddling.

The period immediately after the bombings witnessed extensive international condemnation. However, Iranian discourse covered the terrorist incident more than its Saudi-Arabian counterpart. Elite discourse in both states condemned the attacks, although they differed in how they ascribed blame and responsibility for the attacks. Also, while all the Iranian elite press discussed the terrorist attack in Samarra, the Saudi elite provided brief press statements, leaving the discussions to second-level state actors such as ambassadors and the press. Immediate condemnation came from the Saudi foreign minister and a discourse distancing Saudi Arabia from the attacks in addition to relating the incident to the Shi'i-led Iraqi government's discriminatory practices. In turn, al-Faisal's condemnation discursively constructed the Askari shrine atrocity as a consequence of an Iraqi government that should 'achieve security and stability, consolidation of its national unity, securing equality among all factions' (al-Saud 2006c). While not accusing Iran, it can be argued that the discourse was implicitly blaming the Shi'i-led government that enjoyed significant Iranian support, therefore giving Iran some responsibility for Iraq's insecurity. Iran was represented as an 'important and large country … with its responsibilities for stability and security', while Saudi Arabia hoped that Iran would 'work towards carrying those responsibilities … playing the role of a stabilizing country … not a country that would add to the … volatile situation' in the region (al-Saud 2006c). The Saudi monarch's condemnation followed a few days later during an Arab League meeting in Kuwait. Abdullah's condemnation was a template-based response calling for 'all parties to respect all holy and religious sites in Iraq', alluding to the sectarian violence enacted against Sunni and Shi'i mosques and sites (al-Saud 2006a).

Contrary to Saudi elite discourse, the main pillars of the Iranian elite addressed the Askari bombings in statements. The baseline discourse was that of a 'Zionist and Western conspiracy' against the Islamic world, in a clear reference to the US and Israel. Khamenei was quick to represent the attack as a 'political crime that can be attributed to the Zionist intelligence services and the occupation forces in Iraq' (Khamenei 2006b). While the other strand of the Iranian elite promulgated a similar narrative, their discourses also emphasized Islamic unity, awakening and resistance. Ahmadinejad argued that 'Zionism ... has been plagued by [the] awakening, vigilance, and resistance of the Islamic world' (Ahmadinejad 2006c), citing the 'unification of the Islamic nation' through the 'wave of love of the Prophet and his family in the Muslim world' (Ahmadinejad 2006c). Furthermore, the discourse on the Prophet was intertwined with that on the shrine attacks. Echoing the mantra of the 'occupation forces [disrupting and] prevent[ing] peace and stability [due to] successive failures', the speaker argued that it was the 'establishment of a new parliament and government' that the US and Zionists found troubling and that had ended any chance of stability. That argument was sustained by the claim that 'another goal ... was to divert attention ... from the insulting caricatures' of the Prophet and 'immediately turn their attention to disagreements between Shi'a and Sunnis' (Hadad-Adel 2006). This discourse on division through sedition and sectarian strife was also propagated by Rafsanjani. The US conspiracy sought to create a Greater Middle East. It was being pursued by 'weakening the solidarity of Islam and seeking division ... by creating problems for Muslims', thereby resulting in a rift in the Islamic world (Rafsanjani 2006a).

Iranian editorials followed similar narratives and discourses. As was the case in elite discourse, no explicit mention of Saudi Arabia was made. However, Wahhabism and Salafism were represented as the main culprits behind the bombings, pointing to an implicit representation of Saudi Arabia. The use of the Ominous Triangle (*musalas-i shūm*) phrase from the Taliban period once again defined the perpetrators of the attacks. However, in this instance the denigrated actors were 'Wahhabis, Baathists, and the Hypocrites' in one instance and 'occupying forces, Wahhabis and Baathists' in another (*Resalat* 2006c, 2006d). This trope implicitly represented all Baathists as Sunnis, and therefore as supporters of Wahhabism, which is the official sect of Islam in Saudi Arabia. Iranian editorial discourses mainly included Islamic unity and Western and Zionist conspiracies against Iraq and the Islamic world. Furthermore, they framed the bombings according to their political alignments. Where the conservative-leaning press – such as *Kayhan* and *Resalat* – employed narratives of martyrdom and denigration of Western states, editorials in *Aftab-e Yazd* and *Etemaad* employed a softer tone, discussing foreign intervention as a cause of the bombing but stopping short of denigration.

Saudi representations were perhaps constructed as a by-product of Iranian criticism of the US occupation of Iraq. Editorials in *Resalat* (2006c, 2006d) and *Ettela'at* (2006c) illustrate this. The Askari shrine bombing was attributed to Washington and the Ominous Triangle, which allegedly included Wahhabis (*Resalat* 2006d) and Salafists (in *Ettela'at*) in collaboration with the occupying forces and Baathist remnants. Consequently, since Saudi Arabia was traditionally known to be at the heart of Wahhabi–Salafist thought, it was implicitly framed as having played a role in the incident. In the case of Iraq, the Ominous Triangle intended to disturb the 'positive image of the Iraqi elections and cabinet formation' in a Shi'i-led government. The bombings were also described as a distraction from caricatures that were offensive to the Prophet Mohammad. The newspaper *Aftab-e Yazd* (2006) argued that 'we cannot deny that Western states benefit from the bombings ... diverting the attention of Sunni and Shi'i Muslims from the Prophet Mohammad's caricatures' (*Aftab-e Yazd* 2006). Therefore, this implicated the Salafist school of thought, mainly practised in Saudi Arabia, in a conspiracy against Islam and Muslims.

Sectarian discourse and the Karbala narratives were also employed when discussing the Samarra bombings. The modern-day Ominous Triangle (the Baathists, Wahhabis, and the US) was discursively constructed as the Yazid and Yazidis in Iraq, and the 'Shi'a in Karbala, Najaf, Samarra, and Basra ... [as] the modern-day Imam Hussein and his companions'. These alleged hypocrites, defined as 'Wahhabis and Baathists' were framed as enemies of the Iraqi people, and as such as enemies of peace and of the democratic process in Iraq. This argument was also propagated by the moderate leaning *Etemaad* that discussed the role of the 'radical fundamentalists' (*iftrātiyūn*) in 'collaboration with the US ... because they were not pleased with the current political atmosphere in Iraq' (*Etemaad* 2006). Therefore, by criticizing the role of Wahhabism, Saudi Arabia was implicitly framed as having played a role in the bombings as well as collaborating with 'foreign occupiers' against the Iraqi people and the Islamic world. According to *Aftab-e Yazd*, the occupiers 'seek to ... create sedition among Sunnis and Shi'a ... for future gains and advantage' (*Aftab-e Yazd* 2006). It is these gains that the Iranian editorials used to implicitly frame Saudi-sponsored Wahhabism.

Similar discourses of Islamic unity and the influence of foreign occupation on Iraq were also echoed in the Saudi newspapers. Furthermore, like the Iranian editorials, the construction of an Iranian Other in Saudi editorials was also done implicitly, as part of a greater narrative. The presence of a foreign occupier was argued to have inflamed 'destruction of holy sites', resulting in murder not evident 'during the dictatorships' (*al-Riyadh* 2006a). Also, it was this foreign occupier that had given rise to 'tribal and sectarian strife' (*al-Riyadh* 2006a). However, contrary to Iranian discourse, the presence of a foreign occupier gave rise to a government that has excluded the minority, arguing that 'dialogue ... without interference from anyone' (*al-Riyadh* 2006a) would fix Iraq's ailments. It can be argued that this interference is an implicit reference to Iran's support of a Shi'i-led party, the latter's coming to power, and the dominance of Iraqi politics and its constitution.

The newspaper *al-Hayat* used three strategies to pursue a similar implicit representation of Iranian interference and hegemony. This was achieved, first, by defining Iraq's identity and by rhetorically asking who was seeking to gain from a divided and shattered Iraq. Stressing Iraq's Arab identity, which lay at the 'heart of the Arab world', its political environment impacted on the Arab world since Iraq was 'connected to the Arab arteries and pains' (*al-Hayat* 2006), hinting at the spilling over and expansion of violence across borders, potentially reaching the Arab states such as the GCC. Second, the violence that followed the bombings was deemed to be the 'responsibility of the Iraqi security ... and political forces' led by the Shi'i majority. Third, attributing the extended presence of the occupation to 'Iraqi political forces and sectarian affiliations ... that were victorious by overthrowing Saddam', Saudi editorials called for the Shi'a majority to 'sacrifice a part of the victor's share ... to the losers' (*al-Hayat* 2006). If the victorious were the Shi'a parties supported by an Iran seeking to dominate Iraq, then by not sharing power with the Arab Sunnis they were prolonging the foreign occupation of Iraq and 'delaying the rebuilding of the state and its institutions' (*al-Hayat* 2006). Furthermore, *al-Hayat* framed the Iraqi constitution and government as illegitimate. The Shi'i-led parties were discursively constructed as greedy and sectarian, 'engaged in the race to share the wreckage of the state' and neglecting the fact that the 'sinking ship can only be saved through national unity ... that accommodates all its members' (*al-Hayat* 2006). That is to say, the 'grip of the majority [over the] rights of the victims' who were Sunni had given rise to violence and Iraq's destruction. Therefore, by discursively constructing the Shi'a as the force behind the sectarianism, fragmentation and extended occupation of Iraq, the Saudi editorial discourse also implicitly represented Iran as a malevolent force in the country, since it supported the Shi'i and Iraqi constitution.

Following the Iranian government's line, Iranian clerical discourse blamed the US and Zionism for the Askari shrine bombings, while highlighting a discourse of Islamic unity as a bulwark against sedition. Saudi prayer discourse took a similar line regarding sectarian violence, calling for calm and resistance to sedition. However, taking a closer look at the Saudi sermon that immediately followed the incident, it can be argued that it framed the Iraqi Sunnis as victims of the Shi'a. In other words, a discourse of victimization was constructed, representing the Sunnis as victims and the Shi'a as retaliatory aggressors. The Imam equated the 'unknown ... aggressor' with the Shi'a that retaliated against Sunni places of worship, arguing that 'assaults on the graves' were met 'by attacking the houses of God ... the burning of the Quran ... killing Muslims and preventing prayers' (al-Taleb 2006b). Consequently, the Mecca Friday sermon supported the Iraqi Sunnis, portraying them as victims of Shi'i retribution, while strongly condemning the Shi'a as attackers of the innocent. Although the occupier, i.e. the US, was viewed as causing sedition, the discourse also identified 'poisonous' foreign interference as resulting in sectarian violence, implicitly representing Iran as a culprit in the attacks on Iraqi Sunnis.

In comparison, the Iranian sermon discourse discussed the bombings in two stages. First, a sermon by Emami-Kashani after the incident focused on defining the perpetrators, and it advocated Islamic unity (Emami-Kashani 2006). Second, Rafsanjani's Friday sermon concentrated on the role of Wahhabism, foreign interference and Islamic unity. Like the elite and press, Iranian religious discourse clearly defined the perpetrators. The 'brutal hands of ... the arrogant West, and the leaders of the US and CIA, the Mossad and the Zionists' were behind the explosions (Rafsanjani 2006d). Furthermore, following the discourse of Islamic unity and the prevention of sedition, the Friday sermons expressed the 'sanctity [and] love of the Ahl al-bayt' to both sects. This discourse of unity went as far as to discursively construct the role of Ahl al-bayt in Islamic unity and their service to the Abbasid Caliphs, even though the Shi'a were persecuted by the Abbasids. In the spirit of 'coherence and unity', Emami-Kashani opined that the 'Imams ... were also among the army and the military power of the Abbasid caliph' (Emami-Kashani 2006). The Iranian discourse aimed at showing that regardless of sect, Islamic unity preceded religious convictions.

Shi'i narratives were also employed by Rafsanjani. The bombing of Samarra was juxtaposed with the attacks by the Wahhabis on the shrines in Iraq and the al-Baqi cemetery in Medina in the nineteenth century. Rafsanjani argued that 'once again in the era of freedom and human rationality . . . insane things are occurring', while the 'Wahhabi Salafists came to Karbala, Najaf and Samarra, and went to Baqi, looted and destroyed everything, committing crimes' (Rafsanjani 2006b). This narrative was also used to construct an image of collaboration with 'global arrogance' in a conspiracy to create a 'Greater Middle East' that intended to 'divide and distance Muslims from Islam' (Rafsanjani 2006b). By weaving these discourses into a discourse of Iranian leadership and Islamic unity, and by highlighting the role of 'Sunni and Shi'a in Iran and Iraq . . . gathered in joint unity prayers' while not mentioning Saudi Arabia, an implicit representation was made of Saudi Arabia as having a role in 'hidden hands . . . creating religious and sectarian sedition' in the Islamic world (Rafsanjani 2006b). In linking Wahhabi Salafists to the incident, interweaving it with an eighteenth-century historical context, and highlighting the role of Iran and Iraq in Islamic unity, Saudi Arabia's involvement and collaboration was implicitly represented in the atrocities taking place in the Islamic world.

Conclusion

The first year of the Ahmadinejad administration marked a phase of an overall implicit Saudi–Iranian representation of each other marked by instances of neutral to positive elite representation in 2005 to 2006. Negative representations were therefore left to the editorial and clerical discourse. This phase, marked by Ahmadinejad's victory, reflected a populist narrative and a return to the 1980s rhetoric witnessed in the Khomeini era. However, Iranian discourse also witnessed a two-pronged approach to Saudi Arabia. Ahmadinejad's rhetoric was balanced with Rafsanjani's discourse of Iranian cooperation, unity, and rapprochement. Similarly, Saudi discourse exemplified notions of cooperation, sustained rapprochement, and explicit support for Iran's nuclear programme.

Iranian populist discourse on Israel proved to be contentious for Saudi Arabia. Ahmadinejad's representation of the Iranian Self as an enemy of Israel and championing the cause of the Palestinians implicitly constructed Saudi Arabia as less Islamic and questioned Saudi legitimacy as an Islamic and Arab leader. This came at a time where Saudi domestic discourse was marred with Al-Qaeda's accusations of al-Saud's treachery and subservience to Israel and the West.

Events in Iraq, including the control of a Shi'i-led government and constitution, shifted Saudi representation towards Iran. This shift was illustrated in narratives of sectarianism, Arab losses, and Iranian expansionism, as part of a greater discourse on hegemony that explicitly defined the Saudi Other. Iranian rebuttals on Iraq represented calm and sustained rapprochement across all discourse genres. The bombing of the Askari shrine and the sectarian violence that ensued initiated an Iranian discourse of Saudi Othering, albeit limited to clerical and editorial discourse. Tropes such as the 'Ominous Triangle' (*musalas-i shūm*) from the Taliban period were promulgated by the Iranian editorials. Stopping short of labelling Saudi Arabia by name, Wahhabis were denigrated in references to Saudi involvement in the sectarian attacks, and their collaboration with the US and Baathists. Shi'i narratives of Karbala and discourses of martyrdom during Ahmadinejad's tenure were first cited during this incident. Modern-day Yazid and his supporters were associated with Wahhabism, and Saudi Arabia, against the modern-day Imam Hussein and his followers, i.e. the Iraqi people and the Islamic world. Saudi discourses mimicked Iranian themes of Islamic unity and the negative attributes of foreign occupation. Similarly, Saudi editorial discourse engaged in implicit Iranian Othering. Iranian support for a Shi'i-led government discursively constructed the Shi'a as the force behind the sectarianism, fragmentation, and extended occupation of Iraq. Albeit implicitly, the 2006 Askari shrine bombing was the first sign of Saudi Othering of Iran as a malevolent force in the Arab world, since it supported the Shi'i and Iraqi constitution. It would be the summer of 2006 that would shift all the discourse genres in both countries towards explicitly denigrating representations. The Hezbollah–Israel war of 2006, known as the 34-Day War, would be the 'straw that broke the camel's back'.

Chapter 8

THE IMPACT OF THE HEZBOLLAH-ISRAEL WAR ON SAUDI-IRANIAN REPRESENTATIONS

Introduction

The Levant region, made up of Lebanon, Syria, Iraq, Palestine, and Jordan, proved to be a major arena for Iranian–Saudi rivalry and competition. Wehrey et al. (2009: xv) argue that this 'stems from Saudi perception of the Iranian threat'. Iran's activities in the Levant – mainly in Lebanon and Palestine – cast a shadow on the legitimacy of the monarchy domestically, regionally, and in the wider Islamic world. This chapter examines how Saudi–Iranian discourses began to shift from the start of the Hezbollah–Israel 34-Day War, with initially more neutral and implicit discursive constructions of each other gradually transforming into more explicit and denigrating representations. The discourses of the elite constructed the Other through the employment of historical, political, and nationalistic tropes. In addition, these tropes utilized images of historical and religious significance, such as the infidels versus Islam, Hussain against Yazid, Imam Ali, as well as historicized images of the Israeli–Arab wars that saw the loss of the Arab armies. These images held great significance for both domestic and regional audiences. The religious, historical, and political analogies were easily mobilized and linked to discourses such as treachery and adventurism, leadership and subservience, thereby emboldening the discourse construction of the Self and Other.

The Background to the 34-Day Hezbollah–Israel War

On 12 July 2006, Hezbollah attacked an Israeli border patrol, killing three soldiers, and imprisoning another two. The response was a war lasting thirty-four days,[1] which resulted in the destruction of Lebanese infrastructure and its economy. Arkin (2011: 5) argues that Israel's aim was to 'turn Lebanon's clock back 20 years', after which it was presumed that the Lebanese population would revolt against the Iranian-supported group (Arkin 2011). Hezbollah's True Promise Operation

---

1. Also referred to as the 33-Day War.

(*al-Wa'd al-Sādiq*) was the first Arab–Israeli war in the post-Cold War era (Arkin 2011: 2). It fomented both US support for Israel, along with large scale Arab and Islamic condemnation of Israel. This condemnation involved the regional and Islamic pillars, Iran, and Saudi Arabia. The former fully supported Hezbollah, with the latter exhibiting its support for the Lebanese Sunni-led government of Fouad Seniora, while also attempting to end the war on a regional and international level.

Taking a closer look at the Iranian and Saudi discourse manufacturers and strategies employed by both states during this incident, it can be said that the manufacture and promulgation of the discourses was highly organized, tactical, and tacit. In Iran, the immediate response to the incident was made by the president and foreign ministry spokesman. Khamenei would criticize the silence of the Arab leaders and Islamic clerics without mentioning names, implicitly characterizing their silence as a form of subservience to the West and 'Zionism'. This argument would be continued by Ahmadinejad in his speeches, but with harsher rhetoric. The clerical discourse, as exemplified by the Friday sermons, took on a similar tone to the state narrative, criticizing Israel and the Arab states for their silence without mentioning Saudi Arabia.

It was the newspaper editorials that mainly employed the revolutionary rhetoric and tropes of the Khomeini period. It is interesting to note that the editorials in both states followed the lines of their elite while employing explicit representations of the Other. Iranian editorials, like the elite discourses, refrained from naming Saudi Arabia at the beginning of the war. However, as the war continued with no sign of a resolution, including great material losses for the Lebanese community and Hezbollah's resistance, the editorials shifted from criticizing 'Arab leaders' to naming and shaming specific Arab leaderships, while overall refraining from mentioning Saudi Arabia. This was arguably due to the Iranian nuclear programme and Saudi assistance regarding the threats posed to Iran by the US. The Saudi elite had been overall neutral and at times positive in supporting Iran's rights to peaceful nuclear energy.

Kayhan and *Jomhouri Eslami* used denigrating labels to indirectly represent Saudi Arabia. Phrases reminiscent of the post-revolutionary Khomeinist era such as 'reactionary Arab leaders' (*'sarān-i irtijā'-i Arab'*), 'ivory-throned sheikhs' (*'shiyyūkh-i 'āj nishīn'*), and 'colluding Arab leaders' (*'sarān-i sazeshkar-i Arab'*), were employed to construct an image of US–Zionist subservience and treachery against the Arab and Islamic worlds. Furthermore, conservative-leaning Iranian newspapers employed an in-group strategy to frame Saudi collusion in the Israeli attacks on Hezbollah. To illustrate this strategy, the juxtaposition of Mubarak with the Qur'anic Pharaoh (*Fir'awn*) (*Jomhouri Eslami* 2006a) was mentioned in the context of Israeli collaboration with Saudi Arabia. The intention was to group both leaderships and states together, framing them as complicit in the attacks against Lebanon, with the latter in the service of Israel.

Furthermore, pejorative, and sectarian tropes were applied to make manifest the image of Saudi Arabian silence and its supposed acquiescence with Israeli attacks and the Zionist–US leadership respectively. These discourses and tropes included the 'Ominous Triangle' (*musalas-i shūm*) image discussed in chapter five. This trope was previously adopted during the Taliban era when it was employed to define the collaboration between the US, Pakistan, and Wahhabism, and their involvement in the killing of the Iranian diplomats in Mazar-i Sharif. During the last incident, the trope was deployed mainly by *Ettela'at* and *Kayhan* to highlight Arab silence and subservience. However, where *Ettela'at* defined the Ominous Triangle as composed of the US, Britain, and Israel (*Ettela'at* 2006b), *Kayhan* (2006e) identified it with 'America, Israel, and reactionary Arabs', making a more direct link with Saudi Arabia in its discourse of Saudi subservience and betrayal of Hezbollah, Lebanon, and the Arab and Islamic worlds.

Like Iran, Saudi discourse during the 34-Day War was also structured and organized. The elite discourse was mainly promulgated by the foreign minister, with the king remaining silent, disseminating his views of the war through royal-court statements and Saud al-Faisal. The Friday prayer sermons sought to bolster Saudi leadership and legitimacy, while leaving any direct mention of Hezbollah and Iran implicit. Furthermore, while the Grand Mufti remained silent overall during the war, leading clerics from the Council of Ulama issued a fatwa prohibiting Sunnis from supporting Hezbollah. Saudi editorial discourse in general refrained from explicitly denigrating Iran, largely following the trend set by the discourse promulgated by the king and his foreign minister. Furthermore, the Saudi editorials took three main positions. *Al-Riyadh* adopted a Pan-Arab stance, representing the Arab right to resist occupation. Similarly, *al-Hayat's* editorials had an analytical line that was critical of Hezbollah and Iran. On the other hand, *Asharq Al-Awsat* spun a discourse representing Iran and Hezbollah in a negative context, casting doubt on their regional roles while stopping short of employing the 1980s rhetoric used during the Iran–Iraq war. The difference in stance can be attributed to the audience the newspapers targeted. While *al-Riyadh* targeted a more domestic audience, *Asharq Al-Awsat* had a wider Arab audience since it published its articles from the UK.

The Iranian response to the Israeli attacks on 14 July 2006 initially came from Ahmadinejad and the foreign ministry spokesman. In addition to a condemnation of Israel, he issued a warning to 'the Zionist regime ... not to extend the attacks to Syria', and he framed the attack on Lebanon as an 'attack on the Islamic world' (Ahmadinejad 2006b). Furthermore, a discourse of Islamic unity against Israeli attacks called for 'the regional states to show more unity and integrity'. This was an implicit response to the Saudi royal-court line that stopped short of naming Hezbollah, while its capture of the two soldiers was an 'uncalculated adventure that would extend [its implications] to the entire Middle East'. The Saudi statement blamed these elements, asking them 'to alone take responsibility for their irresponsible behaviour' while arguing that they should carry the 'burden of ending the crisis' and that the international community should make a 'distinction between legitimate resistance and uncalculated adventures'. This condemnation was also aimed at 'elements inside (Lebanon) and those behind them that did not coordinate with Arab nations' (*SPA* 2006). It can be assumed that the Saudi statement was aimed at Iranian adventurism in Lebanon as the backers of Hezbollah, who were 'exposing Arab nations and their gains to grave dangers'. That is to say, the Saudis may have been referring to Abdullah's attempt to revive the 2002 peace initiative. This Saudi statement and Ahmadinejad's response arguably began this exchange in implicit representations of each other, where Iran was viewed as interfering in Arab affairs and as questioning Saudi legitimacy and leadership of the Arab and Islamic world.

Themes and Tropes Regarding the War

Discussions of the Israeli–Hezbollah war in Saudi Arabia and Iran discursively constructed the Self and the Other. Iranian praise for Hezbollah, framing them as continuing Khomeini's line (*'khat-i Imam'*), or as embodying the prestige of facing a powerful traditional army for over a month led to comparisons with the major Arab–Israeli wars that saw Arab states defeated within days. This was an indirect way of constructing an image of the Iranian Self as an Islamic and regional leader, which innately constructed Saudi Arabia as weak and subservient to the West and Zionism. The Saudi and Iranian discourses and the discursive construction of associated tropes were based around main themes that included: Arab silence and subservience; Hezbollah–Iranian adventurism and legitimacy; Israeli hegemony and condemnation; and implicit representations of Hezbollah–Iranian adventurism. Historical and religious comparisons that held great significance for the domestic and external regional audience were used to reinforce these discourses. These included images involving Karbala, Prophet Mohammad, Zionism, and Khomeini. The remainder of this chapter tackles these discourses in turn, emphasizing how the discourse genres constructed the Other through these images that were used to enhance the state's leadership, public loyalty, legitimacy, and status, both domestically and externally.

Arab Silence and Western and Zionist Subservience vs. Hezbollah–Iranian Adventurism and Legitimacy

The theme of Arab silence constructed by Iran versus Hezbollah's adventurism and irresponsibility as represented by Saudi Arabia developed in the early days of the 34-Day War. The official statement from the Saudi royal court along with Saud al-Faisal's remarks on Hezbollah's 'uncalculated adventures' alongside questioning the legitimacy of Hezbollah as a resistance force and 'those behind them' gave rise to the Iranian response and implicit representations of Saudi silence and subservience to the West and Zionism. While the Saudi statements condemned Israel, its criticism of Hezbollah was interwoven into a discourse that questioned implicitly Iran's role in the Arab world and hinted at its meddling in Arab affairs. This is visible in Saudi accusations that certain 'elements', i.e. Hezbollah and Iran, were 'exposing Arab nations . . . and gains to grave dangers', referring to the Arab–Israeli peace process, an initiative of Abdullah since 2002, which he sought to resurrect during the George W. Bush administration.

The Iranian response to the war – which was also possibly a response to the Saudi statements – was an explicit condemnation of the 'silence of some Arab and Islamic governments' (Khamenei 2006f). This response was immediately promulgated by the chief commander of the Islamic Revolutionary Guard Corps

(IRGC), Yahya Rahim Safavi, who added a discourse identifying the subservience and cowardice of 'many leaders of Islamic and Arab countries' (Safavi 2006), thus questioning the legitimacy and role of the Saudi monarchy and their leadership of the Arab and Islamic worlds. Reminiscent of the Khomeini era, both Khamenei and Safavi drew a distinct contrast between Arab and Islamic leaders and their people. However, the trope of US–Israeli subservience was revived. The Iranian elite, represented mainly by Khamenei and Safavi, framed Arab silence and US–Zionist subservience in two main tropes. The first was a silence that was complicit with and that gave way to the formation of a 'New American Middle East', and the continuation of Israeli 'crimes, oppression and violation of human values [intended] to sustain the existence of the Zionist regime … the satanic and cancerous tumour in the Muslim world'. The second was a silence that represented a weakness of the Arab and Islamic leaderships' 'fear of American and Israeli leaders' and therefore 'indifference' to Israel's attacks on Hezbollah. Although Saudi Arabia was not mentioned by either Khamenei or Safavi, the implicit representation challenged Saudi leadership and legitimacy in the Islamic and Arab worlds. These discourses were like bin Laden and Al-Qaeda's accusations of Saudi silence towards the plight of Muslims in general and Palestinians in particular, which also framed Saudi Arabia as a US–Zionist lackey (bin Laden 2004).

Friday sermons followed a similar argument with an implicit representation of Saudi Arabian silence and subservience to the Israeli attacks on Lebanon. When analysing the Friday sermons, it is interesting to observe that, contrary to the post-revolutionary Khomeini era, the Friday imams refrained from mentioning Saudi Arabia or its leaders, thus demonstrating a shift to a more pragmatic position. However, referential strategies were employed to refer to Arab leaders, such as 'some Arab states' or 'some Islamic countries', in an implicit criticism of Saudi Arabia.

The Friday sermons wove the silence of Arab states and subservience to US–Israeli agendas into a narrative of collaboration that harmed Islam, Palestine, and the Arabs. A discourse of victimization that drew on historical narratives was employed. To illustrate this, a sermon by Ahmad Khatami characterized Arab silence as a Zionist collaboration that aimed to fulfil the ambitions of a 'Greater Israel' with 'borders from the Nile to the Euphrates' (Khatami 2006). Khatami interwove the discourse of a 'shameful' Arab silence with a rhetoric based on conspiratorial collaboration with US–Israeli agendas in the Middle East. Hezbollah was represented as a modern-day Saladin, 'the protector of the Islamic world … fighting enemies … against the crusades'. This modern crusade was the Israeli agenda to expand its borders, with Hezbollah the only force protecting Arab and Islamic lands. Even the pragmatic Rafsanjani framed the 34-Day War as a 'scandal [and a] moment of shame and historical disgrace [on the part of] Arab and Islamic countries'. A discourse of 'real Islam' protecting the Muslim world was also promulgated by Rafsanjani, thereby questioning Saudi legitimacy:

> How can people be Muslims, their government Muslim, and see these Muslims being crushed by infidels and sacrificed at the altar while they sit comfortably.
>
> (Rafsanjani 2006c)

The first discourse promulgated by the editorials was one of silence and subservience to the US and Zionism. However – and as was the case in the Friday sermons – the difference lay in the representation and the directness of the references to the Other. The editorials likely followed the Supreme Leader's line at the beginning, referring to both an 'international' silence (*Ettela'at* 2006a) and silence from the Arab countries (*Jomhouri Eslami* 2006b). This reference shifted as the war continued. For example, *Ettela'at* (2006e) used an in-group/out-group reference, in which Saudi Arabia was indirectly referred to by grouping it with the 'silence of important Arab states'. *Kayhan* (2006a), on the other hand, was more explicit, calling out 'Arab states such as Saudi Arabia' as silent and complicit in the Israeli aggression.

As discussed previously, the editorials followed Khamenei's line and argument as a platform for discourse construction and promulgation, and this included Islamic discourses and tropes. Khamenei's (2006c) sermon on Imam Ali's birthday, three weeks into the war, illustrates this argument, when he opined that on this 'day of Eid, our hearts are not happy because of the bloody state of the Islamic Ummah' (Khamenei 2006c). This 'bloody state' was intertwined with the situation in Lebanon and Palestine, and he questioned the silence of Islamic countries and 'division of the Islamic governments', particularly the Arab states, who were 'exhibiting damaging behaviour' (Khamenei 2006c), with 'Arab governments' arms folded and staring idly [at the] action of American and arrogant powers' (Khamenei 2006c).

Khamenei's speech was built into editorials such as those published in *Resalat* (2006b), which defined this silence as subservience to the 'White House and Tel Aviv'. The discourse of Zionist–US subservience was constructed by drawing parallels with the Iran–Iraq war: 'Hosni Mubarak, Saddam Hussein, King Hussain and other Arab leaders were silent and unmoved such that the White House and Tel Aviv viewed them as an extension of themselves' (*Resalat* 2006b). Indeed, just as had occurred during the collaboration against Iran in the 1980s, Arab leaders and Saudi Arabia served the interests of Israel and the US in attacking Shi'i Hezbollah, which was 'reliant on divine power' (*Resalat* 2006b). *Resalat's* representation of Saudi Arabia was therefore based on subservience but framed as a sectarian discursive construction of a war against Shi'i pro-Iranian groups, similar to Saudi aid to Saddam during the 1980s.

The theme of silence and subservience was also attributed to Saudi ulama. Within a week of the war, Abdullah bin Jabreen, a prominent member of the Saudi Senior Clerics Association, issued a fatwa deeming the 'support, joining, or praying' for Hezbollah to be 'impermissible' (bin Jabreen 2006). The senior cleric described Hezbollah as 'rejecters' (*rāfidah*) and advised the Sunnis to 'denounce anyone supporting' Hezbollah, because the '*rāfidah* have always harboured enmity to the Sunnis [and] aspired to show the weakness of the Sunnis, betray them and deceive them' (bin Jabreen 2006). The Iranian response was twofold. First, Khamenei implicitly responded to the Saudi fatwa by highlighting that sectarianism was an 'important tool of the enemies to subjugate the Islamic Ummah ... they are tools and strengthen the enemy' (Khamenei 2006c). This implicitly characterized the

Saudi ulama as a device utilized by the West and Zionism, thus deepening the discourse of subservience and silence. Second, the editorial discourse repeated similar lines, however, the representation was more explicit and employed Islamic narratives to highlight the discourse of treachery, subservience, and enmity towards Islam.

Like Khamenei, the editorials defined sectarian discourse promulgators as 'instruments dividing Shi'a and Sunnis ... sought by the US and Zionist regime'. Furthermore, these 'instruments' were also described as collaborators against Hezbollah and as a group of conspirators that included 'Arab leaders, the UN, famous religious centres, reactionary Arab Fatwa centres, groups claiming to fight the United States such as Al-Qaeda and the Takfiris' (*Jomhouri Eslami* 2006c). The Iranian editorial defined the above out-group as a list of members 'in secret agreement ... with the Zionist regime', thus representing Hezbollah and its supporters – specifically Iran – as undertaking a global war to defend Islam. The editorial emboldened its representation of sectarian conspiracies against Hezbollah and the Islamic world by utilizing the post-revolutionary rhetoric, specifying the 'muftis of Saudi and Egyptian courts [such as] Sheikh Abdullah bin Jabreen ... the largest Wahhabi mufti in the Saudi [royal] court', along with his Egyptian peer, Tantawi of Egypt, who 'blindly followed the Egyptian pharaoh', an allusion to Hosni Mubarak (*Jomhouri Eslami* 2006c). The narrative of royal-court subservience was also adopted, framing both muftis as 'servants' (*jīrahkhur*), releasing 'anti-Islamic fatwas for the US [and] worse than the Sultans' preachers of the dark ages' (*vu 'āz-i asalātīn*) (*Jomhouri Eslami* 2006c). Iranian editorials juxtaposed the Saudi muftis with other Sunni ulama. By labelling Sheikh Yousef Qaradawi as a 'world famous scholar ... proud of Sayyid Hassan Nasrallah', the Saudi muftis were by default depicted as anti-Islamic pariah clerics conspiring in the service of the US and Zionism (*Jomhouri Eslami* 2006c). Also, the comparison made between two of the most renowned Sunni ulama, Qaradawi and Jabreen, in Iranian discourse aimed to stress that 'true' Sunni ulama are supporters of Hezbollah, while the Saudi and Egyptian imams were framed as deviants of the Islamic faith putting forward their leaderships' subservience to the US and Zionism before Islam.

Islamic narratives were also utilized to demonstrate Saudi subservience and silence in the face of alleged US–Zionist attacks against Hezbollah. One such example was the representation of Hassan Nasrallah as the Imam Ali of our time, leading Muslims against the infidels of our time, juxtaposed with the 'War of the Trenches or Parties' (*'Jang-i ahzāb or khandaq'*),[2] that is to say, Hezbollah versus

---

2. The Battle of the Trench (*Harb al-Khandaq*) or Battle of the Confederates (*Harb al-'ahzāb*), was a 30-day siege of Yathrib (modern-day Medina). Prophet Mohammad and the people of Yathrib were besieged by a confederation of Arab and Jewish tribes, outnumbering the Muslims by 10,000 to 3,000. The battle was won by Mohammad and his followers following the advice of Salman Farsi, a Persian companion of the Prophet, to dig a trench around the city, thus weakening the confederates and lowering their morale (see Watt 1974).

'Israel, the US, their European allies, and some conspiring Arab leaders' (*Kayhan* 2006g). Just like the war fought by Imam Ali, the 'Muslims defeated the huge army of idol-worshippers'. *Kayhan* implicitly defined Saudi collaboration with the US and Israel as a conspiracy against the Islamic world and Iranian support for Hezbollah as a victory for the Islamic world. Like the War of the Trenches in which infidels aimed to wipe out Islam within days, the modern-day infidels were intent on 'dismantling Islam in the region' (*Kayhan* 2006g). Thus, Iranian discourse discursively constructed the Iranian Self as the true Islamic and regional leader by defining Hezbollah as a legitimate Islamic army led by a contemporary Imam Ali, and supported by Iran as a modern-day Salman Farsi, the devout Persian companion of the Prophet Mohammad and ally to the Ahl al-Bayt. Consequently, the same discourse questioned the legitimacy of Saudi Arabia as an Iranian Other and its role in Islamic leadership in defence of the Islamic Ummah.

Hezbollah–Iranian Adventurism and Legitimacy

Saudi discourse, on the other hand, constructed a supra-discourse of adventurism. The state discourse as disseminated by the Saudi foreign minister and the Saudi ambassador to the US explicitly referred to Hezbollah while implicitly criticizing Iran. The Friday sermon imams did not mention any group or country, while it was the editorial discourse that used the official Saudi narrative, explicitly representing Hezbollah and its Iranian backers as adventurists. The supra-discourse of Hezbollah–Iranian adventurism spun out state sub-discourse, namely a discourse of Lebanese and Arab sovereignty and legitimacy; Saudi legitimacy and leadership of the Arab and Islamic worlds; a closely related discourse of the Saudi Self and its regional role; and Hezbollah–Iranian regional adventurism. The editorial discourses related the discourse of adventurism to representations of Iranian proxy wars and the destruction of the Arab world.

Discourse of Israeli Hegemony and Condemnation

Arguably, one of the main discourses that led to Iranian accusations of Arab silence and subservience was the calls on the international community by Saud al-Faisal to 'support the Lebanese government's legitimate efforts to preserve Lebanon, preserve its sovereignty' and, most importantly, 'extend its authority over all its national territory' (al-Saud 2006e). A particular discursive construction suggested that Hezbollah was an illegitimate group and was harming the sovereign Lebanese state. Furthermore, Saudi responses to Iranian criticism of Saudi silence and subservience followed two specific strategies. The first was a direct criticism of the international community in elite discourse and Friday prayer sermons. The second was an implicit response embedded within elite discourse, mainly as part of international speeches and press conferences by the Saudi foreign minister.

The Saudi discourse condemned the international silence, mirroring the Iranian narrative. In a press conference by the Saudi foreign minister (al-Saud 2006e), the discourse framed the response of the international community as a 'failure' (*takhādhul*), and it suggested a UN and EU bias in the discourse, that does not take a 'serious position to stop the fighting', representing international silence as a 'real disaster for the Lebanese people'. Saudi mirroring of Iranian rhetoric towards Israel was also a feature. Saudi elite discourse highlighted 'violations of human and national rights . . . targeting of innocents with assassination, arrest and torture' and Israeli disregard for 'international treaties and conventions' (al-Saud 2006e). The Saudi Friday sermons (Sudais 2006b, 2006a) echoed the elite's narrative, further mirroring the Iranian ulama and elite discourse. The sermons framed the international organizations as having double standards, criticizing the 'loud voices that call against genocide [but regularly] chant slogans of freedom', arguing that international silence was a 'propaganda campaign, or a propaganda campaign that seeks the blood of Muslims'. Like Iranian post-revolutionary discourse, its Saudi ulama counterpart framed the attacks on Lebanon and Palestine as a conspiracy against the world of Islam, seeking 'Muslim rivers of blood' (Sudais 2006b).

Saudi responses to Iranian criticism of Saudi silence and subservience were tackled without reference to Iran. The Saudi foreign minister responded both by directly criticizing Israel and implicitly refuting Iranian notions of Saudi subservience and collaboration. Like the Iranian representation of Israel, Saudi elite discourse represented it as a Saudi Other by framing it as a hegemon whose 'blatant aggression' was an 'extension of the Israeli policy of occupation and hegemony . . . in the region' (al-Saud 2006e). Furthermore, and responding implicitly to Iranian claims of US and Western subservience, Saudi discourse framed the 'position of some countries' towards Israel as constituting a bias that 'led the Security Council to fail to take firm decisions to resolve this crisis' (al-Saud 2006e). Therefore, the choice to frame the image of the Saudi Self as an independent state acting against US–Israeli hegemony was an attempt to bolster its legitimacy and leadership domestically and regionally. The Saudi 'conscience is satisfied' as they were undertaking an Arab 'duty . . . that the Lebanese affirm'. Consequently, the Saudi discourse highlighted the Self as leading with Lebanese approval, 'having no one to apologize to' (al-Saud 2006f), in an implicit reference to Hezbollah supporters such as Iran and Syria.

Implicit Representations of Hezbollah–Iranian Adventurism

The Saudi elite proposed a discourse of Iranian–Hezbollah adventurism that 'destabilized the security and stability in the region', in turn highlighting the role of Saudi Arabia as an Arab leader. Implicit references to 'parties' that destabilized the region – i.e. Hezbollah and Iran in Lebanon – highlighted the regional role of Saudi Arabia, Iranian meddling, and a framing of Iran and its proxy as hijacking Lebanese sovereignty (al-Saud 2006d, 2006e). The Saudi 'position on this matter' – i.e. adventurism destabilizing the region – was deemed to be 'reaffirmed by the Arab League', while any issue regarding the Arab–Israeli conflict was one to be discussed 'in accordance with the resolutions of the Arab summits'. Therefore, the Saudi Self was represented as the leader of the Arab world, and it indirectly framed Iranian involvement in Arab–Israeli affairs as interference in Arab affairs. While

Saudi Arabia 'does not accuse any country by name ... intervention from non-Arab states should be positive ... privileged relations with any party should be in the interest of the state'. The Saudi Self was clearly defined in relation to the 'non-Arab' Other, i.e. Iran, while the former's aim was to 'support sovereignty and independence, and extend authority over the entire national territory'. Saudi Arabia's discourse viewed this adventurism as constituting interference in its leadership and the result was an implicit call for an end to Iranian influence in Lebanon (al-Saud 2006e, 2006g).

Discourses Representing the Self, Legitimacy, and Arab Leadership

Saudi discourse also focused on reaffirming its role and legitimacy as the leader of the Middle East and the Islamic world. International speeches constructed an image of pragmatism and moderation when dealing with the Israeli attacks, while simultaneously highlighting Saudi leadership of the Arab world and its standing in the international arena. By juxtaposing the Saudi position with Hezbollah or Iranian adventurism, an image of pragmatism, peace, and leadership was constructed. 'Saudi logic' was claimed to be behind the pragmatism and restraint 'adopted by the Arab League' (al-Saud 2006e). This 'logic', as highlighted by al-Faisal, was a 'strategic decision to seek peace' and positive overtures, in addition to 'methodological measures ... focused on an Arab Peace Conference ... in Beirut'. Hezbollah and its Iranian supporters, on the other hand, were discursively constructed as causing 'chaos and destruction'. This representation of the Saudi Self was a message to its domestic audience, and to the regional and Western states (especially the EU and US), that Saudi Arabia prioritized and cared for the plight of the Arab world, especially Lebanon and Palestine, and that it was a strong Arab leader capable of guiding and swaying Arab states such as Egypt and Jordan, and therefore could achieve peace with Israel through negotiations like the 2002 Abdullah Peace Initiative (al-Saud 2006g). The Other – namely Iran – was inherently constructed as hostile, chaotic, at enmity with the West, and most importantly as meddling in regional affairs.

The Saudi Self's framing in relation to its Arab and Islamic role in the Arab–Israeli Peace Initiative was also visible in the Friday sermons (Sudais 2006b, 2006a). The Saudi imam represented the Islamic nation as one riven by division and despair. Hezbollah's actions were characterized as forging division in the Islamic world, a world that was 'worn out and humiliated', calling for a 'return to the early years of Islam', that is, the Mohammedan era. This was an Islamic narrative similar to the Iranian notion of 'Islām-i nāb-i Muhamadī', and what the Sunnis call the 'al-Salaf al-sālih' era. The juxtaposition was that this Salafi Islam carried with it 'characteristics of strength, eternity and promised victory', implicitly representing the Shi'i Islamic world, that is in support of Hezbollah, as weak, desperate, and divided. The strength of Islam was represented as embodied by Saudi Arabia's 'strong political positions, humanitarian aid, and political aspirations' (Sudais 2006b). Meanwhile, their 'support for the Muslim Lebanese and Palestinian people' and established political team, i.e. Saudi Arabia and its allies in the Arab League, would 'aid the causes of the Muslim Ummah', that is opposed by 'haters' and 'infidels [who] yelled and conspired' against Saudi-led motives. In other words, the Hezbollah–Iran–Syria axis and Western support for Israeli were both represented as enemies of Saudi political positions. In turn, Saudi ulama discourse also legitimized the government's role in negotiations with the US and the EU by employing prophetic scripture (*hadith*) (al Taleb 2006a). Citing a coalition between the pagan Arab tribes of Mecca twenty years before the prophecy. i.e. during the *jāhiliya* era, the Friday imam highlighted that the prophet attended and supported the meeting, since it was an alliance based on the principles of realizing the truth, supporting the oppressed, deterring the oppressor, and making concerted efforts when faced with falsehood (Aal Taleb 2006a). The prophet's attendance enshrined legitimacy and the need to cooperate with any party – i.e. contemporary non-Muslims, the US and EU – to uphold rights and support the oppressed (Aal Taleb 2006a). Therefore, like the Iranian use of the Islamic narrative of Ahl al-bayt, the Sunni ulama of Saudi Arabia employed an Islamic discourse to legitimize the role of Saudi Arabia in negotiations with the West, agree to a ceasefire with Israel, and negotiate an Arab Peace Initiative.

Discourse on the Iranian Proxy War in Lebanon and the Destruction of the Arab Middle East

As mentioned previously, Saudi editorials promulgated the discourse of Hezbollah–Iranian adventurism. However, the tone was more explicit and the representation was that of a proxy group working on behalf of Iran, one which sought to alleviate international pressure on Iran over its nuclear dossier. Furthermore, this proxy war was represented as one that would seek and witness the destruction of the Arab Middle East, recalling, as earlier mentioned, the Arab–Israeli wars fought in 1967 and 1973 (*al-Riyadh* 2006d). It is interesting to note that similar juxtapositions were also made in Iranian discourse. However, the difference between the two states' discourses was that Iran used the wars to frame an image of Arab weakness and defeat within days, in comparison with Hezbollah's resistance for thirty-four days, which they portrayed as a victory and as marking the rise of a new Arab and Islamic leadership. In contrast, the Saudi editorial discourse utilized the narratives of the two wars with Israel to highlight the 'predicament of 1967 that dragged the region into destruction ... with Israel being the victor', while 1973 resembled a 'symbolic victory' for the Arabs (*al-Riyadh* 2006d). The Saudi editorials therefore represented the 34-Day War as one that would lead to the destruction of the Arab region and a divergence from the path of development and regional peace.

Al-Riyadh represented Hezbollah as an Iranian proxy on the first day of the 34-Day War (*al-Riyadh* 2006b). Although this construction was implicit given the rhetorical question, 'Who controls the cards domestically and externally in this game?' (*al-Riyadh* 2006b), this was a clear reference to the notion of a proxy war, underlining Iranian control over Hezbollah. The newspaper *Asharq Al-Awsat* (2006c) interwove the discourse on Lebanese sovereignty with narratives on external influence in the Arab world. Questions were raised about the leadership of the Ummah, asking 'who leads: governments or individuals?' and whether it was 'logical for the Arab countries to have ... a two-headed government'? (*dawlah bi-ra'sayn*) (*Asharq Al-Awsat* 2006c). These questions were also related to a 'group that decided to ignite the region in the service of other agendas', thereby 'exposing the capabilities and resources of the people to destruction and ruin' (*Asharq Al-Awsat* 2006c). The Saudi editorial discourse explicitly represented Hezbollah and its leader, Hassan Nasrallah, as agents and proxies of Iran, with the latter 'practising its wars by proxy' (*Asharq Al-Awsat* 2006d).

It is interesting to note that Iranian support for Hezbollah was also juxtaposed with the former colonizers who had governed Lebanon. While highlighting the position of Saudi Arabia as supportive of legitimate resistance, it was also noted that there was a difference 'between that and uncalculated adventurism', while there were references to 'Lebanese factions that depended on French support and others on Iran'; however, 'French cheese did not result in a fatty meal, nor will Iranian pistachios [be able to] compensate them for the famous cuisine' (*Asharq Al-Awsat* 2006c). What the editorial refers to here is that French support and funds, alongside Iranian promises and aid, would not resurrect Lebanon in the aftermath of its destruction and 'internal divisions' (*Asharq Al-Awsat* 2006c). Therefore, according to the Saudi editorial discourse, its Iranian Other was comparable to the former colonizer, in that they both sought division, destroyed territory, and did not have the capacity and ability to provide significant financial aid. In contrast, the Saudi Self was represented as a legitimate Arab leader, that is 'neutral, an interlocutor', with significant leverage over Western states while having the 'power to stop crises' (*Asharq Al-Awsat* 2006c), thereby constructing the image of a Saudi regional leader and international player.

The proxy war narrative was also utilized to construct an image of an Iranian–US proxy war that had overshadowed the plight of Arabs in Palestine and Iraq. Lebanon was represented as a country that 'after Palestine, always saw the most of the Israeli–Arab conflict' and now it 'not only pays a price for Palestine, but also regional conflicts' (*al-Riyadh* 2006c). These conflicts, according to Saudi discourse, were due to the 'effects of the Iranian revolution, and continuous wars in Iraq'. Therefore, the formation of a Shi'i Islamic government in Iran, and its support for regional Shi'i groups, was depicted as the main reason behind the plight of the Arab world and Islamic Ummah, especially since Iraq was the most 'intense warfront between Iran and the US' (*al-Riyadh* 2006c). This proxy war was represented as creating sectarian and ethnic divisions in the region and making room for regional states to interfere and 'support Sunnis and denounce Shi'i hegemony' (*al-Riyadh* 2006c). It is this interference that the Saudi discourse argued resulted in 'Israel collaborating and supporting groups' acting against Iran, thus making Iraq 'the heart of conflict' (*al-Riyadh* 2006c).

Furthermore, the Hezbollah–Israeli conflict was explicitly represented as an Iranian war to alleviate Iranian regional pressures. These pressures included three contested regional issues. First, the reconciliation process in Iraq led by the Iraqi prime minister, Maliki, was perceived as stemming from 'meetings in Riyadh rather than Tehran' (*Asharq Al-Awsat* 2006a, 2006b), and therefore there were fears of Iraq drifting from the Iranian to the Arab sphere. Second, there was progress in the investigation into the assassination of Hariri in 2005, which would implicate Syria, an Iranian ally, and Hezbollah, an Iranian proxy (*Asharq Al-Awsat* 2006b). Third, Iran's nuclear programme was 'on its way to the UN Security Council' and would result in sanctions being imposed on Iran (*Asharq Al-Awsat* 2006b). Therefore, Saudi editorial discourse constructed Iran as 'planning the much-needed wars and conflicts', to make sure it would sustain its control over Iraq, protect Syria and Hezbollah, and divert attention from its nuclear programme – all with the aim of 'destroying and planning the region's future' (*Asharq Al-Awsat* 2006a, 2006b).

Hezbollah's Historic Victory and Arab Leadership vs. Iranian and Shi'i Hegemony

During the 34-Day War and its aftermath, Iran and Saudi Arabia promulgated opposing discourses. These included Hezbollah's victory and Arab and Islamic leadership, and Iranian and Shi'i hegemony in Saudi discourse. Iranian tropes including Nasrallah's leadership and Hezbollah's support among the Arab masses, while constructing an image of illegitimate and weak Arab leaderships. Furthermore, comparisons were made between Hezbollah's thirty-four-day resistance against Israel and the Arab wars of 1967 and 1973, suggesting the weak status of the Arab states and their subservience to the US. On the other hand, Saudi discourse constructed an image of Iranian and Shi'i expansion and hegemony in the Arab world, representing Iran as meddling in Arab affairs and raising fears of a hijacking of Arab identity.

In the early days of the attacks in Lebanon, Khamenei was quick to claim Hezbollah as an 'exemplary, honest, and honourable Islamic movement [that is] by no means comparable with the past', i.e. with the Arab armies of 1967 and 1973. This movement and its war were represented by Khamenei as one that would bring 'dignity to the Islamic world' (Khamenei 2006f). The Supreme Leader's speeches also characterized the Islamic world as living in shame. Hezbollah was therefore a source of pride, especially since it stemmed from the 'Islamic flag and revolution that was raised in Iran' (Khamenei 2006a, 2006e) with its hand 'in many global issues, especially regional affairs' (Khamenei 2006e). Khamenei's representation of Hezbollah was as an Iranian creation, their victory and resistance attributable to a 'mighty divine power' (Khamenei 2006e). This construction therefore gave rise to the definition of the Self as a strong and divine creation, in comparison to other movements and Islamic or Arab states.

This representation of divinity led to a discourse contrasting the weakness of Arab states with Hezbollah's strength. Since Hezbollah was interpreted as a superior power to Arab countries, Iran was therefore also superior to the Arab states since Hezbollah could be regarded as an extension of the Iranian Self. This was exemplified by Khamenei's sermon in which he argued that the 'courageous and faithful stance of Hezbollah is a symbol of the resistance spirit of the Islamic world' (Khamenei 2006d), thereby drawing a parallel between the Arab populace and their leaders. According to Khamenei (2006d), the 'Islamic and Arab worlds are supportive of Hezbollah...and its leader', discursively representing Hassan Nasrallah as an Arab and Islamic leader but not Saudi Arabia and its allies in the region such as Egypt and Jordan.

Furthermore, the discourse of Hezbollah's victory was reinforced by employing Islamic narratives and relating them to the vision of Khomeini's revolution. The 34-Day War was also represented as a 'great Islamic epic ... with a divine victory bestowed upon them' from God over 'America, the world's greatest tyrant' (Khamenei 2006a). The primordial seed of this victory was related to the vision of the 'late imam', namely Khomeini (Khamenei 2006a). In other words, Hezbollah was a creation of Khomeini, especially since 'the late imam recognized the people's power, discovered it, used it, and relied on people' (Khamenei 2006a). In other words, Hezbollah became a creation of Khomeini's revolution, and his vision of the oppressed versus the oppressor, i.e. Hezbollah versus the US tyrant.

Iranian editorials built on Khamenei's discourse on Hezbollah's victory and the Arab and Islamic leadership. Like the Supreme Leader's discourse, these editorials represented this victory and leadership as the fruit of the Iranian revolution and as the fulfilment of Khomeini's vision. However, their representations and juxtapositions were more explicit: the Iranian discourse aimed to highlight the victory relative to Arab losses to Israel in the region, underlining their weakness as regular armies in comparison to a guerrilla group.

Hezbollah and its cadres were represented as 'honest and sacrilegious warriors [with a] popular and brave leader among the Arab masses' (*Ettela'at* 2006d). This representation of Hezbollah's grassroots support by the masses constructed an image of the Arab leadership's illegitimacy, thus highlighting a Shi'i leader established, trained, and supported by Iran as a neo-Arab leader. In turn, the Iranian discourse arguably represented Iran implicitly as a leader of the Arab and Islamic nations. To strengthen this argument, the editorial discourse – especially in *Kayhan* and *Jomhouri Eslami* – explicitly named, referred to and denigrated the existing leadership of the Arab world, questioning their legitimacy as well as domestic and regional roles. *Jomhouri Eslami* (*Jomhouri Eslami* 2006a) compared Arab leaders, such as Saudi Arabia, to Western-imposed 'scarecrows' (*matarsak*), charged with the sole task of 'serving colonial powers [while holding] a club over people's heads'. In turn, Hezbollah's victory was therefore constructed as a liberation of the Arab masses from 'Western-imposed dictatorships', where Hezbollah's resistance and alleged victory over Israel 'erased the fear' of the masses at the same time that Arab leaders' 'thrones are shaking' (*Jomhouri Eslami* 2006a). An image of cowardice and collaboration was employed as a frame to refer to the Saudi monarch. To give an example, Abdullah was argued to be 'shivering from fear and chaos' as this was the end of the 'mercenary elements that bolster Israel and do anything to defeat Hezbollah' (*Jomhouri Eslami* 2006a). Similarly, *Kayhan* (2006f) interwove this narrative with a historical account, with Hezbollah's victory designed and initiated by Khomeini, which in itself resulted in a 'Saudi state of nervousness [with] Nasrallah the righteous heir of Khomeini and his follower' in leading the Arab and Islamic worlds (*Kayhan* 2006f).

A trope of Arab defeat at the hands of Israel dominated the Iranian editorials, which continued to contrast Hezbollah's successful resistance of Israel over the thirty-four-day period compared with previous Arab wars with Israel (*Ettela'at* 2006f; *Resalat* 2006a, 2006e; *Kayhan* 2006b, 2006f). Although the editorials did not mention Saudi Arabia since it had not participated in the 1967 and 1973 wars, they did discuss Egypt since it was a strong Arab state, a Saudi ally, and had had grievances with Iran since the 1979 Islamic Revolution. In this construction, Arab shame and weakness was the prevalent discursive representation, since 'Israel . . . within six days dragged the armies of a few Arab countries across the mud [and] invaded Sinai' (*Ettela'at* 2006f). The Arab army generals were framed as weak, while a shameful defeat 'forced the commander of the Egyptian army to commit suicide' (*Ettela'at* 2006f). In comparison, Hezbollah was defined as a 'a small army . . . able to extricate the enemy from its soil [without] equipment, facilities, and a regular army' (*Resalat* 2006a), which had led the 'minds of the Arab people to question the philosophy and value of their armies [as Israel] was weaker forty years ago than it is today' but it had still defeated the Arabs (*Resalat* 2006e). As mentioned previously, the contrast made between Arab defeat and Hezbollah's victory was framed around revolutionary Islam and Khomeini. This 'absolute victory' was attributable to 'pure Islamic and Quranic thought', which had been built on Khomeini's *'Islām-i Nāb-i Muhamadī'* (Pure Mohammaden Islam) (*Jomhouri Eslami* 2006a) rather than the 'self-selling muftis of the Saudi courts . . . and not on Al-Qaeda and the ignorant stone-age Taliban puppets' of Saudi Arabia (*Jomhouri Eslami* 2006a). This Islamic victory further represented an extension of a real and legitimate Islamic leadership, beginning with the 'blood of Imam Hussein . . . flowing in the veins of Nasrallah', a victory that was also due to Khomeini's Islamic Revolution (*Resalat* 2006e).

Conclusion

This chapter has argued that the 34-Day War between Israel and Hezbollah had an impact on Iranian–Saudi representations of each other. Discourses in both countries began to shift from the start of the war, where more neutral and implicit discursive constructions of each other gave way to more explicit and denigrating representations. Iranian–Saudi Othering was tiered and hierarchical. Discourses of a silence from Arab and Islamic leaders with subservience to the West and Zionism, and a shift in Arab leadership, were constructed by Khamenei. These were promulgated by Ahmadinejad in his speeches, but with harsher rhetoric. Clerical discourse echoed the state narrative, without explicit mention of Saudi Arabia. However, Iranian discourse mainly employed the revolutionary rhetoric and tropes of the Khomeini period. Post-revolutionary denigrative phrases such as *'sarān-i irtijā'-i Arab'* (reactionary Arabs), *'shyūkh-i 'āj nishīn'* (Sheikhs on ivory thrones), and *'sarān-i sazishkār-i Arab'* (heads of Arab conspirators), were employed to construct an image of US–Zionist subservience and treachery against the Arab and Islamic worlds. Saudi discourse sought to represent the Self and highlight the legitimacy of the Arab leadership. Saudi Othering of Iran revolved around discourses of Iranian adventurism, Iranian–Shi'i hegemony, and expansion.

The 34-Day War had broad regional implications for both Iran and Saudi Arabia. For the former, the war was represented as a victory by a 'resistance axis' that would later become an Iranian discourse hallmark in their war against 'global arrogance'. For Saudi Arabia the war was represented as another Iranian attempt of interference in Arab affairs, especially as Riyadh viewed itself as a leader of the Islamic and Arab world. However, this was not the last time that Iran would be accused of interfering in Arab affairs. The Palestinian file, along with the wars between Gaza and Israel in 2008 and 2009, witnessed another episode of Iranian–Saudi rivalry and discourses of Othering.

Chapter 9

THE GAZA WAR'S IMPACT ON IRANIAN AND SAUDI DISCOURSES

Introduction

The Israeli campaign, Operation Cast Lead, also known as the Gaza War (Cordesman 2009), the Gaza Massacre in the Islamic World (Bregman 2016), or what Hamas referred to as the Battle of Furqan (Kayālī 2009), was a three-week offensive carried out by the Israeli army in the Gaza Strip. The conflict began on 27 December 2008 and ended on 18 January 2009, and it involved the Israeli Defence Forces (IDF) and Palestinian militants, predominantly Hamas. Israel's reasons for launching the offensive included Hamas's decision to smuggle weapons through tunnels and its continual rocket attacks on Israel's southern territories (Cordesman 2009). According to Cordesman (2009: ii), the Gaza War was 'the first major armed struggle between Israel and Hamas, as it distinguished between Israel and the PLO and Fatah', and it was possibly the worst conflict since the Six-Day War in 1967 (Lambeth 2012).

Both Iran and Saudi Arabia played active roles in the Gaza War. From a historical perspective, Iran had always supported Hamas since its creation in 1987, and this was apparent during the Gaza offensive when Iran exerted diplomatic pressure on Egypt to open its border crossing with Gaza as well as international pressure to end the Gaza blockade. Furthermore, Iran continuously and actively supported Hamas due to its Islamic ideology, which was based on opposing the secular Palestinian Authority (PA) that was supported by Saudi Arabia. On the other hand, although Saudi Arabia viewed Hamas as an Islamic group, it also saw it as an extremist faction hindering the Oslo Accord that had the potential to bring stability to the region through a two-state solution. Finally, the Gaza War witnessed the formation of two camps in the Middle East: a pro-Hamas axis led by Iran comprised of Syria and Qatar, and a pro-PA axis led by Saudi Arabia, which included the Persian Gulf states, Jordan, and Egypt. Throughout the Gaza offensive, both Saudi Arabia and Iran adopted active roles and strong stances, which were covered by the newspapers in both countries.

Iranian Discourses: Zionist–US Subservience and Arab Silence

The response to the attacks was immediate, starting with a statement by Khamenei on the second day of the war (Khamenei 2008). Like the Hezbollah–Israel War (i.e. the 34-Day War) in 2006, Khamenei's argument focused on one major theme: the silence and subservience of Arab leaders and the Islamic ulama. Although the reference to Saudi Arabia was implicit, the central point of his criticism was aimed at Egypt and the al-Azhar Islamic seminary. The denigration of the Arab leadership and the 'clerics of the Islamic world' as Iran's Other allowed him to highlight the Iranian Self as leading the Islamic world as well as feeling the plight of the Palestinian people. The statement represented the Self as a continuation of true Mohammedan Islam, bolstering the legitimacy of Iran's regional and Islamic leadership.

It is interesting to note that from the beginning of the war, Khamenei discursively constructed the Arab leaders in three ways, first by questioning the Islamic identity of the silent states and representing them as Israeli collaborators. Khamenei explicitly labelled the silence of 'some Arab governments and those that claim to be Muslim' as 'encouraging silence' (Khamenei 2008), that is, a silence that allowed these countries to 'insolently coordinate and agree to this great catastrophe'. Second, he represented the Arab leaders as acting against the wishes of their people, which was a form of schism between the Arab leadership and its nations. While the 'hearts of the people of Egypt and Jordan and other Islamic countries are aching and bloodied from this massacre', the leaderships' Islamic values were questioned (Khamenei 2008). The juxtaposition of the Iranian leadership and Arab governments constructed the Iranian Other as un-Islamic and lacking in Islamic values as evidenced by their inability to 'answer to the Prophet and the Ahl al-bayt' (Khamenei 2008). This characterization of the Arab governments led to a third construction, namely the silence of the Sunni 'clerics and scholars of the Arab world' (Khamenei 2008). By directly criticizing the ulama of the Arab world in general and the seminary 'leaders of *al-Azhar* in Egypt' in particular, an implicit construction was developed where the Shi'a were represented as the defenders of the Palestinians 'at the hands of war infidels and the hypocrites of the Ummah' (Khamenei 2008). Thereby, Khamenei represented the Iranian Other – i.e. the Arab Sunni clerics – as silent and not 'fulfilling the duty of forbidding the evil and upholding the word of righteousness in front of the unjust' (Khamenei 2008), with the 'unjust' defined as the Arab leaders, such as Saudi Arabia, Egypt and Jordan, the three main countries involved in the Palestinian peace process. Therefore, an Iran led by Shi'i clerics was following a Mohammedan path of upholding the word of righteousness against the unjust US–Zionist and Arab alliance, fulfilling the duty of protecting Palestinians and Islam from 'Zionist aggression'.

Khamenei's speech set down the main themes that the Friday sermons and editorials then took up, including the silence and subservience of Arab leaders and the Islamic awakening of the Muslim world. These themes employed Islamic narratives and tropes, especially as the war coincided with the commemoration of Imam Hussein and the remembrance of the battle of Karbala.

The elite discourse, especially that of Mottaki, the Iranian foreign minister, represented the war as an Arab betrayal of the Palestinians. Speaking at a pre-Friday sermon, Mottaki argued that 'regional countries' were complicit in the attack on Gaza. Stopping short of naming these states, a narrative of Arab treachery and subservience to the West was constructed, claiming that 'those who stabbed the Palestinian movement in the back' had previously assured the Gazan officials that there would be no attack (Mottaki 2009). Furthermore, the Israeli attacks were linked to the 34-Day War with Hezbollah. A similar treachery was identified, with those complicit including the 'US and the Zionist regime of Britain', while highlighting the Iranian role in regional leadership. This role included the failure of the 'Rome conference . . . and the defeat of the Zionist regime', while Iran's Arab Other was negatively represented by underlining Iran's role in 'defending the "dignity of Islam and the interests of the Islamic Ummah"' in a region that was the 'heir to the divine prophets' (Mottaki 2009). The rhetoric of the 1980s war with Iraq was also promulgated at the technocratic level, echoing the Iranian narrative of victimization during the Iran–Iraq war. The Islamic 'sanctities are subject to insults and crimes', with these insults identified with the 'mistakes' the Arab states committed in support of 'Saddam and his crimes', which was further represented as spreading discord in the region by supporting Saddam's war against Iran, 'a war between the Arabs, the Persians, the Shi'ite and Sunni' (Mottaki 2009). Therefore, the Iranian revolutionary narrative stressed Arab treachery, silence, and subservience to a Zionist agenda. In addition, the attack on Gaza was identified as a war on Iran, where the Arabs sought to destroy the region by spreading discord and division among the region's states and the Islamic world, while Iran and its support for the resistance had defeated previous attacks in the 1980s and supported Hezbollah's 34-Day War in 2006.

The representation of the Iranian Self as a leader of resistance alongside the discursive construction of Hamas as an extension of Iranian-led regional resistance was also promulgated in Friday sermons. Rafsanjani (2009) argued that Iran was the main support base and had 'led this field' of resistance that enjoyed the support of 'many Muslim nations'. This Iranian-led resistance was explicitly discussed as based on 'political, cultural, propaganda, financial, and weapons support of any kind', which was available to the 'devout and sacrificial forces and the Islamic Ummah' (Rafsanjani 2009). While the Iranian Friday sermon discourse highlighted support for the resistance, it criticized the Arabs for backing up the Israeli attacks on Gaza. Ahmad Khatami opined that 'some Arab countries are even providing the funds for attacking Gaza' (Khatami 2009). Consequently, the Iranian Self was represented as the leader of the Islamic world, fighting for its rights and freedom against the 'ultimate horror of the US, Europe and Arab states' that were collaborating with Israel against the people of Gaza and the Islamic world.

While the editorials implicitly criticized Saudi Arabia and characterized it as an accomplice in the war on Gaza by referring to them collectively as part of the out-group (i.e. Arab states and Arab leaders) the editorials applied both implicit and explicit constructions of Saudi Arabian complicity in the attacks. When the war on Gaza was launched (*Kayhan* 2008b), *Kayhan* actively pointed its finger at the collusion of Arab leaders with Israel. Like the speeches of the elite and Friday sermons, there was no explicit naming of the Arab leaders but instead a passive grammatical agent referred to 'Arab regimes' and 'Arab leaders' of which Saudi Arabia was a major player (*Kayhan* 2008b). *Kayhan* also emphasized Arab collaboration with the 'Israeli genocide', highlighting the discourse of Arab silence and subservience to Israel by giving Israel a 'green light' to attack Gaza. Collusion was further highlighted and justified by *Kayhan*'s attempt to cite Israeli and Arabic sources when trying to hold Arab leaders accountable for the Gaza attack. Thus, the newspaper applied a strategy to legitimize its argument and demonstrate its unbiased nature. Furthermore, Tzipi Livni, the Israeli foreign minister, was quoted as claiming that 'Arab leaders had prior knowledge of the attack on Gaza' (*Kayhan* 2008b).

In contrast, *Jomhouri Eslami* deployed metaphors and symbols to illustrate Saudi Arabian collusion with Israel in the war on Gaza. The Jordanian, Saudi, and Persian Gulf leaders' subservience and collaboration was described metaphorically as 'golden gifts' ('*hadiyāhā-yi talā-yī*') to the US administration. Furthermore, the editorial discourse represented the Saudi king as colluding and subservient, recalling the role of the monarch in pre-revolutionary Iran, echoing the Shah of Iran and his relationship with Israel prior to 1979 (*Jomhouri Eslami* 2008c). Similarly, the theme of Saudi–Zionist collusion was also represented by implicating the Saudi royal court (*Jomhouri Eslami* 2008a). In a tone like that used during the 1980s, the Iranian editorials depicted the royal courts and monarchs as the 'errand boys of Israel and traitors', discursively constructing an image of the Saudi monarch as an 'errand boy', a state of affairs that was 'shocking [and] shameful'. This denigration of the Saudi Other in Iranian discourse further emphasized the notion of Saudi Arabia as a colluder and betrayer of the Palestinian, Arab, and Islamic worlds (*Jomhouri Eslami* 2008a). This revolutionary Khomeinist rhetoric further constructed Saudi Arabia as a US lackey, corrupt like the former Shah of Iran, and it questioned the Saudi king's legitimacy as an independent Arab and Islamic leader.

The subservience of the Saudi monarchy was also represented through historical juxtapositions. Drawing a parallel between Egypt and the signing of the Camp David Accords (a historic peace treaty concluded between Israel and Egypt in 1979), Iranian editorial discourse situated Arab treachery and subservience within a historical landscape, framing the treachery of the Arab leadership and collusion with the US and Zionism as part of a series of events that began with Anwar Sadat's accession to power and ended with King Abdullah of Saudi Arabia (*Ettela'at* 2009a). Subservience was shown as running through the Arab leadership. It was underlined by their betrayal of the Islamic and Arab worlds, beginning with the Camp David Accord and followed by the Madrid and Sharm el-Sheikh summits. The events of the Arab Peace Process were represented as a scene in a chapter of premeditated events, with the war on Gaza the final treacherous scene planned by Abdullah and Shimon Peres (then Israeli prime minister) at a meeting in New York. Therefore, the Iranian discourse framed Abdullah's subservience to Israel and identified a Saudi–Israeli collaboration as being behind the planning of the Gaza War (*Ettela'at* 2009a).

Silence of the Sunni Clergy

The legitimacy of the Arab ulama was also questioned. Like the 34-Day War in 2006, the editorials questioned the silence of the Arab ulama, mainly the Saudi and Egyptian clerics. Like the monarchy, the Saudi ulama were deemed to be equally to blame for the silence and support of the Israeli attacks on Gaza. However, they were also implicated in the suppression of popular Arab protests. Iranian editorials represented the Saudi ulama as employing religion to suppress the masses. They argued that Saudi Arabia had never had a history of public demonstrations because of clerical edicts such as the fatwa by the mufti bin Baz[1], which called for the banning of demonstrations in support of Gaza (*Kayhan* 2009b). The discourse of clerical silence was also extended to criticism of the main Sunni clerical centres' general silence. While the Saudi muftis were not mentioned by name, the Egyptian muftis were discursively represented as traitors and as colluding with Israel. *Jomhouri Eslami* (2008a) constructed the Egyptian muftis as an out-group that included the Israeli prime minister and the Saudi king. Referring to the presence of Tantawi (the Grand Imam of al-Azhar and earlier the Grand Mufti of Egypt) and the king of Saudi Arabia in a meeting with the then president of Israel, Shimon Peres, in New York before the Gaza attacks, the editorial questioned the status of the Sunni cleric and claimed that '*al-Azhar* has also forged alliances with the Zionists' (*Jomhouri Eslami* 2008a). The construction of the Sunni Other as engaging in treacherous alliances with Israel innately represented the Iranian Shi'i Self as the only legitimate sect and as the ulama that represented a true Islam. The Sunni clerics were further represented as clerics of the court, while Iranians fought for the emancipation of the Islamic and Arab worlds. While the oldest symbol of the Sunni clergy, *al-Azhar*, was queried and constructed based on silence, hypocrisy, and illegitimacy, the Iranian Shi'i ulama who ruled Iran were in contrast depicted as vocal, legitimate, independent, and moral leaders of the Muslim world.

The discourse on Islamic clerical leadership also discussed and drew parallels between Khamenei and the Sunni muftis (*Jomhouri Eslami* 2008b), constructing an image of Khamenei as an Islamic leader who upheld justice in the Islamic world. Using quotes from Khamenei's sermons, the Supreme Leader was represented as a leader of the entire Islamic ulama, advising the muftis that 'for the sake of Islam and Muslims' the clergy should 'forbid people from committing the prohibited' and preach righteousness in the presence of an 'oppressive leader' (*Jomhouri Eslami* 2008b). Khamenei's piety was compared with the aforementioned Sunni mufti Tantawi, with the former represented as an independent cleric who stood for the rights of the Islamic world, while the latter was characterized as under the control

---

1. This refers to a general fatwa against political demonstrations. The Saudi Mufti, Bin Baz, was asked in 1992 of the permisiblity of demonstrations by men and women in against the their rulers and responded with the impersibility of demonstrations and protests due to them being a source of *'fitna'* and *'bid 'ah'* (innnovation) See Maddy-Weitzman, B (1997: 105).

of Arab leaders such as the Saudi monarchy, who were 'relinquishing their religious and Quranic duties' (*Jomhouri Eslami* 2008b).

The discourse of the Sunni clergy's silence used tropes of Wahhabi reticence. Like the Hezbollah war in 2006, the editorial genre wove together the Saudi Wahhabi ulama with Al-Qaeda and the Tantawi of Egypt, defining it as a general silence from the Sunni sect. On this view, the Shi'i school of thought resists and is legitimate while the Sunni school has been taken over by un-Islamic forces that are detrimental to Islam. Questioning the quiet nature of radical Sunni groups, Iranian editorial discourse mocked the lack of sound 'coming from al-Qaeda and [the] Taliban', asking why 'the muftis of Saudi Arabia [were] defending Zionism and Israel rather than defending the rights of the people of Gaza' throughout the three-week war (*Jomhouri Eslami* 2009c). Consequently, the Sunni clergy was constructed and represented holistically by grouping radical terrorist groups with the Wahhabi ulama of Saudi Arabia and the Egyptian mufti. In other words, all Sunni Arab muftis were subservient to their respective leaderships and to Israel, and silent on the plight of Gaza and the Islamic world. This conspiracy against the Islamic world was deemed to target all of Islam as the war on this occasion was 'not the South of Lebanon', a reference to 2006 that underlined that the 'people of Gaza are Sunni' (*Jomhouri Eslami* 2009c). Therefore, regardless of sect, the Sunni scholars were pro-Israeli and anti-Muslim, while the Iranian theocracy was represented as non-sectarian and as the legitimate leader of Islam.

The Sunni muftis' Islamic credentials and legitimacy were also questioned. The Sunni ulama in Saudi Arabia and Egypt were portrayed as 'hired muftis' ('muftiyān-i muzdawir'), and the Iranian discourse employed Islamic scripture to strengthen their construction of the betrayal of Islam and the Muslim world. *Jomhouri Eslami* (2009c) argued that since the prophet mentioned that 'He who hears a man calling out for a Muslim and that Muslim did not obey the call, then he is not a Muslim', the muftis right to issue fatwas was void since 'they do not practice Islam, or identify with humanity and their Arab nationalism' (*Jomhouri Eslami* 2009c). In contrast, the Iranian Self was represented as proud, 'responding to the calls of the prophet' while the 'people of Iran and its seminaries and clerics … showed that the Islamic Republic of Iran stands by the people of Palestine and preserves the ideals of Islam and the revolution' (*Jomhouri Eslami* 2009c). This further demonstrated that the only way to free Palestine was through Islamic movements and an Islamic resistance led by Iran and its revolution.

Islamic Narratives and Tropes of Silence and Subservience to Zionism

The 'pro-Zionist' theme in the Iranian newspapers was further conveyed using symbolism to paint a particular picture for their readers. This symbolism included Islamic comparisons, either drawn from the Quran or Mohammad's narratives, the *hadeeth*. *Kayhan* compared the war on Gaza to that of the battles of Badr and Uhud, the first two wars that Mohammad had fought against the 'infidels' of Mecca. Furthermore, *Kayhan* employed Islamic symbolism and a discourse of martyrdom to identify the Gazan people and Hamas as Islamic warriors and contemporary martyrs. This represented the 'pious and holy warriors of Palestine and the Islamic world' as combating latter day infidels, namely Israel and its supporters. Also, the Arab leadership's treachery was contextualized, as the Arab leaders are engaged in a war of Islam against infidelity. In addition, the Gaza War was compared with the Holy Defence War (*Difa'-i Muqadas*), a reference to the Iran–Iraq war, which was also based on the 1980s discourse of a war of Islam against contemporary infidels, namely Saddam and the Arab leaders who supported him. Therefore, the Gaza War was constructed as a holy war while the resistance represented an extension of a war between good and evil, Islam versus infidelity, with Iran combating the infidels, recalling a Mohammedan struggle and jihad evident in the Uhud and Badr wars (*Kayhan* 2008a).

Islamic references were also employed to represent the Arab leaders in a negative and denigrating light. Egypt's Hosni Mubarak was characterized as a contemporary pharaoh and a 'descendent of the lineage of the pharaohs' (*Kayhan* 2008a). Iranian discourse drew parallels with tyranny and reverence of infidels. Similarly, the Saudi monarch, Abdullah, was represented as '*Āl-i So'ūdī*' (*Kayhan* 2008a), a descendent of Al Saud, which was also a reference to autocracy as the word *Āl* signifies dynasty. Collectively, when both constructions are woven together, they construct an image of a Saudi aristocrat who was collaborating with tyranny in the form of a pharaoh, while Israel oppressed the Palestinian and Islamic worlds. Furthermore, Islamic symbolism was employed to question the Saudi monarch's legitimacy as an Islamic leader and to identify his conspiracy against Palestine. Criticizing Abdullah's attempts to hold a Khatami-like dialogue with the international community, known as the 'dialogue of religion', Iranian editorial discourse constructed a narrative of treachery, conspiracy, and collaboration with 'Zionist regime officials and the Great Satan in the cradle of infidelity and atheism ... to begin the inhumane Zionist attacks' on Gaza (*Kayhan* 2008a). The Iranian Self, in contrast, was interpreted as representing Khamenei as 'the guardian and true leader of all the Muslim world' – a leader who protected the Islamic world from the 'war infidel' (*kafir-i ḥarbī*) and who united the Islamic world 'against a criminal Israel' (*Kayhan* 2008a), while the Iranian Other, i.e. Saudi Arabia and its allies, were pitted against the Palestinian people and, therefore, against Islam.

The discourse of Zionist collusion and treachery was also constructed by employing a religious narrative that referenced the squandering of Islamic wealth as well as un-Islamic conduct and accountability. Weapons such as 'phosphorus bombs and laser-guided armaments' were acquired by the Israelis using the 'deep pockets of the Arabs and *Bayt-ul Māl*', i.e. the Islamic treasury responsible for the revenues and the economic matters of the state or caliphate (*Jomhouri Eslami* 2009b). Verses from the Quran were also cited to provide credibility to the discourse and its construction, thereby framing the Saudi monarchy as having no respect for Islam or the Muslim nations. There were also references to Quranic verses that shed light on 'accountability' (*ihtisāb*) (*Ettela'at* 2009b) for one's deeds and actions, such as 'blocking medical aid and food supplies to the oppressed people of Palestine' by collaborating 'hand in hand with America and Israel . . . thus creating another Karbala' (*Ettela'at* 2009b). This juxtaposition framed Arab collusion as a contemporary Karbala analogous to the collusion of the Arab countries such as Saudi Arabia with the Umayyads against Imam Hussein, namely the oppressed people of Gaza.

The Karbala Narrative: Tropes of Martyrdom and Resistance

The Gaza War coincided with the month of Muharram and the Shi'i commemoration of Karbala, the martyrdom of Imam Hussein, his family, and companions by the Umayyads. The first day of Muharram (2008) coincided with the second day of the Gaza War, with the newspaper *Kayhan* correlating the Gaza War with Karbala by identifying this war with Shi'ism and an Islamic resistance that celebrated the 'martyrs of Gaza', recalling the martyrdom of the grandson of the Prophet Mohammad and his followers (*Kayhan* 2008a). Furthermore, *Kayhan* identified Hamas with Imam Hussein's resistance that resulted in a 'Mohammedan and Ashura-like victory [*Nāb-i Muhamadī*]' (*Kayhan* 2008c).

As the tenth day of Muharram loomed, the Karbala narrative was more potently utilized. Parallels with the Iran–Iraq War were drawn (*Kayhan* 2009d), once again constructing a discourse of martyrdom that wove together Karbala and the Gaza War, thereby emphasizing the treachery of the Arab leaders (including Saudi Arabia), and their inhumane actions towards Palestinian children. In contrast, the image of Khamenei's leadership was framed by juxtaposing the role of the Supreme Leader with Imam Hussein. The editorial began with a story of a thirteen-year-old boy who begged his parents to travel to Tehran during the Iran–Iraq War. When parental permission was attained, the discourse described a second permission sought from Khamenei in his role as president at the time, to issue a fatwa banning poets from reciting poetry mentioning the martyrdom of teenagers on the battlefields of Karbala. The editorial thus combined the discourse of martyrdom, heroism, and Islamic leadership by representing Iran as the source and origin of Islamic sacrifice, with the young children of Gaza now emulating a similar fate, representing the greater struggle for Islam and resistance against 'Zionism' and the 'Great Satan' (*Kayhan* 2009d).

Furthermore, the article compared the Umayyad ban of any support for Hussein with the banning of the demonstrations by the Saudi king. This was further emphasized by quoting Imam Hussein, with the Gaza War compared to a war of 'all of Islam against all of infidelity' that would not stop at the borders of Palestine (*Kayhan* 2009d). Therefore, Iranian discourse identified infidelity with Arab leaders and the 'Pro-Israeli West' staging a war against the free Islamic world that only Iran supported. Imam Hussein was identified with Iran, his followers with Gaza, and the Umayyad with the Arab leaders, the West and Israel.

The use of quotes to emphasize the Karbala narrative in the Gaza War was also evident on the tenth of Muharram (the first month of the Islamic calendar), which was the day of the battle. Representing the war as the 'Karbala of Gaza' (*Kayhan*

2009c), the suffering of the people of Gaza was juxtaposed with Imam Hussein's message of truth and honesty. Like the Ahl al-bayt's suffering under the Umayyad Caliph Yazid, when Gazans spoke the truth, the Arab leaders and Israel sentenced them to death. Like the Umayyad accusing Hussein of heresy and pronouncing his blood permissible when he spoke of righteousness and advice to obey the teachings of the Quran, so were the Gazans sentenced to death by the contemporary Yazid. Quotations were also employed to strengthen this construction, including citing the head of Yazid's army, Amr Ibn Saad, as proclaiming, 'Oh Armies of God mount your horses and go to heaven by killing Hussein ibn Ali!' (*Kayhan* 2009c), with the Arab leaders and Israel symbolized by Amr Ibn Saad and Yazid's slaughter of a righteous Hussein, symbolizing Gaza. The treachery and illegitimacy of the Arab leaders was compared with the treachery of the Umayyad, thus portraying them as hypocrites and citing the hadeeth when constructing a discourse of a false Islam, with the latter represented as a façade by quoting Mohammad's companion Amar ibn Yasser: 'They show Islam but they are not Muslims' (*Kayhan* 2009c). Finally, Iranian editorial discourse attempted to highlight the Shi'i nature of the Gazans and their alignment with Iran by describing the slogans and graffiti on the streets of Gaza. The suffering of the people of Gaza was identified with the suffering and assassination of Imam Ali, the first Shi'i infallible. The walls of Gaza were also depicted as covered with graffiti quoting Imam Ali's famous words as he was struck by the assassin's sword (*Ibn Muljem*): 'I have won by the blessing of the God of the Ka'aba'. The discourse compared the assassin, *Ibn Muljem*, to the Arab leaders, whereby the 'political ancestor' and the modern-day Imam Ali were the people of Gaza, who had been oppressed and betrayed by the Arab leaders (*Kayhan* 2009a).

The 'atrocities' and 'killings' in Gaza were juxtaposed with Karbala using the Shi'i universal phrase 'Every day is Ashura and every land is Karbala' (*Jomhouri Eslami* 2009a). The quoting of Hezbollah's speeches on Karbala on the day of Ashura, combined with the war on Gaza, gave rise to a representation of Hamas and Gaza as an extension of Hezbollah and the Shi'i resistance of Karbala. Hassan Nasrallah's quotes arguing that this era was witnessing the 'oppression and injustice of new Yazids and Yazidis' exemplified this strategy (*Jomhouri Eslami* 2009a), with the Self – namely the Iranian-sponsored groups – described as embodying the 'spirit of bravery, resistance and struggle' (*Jomhouri Eslami* 2009a), which, like the followers of Imam Hussein, would rise up and resist. Therefore, Iran and its sponsored groups were the modern-day Ahl al-bayt, resisting Israel and the treacherous Arab leaders, the contemporary Yazid, and the Umayyads. The Iranian Self was thereby a legitimate and just Islamic leader, while Saudi Arabia and its regional allies were traitors to Islam and the Muslim people.

The construction of the Iranian Self as an Islamic leader fighting Islam's enemies was also achieved by framing the revolution as a basis for all victories. The Iranian revolution was correlated with Islamic resistance, Karbala, and Islamic unity. Although the editorial stressed that the people of Palestine were not Shi'a, over the previous thirty years an Islamic awakening had been achieved by Islamic resistance groups such as Hezbollah and their 2006 victory. This victory was depicted as a Karbala-like triumph that had erased sectarianism. Iranian discourse further emphasized that contemporary argument and discussion was not about 'who is Sunni and who is Shi'a' but rather concerned Islamic unity (*Jomhouri Eslami* 2009a). Thereby the victory in Gaza was also a success for the Islamic Republic. Shi'i narratives were correlated and linked Karbala and Hezbollah's war by demonstrating that Palestinians were Muslims and part of the Islamic world, and they were therefore natural targets of 'Zionists, and their protectors the Europeans and US' (*Jomhouri Eslami* 2009a). Hence, the Arab leadership, including Saudi Arabia, was implicated in conspiring to destroy Islam and the Muslim world.

Saudi Discourses: Iranian Sedition, Hegemony, and Realpolitik

Saudi discourse during the Gaza War revolved around two main themes: Iranian sedition in the Arab world, and hegemony and realpolitik. Each theme gave rise to discourses such as those on inter- and intra-divisions in the Arab region, the promotion of Iranian national interests, and the rebuilding of a Persian empire. These discourses were prevalent in the Saudi editorials. The discourse of the Saudi elite and the ulama focused on their support for the Palestinian people and condemned the strikes on Gaza. Explicit representations of Iran were not articulated by the elite or the ulama. The Saudi editorials framed Iran's support for Hamas and responded to Iranian discourse and representations of Saudi Arabia and the Arab leaders. Let us now consider these discourses in turn.

Iranian Sedition

Saudi editorial discourse discussed Iranian aspirations of Arab division and sedition by arguing that Iran aimed to divide the Arabs by stirring sedition. Furthermore, this Arab division by Iran was represented as a reflection of the Palestinian factions' divisions. That is to say, the Iranian sedition of Arab movements and states sought to destroy Arab unity. Like the Iranian discourse on the Gaza War, the Saudi discourse used the 2006 Hezbollah War to construct and frame an image of Iran. Furthermore, Saudi editorial discourse responded and commented on speeches from pro-Iran groups such as Hezbollah and Hamas. A representative illustration includes *Asharq Al-Awsat*'s criticism of Hamas as an Iranian proxy and the inaction of Hezbollah regarding the Israeli strikes on Gaza (*Asharq Al-Awsat* 2008c). Saudi editorial discourse represented Iran in three ways. First, by creating proxy powers that were 'Iranian bullies' and by depicting Palestine and Gaza as a victim of Iranian meddling in the Middle East. Second, the Iranian-supported Shi'i Hezbollah was represented as hypocritical with a 'mask that has fallen'. Although Nasrallah criticized the Arab states for signing a peace accord with Israel, the Shi'i leader 'had requested that Egypt and the Arab world save Hamas and the resistance' (*Asharq Al-Awsat* 2008c), thereby framing Iranian-sponsored groups as hypocritical and weak and Arab states such as Saudi Arabia and Egypt as strong regional leaders. This argument led to a third representation, namely that 'Iran is the real threat to Arab security' since it sought a war with Egypt and later Saudi

Arabia, weakening the Arab world by destroying its unity. *Asharq Al-Awsat* argued that an Iranian war sought to 'break the bracelet', i.e. to destroy Arab unity, through the devastation of the Arab world by 'first initiating a war with Egypt, and later with Saudi Arabia' (*Asharq Al-Awsat* 2008c).

Framing Hamas as an Iranian pawn, the 'Gaza card' was argued as fulfilling the Iranian agenda of destroying the Arab world. The Saudi discourse described the destruction of the Arab world as being initiated by the US after its invasion of Iraq, while 'Iran has taken it upon itself to destroy the rest of the Arab countries to spread its influence' (*Asharq Al-Awsat* 2009c). Iranian fatwas released by Khamenei were blamed for spreading the destruction of Arab states, while the Saudi discourse labelled Islamist groups such as Hamas as having their 'loyalty bought by Iran' with Iranian control attempting to make them 'superior to states' (*Asharq Al-Awsat* 2009c). This superiority, combined with fatwas 'ordering the Muslim world to defend Gaza' meant that those who 'die defending Palestinians are martyrs'. Therefore, *Asharq Al-Awsat* ultimately accused Iran's leadership of employing Islamic fatwas in aid of their proxies for the sake of causing internal disruption within Arab states as protests would potentially lead to deaths with those killed labelled as martyrs, thereby expanding the Iranian sphere of influence in the region.

The kingdom's editorial genre discursively constructed Iran as having a sectarian agenda, creating an image of a seditionist and sectarian state as evidenced by a sectarian narrative. The Islamic Republic's support for Hamas was characterized as a stepping stone in its expansionist ambitions. Saudi discourse drew a correlation between different Arab states to make the argument that Iran was involved in order to represent the Iranian Other as a chaotic hegemon that had also interfered in the Iraqi political process: 'Iran was not satisfied with dividing . . . Beirut between Sunnis and Shi'a . . . now it seeks to support the Houthi separation in Yemen' (*Asharq Al-Awsat* 2009d).

Saudi editorial discourse further used the 34-Day War to create a representational strategy that blamed Iran for the intra-Arab division and destruction of the Arab world. *Asharq Al-Awsat* (2009) argued that the Gaza War built on the divisions created after the Hezbollah–Israel war in 2006. A specific sectarian narrative was spun, accusing Hezbollah of being an anti-Sunni movement 'engaged in a war against the Sunnis on Beirut' in May and June 2008, under orders from Iran. Consequently, Hamas was 'utilized by Iran' on this occasion to 'strike the Arabs in an unprecedented way' by creating rivalries among Sunni and Arab parties (*Asharq Al-Awsat* 2009b). Therefore, the Saudi discourse framed Iranian proxies as a source of sedition that would attack the Sunni population within their states, as evidenced in the siege of Beirut in 2008, and hence lead to a war that would attempt to destroy the two major Arab countries in the Middle East – Egypt and Saudi Arabia.

Iranian Hegemony and Realpolitik

Another predominant theme in the Saudi discourse was Iranian hegemony and realpolitik, i.e. the use of the Gaza War as a tool to promote its national interests.

As Iran was accused of being responsible for the Gaza War with Israel (*Asharq Al-Awsat* 2008b), Saudi discourse drew on three main arguments to interpret this theme in order to answer the central question: 'Who benefits from this crime?' (*Asharq Al-Awsat* 2008a). The specific arguments revolved around Iran's nuclear dossier, the spread of Iranian ideology, and Iran's leverage in the Golan Heights negotiations (*Asharq Al-Awsat* 2008a). Iran's role was characterized as 'one that in reality was indirect', while the Islamic Republic was labelled as a major actor that had caused a 'tragedy' and committed a 'crime', as a result of which 'Iran is the biggest beneficiary' (*Asharq Al-Awsat* 2008a).

First, Saudi discourse framed Iran's proxy wars to alleviate the pressures of the nuclear programme. By drawing parallels between the Hezbollah War in 2006 and the Gaza attacks, Iran was represented as working on a malign nuclear programme while it sought to keep Israel occupied in a war with Iran's proxies, i.e. Hezbollah in 2006 and Hamas in 2008–2009. This proxy war was argued to include 'other plans to dominate the region' (*Asharq Al-Awsat* 2008a). Saudi editorials further refracted Iran's hegemonic ambitions through the creation of a false sense of national and Islamic resistance. In other words, Iran was using Islam as a device to promote its own interests (*Asharq Al-Awsat* 2008a), thereby questioning Iran's image of resistance, leadership, and Islam.

Meanwhile, a narrative of 'political Shi'ism' was promulgated to demonstrate that Iran's proxy wars aimed to spread its ideology, which was a main goal of its regional interests and hegemonic ambitions (*Asharq Al-Awsat* 2008b). Hamas was characterized as a weak military force while Iranian weapons provided to support the Sunni group were characterized sarcastically as 'flammable fireworks' (*Asharq Al-Awsat* 2008b), drawing an implicit contrast between strong support for a Shi'i Hezbollah compared with the 'fireworks' provided to Hamas. Iran's support for the Hamas kidnapping of the Israeli soldiers was depicted as scapegoating the armed group and its people for the sake of Iranian national interests, raising morale and therefore winning the hearts and minds of the Arab masses. This allowed Iran to capitalize on the use of its proxy by spreading its ideology of 'political Shi'ism'. Therefore, Iran was accused of using Shi'ism as a political tool to garner further support from the masses (*Asharq Al-Awsat* 2008b).

Iran's regional raison d'etre was depicted as characterized by the exploitation of Hamas and Palestine (Asharq Al-Awsat 2009a), while Saudi editorial discourse argued that support for Hamas as a proxy group might lead to total Iranian control over the Palestinian 'dossier', and therefore the end of the Arab Peace Plan, thereby giving Iran the upper hand in the region. Since both Syria and Hamas were both in the Iranian sphere of influence, this would lead to Iran having leverage over Israel, and therefore influence over the US. This leverage would grant Iran 'US guarantees' that would result in an Iranian axis that dominated the region as the resulting benefits would include regaining the Golan Heights while the US might 'hand over Lebanon as an extra bonus' (*Asharq Al-Awsat* 2009a). Therefore, Iran was represented as exploiting the situation and placing nations and the wider region in danger: there was an implicit allegation of Iranian adventurism in pursuit of its regional goals of power and hegemony.

Meanwhile, *al-Riyadh* (2009) defined the Saudi Self in contrast to its Other, Iran, its role in the Middle East, and its impact in the Arab region. By emphasizing Saudi Arabia's fairness and cooperation with Iran, the editorial underlined the king's leadership, pragmatism, and pursuit of peace by discussing his overtures with Iran. Furthermore, the king was framed as endangering the kingdom's position with the US and resisting American pressure, all for the sake of Islamic relations and unity with Iran. In addition, an image of Islamic leadership was projected by claiming that Abdullah was placing the interests of Islam and the region before the kingdom's interests with the US. In contrast, Iran was represented as a manipulator and hegemon that harboured ambitions of becoming the sole regional power. The Iranian leadership was thus framed as an exploiter, taking liberties and abusing détente and rapprochement when relations were normalized with Saudi Arabia. The Saudi Self was a victim of its Other. Iran demanded 'expelling the US from the Gulf and vacating any military bases ... withdrawing all the foreign reserves and boycotting oil sales', which was portrayed as a ploy by Iran to advance its military, financial, and energy interests (*al-Riyadh* 2009). Meanwhile, Iranian regional involvement in Lebanon and the disputed islands with the UAE were used again, along with the concept of Bahraini sovereignty, to illustrate Iranian hegemonic ambitions.

Saudi representations of Iranian hegemony were further promulgated by describing Iran as an agent of division in the Middle East (*al-Riyadh* 2009). The editorial discourse discussed the Iranian aspiration to divide the Arabs and spread its influence in the Middle East using two different strategies. First, it blamed Iran for both Lebanon's 2006 war and Gaza's war with Israel, suggesting that Iran was the cause of the war with Israel and therefore responsible for the destruction of Lebanon and Gaza. This paved the way for a split in Lebanese party politics between the 8 March and 14 March coalitions and for Iranian control over Lebanese politics. Consequently, Iran was framed for sedition through it being responsible for cutting the ties between the two Palestinian factions. Second, the editorial discourse highlighted Iran's intention to sow sedition in the Gulf states and for Iraq to be the fifteenth state, arguing that it had interests in Iraq's south, which had oil and fertile land, and was rich in Arab culture. This would be accomplished by Iran 'agitating the Shi'a in the Gulf to clash with the governments' (*al-Riyadh* 2009).

Finally, sectarian tropes were employed to identify an Iranian regional agenda to 'rebuild a Persian empire' through religious collaboration and ties with Shi'i tribes and sects, that is, the Gulf states such as Bahrain and Kuwait, the tribes located between Khuzestan (Iran) and southern Iraq, as well as the Syrian Alawites and Lebanese Shia (*al-Riyadh* 2009). This framed Iran as having planned the re-emergence of its empire under the guise of religion, a sectarian narrative also supported by the criticism of Iranian religious freedoms as the latter did not allow 'for the presence of one Sunni mosque in the capital Tehran', although Iran had a 25 per cent Sunni population (*al-Riyadh* 2009). Consequently, from a Saudi perspective, the Other was framed as racist, hegemonic, and sectarian, while the Self was lenient and accepting, while projecting true Islamic values and leadership, especially since the Sunni states in the Gulf had smaller Shi'i populations who were allowed to build mosques in their capitals.[2]

Conclusion

The Saudi discourses in relation to the Gaza War included Iranian sedition in the Arab world, and hegemony and realpolitik. Iranian discourses, on the other hand, were an extension of those constructed during the Hezbollah 34-Day War. They represented Saudi Arabia mainly by discussing the silence and subservience of Arab leaders and an awakening of the Islamic world. Furthermore, Iran took advantage of the Muharram and the commemoration of Imam Hussein. This gave rise to Islamic narratives and tropes. Saudi discourse employed tropes and narratives resembling the 1980s Iran–Iraq War. These included the promotion of Iranian national interests and the rebuilding of a Persian empire. Taking a step back, we have seen over the previous four chapters how the Ahmadinejad tenure from 2005–2009 brought about a shift in Iranian–Saudi mutual representations. This shift ended Rafsanjani's period of détente and Khatami's eight years of rapprochement. Iranian factors, such as populism through the election of Ahmadinejad, the first non-clerical president since the exile of Bani-Sadr in 1981, the nuclear crisis, and Iranian regional expansionism were decisive in ending Iranian–Saudi rapprochement. Similarly, Saudi external and domestic forces also played a pivotal role in Saudi–Iranian representations. These included a rise in terrorism, pressures on democratic reform, and the failure of the Saudi-proposed Arab Peace Initiative of 2002.

As the Gaza War came to an end, Iran geared itself up for another round of presidential elections. In the summer of 2009, Ahmadinejad would win a second term after a highly contested election. This election would be a watershed moment for Iran and the survival of the Islamic Republic. However, the related turbulence would not be restricted to Iran. The next year, the world would also witness a domino effect of revolutions occurring across the Middle East. The revolutions – labelled the Arab Spring – would open up a new arena for Iranian–Saudi rivalry and representations of each other. This rivalry would take on an unprecedented form, particularly since the old Arab order was collapsing – the survival of the GCC monarchs was at stake, and Iran was becoming further entrenched in the Arab world.

2. It was claimed that although there are over one million Sunnis living in Tehran, there are no Sunni mosques (Gheissari 2009: 319).

Part 4

Part I

Chapter 10

THE ARAB WORLD RISES: ARAB SPRING OR ISLAMIC AWAKENING?

Introduction

The domino effect of the protests that began with the self-immolation of a Tunisian street vendor, Mohamed Bouazizi, led to a region-wide wave of protests beginning in Tunisia and spreading across authoritarian countries including Egypt, Libya, Syria, and the Arab Gulf region. As the Middle East fell into chaos and turbulence, the protest tremors were felt not only on Saudi Arabia's borders, but also within the kingdom itself. In Tunisia, the Jasmine Revolution saw the end of Zine El-Abidin Ben Ali's two-decade rule and his self-exile to Saudi Arabia. Egypt's Mubarak resigned weeks later, ending the emergency government whose powers he had renewed every three years since the assassination of Anwar Sadat in 1981. Along with Tunisia and Egypt, Morocco also saw the rise of political Islam. The transnational Sunni organization, the Muslim Brotherhood, had begun to dominate the political scene in three North African countries while the flames of change soon blew into the Levant. Protests in Syria began in Deir-e-Zor; within months, chants turned into armed struggle and the opposition called for Bashar al-Assad to step down. The Persian Gulf was no exception to these protests. Bahrain soon caught the Arab Spring wind. As Shi'i-dominated protests began in Manama, there were protests in Riyadh, while the Eastern Province of Saudi Arabia also experienced protests calling for more rights and equality. In the case of Riyadh, stimulus packages and promises of greater accountability and the tackling of corruption calmed the streets. However, clashes continued for months in Saudi Arabia's Eastern Province and Bahrain. In the latter, the protests led to confrontations as the Al-Khalifa monarchy sought assistance from the Gulf Cooperation Council (GCC) sheikhdoms, particularly Saudi Arabia.

The wave of pro-democracy demonstrations that called for the fall of regimes in the Middle East introduced new opportunities and raised concerns for both Iran and Saudi Arabia. In Riyadh, there was a fear of Muslim Brotherhood-style protests, which had already resulted in the fall of three Arab leaders, especially as the demonstrations in neighbouring Bahrain were gaining momentum. For Iran, the rise of the Muslim Brotherhood was an opportunity as the Islamic Republic had forged amicable relations with the Muslim Brotherhood since the Khomeini-led revolution in 1979. Furthermore, the Shi'i protests in Bahrain, once a part of Iran until its independence in 1971, were viewed in Iran with much anticipation. However, the state's main concern was the heart of its 'axis of resistance', namely Syria, as the protestors were calling for the removal of its main axis ally.

Experts have argued that no single group or entity was behind the events of the 'Arab Spring', as it came to be known (Chubin 2012). The fascinating characteristic of this wave of protests was that the protestors – regardless of their specific national locations – had so much in common in terms of the reasons for their disaffection. Economic issues such as unemployment and financial corruption, as well as domestic repression by authoritarian regimes, were the fuel that fed the fire of discontent and energized the revolt against different ruling elites. The concerns raised were not only about the relationship between the rulers and the people, but they also concerned unprecedented questions regarding the citizenry, making the demand that Arab leaders should listen and respond to their citizens instead of just ruling over them (Chubin 2012; Steavenson 2011). In the Arab states of the Persian Gulf, such as Bahrain and Saudi Arabia, issues were not only centred on economic inequality – they also revolved around sectarianism and discrimination. The Sunni versus Shi'i question gave rise to tropes and arguments based on the rivalry and regional struggle for influence between Saudi Arabia and Iran. As Gause (2012) has argued, 'we might be missing the other big story of the Arab Spring – how the rivalry for regional influence between Saudi Arabia and Iran is affected by these domestic political changes' (Gause 2011).

To understand the dynamics of Saudi Arabia and Iran's rivalry and the construction of their respective Self and Other during the Arab Spring, it is imperative to account not only for the geopolitical and regional struggle between both states, but also to discuss the domestic political challenges both countries experienced. Before I examine how Iran and Saudi Arabia reacted towards each other during this highly contested period, I will first explore how both countries had already witnessed protests not long before the advent of the Arab Spring during the Green Revolution in Iran, which emerged in protest to Ahmadinejad winning a second term, and the 2009 riots in the holy city of Medina between Shi'i pilgrims visiting the *Baqi'* cemetery and the Saudi religious police (Committee for the Promotion of Virtue and the Prevention of Vice), as well as the demonstrations in the Eastern Province over the arrest of Sheikh Nimr al-Nimr. This chapter will also discuss the reactions of Iran and Saudi Arabia to the events of the Arab Spring and towards each other. The chapter does not cover all the countries that experienced protests, and I examine those that played a major role in Iran and Saudi Arabia's respective domestic and foreign policies, namely Egypt and Bahrain. This chapter discusses how these rivalries were sharpened and defined amid the construction of Self and Other in the discourse of both countries. Tehran and Riyadh had a lot to both gain and lose from the events of the Arab Spring, which led to their respective manoeuvrings on domestic, regional, and international levels, while shaping how each state viewed the Other.

An Early Spring in Saudi Arabia and Iran

Iran and Saudi Arabia experienced domestic turbulence that gave rise to protests, albeit at different magnitudes. The Shi'i protests in Saudi Arabia began in February 2009 in al-Medina, when the Shi'a commemorate the death of the Prophet Mohammad as well as the martyrdom of the third Shi'i Imam, Hasan bin Ali. Although the Baqi' cemetery incident lasted for a few days, protests erupted in the densely Shi'i Eastern Province of Saudi Arabia in solidarity with the Shi'a arrested and injured at al-Medina. The contested Iranian election results in June 2009 also witnessed nationwide protests. The Green Movement (*Mauj-i Sabz*), i.e. the base supporting the reformist candidate Mir Hussain Mousavi, disputed the election results that saw Ahmadinejad receive 62 per cent of the vote, claiming that votes had been rigged. Consequently, Iran experienced protests and arrests between June and December 2009, which resulted in reformist candidates being put under house arrest.[1] These events shaped discourses of Self and Other in both Saudi Arabia and Iran. In the case of the former, the events in al-Medina led to the mobilization of sectarian tropes and the construction of a Shi'i Other. In the case of Iran, the disputed elections gave rise to protests that resulted in a schism that divided the political spectrum, thus spawning different discourses, representations, and a redefinition of the Iranian Self.

Upending Shi'i Hopes: The 2009 Baqi' Protests

There are always at least two sides to a story, and the Baqi' incident in Medina is no different. The state narrative as reported by local newspapers was that 'citizens were stirring chaos in the vicinity of the Baqi' cemetery as they had hindered hundreds of worshippers from performing their prayers [thus] violating the sanctity of the honourable place by chanting and pelting shoes and empty cartons at the anti-riot police' (*al-Riyadh* 2009e). The government account held that the visitors had 'protested after their demands to open the Baqi' gate were rejected after the deadline [for closure]' (*al-Riyadh* 2009e). The Shi'i protestors, on the other hand, argued that their 'sit-in' was triggered by the Commission for the Promotion of Virtue and the Prevention of Vice (*al-Hay'ah*), the religious police, for having 'harassed the female Shi'i pilgrims, [and] insulted them by using obscenities ... such as infidels, '*rawāfiz*', and offspring of *mut'a*'[2] (*Rasid* 2009). This, coupled with the morality police 'filming the female Shi'i pilgrims' (*Rasid* 2009), led to an initial confrontation between the pilgrims and the authorities. What soon followed were protests that led to the arrest of five Shi'i citizens and the later intervention of the

---

1. It is important to mention that while this chapter takes into account the events of these two incidents in Saudi Arabia and Iran respectively, I will not discuss their causes in depth. For more detailed accounts of these protests please see: Dabashi, H. (2017); Alimagham, P. (2020).

2. For a discussion on Mut'a or Temporary Marriage See Murata (2014).

security forces, which resulted in dozens being injured. Demonstrations then erupted in the Eastern Province of the kingdom. The Shi'a in Awamiyah, Qatif, and Safwa caused a storm that was arguably 'the most serious outbreak of Shia dissent since 1979' (Wehrey 2013: 9).

What followed was a mixed response on the part of Saudi Shi'i political groups. While protests were widespread in the Shi'i towns, the loudest and most vocal came from Awamiyah, long known to harbour mistrust towards the Saudi government. Led by Sheikh Nimr al-Nimr, a cleric known for his strong stance against the state, al-Nimr called for the Shi'i's 'pawned dignity to be restored . . . and if it is not . . . we will call for secession' (al-Nimr 2009). The cleric argued that Shi'i 'dignity is more precious than the unity of this land'. Matthiesen (2009) argues that this left the more moderate voices in a difficult position. Clerics such as Hassan al-Saffar had called for a greater Shi'i role in the Saudi political conversation and advocated for King Abdullah's 'national dialogue' through the Partners in One Nation initiative of 2003, while also holding elected seats after running in the 2005 municipal council elections (Matthiesen 2009). Furthermore, these protests and the violence that ensued cast a dark shadow on the monarch's attempted reforms.

A week before the incident, King Abdullah's call for a ministerial reshuffle saw the dismissal of both the head of the morality police, Abdullah al-Ghaith, and the head of the Supreme Judicial Council, Mohammad al-Luhaydan. Promises were made that the councils would appoint members who were not from the mainstream Hanbali Islamic school of thought, which dominated the kingdom. Although these changes initially raised the hopes of the Shi'a in relation to gaining representation on the Senior Ulama Council and the Supreme Judicial Council, members of other Sunni denominations were appointed with no Shi'i representation. The king was forced to appease the extremists (Keynoush 2016: 196), while excluding the Shi'a, and there was a quick move to calm the situation. Meetings between the king and the Shi'i delegation led by al-Saffar secured the release of all those incarcerated. There were even reports that Ayatollah Sistani in Najaf (Iraq) had intervened and contacted the Saudi monarch to secure the release of the Shi'i prisoners. The king's overture in terms of the prisoner releases could be seen as a form of quick crisis management. The press and media did not dwell on the incidents, covering the initial protests in Medina briefly with hardly any mention made of the protests in the Eastern Province.

Although these protests were arguably the most intense in a three-decade period, the Saudi discourse did not cover the events extensively, with the press editorials focusing on daily aspects of domestic politics. The initial reaction came from the spokesman to the ministry of the interior, who characterized the underlying cause of the incidents as a 'quarrel between a group of worshippers and pilgrims in the courtyard of the mosque'. He said this was a 'completely separate incident to what occurred in the Baqi' cemetery', thereby avoiding a sectarian narrative of the events and even claiming that it was 'difficult to say that these were Shi'a or Sunni before the investigations are over' (*Al-Bawaba* 2009). Other officials, such as the governor (emir) of al-Medina district, attempted to justify the use of force while implicitly sectarianizing the troubles: 'he who comes to the Prophet's mosque to carry out their rituals according to the Sunnah shall be served in every way, and anyone that acts against the Sunnah and enters discrepancies and does not follow the instructions shall be subjected to discipline' *(Al-Bawaba 2009)*.

Known for his support for the morality police and ulama, the late Prince Nayef, then minister of the interior, made comments that reaffirmed the doctrinal commitments to the Saudi brand of Islam and justified the use of force and incarceration. His comments reflected how the state's view of Saudi Shi'a informed his perspective on the incident and suspicion of foreign interference. Nayef presented the Shi'i pilgrims as the perpetrators and cause of the chaos. Underlining the religious identity of the Saudi state and ummah (society or the Muslim community) as based on 'the doctrine of the Sunnis and our righteous forefathers [*al-Salaf al-Sālih*]', 'citizens have both rights and duties; their activities should not contradict the doctrine of the ummah'. Stopping short of labelling 'those affiliated with the Shiite sect, Saudis, or others' as heretics, the minister represented Shi'i rituals at the Baqi' cemetery as 'an insult to the dead, especially the companions of the Prophet or those of his family' and accused the children and female pilgrims of 'tampering with graves'. Consequently, the actions of the morality police were justified since the 'wrong acts must be confronted with force'. All of this was stated while projecting an image of the impartiality and neutrality of the state in enforcing the law regardless of sect and religious background, noting that the 'numbers of Sunnis arrested are no less than the Shi'a Saudi citizens' (al-Saud 2009a).

The Iranian response to the Shi'i protests in Saudi Arabia was characterized by state and media silence in the immediate aftermath of the incidents. This may have been due to Iran's focus on the Palestinian Conference of March 2009 and the government's attempt to avoid any accusation of it provoking sedition and dividing the Arab world along sectarian lines. Any state criticism of Saudi Arabia by Iran could have perhaps justified the Saudi narrative of a rogue state that interfered in Arab affairs with sectarian and seditious tendencies. This was particularly the case since the Saudi government worked hard to not give this a sectarian label, as is evident in the minister of the interior's interview with the local media. The Iranian government's silence therefore created a vacuum that was filled with the seminaries, postponing the state's reaction to the incidents to a later date. Instead, the instant response came from senior Iranian ulama in the city of Qom, while the clerics perhaps strategized their responses by aiming their grievances at the Saudi clergy rather than the Saudi state, questioning the legitimacy of the Wahhabi school of thought and its administration of the holy shrines in Mecca and Medina and going so far as to criticize the Iranian government for its silence.

Grand Ayatollah Makarem Shirazi's statement depicted the Saudi clergy through an Iranian lens: 'we always observe such disorders in Medina [regarding] insults to Iranian pilgrims' (Makarem Shirazi 2009). In addition, the narrative also implied an image of a Saudi state that failed to protect its Shi'i citizens, allowing the clergy to hurl 'insults and harassment . . . at their own people' (Makarem Shirazi 2009). The incident was also used to revitalize the topic of the administration of the holy shrines in Mecca and Medina, particularly as Iran has always advocated international Islamic oversight of the two holy sites. The Baqi' incident, according to the Grand Ayatollah, allowed 'a small group, [an] extremist fanatical minority', i.e. the Wahhabi ulama, who 'consider themselves the owners of the two holy shrines [to] do whatever it wants to freely in these holy places, which belong to all Muslims'. In addition, the Grand Ayatollah urged the Iranian foreign ministry to 'pursue this issue seriously through international channels'. Within this statement, Ayatollah Shirazi sought to define how the Iranian clergy viewed the Islamic ummah. By casting a shadow on the Saudi clergy, the Iranian cleric offered an implicit framing of Iran's view of sectarian non-discrimination and pointed at the Wahhabis of Saudi Arabia as the principal sectarian and divisive force. The discourse on the oversight of Mecca was reminiscent of the 1987 Hajj Incident that had resulted in the early establishing of this discourse. Since then, any incident concerning the two holy shrines in Saudi Arabia resurrected discourses of the Iranian Self as the legitimate protector and leader of the Islamic world, while representing its Saudi Other as a sectarian Wahhabi leadership that sought to control and spread sedition across the Islamic ummah through its control of the two holy sites.

As discussed in Chapter 9, Israel's Operation Cast Lead against Hamas in Gaza was a source of contention between Iran and Saudi Arabia, as Iran was accused of interfering in Arab affairs and sowing division among Palestinians. A meeting between the then Iranian foreign minister, Manouchehr Mottaki, and his Saudi counterpart, Saud al-Faisal, ended with the latter criticizing Iran for 'interference in Arab causes' that had caused 'political disputes' among Palestinian groups (al-Saud 2009b). In an earlier press conference, al-Faisal asked the Arab states for 'unity against Iran's ambitions'(al-Saud 2009c). In response to al-Faisal's comments, the Iranian Friday prayer Imam and member of the Assembly of Experts, Ayatollah Ahmad Khatami, utilized the Shi'i protests to rebut Saudi accusations of Iranian sedition and interference in Arab affairs, emphasizing Iran's role in supporting Palestinians 'to stand up to the criminal Zionists [rather than] 'mobiliz[ing] the Islamic world against Iran' (Khatami 2009). Criticizing the Saudi reforms, Khatami argued that real Saudi reforms should be made 'to confront extremists' since the 'image of Saudi Arabia is not a pleasant one' in comparison to Iran where its 'nuclear power is the pride of the Islamic world'. Like Ayatollah Shirazi, Khatami demanded that the Iranian foreign ministry 'do something to prevent harassment through diplomacy'(Khatami 2009). While the official discourse was silent on the Baqi' incident, the domestic discourse emanating from the ulama assumed the role of responding to events. The government did not want to cause any turbulence at that moment in time, and so responsibility fell on the clerics to respond. This was especially the case since it was an Islamic matter, and Iran views the Self as a legitimate leader of the Islamic ummah. Therefore, by utilizing tropes of 'Western–Zionist subservience', the Iranian clerical discourse wove political events into the Medina incident, thus representing the Saudi Other as being innately un-Islamic and not good enough to lead the Islamic world. Furthermore, by bringing up Iran's nuclear status, the ulama juxtaposed the Iranian Self as a scientifically developed, legitimate leader of the Islamic ummah as opposed to the 'inferior', 'sectarian',

'Western-subservient' Saudi Other. Six months later, it would be Iran that would witness turbulence and incidents because of disputes over the results of its presidential elections.

'Where's My Vote?': Iran's 2009 Protests and the Green Movement

The Iranian elections of June 2009 culminated in the eruption of mass protests against Mahmoud Ahmadinejad's victory. These demonstrations, organized by the budding Green Movement (*Jonbish-i Sabz*), posed a challenge to the Islamic Republic's status quo, possibly the most serious it had experienced since 1979. Scholars have argued that over a million people rallied on the streets of Tehran in protest of the election's outcome (Sreberny and Khiabany 2010: 172). Wearing green, an Islamic symbol commonly seen in Shi'i proceedings as the colour of Ahl-al-Bayt, the street protestors rallied in support of the former prime minister and the then reformist presidential candidate, Mir-Hossein Mousavi.

In addition to the two front runners – Ahmadinejad and Mousavi – other candidates also included the former Majles speaker, Mehdi Karoubi, and the former head of the IRGC, Moshen Rezaie. The former was reform leaning and the latter was a conservative. The elections set a record voter turnout of 85 per cent (Kamrava 2014: 199). Arguably, this gave Iran's system a renewed sense of self-confidence and legitimacy. However, the high turnout also raised voters' expectations. Therefore, when the results were announced with a landslide victory for Ahmadinejad (63 per cent of the vote), Mousavi's supporters raised questions and accusations of electoral rigging, suggesting that tactics had been used to sway the results in Ahmadinejad's favour.

Within hours, protests erupted and continued until after the president's inauguration in August, demonstrations that continued for weeks and that became increasingly violent. Protestors shouted slogans such as 'Where's my vote?' ('*Ra'y-i-Man Kojāst?*') and 'Death to the dictator' ('*Marg bar Dictator*'). This uprising was soon touted as 'the Green Wave' and 'the Persian Awakening' (Khan 2013) while comparisons were made with the coloured revolutions of the Caucasus, such as in Georgia and Ukraine. Starting as a reformist campaign, this movement turned into a confrontation between two poles within the system. Comrades-in-arms who had worked together to bring down the Shah and set up an Islamic Republic were at odds with each other. The pro-Ahmadinejad camp labelled the protests as sedition (*fitna-yi 1388*) fomented by the West and its domestic allies, while the reformists called the elections a departure from the ideals of the revolution and as marking the end of the Islamic Republic (Pargoo and Akbarzadeh 2021). This split led to questions regarding the political health of Iran while casting a shadow on the state's revolutionary Islamic identity. This was evident in the discourses that followed the election results, where religious sermons, political speeches, and newspapers aimed to reinforce the legitimacy of the state and the position of the Supreme Leader, especially after his support for the results. It must be acknowledged that the protests were covered internationally, particularly since demonstrations by the Iranian diaspora were held in foreign capitals around the world (Kamalipour et al. 2010).

The campaign had seen open televised debates between the candidates. Ahmadinejad crossed a line by criticizing Mousavi and hurling accusations of corruption and collaboration with foreign powers. This included Ahmadinejad accusing Mousavi's wife of faking her qualifications, nepotism, and reproving the former Majles speaker Nateq Nouri and his children along with Rafsanjani and his family for abusing their positions to obtain financial power. However, one main area of contention, foreign relations, was a surprising issue that Ahmadinejad used to criticize his opponents. The president accused Rafsanjani of plotting against him in the 2005 elections. According to Ahmadinejad, Rafsanjani sent a letter to King Abdullah of Saudi Arabia assuring him that Ahmadinejad's government would fall within six months, an accusation that Rafsanjani vehemently denied *(IRIB* 2009*)*.

Moreover, the heated debates led to letters of protest being sent to Zorghami, the head of the state broadcasting service, and to the Supreme Leader. In a speech marking the anniversary of the death of Khomeini, Khamenei took a rare position and commented on Ahmadinejad's actions (Khamenei 2009b). Furthermore, the atmosphere was so heated that Khamenei warned of foreign exploitation of the elections, including unrest and turmoil on the streets. The high voter turnout was a sigh of relief for the leadership. Khamenei praised the turnout as historic (Khamenei 2009b). Within 48 hours, the results were announced, and Ahmadinejad was announced the winner. Khamenei, along with members of the clergy, such as Ayatollah Jannati and Musbah-Yazdi congratulated the incumbent president (NY Times 2009). As noted, the results were not accepted by the reformist camp; Mousavi's supporters took to the streets, the Guardian Council received a petition from him, and a recount of 10 per cent of the votes took place. However, the demonstrations continued with clashes between the protestors and the police.

The discourse soon shifted from a celebratory narrative to one of foreign interference, conspiracy, and sedition. Khamenei took to the pulpit after Friday prayers and warned of civil unrest while congratulating Ahmadinejad. The press, especially *Kayhan*, framed the protests as an act of sedition *(fitna)* and a watershed moment equivalent to Imam Ali's turmoil as Caliph. Indeed, since 1979 the Islamic Republic had always been framed as a continuation of Imam Ali's government. In the Iranian discourse discussing the protests, the present Rahbar was depicted as the Imam Ali of the contemporary era and the reformists as modern-day companions who had left their Caliph isolated. In the months following the elections, the Ahl-al-bayt's use of these tropes increased in prevalence and resonance. These tropes, drawn from the well of Islamic references, highlighted a split in the Iranian Self as the two main surviving leaders of the revolution – Khamenei and Rafsanjani – were now divided. The former supported Ahmadinejad and the latter was aligned with the Mousavi camp. Those who shaped the pro-Ahmadinejad discourse represented the split as an act of treachery within the Islamic Republic by comparing it with the turmoil and division among the followers of Imam Ali's caliphate.

The Ashura Protests: the War Between Two Islams

Six months after the elections, the Iranian streets were still witnessing protests, with both sides employing different tropes and repertoires to shape their positions. Yarbakhsh (2013) argues that the 2009 protests reactivated the use of the Karbala paradigm. Once again drawing from motifs present in Islamic history, the Iranian tropes accentuated a clear schism and split in the image of the Iranian Self, which led to the presence of an 'internal Other'. The protests of 26 December, which coincided with the commemoration of Ashura, saw violent clashes between the demonstrators and the state. The opposition had made use of the protests to mark the death of Ayatollah Montazeri, once named as Ayatollah Khomeini's successor and later the spiritual leader of the reform movement, who had passed away a week before. Both parties blamed each other for tarnishing the image of the holy day by 'introducing politics to a religious event' (Yarbakhsh 2014: 82). Fischer (2010) also argues that the Green Movement chants sought to establish parallels between the leading figures of Karbala and the leading figures in Iranian politics, such as Khamenei, Rafsanjani, and Ahmadinejad. As the protestors beat their chests to the chants of 'Oh Hussain' (*'Ya Hussain'*), and 'We are not from the city of Kufa. We are not followers of Yazid', the protestors conceptualized the leading figures of the opposition, namely the presidential candidate Mousavi and the deceased key opposition figure Ayatollah Montazeri as Imam Hussein, with Khamenei and Ahmadinejad as the Umayyad tyrant Caliph Yazid (Fischer 2010). Indeed, the protests were a manifestation of a split in the Iranian Self, as each group was representing itself as the custodian of the 1979 revolution. The response from the state would further highlight and define this fragmented Self and an internal Other. The fragmented Self and representation of an internal Other brought about a split within Iran's revolutionary leadership. The original leaders of the revolution, such as Khamenei and Rafsanjani, who had led Iran since 1981, were now split. Their split was over the domestic political direction of the state. One side was now labelled radical and the other, Green and reformist. This fragmentation also touched upon the essence of the leadership of the Islamic Republic, the *valy-i faqih*. The 2009 protests questioned Khamenei's leadership and in turn, Mousavi's supporters were labelled as seditionists. The internal Other was not challenging the Islamic Republic or the concept of *valy-i faqih* but rather Khamenei's leadership and his support for Ahmadinejad.

In response to the protests, which were labelled by Ayatollah Khamenei as the 'Day of Sedition 2009' (*'rūz-i Fitna 1388'*), the state organized a counter-demonstration in support of the government. Known as the '9th *Dey* Epic'[3] (Tehran Times 2016), this rally would later be observed yearly. The Iranian discourse genres after the 2009 9th *Dey* rally were two-tiered. The first tier was represented by the official discourse, communicated mainly through Ayatollah Khamenei and Ahmadinejad. It interpreted the Green Movement protests as a Western conspiracy

3. Dey is the tenth month of the Persian calendar.

promoted by Israel, Britain, and the United States. In a speech following the Ashura protests, Khamenei opined that 'the riots on Ashura in Tehran [were] influenced by the Zionist and foreign media' (Khamenei 2009a), while Ahmadinejad represented the protests as 'Zionist theatrics . . . a theatre play by the Zionists and the Americans . . . who had purchased the tickets to this play and were the only audience of this play' (Ahmadinejad 2009).

The second tier of the Iranian discourse on the Ashura protests was propagated by the ulama and editorials, with the protests being framed through the lens of Islam, the Ahl-al-bayt, and Ayatollah Khamenei's leadership and legitimacy. This tier of discourse was also multi-layered – the protests were defined as an act of sedition against the Islamic ummah as manifest in the war between two parties, the Party of God (Hezbollah) versus the Party of Satan *(Hizb al-Shaytān)* (Alam Al-Hoda 2009). The former was represented by the supporters of Ayatollah Khamenei and the latter by the Green Movement. This split within the Iranian Self was also manifest as a war of 'Islam with Islam' or a war between 'pure prophetic Islam and impure Umayyad Islam' *('Islam-i Nab-i Nabawī' and 'Islam-i Nāpāk-i Umawī'),* where it is 'not difficult to recognize Imam Ali from Mu'awiyah and Imam Hussein from Yazid' *(Kayhan 2009).* This Islamic trope of Islam versus Islam and Muawiyyah versus Imam Ali was meant to draw a contrast between the sedition that Imam Ali was subject to in his caliphate with the *Vilāyat-i Faqih* position led by Ayatollah Khamenei. In this analogy, the Islamic Republic was the modern-day caliphate of Imam Ali, Khamenei was the modern-day personification of Imam Ali, and Mousavi was Muawiyyah, while his supporters were the Umayyads. By utilizing these tropes, the state and Khamenei aimed to achieve two goals: first, to discredit the legitimacy of the protests and protestors, and second, to assert the legitimacy of both his position and that of the Islamic Republic and its leadership.

Both editorials and Friday sermons emphasized that the target of the protests was Ayatollah Khamenei and that the 'enmity and rejection of the Rahbar' was synonymous with the rejection of 'Islam and the twelfth Imam', the Mahdi. In his sermon to the pro-government supporters on 9th *Dey* rally, Ayatollah Alam-ul-Hoda alluded that the protestors and their leaders were now infidels. The Friday Imam stated that 'rejecting the authority of the Imam of the time' – i.e. Ayatollah Khamenei – meant 'rejecting the Imam Mahdi himself', while to the Iranian ulama, the 'principle of *vilayat-i faqih* is the same as the principle of Imamate, and opposition to this principle is opposition to the principle of Imamate' (Alam Al-Hoda 2009). The sermon intertwined the concept of *vilayat-i faqih* with that of the Mahdi. Since in Qom's mainstream religious thought, Khamenei as *vali-i faqih* is the representative of the Mahdi, then any opposition to him would be opposition to the twelfth Imam himself, and they would thus be characterized as infidels. Mousavi and his supporters were represented as such since they rejected and protested against Khamenei's acceptance of the election results. Therefore, Khamenei and his supporters were the new Self, while the internal Other – i.e. Mousavi and his supporters – were characterized as the Umayyads and infidels.

The Iranian discourse constructed an explicit image of the Green Movement and its leaders; they were not only the enemies of the Islamic Republic but also the enemies of Islam, its leader, and a representative of the infallible imams, Ayatollah Khamenei. Ayatollah Khamenei was depicted as the Imam Ali and Imam Hussein of our times, a Sayyid with a revered genealogy in what *Resalat* argued was 'from the pure lineage of [Fatema] Zahra', the daughter of the Prophet Mohammad *(Resalat* 2009). The internal Other was explicitly defined as seditionists, with the leaders Mousavi and Karoubi compared with Islamic figures such as the Umayyad caliphs, Mu'awiya and Yazid. The Iranian editorial and religious discourse attempted to inform the domestic audience that the comrades and companions of the Ayatollah Khamenei had now deviated from the path. Comparing the leaders of the opposition with the Prophet's companions Talha and Zubair, who had 'lost their way' and fought against Imam Ali in the battle of Sifin was one part of the repertoire the editorials used to make this point of a split in the Iranian Self, given the presence of a domestic Other. It was precisely this fragmentation and split in Iran that the Saudi discourse would highlight and discuss in their own discourse.

Saudi Reaction to Green Movement Protests

The immediate response from the Arab states of the Persian Gulf was one of cautious silence due to Iranian allegations of foreign meddling and the state's growing power, which might bring about retribution. The fear of similar protests spilling over in the region may also have led to a cautious silence. Within ten days the Arab states broke their silence, with the UAE foreign minister backing Iran's claims regarding external interference in Iran's elections, deeming it 'unacceptable' and fearing that it is of 'no interest for any country to be exposed to instability' (Hammond 2009). The Saudi official position was marked by silence. However, the Saudi media, especially the press, played a main role in framing the narrative and discourse in response to the Iranian elections. Since the media is carefully regulated and funded by the Saudi government, this discourse and narrative arguably conveyed the Saudi official position towards Iran and its protests. Also, since the Green Movement protests could inspire demonstrations in Saudi Arabia, the domestic discourse manufacturers remained silent so as not to encourage any domestic protests, particularly since six months earlier Saudi Arabia had seen Shi'i protests in al-Medina and the Eastern Province.

The Saudi editorials covered the Iranian election campaigns, drawing on themes such as instability, societal division, and corruption. The televised debates were described as demonstrating to the Iranian voter that the country was riddled with 'poverty, corruption, financial waste, [and the] falsification of certificates', where 'bread was more important than the bomb' in a 'state that dismisses the multi-ethnic and multi-sectarian fabric of society'. All this occurred while the 'government concentrate[d] on external matters', and it was thus accused of neglecting Iranian citizens while focusing on 'the greater and lesser Satan' and 'their allies Hezbollah, Hamas and Syria' *(al-Riyadh* 2009a) – all of which are issues of no concern to the predicaments of the average Iranian citizen. Furthermore, branding the protests a 'revolution', the Saudi press described the scenes as reminiscent of former revolts, such as the anti-Shah, Islamic Revolution of 1979, and they even compared the

Green Movement protests to the 'Bolshevik and Arab revolutions' that concentrated 'their resources of huge oil reserves [to supporting] the world's free people' and aligning with 'external parties at the expense of their people' based on the 'foundations of Welayat al-Faqih' *(al-Riyadh* 2009a*)*. The mention of 'external parties' was a reference to Iranian support for groups such as Hezbollah and Hamas.

The rifts between the Iranian political camps were represented as reflecting the fragmentation and demise of the three-decade Iranian revolutionary system. The protests were framed as a 'conflict' between Rafsanjani and Khamenei and as underlining the 'friction between the pillars of the Iranian revolution [which is a] cry of pain heard all over the world'. Ahmadinejad's allegations regarding Rafsanjani's corruption were a 'green light' for 'an open bone-breaking battle between the two pillars of the Islamic Republic' *(Asharq-Al-Awsat* 2009a*)*. I contend that the Saudi press tried to show that Iran was imploding internally, where the clerical 'members of the same *hawza* and sect ... regardless of their age' had sought to bring their 'conflict to the fore' because of the actions of the 'children of the revolution' *(al-Riyadh* 2009d*)*, i.e. the second generation. Therefore, the image generated by the Saudi discourse was of an obsolete regime experiencing internal strife that could result in the demise of the state.

As the protests gained momentum, various tropes were used in the Saudi press to emphasize instability. Revelling in Iran's domestic turbulence, the 'semi-official' outlet *Asharq Al-Awsat* argued that the protests were the fruits of Ahmadinejad's 'interventions' in the Arab states, as if karma had now hit Iran. The Iranian president was accused of 'intervening in Lebanon and dividing it into groups', while adopting a hegemonic position by 'putting his hand on Iraq' whose politicians were 'in search of reconciliation [while claiming] to aid the Palestinian cause'. Instead, they were adding to their plight by 'dividing people under occupation', a reference to the Hamas–Fateh strife alongside meddling in the Gulf and Yemen *(Asharq-Al-Awsat* 2009b*)*.

The foreign meddling narrative was also an aspect covered in the Saudi press. Perhaps out of fear of the protests spilling across to neighbouring states, Saudi editorials discussed this theme by employing two strategies: they adopted the Iranian discourse of Western intervention, while also criticizing Iran for its own intervention in the region. The Saudi editorial discourse constructed Western intervention in Iranian affairs along the lines of Western hegemony and fear of an Islamic country rising to prominence. *Al-Riyadh* (2009b) argued that Western interest in the 'Iranian issue, its elections, and reactions [could be] due to its pursuit of a nuclear weapon by an Islamic religious institution'. Furthermore, in an attempt to reflect Saudi pragmatism and non-interference in Iranian affairs, the editorials argued that 'it is not in the interest of neighbouring countries ... for events to go down a dangerous path', i.e. towards a revolution, not because 'Iran does not pose a threat' but because 'Iranian clashes would burn an entire ocean, [thus] the treatment of the crisis must come from the heart of Iran, not from the outside' *(al-Riyadh* 2009b*)*. As for the claiming interference in Arab affairs, the Saudi press framed

Iran as a hegemonic state, seeking to 'establish itself as a trustee and leader of the Islamic world'. To achieve this, it used the cases of Lebanon, Palestine, and Iranian support for the Houthis. These cases were particularly topical as the period from June to August 2009 had witnessed heated events between Saudi Arabia and Iran across the Middle East, such as in Lebanon. The Saudi press criticized Iran for its intervention in the region. Quoting the former president of Egypt, Hosni Mubarak, while Iran 'complain[s] of interventions from external forces in Iran ... Don't interfere with the home affairs of other Arab countries' *(al-Riyadh 2009c; Mubarak and Charlie Rose 2009)*. Therefore, Saudi Arabia constructed the Iranian protests as a product of its interference in Arab affairs, reflecting its neglect of its own people, and being out of sync with its society, given that a 'revolution that is no longer compatible with the state'*(al-Riyadh 2009b)*. These constructions and discourses on Iran would gain momentum as the region began to experience the unpredictable wave of protests later labelled the Arab Spring.

Protests in the Middle East: The Arab Spring

A year into Ahmadinejad's turbulent second term, the Middle East experienced a wave of protests similar to the Iranian Green Movement, but on a larger scale. As earlier mentioned, in December 2010 a Tunisian street vendor, Mohamed Bouazizi, self-immolated in protest at his harassment and the seizure of his goods by the local municipal officials. The repercussions were such that protests spread like wildfire throughout Tunisia, resulting in a regional domino effect. The fear of this contagion reaching neighbouring GCC states was perceived as a real possibility, while the uprisings did spread throughout North Africa, the Levant and the GCC, including Egypt, Libya, Yemen, Syria, Bahrain, and Saudi Arabia. The Arab Spring was likely not anticipated by either Iran or Saudi Arabia (Alsultan and Saeid 2016: 161). However, as Ehteshami (2013), remarks, it escalated the rivalry and cold war between the two states. For Iran, it was a chance to capitalize while for Saudi Arabia the protests were alarming as nearby pro-Western allies of the kingdom were falling one by one.

As I argue above, the protests and events of the so-called Arab Spring resulted in a rapid domino effect. Once the Tunisian protests gained momentum and the government began to fall and falter, protests erupted in other capitals in a similar manner. As a result, the discourse from Iran and Saudi Arabia discussing the events was intertwined: editorials, for example, dealt with multiple events in different Arab states concurrently. Therefore, to discuss Iranian and Saudi rivalry, including how they viewed the events and constructed and framed the discourses and narratives in relation to each other, I will look at each country separately, over a timeline covering the period from December 2010 to June 2013. I will cover the dynamics of Iran and Saudi rivalry and Othering from the protests in Tunisia up to the fall of the Morsi government in Egypt.

Islamic Awakening or Hunger Protests?

The Saudi and Iranian responses to protests in Tunisia did not come until a week into the demonstrations. The press in both states began to cover the events on their international page through news agencies such as the Associated Press (Ebel 2011). Editorials in national newspapers in both countries covered mostly local and regional events. In Iran, the Tunisian protests coincided with the anniversary of the bloody clashes involving the Green Movement, the Ashura protests of 26 December 2009, and the pro-government rallies that followed *(Kayhan* 2009; *Resalat* 2009). Saudi outlets discussed regional events such as the Iranian foreign minister's visit to Saudi Arabia, Saudi Arabia's role in Arab affairs, and a discussion on the GCC security treaty *(al-Riyadh* 2010b; *Asharq-Al-Awsat* 2010a, 2010b). In summary, the newspapers in both states focused on daily issues related to domestic and foreign policy, while remaining effectively silent on the events in Tunisia.

As the clashes in Tunisia became more violent, the Saudi discourse discussed issues of political participation and democracy, initially without mentioning Tunisia. The Saudi daily, *al-Riyadh* (2010a), questioned if 'democracy was suitable for the Arabs', arguing that 'Arab history has not witnessed a system of power sharing' *(al-Riyadh* 2010a). However, once the protests reached the capital, *Asharq Al-Awsat* broke its silence and dedicated an editorial to discussing the events in Tunisia, characterizing the events as a 'political problem . . . a lack of confidence in its government and a loss of credibility' *(Asharq-Al-Awsat* 2010c). Ironically, the solution, according to the Saudi editorial, was for the 'authorities to satisfy people politically through political participation [since it is] not an oil country that can spray money on people to silence them' *(Asharq-Al-Awsat* 2010c). Therefore, the Saudi press's framing was two-tiered. First, as concerns the international community, there was no questioning of the legitimacy of and confidence in the Saudi state. Second, in terms of its domestic audience, the explicit message was that if a state is not resource-rich, its people have the right to protest for their political entitlements because of their poverty. Another coded message was that since Saudi Arabia provided for its people and subsidized their basic needs, there was no reason to protest or ask for any political participation.

By the second week of January 2011, the protests had spread across the border to Algeria, paving the way for the Saudi press to refer to the events as 'fall[-ing] dominoes', a 'virus of protests and chaos' and 'a storm following a long calm' *(Asharq-Al-Awsat* 2011b). However, the argument was maintained that the grievances were not political. These were 'uprisings of sugar, oil, and unemployment' contended Abdulrahman Al-Rashed, the former editor-in-chief of the London-based newspaper *Asharq Al-Awsat (Asharq-Al-Awsat* 2011b). The locally published discourse promulgated a similar narrative. 'Poverty' led to the protests because of the 'mismanagement of state funds', which thereby resulted in the corruption that had caused unemployment as the newspaper *al-Riyadh* argued *(al-Riyadh* 2011b). The argument went further with an attempt to absolve the kingdom of its shortcomings, while also criticizing the state, albeit framed as constructive criticism. By comparing Saudi Arabia to the protest-ridden states, the article 'admit[ted] that in the kingdom we have a problem, and the solutions are slow [to implement, and] we can no longer stay silent'. However, the argument was maintained that the motives behind the protests in Tunisia were not political or due to a 'communist party, or a terrorist organization, but rather by necessity' *(al-Riyadh* 2011b*)*. The significance of the self-criticism was to subtly convey that there were problems in the kingdom, but that people were not against the monarchy, and therefore their grievances were not political but due to life pressures. Here, the Saudi discourse represented the Self as stable and apolitical with no ideological agenda except support for the Al Saud monarchy, thereby distancing the Saudi Self from other protests and Arab currents, such as those that had emerged in Tunisia.

On 15 January 2011, the Tunisian president, Zine El Abidine Ben Ali, fled for Saudi Arabia, which was seen as due to the revolution. The official Saudi discourse remained silent again, and although the press discussed Ben Ali's escape, no mention was made of his arrival in the kingdom. On the other hand, the official Iranian discourse publicized its first reaction to the revolution. The Iranian foreign-ministry spokesman, Ramin Mehmanparast, stressed that the 'developments in Tunisia are an internal issue' (Mehmanparast 2011a). It is important to note that the Muslim Brotherhood of Tunisia – and especially Rachid al-Ghannouchi – has had strong relations with Iran since 1979. Consequently, their ascension to power in Tunisia would have been of the utmost interest for Iran, and any official support for the Islamic group at this point could have worked against any Tunisian pro-Iran groups, so Tehran would be seen as meddling in Arab affairs once again. The meddling narrative could have been exploited by the GCC states, and by Saudi Arabia in particular, given the latest rivalry over the Lebanese elections. The Iranian foreign ministry sent out a neutral message expressing the 'hope that leaders of the intellectual and political currents ... will prevail ... in the interests of the Tunisian people' (Mehmanparast 2011a).

Another interesting aspect was Iran's characterization of the Arab protests. Ben Ali's fall gave rise to three distinct frames. First, the Tunisian revolution and the departure of Ben Ali resembled that of the Shah's fall and departure in 1978 – and for the exact same reasons, namely, 'freedom, work and bread' *(Resalat* 2011*)*. Second, Ben Ali was subservient to Western colonialists, with the alleged proof being he sought 'asylum in Saudi Arabia'. Third, the protests that brought down the Tunisian dictatorship were similar to the Iranian Green Movement protests of 2009 *(Kayhan* 2011c*)*. To the newspaper *Kayhan* (2011a), Ben Ali was another 'Mohammad Khatami who was supported by the reactionary Saudi regime under the pretext of a Dialogue of Civilisations [while he] provided political and media support to counter-revolutionary groups, seditionists, and rioters during the sedition riots of [2009] a month before the elections'*(Kayhan* 2011b*)*. Defining the protests as opposing the 'anti-Islamic policies' of a 'dictatorial government', the Iranian press discourse framed the fall of Ben Ali as a 'domino effect' with anti-Islamic rulers experiencing 'an intifada' *(Kayhan* 2011b*)*. Painting an image of instability, the right-wing editorials, such as *Kayhan*, labelled Arab leaders in countries such as Egypt, Jordan, Yemen, Saudi Arabia and Libya as 'anxious'. The newspaper *Kayhan* constructed the leaderships of these countries as weak by defining them as 'lacking religious democracy' while embracing a 'dictatorial style [of rule that is] politically dependent on foreign countries', with their 'economies dependent on oil ... financially' *(Kayhan* 2011b*)*. On the other hand, the solution was to emulate a regional model that 'should be studied by nations and countries', i.e. the Islamic Republic. While the Saudi and Egyptian Other was defined as unstable and weak with an Islamic façade, revolutionary Iran was an 'efficient and indigenous model of government' built on 'Islamic standards' *(Kayhan* 2011b*)*. The Iranian discourse on the Arab protests framed the Self as a model that the future political parties should emulate after the fall of the current Arab leaderships.

The days that followed in Iran witnessed a deluge of commentary from a vocal clergy and press. The Arab protests not only coincided with the one-year anniversary of the 9 *Dey* protests, that is the day Ben Ali's government fell, but also with the anniversary of the martyrdom of Navvab Safavi, the leader of the Fadā'iyān-i Islam group executed by the Shah in 1956.[4] This allowed the ulama to use the date to associate the protests with Iran's 'history of the revolution' (Noori-Hamadani 2011). Referring to the protests as an 'awakening' *(bīdārī)*, Ayatollah Noori Hamadani coined a phrase that Iran would employ in every subsequent discourse, genre, and narrative construction discussing the events of the Arab Spring (Noori-Hamadani 2011), arguing that 'the awakening of the deprived people of the world and the recent developments ... in Tunisia [are attributable to] the blessings of the Islamic Revolution' (Noori-Hamadani 2011), a mantra that would later be disseminated by Khamenei all the way down the pyramid of Iranian power and across all discursive genres. In practical terms, the Iranian domestic discourse was beginning to frame the Arab protests as rooted in Iran's revolutionary struggles since the anti-Shah movement of the 1950s up to the present. The Iranian domestic discourse represented the Iranian Self as the model revolution and its Islamic leadership as one for the region to emulate.

In contrast to the foreign ministry's neutral and non-interventionist position on the Tunisian protests and Ben Ali's flight, Ahmadinejad wove together a narrative of foreign interference along with Iran's *'Islam-i Nāb-i Mohammadi'*. Speaking at a rally in the city of Yazd, the president warned the 'United States, the Zionists and some European countries not to interfere in the internal affairs of Lebanon and Tunisia and to let the nations of these two countries decide for themselves' (Ahmadinejad 2011b). Ahmadinejad defined the protests as a 'rise against a Western-affiliated dictator' and stated that the protests had an Islamic identity, claiming that the Tunisians employed 'Islamic and humane slogans, a monotheistic view, and justice'. The Iranian president attempted to frame the Tunisian uprising as following an Iranian model since 'they seek justice and dignity and humanity [and the] Tunisian people are seeking to establish relations and the rules of pure Mohammedan Islam' (Ahmadinejad 2011b). Reminiscent of Khomeini's revolutionary discourse, where the mantra of the revolution was of the

---

4. For a discussion on Navan Safavi see Rahnema, A., (2014: 307); Alavi, S.A. (2019).

plight of the oppressed against the oppressor and fighting tyranny, Ahmadinejad's narrative framed Iran as a model for the Islamic world. Tunisia had chosen to follow this model, where the 'eyes of humanity are on Iran' and its development 'means raising the banner of monotheism and suppressing the Pharaohs', thereby raising morale by 'blowing the spirit of hope in the oppressed and deprived nations of the world' (Ahmadinejad 2011b). It would be a matter of weeks before the Iranian-labelled 'Egyptian Pharaoh', Hosni Mubarak, would step down after weeks of clashes and protests, thus opening a new chapter in Iranian–Saudi rivalry and the discursive construction of the Self and Other.

Turbulence in Egypt, the Heart of the Arab World

Ten days after Ben Ali's departure to Saudi Arabia, protests spread to the centre of Cairo. The youth behind the 25 January protests forced Mubarak to step down after a three-decade reign on 11 February 2011. The Arab world now witnessed the fall of two strong leaders with calls for a more democratic system through transparent parliamentary elections (Dodge 2012: 5). Although Egypt's official opposition parties, such as the Muslim Brotherhood, were initially absent from the protests, they later managed to capitalize on the revolution and amass a large share of the political presence on the streets. Other parties, such as the Salafists and Coptic church, who were initially opposed to the protests, also participated in the democratic process (Stein 2012: 23-24). The elections held from November 2011 to January 2012 resulted in 70 per cent of the parliamentary seats being shared between the Muslim Brotherhood and Salafists (Palmer 2018: 140). In 2012, the Muslim Brotherhood candidate, Mohammad Morsi, would be elected president of Egypt.

The pro-democracy and anti-regime waves were of great concern to both Iran and Saudi Arabia. While the Tunisian protests were less vital to the interests of both the Islamic Republic and Kingdom of Saudi Arabia, the turbulence in Egypt was of real significance. As Gause (2014) argues, the Arab Spring questioned the legitimacy of rule in the Middle East (Gause III 2014: 14-15). The combination of democracy and Islamist politics unsettled the Saudi monarchy. Egypt was one of the main Arab allies, and its government's removal was a debacle for Saudi Arabia. The rise of an Islamist power in Egypt posed a threat to Saudi Arabia's leadership of the Islamic world in general and the Sunni Islamic world in particular (Terrill 2011: 9). In addition, with the Muslim Brotherhood at the helm of Arab leadership, there was 'an alternative form of Sunni Islamist politics to the Saudi monarchical model' (Gause III 2014: 14-15).

Since the Iranian revolution in 1979, Egypt had played a major role in countering Iranian regional expansion, including Egypt's position during the Iran–Iraq war, and towards the Iranian-backed groups such as Hamas, Islamic Jihad, and Hezbollah (Terrill 2011: 9). Furthermore, the Mubarak regime and Riyadh were allied with the US in terms of containing Iran's regional influence. The fall of Mubarak could have marked a shift in the regional balance of power in Tehran's favour (Rieger 2014). For Iran, the removal of Mubarak was viewed positively, and his removal sought to benefit from the reversal of the local pro-US status quo, while strengthening Egypt's regional allies (Chubin 2012). This would have allowed Iran to cement and build on the 'victories' of the 2006 and 2009 wars against Israel in Lebanon and Gaza respectively. Consequently, the removal of Mubarak and the rise of political Islamist parties was a major fear in Saudi Arabia, especially since this shift might magnify Iran's regional presence and influence at the expense of the kingdom.

Protests in Cairo: Saudi and Iranian Reactions

Saudi Arabia's reaction towards the political turbulence that hit the Middle East and Egypt, especially in late January and early February of 2011, can be defined as counter-revolutionary (Rieger 2014) with an attempt made to neutralize its effects domestically (Hiro 2019). Saudi Arabia's relentless support for Mubarak was sustained until the day he stepped down. Recuperating at his residence in Morocco, the Saudi monarch contacted both Obama and Mubarak, the former to stress that 'Egypt's stability … safety and security cannot be compromised' and the 'crisis cannot be justified under any excuse', while emphasizing that 'Egypt's gains and capabilities are an integral part of the Arab and Islamic nations' (al-Saud 2011b). In his call to Mubarak, the Saudi message of solidarity was clear. King Abdullah characterized the protests as 'meddling in the security and stability' of an Arab and Islamic nation, defining the revolution as instigated by 'those who infiltrated the people' under the pretext of 'freedom and expression' (al-Saud 2011a). To the Saudis, the Arab Spring was constructed and represented as foreign meddling in the affairs of Arab nations and as driven by an intention to sow discord and sedition.

After Mubarak stepped down on 11 February, Saudi Arabia became alarmed as an ally had fallen due to popular protests. The theme of foreign meddling and sedition was promulgated and given further legitimacy through religious discourse. In a Friday sermon in Riyadh on the day Mubarak stepped down, the kingdom's highest religious authority, the Grand Mufti Abdul Aziz bin Abdullah Al-Sheikh, stated that the Arab 'demonstrations have no real goal and no reality' and had been instigated and 'planned by the enemies of Islam'. These protests seek to 'strike the nation, divide its word, and divide [the] country', arguing that those who did not understand this were 'ignorant' (Al ash-Sheikh 2011b, 2011a). The Saudi ulama aimed to deter the youth from participating in protests, warning them that they have 'dire and bad consequences by shedding blood [and promoting] theft, rape, and living in fear, terror and delusion'(Al ash-Sheikh 2011b, 2011a). To the Saudi people the message was clear: protesting was a sin as it was a foreign plot to spread sedition and anarchy.

In Iran, an opposite atmosphere reigned, with an abundance of optimism in the air. Iranian discourses had already promulgated the supra-theme of an 'Islamic awakening', defining the protests as the 'fruits of the Khomeini revolution in 1979' (Noori-Hamadani 2011). However, this time the foreign meddling discourse argued that there was 'a US and Zionist attempt to stop the awakening of the

Islamic nations and the continuation of the Khomeini revolution' (Khamenei 2011a). Once the Mubarak presidency had fallen, Khamenei led Tehran's Friday prayers as the Egyptian revolution coincided with 22 Bahman, the anniversary of the Islamic Revolution, during which he seized the opportunity to identify the Arab Spring with the Iranian revolution: 'The cry of the Egyptian people today is the familiar cry of the Islamic Revolution'(Khamenei 2011a). In a veiled contrast to the Arab protests, Khamenei remarked that the 'victory of the Islamic Revolution [had] shattered the equations [of] tyrants and arrogant' powers that aimed to 'expand their interests in the strategic Middle East region for years' (Khamenei 2011a). The message to the Iranian people who had experienced the Green Revolution was that the Iranian revolution lived on as an 'attractive model', one that has caused an 'earthquake' in the Arab world.

On the other hand, to Iran's adversaries, the message communicated was that Egypt had returned to its Islamic roots since its people 'considered religious motives as one of the main factors of the revolution [and that] Westerners are very worried about the revelation of the Islamist motive for the uprising of the Egyptian people among the nations of the region', thus missing out the notion of the revolution as due to 'economic factor[s]' (Khamenei 2011a). The Supreme Leader represented the Egyptian uprising as a watershed event that had caused the 'US and Zionists panic'. Thus, he constructed a narrative of foreign intervention, alleging that the US and Israel were 'look[ing] for a way out of this situation', i.e. the protests, and had therefore started a campaign 'to deceive the [Egyptian] people' (Khamenei 2011a). To the Arab world, the Supreme Leader's sermon represented the Arab leaderships as 'servants [who] would not be rewarded by the Americans'(Khamenei 2011a). The theme of Western subservience was employed once again to construct an image of weak, subservient Arab leaderships that would be neglected and betrayed by the US, and this image was now backed up by their being toppled one by one. In addition, in referring to the role of the Egyptian ulama of al-Azhar and mentioning scholars like Sheikh Mohammad Abdu, Khamenei called on religious figures to 'play a historical role in the uprising' (Khamenei 2011a). The rise of al-Azhar and its religious scholars would have led to a Sunni political-Islamic collaboration that would pose a threat to Saudi Arabia's leadership of the Islamic world, especially if it were a leadership that was on friendly terms with Iran, such as the Muslim Brotherhood.

The Iranian representation of the Arab Spring as an Islamic awakening was a matter of great concern for Saudi Arabia. Even before the fall of Ben Ali and Mubarak, the Saudi press framed the involvement of the Muslim Brotherhood as reflecting sinister 'ambitions to takeover and change' the social structure of the state. These 'ambitions', according to the Saudi editorial, were rooted in the 'success of the Khomeini revolution' *(Asharq-Al-Awsat* 2010d*)*. Consequently, Saudi newspaper discourse constructed the protests as a negative extension and implicit reference to Khomeini's 'export of the revolution', the latter being a trope dominant in post-revolutionary discourse. To their domestic audience, Saudi discourse depicted the revolutions as 'chaotic' and potentially leading to 'multiple war fronts' that would spread across the whole region *(al-Riyadh* 2011f*)*. The reason for this chaos was a 'failure of republics' since monarchies in Egypt were replaced by 'dictatorships' and from there on, chaos ensued *(al-Riyadh* 2011f). With the fall of Mubarak, the Saudi domestic press implied that if the revolutions reached the kingdom, the latter would be replaced by a chaotic dictatorship, a construction also used to implicitly represent Al Saud as a symbol of and key to stability *(al-Riyadh* 2011f).

While there was no official Saudi reaction to the Iranian sermons and speeches concerning an Islamic awakening in the Arab world, the Saudi press discourse was mobilized to respond. Editorials referred to Khamenei's narrative of the Egyptian uprising as an 'extension to the Khomeini revolution', retorting that this was a set of 'fabrications that have no relationship to the events in the entire region' *(al-Riyadh* 2011d). The newspaper *al-Riyadh* emphasized the 'pure Arab character' of the revolutions and that the Arab Spring could not be related to Iran because of the 'repressed uproar' of the 2009 protestors, which the Saudi discourse alleged was suppressed by a 'Supreme Leader or Sultan', i.e. by Khamenei who 'does not endorse the will of a popular counter-revolution' in Iran *(al-Riyadh* 2011d). Furthermore, the reaction to the Iranian Islamic awakening discourse was to associate Iran and the Muslim Brotherhood with ignorance and terrorism. Iran was viewed as 'exploiting' the protests to 'import their model through weaponizing the people' of Egypt, with its 'history of moderate Islam', while politicizing it in the process. Saudi editorials also bolstered the image of Saudi leadership of the Islamic world and underscored its prestige. Khamenei's speech was understood by the Saudi media discourse as an attempt at bolstering Iran's position of Islamic leadership and its supposed role as the 'epicentre' of Islam *(al-Riyadh* 2011i). The response was to emphasize the 'purely Arab' nature of the protests; and although Arabs do not make up the majority of the Islamic world, 'it does not make [non-Arabs] its leaders', i.e. stating that Iran seeks to 'hijack the leadership and thought of [those] who guide the Islamic world politically and religiously', in reference to the Saudi leadership *(al-Riyadh* 2011i).

Cushioning the Blow: The Saudi Domestic Reaction to the Arab Protests

The wave of protests was fast approaching the Persian Gulf. In Saudi Arabia, activists began mobilizing. Its first signs were evident by 21 December 2010, some four days after the initial spark that led to Tunisia's demonstrations. Saudi activists gathered to plan a peaceful sit-in to demand employment, health care and education reforms as well as an end to corruption (Human Rights Watch 2011b). On 28 February 2011, protests in Jeddah resulted in the arrest of thirty to fifty demonstrators who had gathered to protest against the government's handling of the floods that saw ten deaths (AlSharif 2011). Gaining momentum, on 9 February a group of Saudi academics and activists formed the Islamic Umma Party *(Hizb al-Ummah al-Islamī)*. In a petition to the royal court asking for their party to be recognized, the group outlined their manifesto, in which they wished to: promote democracy, political participation, and elections; reform the judiciary; gain the right to free speech and peaceful protest; promote civil society; and implement

Islamic values in the kingdom's foreign policy. Most likely regarded as opposing the state and monarchy, seven of the signatories were arrested (Human Rights Watch 2011b).

By March, social media activists had also joined in. Protest movements such as the Free Youth Coalition ('*i 'tilāf al-shabāb al-ahrār*') (Khatib and Lust 2014: 311) began calling for political reform and to organize Friday protests known as the Day of Rage. As Lacroix (2014: 12) observes, online activists set up webpages that framed the protests using rhetoric related to Islamic conquests (Lacroix 2014). Citing the Battle of Hunayn, where the Prophet Mohammad fought the Hawazin tribe during the conquest of Mecca, the activists called for reform of the state. The monarchy was represented as the infidels of Mecca, and the Free Youth Coalition movement as intending to bring the kingdom back to Islam. It is no secret that the wave of protests alarmed the state and made the monarchy nervous. The state moved rapidly to appease the public and deter further dissent. On 22 February, the royal court announced an aid package worth $37 billion. To alleviate economic pressure and tackle unemployment, the funds targeted state employees, youth, and the poor. The resources aimed to increase salaries for all government employees by 15 per cent, offer interest-free loans for those seeking marriage or to assist first-time house buyers and builders, and start small businesses, in addition to providing funds for social initiatives and students studying abroad (Hiro 2019). However, all this did not stop protests from appearing on the streets of the kingdom. The protests had now come home.

Trouble Comes Home: Days of Rage in the GCC

The wave of protests spreading from North Africa inspired activists and opposition parties in the GCC to mobilize. On 14 February 2011, the Bahraini Shi'i party, Al-Wefaq, called for demonstrations in the capital city of Manama in what came to be known as the Pearl Roundabout protests. Demanding a reform of the laws, such as a constitutional monarchy, a fully elected government, and an end to sectarian discrimination, the protestors camped on the roundabout in defiance of government requests to evacuate. Clashes erupted and the security forces cleared the square, leaving four dead and several casualties. The dead would be labelled martyrs, and on 22 February their funerals were a public show of defiance under the banner of Martyrs Day, accompanied by slogans calling for regime change. As the numbers demonstrating were in the tens of thousands, the state allowed the people back to the square and released political prisoners, which raised the ceiling of public demands. On 3 March, the protestors called for the ousting of the prime minister, Khalifa bin Salman Al-Khalifa, Bahrain's longest serving prime minister (over four decades). Citing an 'external plot [based on] subversive designs' (Al-Jazeera 2011), on 13 March the King appealed to the GCC to invoke an article requesting the assistance of the Peninsula Security Shield forces. The next day, 1,200 Saudis, 600 Emiratis, and a small number of Kuwaitis and Qatari forces arrived in Bahrain. Declaring a three-month national emergency, the Bahraini monarch imposed extraordinary measures including a curfew, martial law, and a total ban on protests.

Parallel protests were underway in Saudi Arabia. In addition to limited protests in Riyadh and Jeddah, the Shi'a in the Eastern Province protested both for their own demands and in solidarity with their kin in Bahrain. The Shi'a protested in thousands, demanding the release of detainees who had been held without charge for the 1996 Khobar bombings. These protests gained momentum, and like their Bahraini kin, their calls for reform became more intense and included three petitions: a youth petition by journalists, and two others named Toward a State of Rights and Institutions, and a National Declaration for Reform. There were also calls for the democratization of the state with an elected parliament, a constitutional monarchy, and revision of the Basic Law of 1992, which recognized only Sunni Islam as the state's source of authority (Wehrey 2013).

By March, the protests had spread to Riyadh along with weekly demonstrations held at the ministry of the interior, demanding the release of detainees. A further stimulus package of $93 billion in state assistance and increased funding for the security and religious police was issued by the king, although it stopped short of any political-reform measures. Threats and warnings by the security services fell on deaf ears. By the second week of March, both Bahrain and Saudi Arabia were facing protests that were gaining momentum. The Bahraini protests were contagious, and they were now affecting the Eastern Province of Saudi Arabia. On 8 March, calls were made to abolish the Al-Khalifa Bahraini monarchy. This, along with the Friday prayer Day of Rage in the Saudi Shi'i towns of Qatif, Safwa, and Awamiyah, was an indicator of the 'contagion of democracy' (Hiro 2019: 251), thereby unnerving both monarchies. The Shi'i identity of the protests may have ultimately led to government claims of Iranian meddling. These claims of meddling in Saudi domestic affairs would become a major part of Saudi discourse on Iran, especially as the protests began to take off in Bahrain, and claims of meddling became a dominant trope across all Saudi discourse genres.

The Arab Spring Engulfs the GCC: the Battle for Bahrain

Discourse construction in the Bahraini protests in both Iranian and Saudi Arabian genres were two-phased. Before the GCC Peninsula Shield Forces (PSF) entered Bahrain and after, Saudi discourse framed the protests with Iran in mind, while Iran utilized the military intervention in Bahrain to construct Saudi Arabia as its Other. This was the first sign of explicit rivalry in the Arab Spring. In addition, the regional and international response to the Bahraini protests shaped the discourse construction and framing in Iran and Saudi Arabia. Through its secretary of state, Hillary Clinton, the US administration expressed 'deep concern' and urged restraint, while stressing that 'political and economic efforts' were needed to respond to people's demands (Clinton 2011b) with similar messages echoed by the White House a day later (Obama 2011). Regionally, there was a clear contrast in the official discourses from Iran and Saudi Arabia. The initial response came from Iran on the third day of the protests. In a line similar to the US calling on the

Bahraini government to 'exercise restraint', the Iranian foreign-ministry spokesman, Ramin Mehmanparast, defined the protests as 'bloody incidents' and the government's treatment as 'violent' in nature in response to the 'demands of the Bahraini people', calling for the 'fulfilment of a political process' and respect for the 'right of people to express their views' (Mehmanparast 2011b). The Saudi reaction was multi-tiered, shaping a discourse on all levels of a foreign intervention in GCC affairs, as well as a discourse of protection and the unity of Bahrain in the face of adversity. In an allusion to a foreign threat, Prince Nayef expressed Saudi support for Manama and offered protection from anything that affected the 'security, stability and national unity' of Bahrain (al-Saud 2011c). The Saudi monarch went a step further and 'confirmed the readiness of the Saudi forces to support Bahrain's security and stability' *(Elaph* 2011a). A more explicit response came from an 'unnamed government official' via a Saudi government statement. The message was explicit and clear: 'Saudi Arabia is closely following the situation in Bahrain', while the kingdom 'absolutely rejects foreign interference in the affairs of Bahrain', noting that Saudi Arabia stood by Bahrain 'with all its capabilities' *(Elaph* 2011b). The news outlet *Elaph* (21 February 2011) claimed that alleged Gulf sources had stated that Saudi Arabia had two brigades 'on alert in the city of Dammam, about half an hour away from Manama' *(Elaph* 2011b). It was clear that the Saudis were deeply concerned regarding the threat the Bahraini protests posed to both itself as well as to Saudi Arabia. The official discourse on the protests was securitized and framed in terms of regime instability, thereby posing an existential threat to their survival and a foreign threat that should be eliminated at any cost.

The Saudi press was silent on the protests in the country and its domestic problems. Rather – and following the securitization framing – the Saudi press represented the Bahrain protests as threatening chaos, stressing that without national security the region would be 'without stability and comprehensive development' *(al-Riyadh* 2011k). By concentrating on the shortcomings of the other Arab states, such as Egypt and Tunisia, the Saudi discourse portrayed itself as an island of peace while the 'upheavals ... in the Arab world' were due to 'the accumulation of problems and neglect of the [Arab] governments' *(al-Riyadh* 2011k); in other words, the Saudi monarchy never neglected its people or its duties. With regard to Bahrain, on the other hand, the Bahrainis were defined as a society that 'is not spoiled, [with] poverty-stricken villages' prevalent *(al-Riyadh* 2011k). Thus, their aid and security was a responsibility of the 'rich countries of the GCC' to 'deter any foreign intervention that seek[s] to take advantage' of Bahrain's economic conditions. From the early days of the Bahraini demonstrations, the Saudi discourse framed the protests as an issue for domestic and GCC collective security, while a deterioration in Bahrain's security would mean that 'the entire Gulf region will suffer testing consequences' *(al-Riyadh* 2011k).

The Iranian press discourse discussed the Bahraini protests through the supra-discourse of an Islamic awakening. Unlike the government in the first days of the protests, the editorial press discussed Saudi Arabia and its regional position. Framing Riyadh's position as in fear, Saudi Arabia was represented as a 'trembling' state, one 'awaiting a wave of justice, anti-arrogance, and Islamism to cross its borders' *(Kayhan* 2011a*)*. To its readership, the press represented Saudi Arabia as a monarchy that was nearing its end, and it stated that 'amazing things will happen both within the Saudi government and in society'. Furthermore, the 'fall of Bahrain' and the rise of 'those who lived all their lives to take revenge on the US' would see the 'whole military geography of the region collapse'. Alluding to the US 5th Fleet stationed in Bahrain, Iranian discourse projected the end of the US regional presence and the Saudi monarchy, implying the rise of Iran using a veiled reference to the Shi'i majority taking over in Bahrain. To Iran, the 'collapse of the US pillars' in the region was imminent, while the coming Islamic awakening was a continuation of Khomeini's 1979 Revolution *(Kayhan* 2011a*)*.

By the first week of March, the events in Bahrain were starting to take a more sectarian turn. On 2 March, there were protests involving secondary school students (Howard and Hussain 2013). The next day, there were clashes in different areas, such as in Hamad town; confrontations erupted between naturalized Bahrainis of Syrian origin and indigenous Bahraini Shi'a, marking the first sectarian clash since the demonstrations had begun in February *(Howard and Hussain 2013)*. Similar protests continued with demands for an end to granting citizenship to Sunnis from other countries alongside clashes between parents of pupils in front of their schools (Howard and Hussain 2013). In Saudi Arabia, protests emerged in the Eastern Province towns of Qatif and Awamiyah; Saudi and Bahraini protestors began planning a 'Day of Rage' for 11 March.

GCC meetings were held in Saudi Arabia and statements were made to the domestic, regional, and international community. Speaking from Mecca, the Saudi foreign minister, Saud al-Faisal, laid out clearly the kingdom's position and view of the protests. Rejecting US calls for tolerance and the right to protest, al-Faisal condemned in clear terms US 'foreign interference in [Saudi] internal affairs', stressing that 'the principle of dialogue … is the best way to address the issues facing society' and promulgating the Saudi fatwa that deemed protests as 'forbidden since they violate the Koran and the way of the Prophet'[5], stressing that, 'We will cut off any finger that comes near the kingdom' (al-Saud 2011d). In the first official Saudi reference to any Iranian interference, al-Faisal claimed that the Saudi state 'will not tolerate any interference in our internal affairs by any party' and that if confirmed, the 'kingdom will deal with them decisively'. The Saudi official view of Iran is that it should 'deal with the demonstrations in its own country [since] the kingdom does not have demonstrations like those in Iran' (al-Saud 2011d). The Saudi discourse constructed the image of protests as non-Islamic acts, thereby framing those protesting and their supporters, including Iran, as deviating from the teachings of Islam. Moreover, Iran was constructed as a country in turmoil and chaos since it had experienced protests and demonstrations. This was perceived as reflecting a disgruntled society, as opposed to Saudi Arabia, which was represented as socially quiescent, while any internal turbulence was artificially instigated through foreign intervention and encouragement.

---

5. In addition to Bin Baz's fatwa of 1992, in 2011 the the Council of Senior Scholars in Saudi Arabia issued a statement on 6 March, 2011 prohibiting protests.

On 10 March 2011, the GCC states announced a Marshall Plan-style pledge of $20 billion to the governments of Bahrain and Oman in support of their development, with a statement implicitly alluding to Iran's interference in Bahrain's internal affairs by supporting the opposition:

> The Ministerial Council (foreign ministers) of the Gulf Cooperation Council (GCC) today confirmed that its countries and peoples categorically reject any foreign attempt to intervene in their internal affairs, announcing that it would instead face with firmness and decisiveness whoever tries to tamper with their security and interests or spread the seeds of rift and sedition among their peoples.
>
> (*al-Jazirah* 2011; GCC 2011)

On 13 March, the Bahraini monarch formally requested the support of the PSF to help quell the protests and restore public order (NY Times 2011b). It was this watershed moment that shifted the discourse production in Saudi Arabia and Iran on their mutual Others.

The general representation of Iranian–Saudi rivalry, i.e. its discourse in the context of Bahrain, arguably drew on narratives of hegemony, Western double standards, and sectarianism. However, if we take a deeper look at the discourse construction on Bahrain, an evolution in both Iranian and Saudi discourse over the course of events is visible, that is to say, as events in Bahrain unfolded and elites reacted, the main themes were constructed and the press then fleshed out the narratives through the employment of specific metaphors and imagery. To illustrate this, in the case of Bahrain, Saudi discourse first began with official comments on foreign intervention in Bahrain's domestic affairs and GCC military involvement, especially regarding Saudi Arabia's protection of its neighbour. As the protests gained momentum and the international community reacted, a second shift took place resulting in a discourse laying blame on a foreign entity – namely Iran – alongside the Saudi foreign minister's warning to the international community not to interfere in Gulf domestic affairs, while underlining Iranian expansion, chaos, and hegemonic ambitions. The third shift came after the PSF entered Bahrain. This was evident from the response shown by the international community, most notably the US, where the secretary of state, Hillary Clinton, cautioned the GCC states against using force (Clinton 2011a). Since Riyadh did not want to directly antagonize Iran, the main role of the discourse construction was left to the Saudi press, while the state attempted to respond to Iranian reactions to and comments on Bahrain.

As for Iran, the discourse on Bahrain also involved themes encompassing Western double standards, hegemony and expansion, democracy and the Islamic awakening, sectarian rivalry, and a war on Shi'ism, besides human rights violations. However, it is interesting to note that the discourse also developed as a reaction to Iranian domestic events. On 14 February 2011, the Green Movement called for a Day of Rage in solidarity with the Arab Spring movements. The Iranian state discourse was silent, focusing instead on replying to the Saudi discourse in response to the uprisings that had already begun in the kingdom. The incidents in Iran resulted in arrests and what the UN termed 'human rights issues' (Human Rights Council 2011). By 14 March, i.e. the day the PSF entered Bahrain, the United Nations Human Rights Council held Iran accountable for human rights abuses (Human Rights Council 2011). I argue that it is this event that triggered the Iranian discourse towards Bahrain which led to Iran's representation of Saudi Arabia's involvement becoming more potent. This, along with the GCC accusation of Iranian interference, formed the foundation for Iran's discourse on Saudi Arabia. However, the press took a leading role in forming explicit representations of Saudi Arabia that employed tropes, metaphors, and imagery, all of which echoed the post-revolutionary era.

Saudi Themes and Tropes on Bahrain's Protests

As discussed above, Saudi opinions on the protests in Bahrain and, to a lesser extent, domestic demonstrations, highlighted foreign interference in the domestic affairs of the GCC states in general and in Bahrain in particular. Saud al-Faisal's remark arguing that the Riyadh would cut off 'the finger that is laid on the kingdom' (al-Saud 2011d). served more than one purpose. The first was a response to the US, and the second a reaction to Iran's 'Islamic awakening' discourse. In the latter context, the Saudi foreign minister's comment was a reply to Iran's posturing and projection of regional and Islamic leadership, adding to the fears that the kingdom might end up on a path similar to that of Egypt and Tunisia. Although the Saudi ulama released a fatwa deeming any protests as impermissible as they were in effect 'acts of sedition', protests in Saudi Arabia nevertheless took place. Therefore, like Iran, it was left mainly up to the media to shape the discourses and narratives on the protests. These included three main themes, namely Iranian hegemony and expansion, sectarian rivalry, and Western hypocrisy and double standards.

Iranian Hegemony and Expansion   Even though the Saudi press defined the protests as an inalienable right of Bahrainis to express themselves, admitting to 'poverty' in Bahrain 'may require an immediate solution' as it could result in 'seeking religious, ethnic, political and sectarian solutions' *(al-Riyadh* 2011k). The editorials warned that such solutions would lead to instability and the 'fulfilment of Iran's ambitions' as the protests would spread and the GCC would 'undergo difficult outcomes' that would 'serve Iranian interests' *(al-Riyadh* 2011k)). Moreover, the theme of hegemony and expansion was made more potent and highlighted as editorials evoked the 'Shi'i crescent' narrative. As the GCC meeting on 13 March discussed the protests in Bahrain (and Oman), the Saudi press echoed the narrative on foreign interference by employing sectarian tropes claiming Iranian 'fingerprints with the Houthis in Yemen, destabilizing Egypt, then the infatuation that the Arab protests are an echo of Khomeini's revolution' *(al-Riyadh* 2011c)). The Saudi press represented the protests in Bahrain as an Iranian ploy to sideline the 'Arab identity of the protests' and cause 'sedition in the social fabric of society' *(al-Riyadh* 2011j); *Asharq-Al-Awsat* 2011c). The sedition narrative was also extended to reference the

Western powers, where they were accused of pursuing destabilizing motives through 'creative chaos' *(al-Riyadh* 2011h) and their 'hatred towards us [Arabs]', and the 'Christian crusades ... and colonization' that saw the West 'looting our resources and starting wars' in the Middle East *(al-Riyadh* 2011g).

The trope of Persian ambition became more potent as the reactions from Iran gained momentum, resulting in a GCC–Iranian clash on the diplomatic stage. In March 2011 both Kuwait and Bahrain accused Iran of terrorism after Kuwait arrested a 'spying cell', accusing Iran of planning domestic attacks (CNN 2011). This fortified the Saudi representation of 'Iranian hegemony and Persian ambitions' in the Persian Gulf. The Saudi press used the terrorism accusation and employed the trope of Persian Empire revivalism to highlight issues of contention between the GCC and Iran, including the contested 'three Islands', claiming that the 'GCC is Iran's first and foremost target' as it sought to 'take over territory starting with the three UAE Islands and also Bahrain' through 'spy operations and their Hezbollah proxies' in Kuwait. This equated Iran's actions to those of Saddam, a similar comparison to one Ahmadinejad had made a little earlier when describing PSF operations in Bahrain (Ahmadinejad 2011a; *al-Riyadh* 2011e).

Saudi editorial representations of Iran also painted an image of Iran as a 'failed state' with a 'false image of grandeur' *(al-Riyadh* 2011e). This was matched by the claim that Iran highlighted issues in the GCC – particularly regarding Saudi Arabia and Bahrain – as a way of 'escaping forward' from its own 'domestic troubles' and the reality of a 'failed unstable Iranian state' *(Asharq-Al-Awsat* 2011c; *al-Riyadh* 2011a). By exporting its problems abroad, the Saudi discourse suggested that Iran distracted the attention of its people and employed 'propaganda methods to distort the image of Saudi Arabia'. In turn, I argue, a manoeuvre occurred whereby the Saudi discourse on Iran also formed a strategy to distract from its own domestic problems by constructing Iran as its Other. Both Iran and Saudi Arabia constructed and demonized the external Other to distract from internal tensions.

Sectarian Rivalry   There is an overlap between the discourse on hegemony and expansionism and sectarian discourse. However, in the Saudi discourse, sectarian tropes were employed not only to highlight Iranian hegemonic ambitions, but also to construct the image of a discriminatory Iran as opposed to Saudi Arabia as a state that viewed all nations as equals. According to the Saudi press, Iran's defence of the Shia of Bahrain, in light of the foreign minister's comments that '[Iran] will not remain indifferent ... to the crisis in Bahrain' *(IRNA* and Salehi 2011) was construed as a 'ploy by Iran [to use] a method of divide and conquer' *(al-Riyadh* 2011j). The Iranian position on the Shi'a of Bahrain was represented as an Iranian fear from 'social coexistence' between Bahraini ethnicities and sects, as this would serve as a 'template of Arab–Islamic [coexistence] that threatens Iran's [seditious] modus operandi'. Therefore, *al-Riyadh* argued that 'Iran exported its revolution and invested all its wealth' to plan for sectarian sedition. Furthermore, Iran's sectarianism was depicted as a 'double standard', accusing the country of 'oppressing its minorities ... while defending the rights of the [Gulf] Shi'i minorities that identify with their natural Arab identity before a religious one', criticizing Iran for 'not allowing Sunnis to build mosques; nor do the mullahs allow them to practice freely through fatwas' (*al-Riyadh* 2011l). Therefore, the Saudi editorials represented Iran's calls for an Islamic awakening as hypocrisy while constructing an image of a seditionist state seeking to divide the GCC and Arab world along sectarian lines, thus calling Iran's legitimacy and leadership into question. This was complicated further as the Arab Shi'a protesting in Bahrain and Saudi Arabia were represented as 'Iranian pawns' being used to 'spread sedition [and fulfil] expansionist ambitions' (*al-Riyadh* 2011l, 2011c). The Saudi discourse attempted to redefine the Bahraini protests as a 'silencing of the Sunni Bahraini population' as it is not just the Shi'a who were the inhabitants of Bahrain. This was a response to earlier comments made by the Iranian foreign minister, Salehi, alleging sectarian persecution in Bahrain. The Saudi response to the purported Saudi cleansing of Shi'a in Bahrain was used to highlight 'Iran's sectarian nature', versus a more responsible Saudi Arabia that was in Bahrain 'to stop the protests slipping into a sectarian civil war ... and to send a strong message' to Iran that Saudi Arabia is responsible for the GCC and is the protector of the Sunni faith (*al-Riyadh* 2011l).

Western Hypocrisy and Double Standards

The Saudi and GCC reactions to the protests in Bahrain were criticized by the Western governments, the UN, and the international community. Human rights agencies also criticized the clashes in Bahrain (Human Rights Watch 2011a; Amnesty International 2011). As a result, the response in the official Saudi discourse used veiled allusions to Western intervention in GCC domestic affairs. The state-sponsored press, however, presented a more structured response to the Western positions, particularly in relation to the US and EU. Saudi editorials represented the US and EU positions as double standards of sorts. They highlighted their silence on 'crimes' committed by Western governments, such as the United States. The narrative of Western hypocrisy was promulgated just as the GCC meetings and clashes in Bahrain gathered pace. The positions of the US and EU were represented as 'hysterical' while their encouragement of Arab movements became a conspiracy fomented by 'secret intelligence services', with the 'US congress [and] US security apparatus targeting any Muslim under the guise of Islamic terrorism ... spying and questioning any Muslim student, visitor, or diplomat that mentions bin Laden or Al-Qaeda' (*al-Riyadh* 2011g). As for Europe, the French authorities were criticized for their treatment of 'Maghreb Arab soldiers' in Vietnam, with the British giving 'refuge to seditionist imams [while] collaborating with terrorist organizations ... to utilize them as weapons of pressure against their countries of origin' (*al-Riyadh* 2011g), in an implicit reference to Saudi opposition leaders resident in the UK.

The hypocrisy trope was also used with regard to US positions on Iran. The US secretary of defence, Robert Gates, after visiting the GCC on 12 March 2011 made a statement encouraging reform to ensure a quick end to the protests because 'there is clear evidence that ... the Iranians are looking for ways to exploit it and create problems' in Bahrain (NY Times 2011a). These US calls for reform were criticized in the Saudi press, arguing that US officials should have criticized Iran rather than Bahrain. The US position on GCC reform was cast as hypocritical and naïve, asking 'if the US is aware of what is happening on the ground', questioning 'US effectiveness' while going so far as to claim that the country was 'weak, specifically towards Iran that has an oppressed minority' *(Asharq-Al-Awsat* 2011a). Therefore, Saudi discourse on US double standards gave rise to an image of US naivety, hypocrisy, weakness, and silence towards 'belligerent states' in reference to Iran, and vocal against 'benevolent states' like Saudi Arabia.

Similarly, the US criticism of Hillary Clinton's PSF mission to Bahrain was also characterized as reflecting Western double standards and comparing them to Iranian narratives on Bahrain. In an article in *Asharq Al-Awsat*, the editor-in-chief contrasted Clinton's remarks on Saudi troops in Bahrain to those of her Iranian counterpart, Salehi. In an implicit allusion to US hypocrisy and collaboration with Iran against Saudi Arabia, the editorial argued that this 'statement made by the secretary of state seems to have come from the Iranian foreign minister', alleging that 'either the secretary is ignorant or seeks to score public opinion points' *(Asharq-Al-Awsat* 2011a), thereby, framing Saudi Arabia as a target for US personal interests and highlighting American naivety regarding events in the Middle Eastern region.

Iranian Themes and Tropes on the Bahrain Protests

The representation of Saudi Arabia in Iranian discourse during the protests in Bahrain followed on from the initial Iranian speeches made by Khamenei, the latter hinting that the region was undergoing an Islamic awakening, with Iran as its role model and the primordial seed of the movement stemming from Khomeini's 1979 Islamic Revolution. As events in Bahrain unfolded, the discourse and its main themes were already set in motion across all genres, i.e. media, political, and religious discourses. The difference in framing Saudi Arabia with regard to Bahrain was influenced by the timing of the events. Furthermore, the response to the Bahrain revolution was multi-staged. The initial reaction came from Iranian officials as the protests gained momentum. The second stage of discourse production emerged during the GCC meetings and the PSF's entry into Bahrain, while the third stage was in reaction to the international discourse on Iran. These included discourses emanating from Saudi Arabia, the GCC, in addition to the UN and international community, particularly in relation to human rights issues vis-à-vis the Green Movement demonstrations and the arrests of its leaders. The supra-discourse on Bahrain and Iranian representations of Saudi Arabia can be attributed to a speech made by Ayatollah Khamenei on the Iranian New Year. On 21 March 2011, Khamenei gave a speech outlining Iran's position on Bahrain (Khamenei 2011b). Furthermore, the Iranian elite – namely parliamentary members, the diplomatic service, and press – had already begun constructing the Iranian discourse on Saudi Arabia and its involvement in Bahrain. The Supreme Leader's New Year sermon only sought to legitimize, embolden, and promulgate the discourses of and narratives by the other Iranian discourse manufacturers. These gave rise to three main themes and tropes, namely: sectarian war, the end of the GCC and regional stability; invader and Zionist subservience; intifada, Karbala, and genocide.

Sectarian War, the End of the GCC, and Regional Instability   Framed in terms of Islamic eschatology –i.e. 'the end of times' – and Mahdism, the Iranian discourse on Bahrain was communicated as a fulfilled prophecy where the 'rise of the Mahdi' would come after the groundwork had been prepared for his rise. A Friday sermon (Emami-Kashani 2011) claimed that Iran was a model for the Arab protests and that the Islamic awakening had already been prepared for in Iran, in terms of the arrival of the Mahdi (Emami-Kashani 2011). The Arab protests, of which Bahrain was a major part, was a hallmark of this prophecy, since its Shi'a majority would be 'liberated from tyranny'. The Iranian press framed this rise as one that 'Saudi Arabia fears' *(Kayhan* 2011a*).* As the PSF entered Bahrain, the outcries from Iran became louder and echoed across all discourse genres. The foreign ministry framed the military excursion as a 'killing of the Shi'a [that] Iran cannot stand by and watch'(Salehi 2011). Abdolahian, the deputy foreign minister for Arab affairs, warned that the actions of the PSF could 'spiral out of control [and] spill over' to other countries, jeopardizing regional stability. The diplomat contended that if Saudi Arabia did not withdraw from Bahrain, then it risked the survival of the GCC (Abdolahian 2011).

On the same day, Iranian Majles members issued a statement condemning the PSF and Saudi Arabia in the harshest of terms. Representing Saudi Arabia as an aggressor with a sectarian agenda and slavishly following US orders to invade Bahrain, the MPs framed Iran as the defender and protector of Shi'ism, the Bahraini revolution, and democracy. To the parliamentary members, 'Saudi Arabia was a tool in US hands ordered to invade Bahrain' *(IRNA* and Majles 2011*).* The Majles speaker, Ali Larijani, branded the incursion as a 'green light' to end the protests in Bahrain (Larijani 2011). Through press editorials, the Iranian argument acquired a further hue, stressing the silence of the West and its fomenting of a conspiracy against Bahrain *(Kayhan* 2011a*)* – a trope also used in the Saudi discourse on Bahrain. Iran's criticism of the West regarding Bahrain was arguably due to the UN and EU positions on Iran's handling of the Green Movement protests. In a letter to his German counterpart, the head of the National Security Committee in the Iranian parliament – Alaadin Boroujerdi, criticized 'Western silence on Bahrain, double standards and human rights abuses', which was an indirect response to Ban Ki Moon's allegations relating to Iran (Boroujerdi 2011). Using Saudi Arabia as an example of human rights abuses, the Iranian legislator rhetorically argued 'Why should Iran adhere to Western human rights [while it is] silent on Saudi atrocities in Bahrain?' Furthermore, emphasizing Saudi Arabia's political system, Boroujerdi chastised Saudi Arabia for not being a democracy, and therefore as willing to 'kill Bahrainis seeking democracy and freedom' (Boroujerdi 2011). The parliamentarian implicitly framed Iran as a democracy and therefore as fighting for the human rights of Bahrainis, while explicitly criticizing Saudi Arabia.

The Iranian Self was a protector of democracies and those fighting for this, thus spelling the 'end of the GCC regimes' (Boroujerdi 2011).

Invader and Zionist Subservience   Perhaps the most prominent representation of Saudi Arabia by Iran came from its president. In an initial reaction to the GCC's decision to send PSF troops to Bahrain, Ahmadinejad compared the action to Saddam's invasion of Kuwait in 1990 (Ahmadinejad 2011c). Warning the Saudi monarchy that they could 'suffer a similar fate', Iran's characterization of Saudi Arabia as an invader strengthened the image of a kingdom seeking to destabilize the region while hinting at the end of the other GCC monarchies. Furthermore, Ahmadinejad's comments framed Saudi actions as US orders to invade Bahrain, thus implicitly defining Saudi Arabia as subservient to US hegemony and regional control (Ahmadinejad 2011c). This Iranian president's casting of Saudi subservience to the US identified the kingdom as 'causing sedition [while] working in favour of Zionism'. Furthermore, in his 'brotherly advice' to the Saudi leadership, Ahmadinejad highlighted Iran's role and position as a regional leader, thereby questioning the leadership and legitimacy of Saudi Arabia. By contrasting King Abdullah with Saddam, Ahmadinejad reminded Saudi Arabia of Iraq's fate, and of the US's false promises of protection and alliance, leaving an image of Saudi naivety and weakness.

On the other hand, while arguing for the 'end of the era of aggressive regimes' through an Islamic awakening – with Iran as the Arab movement's role model – Ahmadinejad represented Saudi actions as a means through which 'some [GCC] rulers attempt to hijack the revolution through US assistance' (Ahmadinejad 2011a), amounting to a discourse of conspiracy and collusion between the US and Saudi Arabia as opposed to Islam and democracy. It is this conspiracy that the press further suggested would see 'the end of the US in the region' and a fear of a rise of an 'Iranian regional power', as a result of this 'Islamic awakening', thus alluding that this might result in the end of the GCC and Saudi leaderships *(Kayhan* 2011a*)*.

Intifada, Karbala, and Genocide   By April 2011, the UN and EU had ruled in favour of a motion to appoint a human rights envoy to investigate alleged human rights abuses in Iran, mainly in relation to the Green Movement protests. Regarded as reflecting the 'double standards' of the UN and Western states in Iranian discourse, reactions to the Bahraini protests were strategized to highlight and rebuff such allegations and accusations, including using Shi'i tropes relating to the Ahl-al-bayt. The Karbala narrative was employed to highlight a sectarian angle to the PSF in Bahrain (Jannati 2011). The press built on the Karbala narrative by referring to the Bahraini protests as an 'intifada', drawing parallels with the Palestinian fight to liberate their lands from 'Zionist aggressors'. Moreover, Bahrain in Iranian discourse was a war between Islam and infidels, while also representing Saudi treachery against Islam and Iran. The editorials employed symbolism and metaphors to shape, shade, and colour their image of 'Saudi atrocities' in Bahrain and respond to Saudi allegations of sectarianism, Iranian propaganda, and human rights abuses. In the case of Bahrain, these discursive constructions were innovative; however, in the context of Saudi–Iranian rivalry since 1979, the tropes employed represented a continuity in the Iranian representation of its Saudi Arabian Other.

Press editorials argued that Iran protected all political and religious movements and not just the Shi'a. Khamenei had argued that Palestinians and Egyptians were Sunnis, and Iran had supported the latter against Mubarak and the former since the 1979 Islamic Revolution. Both the press and Khamenei therefore argued that Saudi Arabia was silent over Lebanon in 2006, Gaza in 2009, and complicit in a 'Bahraini genocide' against an 'intifada' in the service of the US and Zionism (*Kayhan* 2011a). By employing the genocide trope while citing Saudi human rights abuses in Bahrain, Iranian discourses constructed Riyadh's position towards Iran as a conspiracy against the Islamic Republic for Tehran's support of democracies, humanity, and the oppressed. This was clear in a second parliamentary statement signed by Iranian legislators questioning Saudi legitimacy and their Islamic credentials and leadership. Framing the Saudi role in Bahrain as one based on double standards, pillaging, and human rights abuses against the Shi'a of Bahrain resulted in the PSF's presence resembling an occupation akin to the Israeli occupation of Palestine. Therefore, in Iranian discourse, the Bahraini protests were an 'intifada', Bahrain was Palestine, while Saudi Arabia became Israel invading Islamic lands (*Donya-yi-Iqtisad* and Majles 2011).

Conclusion

Although the protests in the Arab world began in December 2010 in Tunisia, both Iran and Saudi Arabia experienced domestic turbulence a few months prior. The Baqi' protests in Saudi Arabia and the Green Movement in Iran shaped the discourses of Self and Other in both countries. In the case of Riyadh, the Baqi' protests brought about sectarian tropes and the construction of a Shi'i Other, while in the case of Iran, internal protests disputing the elections resulted in a domestic divide in the political spectrum and a 'split Self', the latter involving a redefinition of the Iranian Self. This Iranian divided Self came about as the two leading members of the revolution who had also ruled over post-revolutionary Iran since the 1980s – namely Khamenei and Rafsanjani – were on opposing sides. To the Iranian Self, the division suggested a modern-day Imam Ali caliphate, as 2009 had led to a 'war of two Islams'. For Saudi Arabia, the split in the Iranian Other was viewed with caution at the governmental level. In the domestic non-state discourse, however, the Iranian Other was constructed as an imploding state with a divided seminary and clergy, representing an Islamic Republic nearing its end.

The protests that spread across the Arab world were viewed from two different angles. In Iran, the protests were an 'Islamic awakening', while in Saudi Arabia the 'Arab Spring' was a source of grave concern. Iranian discourse represented this Islamic awakening in the Arab world as rooted in the Islamic Republic's revolutionary struggle, with the Iranian Self as the model revolution, and Iran having the Islamic leadership that countries like Tunisia and Egypt sought to emulate. For Saudi Arabia, the protests were viewed as foreign meddling. The Iranian discourse on the Arab uprisings and its diplomatic activity were represented by Saudi Arabia as interference in the affairs of Arab states, with Iran depicted as attempting to sow discord and sedition. The protests in Saudi Arabia and Bahrain were a case in point. In the case of the Eastern Province, Iranian meddling in Saudi domestic affairs would be a major part of Saudi discourse towards Iran, a representation that became a dominant trope when discussing Bahrain, with the Saudi media taking charge of Riyadh's representation of its Other. These Saudi editorials' construction of the Iranian Other focused on central themes and repertories such as Iranian hegemony and expansion in the Middle East and its sowing of sedition and sectarian tensions. By the same token, Iranian discourses used similar tropes to characterize the Saudi Other, such as the Saudi fomenting of a sectarian war and Iranian efforts at achieving regional stability, while also deploying the early post-revolutionary rhetoric of the 1980s that represented the Saudi kingdom as subservient to the West and 'Zionism'. These tropes of sectarianism, rivalry, sedition, and subservience would continue as the Arab Spring extended to the Levant. The protests that reached Syria in the Spring of 2011 were an opportunity for Saudi Arabia and a source of serious concern for Iran. These opportunities and concerns enhanced the rivalry between both states, bringing with them a plethora of discourses, tropes, and themes.

Chapter 11

THE ARAB SPRING AND SYRIA AS THE HEART OF THE AXIS OF RESISTANCE

Introduction

The Arab Spring had spread to Syria by the first week of March 2011. The arrest of youths in the city of Deir-e-Zor was the spark that led to widespread protests. By April, Syrian protests eclipsed the Arab movements, particularly in the Persian Gulf region. Both Iran and Saudi Arabia maintained their support for the Assad government initially; however, by August the Saudi monarch had taken a sharp turn, labelling Assad's response a 'killing machine that has to stop' (al-Saud 2011a). The rise of the Syrian protests and their effects on Iranian–Saudi relations was gradual, that is to say, as the protests gained in intensity, so did the reactions from Tehran and Riyadh. Furthermore, regional events also shaped the policy towards Syria. For instance, the election of a Muslim Brotherhood president in Egypt in June 2012 was viewed as an opportunity for Iran and a concern for Saudi Arabia. While the former had enjoyed historic relations with the Muslim Brotherhood, particularly in Tunisia and Egypt, Riyadh was cautious as it did not want a Sunni political movement that adhered to political Islam to export its revolution to the kingdom. This chapter examines the impact on Iranian and Saudi constructions of Self and Other of the civil war in Syria, the rise of armed opposition groups, the attacks on Shi'i shrines (such as Sayyida Zainab), the involvement in Iran and its regional allies, as well as inter-Arab tensions that saw Syria's dismissal from the Arab League and the emergence of the Takfiri narrative. For Iran, Syria was the heart of its 'axis of resistance', an ally that had aided Iran since the 1980s Iran–Iraq war, while supporting Iranian-aligned groups such as Hamas and Hezbollah, the latter during their war with Israel in 2006. For the Arabs, Syria was the 'heart of the Arab world' and one of the three major Arab powers along with Iraq up to 2003 and Egypt, even after the fall of Mubarak. Consequently, the stakes were high and the fight to either sustain Assad's rule or effect his removal was a major objective for both Tehran and Riyadh.

It would be this war that would also drastically shape the discourse on regional and Islamic legitimacy and leadership. In every stage of the events related to Syria, discourses of Self and Other would evolve, while the discourse manufacturers and promulgators would employ tropes and narratives that highlight and accentuate the Self and Other to both their domestic and international audiences. In this chapter I argue that supra-discourses e.g. of 'Zionist' attributions and Western subservience, sedition, and hegemony were dominant. In Saudi Arabia the discourses on Iran brought about themes of Iranian terrorism and sectarianism as Hezbollah and the Islamic Revolutionary Guard Corps (IRGC) came to the aid of Assad and repelled the Syrian armed opposition from cities and villages. Furthermore, to highlight the Self and the leadership of Saudi Arabia, Riyadh's role was emphasized by highlighting Assad's 'killing machine' and the war's casualties alongside the Arab League's lack of influence over the Syrian issue. Iranian discourses on Saudi Arabia revolved around a US–Israel–Saudi conspiracy to weaken Iran and its 'axis of resistance'. As the armed struggle gained pace, the conspiracy discourse shaped Iranian tropes of Saudi subservience to the West and Israel, along with Riyadh's quest to destroy Syria through terrorism and extremism amid the Takfiri narrative. Furthermore, with the first major IRGC deaths in the war and Israel's involvement in Syria, I argue that tropes of sectarian and 'Zionist' wars were employed, shaping the Self as fighting to protect the Shi'i and Islamic world from Saudi-led Wahhabi sedition and its destruction.

Syria: A View from Iran

A Conspiracy Against Syria

The first Iranian reaction to the Syrian revolution framed the protests as a 'conspiracy in Syria' to bring down the pro-Iran government of Bashar al-Assad, and distancing Iran from any intervention in the country's domestic affairs (*Ahmadinejad 2011a*). This assertion of a conspiracy by the Iranian president framed the 'supra-narrative' of Iran's discourse on Syria. Iran's editorials took their cue. *Kayhan* first constructed an image of foreign intervention as reflecting 'Western plans for Syria' (*Kayhan* 2011b) and an attempt 'to weaken Syria', with the final aim being to 'weaken Iran and benefit Saudi Arabia' (*Kayhan* 2011b). The reason underlying the conspiracy was the intention to degrade the 'axis of resistance', reminding the audience of Syria's position in the '33-Day War and Gaza', which was supportive of Hezbollah and Hamas respectively, in a bid to legitimize any Iranian support for Assad against the protests; this contrasted with Iran's strong support for other Arab movements protesting in the Middle East. Khamenei highlighted this discourse legitimizing Iran's supportive position towards the Syrian government, drawing a comparison with Tehran's stands on Egypt and Bahrain. In his first speech discussing Syria, Iran's Supreme Leader explained Iran's position arguing that 'Syria differs from other Arab protests' in that it was a conspiracy wherein 'Western governments aim to hijack the Islamic awakening' (Khamenei 2011). It was because of this US interference that Iran's ambassador in Damascus, Mohammad Sheibani, rebuked the American ambassador in Syria for visiting the city of Hama during the July 2011 protests (Sheibani 2011).

Breaking the 'Axis of Resistance'

The second phase of the Syrian revolution was marked by the Arab League suspending the country's membership. Arab states, including Saudi Arabia, censored Damascus for its heavy-handed retaliation to the protests. Assad's unwillingness to shift his position from Iran's 'axis of resistance' could be a possible explanation for why the Saudi support ended. In Saudi Arabia, King Abdullah's speech framed Assad as a 'killing machine' (al-Saud 2011a), and thereby, signalling support for the opposition, a move that was counter to Riyadh's previous stance on the various Arab Spring movements, with the exception of Libya (Phillips 2020: 360; Antonopoulos and Cottle 2017; Mason 2014). Iranian discourse framed the Saudi anti-Assad speech and policy as a failed attempt to 'separate Syria from Iran and Hezbollah', deepening the conspiracy narrative by labelling it a front that involved 'Saudi Arabia, Israel and the US' and that sought 'to destroy the axis of resistance' (Velayati 2011; *Kayhan* 2011a). On the international stage, Iran's president argued that while Syria needed reform, 'killing each other is no good' and that 'both sides should talk' (Ahmadinejad 2011a). However, the bottom line was that Iran was not going to give up its ally, especially after accusations of being a 'menace' to others in the region, specifically by Saudi Arabia (Chubin and Tripp 2014).

Calls for Assad to step down echoed throughout the international community. The Arab League attempted to initiate dialogue and negotiate a transition of power from the government to the different Syrian parties. By the autumn, meetings between Arab League members took place to send observers to monitor the deteriorating situation. Iran initiated its own diplomatic and political manoeuvres to preserve its ally in Damascus. However, in the chaotic diplomatic tug of war over Syria, Iran and Saudi Arabia became entangled because of US accusations of an IRGC inspired assassination attempt on the Saudi ambassador to Washington, Adel al-Jubeir (Sherrill 2018: 180). This accusation added a new dimension to the Iranian narrative of a foreign conspiracy attempting to weaken the Iranian axis of resistance, namely a Saudi attempt to create sedition within the Islamic world (*Kayhan* 2011c). It was this allegation that introduced the IRGC into the discourse on Saudi Arabia in the context of Syria. Iran's then defence minister, Ahmad Vahidi, framed the US allegations as a 'wider war with Iran' (Vahidi 2011). In addition, the head of the IRGC aerospace division, General Amir Ali Hajizadeh, raised the issue of a US threat against the IRGC Quds Force (Hajizadeh 2011). This narrative was also promulgated among the top ranks of the IRGC: General Salami (Salami 2011), then deputy head of the IRGC, observed that the US was seeking to assassinate IRGC officers for what Iranian diplomats had called 'falsified scenarios' while attempting to foment 'sedition and tarnish Iran's image' (Abdolahian 2012).

The allegations of the Quds Force's assassination of Adel al-Jubeir along with the rise in armed clashes in Syria between foreign supported groups and Assad, as well as the threat to Iran's position in Syria, paved the way for Qassem Soleimani's entry into Syria and the Arab Spring. Soleimani became the flagbearer of Iran's activities in Syria. In a speech in his hometown of Kerman, the head of the Quds

Force tacitly defined Iran's policy on Syria. Stopping short of naming the GCC leadership and Syria, Soleimani propagated the Iranian narrative that 'Hezbollah broke Zionism and the US', leading to 'the masses not fearing US hegemony', which in turn has given rise to 'a movement that began in mosques' and has led to an Islamic awakening (Soleimani 2011). The threat posed by the US to the Quds Force also initiated an open discussion of Soleimani's leadership. In a Friday prayer sermon in Tehran, Ayatollah Jannati constructed a heroic image of the Iranian general as a man who 'instilled fear in the US and Israel', saying that the 'US shivers when they hear his name' (Jannati 2011). Moreover, the cleric warned the Al Saud monarchy that they 'shall soon suffer the same fate as the Pharaohs of Egypt and Libya', namely that the masses would soon uproot the Saudi monarchy (Jannati 2011). The threat against the Quds Force and the accusation of an assassination attempt gave rise to a sense of Iran and its allies being internationally targeted. The calls for the ousting of Bashar al-Assad coupled with accusations of an Iranian plot to assassinate a Saudi ambassador in Washington, while naming the Quds Force as the perpetrators, led the Iranians to believe that they were the ultimate target. Consequently, any attack on a member of the axis of resistance, i.e. al-Assad, was viewed as targeting the Iranian Self. This latter dynamic gave rise to the construction of the Saudi Other in Iranian military and clerical discourses.

By the end of December 2011, the situation in Syria had become so violent that Arab League monitors were deployed there *(Times 2011)*. Two days later, Iranian engineers were kidnapped in Homs by opposition groups who claimed that they were IRGC affiliates *(Reuters 2011; Hasan 2011)*. This all occurred as suicide bombings were beginning to target the heart of the Assad government in Damascus *(BBC 2011)*. Iranian editorial discourse framed these attacks as having been instigated by 'US and Saudi-sponsored groups' *(Kayhan 2011e)*, attacks that were given a sectarian tone by the claim that 'Sunni-backed Saudi parties' had sought to create an 'anti-Syrian base' that would ensure the fall of a Shi'i government in Damascus. On the basis of these attacks and discourses, Ahmadinejad opined that the US utilized the Arab Spring to impose 'American Islam' in opposition to 'Iranian revolutionary Islam' (Ahmadinejad 2011b). In short, Iranian discourse was implicitly constructing an image of a false US brand of Islam versus Iranian Mohammedan Islam *('Islam-i Nāb-i Mohammadī')*, which emanated from the Islamic Revolution. Therefore, by early 2012, the violence in Syria, along with Iranian support for Assad, which was being contrasted with Western and Arab support for the opposition, had given rise to a discourse of sectarian rivalry. Within this discourse, the Syrian revolution had become a war with US and Saudi powers battling against Iranian revolutionary forces.

Terrorism, Bloodshed, and Al-Qaeda

Following two failed monitoring attempts, the Arab League suspended its activities in Syria by the end of January 2012. The bloodshed in Syria had increased drastically, while Iranian Arabic speaking media outlets such as al-Alam were shut down by the GCC-owned Arabsat satellite network, accusing Iran of interference and propaganda against the GCC and the people of Syria *(Al-Alam* 2012*)*. As international pressure – emanating in particular from the GCC – mounted on Assad to step down, Iran's support for Damascus became more explicit. In a press interview with Arab media, the former Iranian foreign minister and the Supreme Leader's foreign affairs adviser, Ali Akbar Velayati, argued that the international community's main aim was not political reform but was 'to overthrow the Assad government' through bloodshed, whereas Arab states were fomenting propaganda and sedition that would lead to civil war (Velayati 2012b). This civil war, Velayati insisted, was a 'partnership between domestic groups [and] investors', stressing that the Syrian opposition armed groups were 'outlaws' receiving 'aid from foreign parties' as well as military training (Velayati 2012b). Highlighting a discourse focused on foreign intervention, chaos, and civil war, Velayati defined Iran's position and role in the context of the Syrian civil war: 'Syria is the golden ring of the axis of resistance'; it is Iran's 'red line and we will not let anyone from the regional or international parties interfere in Syria or overthrow the regime' (Velayati 2012b). This was the first time a high-ranking Iranian official, especially a person like the Supreme Leader's adviser, had openly defined Iran's stance on the Syrian revolution since it had started in March 2011. The position articulated was that Iran would protect Assad and Iranian interests in Syria against any foreign or domestic intervention that would alter the status quo. Days later, in a meeting with the Palestinian group Islamic Jihad, Khamenei supported and echoed Velayati's position, adding that the conspiracy against Syria was due to its 'position of resistance' against Israel because Syria supported 'Palestinian and Lebanese Islamic resistance'. While Iran was behind 'reforms in favour of the Syrian people' it also opposed 'interference in Syria's internal affairs' (Khamenei 2012b). The Supreme Leader framed the upheaval in Syria as a US design that unfortunately some regional countries had participated in (Khamenei 2012b). According to Khamenei, Iranian policy was that 'wherever any nation or group fights against the Zionist regime, we will help and we have no hesitation in saying this', arguing that Iran had become involved in the 34-Day War and the 22-Day War against Israel in 2006 and 2009 respectively (Khamenei 2012a). Therefore, since Syria was the part of that 'axis of resistance', Iran represented its support for al-Assad as its solemn duty. Iran's position now defined Syria as being part of the Iranian Self, and so targeting Syria entailed targeting the Iranian Self; by default, Syria's Other was synonymous with Iran's Other or a 'common Other'.

The international community adopted a stronger pro-opposition stance, marked by the Arab-League-sponsored motion to the UNSC in February 2012 and the subsequent Friends of Syria Group conference in Tunisia on 24 February *(Reuters* 2012*)*, while there was an increase in terrorist activities such as the Aleppo bombings in the same month, and growing anti-Assad rhetoric from the Saudi monarch (al-Saud 2012b). Meanwhile, Iran dug its heels in with its rhetoric and increased support for Assad. Saudi Arabia accused Iran of sending frigates to Syria to jam the opposition's frequencies and communications *(Alarabiya* 2012*)*. As meetings were underway to raise financial support for the opposition, the Iranian discourse drew parallels with the Camp David meetings of 1978 that led to a normalization of relations between Israel and Egypt. In a speech to the IRGC, Velayati used Khomeini-era tropes to frame the meeting as a conspiracy against both the Islamic awakening and Assad, a conspiracy sponsored by 'reactionary Arabs', arguing that this was due to Bashar al-Assad's position, as he had 'always stood against Israel and the Camp David accords' (Velayati 2012c). This narrative was also adopted by Iranian editorials framing the Tunisian meeting on Syria as a 'reincarnation of Camp David' supported by Saudi Arabia and Qatar, who were currently 'funding terrorists in Syria' *(Kayhan* 2012c*)*, a trope that would be propagated as the bombings and violence increased in propensity.

By March 2012, hard-fought battles for cities like Baba Amr saw clashes between the Syrian military and the Free Syrian Army (FSA) *(Guardian* 2012*)*. Iranian editorial discourse constructed the war as one between 'Saudi Arabia and Qatar-sponsored Al-Qaeda' against the Syrian government. The image of terrorist sponsorship was compounded by Iranian press claims of 'Zionist sponsored groups', projecting an image of Saudi Arabia as not only a sponsor of terrorism but also as a (subservient) collaborator with Israel (*Kayhan* 2012). As Syrian government troops pushed back the FSA from cities like Baba Amr, the victory was constructed as a win for Assad against 'Saudi-sponsored terror with Zionist backing', the latter intending to destroy Syria and its people *(Kayhan* 2012d*)*. This representation would become dominant in Iranian discourses as officials defended their support for Assad as humanitarian and not military. Fending off the accusations of Iranian military support for Assad, diplomats such as the Iranian ambassador to Syria, Mohammad Rouf Sheibani, characterized the Western understanding of Iranian support for Assad as a 'misinterpretation', later laying the blame for the death toll in Syria on 'Arab states' who sent weapons to the country, and who are thus 'responsible for killing people' (Sheibani 2012).

On 25 May 2012, Syria witnessed one of its bloodiest massacres in the town of al-Hawla. Both Iranian and Arab media characterized the bloody incident in line with whatever side they supported. While the anti-Assad media uncovered that Assad had caused the massacre, the Iranian discourse represented the al-Hawla atrocity as a 'terrorist attack' (Mehmanparast 2012). In an interview with the French media outlet France 24, Ahmadinejad distanced Assad from responsibility for the incident (Ahmadinejad 2012a). A foreign-ministry spokesman condemned the attacks, calling for an investigation (Mehmanparast 2012). However, Iran's military cadres alluded to 'Saudi use of Israeli weapons to kill innocent Muslims in Syria' (Firouzabadi 2012a). In contrast, editorial discourse depicted the al-Hawla massacre as similar to the 'Israeli attacks in Lebanon', drawing historical parallels with the 'Qana massacre' in the 2006 Hezbollah–Israel war *(Kayhan* 2012i*)*. Another juxtaposition used was a reference to the UNRWA school bombing in Gaza during the 2009 Israel–Hamas war. In Lebanon and Gaza, Israel was accused of being the perpetrator, whereas in the al-Hawla incident, Qatar and Saudi Arabia were accused of funding 'Syrian terrorists', leading to the death of innocent people *(Kayhan* 2012i*)*. To its domestic audience, Iranian editorials conveyed the image that al-Hawla was a 'Western conspiracy to blame Assad', while the perpetrators were supported and funded by the GCC states such as Qatar and Saudi Arabia, as both sought 'a military role in Syria' by forging a relationship between 'terrorists . . . and Saudi Arabia' *(Kayhan* 2012i). In addition, this 'Saudi attack' on Syria and 'its aid in a conspiracy against' the Assad government was framed as 'retribution and revenge' for Iran's and Hezbollah's victory in the 34-Day War of 2006, as well as an attempt to compensate for Riyadh's regional losses after the fall of Mubarak *(Kayhan* 2012h). It is these post-2006 losses that Iran framed as being the basis for a Saudi conspiracy to take revenge in order to rebuild its image and regain its losses in the Arab world. This narrative of revenge, according to Iranian press discourse, included an attack on Iran after the fall of Syria *(Kayhan* 2012g).

To the domestic audience, Iranian editorials represented the attacks on Assad not only as an anti-Syrian conspiracy but also as a holistic plan that aimed to cripple and destroy Iran. Highlighting the sanctions imposed by the Obama administration and the EU on Iranian oil, *(DW* 2012), Iranian editorials framed the concurrent measures against Iran and Syria as dual pressure on both states, since the 'Islamic awakening' began in Iran while Western and Arab states had failed to stop the uprisings. Therefore, the attacks on Syria were a form of retribution since the Arab movements were due to the 'Islamic Republic's spiritual support and influence in the regional equation' *(Kayhan* 2012g). On this basis, a partnership had emerged between 'Wahhabism and Israel in Syria'. This 'pan-Wahhabism' was defined as a collaboration between 'Al-Qaeda, Saudi Arabia, and Israel', which had created the FSA. According to *Kayhan*, the FSA in turn had one aim, namely to help 'Israel to compensate for its losses in the Middle East region', while allowing 'Saudi Arabia to play a major role in aiding Zionists in deepening the rifts' in the Islamic world *(Kayhan* 2012g). Therefore, the argument went that by using terrorism, Saudi Arabia and Israel were creating sedition in the Islamic world in an attempt to stop the Islamic awakening in which Iran is the spiritual leader. Within the Iranian discourse, their tools were terrorist groups such as Al-Qaeda and their battleground was Syria, the 'golden ring of the axis of resistance' (Velayati 2012a). This discourse and image later became the public and ideological basis for Iran's aid to Damascus, especially as the threat to the survival of Assad's regime increased with the volume of the opposition's attacks and the armed opposition's march towards Damascus.

On the eve of the anniversary of the 34-Day war, a large explosion shook central Damascus *(Times* 2012). Iranian press discourse defined the attack as a 'terrorist operation' *(Resalat* 2012; *Kayhan* 2012f). *Kayhan*, Iran's ultra-conservative leaning newspaper, labelled the incident as bearing the 'footprints of US and Saudi Arabia in a terrorist operation' *(Kayhan* 2012f). Among widespread Iranian condemnation, the elite discourse shifted and began alluding to Saudi Arabia's relationship to the attack. The parliamentary speaker, Ali Larijani, argued that 'countries with no scent of democracy' sought to 'conquer Syria by sending money and weapons' with some countries being 'too small', while 'others do not allow women to drive', clearly hinting at Qatar and Saudi Arabia (Larijani 2012). As the dates coincided with the 34-Day War, the editorials promulgated a narrative of retribution and revenge 'for the victory against Israel' in the summer of 2006, with the attack being 'orchestrated by Zionists, the US, and reactionary Arab countries' *(Kayhan* 2012l). Furthermore, metaphors were employed by Iranian editorials branding the explosion as conceived by 'Arabistan's Terror Democracy' (*'Arabistan-i Terror-crat'*), a new coinage by the Iranian press discourse for Saudi Arabia, which was funding a Syrian opposition composed 'mostly of terrorists imported and affiliated with Al-Qaeda and Saudi-backed Salafi groups' (*Kayhan* 2012b). These groups, according to the Iranian military leadership, would only cease their activity when 'Syria's friends deal decisive blows to enemies and reactionary Arabs', implicitly warning the Arab world that a retaliation was in the making, while explicitly informing the Iranian people that 'Iran and Hezbollah are still not in Syria' (Jazayeri 2012a). This was followed by the Majles' statements pledging support for the Syrian government as the Syrian foreign minister visited Tehran, requesting aid and assistance (Majles 2012). The Iranian discourse represented Saudi Arabia's efforts in Syria and its support for the armed opposition as support for Islamic terrorism. This was compounded by employing the sectarian tropes of Salafism and Wahhabism as symbolized by references to Al-Qaeda. Furthermore, by contrasting the image of a terrorist group, such as a 'Saudi-backed' Al-Qaeda, with 'Syria's friends', i.e. Hezbollah and Iran, the Iranian discourse set up an opposition between Saudi-led terrorism and a legitimate Iranian-led axis of resistance.

With more domestic voices demanding support for Syria, a shift occurred in the Iranian discourse on Syria and its civil war. The press began framing the Syrian civil war as a war between two fronts, as Iranian Islam versus US Islam, bringing back the narrative of Mohammedan Islam (*'Islam-i Nab-i Mohammadi'*) versus infidelity (*Kufr*), and the axis of resistance versus Zionism (*Kayhan* 2012e), a trope first employed by Ahmadinejad in relation to Syria. This happened because Iran viewed the Syrian issue as hijacking what it termed 'an Islamic awakening'. This hijacking was apparently undertaken by the US and Saudi Arabia, and so the Iranians construed this as a war between an Iranian Islam that was pure, and an infidel-sponsored form backed by the United States and led by Saudi Arabia. The Friday prayer sermons repeated the narrative that the 'US, Saudi Arabia, Israel ... have all joined hands against Syria', adding that 'they send weapons' because it 'is all about Israel and the resistance' (Jannati 2012). Iran's Qom-based ulama, such as Ayatollah Makarem Shirazi, clearly implicated the Saudi monarch, calling on 'the Custodian of the Two Holy Mosques to stop supporting Israel and the US in the Syrian unrest and [furthering] the disintegration of this Islamic country in favour of Israel'. They criticized the Saudi monarch's leadership and questioned Saudi legitimacy for acting as a 'servant of the US and Israel', that is, by 'claiming to be Muslim [while] joining hands as servants' with the US and Israel (Makarem Shirazi 2012). It can therefore be argued that the Iranian populace was being prepared for a more active and overt role in Syria. This was evident in the official, editorial, and religious discourses on Syria, which represented the events as an existential threat that not only targeted Assad and the axis of resistance but also Iran and the Islamic world. This was visible in the press moving to characterize the Syrian civil war as representing a dichotomy, namely a 'US front' versus an 'Iranian front', with the war in Syria an extension of the battle between 'arrogance' (*istikbār*) and the 'oppressed' (*mustazafān*), and 'Zionism' versus Islam (*Kayhan* 2012a). This discourse became more prominent with the expulsion of Syria from the OIC in August 2012, an action that Ahmadinejad criticized as aiding 'those supporting the US against Syria'. Ahmadinejad went as far as to project an image of Assad's adversaries as lackeys and agents of the US (Ahmadinejad 2012b). On Quds Day, the last Friday of the month of Ramadan, Tehran's Friday sermon represented the OIC suspension as a prelude to the fall of Syria and hinted that Iran was the ultimate target. Ayatollah Khatami argued that the suspension would lead to 'Al-Qaeda attacking Syria's neighbours' once Assad falls, warning that the 'US and its allies should not think of coming near Iran' (Khatami 2012). The discourses of the two Islams, namely of the 'oppressed' versus the 'oppressor', alongside the use of tropes based on subservience to Israel and the West, were reminiscent of the post-revolutionary Khomeini era. In addition, the trope of a US-funded Islam with 'Zionist' fingerprints and Saudi Arabian involvement destroying Syria was an attempt to construct an image of Saudi-led terrorism and a deviant form of Islam, one marked by terrorism and extremism (e.g. in the vein of Al-Qaeda), which Iran would later label the Takfiris.

Iran Prepares for War: The Takfiri Narrative

In the summer and autumn of 2012, the rebels scored successes leading to a withdrawal of government forces in northern Syria, particularly around Aleppo. In August, Obama authorized covert support for the Syrian armed groups(*CNN* 2012). In December the US recognized the Syrian National Coalition (SNC) as the official representative of the Syrian people (*Al-Jazeera* 2012b), which in turn gave legitimacy to the opposition armed groups including the FSA. By then, suicide bombings by Al-Qaeda had also taken a toll on the Syrian government. The June and October 2012 bombings of the Shi'i Sayyida Zainab shrine in Damascus are a case in point. The October attack specifically struck a nerve with the Iranians and resulted in the formation of Shi'a armed groups in defence of the holy shrine. It was these sectarian targeted attacks that gave rise to a discourse of war and the Takfiri narrative, which was according to Iran, defined by Saudi-led Wahhabi militant-terrorist groups. Through the emerging discourse on Syria, the state was preparing its citizenry for war in Syria against the Takfiris, and Iran used this label to define anti-Shi'i groups, such as Al-Qaeda, and their backers and supporters. The importance of this episode concerns how the war now shifted from protecting the axis of resistance (i.e. the Iranian view) and bringing democracy to Syria (the Saudi view) to a sectarian war. In this war, Iran perceived itself as the protector of Ahlulbayt and Shi'ism against 'Saudi-led Takfiri terrorism'.

The Friday imams warned that 'regional governments' – a veiled reference to Saudi Arabia and other GCC countries – would suffer consequences similar to Syria as 'the fire will burn' the Gulf states, with sermons revolving around themes such as sedition and 'fratricide by encouraging and mobilizing the youth to kill Muslims' (Sidiqqi 2012). The radical cleric Ayatollah Ahmad Khatami argued that the 'enemies of Islam' – implicitly referring to Saudi Arabia – created the FSA which was a 'helpless servant of the West'. It was this FSA that the cleric argued 'entered a house near the Sayyida Zainab shrine, killed the family and hung a three-year-old boy' (Sidiqqi 2012). Preaching during Muharram, religious allegory was employed in the form of the Karbala narrative. The cleric drew parallels with Imam Hussein, his family and companions and the Umayyad army of Yazid, stating that 'the FSA beheaded a little girl' and showed the 'arrogant face' of Shimr and Omar ibn Saad (Sidiqqi 2012; Emami-Kashani 2012). Saudi Arabia, its allies, and the FSA were represented as the enemies of Islam and the Shi'a, while Saudi Arabia became the Yazid, the FSA the Umayyad army, and Syria a modern-day Karbala. These discourses were aimed at an internal audience by preparing the Iranian people for official Iranian military involvement in Syria and to begin recruiting the youth as *'mudafeen-i haram'* (defenders of the shrine) for the upcoming war to 'defend the Sayyida Zainab'.

The Iranian press went further, identifying and defining the FSA and their animosity towards the Shi'a. Editorials observed that the FSA were 'Saudi supported Wahhabis [and] armed Salafis' in Syria *(Kayhan* 2012k). According to Iranian discourse, these militants were 'the most important terrorist group and will be a threat to other countries if Syria falls'. This group was portrayed as a tool of US policy, which was 'prolong[ing] the Syrian crisis' because the US 'cannot accept a government empowered by Hezbollah and Iran' *(Kayhan* 2012j). These Salafi terror outfits were called out as the 'al-Nusra Front', the Syrian brand of Al-Qaeda. Their duty, according to *Kayhan*, was to 'create terrorism through Saudi support' with the sole aim being to 'create a neo-Taliban state and sectarian warfare' *(Kayhan* 2012k).

This notion now began to take the lead in Iranian military discourse, following the tropes dominant in the press and clerical discourse. Iran's Chief of Staff, Major General Hassan Firouzabadi, accused the 'US supported Al-Qaeda in Syria' and the 'hypocritical regional governments' for their role (Firouzabadi 2012b). The IRGC spokesman argued that the countries that sponsor terrorism in Syria would later 'fall victim to Syrian terrorists', since 'reactionary governments' sought to 'destroy the resistance in the name of Islam' (Jazayeri 2012b). It is these Al-Qaeda affiliated groups with alleged Saudi backing that the secretary general of Hezbollah, Hassan Nasrallah, openly announced were 'funded by Saudi Arabia' and intended to 'foment sedition'. He branded them Takfiris, a term that would be employed to refer to anti-Shi'i groups in Syria (Nasrallah 2013a). According to *Kayhan*, these Takfiris had a plan to establish a 'global caliphate' that was 'designed by Western intelligence' in an attempt to 'bring together extremist groups to prevent the spread of Shi'ism [by] shedding the blood of believers' *(Kayhan* 2013b). The identity of these groups was portrayed as being 'similar to Wahhabism', the predominant Saudi religious doctrine, which was depicted as a current that 'presents itself as religious but is hypocritical [since it is] in alliance with the West, just like the Saudi king' *(Kayhan* 2013b). At the official level, the role of these Wahhabi groups – according to the Iranian political elite – was to 'create divisions and problems in today's Islamic world … They are Takfiris'. In addition, these groups have 'divided the Islamic world', while what was visible in Syria was 'an example of this extremism' (Larijani 2013). The Iranian discourse constructed three distinct frames. First, one of Saudi Arabia as the creator of Wahhabism and the Takfiri groups. Second, a frame wherein these groups had been sent to destroy Syria and fight a sectarian war with US funding and backing. Third, one of the Takfiri groups – if they succeeded in Syria – returning to Saudi Arabia and the GCC region and destroying these 'reactionary countries'. Therefore, to the domestic and regional audience, the Iranian discourse represented Tehran's position on Syria as reflecting the duty of Iran and its allies to protect Syria, Shi'ism, and the Arab and Islamic world from alleged 'Saudi-led terror groups'.

Sectarian and 'Zionist' Wars

On 30 January 2013, Israeli planes struck a convoy on the outskirts of Damascus, which was followed by Israeli claims that Hezbollah was smuggling missiles back to Lebanon *(Reuters* 2013d*)*. Days later, the then head of Iran's Supreme National Security Council (SNSC), Saeed Jalili, met with Bashar al-Assad, and his later comments marked a shift in the Iranian tone. Jalili claimed that the 'Islamic world will not allow the invasion of Syria by enemies, especially the Zionist regime' (Jalili 2013). However, another attack targeting a high-ranking IRGC officer would later strike the heart of the Iranian military establishment. A second strike that took place less than two weeks after Israel's strike on the alleged Hezbollah convoy resulted in the assassination of an Iranian general, Hasan Shateri *(Reuters* 2013b*)*. The attack was said to have carried out by a 'rebel group' on the road between Syria and Lebanon *(Guardian* 2013*)*. Iran was now formally involved militarily in the Syrian civil war.

The death of General Shateri, labelled the 'Engineer of Lebanon's reconstruction' (IRGC 2013) in the aftermath of the 33-Day War with Israel, raised the scope of the 'Zionist' discourse in the Syrian war, drawing in tropes of international terrorism and an Israeli conspiracy in the Syrian war by targeting Iran and its 'axis of resistance'. In his statement of condolences, Ahmadinejad characterized the perpetrators as 'mercenaries' that had utilized the 'dirty hand of terror' and had assassinated a person 'who represents the government of the Islamic Republic of Iran'. According to the president, these 'mercenaries' had participated in 'international terrorism and a conspiracy of global arrogance [*istibar-i Jahani*] and criminal Zionism due to the growing fear of the flourishing of the holy system of the Islamic Republic of Iran' (Ahmadinejad 2013). The IRGC echoed the president's discourse. In a statement the IRGC claimed the attacks were carried out by:

> the mercenaries of the Zionist regime ... [and] showed that the enemy is afraid and angry from the sphere of influence of the revolution, and the connection of the Iranian nation with the Muslim nations, especially the front line countries of the Islamic and anti-Zionist resistance.
>
> (IRGC 2013)

The Iranian discourse as a reaction to the Shateri incident served three purposes. First, by accusing the 'Zionists' and 'global arrogance', i.e. Israel and the US, as well as using the trope of 'international terrorism', the Iranian officials, and particularly the IRGC, legitimized Iran's activities and presence in Syria. Second, these tropes of 'Zionism' and 'international terrorism' were also redefining Iran's Other in the case of Syria to include a collaboration between Israel, the US, and the armed opposition groups. Third, the definition of the Other to include Israel and the US allowed Iran to both decrease the negative image of a weakness that may have been created due to the attack being carried out by rebels. The allusion to Israel also allowed the Iranian discourse to highlight the Iranian Self as a regional and Islamic leader, and as a custodian of the Islamic world with a 'sphere of influence' and an 'Islamic and anti-Zionist resistance'. This war on 'global terrorism' would take a sectarian turn as the anti-Assad armed groups attacked Islamic sites revered by the Shi'a.

Heritage sites began to be increasingly targeted in the Syrian war. This included Shi'i mosques that had been targeted since the beginning of the unrest in Syria. Dubbed 'the war of holy tombs' (Mousavian 2012), rebels belonging to al-Nusra, the Syrian branch of Al-Qaeda, had targeted two main Shi'i shrines. The first belonged to the tomb of Ammar ibn Yasir, who was one of the companions of the Prophet Mohammad (Blank and Noone 2018: 486). The second, the grave of Hujr ibn Adi, was another companion of the Prophet and a supporter of Imam Ali against the Umayyad Mu'awwiya (Abbas 2021: 165). In the case of the tomb of Hujr, it was alleged that the al-Nusra exhumed the body and desecrated the grave (Tschannen 2013). It was in reaction to tomb of Hujr that the Iranian discourse genres used sectarian narratives and tropes, and they explicitly framed the attack as one conducted by Wahhabism in collaboration with 'Arab funding' and 'Zionist–US support'.

In an immediate response to the incident, Ayatollah Khamenei gave a sermon that highlighted the role of foreign interference while referring to Sunni-Wahhabi thought as the cause behind the incident. Khamenei argued that 'these people are the ones whose ancestors destroyed the graves of the imams in Baqi'' (Khamenei 2013). The 'ancestors' to whom Khamenei was referring were fighters in the Wahhabi army that conquered al-Madina in 1806, and King Abdulaziz ibn Saud who granted his ulama permission to destroy the cemetery in 1925 (Ende 2010). Khamenei framed the destruction of the shrines as a form of sedition by the 'evil Takfiri movement'. This included al-Nusra, who he defined as 'instruments of the policies of the British and American intelligence services' (Khamenei 2013). The official Iranian discourse, through Khamenei, began to construct the Syrian war in a sectarian light, as a supra-discourse that constructs a common Other: i.e. Takfiris, foreign states such as the US and Britain, and the Saudi monarchy. Khamenei's speech constructed two frames in relation to the war: first, that the Syrian war was sectarian in nature and was implicitly a continuation of the actions against the tombs of the infallible imams in *al-Madina* that began in the early 19th century and that continued under ibn Saud; and second, that the Takfiri groups, Wahhabi thought, and the Al Saud were 'instruments of the British and American intelligence services' (Khamenei 2013).

Building on Khamenei's implicit reference to Saudi Arabia, the editorials and Friday sermons were more explicit in their construction of the Saudi Other.

Kayhan (2013) argued that the attack on the shrine was a 'calculated American–Israeli plan' that employed 'religious warfare' to bring down Assad (*Kayhan* 2013a). The editorial discourse framed the war as sectarian sedition. It drew on tropes of foreign intervention and argued that 'the attack on the shrine of the great Shiites brings the Shiites and Alawites of Syria against the Sunnis and encourages the Sunnis to fight the Shiites' as part of a plan devised by 'intelligence services of the United States, Britain, France, Turkey, Saudi Arabia, Qatar, and the Zionist regime' (*Kayhan* 2013a). Furthermore, by drawing on events from recent history, *Kayhan* reminded its domestic audience that the incident in Syria was 'similar to the actions in Iraq' and the 'Wahhabi elements that have used explosives on the shrines' (*Kayhan* 2013a). The editorial was referring here to the Askari Shrine bombing of Samarra in Iraq, arguing that like then 'many hands are intertwined' (*Kayhan* 2013a) to destroy the shrine of an infallible. To the domestic audience, the Iranian discourse had used the Shrine of Hujr incident to define the Syrian war to its people as a war that was targeting Islam by causing sectarian sedition. This trope of a war to divide Islam served two purposes. First, it further legitimized Iran's role in Syria on a domestic level. Second, by framing the perpetrators as Wahhabis funded and directed by foreign and Arab intelligence services, predominantly US, Israel, Britain and Saudi Arabia, Iran aimed to project an image of the Self as a legitimate Islamic leader that seeks to defend Syria from an international plot to divide the Muslim world along the lines of sedition and sectarianism, while defining the Saudi Other as a seditionist and sponsor of 'Takfiri Wahhabi terrorism', which is subservient to foreign-intelligence services. These discourses of foreign intervention, sectarianism, and sedition would also be employed in Saudi Arabian discourse.

Saudi Narratives and Tropes on Syria

The Saudi discourse on Iran during the Syrian protests and later civil war shifted as the events evolved and the war progressed. Like Iran, Saudi discourse genres discussing the events in Syria were shaped gradually i.e. Saudi discourse construction representing Iran in light of the events in Syria was strategized, i.e. the discourse genres were reactionary. The themes, tropes, and construction of the Self and the Other developed as a reaction to events related to the Syrian war. The Saudi themes that emerged in the discourse included the fear of a state falling, the Saudi monarchy calling for a stop to Syria's 'killing machine', Iranian terrorism and sectarianism, and the death of the Arab League. Saudi Arabia constructed the Saudi Self and its Other through these themes and discourses for both domestic and international audiences.

Fear of a State Falling

Saudi press editorials began discussing the events in Syria the third week after the protests that began in Deir-e-Zor (*Asharq-Al-Awsat* 2011). Editorials such as those published in *al-Riyadh* and ASAA focused on the protests as a natural reaction to the wave of protests that were sweeping the Middle Eastern and North African region. At first they called on Assad to take a serious and sincere approach to popular demands and the need for reform *(al-Riyadh* 2011d). Gradually, they began criticizing the violence and steps that the Assad government was taking in reaction to the protestors. As the protests intensified and clashes became more violent, the discourse began framing the Syrian protests as a watershed event and alluded to the 'Iranian fear' that Iran may lose its most important ally *(al-Riyadh* 2011f). The press discourse also brought Hezbollah into the equation. The loss of Assad also meant a weaker Hezbollah, and the discourse stressed that 'Iran would be the next to fall' *(al-Riyadh* 2011f). The discourse on Iranian fear was further expanded to include the beginning of a sectarian narrative. To the Saudi audience, local editorials argued that the fall of Assad would result in a Sunni-governed state, and this would raise fear in the Shi'i governments of Iraq and Iran. Therefore, in Iraq 'a Sunni Syria would act as a tributary *[rafid]* for the Iraqi Sunnis' *(al-Riyadh* 2011f). For Iran, the fall of Assad would impede the state from fulfilling its 'regional ambitions', i.e. the 'Shi'i Arc' *(al-Riyadh* 2011n), because a Sunni leadership in Syria would deprive 'Iranian allies, such as Hezbollah, of financial and military support' *(al-Riyadh* 2011n).

Stopping the 'Killing Machine'

On 7 August 2011, the Saudi monarch finally voiced his condemnation of Assad and his government, calling on the Syrian president to 'stop the killing machine' *(al-Saud* 2011a). Following months of discussions and support, both on the financial and political fronts, and led by Saudi Arabia and Qatar, the Arab states – and especially the GCC – began lobbying against Assad while supporting the Syrian opposition. The Saudi press continued its criticism of Iranian support for Assad, claiming that Iran had been funding him and sending arms and support to quash the protests *(al-Riyadh* 2011c). The condemnation also targeted Nouri al-Maliki's pro-Iranian government in Iraq, observing that 'Iran ordered the Iraqi government to pay $15 billion to support' the Syrian regime *(al-Riyadh* 2011c), framing this support as based on a pro-Shi'i nexus comprised of Iran, Assad, and Iraq against the Syrian Sunni population. This collaboration was also supposedly compounded by the Iranian leadership ordering 'Hezbollah to go to Syria and join Assad' while the 'Arab states remained silent' *(al-Riyadh* 2011c). Consequently, the Saudi discourse represented the monarch's speech as a show of leadership and bravery, one that 'broke Arab silence', thereby projecting an image of the Saudi king as leading a fight for the 'freedom and rights [of the] oppressed people of Syria' *(al-Riyadh* 2011h). It was this discourse of Saudi leadership and its emancipation of Sunni Syrians that was the soil and substrate that gave rise to the first signs of the ethno-sectarian narratives that emerged during the Syrian revolution.

Furthermore, as Iran increased its vocal support for Syria, other regional states, such as Turkey, entered the Syrian arena. Saudi editorials framed Syria's proponents and Iran's involvement as one of ethno-sectarian rivalry, drawing historical parallels between sixteenth century Iran (led by the Safavids) and the Turks (led by the Ottomans). This Safavid–Ottoman rivalry was contrasted with a modern-day sectarian war between the two countries *(al-Riyadh* 2012g*)*, while stressing Syria and its people's identity as being 'Sunnis that are anti-Iran, [against] Hezbollah and the Shi'i-led government in Iraq' *(al-Riyadh* 2012g*)*. This Saudi sectarian narrative was possibly aimed at comments made by Ahmadinejad and Iranian Friday imams that highlighted aspects of Mahdism and Islamic eschatology when discussing events in Syria (Emami-Kashani 2011). The Iranian discourse framed the events in Syria as a preparation for the Mahdi, with Iran at its forefront. The Saudi argument was explicit, namely that 'the Syrian revolution is one against Iran, the Shi'i thought of *Valy-i Faqih,* and Khomeinism' *(al-Riyadh* 2011r*)*. To the Saudis, the Syrian protests were a sign of a 'fracturing of the Persian–Shia alliance' and an end to the Shi'i crescent that would be eclipsed by the 'rise of a Sunni-led government and majority in Syria' after Assad falls *(al-Riyadh* 2011g, 2011o*)*.

Iranian Terrorism and the Sectarian Agenda

By October 2011, the UNSC had failed to adopt a draft resolution on Syria condemning the government's crackdown on the protests. China and Russia had vetoed the resolution, with Russia arguing that the 'non-acceptability of military intervention' was not being considered (UN 2011b). This was seen by the Saudis as a victory for Iran and Assad, especially since the Russian envoy to the UN stated that 'the Syrian opposition had not hidden its extremist bent', and that the non-armed groups were 'not patriotic' (Churkin and UN 2011), thus implying that the GCC-backed groups were not patriotic enough to be recognized as the legitimate opposition to Assad. The Saudi press framed this faltering at the UNSC and the Arab League as based on 'Arab failure' in Syria, a framing that was used to subtly represent Saudi failure, since the kingdom had always been thought of as the leader of the Arab and Islamic world. The significance of the Saudi press in criticizing Riyadh's position on Syria was that the media were implicitly encouraging the government to take on a more explicit and practical role there. Editorials blamed the tensions in Syria on non-Arabs, characterizing Syria as embodying the rivalry between two non-Arab states, Turkey and Iran. The latter was referred to as the 'godfather of global Shi'ism', which was suffering from a false sense of grandeur while believing that it is 'suitable to rule the Islamic world' through an 'export of the revolution' *(al-Riyadh* 2011m*)*. The Saudi press argued that on this occasion, Iran had set its eyes on Syria, employing the concept of *taqiya,* which alludes to the Iranian and 'Shi'i doctrine of deceit' *(al-Riyadh* 2011m*)*. The trope of *taqiya* and 'Iranian doctrine' in Saudi discourse was an attempt to cast Iran and Shi'ism in a hypocritical and non-Islamic light, as the discourse attempted to represent the Islamic Republic as deceitful. Saudi discourse was informing its audience that Iran would do anything and under any pretext while employing Islam as a front to further its cause and aspirations.

On 12 October 2011, the US government accused Iran of an assassination attempt against the Saudi ambassador on American soil *(CNN 2011)*. The Saudi press argued that 'Iran was proficient in terrorism' *(al-Riyadh* 2011k*)*, especially given that Iran had 'suffered losses . . . [and was] seeking revenge for losses during the Saddam-era war through assassinations in Iraq' after 2003, while even targeting 'all Arabs, even those that belong to the Shi'i sect' *(al-Riyadh* 2011k*)*. The Saudi media constructed an image of Iranian malevolence, belligerence, and indifference towards Arabs as a whole, regardless of sect, explicitly labelling Iran as a 'terrorist state' *(al-Riyadh* 2011q*)*. On the other hand, the Saudi Self was depicted as a 'peaceful leader' that has 'mastered diplomatic relations and welcomed [Iranian] presidents and clerics', while Iran had sought to 'push matters towards chaos' *(al-Riyadh* 2011q*)*. A month later, on 18 November 2011, the UNSC voted by 106 votes in favour of Saudi Arabia, condemning Iran for 'plots against the Saudi ambassador' (UN 2011a). This gave rise to a more demonized representation of Iran in the Saudi press, positioning the Islamic Republic alongside Al-Qaeda *(al-Riyadh* 2011l*)*. In short, Iran was referred to as a 'terrorist state', defined as a pariah and menace to the region and the wider Islamic world *(al-Riyadh* 2011j, 2011l*)*, a representation that was reinforced by drawing on previous as well as more recent accusations against Iran. Less than a month after the al-Jubeir allegation, Bahrain accused Iran of planning terrorist activities on its soil *(Guardian* 2011*)*. According to officials, a 'Bahraini Iranian-funded terrorist cell [was caught] planning attacks on the King Fahad bridge' *(al-Riyadh* 2011l*)*. Alleging that the 'terrorist cell' was backed by 'IRGC training and funding', the incident was used to draw parallels with the 'failed plot to assassinate' the Saudi ambassador. This gave rise to narratives of victimization and international prestige. Saudi Arabia was framed as a 'victim of terror [perpetrated] by different terrorists from various powers', which had led the monarch to set up the King Abdullah Centre for Dialogue and funded a UN anti-terrorism and cultural dialogue programme *(al-Riyadh* 2011l*)*, thereby implicitly representing Iran as a sponsor and organizer of terror. Therefore, for the Saudi domestic audience, Iran was portrayed as a hostile actor in the international arena, while Saudi Arabia was an internationally responsible and peaceful one, highlighting the kingdom's regional and Islamic leadership, which included labelling the king as the 'Father of the Arab World' *(al-Riyadh* 2011i*)*. This was a position that both Iran and Saudi Arabia had been competing for since 1979 and a trope that fed into the discourse, especially as the Arab League and international community failed to remove Assad or curb the violence in a country that was sliding from a revolution into a full-blown civil war.

The Death of the Arab League: The Kingdom Takes Charge!

The Arab League approached the Assad government in an attempt to curb the violence and regime clashes with the opposition. Although the Syrian government was suspended from the Arab League, and Arab states including GCC members had withdrawn their ambassadors from Damascus, attempts were still being made by the Arab League to monitor the situation and send in observers, much to the dismay of Saudi Arabia. Saudi discourse, especially the press, described the Arab League's role as 'lacking courage', constructing an image of weakness, describing their moves to negotiate with Assad as being 'at the expense of the Syrian people' (*al-Riyadh* 2011s). Furthermore, this supposed weakness was represented as a negotiation between two fronts, the Arab League on behalf of the Syrian people versus the Syrian regime and its backers in its 'foxhole', namely Iraq, Iran, and Hezbollah. The former group was characterized as 'sterile' and 'dead' against a dictatorship that was defined as the 'heart of the Shi'a axis that plans to prove its presence on Arab lands' (*al-Riyadh* 2011s). This construction of a Shi'i hegemonic presence was represented as a 'Persian conspiracy' that ran through Baghdad, forming a 'Shi'i bridge' enabling the 'fulfilment of long term [Persian] ambitions [facilitated by] Arabs who have betrayed their patriotism', in an allusion to Maliki and Assad (*al-Riyadh* 2011s). Therefore, the Saudi editorial discursively constructed pro-Iran Arab leaders as treacherous, betraying their Arab patriotism in service to the Shi'i sect deployed by Iran to fulfil 'figments of the Mullah's imagination' in pursuit of an 'expansionist Persian empire'. This trope of Persian expansion was applied to Syria and Iraq, since both are significant 'geographically, and with human resources and wealth' and can be 'utilized to fulfil their [Persian] dreams' (*al-Riyadh* 2011b). It is these Persian 'dreams' that the editorials were telling their Saudi audience that the Arab League was failing to stop, while stating that the GCC is 'at the heart of this quagmire'. This image of the GCC states as being at the centre of an Iranian threat gave rise to a specific discourse on Saudi Arabia's regional role, bringing in a trope of a 'joint Gulf vision and policy' (*al-Riyadh* 2011p) to counter regional problems. This trope alluded to Saudi Arabia's role and leadership of the Arab world in a fight against the Iran–Syria axis, especially since the monarch called for the GCC to become a 'union . . . in the face of current threats' (*al-Riyadh* 2011e; *al-Saud* 2011b). The press used this call to establish a union as an opportunity to describe the king as the 'grat father to all Arabs' (*al-Riyadh* 2011a). This union, led by the Saudi monarch, included standing in the face of 'Iranian expansion' by forming an Arab–Sunni 'army of 500 thousand' with Saudi leadership and Abdullah at its helm (*al-Riyadh* 2011p). The call to establish a union and an Arab–Sunni army to confront Iran marked a shift in Saudi discourse. Not since the Iran–Iraq war had Saudi Arabia called for a military confrontation with Iran. Since the Iraqi invasion of Kuwait in 1990, the Saudi domestic discourse had argued for resisting Persian expansionism, but it had not issued an explicit call for war. In this instance, there was a return to the rhetoric and Arab hostility towards Iran of the 1980s. Now, Saudi Arabian discourse was preparing its domestic audience for a confrontation with Iran, seeking a justification for any military intervention, while at the same time legitimizing Riyadh's role in Syria as the kingdom's duty while the monarch in particular was represented as 'the great father of all Arabs' (*al-Riyadh* 2011p).

By the end of December 2011, the violence and destruction had reached the Syrian capital itself. Two suicide car bombs exploded outside Syrian intelligence buildings on 23 December. The states allied with Syria accused 'terrorist armed groups' such as Al-Qaeda (Kepel and Randolph 2020). The Arab press, on the other hand, particularly the Saudi editorials, represented the bombing as a 'tactic to quell the protests . . . and blame Al-Qaeda' (*al-Riyadh* 2012f). Three days later, the Arab League monitors, among them Saudis and other GCC observers, arrived in Syria

(Davis 2016: 186). However, their mission was short-lived. On 22 January 2012, the Saudi observers withdrew from Syria, suspending the mission citing 'the critical deterioration of the situation' (Samir and Solomon 2012).

The Saudi foreign minister, Saud al-Faisal, argued that the reason Saudi Arabia 'withdrew its monitors was because the Syrian government did not execute any element of the Arab resolution plan' *(al-Saud* 2012e*)*. However, the Saudi editorials had already forecast the mission's failure a week before. The newspaper *al-Riyadh* (2012a) argued that 'Saudi Arabia was against such a move [i.e. sending Arab monitors]', underlining that it was 'Qatar's suggestion [and that the] Arab League was not powerful enough', and urging for the Syrian file to be 'sent to the UNSC' *(al-Riyadh* 2012d*)*. The Saudi decision to withdraw from the Arab League mission cemented the specific 'death of the Arab League' narrative, framing the organization as incompetent and having 'never solved any Arab problems', going as far as to call for a military solution by the 'Free Syrian Army and opposition … and to refer Syria to the UNSC' *(al-Riyadh* 2012i*)*. Riyadh's denigration of the Arab League was due to its frustration with both the US and Saudi Arabia's Western allies, as well as with members of the Arab League, particularly since Iran was gaining traction and increasing its support in Syria. Furthermore, since Riyadh had lost its historic allies in countries such as Tunisia and Egypt, while Iran was capitalizing on its relationship with Islamic groups such as the Muslim Brotherhood in Egypt, Riyadh was acting to impose and reaffirm its position of leadership and dominance in the Arab world. On 31 January 2012, the Arab League briefed the UN on a resolution to be drafted and coordinated with the US, EU, and several Arab states, one part of which supported a political transition in Syria. This resolution was vetoed on 4 February 2012, once again by China and Russia (UN 2012), which further agitated the Saudi press and encouraged the government to take bolder steps against the Assad government and its allies.

In a televised address, King Abdullah criticized the UN veto, stating that 'what happened at the UN is absolutely regrettable' and that 'the world's confidence in the UN has undoubtedly been shaken' *(al-Saud* 2012b*)*. The failure of the Arab League and the UN to adopt a resolution fomented Saudi Arabia taking an assertive position on the world stage. Saudi Arabia's top diplomat called on the Arabs to 'give all forms of support' to the Syrian opposition *(al-Saud* 2012d*)*. Saud al-Faisal's reaction framed the Arab League as weak and sterile, labelling them as 'onlookers to what is happening to the brotherly Syrian people', while Arab countries were not active enough, criticizing their 'half measures, … granting the Syrian regime one period after another … to commit massacres against its people' *(al-Saud* 2012d*)*. Through its foreign minister, the Saudi government was explicitly calling for an all-cards-on-the-table approach to the Syrian revolution. Consequently, through its monarch and foreign minister, Saudi Arabia was constructing an image of regional and Arab leadership on Syria, thus propagating an image of concern, humanity, and dignity for the Syrian people. Both Iran and Saudi Arabia had been competing for this position, especially since Iran claimed that the Arab Spring was an Islamic awakening with its origins in the 1979 Islamic Revolution.

As the anniversary of the start of the Arab uprisings drew close to a year, the Saudi discourse attempted to bolster the image of the monarch and the kingdom's leadership and humanity. Highlighting the position of the Saudi leadership on the world stage, King Abdullah criticized Russia's position on Syria. He condemned the Russian veto on Syria, as it was 'absolutely impossible for the kingdom to abandon its moral and religious position' towards the Syrian people. The king demanded that 'it was best if Russia coordinated with the Arabs before using its veto', snubbing overtures of dialogue made by the Russian president, Medvedev while arguing that 'now, any dialogue on current events is useless' *(al-Saud* 2012a*)*. The monarch's reaction resulted in the Saudi press developing a trope focused on Arab leadership, framing the Saudi aggressive response to the Russian president as defying a world power. Commenting on Russian calls for dialogue, the editorials stressed that the 'kingdom would never start a dialogue that does not address humanitarian conditions, suffice to say with the [Russian] government, which has implemented a policy [that Saudi Arabia] does not agree with' *(al-Riyadh* 2012l*)*. This policy included military aid such as 'Russian frigates and the [presence of the] Iranian navy in Syria's waters . . . in support of the Syrian regime' *(al-Riyadh* 2012h*)*. The editorial criticized 'Arab shortcomings [since the] Syrian regime supported by Russia and China, in alliance with Iran' continued its 'criminal acts' that could only be solved by 'strong deterrence'. This call for armed deterrence by the Saudi domestic press was justified by representing 'the Syrian people [as] standing alone', given that it was a 'crime to leave them to face death without a fruitful and effective Arab mobilization' to confront Assad and Iran *(al-Riyadh* 2012c*)*. This trope of mobilization and a confrontation with Assad and his allies was deployed to accentuate Riyadh's leadership and its calls for Arab mobilization and support for armed opposition groups in Syria against the Iran–Assad nexus. It is this image that was being constructed and invoked in dichotomies such as a clash between Syrian–Iranian oppression and barbarism versus Saudi humanity, leadership, and legitimacy in the Arab and Islamic world, with Saudi Arabia playing the role of a responsible actor in the international community.

Exporting (Syria's) Revolution: Hezbollah Goes to War

As many analysts predicted, the Syrian revolution and the armed conflict that ensued as a result of the clashes between the government and the opposition groups began to spill over Syria's borders (Young et al. 2014). In May 2012, the Lebanese areas of Jabal Mohsen and Darb-al-Tibanah experienced armed clashes resulting in tens of fatalities and hundreds of injured *(Daily Star* 2012*)*. Clashes between Sunnis and Alawites in Lebanon were framed by the Saudi media as a conspiracy by Assad's allies, particularly Hezbollah, to 'export Syria's revolution' as Assad and his allies wanted to 'weaken the Sunnis in Lebanon because they are the main supporters of the revolutionaries in Syria' *(al-Riyadh* 2012m*)*. The Saudi argument was that the Alawite government in Syria sought the assistance of secret militias trained by the IRGC and Hezbollah, and they recruited Lebanese Alawites in addition to Syrian Sunni agents in order to retrieve senior opposition figures and scare the Syrian opposition from seeking refuge in Lebanon *(al-Riyadh* 2012m*)*. In a telegram to the Lebanese president, the Saudi monarch claimed that the spillover would potentially 'break out into sectarian strife, [thus] returning [Lebanon] to the spectre of civil war'. King Abdullah framed the events in Lebanon as conspiracies that play out in 'the interest of foreign parties that do not want good for Lebanon' (al-Saud 2012c), an allusion to the Assad government and its allies, Iran and Hezbollah.

Drawing on the king's telegram and using it as a canvas to sketch an image of Iranian meddling in Arab affairs, Saudi editorials promulgated the trope of a foreign conspiracy, sedition, and sectarian strife – all tropes employed since the beginning of the Arab Spring, particularly in Bahrain. Editorials discussed the Lebanese clashes and made two main frames with the Iranian–Hezbollah–Syria axis their focal point. First, the sectarian clashes were framed as a 'test for Sunni powers' against the Syrian government and its allies. The second frame taken was a warning by Assad's allies to the Lebanese government 'not to be sympathetic to the Syrian opposition', or else Lebanon would face a civil war fomented by 'Hezbollah that has weapons and is the major and most important power' in the country *(al-Riyadh* 2012e*)*. These frames served to construct, for the Saudi domestic audience, an image of Iran and its allies as sectarian seditionists seeking to export Assad's revolution to alleviate the pressure from Damascus, and also for Iran and its proxies to maintain control over Lebanon.

Saudi Arabia Pushes Back

The summer of 2012 witnessed a rise in opposition attacks in Damascus, with some media outlets referring to the armed clashes as a 'street war' *(al-Riyadh* 2012o*)*. On 14 July 2012 armed clashes between Syrian security forces and armed opposition groups took place in the capital. The Saudi press framed the battles as the 'beginning of the end' for Assad *(al-Riyadh* 2012o*)*, an anticipation of both the end of the regime and the fall of the capital, which was reinforced after the Al-Qaeda bombing of the National Security headquarters on 18 July 2012 that saw the assassination of Syria's top security chiefs and generals *(al-Riyadh* 2012o*)*. While the pro-Assad media accused Al-Qaeda of involvement, Saudi editorials spun a conspiracy narrative, depicting the attacks as a 'regime-planned mission' because the generals were planning a coup against Assad *(al-Riyadh* 2012p*)*. This also marked the beginning of an innovative Saudi trope that wove together a narrative of a collaboration and links between Al-Qaeda, Iran, and Syria.

By drawing on a supposed Iranian history of GCC 'meddling', the Saudi editorials pushed a narrative based on Iranian terrorism, accusing it of the longstanding use of proxies in the Gulf via 'fifth column' Shi'i groups *(al-Riyadh* 2012b*)*. These groups, according to the editorials, also included the 'Houthis and Al-Qaeda in Yemen' in addition to the 'bombings in Iraq' perpetrated by 'Al-Qaeda linked groups' *(al-Riyadh* 2012b*)*. These editorials appeared just as the FSA detained forty-eight Iranians thought to be pilgrims visiting Shi'i shrines in Syria but who were accused by the Syrian opposition as being IRGC officers aiding Assad *(Al-Jazeera* 2012a*)*, an allegation that Iran vehemently denied (Vahidi 2012).

Citing this incident, the Saudi media discourse amalgamated the trope of Iranian and Al-Qaeda terrorism with one based on sectarian war in Syria, namely the FSA versus Assad's forces. This was depicted as a Sunni–Shi'i war, a framing by the Saudi press in which the Sunnis were limiting 'Persian expansionism', while Iran aspired to 'convert Syria into a Shi'i state' *(al-Riyadh 2012g)*. In the press, Saudi Arabia was represented as a leader and unifier of the Islamic world, as illustrated in the coverage of the OIC conference in Mecca on 15 August 2012, at which the Iranian president, Ahmadinejad, was seated next to the king. As the Saudi king spoke of Islamic unity, the domestic press represented the monarch as a 'unifier of faith and sects', a 'promoter of Islamic dialogue between Sunnis and Shi'a' with a goal of 'breaching divisions and sedition' *(al-Riyadh 2012a)*. Therefore, the Saudi Self, represented by the king, was explicitly constructed as a leader of Islam, falling back on tropes fortifying Saudi legitimacy in the Islamic world, while implicitly characterizing Iran as a seditionist state with hegemonic aspirations to reconstitute a Persian empire, while suffering from delusions of grandeur.

Sectarian War in Syria

On 16 September 2012, IRGC Brigadier General Ali Jafari confirmed in a speech that the Iranian military was officially involved in Syria (Sharif and IRGC 2012). The Saudi discourse emphasized Iran's activities in Syria, claiming that Tehran was 'utilizing Iraqi airspace' as an air corridor to supply Damascus with weapons *(al-Riyadh 2012n)*. US reports claimed that Iran had sent 150 officers to strengthen the Assad government's military expertise *(Telegraph 2012)*. Furthermore, by October 2012, attacks on Damascus were being directed at Shi'i religious sites, including the Sayyida Zainab shrine. Although Saudi discourse did not mention the Al-Qaeda attacks on the Shi'i holy site, the Saudi press did promulgate a sectarian narrative characterized by Iranian meddling in Iraq and Iran coercing the Baghdad government into aiding Assad, while accusing Assad of a historical relationship with Al-Qaeda going back to the early days after the fall of Saddam *(al-Riyadh 2012k)*. Saudi editorials argued that the use of the Al-Qaeda narrative by Iran and its allies was a propaganda tool intended to falsely propagate the spectre of a radical Sunni state should Assad fall, thereby hindering US support for the Syrian opposition *(al-Riyadh 2012k)*. Furthermore, the Iranian government was construed as meddling in Iraq's security by 'utilizing Al-Qaeda [as a tool] and making Iraq a scapegoat due to the lack of [internal] security [while] instilling fear in the hearts of Iraqis', thus framing Iran as hijacking the Iraqi nation and state by deploying terrorism and sectarianism *(al-Riyadh 2012k)*. This trope of Al-Qaeda and terrorism as an Iranian tool was also employed when discussing Syria. An *al-Riyadh* (2012j) editorial, for example, rhetorically asked 'What would happen if Al-Qaeda formed an alliance with the Damascus regime?' The Saudi editorial argued that although the 'FSA had pledged to protect minorities' in Syria, the increase in terrorist activity was similar to 'Iranian tactics in Iraq [whereby] Iran employed [Al-Qaeda] although they were in conflict'. The conclusion was that 'Syria follows the same path in terms of creating chaos' *(al-Riyadh 2012j)*.

Multiple actors became involved in the Syrian civil war in 2013. Israel began targeting pro-Iran groups, beginning with a Hezbollah convoy on 30 January 2013 *(BBC* 2013b). A second attack resulted in the killing of an Iranian general less than a month later *(Reuters* 2013c). Saudi officials remained silent, while the country's press editorials questioned 'Iran's silence', framing Iran as a 'paper tiger' marked by fearfulness and as a country that could 'never win a war against Israel and its allies' *(al-Riyadh* 2013b). The Saudi press discursively constructed an image of a weak Iran that was more talk than action, terrorizing Syrians and waging a war to protect Assad, all in aid of protecting Iranian interests in Syria *(al-Riyadh* 2013d, 2013h). This narrative of Iranian weakness was reinforced by drawing parallels with alleged Iranian activities in the GCC. The Iranian axis was criticized as 'stirring instability' inside GCC states by employing a 'Bahraini terror cell' *(al-Riyadh* 2013j), while the Iranian-backed Iraqi Shi'i groups threatened Saudi Arabia *(al-Riyadh* 2013g). The Saudi editorials were implying that Iran and its allies spoke of enmity and bravery in the face of Israel while attempting to intimidate their Muslim and regional neighbours rather than responding to Israeli attacks on Iranian interests. Saudi Arabia employed a similar strategy of Othering to Iran where the latter had accused Riyadh of attacking Bahraini protestors rather than aiding and protecting the Palestinians in Gaza from Israeli attacks. In this case, a similar trope was employed by Saudi Arabia as the press accused Iran of attacking Muslims rather than responding to Israel's attacks on Iranian targets.

By spring 2013 the war in Syria had taken a more radical turn. The al-Nusra Front, the Syrian brand of Al-Qaeda, had begun to desecrate Shi'i shrines, such as the Hijr ibn 'Adi mausoleum (Tschannen 2013). By then, the Syrian opposition had congregated under an official umbrella, the National Council for the Syrian Revolutionary and Opposition Forces, gaining formal recognition at the Arab League Doha summit on 26 March 2013 *(Reuters* 2013a). On 4 April, Hezbollah formally entered the Syrian civil war, participating in the al-Qusayr offensive (Phillips 2020), in a border town in Homs province close to Lebanon. While Saudi officials were mainly silent, their reaction came after the fall of Qusayr to Hezbollah, deeming it a great victory for Hezbollah and, by default, Iran.

What was striking was the sectarian call to arms in the Saudi press. Saudi press discourse constructed the Qusayr battle using a sectarian frame, characterizing the Shi'a, led by Hezbollah, as attempting to 'ethnically cleanse Sunnis [and] replace them with Shi'a on the border' (al-Riyadh 2013b). Meanwhile, editorials called on 'Sunnis in Lebanon, Iraq, and Syria to form an alliance . . . at the borders' in support of the Syrian opposition *(al-Riyadh* 2013b). Indeed, the Saudi media started to call explicitly for a sectarian war. Responding to Nasrallah's remark that 'Qusayr was Karbala', while 'Hezbollah soldiers were the companions of Imam Hussein' (Nasrallah 2013b), Saudi discourse saw this as reflecting a sectarian anti-Sunni war directed by Iranian orders, observing that 'Hezbollah takes orders from Iran' just like 'mercenaries who fight for whomever pays' *(al-Riyadh* 2013e). The Saudi press went further, arguing that the 'Sunnis in Lebanon will find themselves drawn into battle', underlining that 'radical Islamic groups' such as Jaish al-Islam existed in Lebanon. Furthermore, the press opined that this allegedly Iranian-led war would spread radical groups across the region, such as the al-Nusra Front and Al-Qaeda in Iraq, which could – along with Lebanon-based radical groups – form a 'triangle with negative repercussions for these countries' security' (al-Riyadh 2013f). Furthermore, the FSA's defeat was attributed to Iran; by labelling Nasrallah as 'an Iranian citizen living in Lebanon', Hezbollah's victory was framed as an Iranian triumph, as his 'patriotism is questionable' (al-Riyadh 2013e). The rebel's defeat also inspired terror labelling, going as far as equating Hezbollah with groups such as Al-Qaeda, labels that were reinforced by drawing parallels with historical events that allegedly involved Hezbollah, such as the 'assassination attempt on the Emir of Kuwait in 1982', and incidents in Bahrain, all the way to 'Bulgaria and Nigeria' (al-Riyadh 2013a), where Hezbollah were accused of being involved in the Arab Spring and in a bus bombing in Burgas, Bulgaria, which involved Israeli tourists (BBC 2013a). These parallels were used to discursively construct an image of international terror, menace, and regional disruption, all due to Iranian sponsorship and machinations.

The loss of Qusayr to Assad and his Iranian-backed allies also mobilized the voice of the Sunni ulama, leading to a statement on 1 June 2013 calling for aid to Sunnis in Syria (Al-Jazeera 2013). The Grand Mufti Yusuf Qaradawi, once renowned for breaching the sectarian divide and especially for holding talks with the Shi'i ulama in general and their Iranian counterparts in particular, now issued a statement calling on 'Sunni Muslims to go to jihad in Syria' and to 'join the battle against Assad' (Al-Jazeera 2013). Qaradawi, a cleric who once supported Hezbollah in its war against Israel in 2006, now labelled them the 'party of Satan' ('hizb al-shaytan'), claiming that the Iranian-backed group wanted to 'exterminate Sunnis' (Al-Jazeera 2013). The Saudi ulama chimed in. The Grand Mufti Al-Asheikh praised the Egyptian cleric and backed the narrative demonizing Hezbollah, the Shi'a, and Iran (al-Jazirah 2013). Meanwhile, the Saudi press capitalized on the sectarian momentum, framing the Shi'a as two groups, 'apolitical Shi'a', which the kingdom respected, versus 'political Shi'a', namely Iranian-backed Shi'a (al-Riyadh 2013c). The latter were explicitly characterized as being part of a sectarian war to 'exterminate Sunnis', and therefore as calling for a 'unified Sunni front of ulama against Iran's agenda and its proxies' (al-Riyadh 2013c). This Hezbollah victory drew on historical allegory, comparing the Shi'a with the Mongols' invasion of Syria in the thirteenth century. However, according to the Saudi press, these 'neo-Mongols' had one goal in sight, 'to create a Shi'i state' by 'recolonizing Syria' while setting their eyes on 'Iraq and their next target', comparing 'Iranian ambitions for a Persian empire' with the Mongols (al-Riyadh 2013i). While historical and Islamic tropes were previously used in Saudi discourse to represent Iran as a hegemonic power that sought a rebirth of its Persian empire, the juxtaposition with the Mongol invasion of the Islamic world was innovative. What the Saudi discourse was implying was that, like the Mongols who sacked Baghdad and Aleppo and destroyed the Abbasid Caliphate, Iran was now attempting to destroy the Arab and Islamic world.

Conclusion

The construction of the Self and Other with regard to the events in Syria had one central feature: the discourses evolved as time passed, the number of actors on the ground increased, and events gained momentum. Another feature of the discourse construction of the Self and Other – predominantly in the Saudi discourse – was the strategized feature of the discourse, that is to say, the genres' representation of the Self and Other were reactionary. In the case of Saudi Arabia, the constructions began with the cautious silence of the elite Saudi discourse while diverting the discussion on Syria to the non-state discourse, i.e. the press. These constructions began by advising the Assad government to reform; they then criticized the violence and, as the protests intensified, the Iranian Other was brought into the discourse construction. Therefore, with the discourse on the Iranian Other came narratives and tropes on the demise of Iran, Hezbollah and the IRGC, while focusing on a Sunni-governed state in Syria. However, as the clashes in Syria intensified and Iran and its allies made gains, for the first time since the 1980s, Saudi domestic discourse began to explicitly call for war in order to control Persian expansionism. The construction of the Iranian Other in Saudi discourse used the narratives of terrorism and sedition. Like its Iranian counterpart, Saudi Arabia used the terrorist discourse to position the Islamic Republic alongside Al-Qaeda, while promulgating a demonized representation of its Other in Saudi domestic discourse, framing the Arab and Saudi Self as a victim of Iranian-sponsored terror. Furthermore, the Saudi discourse employed historical and Islamic narratives, particularly when Iran and its allies made gains on the front line. The victory over the FSA in al-Qusayr redefined Iran's image in the Saudi discourse, not only as a hegemonic power that desired a return to a Persian empire, but as an invader seeking to destroy the Islamic world as did the Mongol invasions of the thirteenth and fourteenth century in Iraq and the Levant.

The Saudi Other in Iranian discourse was reminiscent of the post-revolutionary Khomeini era. As the war intensified, so did the discourses representing the Saudi Other relative to the Self. The armed struggle and bombings in Damascus gave rise to Iran's explicit othering of the kingdom and this in turn propelled the representation of the Self as a leader and protector of the region, the Shi'a, and the Islamic world, while representing the Saudi Other as a greedy seditionist bent on aiding the international community in looting Syria. Furthermore, the attacks on the Shi'i shrines in Syria by the al-Nusra Front led to a discourse justifying the Iranian presence in Syria and preparing the populace for an overt Iranian role, i.e. of defending the Ahlulbayt shrines from the 'Takfiris'. The Takfiri narrative also resulted in a discourse of two Islams, of a war between the oppressed and the oppressor, and between a US-funded Islam that had 'Zionist' fingerprints, which was being used by Saudi Arabia to destroy Syria, versus a pure Islam that was led and protected by Iran. It was this war against the Takfiris that Iran used to construct an image of Saudi-sponsored terrorism and a deviant form of Islam through the employment of the Wahhabism trope and Riyadh's alleged association with Al-Qaeda and other armed groups. The war in Syria saw the use of a polarized rhetoric and pattern of demonization that had not been witnessed since the immediate post-revolutionary era. However, in the summer of 2013, the Ahmadinejad presidency ended, and Iranians elected a pragmatic president who was known for his alignment with the 1990s-era moderate camp of Rafsanjani and Khatami. It would be Iran's new moderate administration that attempted to recalibrate ties with Riyadh, lessen the rhetoric used in official discourse, while trying to reverse Ahmadinejad's confrontational foreign policy in relation to the region and the wider world, particularly concerning Saudi Arabia.

Chapter 12

IRAN GOES NUCLEAR AND THE FIGHT TO SAVE ISLAM

Introduction

Relations between Iran and Saudi Arabia experienced a gradual decline in the first term of the Ahmadinejad presidency, before taking a significant turn for the worse in Ahmadinejad's second term, particularly as the Arab Spring protests enveloped the Arab world and sharpened the rivalry between both states. Furthermore, Tehran's relations with Riyadh were not the only ones under strain. The period of the Ahmadinejad tenure saw a heated debate in the international community over Iran's nuclear programme as well as the imposition of multiple UN and US sanctions on the Islamic Republic. Furthermore, the war in Syria had now taken its toll, with a rise in militant and terrorist groups, including the Syrian version of Al-Qaeda – the al-Nusra Front – and a new group calling itself the Islamic State in Iraq and al-Sham (ISIS), or to use its Arabic moniker, *Daesh*.

This chapter examines Iranian–Saudi relations after the victory of Hassan Rouhani in the Iranian presidential elections and his attempt to recalibrate relations with Riyadh and the region in a manner similar to his predecessors Rafsanjani and Khatami. In this chapter I discuss the impediments and factors that prevented both states from establishing détente and rapprochement. In Iran, the factionalism in the country's domestic politics affected any attempt at rapprochement, while in Riyadh Iran was mistrusted due to its expansion in the Middle East and its nuclear programme, especially as the US attempted to thaw relations with Tehran and negotiate a nuclear deal. While at first there were positive signs of a possible détente, this would later prove difficult. In this chapter I argue that while figures such as Rafsanjani helped promote positive overtures and discourses directed at Riyadh, the legacy of the Ahmadinejad presidency, the nuclear dossier, and the rise in Islamist terrorism in Iraq and Syria would hinder efforts at rapprochement. Focusing on events such as the Iranian elections and Rouhani's victory, the P5+1 nuclear negotiations,[1] ISIS and Iran's presence in Iraq,

---

1. The P5+1 refers to the UN Security Council's five permanent members (known as the P5). These are China, France, Russia, the United Kingdom, and the United States, plus Germany.

and the formation of the Popular Mobilization Units (PMUs) under Iran's training and leadership, this chapter discusses discourses of Self and Other in the war against ISIS over a period in which Iran endeavoured to reach a nuclear deal.

A Victory for the Moderates: An Attempt to Rebrand Iran

The Iranian elections on 14 June 2013 resulted in the ascendency of the cleric Hassan Rouhani to the presidency. Branded a moderate, especially given both his tenure as the secretary general of the Supreme National Security Council (SNSC) under the Khatami leadership and his closeness to Rafsanjani, Rouhani won the elections with 50.7 per cent of votes cast. Rouhani aimed to rebrand Iran's image, ease sanctions, and break international isolation after Ahmadinejad's tenure, and these electoral promises secured his victory. Moreover, his credentials included a Western education, experience in the Majles during the 1980s, and his role as a Rafsanjani acolyte in the 1990s and as a chief nuclear negotiator in the heydays of Khatami's international rapprochement, including with the West and the Arab Persian Gulf states, especially Saudi Arabia. Iran's foreign policy during the Ahmadinejad era, including Iran's presence in Syria, support for the Arab Spring in Bahrain, and expanding influence in Lebanon and Iraq, upended the Saudi détente and rapprochement that was diligently pursued during the Rafsanjani and Khatami administrations.

Rouhani's victory recalled Khatami's 1997 landslide victory. With a turnout of over 72 per cent, Rouhani's conservative opponent, the Tehran mayor Mohammad Ghalibaf, immediately conceded defeat with 16.5 per cent of the vote (Monshipouri 2016: 166). Bearing strategical similarities with the Khatami campaign, Ehteshami (2017) argues that Rouhani received support and endorsements from both Rafsanjani and Khatami (Ehteshami 2017: 94). Rouhani made changes to the cabinet to remove both the legacy of Ahmadinejad's tenure as well as the influence of IRGC-affiliated ministers in favour of those closely aligned with Rafsanjani. However, as Sultan and Saeid (2016: 166) argue, the eight years of the Ahmadinejad presidency 'had more profound consequences than that of any other president in post-revolutionary Iran'. Regarding Iran's foreign policy, the consequences of the Ahmadinejad presidency could be observed as Iran attempted to recalibrate its relations with Saudi Arabia. Although the Rouhani administration intended to rebrand Iran's image and re-establish relations with Saudi Arabia, the factionalism in Iran's domestic politics affected any attempt at rapprochement. Iran's expansion and presence in the Middle East after the fall of Saddam, especially given the events of the Arab Spring, Bahrain, and Syria, only bolstered competition and rivalry with Riyadh. The pushback by Saudi Arabia in the international arena, alongside political dynamics dating back to the 1980s, compounded Iranian conservatives' suspicion of Saudi rapprochement, a suspicion that was entirely mutual. To the hardliners in Iran, the rivalry with Saudi Arabia was a sign of resistance against Zionist subservience and Islamic leadership. Similarly, Saudi

Arabia viewed Iran's expansion as a form of interference and a threat to the Saudi self-image as leader of the Arab and Islamic world. Consequently, Rouhani's priority was to break Iran's isolation, and he started by re-establishing relations with Iran's rival, while promoting the line that the newly elected president would be the 'true face of Iran' (Rouhani 2013b).

Rouhani's intention to mend Iran's relations with the GCC in general, and Saudi Arabia in particular, were made public during his campaign and aimed directly at the Arab public through Arab media. Two days before the elections, the newspaper Asharq Al-Awsat secured an exclusive interview with the candidate through email correspondence. In response to a question on 'deal[ing] with key regional players, including Saudi Arabia ... and accusations of Iranian involvement in the unrest in Bahrain', Rouhani made his intentions explicit, stating that if elected, his major priority in the future administration would be to improve and expand relations with neighbouring countries, while on the topic of Saudi Arabia, he stated:

> I plan to reverse the recently exacerbated [and] unfortunate rivalry the two countries into mutual respect and mutually beneficial arrangements and cooperation to enhance security and restore stability in the region.
>
> (Rouhani and *Al-Majalla* 2013)

With regards to Bahrain, Rouhani's response aligned with Riyadh's call: 'My future administration neither intends to intervene in any other country's internal affairs nor to permit others to do so in Iran', highlighting that while 'Bahrain is of concern' for Iran, the 'political independence, national integrity and security of Bahrain are important factors for the stability and security of the region'. Rouhani pragmatically emphasized that 'the aspirations of Bahraini people to seek their legitimate rights ... should not be compromised', and he further stressed that, if elected as president, he would engage closely in diplomatic interaction and cooperation with all countries in the region to remove the clouds of misunderstanding and rivalry' *(*Rouhani and *Al-Majalla* 2013*)*. Rouhani's narrative and viewpoint recalled the days of Rafsanjani and Khatami, marking his intention to change rivalry to détente and a rapprochement that called for Islamic unity, greater cooperation, and joint regional and Islamic leadership.

In his first post-victory public appearance and press conference, Rouhani emphasized his intentions to improve relations with Saudi Arabia. The president-elect framed Saudi Arabia as a 'priority of the new government', using keywords such as 'friendly and close relations with all its neighbours' to describe the regional states, and highlighting fraternal relations defining the Arab state as 'not only neighbours but also brothers', and highlighting the kingdom's position in the Islamic world since 'hundreds of thousands of Iranians go on pilgrimages to the House of God', reminding the Saudi monarchy that it was he who 'signed the first security agreement between Iran and Saudi Arabia in 1998', hinting to Riyadh that they now had a friend in office to rebuild relations with. Rouhani's tone was optimistic, expressing his hope that the next government would have good relations with Iran's neighbours, and especially with Saudi Arabia (Rouhani 2013a).

Cautious Saudi Optimism

Rouhani's election was met with cautious optimism within Saudi Arabia. Initial reactions from the monarch and his crown prince included telegrams relaying the 'most beautiful congratulations ... [and] progress and prosperity for the brotherly people of Iran', while praising the keenness that the president-elect had expressed in his statements for cooperation and improving relations between the two countries (al-Saud *and SPA* 2013). Domestic newspapers were divided in their opinion of the newly elected Iranian president. In *Asharq Al-Awsat*, Abdulrahman Al-Rashid, a former editor-in-chief of the publication, referred to Rouhani as 'our old friend Rouhani', reminding the readers that it was Rouhani who, in the 1990s, had led the Iranian security and intelligence council, penning a security pact with Nayef, the minister of the interior, and framing the president as a peace-loving pragmatic leader who had 'withdrawn support from Saudi Hezbollah' and had opted for security cooperation with the kingdom (*Asharq-Al-Awsat and Al-Rashid* 2013). Meanwhile, *al-Riyadh* (Al-Dakhil 2017) warned against 'excessive optimism' as the newly elected president's promises were 'reminiscent of [the] Khatami presidency, [which marked] an era of greater calm and development in Saudi–Iranian relations'.

In contrast, other Saudi pundits viewed Rouhani's victory with scepticism. The editor-in-chief of *Asharq Al-Awsat* argued that 'caution is also very imperative today' as the 'president is not everything in Iran, since it has become a military state wearing the turban of the Valy-i Faqih [and] no matter how moderate a president is, his powers are limited' (*Asharq-Al-Awsat* 2013b). Moreover, the criticism of a 'moderate president' was taken further, arguing that 'Hezbollah was created during Rafsanjani's tenure', while Iran 'penetrated our region during the reformist Khatami's tenure', thus framing his 'Dialogue of Civilisations' as a façade that was used to 'divert attention, while the Revolutionary Guards were enhancing Tehran's influence in an unprecedented way in our region' (*Asharq-Al-Awsat* 2013b). Similarly, both state and non-state actors made similar arguments. The chairman of the Saudi Shurah Council's foreign affairs committee, Abdullah Al-Askar, opined that while Rouhani 'will not speak out as harshly as Ahmadinejad', he would 'work within the framework set by Khamenei', making a humorous comparison between the two as the 'difference between Coca-Cola and Pepsi' (*Reuters* and Al-Askar 2013). It was clear that the optimism and narratives of brotherhood and the neighbourly relations of the Khatami era were not going to work. Saudi Arabia preferred a 'trust but verify' approach, while its chief diplomat, Saud al-Faisal (*Reuters* and Al-Askar 2013), coupled any improvement in foreign relations with Iran with gestures of good faith, including cutting support for Assad and Iran's nuclear programme. The latter would be a cause of great concern to the Saudis especially, as the US and Iran broke the ice and initiated their first leadership level contact between Rouhani and Obama in September 2013.

'Heroic Flexibility': A Thaw in US–Iran Relations

The Rouhani presidency was won on the promise of breaking Iran's international isolation, which was in place because of its nuclear programme and the resultant sanctions. During his campaign, Rouhani stated explicitly that 'it is easier to talk to the Americans [rather] than the Europeans', framing the relationship between the EU and the US as that between members of a village with the US being its 'head' (*kadkhodāh*) (Rouhani 2013d). He said, 'Dealing with the head is always easier' (Rouhani 2013d), since the Europeans would seek American approval at every step. It is important to mention that Khamenei had secretly approved talks with the Americans in Oman during the final months of the Ahmadinejad presidency. Rouhani's mission was to take the negotiations into the next phase, including to normalize relations with the international community and begin explicit negotiations with the P5+1 to reach a comprehensive deal that would see an end to negotiations and detrimental sanctions. This required a courageous step from both the Iranian and US leaderships to break the ice, and it was a major area of contention in Iranian–Saudi rivalry and relations.

Both Iran and the US sought to justify to their audiences and allies – such as the latter's Middle East partners – the reason behind the decision to enter into talks. Obama framed the necessity for talks as part of a regional security framework, one in which negotiations would reduce tension and might, in future, include an extended cross-regional dialogue that could include the GCC (Obama 2015). On the Iranian front, Rouhani's critics, predominantly the conservative groups, stepped up opposition against the nuclear negotiations. Khamenei's support in the latter months of the Ahmadinejad presidency had been crucial in sidelining these critics. Furthermore, after forty years of enmity, the Iranian state had to give solid reasons for its change in direction from animosity to discussions with the US. The answer was in the Iranian framing of this change as one of heroism and flexibility. In a speech on 17 September 2013, Khamenei branded Iranian overtures as marking 'heroic flexibility' *(ISNA 2013)*. Iran's change in position was, therefore, not framed out of necessity and dire economic consequence but was instead based on pragmatic heroism. In addition, Rouhani sought to show Iran's 'true face to the world' as he set off on his first foreign trip to address the UN General Assembly (Rouhani 2013c).

Backed by Khamenei, Rouhani argued that Iran had 'in recent years ... been presented in another way', and he was going to show the world the true face of 'a great and civilized nation [while communicating] the voice of the oppressed people of Iran' with the aim of ending the 'sanctions [that] are an illegal and unacceptable path' and urging the West to 'opt for talks, cooperation, and mutual interests' (Rouhani 2013c). In his UN speech, Rouhani reaffirmed Iran's position of 'heroic flexibility', calling its interlocutors to resolve matters through 'mutual respect' (Rouhani 2013b), thus framing Iran's position as one of strength rather than of weakness or desperation. Furthermore, the president aimed to convey an image of Iran as a responsible actor within the international community, and so he highlighted the 'pursuit of two common objectives': the peaceful nature of Iran's nuclear programme and Iran's right to enrichment to pursue nuclear technology (Rouhani 2013b). Intriguingly, in an echo of his predecessor, just like when Mohammad Khatami asked the world to join Iran in a 'Dialogue of Civilisations' at his first UN speech in 1997, Rouhani 'invite[d] all states to start thinking about a coalition for peace' by joining 'The WAVE: World Against Violence and Extremism' (Rouhani 2013b). Although part of the speech laid the blame on the US for arming Saddam with a chemical arsenal during the Iran–Iraq war, establishing Al-Qaeda, and aggravating the issue of Israel and the 'brutal oppression of the Palestinian people', these acts did not deter diplomatic efforts between Iran and the US.

The US secretary of state, John Kerry, met with his Iranian counterpart, Javad Zarif, on the sidelines of the United Nations General Assembly in New York (Jett 2017: 357). The Kerry–Zarif talks are believed to have been crucial for the events that followed, and they led to Obama's fifteen-minute call with Rouhani. Consequently, Obama announced that he and Rouhani had requested that their teams work towards resolving the nuclear issue and move towards an agreement on Iran's nuclear programme. The crucial point was Obama's reasoning that, while obstacles remained, there was an air of positivity that both parties could 'reach a comprehensive solution' *(Reuters* 2013b*)*.

As Hiro (2019) has argued, Iranian and US officials had two further secret meetings in Muscat (Oman) in October that cleared the way for the resumption of talks between Iran and the P5+1. After two rounds of talks in October, the new Iranian delegation headed by Zarif reached an interim deal with the P5+1 on 24 November 2013. In return for lowering enrichment to a maximum of 5 per cent and giving IAEA inspectors access to Iranian nuclear facilities, Iran would receive $7 billion of its frozen assets. The Joint Plan of Action would also set a roadmap for a final deal, later referred to as the Joint Comprehensive Plan of Action (JCPOA), with the aim of settling the nuclear dossier, easing tensions, and bringing Iran back into the international community. Catching it off guard, this détente and rapprochement between Iran and the 'Great Satan', i.e. the US, raised concerns among the Saudi elites.

Fear of a Grand Bargain

The Obama–Rouhani phone call raised the prospects of a thaw in US–Iranian relations after four decades of enmity, while also raising the alarm in the Saudi kingdom. Indeed, the Obama administration viewed the warming of relations with Iran as part of a grand strategy to alleviate regional instability in the Middle East, the lynchpin of which was, according to the Americans, deterring Iran from ever possessing nuclear weapons and maintaining deterrence; in order to achieve this, dialogue and negotiations had to take place with Iran. Although the Saudis benefited from a nuclear-weapon-free Iran, they did not have a seat at the negotiating table, thus heightening their fear that a 'grand bargain' might be negotiated between the US and Iran. In such an outcome, the Obama administration might award Iran geopolitical concessions, namely allowing it to expand its power and presence in Syria, Iraq, Lebanon, and the Persian Gulf in exchange for a nuclear deal (Gause 2013). Saudi Arabia was apprehensive of any geopolitical concessions in favour of Iran, not only because it would add to Iran's regional leverage and fears of a 'Shi'i crescent', but also because it reminded Riyadh of the pre-revolutionary era in which Iran had strong ties with Washington, when the former was dubbed the 'policeman of the Gulf'.

The Saudi response to the thaw in relations was framed from the outset by the kingdom's disappointment over the Palestinian–Israeli conflict and, mainly, with US reactions to the ongoing Syrian civil war and the alleged chemical-weapons attacks in August (Kozhanov 2021: 118). The US and Russia had reached a deal that resulted in a dismantling of Syria's chemical-weapons stocks and programme. This move, according to Saudi Arabia, was not the response they had hoped for after Obama had announced that Assad had crossed a red line in the summer. Therefore, Saudi Arabia strategized its response, using its discourse and actors. This was true of both its response to the international community in general and to the US in particular, and it did so by highlighting their position and relevance on the world stage. This was accomplished on three levels: official discourse from the Saudi elite, semi-state actors, former officials such as members of the Shura Council and former ambassadors, and the press.

In a novel step, one never undertaken by any other state, Saudi Arabia rejected a UN Security Council seat (Kozhanov 2021: 234; Ehteshami and Horesh 2019). This was preceded by the Saudi foreign minister's, Saud al-Faisal's, absence from the UN General Assembly annual speech. Instead, the Saudi ministry of foreign affairs issued a statement outlining the reasons behind the kingdom's position. On the surface, the statement was aimed at the UN Security Council, while in essence it was directed at the US. Accusing the Security Council of 'double standards [that] prevent it from performing its duties and responsibilities', which had resulted in 'continued disruption of peace ... [and the] expansion of injustice against people, the violation of rights, and spread of conflict and wars in the world' (Saudi Foreign Ministry 2013). The Saudi statement implicitly blamed the US for 'allowing the Syrian regime to kill its own people and burn them with chemical weapons ... without any deterrent or punishment' (Saudi Foreign Ministry 2013).

This aggravation of the US–Russia deal over Assad's chemical weapons was compounded by the Obama–Rouhani call. The kingdom's intelligence chief conveyed that the Saudi UN move was really aimed at the US. In a meeting with European diplomats, Bandar bin Sultan argued that the snub 'was a message to the US, not the UN' (Knickmeyer 2013). Once a career diplomat and close friend of the US, he emphasized that the 'shift away from the US is a major one', whereby the kingdom would reduce its cooperation with US intelligence in Syria and seek other allies. This was the first explicit sign of Saudi frustration with the Obama administration, since the kingdom had invested heavily in ousting Assad and felt let down by the US intention of achieving friendlier relations with Assad's main backer, Iran, thereby increasing Saudi fears of a US–Iran deal at its expense.

The Saudi fear of a thaw in Iranian–US relations was formulated in terms of the identification of a hidden agenda and Saudi scapegoating. The chairman of the

Shura Council's foreign affairs committee, Abdullah Al-Askar, argued in a statement to Reuters that 'I am afraid in case there is something hidden', stressing that 'America and Iran reached an understanding [with European diplomats] . . . at a cost to the Arab world and the Gulf states, particularly Saudi Arabia'. This narrative of Arab and Saudi scapegoating was also promulgated in the Saudi press. In their editorials, Saudi journalists, such as Tariq Al-Humaid, argued in *Asharq Al-Awsat* that the warming of Iranian–Saudi relations was 'political naivety' on Obama's part, while dialogue and sanctions relief would lead to Iran 'acquiring nuclear weapons and changing the rules of the game in the region', adding that Obama was 'saving Hezbollah and easing its mission' in the Middle East in general and in Syria in particular *(Asharq-Al-Awsat* 2013a). In contrast, Iranian signals to the US were branded as Iranian 'hypocrisy'. The newspaper *Asharq Al-Awsat* argued that 'billboards in Tehran' demonizing the US, were a form of 'Iranian political propaganda' that had now ended as 'Iran seeks to open its doors to the US', and they therefore 'erase[d] four decades' of anti-US slogans *(Asharq-Al-Awsat* 2013a). The Saudi press projected two notions to its domestic audience. The first was that the US was naïve in its dealings with Iran, where the region was being scapegoated in return for good relations, which would, however, permit Iranian regional expansion. Second, Iranian enmity towards the US was hypocritical political propaganda, which would be erased and reversed when it suited Iran's interests. There was a genuine fear in Riyadh that the US was leaning towards détente and rapprochement with Tehran at the expense of its relationship with the kingdom. To Saudi Arabia this rekindling was reminiscent of the pre-revolutionary era, when the Shah enjoyed military supremacy and a strong relationship with the US, and was dubbed the 'policeman of the Gulf'. It was this image of regional control with Washington's blessing coupled with nuclear energy and regional expansion that instilled anxiety in Riyadh, thus leading to its UN posturing and outspoken statements on Syria. It would also be these Saudi threats that would lead Washington to make gestures to appease Riyadh.

Fortifying the Relationship: Washington Appeases Riyadh

The Saudi threats of shifting away from their alliance with the US and the dismissal of the UNSC seat seemed to work. On 4 November, John Kerry flew to Riyadh to meet with the monarch and his Saudi counterpart, Saud al-Faisal, in a bid to reassure the kingdom of US commitments towards Saudi Arabia and the region. Kerry's mission was also intended to assure the Saudis that the developments between Iran and the US would not come at the expense of Washington's allies. In a nutshell, Kerry sought to mend and reinforce the eighty-year-old bridge between the two states. This was accomplished by highlighting the image of Saudi Arabia and its importance. Branding Saudi Arabia as a 'senior player' in the Arab world, Kerry also sought to resolve the dispute with the Saudis over Iran's nuclear programme. Regarding the Syrian crisis, Kerry doubled down on the fact that 'there were no differences' with the kingdom, stressing that its ties with Riyadh were 'strategic' and 'enduring', emphasizing that Obama 'will use all elements of US power, including force' to secure US interests in the Middle East (Kerry and al-Saud 2013). These core interests were defined as shared with Saudi Arabia, and on the issue of Syria, the 'US appreciates Saudi Arabia's leadership' and its collaboration towards a 'negotiated political settlement [to] counter violent extremist groups'. On Iran, Saudi Arabia's main concern, Kerry stressed that the US 'would not allow Iran to acquire nuclear weapons', and that both countries 'are in close agreement'. Kerry went further to highlight that 'nothing ... will alter or upset or get in the way ... between the US and Saudi Arabia and the relationship in this region' as they negotiate with Iran (Kerry and al-Saud 2013).

Saudi Arabia took this opportunity to reinforce the kingdom's image domestically, regionally, and on the world stage. Satisfied with the US remarks, Saud al-Faisal reciprocated the comments of his American counterpart while playing down the recent tensions. Sharing Kerry's opinion, al-Faisal asserted that the kingdom 'accepts the assurance of the secretary that they will not allow the development of ... atomic weapons in Iran' (Kerry and al-Saud 2013). Saud al-Faisal framed the kingdom as a power that was of strategic importance to the US, and he stressed that both states were 'friendly countries' with relations built on 'sincerity, candour, and frankness' (BBC 4 November 2013). The foreign minister dispelled 'media reports about Saudi–US relations ... as dramatically deteriorating', while also underlining that the relationship was 'historic ... based on independence, mutual respect, common interest, and continual cooperation on regional and international issues'(Kerry and al-Saud 2013). The Saudi–US relationship was characterized as one of equals and on par, 'based on sincerity and frankness ... rather than courtesy'. In addition, the kingdom's 'declination of the membership of the [UN] Security Council' was toned down but not elaborated on (Kerry and al-Saud 2013). However, the fault of the UN was raised in terms of their 'failures to deal with political issues, [and] crises' in the Middle East (Kerry and al-Saud 2013), predominantly Syria. Saud al-Faisal also drew on the grievance over Syria when discussing Iran's nuclear deal.

During the press conference with Kerry, Saud al-Faisal also defined the kingdom's position on the P5+1 negotiations with Iran. Riyadh viewed the talks as 'based on good intentions', while to 'bolster the negotiations with Iran' they should include 'Iran's presence in Syria'. Riyadh viewed Syria as in a state of civil war. Tehran was defined by al-Faisal as an invader and 'Syria an occupied land' (Kerry and al-Saud 2013). The foreign minister lambasted Tehran's presence there as a means 'to help the regime hurt the Syrian people'. One remedy, according to al-Faisal, was to test Iran and for Tehran to prove its 'good intentions' to its neighbours. These gestures, according to Riyadh, would be for Iran to 'get out of Syria and get its ally, its Lebanese ally Hezbollah, out of there too' (Kerry and al-Saud 2013). The press conference was a public relations exercise for Riyadh to not only highlight the position and image of the Saudi self but also to define its rival and Other, Iran. It was evident that Saudi Arabia was highlighting its image as a force for peace versus an image of Iranian belligerence in the region. The kingdom projected an image of being a regional power and its relationship with the US as a necessity that Washington could not do without. Implicitly, Riyadh informed its audience that it had 'forgiven' the Obama administration for its trespasses as the kingdom was the region's main power regardless of Iran's nuclear achievements, in an effort to downplay Iran's upcoming nuclear deal. This would be a tactic that Iran would also undertake as it highlighted its regional presence and downplayed the nuclear negotiations as they moved forward in their talks with the P5+1 and signed the Joint Plan of Action (JPA). Saudi Arabia's posturing and articulation of its external image in such a manner as rejecting a UN seat was a rare occurrence. In the past it had asserted its image to Iran and the region, but never to the US and the West. Also, this was the first time that any country had rejected a seat at the UNSC, and so they had set a precedent.

The Interim Nuclear Deal: The Joint Plan of Action

The JPA interim nuclear accord was signed in Geneva on 24 November, with the Supreme Leader lauding the negotiators and stating that they 'deserved to be appreciated and thanked' (Khamenei 2013). The Iranian president framed the JPA as a route to improving the wellbeing of the Iranian economy and society. Speaking in a televised address, Rouhani repeated his famous slogan 'Nuclear energy is our absolute right', representing this as an inalienable right for all Iranians that allowed them to 'progress, develop, and improve people's livelihood and welfare'. However, as the Iranians rejoiced, the voices from Riyadh were hesitant and sceptic. Iran was inching closer to being part of the 'nuclear club'.

Following the tensions and narratives of scapegoating and Iranian hypocrisy, Saudi Arabia joined the P5+1 and the international community in welcoming the interim nuclear agreement. The Saudi official statement contained a hint of scepticism, stating that 'if there is goodwill' then the JPA 'could be an initial step towards reaching a comprehensive solution for Iran's nuclear programme' (Saudi Cabinet 2013). Alluding to the alleged clandestine nature of Iran's nuclear programme, it hoped the agreement would lead 'to the removal of weapons of mass destruction, especially nuclear weapons, from the Middle East and the Arab Gulf' region (Saudi Cabinet 2013).

Despite the initial gesture, Saudis were concerned that the US would sell them out to the Iranians (Al-Sultan and Saeid 2016). The thaw in relations between Tehran and Washington was a concern for Riyadh, especially since any US–Iranian agreement could tilt the balance of power in Iran's favour, empowering Tehran and allowing it to expand. Domestically, this worry was remarked on by Saudi Arabia's Shura Council member, Abdullah al-Askar:

> I am afraid Iran will give up on something to get something else from the big powers in terms of regional politics. And I'm worrying about giving Iran more space or a freer hand in the region ... The government of Iran, month after month, has proven that it has an ugly agenda in the region, and in this regard no one in the region will sleep and assume things are going smoothly.
>
> (*Reuters* and Al-Askar 2013)

Consequently, the Iranians, like the US, sought to reassure Riyadh of the peaceful nature of their nuclear programme and attempted to resume relations. Iran employed a two-pronged approach. The first included semi-state actors with positive ties to Riyadh, principally Rafsanjani, as well as the foreign minister, Javad Zarif. In what seemed to be a mimicking of Kerry's discourse on Saudi Arabia, the official Iranian discourse praised and recognized the Saudi leadership regionally, in terms of Islam, and on the world stage.

In a bid to brief the GCC states and allay their fears, Iran sent Zarif on a whirlwind Gulf tour that included Kuwait, UAE, Qatar, and Oman. Furthermore, while Zarif was not able to secure a visit to Riyadh, he made a point of mentioning Saudi Arabia in every one of the Gulf capitals he landed in. Tehran's message focused on Iran's desire to reduce tensions and strengthen relations with the kingdom. In Kuwait, Zarif stressed to the late emir, Sheikh Sabah Al-Ahmad Al-Sabah, that Saudi Arabia was an 'influential regional country'. A similar comment was made in Oman, which emphasized that Iran's 'relations with Saudi Arabia should expand' while highlighting Riyadh's position as 'an extremely important country in the region and the Islamic world' *(Reuters* 2013a*)*. Iran endeavoured to please Saudi Arabia by affirming the kingdom's regional leadership as well as its weight in the Islamic world. However, the messages fell on deaf ears; Saudi Arabia would not open the door to Iran's attempts at rapprochement.

On his return to Iran, Zarif made a final overture on social media. Posting on his Facebook account, Zarif once again confirmed, affirmed, and confessed to Saudi leadership and Iranian readiness to begin talks: 'We are ready to consult and talk with Saudi officials whenever the brothers are ready ... we consider it in the interest of the two countries, the region, and the Islamic world'. Zarif stressed that that the 'security and tranquillity in the Persian Gulf have always been and will be a priority' (Zarif 2013). However, there was no immediate response to Zarif's offer. The kingdom was clearly bitter over Tehran's expansion in Syria and increased power in Iraq, and so Iran pursued an alternative route through Rafsanjani, the architect of Iran's rapprochement with Saudi Arabia during the 1990s.

Rafsanjani had made explicit overtures to Saudi Arabia in his press and media interviews parallel with the advances made by the Rouhani administration. In an interview with the newspaper *Entekhab* (Rafsanjani 2014b), the former president and Majles speaker stated that he would volunteer to go to Saudi Arabia to help improve and rebuild relations with Riyadh. Rafsanjani, known for his explicit approaches to the Saudi monarch shortly after the liberation of Kuwait in 1991, argued that 'Iran–Saudi relations have never been so stressed in any period' and that if 'negotiations were to take place to solve the problems, a plan must be drawn up to identify what each side wants'. The pragmatic cleric expressed the grievance that Riyadh had and the solution to remedy these unresolved issues. This solution would include 'expert negotiations' aimed at 'resolving outstanding issues' starting with 'Bahrain and Lebanon first ... [then] Syria and Iraq' (Rafsanjani 2014b). Rafsanjani was proposing an explicit roadmap; namely, if matters in Manama and Beirut were resolved, then the two parties could discuss Yemen, and once that was settled, then they could discuss a compromise over Syria (*Al-Monitor* and Hashem 2014).

Zarif's tour and Rafsanjani's remarks and efforts led to a slight thaw in relations between Riyadh and Tehran. Zarif's comments to the GCC leaders and admission of Saudi Arabia's leadership role, along with Rafsanjani's proposed roadmap out of the regional impasse, had borne fruit. On 3 March 2014, a newly appointed Saudi ambassador, Abdulrahman al-Shehri, presented his credentials to the Iranian president. Rouhani stressed that Tehran was determined to advance 'cordial and brotherly relations', not only with Riyadh but also with all Islamic countries. Framing the thaw in relations between Tehran and Riyadh as an avenue 'which opens horizons between the two countries', the Saudi ambassador labelled Rouhani's presidency as a 'wise leadership' that will allow for an 'unprecedented development' in relations between the two states (Al-Shehri 2014). In later interviews, Rouhani sustained this dynamic with Riyadh, arguing that the kingdom 'is not an obstacle, and we have no problems with them'. As Riyadh was rekindling relations with Iran diplomatically, Tehran was sustaining the language of détente. The Iranian official discourse, through Rouhani, framed relations with Saudi Arabia as based on collaboration and joint leadership in the face of regional threats and opportunities. Iran called on the kingdom to find a solution to 'regional problems . . . and understand the best route to peace in the region'. This could only be achieved through 'peace and brotherhood and elimination of terrorists' from the region (Rouhani 2014).

Rouhani's remarks, although welcomed in Riyadh, did not reap the results Iran had hoped for. The Iranian foreign minister had announced that he was willing to travel to Riyadh as soon as he was invited (Kamrava 2020). Zarif's Saudi counterpart, Saud al-Faisal, stated that the kingdom had already 'issued an invitation to the Iranian foreign minister, Mohammad Javad Zarif, and that Riyadh was willing to receive him any time he sees fit to come', calling Iran a 'neighbour' and expressing Riyadh's willingness to 'negotiate [and] talk with them' *(Reuters and al-Saud 2014)*. With all the signs of thaw and overtures from Iran, and the welcoming remarks from Riyadh, the visit, however, never materialized. Although Rouhani had a strong voice in shaping Iran's foreign policy, the final decision to meet the Saudis was in the hands of the Supreme Leader. Furthermore, conservative voices, especially hard-line ones, had an effect on any potential rapprochement with Riyadh.

Iranian conservative parliamentary members, such as Mohammad Hassan Asafari, stated that the 'invitation was not enough', arguing that if Riyadh was serious about détente, it should 'drop its support for Takfiri movements' (Asafari 2014). This call was echoed by Khamenei in a meeting held with the Kuwaiti emir, Sheikh Sabah Al-Ahmad Al-Sabah, urging him to relay the message to the Saudi monarch that they will stop their support for the armed Syrian opposition because 'in the not-too-distant future, these groups will turn against their very supporters' (Khamenei 2014a). The signs from Khamenei and the conservative factions of Iranian politicians were enough for Zarif to make the trip to Riyadh. On 3 June Zarif turned down an invitation to a meeting of the Organization of Islamic Cooperation (OIC) held in Saudi Arabia, as it coincided with the nuclear talks *(Reuters 2014a)*. Iran was now speaking from a position of strength. Tehran was in direct talks with its main adversary, the US. However, Iran would soon become entangled in a quagmire that would threaten the security of the region and the international community. ISIS was making vast gains on Iran and Saudi Arabia's doorsteps.

The Rise of ISIS: Rivalry and Mutual Threat

Taking advantage of the civil war in Syria and the sectarian unrest in Iraq, ISIS made substantial advances in both countries. Initially, the Iranian media had downplayed the threat (Esfandiary and Tabatabai 2015). The fall of Mosul to ISIS on 10 June was described as 'unexpected' with the governor of Ninawa province characterizing it as 'a questionable event' (*Resalat* 2014b), since the city fell to ISIS after just four days of clashes. Residents had been displaced and had fled in thousands to the Kurdish regions of Iraq as ISIS was relentless in its fight to take over Iraq by heading south towards Samarra and Kirkuk. As the international media reported the fall of Mosul and the ISIS advance towards Samarra, Iran's major newspapers, such as *Kayhan* and *Resalat*, announced that '5,000 ISIS troops along with some tribesmen attacked the city' (*Resalat* 2014a). As *Kayhan* remarked, the 'Iraqi army and security forces repelled an ISIS militant attack on the city of Samarra, killing at least 100 militants' as Iraq's ground forces entered 'Samarra with 300 armoured vehicles and a large number of troops ... and launched heavy attacks on terrorists' (*Kayhan* 2014a).

The Iranian government's view of ISIS was clearly defined by its Supreme Leader. In a meeting with Kuwait's emir, Sabah Al-Ahmad Al-Sabah, on 1 June, Khamenei argued that regional states 'underestimate the danger of the Takfiri groups', i.e. ISIS, accusing local states of 'supporting these Takfiri groups', predicting that these countries will 'be the victims ... and will have to destroy them at great cost'. In a veiled reference to Saudi Arabia, Khamenei interpreted the regional support for Islamic terrorism and the 'killings and crimes in Syria and some other countries', i.e. Iraq (Khamenei 2014e). Iran's government line downplayed the fall of Mosul. Ali Shamkhani, the Secretary of the Supreme National Security Council (SNSC), limited his comments to the fact that 'ISIS terrorist elements ... in Iraq is a warning signal for the security of the region', and he said it calls for 'serious attention by governments and the international community' (Shamkhani 2014). The deputy foreign minister, Amir-Abdollahian, assured the Iranian people that ISIS was 'no threat against the geographical borders of the Islamic Republic of Iran' (Abdolahian 2015). Iranian parliamentarians, however, sought to project an air of calm as regards the worrying situation next door, while exploiting the crisis to highlight Iranian military power and identify regional conspiracies and a hidden agenda against Iraq. By drawing parallels with ISIS and Israel, Esmail Kowsari, a conservative member of the parliament's National Security and Foreign Policy Commission, stressed that the 'Iranian Armed Forces are vigilant and ISIS is not a force that can create a problem in Iran', arguing that Iraq's terrorist crisis was due to Westerners and Israel and their goal 'to divide and divide Iraq' (Kowsari 2014).

The former IRGC officer turned legislator framed ISIS as 'mercenaries who receive money and carry out the goals of others', implicitly referring to countries such as Saudi Arabia, and how 'their hands will be cut off from Iraq as soon as possible', emphasizing that a 'group like ISIS ... would not dare create a problem inside Iran' (Kowsari 2014).

To its domestic audience, the Iranian ulama's discourse represented the ISIS attacks in Iraq as an extension of the war against the Islamic Republic and the Iranian-led 'axis of resistance' in Syria. In his Friday prayer sermon, Ayatollah Emami-Kashani argued that the 'enemy still has greed *[ṭama ']* towards the Islamic Republic' while the 'awakening of the nation, unity of the people and the *Valy-i Faqih* will throw all the conspiracies in the dustbin of history' (Emami-Kashani 2014). The jurist defined these 'enemies' as those that aided the rise of ISIS, such as the 'Takfiri groups that were once known as the Taliban, Al-Qaeda, and now ISIL (ISIS)' and were 'defeated with humiliation', depicting ISIS as an evolution of groups that had 'already entered Iraq' and were seeking the destruction of Iran and its allies (Emami-Kashani 2014). Speaking to Iraqis in Arabic, the Friday imam promulgated Iran's narrative of Islamic unity, sacred defence, and 'Zionist conspiracies' (Emami-Kashani 2014). Constructing the war against ISIS within an apocalyptic frame, the cleric emphasized that the youth must defend their land and gather around the 'Imam Zaman', i.e. the Mahdi, who is 'revered not only by the Shi'a but also by a large number of Sunnis' (Emami-Kashani 2014). The use of Islamic eschatology and Shi'i tropes of the Mahdi were reminiscent of the turbulent post-Saddam era in Iraq, particularly the bombing of the Askari shrine. Furthermore, discourses on 'Zionism' and plots to destroy the Islamic world could be traced back to the military confrontations between Hezbollah and Israel in 2006, and Gaza and Israel in 2009.

Iranian editorials employed two tones when discussing ISIS advances in Iraq. Newspapers aligned with Rouhani and Khatami, such as *Etemaad*, defined the rise in terrorist attacks as due to fundamentalism and hatred bred by fanaticism. Without mentioning names, or denigrating states, editorials in *Etemaad* argued that the 'first culprits' of the Iraq crisis were 'the most powerful ... ruling governments in the region' that have 'all the oil and gas' and were 'directly and indirectly involved in the formation of these catastrophes' (*Etemaad* 2014). However, instead of demonizing the Other and naming the regional states, moderate-leaning editorials argued that open and practical dialogue between the major regional states could 'alleviate these problems' (*Etemaad* 2014). Echoing the pragmatic narratives of the Iranian government since Rouhani's election, *Etemaad* called for 'Islamic unity between Muslims' and an effort to 'isolate [the] terrorism that has tarnished Islam'. The solution according to the reformist press was to strengthen 'the discourse of moderation and reform ... and democracy ... alongside religiosity'. The Islamic world, according to the moderate Iranian press, needed a saviour, 'a great asset to the Islamic world' such as Sayyid Mohammad Khatami, the former president of Iran, who enjoyed 'many admirers among democrats, and other figures in other Islamic countries' (*Etemaad* 2014). *Etemaad* was now constructing a narrative opposed to the conservative press, the latter viewing Islam's solutions through the sole leadership of the Valy-i Faqih. That is to say, the Iranian moderate press argued that the problems of the Islamic world required a leader who enjoyed a wide consensus among Muslims, implicitly referring to the Sunnis in general and Saudi Arabia in particular.

Conservative newspapers started defining ISIS and its origins and framed its rise as drawing on a sectarian, Saudi and Wahhabi-led agenda with US collaboration. Kayhan did not hesitate to frame Saudi Arabia as sponsoring the terrorist group. Citing 'documented reports', the editorial argued that ISIS had 'strong and full support from the Saudi government' as 'satellite imagery ... showed a convoy carrying weapons from Saudi Arabia to Anbar province and then flowing to Fallujah and Ramadi' (*Kayhan* 2014b). The reason behind this Saudi support, according to the conservative press, was that the US and Saudi Arabia were 'concerned and angry at Assad's re-election' which was highlighted as a 'victory for the resistance front'. The ISIS attacks were, therefore, constructed as Saudi and US revenge against the Shi'a through the 'capture and destruction of the shrines of Imam Hadi and Imam Askari in Samarra', a line of thought more 'attuned to Wahhabism in terms of belief than to ISIS' (*Kayhan* 2014b). As far as the Iranian press discourse was concerned, ISIS members 'belonged to the Hanafi sect ... which forbids the destruction of graves', reminding readers that the aim was to recreate the 'destruction of the holy shrine of Hujr ibn Ady in Syria' as carried out by the al-Nusra Front who were 'more in line with Wahhabism and their history and beliefs' (*Kayhan* 2014b). In addition, Iran was implicitly included as part of the Iraqi forces' military achievements and part of the 'resistance front [that had] thwarted the terrorist plot and dealt a fatal blow' to ISIS (*Kayhan* 2014b).

As ISIS made gains, the hypothesis put forward in the conservative press sought to strengthen the narrative of Saudi involvement. One assertion was that the 'conflict is internal in nature and relates to the results of the recent Iraq parliamentary elections' and that the loss of the Sunni parties had led the 'three Sunni provinces [to] deal with ISIS' and begin the process of forming a Sunni state (*Kayhan* 2014c). A second argument adopted a more regional perspective, portraying Saudi Arabia as involved 'in a war with the resistance bloc', accusing the kingdom of 'sustaining its ten years of advances with the formation of terror squads in Iraq' and its 'role in Syria for the past three years', i.e. since 2011. A third hypothesis put forward was that the rise of ISIS and its attacks in Iraq were the 'product of joint actions by Saudi Arabia, Turkey, Jordan, Qatar, and the Zionist regime aimed at intimidating Iraq' from joining the Iran-led axis of resistance, hence 'separating [Iraq] from Iran' (*Kayhan* 2014c). The conservative Iranian press discourse constructed an image of the Saudi Other as being a supporter of terrorism, a seditionist – in terms of dividing Iraq and fanning sectarianism between Muslims – and a collaborator in a 'Zionist-led conspiracy' to destroy the Iranian-led 'axis of resistance'. This characterization of Saudi Arabia and its relationship with ISIS and the axis was aimed at the domestic audience, preparing Iranians for Tehran's war with ISIS and for Iran's protection of the Islamic world.

By 16 June, ISIS had seized the strategic city of Tal Afar along the main highway linking Mosul to the Syrian border (*BBC* 2014). Iran acted swiftly and sent its chief military strategist and head of its Quds Force, Qassem Soleimani, to Iraq (News and Hendawi 2014). *The Guardian* had reported on 13 June that Iran had 'sent 2,000 advance troops to Iraq in the past 48 hours to help tackle a jihadist insurgency' (*Guardian* 2014a), an allegation the Iranian president vehemently denied (Rouhani *and ISNA* 2014). The gravity of the crisis in Iraq had, however, sunk in. Rouhani was not only willing to support Iraq militarily, but he went as far as hinting that Iran could collaborate with the US to tackle ISIS. Rouhani mentioned that Iran could 'think about it if we see America starting to confront the terrorist groups in Iraq or elsewhere' (Rouhani *and ISNA* 2014). The Obama administration reciprocated Iran's signalling of possible cooperation (*BBC* 2014). The Pentagon confirmed that it was willing to enter into discussions with Iran over ISIS without any military cooperation, while other administration officials emphasized the informal nature of any talks, rejecting earlier propositions by the US secretary of state of a possible military collaboration with the Islamic Republic (*Guardian* 2014b). In a similar move, Iran's deputy foreign minister, Hossein Amir-Abdollahian, downplayed any prospects of collaboration, arguing that 'Iran had had no negotiations with the Americans over mutual cooperation in Iraq' (*Guardian* 2014b; Abdolahian 2014a).

Amid talk of possible cooperation, Ayatollah Khamenei characterized the events in Iraq as a 'confrontation between American Islam and pure Muhammadan Islam ['Islam-i Nab-i Mohammadi']', whereby the former was represented by '*Taghut* [tyranny] and Zionism' including the US, and the latter was represented by Iran and its allies (Khamenei 2014c). Furthermore, speaking at a meeting with the judiciary (Khamenei 2014d), Khamenei made a set of remarks that included his acknowledgement of the ISIS crisis and America's role and involvement in recent developments in Iraq. According to Khamenei, ISIS was a result of US conspiracies to 'deprive the Iraqi people of the country's achievements' in the elections, which has caused 'US dissatisfaction with the current status quo in Iraq' since the 'US seeks to dominate Iraq and [force] people to obey US rule' (Khamenei 2014d). What Khamenei was implying was that a victory for pro-Iranian groups in Iraq, led by Nouri al-Maliki, had resulted in the US creating the current terrorist crisis in Iraq. Toning down talk of a 'sectarian war', the Ayatollah constructed the crisis as a collaboration between the US, remnants of the Saddam regime, and Takfiri elements. This war, according to Khamenei, was 'sedition' and 'not a Shiite–Sunni war, but a system of domination … to disrupt the stability and peace of Iraq and threaten its territorial integrity' (Khamenei 2014d). He further argued that Iraq was undergoing a 'struggle between two camps', namely a pro- and anti-American camp, and he framed the war on ISIS as one between a pro-US side, which used ISIS as a tool, and a group defending the independence of Iraq, which – by its very nature – was in favour of the Islamic Republic (Khamenei 2014d). In a later speech, Khamenei emphasized that the 'events in Iraq … are a war of terrorism against the opponents of terrorism … a war of humanity against barbarism and savagery' (Khamenei 2014b). As for any American aid in the fight against ISIS, Khamenei's message was the polar opposite of Rouhani's, arguing that, 'We [namely Iran] oppose the involvement of the Americans and others in the

internal affairs of Iraq' since its 'government, people, and the religious authority ...
have the ability to end this sedition' (Khamenei 2014d).

The Iraqi forces led by Qassem Soleimani and Quds Force advisers were making
minor gains against ISIS, while the terrorist groups were making advances towards
the Kurdish region, thereby threating Iran's borders and Iraq's territorial integrity.
In early August, the terrorist group seized control of the Mosul dam, prompting
Obama to order airstrikes against ISIS in Iraq (Pittard, Bryant, and Petraeus 2019).
On 12 August, ISIS captured the town of Jalawla, less than forty kilometres away
from the Iranian border (Dougherty 2019: 216). Iran moved swiftly and repelled
the terrorists in a joint Kurdish counter-offensive (Uskowi 2018: 100). The episode
sparked Iranian fears of a compromise of Iraq's territorial integrity and Iran's
borders.

Talks of Iraq being divided into three parts – Shi'i in the south, Sunni in the
middle, and Kurdish in the north – had first surfaced at the beginning of the US
invasion in 2003 and had been floated by Paul Richter as late as in July 2014
(Esfandiary and Tabatabai 2015: 7). Furthermore, ISIS was making its way south
towards the Shi'i holy cities of Karbala and Najaf that house the shrines of Imam
Hussein and Imam Ali respectively. The initial reaction from Tehran came from
the minister of the interior, Rahmani Fazli, in an interview with the newspaper
Entekhab (Rahmani-Fazli and *Entekhab* 2014). The minister reported that the
Iranian president had declared that Najaf Karbala was 'our red line' and that 'there
would be no restrictions on operations'. Given the worsening situation on the
ground, Iran sought to project a discourse of Shi'i leadership and political
pragmatism. The minister emphasized that it was Iran's 'strong belief and faith,
along with the prudent and intelligent leadership [of] Iran and Hezbollah' that
solved the 'political differences in Iraq ... and supported the Iraqi government', as
well as aiding 'Kurdish officials after they requested help from Iran' (Rahmani-Fazli
and *Entekhab* 2014). This had led the Islamic Republic to 'organize their forces and
provide [military] advice' (Rahmani-Fazli and *Entekhab* 2014). The 'prudent and
intelligent leadership' that the minister referred to was the source of tensions
between the two Iraqi Shi'i political leaders, Nouri al-Maliki and Haider al-Abadi,
an issue that required domestic, regional, and international negotiation in order
for Nouri al-Maliki to step down for Haider al-Abadi. In addition to Iran's image
of Islamic leadership and as protector of the Shi'a, the official discourse constructed
an image of itself as having a pragmatic and positive role in Iraq, as being a problem
solver rather than an agitator, thus countering the Saudi discourse that Iran was
interfering in Iraq's affairs, causing sedition among its politicians and weakening
its Iraqi government.

The rise of ISIS and its threat to the regional states, including the GCC, may
have contributed to the relationship between Saudi Arabia and Iran warming. Iran
managed to convince Nouri al-Maliki to abdicate, allowing Haider al-Abadi, a
candidate more to Saudi Arabia's liking, to take office. In this way, Iran's withdrawal
of support for Maliki was part of their mission of Saudi–Iranian rapprochement as
it removed any obstacles that could allow the US to increase their support in the
war against ISIS. Nouri al-Maliki had previously accused both the US and the

Arab states, namely Saudi Arabia and Qatar, of creating and aiding terrorism and ISIS in Iraq *(Illahi 2020)*. In addition to domestic pressure, especially from the Shi'i ulama in Najaf, it is quite possible that there may have been an unofficial agreement between Iran, Saudi Arabia, and the US to replace Maliki (Zarras 2018: 126).

On 25 August, Iran announced the appointment of Hossein Sadeghi as its ambassador to Riyadh (Partrick 2016: 35). Sadeghi had previously served in Saudi Arabia during the Khatami era and was also an ambassador to Kuwait during the turbulent 1980s (Marschall 2003). The Iranian foreign ministry explicitly reaffirmed their wish for regional rapprochement, declaring that 'Iran's relations with the regional countries including Saudi Arabia are taking their normal course' (Afkham and *Fars* 2014). The next day, the Iranian deputy foreign minister, Abdollahian, visited Riyadh and met with the foreign minister, Saud al-Faisal. The meeting coincided with Iran's efforts at forming a new government in Iraq since Zarif was also on a tour of Iraq to meet its Shi'i and Sunni ulama, and its minority political leaders and representatives (Walsh 2017: 111). In a later interview with Abdollahian, the diplomat highlighted that Saud al-Faisal 'aimed to put relations with Iran on a path to normality'. The meeting was described as 'positive in terms of protocol and the various discussions that took place' (Abdolahian and Shargh 2015). Legislators in the kingdom, such as the head of the Shurah Council's foreign policy committee, described the meetings with Iran as characterized by an atmosphere of positivity, while also sustaining the narrative of Iranian regional meddling and sectarianism. In a rare confession, Abdullah al-Askar argued that Iran had a role to play in the region, remarking that 'it is very important for Iran and Saudi Arabia to talk because both play a role in the region', thereby implying the necessity for regional cooperation *(Al-Arabiya* and Al-Askar 2014*)*. However, al-Askar also remarked that there was a need to 'tell them [Iran] frankly about their meddling in Syria, Iraq, and Yemen, and elsewhere', accusing the Islamic Republic of 'backing all these sectarian groups … to shake the ground underneath regional countries' *(Al-Arabiya* and Al-Askar 2014*)*. The threat of ISIS to both Iran and Saudi Arabia had led to diplomatic overtures on both sides and a reframing of the image of the Iranian Other in Saudi discourse. Although the official discourse was cautious, there were positive signs of détente.

Nevertheless, the meeting in Riyadh bore fruit. At a joint press conference with his Finnish counterpart on 30 August, the Iranian chief diplomat expressed his desire to meet with his Saudi peer: 'The first opportunity for talks between me and his Excellency (Foreign Minister Prince) Saud al-Faisal is on the sidelines of the United Nations General Assembly, and we hope to be able to use the opportunity', suggesting that it would open a door 'to visit[ing] Saudi Arabia and welcom[ing] Saud al-Faisal] to Iran' *(AP News* 2014*)*. Indeed, on 22 September on the sidelines of the UN General Assembly sessions, both foreign ministers met for talks, with the chief diplomats describing the talks as marking a 'a new page in relations between the two countries'. In a live press conference after the discussions, the ministers made positive statements that signalled their intent to start a new chapter in foreign relations *(Al-Arabiya* 2014*)*. In addition to the kingdom's regional and international position, Saud al-Faisal acknowledged Iran's regional weight, observing that both countries are 'influential in the region' while hoping for 'common cooperation [that] will undeniably have an effect on restoring peace' – a message that was echoed by his Iranian counterpart *(Al-Arabiya* 2014). On pressing matters, such as the threat of ISIS and the Syrian crisis, the Saudis were now extending their hand in order to cooperate with Iran, maintaining that both states 'can deal with the regional crisis successfully by using this precious opportunity to avoid the mistakes of the past' *(Arab News* 2014). The threat of ISIS was so great that the Saudi minister now reinterpreted Saudi Arabia's narratives of Iranian regional meddling, sedition, and threat to having been mere 'mistakes and errors of the past'. However, this Saudi position would not last for long.

Signs of a thaw in Iranian–Saudi relations had ended by mid-October. At a press conference hosting his German counterpart in Jeddah, Saud al-Faisal – who had praised a new chapter in relations only three weeks beforehand – lambasted Iran for its 'policy in the region and not … as a country or people' *(Al-Arabiya* 2014). Iran was once again an 'occupying force' in Syria and 'part of the problem, not the solution'. In a major turn, the Saudi state once again framed Iran as an invader and not as a partner with whom Saudi Arabia could cooperate in order to solve the region's problems. 'If Iran wants to be part of the solution' it has to 'pull its forces from Syria. The same applies elsewhere … Yemen or Iraq' *(Al-Arabiya* 2014). One explanation for such a sudden reverse in position and narrative is three main events that occurred consecutively and that may have thrown Saudi Arabia off-balance. These include the Houthi takeover of Sanaa, the death sentence issued against the militant Shi'i cleric Nimr Baqer al-Nimr, and the gains Iran made through its support for Iraq and the Popular Mobilization Units (PMU) in Iraq.

As the two ministers met in New York, the Houthis had taken over the Yemeni capital, Sanaa, a day before. By October, the Houthis had replaced the Yemeni prime minister and had upended an agreement that was signed after the Arab Spring clashes between Abdulrabu Mansour Hadi and Ali Abdullah Saleh. Conflict erupted in Sanaa again, and Saudi Arabia's archenemies, the Iranians, aligned with the Houthis, who were gaining power and momentum in the Yemeni capital. The Houthi takeover was described by the Iranian Supreme Leader's adviser, Ali Akbar Velayati, as 'successive victories' that 'came in a thoughtful and planned manner', and he defined the group as 'part of the successful movements of the Islamic awakening' (Velayati 2014b), a phrase that reminded the Saudis of the Arab Spring. Velayati's representation of the Houthi takeover of Sanaa contradicted the dialogue and narrative of Islamic leadership, collaboration, and unity amid a growing ISIS crisis. The Saudi press reflected the views of the state. The newspaper *Asharq Al-Awsat* represented the Iranian adviser's statement as unacceptable as having the Houthis next door in Yemen was like living with a 'neo-Hezbollah', arguing that Velayati 'hopes that the Houthis … will play the same role as Hezbollah in Lebanon' *(Asharq-Al-Awsat* 2014). The Saudi discourse was once again projecting the image of a 'meddling Iran', contending that, through their 'affiliation with the Houthis, that there was 'evidence that Tehran is once again plaguing the region with its sedition and sectarianism' *(Asharq-Al-Awsat* 2014).

The death sentence passed against the Saudi Shi'i cleric, Sheikh Nimr al-Nimr, aroused different levels of Iranian anger and criticism on the part of state and non-state actors. On 15 October, the Specialized Criminal Court in Riyadh sentenced the cleric to death on charges of 'disobeying the ruler', 'inciting sectarian strife', and 'encouraging, leading and participating in demonstrations' (Amnesty International 2014). The Iranian foreign ministry through Amir-Abdollahian described al-Nimr's clerical status as an Islamic scholar and stated that his sentence would have global repercussions for the kingdom, distancing al-Nimr from his Shi'i identity and arguing that 'if the death sentence is true it would ... hurt the feelings of the Islamic world and trigger an international reaction' (Abdolahian 2014b). Abdollahian appealed to the 'pragmatic' nature of the Saudi officials so as to 'prevent tension from further escalating in the Islamic world' if the sentence were carried out (Abdolahian 2014b).

The Majles members also denounced the death sentence. The head of the parliament's National Security and Foreign Policy Commission, Aladin Buroujerdi, argued that the Saudi 'decision ... will transfer the Yemeni crisis to the eastern region' of the kingdom. The parliamentarian stated that since the Shi'a revered their ulama, 'a serious security crisis will occur' because Riyadh has its 'largest province of Saudi Arabia bordering Yemen where Saudi Shia live', in addition to the Eastern Province that includes 'one of the most important cities ... al-Qatif' (Boroujerdi and Emrooz 2014), thus warning of the risk of an uprising on both Saudi borders. Another legislator, Mohammad Saleh Jokaar, launched an attack on the Saudi government, contending that the execution of al-Nimr would 'inch the Saudi regime closer to their downfall' since the 'regime is more unstable than at any other time' (Majles 2014).

The ulama in Qom also chastised the Saudi monarchy and government. Ayatollah Makarem Shirazi warned Saudi officials that 'such acts would seriously hurt the sentiments' of the Islamic world, and 'Saudi Arabia knows that if it carries out the sentence [it will] invoke the hatred and anger of all the freedom-loving Shia and Sunnis' and that turning the Muslims 'against them and [Saudi Arabia] will pay a heavy price', further warning of 'unpredictable consequences' (*Jahan News* 2014). The Grand Ayatollahs of Qom also called on the foreign ministry to act. Ayatollah Safi Golpayagani requested that Zarif 'take swift and appropriate action to overturn the death sentence', lamenting that 'the death sentence of this militant cleric has caused great sorrow and regret for all free Shiites and Muslims' (*Jahan News* 2014). The jurist sought to remind the Saudi government that 'Islamic scholars have considerable influence', warning the 'Saudi rulers' of the 'consequences of such an oppressive ruling' (*Jahan News* 2014).

The Iranian leadership also attempted to appeal to the king through its relationship with the former president Akbar Hashemi Rafsanjani. Rafsanjani attempted to mediate and sent a letter to King Abdullah requesting a pardon for Sheikh al-Nimr. In contrast to the sharp tone of the Qom ulama, Rafsanjani pleaded with the brotherly and Islamic nature of the Saudi monarch, arguing that 'at this time' – i.e. during the ISIS crisis – 'sedition has sought to attack the very essence of the Islamic ummah' (Rafsanjani 2014a). Rafsanjani argued in his letter that the Saudi king's pardon would 'cause despair for those that create division among the Muslims and strengthen the unity of Shi'as and Sunnis in the Islamic world' (Rafsanjani 2014a). The letter emphasized a discourse of Islamic unity reminiscent of the Rafsanjani and Khatami-era discourses towards Riyadh, and it implied that the Saudi monarch was a saviour of Islam rather than just saving a single Shi'i cleric. The Ayatollah requested that the king contemplate the 'unity and the strengthening of the Islamic sects [that would] result from cooperation and solve the problems of the Islamic world' (Rafsanjani 2014a). Nevertheless, Rafsajani's request fell on deaf ears. The king neither issued a pardon nor reversed al-Nimr's sentence.

The military advances by Iran-backed forces in Iraq against ISIS may also have irritated Saudis and reversed the process of détente. The image of Qassem Soleimani was now associated with the Iranian leadership in the war against terror. After a series of ISIS gains in September 2014, Soleimani-led forces were responsible for breaking the siege, liberating, defending, and saving Kurdish towns in the battles of Amerli and Suleiman Beg. In interviews, Kurdish Peshmerga commanders confirmed the role of Iranian military assistance, advice, training, and arms in their victories *(Reuters* 2014b*)*. By October, Iran began to highlight its role in Iraq, projecting the image of a protector while highlighting Iranian sacrifices for Iraq's stability and liberation from ISIS. In a meeting with the French foreign minister, Dominique de Villepin, Velayati emphasized Iran's regional role and burnished Iran's prestige as a regional power; one that had 'helped Syria and Iraq to battle terrorism and ISIS' (Iran and Zarif 2014; Velayati 2014a). The Majles speaker, Ali Larijani, also echoed Iran's regional role and argued that if the country had 'not been involved in the Iraqi issue … Iraq could have spun out of control' *(Larijani and CNN* 2014; *Guardian* 2014c*)*. IRGC commanders started confirming Soleimani's presence in Iraq, representing the recent victories as a result of Iranian assistance and Soleimani's leadership, stating that 'if it wasn't for Iran's help, Iraq's Kurdistan would have fallen into the hands of Daesh (ISIS)' (Javani and *ABNA* 2014a, 2014b). A senior adviser to Ayatollah Khamenei, Yadollah Javani, argued it was the 'presence and assistance of the Islamic Republic [that] prevented Baghdad from falling'. The official argued that it was 'Soleimani [who] was risking martyrdom' to fight ISIS, protect Iraq, and 'not let insecurity come close to our [Iranian] borders' (Javani and *ABNA* 2014b).

On 24 October, the Soleimani-led Operation Ashura took place, a battle aimed at retaking the strategic town of Jurf Al-Sakhar – both because it was close to Baghdad and because it threatened the holy cities of Najaf and Karbala, which Rouhani had referred to earlier as Iran's 'red line'. Threats by ISIS to carry out attacks against the Shi'a commemorating the Day of Ashura had drastic effects on the Shi'a. The battle was framed as a liberation from ISIS and their threat to the Shi'a and their shrines. The significance of the holy city of Najaf to the Shi'a could be compared with the Vatican's significance to Catholics. Photographs of Soleimani on the battlefield were circulated in the two days it took to retake the town (Dougherty 2019: 122). Although the presence of Iranian forces was questioned, no one queried the assistance, advice, and leadership of the head of the Quds

Force. Consequently, Iran highlighted three main messages to the region – and indeed the world – in its role in the fight against ISIS and its aid to the Kurds and Shi'a. The first was to reassure Iran that their government and military were protecting the country by fighting ISIS in Iraq and protecting Iran's borders. The second message was that Iran was the main protector of Shi'ism, including its shrines and scholars. Finally, the third was of Iran leading the regional fight against terrorism, as opposed to the GCC, and especially Saudi Arabia. The official Iranian discourse sought to refute Saudi narratives of Iran as an occupying force. Iran's 'boots on the ground' in Iraq and Syria were constructed in the internal discourse as being there not due to hegemonic intentions, their meddling in Arab affairs, or the promotion of sectarian sedition, but rather due to the fight against terrorism. In addition, since Iran had generals and advisers on the ground, this underlined the state's image as the leader and protector of the region and the Islamic world.

Conclusion

Rouhani's victory brought with it the hope of improving relations with Saudi Arabia. However, as Al-Sultan and Saeid (2016: 178) argue, the newly elected president's endeavours at rapprochement with the kingdom were a case of 'one step forward and two steps back'. Although the Rouhani administration aimed to rebrand both the image of the Iranian Self and its relations with Riyadh, factionalism within Iran's internal politics stifled any such overtures. The Ahmadinejad era's expansion in the Middle East after the Arab Spring, particularly the uprisings in Bahrain and the war in Syria, had increased tensions between Riyadh and Tehran. An international pushback by Riyadh in addition to 1980s-era rhetoric compounded the suspicion of conservatives in Tehran, in turn creating mutual suspicion and wariness regarding rapprochement. Rouhani's narratives of brotherhood and the 'neighbourly relations' of the Khatami and Rafsanjani eras were not working because Riyadh now preferred a 'trust but verify approach'. As the Rouhani administration entered negotiations with the P5+1 and talks with the US were being prepared, the Saudi press projected images of US naivety in its dealings with Iran and represented the talks as scapegoating the region in return for improving relations with Tehran and allowing Iranian regional expansion. As the talks progressed and Riyadh's fears of a US–Iran deal at its expense increased, the kingdom projected a certain image of the Saudi Self and its regional and international leadership by rejecting a UN seat, which forced Washington to appease Riyadh. In its official discourse Iran aimed to please Saudi Arabia by affirming its regional leadership and its weight in the Islamic world, a discourse that was employed in the 1990s in post-war Iran. This too fell on deaf ears.

As the Iranian P5+1 talks commenced, ISIS had managed to take advantage of the civil war in Syria and unrest in Iraq, and it had expanded its control over areas in both countries. The Iranian discourse on takfiris was cited by the Supreme Leader as the reason behind the ISIS atrocities. The Iranian discourse on Takfiri groups constructed the image of the Saudi Other as the creator and backer of ISIS, bringing in troposes based on Al-Qaeda, Wahhabism, and 'Zionist conspiracies' creating sedition in the Islamic world while trying to destroy the Iranian-led 'axis of resistance'. Indeed, the Iranian Self and its role in Syria and Iraq was represented as an Islamic calling rooted in eschatology and the Mahdi, just as the Iranian discourse projected an image of regional leadership and the Islamic Republic as a protector of the Muslim world. For Saudi Arabia, ISIS was also a threat. However, like Iran, it blamed its Other for the rise of ISIS. The official discourse employed narratives of Iranian regional meddling and sectarianism, particularly in Syria, Iraq, and Yemen. Simultaneously, Saudi Arabia acknowledged that ISIS was a common threat to both Tehran and Riyadh, and it represented itself as a pragmatic Islamic leader that put Islam before itself, thus agreeing to hold talks with Iran.

Saudi Arabian and Iranian discourses shifted once again as Iran made military progress in Iraq with the Quds Force and the PMU along with the Houthi advances towards Sanaa and the death sentence issued against the Shi'i cleric al-Nimr. Saudi Arabia's discourse on Iran was reactive and represented the Iranian Other as an invader who occupied three countries in the Middle East: Syria, Iraq, and Yemen. By the end of 2014, Iran had used the war on ISIS and its nuclear programme to promulgate an image of prestige, leadership, and the Islamic Republic as the main protector of the Shi'a and their shrines and scholars. Iran's military and domestic discourse promulgators highlighted an image of the Iranian Self as leading a war against regional terrorism in opposition to their Saudi Other, while the official state discourse in Iran was attempting a détente with the Saudi kingdom by responding to actors such as Rafsanjani and his relationship with King Abdullah. However, these overtures would soon come to a dead end, particularly after the Saudi monarch died and a new king ascended the throne, bringing with him a young prince who would attempt to rebrand the kingdom and its regional and international image.

Part 5

Chapter 13

YEMEN: A NEW SAUDI MONARCH AND A PROXY WAR

Introduction

The start of 2015 brought bad tidings for the Persian Gulf region, and especially for Saudi Arabia. On 23 January, the Saudi monarch, Abdullah bin Abdulaziz Al Saud died, ushering in a new monarch and administration. His successor Salman had been the crown prince since 2012. In a premeditated move by Abdullah, the monarchical Allegiance Council resolved any issues related to the line of succession. The council had agreed that once Salman ascended the throne, his brother Muqrin would be named crown prince, thus elevating Mohammad bin Nayef to the role of deputy crown prince, and thereby easing the line of succession to the second generation. Furthermore, one of Salman's first decrees as king was to appoint his son. Mohammad bin Salman, known also by the acronym MBS, became defence minister, a promotion from his former role as chief of the crown prince court with the rank of state minister.

The death of Abdullah bin Abdulaziz significantly influenced Iranian–Saudi relations. The late monarch had built a personal relationship with Rafsanjani spanning two decades, all the way from his first personal encounter with the late president and Majles speaker at the OIC meeting in Senegal in 1991. This relationship between the two leaders led to Tehran's relationship with Riyadh being resumed, and it ushered in an era of détente and rapprochement. The death of Abdullah and the gradual side-lining of Rafsanjani from Iranian politics would have severe repercussions on Iranian–Saudi relations. This was particularly the case as a young prince was on the rise amid domestic and regional turbulence. Three months into his role as king, Saudi Arabia entered a war with the Iranian-aligned Houthis in Yemen. The Houthi movements in Yemen and the group's control over Sanaa from the pro-Riyadh Hadi government would be the last straw for Riyadh. Furthermore, in July of the same year, Iran was to sign the nuclear deal, also known as the Joint Comprehensive Plan of Action (JCPOA) with the P5+1 and have its international sanctions removed and funds unfrozen. This would lead to further tension between Iran and the kingdom. However, it would take two major incidents that would push the relationship to the pre-détente phase of the 1980s. The first was a hajj incident that would lead Iran to boycott the pilgrimage once again, this time for a year. Second, the execution of the Shi'i cleric in Saudi Arabia, Nimr al-Nimr would foment an uproar on Iranian streets, an attack on the Saudi diplomatic offices, and Riyadh's severing of diplomatic relations with Tehran – a situation that is still current at the time of writing.

This chapter will therefore examine Iranian–Saudi relations, their rivalry, and representations of Self and Other since the death of King Abdullah, with a focus on three main events: the Yemen war, the hajj stampede in 2015, and the execution of Nimr al-Nimr, which ended with the severing of diplomatic ties. In this chapter I argue that under the leadership of King Salman, Saudi Arabia aimed to reaffirm its image of leadership by representing the Houthi takeover of Sanaa as an Iranian expansion and preparing its domestic populace as well as the Arab world for a war against the Islamic Republic with Saudi Arabia at its helm in Operation Decisive Storm. Furthermore, I argue that while Iran attempted to maintain overtures of rapprochement towards Riyadh, its representation of its Saudi Other included tropes of military inferiority, US subservience, and sedition. In the case of the hajj, I argue that the discourse from the hajj incident of 1987 was reintroduced in both countries. For Iran, this included international Islamic oversight of the hajj and the shrines. On the other hand, Iran was framed as politicizing the hajj to serve its own agenda. These discourses of hegemony, expansion, leadership, and legitimacy would also be employed as both countries represented each other in the aftermath of the al-Nimr execution, and as Iran entered the 'nuclear club'.

Death of a Monarch: The End of Rapprochement?

The death of King Abdullah brought with it a decline in hopes of Iranian–Saudi rapprochement. Saudi Arabia's relationship with Iran was at its warmest during Abdullah's era, especially given the fraternal relations he maintained with Rafsanjani. The Iranian response to Abdullah's death was a clear reflection of the schism in the Iranian power structure. As Rouhani sent a telegram of condolences, Zarif attended the funeral. The president offered his 'condolences to the Saudi government, people, and family' of King Abdullah, wishing for 'forgiveness for the deceased [and the] success of the Saudi nation and government' (Rouhani 2015b). The spokeswoman for the Ministry of Foreign Affairs, Marzieh Afkham, also gave her condolences on national television (Afkham 2015). Rafsanjani also sent a telegram, offering his 'condolences to the people and officials of the friendly country of Saudi Arabia' and sought to continue sending his message to Salman as he ascended the throne:

> I wish His Excellency success in strengthening the unity of the Islamic world [and] happiness, coexistence, and brotherhood of the two nations of Iran and Saudi Arabia in the shadow of the high teachings of Islam.
>
> (Rafsanjani 2015)

By invoking narratives of brotherhood, unity, Saudi Islamic leadership, and coexistence, the former president attempted to signal to the new Saudi monarch a continuation of Abdullah's legacy and his relations with Iran. This was, however, short-lived. In a Friday sermon, the chairman of the Guardian Council, the conservative leaning Ayatollah Jannati,[1] celebrated Abdullah's death on the pulpit. Employing Islamic symbolism, the ayatollah referred to the late king as a 'Saudi Qarun' (Korah in Hebrew), i.e. a metaphoric representation of greed and tyranny, while declaring that the late king was 'very hostile to the Shi'a and supported the Takfiris'. Furthermore, this enmity with the Shi'a was constructed as being systemic, as 'so many books were written slandering the Shi'a during his era', declaring his death a 'punishment for his deeds' (Jannati 2015). Furthermore, the revolutionary cleric declared that the 'Shia and Islamic world should be congratulated [and] condolences should be sent to Israelis and the US', thereby constructing an image of Abdullah as an enemy of the Shi'a in particular and Islam in general, while affirming the image and trope of 'Western and Zionist subservience' (Jannati 2015).

As reformist journalists pushed back against Jannati's rhetoric, the conservative press spared no time or expense in constructing an image of a fragile kingdom, one that was having a 'Game of Thrones' moment replete with deep US concerns about Saudi Arabia's stability. The leading reformist journalist, intellectual, and adviser to Rafsanjani, Sadegh Zibakalam, sent an open letter to the chairman of the Guardian Council criticizing his sermon and rhetoric towards Saudi Arabia. In what may have been an indirect message from Rafsanjani to his political rival, Zibakalam argued that Jannati's comments were 'both amazing and unfortunate' (Zibakalam 2015). The amazement was that as 'the president ... has officially expressed his condolences ... and the foreign minister ... attended the funeral ... one of our religious leaders described the incident as blessed'. Furthermore, Zibakalam's incredulity was compounded as he reminded the cleric that his position as a Friday prayer Imam was as part of an 'informal government body' and his status as the chairman of the Guardian Council represented the system and not a personal opinion, thus portraying the senior cleric as naïve and boyish. The 'unfortunate' part of the sermon according to the adviser was that 'such words were used at a time where dimensions of the conflict between Shi'as and Sunnis go beyond normal rivalries and tensions', referring to the civil war in Syria and the ISIS crisis in Iraq. The reformist camp's rebuke of a senior cleric like Ayatollah Jannati was a clear sign of the difference in opinion and understanding of Iranian–Saudi relations and rivalry. Although Zibakalam was a prominent figure, this was an exceptional development since an intellectual does not normally rebuke a senior figure in the Iranian clergy and in politics. The writer reminded conservatives that this was 'an insult and ridicule of the death' of the king 'with the title of Custodian of the Two Holy Mosques [who] had great status and respect among his country and Arabs' in general (Zibakalam 2015). Zibakalam further represented Jannati's narrative of Shi'i–Sunni unity as 'hypocrisy', emphasizing the late king's

---

1. In 2015 Ayatollah Jannati was a member of the Guardian Council and from May 2016 he became chairman of the Guardian Council.

image as a 'reformist and moderate among the Saudi leaders and princes ... in comparison with other Saudi clerics and leaders such as Turki or Bandar [Al Saud]' (Zibakalam 2015). To the reformist camp, the death of the king was represented as an opportunity to achieve the peace that existed earlier. The reformist position on the death of King Abdullah showed how polarized the views were among the two main political camps in Iran. Furthermore, the disdain for Saudi Arabia among conservatives had deepened to such an extent that they would not even give their condolences, a compulsory Islamic act when a Muslim dies. Basically, in the conservatives' eyes, the Saudi monarch had lost his Islamic credentials.

The conservative press in Iran projected an image of a fragile and ailing Saudi kingdom. They employed tropes of internal coups, a worried US, and the rise of a new generation of princes. In relation to the wider region, the radical-leaning editorials also discussed the Houthi-Ansarallah rise in Yemen as well as a Saudi power in decline, and the opportunity to expand the Islamic Revolution and foment a regional awakening. The king's health was questioned in the press. An image was constructed of a frail and ageing king suffering from a variety of diseases, including Alzheimer's (*Kayhan* 2015d). As a result, the Saudi palace administration was represented as subordinate to the US. The editorial argued that the Americans were 'interfering in the details of Saudi Arabia's affairs and assigning tasks to the king and princes' because the US 'is not certain of the course of events' (*Kayhan* 2015d). By also using a narrative of an internal coup, the *Kayhan* editorial argued that Salman 'fired' Abdullah's son, Mut'ib, the head of the National Guard, and was attempting to 'select Salman's son as the crown prince's successor' (*Kayhan* 2015d), a move that would later be proven true.

The image of Saudi weakness was extended to the Yemen crisis and the monarch's death was interpreted as having been beneficial to the Houthis. Using a sectarian trope, the Iranian discourse implicitly highlighted Iranian power over Yemen by describing the sectarian demographics of the latter. The editorial argued that 'half of Yemen is comprised of Zaydi Shi'a' who live on 'two-thirds of [the country's] territory', thus 'playing a key a role in Saudi Arabia's regional position' *(Kayhan* 2015d). The Houthi takeover of Sanaa in September and its expansion within Yemeni political structures was attributed to Saudi weakness and Iranian regional prominence. The editorial explicitly argued that 'the Islamic Revolution in Iran brought Saudi Arabia's role in the Persian Gulf and the Strait of Hormuz close to zero', while the 'victory of Ansarallah ... over the Saudi-affiliated regime in Yemen' was represented as a serious blow to 'Saudi Arabia's importance to the West' and marked a decline in its 'geopolitical and religious status' (*Kayhan* 2015d). The narrative being promulgated to Iran's domestic populace concerned the 'victory of the Twelver Shi'a in the north' i.e. Iran in 1979, and the 'victory of the Zaydi Shi'a in the South' i.e. Yemen, which would lead to a change in the 'future of the region [to the] detriment of Saudi Arabia' *(Kayhan* 2015d). To ordinary Iranians, Saudi Arabia was constructed as a weak state and a regional failure nearing collapse, while Iran was maintaining its strength, expanding its regional presence, and spreading its revolution to other countries. Saudi Arabia specifically feared this image, and this is precisely why in March 2015 Saudi Arabia decided to go to war in Yemen.

War in Yemen: Operation Decisive Storm

Two months into Salman's reign, Riyadh launched a military campaign against the Houthis in Yemen. Launched on 26 March with the name Operation Decisive Storm (*'āsifat al-ḥazm*) in relation to the quote and proverb by King Abdul Aziz, the founder of the kingdom *(Al-Khaleej* 2015), the mission lasted for approximately four weeks, ending on 21 April. On the same day in March 2015, Iran and the P5+1 were preparing for nuclear talks in the Swiss city of Lausanne. These negotiations led to the signing of a preliminary framework agreement that formed the basis of the JCPOA, later signed in July 2015. Much to the anxiety of Saudi Arabia and its GCC neighbours, Iran was inching towards a nuclear agreement. The framework would pave the way to lifting the sanctions against Iran, unfreezing $100 billion of frozen Iranian assets, and removing all imposed sanctions (Northam 2015). From a nuclear standpoint, Iran would be allowed to enrich uranium, an issue of contention between Iran and the international community. Iran's regional adversaries viewed this as a form of Western capitulation and leniency towards Tehran, particularly by the Obama administration. Ikonomou (2020: 84) argues that 'Saudi Arabia continues to see the ... JCPOA as an unacceptable deal, risky, and harmful to its national interests. The kingdom ... did not want a solution to the Iranian crisis without Iran's humiliating defeat' (Ikonomou 2020). Therefore, as Iran's nuclear crisis gradually neared a breakthrough, and Tehran was achieving its goals, Saudi Arabia was witnessing a possible Bahrain and Syria scenario on its borders, and the rise of yet another pro-Iran group in its immediate vicinity – the Houthis. This led to Riyadh calling for a coalition of Islamic (Sunni) states, sparking a war with the Houthis. The mission was supported by the GCC, except for Oman, which chose to stay out of the coalition but offered its airspace, as did four other Arab countries – Morocco, Egypt, Jordan, and Sudan. Therefore, the states forming the coalition gave it an innate Sunni identity. The coalition's aim, according to Saudi Arabia's 'responsibilities towards the Yemeni people', was to 'provide immediate support by all means and measures necessary to protect Yemen and its people from the aggression of the Houthi militias supported by regional powers whose aim is to extend their hegemony over Yemen and make it a base for their influence in the region' (al-Jubeir 2015b).

The phrase 'regional powers' was a veiled reference to Iran. Saudi Arabia feared a rise in Iranian influence on its southern border. On 22 January, the Houthis had pressured Hadi to resign, after which he escaped to his hometown of Aden. The Houthis also named a revolutionary committee on 6 February to carry out the duties of the president along with the main political party, the General People's Congress. Within a week, Sanaa had announced that it had negotiated trade deals with Iran. These included direct flights to Tehran from Sanaa, provision for a 165MW power station, Iranian access to Yemeni port facilities, the extension of the port of Hudaida, and the signing of an oil deal with Tehran's National Iranian Oil Company (NIOC) (*Al-Jazeera* 2015). The trade deal between Iran and Yemen was similar to those signed with Damascus and Iraq. As the Middle East expert Bruce Reidel (2015) has argued, an Iranian foothold in Yemen was of great concern to King Salman, particularly since Yemen 'has always been the soft underbelly of Saudi Arabia' (Riedel 2015). Furthermore, the Saudi decision to wage war on the Houthis was also due to a worry that Iran would now have a role in the decision-making process in Sanaa, thus making Sanaa Iran's fourth capital of influence in the Middle East after Baghdad, Damascus, and Beirut (Riedel 2015). Saudi Arabia planned to stop this from happening at all costs.

The Saudi monarch's speech to the Arab League (al-Saud 2015c) on the day the military operations in Yemen started was an exercise in redeeming and rebranding Saudi Arabia's image of leadership, legitimacy, and power. Representing the status of the Middle East as a region going through the 'painful reality [of] terrorism, internal conflicts, and bloodshed', Salman implicated Iran in his speech, arguing that this 'regional power [formed an] alliance between terrorism and sectarianism', as well as 'blatant interventions in our Arab region ... [that have] undermined security and stability in some of our countries' (al-Saud 2015c). The Arab countries Salman was referring to were Syria, Iraq, and – more recently – Yemen. According to the king, 'external intervention'– a tacit reference to Iran – had helped facilitate the Houthi militias. This image of Iranian meddling in Yemen and the interpretation of the Houthis as a destabilizing 'militia' , served one purpose, which was to project an image of Iran that aimed to 'overthrow the legitimate authority, occupy the capital, Sanaa, and disrupt the completion of the implementation of the Gulf initiative' which had been adopted to 'preserve Yemen's security, unity, and stability' (al-Saud 2015c) . The king's speech argued that Iran was meddling in the affairs of yet another Arab state, this time on the kingdom's doorstep. Indeed, the monarch was preparing the Arab League for war with Saudi Arabia at its helm by propagating a discourse rebranding Riyadh's image as a leader and protector of the GCC region, and as the state that would finally stand up to Iranian interference.

Furthermore, the Arab League speech represented Saudi Arabia as a regional leader tasked with 'bringing Yemen ... to safety' under the support of the GCC and the Arab League. Through Riyadh's leadership with Salman at the helm, and given the 'brotherly and friendly countries participating in [Operation] Decisive Storm', Saudi Arabia promoted itself as the force that would liberate Yemen from the Houthis, 'supported by regional powers whose aim is to extend their hegemony over Yemen' and who are trying making it a 'base for their [i.e. Iran's] influence in the region' (al-Saud 2015c). The king's speech went as far as implying that this alleged Iranian support for the Houthis posed a 'great threat to regional security and stability' as well as being a threat to both 'international peace and security' and a chance to 'confront terrorist organizations'. Additionally, Iran was represented as a 'bully', a 'rebel against legitimacy', and a 'promoter of ... terrorism ... sowing the seeds of sectarianism' (al-Saud 2015c). Therefore, the Saudi monarchical discourse was projecting an image of the kingdom as a force for peace, a defender of the oppressed, and a force against discrimination and terrorism. This would be accomplished by an Arab 'coalition of the willing' with Saudi Arabia at its helm and the young Mohammad bin Salman as its executor. Even though Saudi Arabia had called for the establishment of an Islamic coalition during the reign of King Abdullah, this was the first time that it had wanted to create a force that would counteract Iran specifically.

As the Saudi press cheered on the military operations, they projected an image of Saudi Arabia's regional and Islamic leadership and legitimacy, while highlighting Iran's role in Yemen and applying familiar narratives and tropes of Iranian sectarianism, terrorism, and foreign meddling in Arab affairs. Published editorials aimed at the local Saudi audience, such as in *al-Jazira*, emphasized that Saudi Arabia was at war with 'a terrorist organization ... an agent that carries out the orders of his obeyed Iranian Khomeini master' (*al-Jazirah* 2015d). Editorials further described the king as a man of mercy, wisdom, and patience, arguing that the 'king was forced to take this historic decision [as] he preferred dialogue [and a] situation that would spare Yemen the scourge and horrors of war' (*al-Jazirah* 2015f). However, the king's decision to launch Operation Decisive Storm was not only 'a lesson for the Houthis and their allies in Yemen [but] rather a lesson for Iran', which had been 'meddling in Arab affairs, weaving plots ... stirring differences ... using sectarianism and money at times' (*al-Jazirah* 2015c). Domestically, the message was that the 'large-scale military operations that are taking place in Yemen now are, in fact, a war against Iran'. The war was represented as a Persian–Arab war, where the 'mullahs of Tehran [have to] leave the Arabs alone' (*al-Jazirah* 2015c). The trope of Persian deception was employed, asking 'Arabs that are deceived by Iran' to 'review their alliances' with the Islamic Republic, because Tehran's 'goals are clear and its ambitions are limitless' (*al-Jazirah* 2015e). Iran was constructed and explicitly referred to in the Saudi press discourse as 'an enemy who passes its evil intentions [and employs] religion to hide its evil intentions' while playing to 'the tune of sectarianism and the Palestinian cause' to the 'fools that believe them' in order to 'build a Persian empire' (*al-Jazirah* 2015e). The call for military confrontation with Iran surfaced with the war in Syria and had its origins in the Iran–Iraq war. However, the specific call for a war against Iran was a shift in the discourse as the press now defined the war with the Houthis as in effect a war with Iran.

To the Arab world, the message from Saudi newspapers such as Asharq-Al-Awsat was even more explicit and precise. First, through King Salman's leadership, Saudi Arabia had led 'an alliance of ten countries [consisting of] remarkable Arab, Islamic, and international support' to not only 'rescue Yemen' but also to carry out an 'unprecedented rescue of the region as a whole' (*Asharq-Al-Awsat* 2015a). Thus, Saudi editorial discourse deployed the image of the Custodian of the Two Holy Mosques, King Salman bin Abdulaziz, as a rescuer and messiah. Second, it announced that Salman's mission was to confront Iranian expansion, and the 'crude propaganda' that it employed in 'four Arab capitals [through] Iranian military leaders headed by Qassem Soleimani' (*Asharq-Al-Awsat* 2015a). The Saudi editorials were clear in pointing to images of Iranian-led missions in Iraq and Syria pronouncing them as 'propaganda images' and alluding to these sites of destruction and rubble in the aftermath of Iranian-led battles as 'propaganda tourism sites' that Iran utilized for its own power projection. The Saudi discourse argued that Saudi Arabia sought to 'change the rules of the game', and return these countries to the Arab fold, through Operation Decisive Storm (*Asharq-Al-Awsat* 2015a). Furthermore, these military operations were the 'beginning of a new dawn for the region' cementing the notion and image of 'Saudi leadership [and its] management of a Gulf Arab coalition [along with] Islamic and international support' (*Asharq-Al-Awsat* 2015a). In essence, through this military operation and the discourse being articulated, Saudi Arabia attempted to underline its image of legitimacy, of Arab and Islamic leadership, and its role as a responsible actor on the world stage, which seeks to fight terrorism and impose regional order. This rebranding of the image of the Self as an Arab and Islamic leader, and as a liberator of 'occupied Arab lands' came amid a weakened Saudi image due to the fall of Saddam, Iranian regional expansion, and the ramifications of the Arab Spring. The message was that 'today . . . our region has changed . . . the time for procrastination and manipulation of homelands has ended' and that Saudi Arabia was 'taking a historic and practical stand to save the region as a whole, under the leadership of King Salman bin Abdulaziz' (*Asharq-Al-Awsat* 2015a). To the domestic audience, the Saudi editorial discourse represented the king as a liberator of Iranian-occupied lands and as a figure who would return Saudi Arabia to its original position as a leader of the Arabs and Muslims and defender of their lands. This was designed to maintain the image of the kingdom given that Assad was still in power, Hezbollah had control over Lebanese domestic politics and was branching out in Syria, Iran was still influential in Iraq, and now an Iran-aligned group had just taken over Sanaa from a pro-Saudi government.

The initial Iranian reaction to both the Saudi military strikes on Yemen and speeches from its officials came from the foreign ministry. The foreign-ministry spokeswoman Marzieh Afkham argued that 'resorting to military action would complicate the situation and widen the scope of the crisis', especially since 'Yemen is embroidered in an internal crisis and counter-terrorism' a reference to Al-Qaeda in the Arabian Peninsula (AQAP) (Afkham and *Fars* 2015). The solution, according to Iran, was political, calling for an 'immediate cessation of airstrikes and hostilities against the country and the Yemeni people'. Where Saudi Arabia framed the military operations as a war to return 'legitimacy to Hadi [and to] free the Yemeni people from the Houthis', Iran framed the war as one against Yemen as a country and its people. Tehran argued that there was a dire 'need to implement national agreements reached between the Yemeni parties and groups in the first place', defining the Saudi-led strikes as an act of 'aggression that will only result in the spread of terrorism and extremism and accelerate insecurity throughout the region' (Afkham and *Fars* 2015). In other words, Tehran asserted that the Saudi-backed government had backtracked on the inter-Yemeni national agreements and that Saudi Arabia's actions would cause instability and terrorism. In an interview for the Arabic speaking news network Al-Alam, (Zarif 2015) the Iranian foreign minister, Zarif, echoed calls for an 'immediate end to Saudi military operations against Yemen', declaring that its actions were a 'violation of Yemeni sovereignty' that would 'result in nothing but bloodshed'. Iran's chief diplomat sent out a loud message to both the Arab nations and the Saudi coalition: 'We [i.e. Iran] will do our best to contain the crisis in Yemen' advising the Saudis that this military operation 'will not benefit any country [and] will cause more regional tension' (Zarif 2015).

The initial response from the Majles came from Alaedin Boroujerdi, the head of the Iranian parliament's National Security and Foreign Policy Committee. The legislator accused Saudi Arabia of 'irresponsibility' and projected an image of Riyadh's 'carelessness' in being a regional actor that has 'fanned the flames of a new war' (Boroujerdi 2015). This was perhaps a veiled response to Saudi Arabia's official line on Iranian meddling. The parliamentarian sustained his construction of Saudi Arabia's 'carelessness' and irresponsibility' by subtly warning Riyadh of collateral damage in this new war: 'The smoke of this fire will go into the eyes of Saudi Arabia as war is never limited to one place only' (Boroujerdi 2015), metaphorically alluding to Yemeni and possibly domestic reactions in Saudi Arabia and the region. Furthermore, Boroujerdi cast a shadow on Saudi Arabia's leadership of the military operation, employing the trope of Saudi subservience to the US. Accusing the US of supporting the war, Boroujerdi argued that there was 'no doubt that Saudi Arabia ... would not get involved without America's permission' and that 'America has ... started another crisis and massacre in the Islamic world' (Boroujerdi 2015). Therefore, what the Iranian legislator was alluding to was that the war on Yemen was led by the US. The legislator was accusing the US of perpetrating massacres in the Islamic world, while Saudi Arabian military operations served the US and its enmity to Islam. This representation of Saudi Arabia and the response to Saudi charges against Iran aimed to represent the Saudi Other as weak, subservient to the US, and as a perpetrator of US-inspired crimes in the Islamic world, particularly in Yemen.

As the military strikes on Yemen gained momentum, the narrative and trope of Saudi Arabian subservience to the US and Zionism was promulgated in Iranian discourse. Ten days into Operation Decisive Storm, 262 members of the Iranian parliament issued a joint statement condoning the Saudi-led strikes on Yemen (Majles 2015). In their first meeting after the Persian New Year, the statement described the strikes as 'killing the innocent people of a neighbouring country', 'killing Muslims', and 'severing instead of promoting the unity and dignity of Muslims' (Majles 2015). The statement questioned the Islamic credentials of the Saudi monarch, arguing that the military operation 'goes against the title of the Custodian of the Two Holy Mosques' proving that the king 'has served the enemies of Islam' (Majles 2015). In this statement, Iranian discourse made its first reference to and criticism of the new Saudi monarch. Furthermore, by adopting Boroujerdi's metaphor, the Iranian legislators explicitly contended that the 'Al Saud regime must know that the burning fire will spread and inflict a heavy defeat on the Islamic world' referring to the Saudi-led coalition as 'fictitious' while 'complicat[ing] the problems of the Islamic world and the region', since the mission is supported by 'the United States and Zionist regime' (Majles 2015). The Iranian narrative characterized the operation as a 'Saudi invasion of an independent nation and country', one that implemented the 'mercenary policy of the United States and its allies' (Majles 2015). Therefore, it appears to be the Iranian Majles members who openly denigrated the Saudi monarch and accused Saudi-led forces of being subservient to the US and Israel, who were in conflict with the Islamic world.

The conservative press, including *Kayhan*, identified the reason behind the Saudi attack on Yemen as due to four interrelated events that all related to Iran. By employing religious stereotypes and the Ahl al-bayt narrative, the first Iranian editorial to discuss the Saudi military strikes represented the Al Saud as 'camel-riding bandits' on an historical mission to continue the 'lost wish of their ancestors Abu Lahab, Abu Jahl, and Abu Sufyan', the uncles of the Prophet Mohammad, who were his staunch enemies at the beginning of his life as a Prophet (*Kayhan* 2015c). The Saudi coalition attack on Yemen was compared with the 'infidel wars against Islam' with the Yemenis representing 'true Mohammedan Islam' (*'Islam-i Nab-i Mohammadi'*) and the Al Saud as the infidels of Quraish who were using 'American-donated and Israeli-leased fighter jets [in a bid to] oppress the Muslims of Yemen' (*Kayhan* 2015c). The second event was the 'uprooting and suppression of Western and Hebrew-sponsored ISIS and Takfiris' by the 'sons of Ruhollah [Khomeini] in Syria, Iraq, and Lebanon' (*Kayhan* 2015c). Third, the success of Iran in the nuclear talks in Lausanne had seen it resisting 'twelve years of [US] imposed illegitimate demands' (*Kayhan* 2015c). Consequently, the conservative editorial represented the war on Yemen as retribution for Iranian regional successes. Furthermore, the Iranian discourse depicted the Houthi movement in Yemen since the Arab Spring of 2011 and up to the takeover of Sanaa in September 2014 as an 'Islamic Revolution ... modelled on the Islamic Revolution in Iran' (*Kayhan* 2015c). The conflict led by Saudi Arabia was interpreted as a 'proxy war' characterized by a 'brutal attack ... on the Muslim people ... by the US and its allies'. The aim, as highlighted in the *Kayhan* editorial, was 'to prevent the rise of another Islamic Iran, which cannot be stopped' (*Kayhan* 2015c). Iranian discourse represented the Houthi takeover of Sanaa as emulating the 1979 Islamic Revolution, with part of their discourse on the Islamic awakening born out of the Arab protests in December 2010. Meanwhile, the Saudi Other was represented as a force that was against both this Islamic awakening and Islamic governments in general.

Discourses on Saudi Arabia in the Iranian media – aimed at the domestic audience – sought to discredit Riyadh by portraying the kingdom as a fragile state with a weak leadership. The war was attributed to the Saudi defence minister, Mohammad bin Salman, who was represented as a 'young and inexperienced' prince who was employing a barbaric strategy as the airstrikes 'killed and wounded hundreds of Yemeni civilians, most of them women and children ... much of Yemen's infrastructure destroyed ... in the UN-approved attacks' and courtesy of a 'green light from the West' (*Kayhan* 2015a). The reason behind the attacks was portrayed as Saudi Arabia's 'enmity with Shi'ism' (*Kayhan* 2015a). According to the Iranian press, since Hussain al-Houthi, the former leader of the movement, adopted the revolutionary slogan 'Allah Akbar, death to America, death to Israel, curse the Jews, and victory to Islam', this 'official slogan ... led Al Saud and the US ... to seriously confront the Houthi movement' (*Kayhan* 2015a). Therefore, the Iranian editorials' discourse began representing the war in Yemen as a sectarian war, one pursued with a UN, Zionist, and US blessing, a narrative that was promulgated after Khamenei's first remarks on the war in Yemen.

Khamenei's remarks came two weeks after the war had begun. By that time, the Saudi monarch had given his speech at the Arab League summit in Sharm al-Sheikh (Khamenei 2015b) and Saudi state and non-state actors had promulgated their discourse, framing the war as a result of Iranian threats, hegemony, expansion, and meddling on Riyadh's doorstep. Iran's Supreme Leader defined Operation Decisive Force as a 'mistake' comparing the Saudi government's decision to go to war in Yemen with 'what the Zionists did in Gaza' (Khamenei 2015b). The Ayatollah went as far as representing the Saudi-led war as a 'crime and genocide [in which] children are killed, [and the] houses, infrastructure, and wealth of a country is destroyed' (Khamenei 2015b). Furthermore, aimed at the Iranian domestic audience, the Grand Jurist constructed an image of Saudi weakness and incapability. Khamenei forecasted that the 'Saudis will suffer ... [they will] lose and not win anyway [and the] reason is very clear' (Khamenei 2015b). Comparing the Saudi armed forces with Israeli military capabilities, he argued that the Israelis 'lost in Gaza while the military capabilities of the Zionists are many times greater than that of these so-and-so Saudis' and their opponents were the people of Gaza (Khamenei 2015b). Therefore, Saudi Arabia's failure was imminent since the 'other side is a country of tens of millions, a nation, a vast country'. Saudi Arabia's chances, according to the cleric, were 'below zero', representing Saudi Arabia's demise as 'noses that will definitely be rubbed in the sand' (Khamenei 2015b). As for Saudi's decision to attack Yemen, Ayatollah Khamenei ascribed this to naïve governance, regional politics, and international relations. Referring to the Saudi administration as a 'few inexperienced young people [that have] taken over the affairs of that country', in an implicit reference to MBS, and as a result this had 'allowed savagery to overpower aspects of sobriety', which would be to 'their detriment' (Khamenei 2015b). Furthermore, to refute Saudi allegations of Iranian interference and meddling in Arab affairs, Khamenei hinted at double standards, where 'sitting here and saying a few words is regarded as interference', as opposed to 'criminal planes that have made Yemeni skies insecure; is that not interference?' To the Iranians, the Saudi-led war in Yemen was a real kind of interference and it had one goal, namely 'to generate power, controversy, [and] to replicate ... the very poor and miserable situation in Libya today' (Khamenei 2015b). By constructing an image of Saudi Arabia as militarily interfering in the affairs of Yemen and framing the method as based on genocide and crime, Khamenei projected an image of Iran as a protector, saviour, and a regionally responsible and mature actor. This representation of Saudi Arabia and their actions in Yemen recalled the discourses and tropes employed in Syria and Iraq, particularly as the Shi'i shrines had been attacked and ISIS had taken over swathes of land in the Levant and Iraq, thereby threatening other Shi'i sites.

Taking their cue from Khamenei's speech, the Friday prayer sermons promulgated the narrative of a Saudi proxy war in Yemen. The revolutionary cleric, Ayatollah Ahmad Khatami, repeated the Supreme Leader's definition of the Saudi-led operations as a 'proxy war on behalf of the Zionists [that is] turning an Islamic country into ruin' (Khatami 2015). Quoting Khamenei in his sermon, Khatami trivialized the strength of the Saudi military by juxtaposing the war in Yemen with the 'Zionist defeat in Yemen', implicitly constructing an image of the war as one of oppressors versus the oppressed, that is, a coalition led by Saudi Arabia against 'one million Basij fighters who are familiar with guerrilla warfare', branding the latter as 'revolutionaries' (Khatami 2015). This juxtaposition, therefore, drew implicit comparisons with the Iranian Basij forces that were created in the early years of the revolution to fight against Saddam in the Arab and Saudi supported eight-year Iran–Iraq war. The Iranian advice from the pulpits of Tehran was clear: 'You [i.e. Saudi Arabia] have failed in this arena; retreat before you tarnish your reputation even further' (Khatami 2015).

The Next Phase: Operation Restoring Hope

After three weeks of an intense bombing campaign across Yemen, on 22 April Saudi Arabia announced that it had achieved its goals. However, the Saudi spokesman, Ahmad Al-Asseri, emphasized that the coalition would continue to target the Houthi, 'removing the threat to Saudi Arabia and neighbouring countries' (*Reuters* and Asseri 2015). The next phase would be termed Operation Restoring Hope and its main goals were to 'continue to protect civilians ... fight terrorism ... facilitate the evacuation of foreign nationals and to intensify relief and medical assistance to the Yemeni people' (*Reuters* and Asseri 2015). Riyadh represented the ground offensive as a 'combination of political, diplomatic, and military action' (*Reuters* and Asseri 2015). Although during the air campaign there were 150,000 troops amassed on the Saudi–Yemen border, it was not immediately clear if a boots-on-the-ground approach would be undertaken (Stephens 2013).

Even after a continuous bombing campaign, the Houthis and their domestic allies still showed signs of resistance. It was imperative that the Saudi government justified the continuation of the war. To its wider domestic audience, press editorials such as those featured in *Asharq-Al-Awsat* argued that the main goal of the operation had been achieved, namely 'drawing a red line for Iran' (*Asharq-Al-Awsat 2015b*). The military campaign was represented as a great success courtesy of the Saudi leadership, arguing that Riyadh had now 'removed a real danger from the Saudi and [Persian Gulf] borders'. It had 'pulled out Iranian roots in Yemen', thereby sending 'a stern message to Iran and its followers' that Saudi Arabia had the ability to independently 'preserve its security [and does] not need the international community or others to intervene and defend' the kingdom (*Asharq-Al-Awsat* 2015b). This image of Saudi regional leadership and power was compounded by references to international legitimacy. The editorial argued that Operation Decisive Storm had 'become an international ruling issued by the Security Council, and under Chapter VII', thereby justifying Saudi actions that had been criticized by the international community such as the bombing of public places (*Asharq-Al-Awsat* 2015b). They had also constructed an image of accountability by arguing that 'the international community is watching' the coalition's actions in Yemen (*Asharq-Al-Awsat* 2015b).

Local publications, such as *al-Jazirah*, represented the end of the mission as a 'lesson to be learned' by the Houthis and their allies and as a warning not to take advice 'from Qom in Iran and the southern suburbs of Beirut' (*al-Jazirah* 2015b). Operation Restoring Hope was framed as an 'one-time opportunity' for Yemen, a 'way out of a dark tunnel', and an 'end to a disaster' (*al-Jazirah* 2015b). Therefore, the next phase of the Saudi-led operation was communicated as reflecting Saudi compassion and appreciation of 'Yemen, [and] its different denominations', which was an implicit reference to the Zaydi Shi'a, and 'history [which is] dear to the kingdom'. Saudi actions were, it was argued, a brotherly act highlighting a special relationship between Riyadh and Sanaa, 'which no other country has stood by' (*al-Jazirah* 2015b). To the Saudi audience, the war was portrayed as a gesture of good faith and kindness from the 'kingdom towards its Yemeni sister', whereas no other state had considered the 'political, military, security, economic, and financial support' that Riyadh had offered. Emphasizing the Saudi leadership, the editorial discourse argued that it was only the 'kingdom that ... protected the Yemeni people from foreign conspiracies, [thus] preventing its collapse' representing Riyadh as a regional leader and Yemen's protector by arguing that 'what affects the interests of Yemen affects the kingdom and vice versa' (*al-Jazirah* 2015b). This leadership was attributed to 'Salman [who had] been more keen on preserving the interests of Yemen [and] most capable of defending it', shaping the narrative of Saudi Arabia's need to maintain the war by encouraging the monarch to 'continue with the operation to restore the hope' of the Yemenis, especially since 'your brothers in the coalition encourage your leadership' (*al-Jazirah* 2015b).

A week into Operation Restoring Hope, on 29 April, King Salman issued twenty-five decrees (al-Saud 2015a) one of which included a cabinet reshuffle. Saudi Arabia had undergone another transformation; a new leadership was emerging, and the baton of power was being passed to the next generation. Muqrin bin Abdulaziz was declared to have stepped down for Mohammad bin Nayef. This had given MBS an automatic promotion to the rank of deputy crown prince, inching him closer to the throne. Similarly, the old guard was also changing. Saud al-Faisal, Saudi Arabia's foreign minister for the past four decades, had allegedly asked to be 'relieved from his duties due to health conditions' (al-Saud 2015a). This ushered the first non-royal into the position. Adel al-Jubeir, the former Saudi ambassador in Washington, and someone who was personally bitter at the Iranian regime because of the alleged assassination attempt, was now the foreign minister. The Saudi editorials represented the shifts as marking a progression from one generation to another and a new dawn and era in the kingdom. Furthermore, the stepping down of the crown prince, Muqrin, was framed as a gesture of goodwill and an organic development unique to Saudi Arabia. Citing a royal gathering at Muqrin's palace with all the senior royals present including Saud al-Faisal, he gave allegiance to the next line of ascension with the Saudi editorial discourse dispelling any rumours of turbulence within the monarchy (*al-Jazirah* 2015a, 2015g). The Saudi editorial discourse represented the Saudi monarchical system as a mature and civilized system that handed over power willingly and peacefully without strife or confrontation. This was a veiled reference to the other Arab states that had experienced civil wars and protests and an implicit representation of a long-held Saudi opinion that democracy does not suit the kingdom.

Officially, Iran extended its greetings regarding al-Jubeir's appointment via the foreign minister, Zarif. However, the Iranian newspaper editorials reported these shifts in a different way. While *Kayhan* treated this reshuffling as an internal coup *(Kayhan* 2015b), the more reformist *Etemaad* depicted the event as orchestrated by Western intelligence agencies *(Etemaad* 2015*). Kayhan* criticized Zarif for his message to Saudi Arabia, branding the latter as 'germs of corruption and filth in the child-killing regime of Al Saud [who are involved in] shameful crimes ... in the oppressed Yemen [as witnessed by] the daily massacre of Muslim women, men, and children in that region', with Saudi Arabia displaying an 'obvious allegiance to the Zionists, a pawn for the United States' and providing 'financial and logistical support to ISIS' *(Kayhan* 2015b). The military discourse ignored Riyadh's monarchical politics and reshuffling, thus focusing on the war in Yemen, particularly the Houthi takeover of Sanaa and its relationship to Iran and Iran's regional leadership. In an interview with the news outlet Dowlat Bahar, the then IRGC chief, Ali Jafari, branded the takeover of Sanaa as a 'Shi'i crescent being formed' (Jafari 2015). This 'crescent', according to the IRGC general, meant the 'empathy and unity of the Muslims of the region, such as in Iran, Syria, Yemen, Iraq, Lebanon, and other resilient countries in the region', as comprising the 'axis of resistance' (Jafari 2015). This Shi'a crescent was first mentioned in a speech by King Abdullah of Jordan after the fall of Saddam in 2003. The notion sparked fears of Iranian and Shi'i regional domination and expansion, a trope that Saudi Arabia had promulgated regularly in their discourse genres. To allay that fear, Rouhani was quick to refute Jafari's claims, arguing that 'we do not have a Shi'a crescent ... rather we have the full moon of Islam' (Rouhani 2015c).

The Iranian discourse on Saudi Arabia in Iran was fragmented, i.e. there was a split in the Iranian Self with regard to the Saudi Other. The military and press discourse supported the Houthi takeover of Sanaa and denigrated Riyadh, while the official government maintained its diplomatic overtures towards the kingdom, much to the dismay of the conservative press. Iranian support for the Houthis in Yemen, and defining them as members of the 'Shi'i crescent', raised questions for the Saudi regional leadership. Darwich (2020: 104) argues that the 'Saudi kingdom is concerned with its image and standing as a "leader" in the region' (Darwich 2020). Therefore, one of the main aims of the Yemen war was for Saudi Arabia to re-establish, rebrand, and tighten its grip on regional leadership in general and the GCC in particular. Two summits held in Riyadh after the signalling of an end to Operation Decisive Storm reflect this image of regional leadership.

At a GCC summit held on 6 May 2015, the Saudi monarch implicitly identified Iran as the reason why the region was 'exposed to foreign ambitions that seek to extend its hegemony' (al-Saud 2015b). By then, the Houthis had intensified their attacks on Saudi Arabia. On 5 May, for instance, the Houthis attacked the Saudi city of Najran, looting the base and wounding soldiers (al-Saud 2015b). King

Salman proclaimed that Iran sought to 'sow sectarian strife and create a fertile environment for terrorism and extremism' (al-Saud 2015b). Chairing the GCC conference with the French president, François Hollande, as the summit's 'first guest of honour', the Saudi monarch maintained that 'Decisive Storm has achieved its goals, and (Operation) Restoring Hope' would lead to the 'preservation of Yemen' (al-Saud 2015b). The task of maintaining the Yemeni state would be completed with the help of the Saudi leadership and 'the process of restoring hope by pushing all Yemeni parties to dialogue [alongside the] establishment of a centre for humanitarian and relief works to be located in Riyadh' (al-Saud 2015b). Consequently, the image of Saudi regional leadership was fortified by highlighting Saudi reconstruction and humanitarian initiatives, as well as leading the Yemeni National Dialogue through full compliance with UN Security Council Resolution No. (2216) (al-Saud 2015b) . The king's emphasis on Riyadh's political initiatives was intended to bolster the image of a Saudi Arabia that was a regional leader and responsible international actor, in contrast to an Iran that was framed as a hegemon and seditionist entity in the king's discourse.

The final statement of the Riyadh conference in Yemen held on 17 May repeated the aforementioned argument, arguing that the participating states 'fully support the efforts of the UN and the ... GCC led by the Custodian of the Two Holy Mosques, King Salman bin Abdulaziz Al Saud, King of the Kingdom of Saudi Arabia [who had] rushed ... to intervene and support the constitutional legitimacy', 'reject the coup' and 'stand by the Yemeni people' (*SPA* 2015). The declaration also gave Saudi Arabia and its allies the green light to 'intensify the process of support ... in the valiant city of Aden and Taiz and throughout Yemen', that is to say, a full invasion of Yemen with an 'Arab coalition led by Saudi Arabia' (*SPA* 2015). The kingdom-led coalition was represented as 'advocates of peace [and a] source of hope, as a defender of Gulf and Arab rights [and the] unity, security and stability of Yemen and the unity of the common Arab destiny' (*SPA* 2015). In the final statement, Saudi Arabia announced that the major military aim of the mission was 'the complete withdrawal of the Houthi militia and Ali Abdullah Saleh from the capital, Sanaa, and all Yemeni cities in the south and north'. The Saudi coalition's intention was to push Iran back as it 'constituted a threat to the security of Yemen, the Gulf' while seeking the 'implementation of a foreign agenda that threatens Arab national security and makes Yemen an arena for the influence of these forces in the region' (*SPA* 2015), allegations that were refuted and responded to throughout Iranian discourse, especially through the president's speeches.

As the Saudi state discourse highlighted the role of the kingdom as a regional leader, depicting Iran as a belligerent state that meddled in the region and in this instance in Yemen, Iranian official discourse, such as through Rouhani, pushed back, refuting Saudi allegations and Saudi depictions of Iranian actions. Rouhani's speech in the city of Gilan on 15 April refuted Saudi allegations, while at the same time highlighting Iran's position and image domestically and regionally (Rouhani 2015a). In strongly criticizing Riyadh, Rouhani took a more explicit position compared with his previous statements, particularly compared with his post-election speeches of June 2013 that called for regional rapprochement and détente.

Framing Saudi Arabia as a hegemon, Rouhani explicitly called out the Saudi monarchy, describing a delusionary Saudi hegemonic state, and arguing that the 'Al Saud are under the illusion' that they can continue 'dominating the region yesterday with dollars and today with bombs' (Rouhani 2015a). By employing dichotomies of 'oppressor' versus the 'oppressed', and 'Western subservience' versus 'sovereignty' and 'regional stability', the Iranian presidential discourse juxtaposed an image of the Saudi Other as a hegemon pursuing an 'invasion of Yemen' with the 'killing of defenceless people' (Rouhani 2015a). These images in the official discourse were constructed to counter the images and tropes of Iranian hegemony, sectarianism, and expansionism promulgated in the Saudi Arabian discourse, particularly in the king's speech.

On the other hand, Rouhani reflected on an image of Iran as a responsible regional actor, one that sought the 'security of the whole region' and the creation of 'regional stability' (Rouhani 2015a). By advising Riyadh to 'interact with regional countries and respect their votes' rather than use 'American-donated planes to drop bombs ... on the oppressed people of Yemen', Rouhani's narrative underlined Saudi belligerence and subservience to the West by accusing the monarchy of 'destroying the infrastructure of a weak country [while] kill[ing] women and children' (Rouhani 2015a). In return, the Iranian president emphasized that Iran did not have an 'ultimate goal of regional domination of the Shi'a over the Sunnis' as promulgated in Saudi discourse; instead, its intention 'was to make the nations of the region proud', sustaining the image of a non-sectarian Iran that saw 'no difference between Shi'a and Sunnis, Turks, Arabs, Persians and Baluchis' (Rouhani 2015a).

The 2015 Hajj Stampede

Iran–Saudi relations became polarized and increasingly tense after the new monarch's ascension to the throne in Saudi Arabia, which Han and Hakimian (2019: 6) have attributed to 'Iran's imminent nuclear deal with the world powers, regional proxy battles, and disagreements over production quotas in OPEC due to the decline in oil prices' (Han and Hakimian 2019). Moreover, Calebrese (2020: 74–75) contends that three consecutive events across 2015 and 2016 shaped and reinforced the rivalry between Tehran and Riyadh under King Salman's leadership, including the hajj stampede in September 2015, the execution of the Saudi Shi'i cleric, Nimr al-Nimr, and the participation and speech made by Prince Turki al-Faisal at the Mojahedin-e Khalq (MeK) annual rally held in Paris in July 2016 (Calabrese 2020; al-Saud 2016).

On 24 September 2015 in Mecca, millions of pilgrims gathered in Mina to 'stone the devil' as part of their hajj ritual. In one of the worst tragedies to occur since the Al-Ma'aisim tunnel incident in 1990 *(Time* 1990*)*, over 2,000 pilgrims were killed during the stampede (Gladstone 2015). Of those who died, more than 464 were Iranian pilgrims (Sadeghi-Boroujerdi 2019: 111), approximately a quarter of the fatalities. There were conflicting reports as to the cause of the stampede. However, Iranian media pointed the finger at MBS, arguing that the convoy of the 'deputy crown prince . . . caused a panic among millions of pilgrims and started the stampede' *(Fars* 2015*)*. Iranian media also contradicted the Saudi death toll, arguing that the fatalities could be as high as 4,700 *(*Nobakht and *IRIB 2015)*.

In an immediate reaction to the tragedy, the Iranian discourse, led by the Supreme Leader, depicted it as due to Saudi 'mismanagement, and improper measures'. In a statement on 24 September 2015, Ayatollah Khamenei argued that Riyadh 'should accept its heavy responsibility . . . [to] meet its obligations based on the principles of truth and fairness' (Khamenei 2015a). Further alluding to Saudi mismanagement, the official Iranian discourse also implied a Saudi cover-up. The Saudi foreign minister, Adel al-Jubeir, rejected Iran's criticisms. In a joint meeting alongside his US counterpart in New York, al-Jubeir argued that the 'Custodian of the Two Holy Mosques has directed the launch of a thorough investigation that will be transparent', emphasizing an image of accountability and emphasizing that the kingdom would 'reveal the facts when they emerge; [and] if mistakes were made, those who made them will be held accountable' (al-Jubeir 2015a). The minister also reprimanded Iran for its allegations, arguing that it 'should know better [than to] play politics with a tragic event'. As for Iranian allegations of negligence, the Saudi counter-narrative proclaimed Saudi prestige and 'a long history of expending tremendous resources to care for the pilgrimage' (al-Jubeir 2015a). Alleging that Iran was exploiting the incident for its own interests, al-Jubeir stressed that Saudi Arabia was a responsible actor that would address any shortcomings revealed in the inquiry.

However, as the days passed, official Iranian narratives began to diverge. Iran's secretary of the Supreme National Security Council (SNSC), Ali Shamkhani, framed the incident as a direct result of the misappropriation of the workforce, weaving in tropes from Bahrain and Yemen (Shamkhani 2015). Moreover, Shamkhani drew on discourses relating to mismanagement, weakness, and the shifting security priorities of the Saudi state. Shamkhani argued that the 'weak management of the Saudi government and lack of capability of the Saudi hajj officials' along with a 'change in Saudi Arabia's security preferences and seeing its security in the war on the Yemeni people . . . and [Saudi Arabia] suppressing the Bahraini people [had resulted in] this tragedy'. Furthermore, Riyadh was also framed as complicit in targeting Iranian officials attending the hajj (Shamkhani 2015). The senior adviser to the Supreme Leader, Ali Akbar Velayati, contended that the incident was 'suspicious because some high-ranking technical, scientific and political figures of the Islamic Republic of Iran have gone missing or been martyred' (Velayati 2015). Velayati was hinting at the disappearance of the Iranian Ambassador to Lebanon, Ghazanfar Roknabadi, who was later announced as having been killed during the stampede with his body later recovered and returned to Iran. In 2004, Shamkhani received the Order of Abdulaziz Al Saud, the highest medal awarded in Saudi Arabia, for his 'prominent role in designing and implementing a policy of détente and developing relations with Arab countries of the Persian Gulf (Shafaqna 2013).

For both Iran and Saudi Arabia, the events of Mina in 2015 brought back memories of the hajj of 1987 that saw hundreds of Iranian pilgrims dying in clashes with Saudi security forces. Since then, Iranian voices across the different discourse genres had argued that there should be international Islamic management of the Grand Mosque. During a Tehran Friday prayer sermon, Ayatollah Emami-Kashani repeated the discourse of Riyadh being 'incapable of organizing the pilgrimage', arguing that the 'running of the hajj must be handed over to Islamic states' (Emami-Kashani 2015). This notion of Islamic oversight of Mecca and Medina was sustained as both Iran and Saudi Arabia failed to reach an agreement over the 2016 hajj. On 26 May, the hajj ministries of both states had entered discussions to reach a deal on hajj arrangements. Both parties blamed the other for the impasse. The Iranian delegation walked out of the negotiations two days into the talks. On 30 May 2015, the Iranian government issued a ban on Iranians attending the hajj, citing lack of security assurances. This led to a ban on Iranians performing the hajj the next year.

The hajj dispute brought with it the tropes of Islamic leadership and 'Islamicness'. While the Iranian officials framed the ban as being due to a lack of safety of Iranian pilgrims, the Saudi discourse argued that Iran had once again attempted to 'politicize hajj rituals' (Khamenei 2016a). In a statement issued by the ministry of hajj and religious affairs, Saudi clerics questioned Iran's Islamic credentials. The Saudi ulama laid the blame on the Iranians, opining that 'the Iranian government will be will be responsible in front of Allah Almighty and its people for the inability of the Iranian citizens to perform the hajj this year' (Khamenei 2016a). As the hajj of 2016 took place, Iranian discourse once again criticized Saudi Arabia, particularly since Iranian pilgrims were absent. In a speech to the families of the victims of the 2015 hajj stampede, Khamenei once again identified Riyadh's lack of transparency, rhetorically asking, 'If they are telling the truth and are innocent in this incident, they must let an Islamic-international fact-finding committee investigate the realities of the issue on the ground and shed light [on them]' (Khamenei 2016a). The Supreme Leader added that the 'Saudi rulers' refusal to offer a simple verbal apology was indicative of their ultimate impudence and shamelessness' (Khamenei 2016a). Khamenei questioned the Islamic leadership of the Al Saud, framing Iran as an Islamic leader that would 'stand courageously against the Al Saud's ignorance and misguidance and [that] expresses its Quranic and rightful positions' (Khamenei 2016a). According to Khamenei, the Saudi 'government is not qualified to manage the two holy mosques' (Khamenei 2016a).

The response from Riyadh came predominantly from its clergy. Its most senior cleric, Abdul Aziz al-Sheikh, the Grand Mufti, questioned the 'Islamicness' of the Iranian leadership. The Saudi mufti labelled Iran's leaders as 'not Muslims'. Using tropes of infidelity (*kufr*), he underlined that 'we have to understand that they [Iran's leaders] are not Muslim ... they are the sons of the Magi', i.e. Zoroastrians, such that Khamenei's comments were 'not surprising' (Al Ash-Sheikh 2016). The clerical discourse drew in tropes of the historical enmity between Persians and Islam. According to the Grand Mufti, this Zoroastrian *kufr* was the reason behind Iran's 'hostility towards Muslims', an enmity that 'is an old one ... especially with the Sunnis' (Al Ash-Sheikh 2016). The Saudi clerical discourse highlighted the image of the Saudi Self as Islamic versus the Iranian Other as an infidel. Therefore, to the Saudi domestic audience, Iranian hostility and a polarizing narrative aimed at the Al Saud was embedded in their historic enmity towards Islam. The clerical discourse framed Al Saud as the true Muslims and as the protector of Sunnis, and the Iranian leadership as the enemies of this form of Islam and as its 'custodian', i.e. the Saudi monarch. The hajj stampede was the incident that initiated a deterioration in the relations between Tehran and Riyadh. However, the execution of a vocal Shi'i cleric, as briefly discussed in the previous chapter, would lead to a complete severing of these relations.

Severing Diplomatic Ties: The Execution of Nimr al-Nimr

The second event that led to a deterioration in Iranian–Saudi relations was the execution of the Saudi Shi'i cleric, Nimr al-Nimr. On 2 January 2016, the Saudi king gave the order to execute Shi'i and Sunni Saudis on charges of terrorism, some of whom were affiliated with Al-Qaeda. This also included carrying out a death sentence issued against the cleric in 2014, an incident that led to an escalation of the crisis and unrest on the streets of Iran. Iranians demonstrated against the execution; matters got out of hand and the aggravated protestors attacked the Saudi diplomatic missions in Tehran and Mashhad (NY Times 2016). As the rioters ransacked the Saudi embassy, there were rumours of a Saudi airstrike on the Iranian embassy in the Yemeni capital, Sanaa (Stutser 2016). Moreover, in retaliation for the embassy attacks in Tehran, Saudi Arabia severed its diplomatic relations with Iran. Officials from both countries chimed in and traded further accusations and allegations.

In Iran, moderate voices such as Rafsanjani had no effect under Salman's tenure. Previously, Rafsanjani's advice and backdoor communication with Riyadh had carried weight and the 2014 sentence levied against al-Nimr was not carried out. However, with Salman at the helm along with MBS, Rafsanjani's good relations with Riyadh were not enough to stop the sentence from being carried out. Different scholars have suggested different reasons underpinning Riyadh's decision to execute al-Nimr. Zaccara (2016: 371–72) argues that Riyadh carried out the execution in that moment with Iran in mind. First, Saudi Arabia was growing wearisome and was 'feeling betrayed' by the Obama administration, particularly as Obama took steps to thaw relations with Iran (Zaccara 2016). Therefore, Riyadh decided to take matters into its own hands and build a coalition that would confront Iran regionally. By the end of 2015, Saudi Arabia announced the formation of the Islamic Alliance to Fight Terrorism (IMAFT). This alliance was comprised of thirty-four countries at its launch and by December 2016, a total of forty-one Sunni countries were members (Shahab Ahmed 2019). Neither Iran nor Iraq nor Lebanon were invited to join, leading the Iranians to speculate that it was a Sunni alliance against Iran and its allies. The coalition was to 'fight Shi'i terror' and not ISIS per se.

Another reason for Riyadh's decision to execute al-Nimr at that time was its apprehensiveness over the Iran nuclear deal. The JCPOA was about to be implemented on 16 January 2016, meaning that Iran would have been empowered to support its regional allies, including in the ongoing wars in Syria and Yemen. Therefore, executing al-Nimr was seen as deliberately antagonizing Iran. Fraihat (2020: 55–56) has also argued that al-Nimr's execution was deliberate and carried out in the knowledge that Iran would react in a hostile manner. According to Fraihat, Riyadh intended to send out three messages (Fraihat 2020). The first message was that it did not fear Iranian threats. Second, it wanted to communicate a message to the US that Riyadh did not trust the Obama administration, and that the latter's pressure on and warnings to not execute al-Nimr did not work. The third was a message to the Saudi domestic audience warning them that dissent against the state would result in a death penalty. Consequently, executing al-Nimr was a tactical measure aimed at bolstering the image of the Saudi Self, first domestically to warn against any thoughts of anti-state uprising and opposition, and second to the international community, principally the Obama administration and Saudi Arabia's Other, Iran.

The cleric al-Nimr was one of forty-seven individuals executed on charges of engaging in 'terrorism' and 'adopting Takfiri ideology' *(SPA 2016)*. After al-Nimr's execution, Iranian protestors stormed the Saudi embassy in Tehran. The Saudi government immediately severed diplomatic ties with Iran. In a show of solidarity Bahrain followed suit, and other GCC countries, such as Kuwait, recalled their ambassadors for discussions.

The first response came from the Iranian foreign-ministry spokesman. It condemned the execution and stated that the 'Saudi government supports terrorists and Takfiri extremists, while talking to its critics at home with the language of execution and suppression (Jaberi Ansari 2016). This was followed by a speech by the Supreme Leader, Ayatollah Khamenei, who attributed the execution to Saudi officials. Stopping short of charges of terrorism, Khamenei framed the execution as a 'major crime' against a 'pious and innocent scholar' who was an 'innocent martyr' rather than 'a terrorist', as the Saudis had labelled him (Khamenei 2016b). Khamenei represented the incident as a norm for Riyadh, a 'crime [among] similar crimes committed by the Saudi regime in Yemen and Bahrain' (Khamenei 2016b). Khamenei was implying that Riyadh had targeted Shi'i communities as in the case of Yemen and Bahrain. Furthermore, al-Nimr's execution was discursively constructed as a human rights violation, bringing in tropes of the hypocrisy of both the international community and the Islamic world. Khamenei criticized 'the silence of the self-proclaimed advocates of freedom, democracy, and human rights', attributing their deafening response to 'their support for the Saudi regime' (Khamenei 2016b). The Supreme Leader represented the international response, especially that from the Muslim world, as being subservient to Riyadh, claiming that the 'Muslim world and the entire world must feel responsible for this issue' (Khamenei 2016b).

The Saudi discourse on the al-Nimr incident was a reaction to Khamenei's sermon. Indeed, the Saudi discourse towards Iran in relation to this incident focused on three main images: the first was that Iran and its officials were irresponsible international actors; second, the Iranian government had a history of attacking diplomatic missions; and third, Iran supported terrorists. The initial Saudi response came from the foreign minister, Adel al-Jubeir, who asserted that Iran had a 'long record of violations of foreign diplomatic missions' (al-Jubeir

2016). He drew historical parallels and mentioned previous incidents such as the 'occupation of the US embassy in 1979, [and] the attack against the British embassy in 2011' (al-Jubeir 2016). Riyadh's initial message to the international community framed Iran's actions as a 'flagrant violation of all international agreements, charters, and treaties'. Iran was represented as an irresponsible international actor, with leaders who 'issue aggressive statements' that had caused the attacks. Moreover, al-Jubeir's statement represented Iran as a supporter of international terrorism; one who has 'provide[d] safe havens on its territories for Al-Qaeda leaders since 2001 [and] provided protection for a number of those involved in the al-Khobar Towers explosion in 1996' (al-Jubeir 2016). In his statement, al-Jubeir was implicitly framing Tehran's distress as being over the loss of its proxies in the kingdom rather than simply protesting the execution of an innocent Shi'i cleric. Saudi Arabia had used the discourse of the Iranian sponsorship of terror previously in the context of Hezbollah and of Iran's alleged role in Bahrain during the Arab Spring, in the Syrian war, and in the alleged assassination attempt of Adel al-Jubeir during his tenure as ambassador in Washington.

As the GCC and Islamic countries severed diplomatic ties with Tehran, the official Iranian discourse attempted to cushion the blow to its image, especially as it was about to begin implementing the JCPOA. The official Iranian discourse was two-tiered. The first tier was aimed at the domestic populace and the other at the international community. The official and domestic discourse was now similar, particularly as chances for détente had withered away. At a meeting with a Danish delegation, the Iranian president argued that Saudi Arabia's 'severing of diplomatic relations with . . . Iran' was Riyadh's attempt to 'conceal its criminal act of beheading a religious leader' (Rouhani 2016). Rouhani echoed Khamenei's framing of the international community's hypocrisy. By invoking the trope of human rights, the president observed that 'European countries that always react to human rights issues, fulfil their human rights responsibilities on the matter' (Rouhani 2016). As for the Saudi allegations of Iranian support for terrorists and terrorism, Rouhani's speech responded to al-Jubeir's allegations. Iran was a responsible actor that believed in 'diplomacy and negotiations as the best solution to settle the differences between nations' and Tehran believed 'that the regional situation is not stable', and called on Saudi Arabia and Iran to 'cooperate with each other to confront terrorism, which is endangering the region' (Rouhani 2016). The domestic discourse, however, criticized Riyadh, utilizing tropes of sectarian strife.

In a cabinet meeting aired on domestic media outlets, the Iranian president discussed the execution of al-Nimr and the local reaction, namely the attack on the Saudi diplomatic mission. The attacks on the Saudi missions were defined as acts of 'ignorance' and those who participated were branded 'criminals' who were 'distant from Islamic and Iranian culture, as well as the law' (Rouhani 2016). The attacks were also defined as being 'against legal and religious laws'. Rouhani admitted that the attacks on the Saudi mission had dented Iran's cultural prestige. The attacks were considered an insult to the political system's reputation as well as to Iranian culture and society. On the other hand, Saudi Arabia's attacks on Iran were framed through the lens of 'Iranophobia' and accusations of sectarian tropes.

Although recognized by Rouhani as an 'Islamic country', the Saudi government was charged with being a 'sectarian state that had attempted for so long to introduce and fan Shia–Sunni strife', as well as employing particular rhetoric and creating an atmosphere of 'Iranophobia' (Rouhani 2016). This, according to Rouhani, was to skew 'world public opinion', especially as the JCPOA was close to being implemented and the sanctions on Iran removed. Rouhani remarked that the 'childish acts of novices in a certain government' were creating 'obstructions' for Tehran (Rouhani 2016). It was these allegations that MBS attempted to dispel in his media interviews.

In a press interview with *The Economist* (6 January 2016), Bin Salman discussed the al-Nimr execution and Iran's reaction. The questions focused on why the executions took place, why a Shi'i cleric was among Al-Qaeda affiliates, and Iran's role and reaction. The response was framed in terms of highlighting the Saudi Self as a responsible international actor; one that followed a judicial process, with the accused parties having full rights. MBS related the executions to 'terrorism' and the cases 'went through three layers of judicial proceedings' and were 'made public [and the] court doors were also open for any media people and journalists' (al-Saud and *Economist* 2016). As for the Shi'i identity of al-Nimr, MBS dispelled any hint of sectarianism, arguing that the 'court did not ... make any distinction between whether or not a person is Shi'ite or Sunni'. As for Iran's reaction, the prince opined that it was a 'strange thing' that Iran was protesting about a 'Saudi citizen who committed a crime in Saudi Arabia', framing the demonstrations as a form of Iranian hegemony and as an intrusion into Riyadh's domestic politics. MBS further observed that 'it proves that Iran is keen on extending its influence over the countries of the region' (al-Saud and *Economist* 2016).

The issue regarding the severing of diplomatic relations was portrayed as a defensive measure by Riyadh, amid allusions to Iranian narratives of Saudi pressure on Tehran. MBS defined the action as a face-saving measure to save 'Iran from ... embarrassment' as the 'Saudi mission was set ablaze and the Iranian government was watching', asking what if 'a diplomat, or their families are attacked?' (al-Saud and *Economist* 2016). As tensions grew between the two states, so did fears of a regional war. Saudi Arabia had created a coalition composed of Sunni countries to fight terrorism. When MBS was asked if the incident would result in a war, he responded that Saudi officials 'do not foresee [war] at all' as it would create a 'major catastrophe in the region, and it w[ould] reflect very strongly on the rest of the world' (al-Saud and *Economist* 2016). Asked if he considered Iran to be Saudi Arabia's 'biggest enemy', the response was that 'we hope not' (al-Saud and *Economist* 2016). The interview was a public relations opportunity to highlight the Saudi Self versus the Iranian Other. Saudi Arabia was explicitly defined as a responsible state, i.e. one that followed rules and regulations, a responsible actor that tried individuals based on the crime committed and not on sectarian or religious identity. From a foreign policy perspective, MBS framed Riyadh as a responsible and peaceful regional actor, one that did not seek war with Iran. However, Tehran's criticism of Riyadh over the executions was framed as a hegemonic move by Iran and a form of interference in Saudi and regional affairs.

MBS's discourse on Iran aimed to show the benign face of the kingdom towards its chief adversary; however, it would not be long before MBS's narrative on Iran shifted as he asked for the war to be taken to Tehran rather than wait for it to come to Riyadh.

Conclusion

The death of King Abdullah and the ascension of Salman as monarch resulted in the Iranian efforts at rapprochement becoming sterile as the relationship between Rafsanjani and Abdullah ended due to the death of the latter. The rise of Salman and the new administration in Saudi Arabia, namely, MBS and the new foreign minister, Adel al-Jubeir, marked a shift in the discourse of the Saudi Self and the Iranian Other. The death of Abdullah coincided with the Syrian war entering its fourth year; Iran and its allies were deeply entrenched in Syria, which frustrated Saudi Arabia. With Assad beginning to make significant gains with Iran and its allies along with Russia, this led Saudi Arabia to view Assad's resistance and Tehran's support as part of a growing Iranian influence in the Middle East. The September 2014 Houthi overtaking of Sanaa, and the Iran-aligned group pushing the pro-Saudi Hadi government out, was a severe blow to Riyadh as it left the country with a pro-Iran ally on its immediate borders. Therefore, Saudi Arabia aimed to shore up its image and take a more confrontational stance towards Iran, establishing a coalition with itself at the helm. The war in Yemen, dubbed Operation Decisive Force and Operation Restoring Hope formed the basis for a multitude of newly triggered discourses, tropes, and narratives constructing and representing the Self and the Other.

The Houthi takeover of Sanaa brought with it Saudi discourses of Iranian expansionism, Persian empire, and narratives that alluded to a sectarian war and a Shi'i crescent. Similarly, Iran's representation of Saudi Arabia in the war in Yemen brought in discourses that recalled those present during the wars of Hezbollah and Gaza of 2006 and 2009 respectively. Saudi Arabia was therefore represented as an equivalent to Israel, and tropes of the oppressor versus the oppressed were employed. Furthermore, Saudi Arabia's construction of Iran as being the cause of the war in Yemen led the Iranian discourse promulgators to react and represent Saudi Arabia as subservient to the US, while characterizing the war as an American-led war and Saudi Arabia as a perpetrator facilitating the massacring of Muslims. Moreover, the discourses on the hajj incident of 2015 invoked Saudi discourses of animosity and the demonization of Iran. This polarized representation of the Iranian Other reached its peak in the hajj incident, bringing with it tropes and narratives reminiscent of Iran in the 1980s post-revolutionary period, particularly those relating to the hajj of 1987. The redeployed tropes from 1987 included questioning Saudi Arabia's Islamic leadership, its legitimacy, and calling for international and religious oversight of the Holy Lands in Mecca and Medina. This therefore resulted in a reactionary Saudi discourse of the Iranian Other as politicizing the hajj rituals and accusing Tehran of sectarian sedition and of dividing the Islamic world. These tropes became dominant as both countries exchanged rhetoric in reaction to the execution of the Shi'i cleric Nimr al-Nimr.

The al-Nimr execution had a profound effect on Iranian–Saudi relations, which led to the severing of diplomatic ties because of protests in Iran and the ransacking of the Saudi diplomatic missions. This incident led the official Saudi discourse, namely that of MBS and al-Jubeir, to construct a discourse on Iran that mimicked the Iranian discourse and used historical tropes. The Saudi discourse constructed three images of the Iranian Other, which included: Iran as an irresponsible international actor, a history of attacking diplomatic missions, and harbouring and supporting terrorism. Incidents such as the 1979 US Embassy Hostage Crisis and the 1996 bombings of the al-Khobar tower were examples of such tropes. Moreover, the severing of diplomatic relations coincided with the signing and the implementation of the JCPOA, particularly since Saudi Arabia had become worried, feeling betrayed by the Obama administration and its slight thaw in relations with Iran. The Iranian discourse characterized Riyadh's apprehension and severing of diplomatic relations as a defensive measure by Saudi Arabia. Discourses of Iranophobia were employed by Iranian officials to portray Riyadh's treatment of the JCPOA, to which Saudi Arabia utilized the trope of terrorism when representing the Iranian Other. The trope of terrorism gained dominance in Saudi discourse after the al-Nimr incident. In effect, the Saudi Self was represented as a victim of this terrorism, while also seeking to repel Iranian charges of Saudi sectarianism. It is these discourses representing the Self and Other in both countries since 2015 that have led to an exchange and mutual representations of each other as sectarian, as interfering in each other's domestic affairs, and as working towards regional expansionism.

In early 2016, the Obama administration was getting ready to hand over the reins to a new presidency. As the US election campaign was in progress, a new populist voice was being heard in US politics. The rise of Donald J. Trump, a businessman turned politician, would upend US foreign policy and relations with the international community. Trump's victory in November 2016 would spell positive tidings for the GCC states, particularly Saudi Arabia. MBS would find an ally in Washington, not only through a fresh alliance with the newly elected US president, but also with his son-in-law, Jared Kushner. For Iran, this would jeopardize the recently signed nuclear deal with the P5+1. Furthermore, this would reverse the slight thaw in relations and the glimpse of détente between Washington and Tehran, especially as the new Republican president adopted a 'maximum pressure' campaign against Iran, much to the pleasure of Saudi Arabia. The Trump administration would push not only Iran and Saudi Arabia towards conflict, but would also put the whole region in danger. It would also be this US administration that would embolden MBS and enhance Saudi Arabia's rhetoric towards Iran.

Chapter 14

A COLD WAR TURNS HOT: THE TRUMP PRESIDENCY AND MOHAMMAD BIN SALMAN

Introduction

The election of Donald Trump in November 2016 was a crucial moment, not just for the US but for the world at large. Never in the history of the US had a businessman known for reality television, beauty pageants, and real estate, ever become the commander-in-chief. The year 2017 not only opened a new chapter in the US, but also witnessed major events in the Persian Gulf region. In Iran, the death of one of the main pillars of Iranian politics and the Islamic Revolution, the former president and Majles speaker, Akbar Hashemi Rafsanjani, a crucial figure in bringing about détente and rapprochement with Saudi Arabia had been lost. In the GCC, the war in Yemen had now escalated and entered its third year. Domestically, Saudi Arabia witnessed a rise in hyper-nationalism with the increasing dominance of MBS over Riyadh's politics and its machinations, alongside his plans to develop Saudi Arabia through his Vision 2030. The rise of MBS coincided with the end of the Obama administration and the onset of the Trump presidency. The reciprocated visits by MBS and Trump, where the latter made Riyadh his first foreign destination, helped to recalibrate the kingdom's relationship with Washington. This collaboration gave rise to the formation of a type of Islamic NATO with MBS at its helm, and a new 'war on terror' with extremism as its focus and Iran as its main target. This collaboration would also push MBS closer to the throne as he was promoted to crown prince, replacing his cousin Mohammad bin Nayef. The same year also witnessed a Saudi-led blockade of Qatar and the resignation and alleged kidnapping of the Lebanese Premier, Saad Hariri, in Riyadh.

For Iran, the year was exceptionally challenging in terms of both the administration and image of the Islamic Republic. The summer of 2017 saw an ISIS attack in Tehran, targeting symbolic landmarks such as the parliament and Ayatollah Khomeini's mausoleum. Iran's reaction was to launch a missile strike on ISIS targets in Syria, the first of their kind for Tehran. These attacks also brought about accusations of a Saudi- and US-led conspiracy that was supposedly sponsoring ISIS against Iran. Riyadh also witnessed attacks. The Houthis initiated their own missile attack targeting King Khaled airport in Riyadh, an incident blamed on Iran. These attacks, in addition to MBS's fight against extremism, saw the use of discourses juxtaposing Khamenei and Iran with Hitler and Nazism respectively, as well as a narrative based on 'taking the war to Tehran'. The advent of the Trump administration also put the JCPOA in jeopardy. Riyadh's dissatisfaction with the Iran nuclear deal negotiated by the Obama administration was now echoed and supported by Trump. As a result, Saudi Arabia had forged a new alliance with Washington calling for additional pressure on Iran.

In this chapter I argue that one of the main Saudi Arabian aims was to construct a unified Self with the new US administration, which I view in turn as an effort generated by Riyadh and shaped by MBS to produce a unified 'common Other', namely Iran. In this chapter we will see some new and unique discourses that produced this dynamic as well as the resurrection of tropes reminiscent of the early post-revolutionary and Khomeini era. These new and resurfacing discourses illustrate innovations in how Iran and Saudi Arabia represented each other and interacted with the US. A detailed discussion of the Trump campaign and presidency and its interaction with Saudi Arabia is therefore imperative to give much needed context to this Self-and-Other dynamic. The uniqueness of the Trump presidency and its relationship with MBS was such that the former explicitly towed the line of Riyadh in its confrontation and rivalry with Iran. It is this confrontation and synergistic relationship that gave rise to different tropes and narratives employed by Saudi Arabia and responded to by Tehran, including those based on hegemony, fascism, sectarianism, Western–Zionist subservience, as well as images of irresponsibility, immaturity, and naïveté as an international actor.

The Death of Rafsanjani: the Demise of Rapprochement?

The death of Rafsanjani coincided with the anniversary of the severing of diplomatic ties between Riyadh and Tehran over the ransacking of the Saudi embassy in Tehran during protests against the execution of the Shi'i cleric Nimr al-Nimr. While the kingdom did not send an official telegram to Iran, an Iranian news outlet, Entekhab (24 January 2017), reported that the Saudi monarch sent a personal letter addressed to the 'honoured family of Akbar Hashemi Rafsanjani' via the OIC on 12 January, expressing his condolences *(Entekhab* 2017a*)*. This letter overlapped with Kuwaiti overtures to establish dialogue and rapprochement between the GCC and Iran. The Kuwaiti foreign ministry announced the same day that its deputy foreign minister, Khaled Al-Jarallah, would 'relay a message to Iran from the GCC member states'. Stopping short of elaborating on the contents of the letter, the Kuwaiti diplomat proclaimed that the groundwork had already begun with 'Iranian brothers to set a proper date to deliver the message' *(KUNA 2017)*. As the Iranian press announced the Saudi letter to the Rafsanjani family, Iranian media outlets also disclosed mediation efforts between Iran and Saudi Arabia. The Iranian Student News Agency (ISNA) cited a report from the Lebanese newspaper *Al-Akhbar* highlighting the Kuwaiti delegation's visit as an attempt to mediate between Iran and Saudi Arabia *(ISNA 2017a)*. This mediation announcement came at a time when Iranian officials once again expressed a desire for rapprochement with Riyadh. While Saudi Arabia was not interested in rapprochement at that point, the condolences communicated to Rafsanjani's family were an attempt at sending an implicit message to the Iranian audience. In other words, Saudi Arabia had no grievances with the Iranian people; it respected certain major figures in the Iranian political arena, and its issues were rather with the Velayat-e Faqih and those who had shown animosity towards the Saudi state. Therefore, although Iran's position on al-Nimr's execution was based on a Shi'i standpoint, the monarch's note was an attempt to underline his Islamic leadership by conveying an image based on Islamic equality and non-sectarianism, thereby shifting the issue with Iran from a sectarian position to a political one in relation to the Islamic world in general and the Iranian domestic population in particular.

The reformist Iranian press projected a positive image of Iranian–Saudi rapprochement in the near future through regional mediation *(Etemaad 2017)*. The editorial quoted the Saudi foreign minister, Adel al-Jubeir, who had initially suggested that solving the problems between Iran and Saudi 'did not require a mediator [and] Tehran knows what to do' (Adel al-Jubeir 2017). In addition, the outlet represented the Saudi remarks as reflecting the implicit readiness of Riyadh to settle its differences with Iran *(Etemaad 2017)*. Furthermore, senior Iranian security and diplomatic officials welcomed the mediation, including the prospect of the easing of tensions and good relations with Saudi Arabia. From a security perspective, Ali Shamkhani, the secretary of the National Security Council, emphasized that Iran 'does not seek to overthrow' the monarchy, 'on the contrary it looks to curb efforts to overthrow the Saudi government' (Shamkhani 2017). From a diplomatic standpoint, Tehran's senior diplomat, Javad Zarif, framed the mediation efforts as an opportunity for Iranian–Saudi cooperation, and he projected an image of Iranian pragmatism and the Islamic Republic as a responsible actor and regional leader. On 18 January in Davos, Zarif reminded the international community, and the Saudis in particular, that both states were capable of sharing the region's leadership and should be cooperating in order to solve its problems. Citing the efforts made to end the impasse over the Lebanese elections for instance, Zarif argued that both states 'can in fact work together to put an end to the miserable conditions of the people in Syria, Yemen, and Bahrain and elsewhere in the region' (Zarif 2017f). Zarif stressed that he did 'not see any reason why Iran and Saudi Arabia should have hostile policies towards each other' (Zarif 2017f). Through its foreign minister, Iran extended its hand once again in a seeming effort to turn a new leaf and settle outstanding differences, including both the Syrian and Yemeni crises, the latter entering its third year and becoming a war of attrition. The Saudis were also beginning to warm to the idea of mediation, which included extending an invitation to the Iranian hajj committee to discuss Iran's return to the annual pilgrimage after its boycott following the stampede of September 2015.

The election of Donald Trump in November 2016 signalled to the Iranians that the somewhat favourable position that Obama had towards Iran might shift and could be exploited by Saudi Arabia and certain other GCC countries. Therefore, the Islamic Republic aimed to build rapprochement and détente with Riyadh pre-emptively. Zarif's discourse of joint leadership with Saudi Arabia recalled the Rafsanjani–Khatami-era narrative of the pragmatic Iranian Self by suggesting joint Riyadh–Tehran leadership of the Islamic world. The emphasis in the official Iranian discourse on the pragmatic Iranian Self also came about as Obama had explicitly signalled in an interview with *The Atlantic* that both Iran and Saudi Arabia should learn to share the region in what he referred to as a 'cold peace' (Obama 2016). Zarif's discourse towards Riyadh also signalled to the international community as well as to Washington that Iran aimed to sustain its rapprochement and détente overtures, and it was not seeking regional animosity, especially with Saudi Arabia. The discourse thereby underlined the Iranian Self as a responsible regional and international actor, particularly after signing the JCPOA and attaining nuclear status. To Saudi Arabia, Zarif was implying that this rivalry was creating regional tensions and that détente and rapprochement could put an end to regional crises, such as Lebanon. Consequently, by highlighting the Iranian Self as a pragmatic and sensible regional leader, the official Iranian discourse implicitly constructed its Saudi Other as irresponsible and not wanting to 'share' the region. However, while the Iranians were attempting to establish mediation with Riyadh, the US president elect, Trump, would emerge both as an impediment to Iranian–Saudi relations and as a new factor in their rivalry.

Candidate Trump, Saudi Arabia, and Islam

At the same Davos conference at which Zarif highlighted his country's readiness to cooperate and attempted to lay to rest any hostile policies between the two capitals, the Saudi foreign minister openly called for more hostile policies towards Iran, framing the Islamic Republic as a sponsor of terror that was a regional menace seeking nuclear proliferation. Iran's backing of Hezbollah, its presence in Syria, and accusations of direct support of the Houthis in their war with Saudi Arabia, were examples of the tropes utilized by al-Jubeir to counter Zarif's image of the responsible and pragmatic Iranian Self. Adel al-Jubeir sought to construct a Saudi Arabia that had fallen victim to Tehran, thereby shaping an image of a belligerent Iranian Other. At the same time, the Saudi foreign minister was sending a clear message to the new US administration. On the same day as Trump's inauguration, the Saudi chief diplomat emphasized his country's position towards the Trump administration. In addition to recalibrating the kingdom's relationship with the US under a new administration, al-Jubeir argued that Riyadh hoped to see 'more American engagement in the world, more American engagement in the region, rebuilding relations with allies, a serious effort to destroy ISIS, a serious effort to contain Iran', further expressing the hope that 'change will happen' (al-Jubeir 2017).

To the international community – and more precisely to the new US administration – the official Saudi discourse constructed Iran as the key problem for the world, the region, and Saudi Arabia as well as the US. The foreign minister argued that 'Iran has been single-handedly the most important supporter of terrorism in the region', hinting that Iran might be behind Al-Qaeda and ISIS since he found it interesting that 'virtually every country in the world has been attacked by Al-Qaeda and Daesh, except Iran. Why?' (al-Jubeir 2017). On Iran's nuclear programme, the official Saudi discourse tried to cast doubt on the JCPOA, arguing that Iran was seeking nuclear arms and emphasizing that 'a number of countries, including Saudi Arabia' have concerns over the JCPOA, in an allusion to Israel. However, Saudi Arabia had its own outstanding issues with the US. On 26 September 2016, the US Senate passed the Justice Against Sponsors of Terrorism Act (JASTA) that enabled the families of the victims of the 9/11 attacks to sue the Saudi government, which was initially vetoed by Obama (Khatib and Maziad 2018). Amid these issues, al-Jubeir tried to signal that the US and Saudi Arabia had a common enemy, while the Saudi discourse tried to align its position with that of the United States and create a common anti-Iran front by constructing a common Other. Saudi Arabia argued that the US had 'the most to lose' from the JASTA Act and hoped that 'wisdom will prevail, and Congress will do the right thing' (al-Jubeir 2017). In addition, al-Jubeir signalled a recalibration and a new strategic partnership with the US under Trump, the same Trump who had been vocally against Saudi Arabia during his election campaign and held it accountable for 9/11.

Trump's antagonistic views on Muslims in general and Saudi Arabia in particular were visible both in his campaigning and during his first hundred days in office. Speaking in the aftermath of a mass-shooting attack by a couple of Pakistani origin in California, Trump called for 'a total and complete shutdown of Muslims entering the United States until our country's representatives can figure out what is going on' (NPR 2015). Speaking at a rally in Mount Pleasant, South Carolina, Trump called for the nationwide surveillance of mosques, a similar idea to the one he proposed after the Paris shootings, where he went as far as suggesting shutting down some mosques (NPR 2015). Less than ten months before the 2016 elections, Trump targeted Saudi Arabia. The business tycoon turned politician openly charged that 'It wasn't the Iraqis that knocked down the World Trade Centre ... You may find it's the Saudis, okay? But you will find out' (Trump 2017b). On the Fox news network, Trump argued once again that it was not Iraq that attacked the World Trade Centre, 'it was Saudi – take a look at Saudi Arabia', asking the Obama administration to 'open the documents', in a reference to the 2002 redacted Joint Inquiry report into the 9/11 attacks (Trump 2017b; Hiro 2019: 314).

In his early campaign, Trump criticized the Saudi–US military and defence relationship. As early as in 2015, Trump charged that 'Saudi Arabia should be paying the United States many billions of dollars for our defence of them. Without us, gone!' (Trump 2015). As Saudi Arabia was embroiled in the war in Yemen, Trump projected an image of Saudi weakness and their dependence on US military capabilities. Hiro (2019) observes that later in his campaign in March 2016, Trump referred to Riyadh as a 'monetary machine' and stated that the US is 'not being reimbursed for our protection of many of the countries ... including Saudi Arabia' (NY Times and Trump 2016), representing Riyadh as a source of wealth that the US should exploit, arguing that the 'amount of money they [Saudi Arabia] have is phenomenal', highlighting that 'without us, Saudi Arabia wouldn't exist for very long ... I would say at a minimum, we have to be reimbursed, substantially reimbursed, I mean, to a point that's far greater than what we're being paid right now' (NY Times and Trump 2016). This 'existence' referred to US protection against both domestic and external threats, opining that 'whether it was internal or external [opposition, Saudi Arabia] wouldn't be around for very long' (NY Times and Trump 2016). Trump's construction of an image of Saudi Arabia as militarily weak and dependent on US protection, and that should therefore be exploited for its wealth would later become a dominant construction in the Iranian Othering of Saudi Arabia. Trump's construction of Riyadh was arguably the first primordial element in the Iranian construction of the Riyadh 'milking cow' (Khamenei 2017b).

The response from Saudi Arabia was overall silence. With the exception of an isolated response from CNN, Adel al-Jubeir depicted the relationship between Riyadh and Washington as an alliance, where 'the kingdom of Saudi Arabia is an ally that carries its own weight', thus highlighting a discourse of self-reliance that was reminiscent of the 1990s era in which Saudi Arabia invited in the US forces to protect Riyadh from Saddam, in a moment when King Fahd emphasized the kingdom's self-reliance and military standing *(CNN* and Al-Jubeir 2017*)*. Drawing on historical narratives, al-Jubeir reminded both the US and the Saudi domestic audience that during 'the Gulf War to liberate Kuwait', Riyadh 'assumed the lion's share of the financial burden of that war' *(CNN* and Al-Jubeir 2017*)*. The Saudi foreign minister emphasized that 'We've always supported ourselves. We have not relied on anyone to provide any assistance to us'. As for how the kingdom perceived Donald Trump, the Saudi response was diplomatic: 'At least he likes us ... He provides great products and people enjoy buying them and living with them' *(CNN* and Al-Jubeir 2017*)*. It would be these US products and contracts that the kingdom would later purchase and negotiate with Trump, which would lead to a recalibration of the relationship and alliance between both states.

President Trump, Saudi Arabia, and the Common Iranian Other

Trump's presidency caused a substantial reversal in US foreign policy, evident in the changed position towards the Iran nuclear deal, which Trump cited as the 'worst deal ever' (*The Times* and Trump 2017) while adopting an aggressive position towards Iran, which fitted in with Saudi Arabia's call for harsher measures at Davos. The bellicose nature of Trump's tone became evident during the first two weeks of his presidency, especially after Iran's testing of its 'Khorramshahr' medium-range ballistic missile on 29 January 2017. Trump tweeted that 'Iran is playing with fire [and] they did not appreciate how "kind" President Obama was to them', signalling a change in era, ending his tweet by stressing 'Not me!' (Trump 2017c). Trump's Iranian narrative and signalling of a much-altered post-Obama relationship was an implicit message to his domestic audience, Israel, the international community and, most specifically, Saudi Arabia. Trump was now towing the Saudi line, establishing a common Iranian Other with Riyadh.

Trump's position towards Iran was evident in the 'Muslim ban' that he ordered a week into his presidency. Iran, along with other Muslim countries, was placed on the list due to allegations of its sponsorship of terrorism. While Saudi Arabia was not on this list, Trump had implicated Riyadh for being behind the 9/11 attacks (Hassan 2017)[1]. The silence from Saudi Arabia and the GCC states was deafening, however, while the response from Iran was more confrontational. In an implicit response to the Muslim ban, Iran's reaction was a missile test to buttress its image of military prowess and scientific supremacy, while Trump's response was a set of new sanctions against members of the IRGC and the entities that supported the Iranian missile programme.

Iran's official response – communicated primarily through its foreign ministry – aimed to dampen the aggressive image projected by the sanctions and by Trump's discourse. This was accomplished by Iran expressing the peaceful nature of the missile test and its objection to the new US sanctions *(Reuters* 2017a). As for the Muslim ban that Iran was included in, the Ayatollah opined that Trump's actions 'fully displayed and manifested ... reveal[ing] the naked truth about America during and after the elections, [Trump] is showing the truth about the United States ... what American human rights mean; they detain innocent children: this is their human rights!' (Khamenei 2017c). In other words, the Ayatollah was subtly preparing Iranians for a more confrontational US administration, one that would use 'iron fists' without 'velvet gloves' (Khamenei 2017c). Khamenei's discourse was aimed at domestic, regional, and international audiences. While the Supreme Leader's words explicitly targeted the US, it was also a message to the Islamic world, and it constructed an image of Islamic leadership and defiance of US enmity towards Islam and Iran. In addition, another image was developed, namely one based on a strong, advanced, self-reliant Iran acting as the custodian of the Islamic world as opposed to a silent and quiescent Saudi Other. This implicit discursive construction attempted to portray Riyadh as subservient and dependent on the US and as weak, lacking prestige, and scientifically primitive. To that effect, while Iran was fending off and countering the new Trump administration's aggressive posturing, Riyadh was attempting to recalibrate its relationship with Washington, which would become evident after Trump's volte-face in terms of his relations with the Saudis and the synergy he displayed with Riyadh in its enmity towards Iran.

Quincy Meeting 2.0: bin Salman Meets Trump

Trump's reversal of Obama's foreign policy towards Iran was a welcome sign for Riyadh. In relation to Yemen, Trump had gone as far as to approve a mission

---

1. On 27 January, Trump signed an executive order entitled 'Protection of the Nation from Foreign Terrorist Entry into the United States'. The order included a ban on the arrival of citizens from seven countries including Iran, Syria, Sudan, Yemen, Iraq, Libya, and Somalia. Iraq was later removed from the list. Saudi Arabia, which Trump accused of being behind the World Trade Centre terrorist attacks, was absent to the surprise of many.

against a suspected Al-Qaeda base just days after his inauguration, which was another positive sign for the Saudis in terms of a reversal of US policy on the conflict. This became the basis for a high-level Saudi visit to Washington, and a 'historical turning point' in US–Saudi relations. The deputy crown prince, Mohammed bin Salman, met Trump on 14 March, agreeing to arms sales, including a guided munitions sale blocked by the previous administration, with discussions including opportunities for US companies to invest in Saudi Arabia, and Riyadh's investment in the US economy potentially leading to job creation (*Guardian* 2017).

The official Saudi discourse on this visit was articulated by Mohammad bin Salman and his retinue. The prince's narrative and discourse construction arrived via a royal-court official. One of the deputy crown prince's special advisers, speaking anonymously, shaped the discourse on Iran and the Muslim travel ban in his meetings with the new US administration (*Reuters 2017c*). Regarding the Muslim travel ban that included Iran, the Saudi reaction conformed with the Trump narrative. Mohammad bin Salman's position now was that Trump's executive order was not aimed at Islam or Muslim countries and he 'expressed his satisfaction after the meeting on the positive position and clarifications he heard from President Trump on his views on Islam' (*Reuters* 2017c). This discourse based on appeasing Trump helped to construct the image of a common US–Saudi Self and Iranian Other as evidenced in the discussion of regional matters, most specifically those on Iran. The conclusion of the MBS–Trump meeting was an identical view of the 'the danger of Iran's regional expansionist activities' (*Reuters* 2017c). The threat of the JCPOA as 'very dangerous' (*Reuters* 2017c) was now a shared set of official narratives that bolstered the discursive construction of a common Iranian Other. In addition to appeasing Trump on the travel ban and the joint position on the JCPOA, the support for a common Othering of Iran was also bolstered by Saudi promises of investment and arms sales. In this 'historic visit', MBS attempted to construct an image of both himself and the Saudi Self as a strategic partner to Trump and the United States in relation to a shared rivalry with Iran.

Domestically, the Saudi media constructed the Saudi leadership represented by MBS in the image of a prince who succeeded in 'putting things Obama spoiled back on the right track', achieving a historic turning point that 'restored the special relationship between the two countries' that began 'between King Abdulaziz and President Roosevelt on the Cruiser Quincy after the end of World War II' (*Asharq-Al-Awsat* 2017). To the Saudi domestic audience, bin Salman was subtly represented as the reincarnation of his grandfather, the modern day 'bin Saud' who founded the third Saudi state and its first king. As for Saudi Arabia's international position, the Saudi editorials argued that the 'White House has shown great interest' in the crown prince and that 'the president brought the meeting forward two days ahead of schedule [and] gathered the White House staff including the Vice President' on short notice (*Asharq-Al-Awsat* 2017). Mohammad bin Salman's mission was deemed a success since he 'convinced Trump ... to correct the situation and confront Iran's hegemony and [challenge] terrorism' and Tehran's 'military expansion in Iraq, Syria, and Yemen' (*Asharq-Al-Awsat* 2017). In short, this meeting boosted bin Salman's image, morale and position in the region and paved the way for Trump to choose Riyadh as the destination for his first foreign trip. This trip was also the preamble to Saudi Arabia constructing an image of itself through that of bin Salman and his shaping of the Iranian Other.

Bin Salman's Definition of the Saudi Self vis-à-vis the Iranian Other

As Trump's anti-Iran discourse and his dismay at Obama's negotiation of the JCPOA gained momentum, his new-found ally, the deputy crown prince, propagated a similar narrative domestically, highlighting Saudi prestige and prowess at developing the kingdom and transforming its economy away from being hydrocarbon dependent to a non-oil-based economy through Vision 2030. Furthermore, while highlighting the Saudi Self through Vision 2030, bin Salman defined Iran as an Other, employing tropes of Islam and Shi'ism that, up until then, had only been heard and used in Saudi religious discourse, while it can be argued that the ambitious prince's intention was to promote the image of the Saudi leadership on a domestic, regional, and international level.

In an interview with the Saudi news channel *Al-Arabiya* (2017), MBS discussed his plans for the kingdom under Vision 2030 and the launch of a 'national transformation' and fiscal-balance programmes. The deputy crown prince argued that part of his plan was to improve the functioning of government bodies that were marred by years of inefficiency and bureaucracy, while streamlining their function by including 'indicators and objectives for twenty-four government [and] several other bodies' to enhance accountability. Highlighting his project as a 'great achievement' that had resulted in a reduction of a 'budget deficit [more] than what local and global experts had expected for 2015, 2016, and 2017' (al-Saud and *Al-Arabiya* 2017), MBS argued that 'non-oil reserves have nearly doubled' since the launch of Vision 2030 under his guidance in 2016. As for the drop in oil revenue with the advent of a global slowdown, bin Salman attributed the stability of the economy to his leadership. Praising the 'directives of the king and the work of government bodies, officials, and employees', the transformation programme led by the prince 'was able to protect many indicators and rates from being negatively affected, including the unemployment rate' (al-Saud and *Al-Arabiya* 2017). An image of the Saudi Self as a significant regional and world economy was projected by bin Salman alongside ideas for 'developing ports and participating in industrial cities along the Red Sea', and 'enhancing Saudi and Gulf exports to Europe', constructing an image of Gulf leadership in which Saudi Arabia could strengthen its Vision 2030 while sending 'forty per cent of the region's exports to Europe' (al-Saud and *Al-Arabiya* 2017). Through MBS's ambitious Vision 2030, Saudi Arabia projected a transformation of its own economy alongside its aim of becoming a regional economic powerhouse, while acknowledging the risks of not just an economic but also a political and geographical nature, most notably the Yemen War and Iran. The Saudi discourse suggesting prestige through financial prowess courtesy of being a global energy provider and regional leader was not a new narrative. Throughout its history, the official Saudi discourse had sustained and maintained an image of the state's economic, geographic, and religious leadership. However, what was different after the ascent of MBS was that the kingdom's official discourse took a more explicit position on the Saudi Self's Other. Instead, this position was not defined by the Saudi state but through an image of MBS and his vision for Saudi Arabia. After bin Salman had come to power, Saudi Arabia's image was synonymous with the image of MBS. Consequently, and as later events would show, the discourse on Saudi Arabia's Other, i.e. the Islamic Republic and its leadership, was developed around the person of MBS.

Against such a stable and strong projection of the Saudi Self with the deputy crown prince at the helm, MBS explicitly constructed an image of the Other based on both the Houthis and Iran, while implicitly contrasting them with a prosperous Gulf. With regard to a worsening and remorseless war in Yemen, MBS – who also acted as defence minister – argued that Saudi Arabia 'had no choice ... the other scenario was much worse' (al-Saud and *Al-Arabiya* 2017). The alternative scenario that MBS was highlighting referred to 'threats inside Saudi Arabia and in regional countries and on international borders and crossings' (al-Saud and *Al-Arabiya* 2017). In addition, to bolster the image of the Other, demonizing strategies were pursued. The Houthis were compared side by side with ISIS. The defence minister contrasted his war in Yemen with 'another coalition in northern Saudi Arabia, Iraq, and Syria fighting ISIS'. By highlighting the war against ISIS, MBS was also attempting to construct an image of regional leadership and military prestige, equivalent to the US-led international coalition against ISIS. Moreover, MBS attempted to emphasize the prestige of the Saudi-led coalition through self-aggrandizement by comparing the number of countries in their respective coalitions. He argued that while the Saudi-led coalition are made of 'only ten countries in the region', they had 'managed to gain achievements in a lesser time frame compared with operations' than the US-led 'coalition that consists of sixty countries ... since 2014' (al-Saud and *Al-Arabiya* 2017).

On Iran, Riyadh's demonizing strategies were also visible in MBS's discourse towards Iran and its Supreme Leader. In a very rare occurrence hardly ever witnessed in Saudi monarchical discourse, MBS was now directly and explicitly targeting Iran and its Supreme Leader, a phenomenon not witnessed by any of the previous Saudi monarchs and crown princes. This discourse construction was previously limited mainly to the media and the clerical genre of Saudi discourse. This new MBS-generated discourse ranged from representing Iran as an extremist state and an expansionist hegemon to challenging discourses on Iranian legitimacy and leadership. On extremism, the deputy crown prince observed that there was no room to 'communicate with someone', i.e. Khamenei, 'or a regime'; this included the Rouhani administration, which was 'based on an extremist ideology' (al-Saud and *Al-Arabiya* 2017). Furthermore, MBS's discourse on Iran drew from the well of Islam by employing religious and sectarian narratives rooted in the Shi'i belief of the occultation of the Mahdi. These beliefs included the cornerstone of the identity of the Iranian revolution, which culminated in Khomeini's legacy. The latter, MBS argued, was radical and fundamentalist, while it was 'difficult to convince these [Iranians] of anything' since their religious doctrine 'stipulates that it must control Muslims in the Islamic world and spread the Twelver Ja'afari sect across the Islamic world so Imam Mahdi comes' (al-Saud and *Al-Arabiya* 2017). Furthermore, in this interview the prince portrayed Iran as an irresponsible actor who others did not trust vis-à-vis an image of a responsible and pragmatic Saudi Self. For example, MBS remarked that 'when there's a problem between me and another state, we begin by solving it, these include economic problems', and 'we' – that is Riyadh – 'communicate [and] understand how to address the problem' (al-Saud and *Al-Arabiya* 2017). The prince brought Yemen into the equation, while highlighting an image of a dogmatic and rigid Tehran, and he thus characterized his Iranian Other as one that lacked the ability to communicate, while supporting a war against the kingdom.

As mentioned above, the discourse on Iranian expansionism and hegemony was also intermixed with Shi'i narratives of occultation and Mahdism. MBS represented Iran as being led by expansionist zealots with Tehran's 'logic . . . based on the notion that Imam Mahdi will come and that they [Iran] must prepare the fertile environment for his arrival and they must control the Muslim world' (al-Saud and *Al-Arabiya* 2017). Their goal, according to the young prince, was to 'reach the Muslims' *qibla*' (al-Saud and *Al-Arabiya* 2017), which can be defined as invading Saudi Arabia and taking over Mecca and Medina. This, according to MBS, came at the expense of the Iranian regime having 'deprived their own people of development for more than thirty years and put them through starvation' (al-Saud and *Al-Arabiya* 2017). Interestingly, this represented the first time in the history of the two states' relations since 1979 that a Saudi leader explicitly argued that 'We will not wait until the battle is in Saudi Arabia but we will work so the battle is there in Iran and not in Saudi Arabia' (al-Saud and *Al-Arabiya* 2017). Not even during the Iran–Iraq war, or the events of the 1987 hajj, had a Saudi leader used such sectarian rhetoric. The discourse otherwise has always been based on the supposedly non-sectarian Saudi leadership of the Islamic world, and so MBS's rhetoric was a sign of a move away from his predecessors' public stance on Iran. Saudi Arabia, therefore, had begun a discourse of war against the Islamic Republic, which sparked a harsh response from Iranian officials.

The Discourse of Terrorism, Insecurity, and Obsession when Defining Saudi Arabia as Iran's Other

The Iranian response to bin Salman's narrative of Iranian aspirations to hegemony and Shi'i expansionism was met with the Iranian construction of Saudi Arabia as the originator and promoter of terrorism, which was strategized mainly by the defence and foreign-ministry officials. The former, represented by the minister of defence, Brigadier General Hossein Dehqan, openly threatened Riyadh with military action if they made an 'ignorant move' towards Tehran (Dehghan and *Al-Manar* 2017). The minister argued on the pro-Iran Lebanese TV channel Al-Manar that Iran 'recommends them [the Saudis] not to make any ignorant moves', because 'if they do, we will not leave anywhere intact except Mecca and Medina' (Dehghan and *Al-Manar* 2017).

In contrast, the foreign-ministry officials constructed a counterargument to bin Salman's claim, arguing that the prince's comments were 'testament to the promotion of terrorism and the pursuit of the destructive policies of the Saudis in the region and the issues of Iran' (Ghasemi 2017a). Baharam Ghasemi's response to MBS's comments was framed in terms of defining the Iranian Self. In other words, the Islamic Republic had shown in both 'deeds and words to try to use common ground to reach an understanding and cooperation ... in West Asia', arguing that bin Salman's 'statements are far from political wisdom and are considered ... a strategic mistake' (Ghasemi 2017a). Moreover, as the Iranian spokesman attempted to implicate the prince's naivety regarding international relations and regional politics, the Iranian Self was defined as a responsible regional actor and Islamic leader promulgating the notion that what was of great significance to Iran was 'the unity of the Islamic world and the convergence of countries' in fighting terrorism (Ghasemi 2017a). This terrorism was defined as 'foreign intervention' resulting in 'the rise of extremist ideology and Takfiri terrorism', which originated in and was fuelled by the 'Wahhabi sectarian ideology in Saudi Arabia' (Ghasemi 2017a). The official Iranian discourse first aimed to construct MBS as a naïve and immature actor devoid of pragmatism while jeopardizing opportunities for peace and cooperation with the Islamic Republic for personal motives. In constructing this Saudi Other through its criticism of MBS, the discourse of the Iranian foreign ministry innately constructed the Iranian Self as a responsible, cooperative, regional actor that sought regional collaboration and neighbourly relations. This also emphasized Iranian legitimacy and leadership, thereby countering MBS's negative image of Iran in the Saudi media. Furthermore, and in a very rare move, the foreign ministry adopted sectarian tropes to highlight Saudi identity as the source of regional Wahhabi terrorism and extremism. This narrative was previously visible mainly in media and ulama discourses. For instance, in the cases of the Taliban of the 1990s where a 'silent Othering' occurred, i.e. implicit references to Iran were made, or there was a refrain from criticizing Iran evident in the official state narrative, alongside explicit Othering by the press and in the Friday sermons. More recently, the sectarian trope of Saudi Wahhabism was utilized by the press and sermons to emphasize Saudi Arabia's role in the Syrian civil war. This shift in the Iranian foreign-ministry discourse on Saudi Arabia was a reaction to the direct denigration of the Supreme Leader by a member of the Saudi monarchy, whereas during the 1990s both states had aspired for détente.

The foreign ministry's discourse in response to MBS's call to take the war to Iran was internationalized through a letter that Iran had sent to the UN secretary-general and members of the UN Security Council. This action was an attempt to affirm the Iranian Self as a responsible international actor juxtaposed with the image of a belligerent Saudi Other. Iran's envoy, Gholamali Khoshroo, interpreted MBS's statements through the lens of terrorism. Drawing on historical events as well as incidences of terrorism in Iran, the ambassador framed Saudi Arabia as a sponsor of terror courtesy of the 'admission of the long-known complicity [of Riyadh in] acts of terror and violence inside Iran' (Khoshroo 2017). The ambassador was referring to events such as the Jundallah attacks in Balochistan and the terrorist attacks by Arab separatists in Khozistan (Habeeb 2012: 46; Chalk 2013: 323). Moreover, the Iranian diplomat attempted to define the prince's 'unveiled threat against the Islamic Republic of Iran [as] being in violation of ... the UN Charter', and therefore an illegal act from an international perspective' (Khoshroo 2017), thus emphasizing the image of the Saudi Other as both a leader of terrorism and an irresponsible actor. Saudi accusations of Khomeini-era hegemonic intentions were countered by framing Riyadh as being in a state of paranoia, arguing that for the 'past four decades [both the] region and the world have suffered ... as a consequence of Saudi insecurity and misplaced obsession with Iran' (Khoshroo 2017). This discourse of Saudi insecurity and obsession was also compounded by drawing on historical illustrations going back to post-revolutionary Iranian constructions. These included 'the kingdom's unreserved support and financing of Saddam Hussein's aggression against Iran from 1980 to 1988' leading to 'hundreds of thousands of Iranians who became victims of Saddam's ... use of chemical weapons', finally resulting in Saddam attacking Kuwait and Saudi Arabia, thus 'biting the hands that had fed and sustained him' (Khoshroo 2017). By emphasizing the Saudi role in the Iran–Iraq war, the Iranian discourse represented Saudi Arabia as a belligerent actor with a history of enmity towards Iran and as an irresponsible regional actor that supported war with an emphasis on the state's insecurity and obsession with Iran.

Nevertheless, through the 'misplaced obsession' narrative, the Iranian letter characterized Saudi Arabia as a leading sponsor of terror – one that caused regional and global instability. Just as MBS highlighted Iran's role in Yemen and the wider region, Iranian discourse cast light on Riyadh's hand in the creation of Al-Qaeda and the Taliban in the 1990s, 'terror and instability in Iraq since 2003', their support for ISIS, al-Nusrah and 'other terrorist organizations in Iraq and Syria [through the] formation, financing, and arming' of these groups (Khoshroo 2017). Furthermore, the Iranian diplomatic discourse drew on tropes of genocide and acts of war. In the case of Yemen, Saudi Arabia was described in the Iranian letter to the UN as a 'source of blatant and open aggression, starvation and genocide against the people of Yemen' (Khoshroo 2017). This trope aimed to counter the Saudi narrative defending the kingdom's borders through a war against 'terrorist activity' and a 'coup against legitimacy' by the Houthis (al-Saud and *Al-Arabiya* 2017). In this way, Iran constructed two defined images of leadership: the Iranian Self as a responsible, regional, and global leader seeking 'to promote regional stability, combat destabilizing extremist violence and reject sectarian hatred', against Saudi Arabia as its irrational Other. The second image represented the monarchy as an irrational actor that sought to 'attain security at the expense of the insecurity of others' while not 'heed[ing] the call of reason' (Khoshroo 2017). This discourse on Trump's first foreign trip as president to Saudi Arabia was aimed at the international community, and it focused on the regional leadership and the suggestion that terrorism would be further exacerbated by Iran and its regional allies.

Trump Visits Saudi Arabia: a Renewed Call for the 'War on Terror'

It has been the norm for a newly elected US president to visit a neighbouring country on their first foreign trip. Trump unconventionally chose to visit Saudi Arabia on his first tour as president, then stopping off in Israel and the Vatican. In what the king labelled a historic visit (al-Saud and *SPA* 2017), Riyadh and Washington signed contracts and memoranda of understanding that included the sale of arms valued at $380 billion over a period of ten years (Garrett 2018: 193). The visit was marked with celebrations and the traditional tribal dance of the *'ardha*, where Trump was witnessed brandishing a sword, locking arms, and dancing the Bedouin tribal dance of loyalty and war. The aim of all the pomp and circumstance was to show Trump's support for the kingdom against Iran. For Trump, this was an attempt to fulfil a pillar of his presidential campaign, i.e. to generate foreign investment and create jobs.

The highlight of this 'historic visit' was a summit involving fifty-five Arab and Islamic countries chaired by King Salman. At this conference, the speeches made by the king and Trump had one goal: to discuss extremism and fight terrorism. The target of the speeches was Iran. Building on the discourse of Iranian expansionism and terrorism, and the MBS trope of fighting 'Iranian-sponsored terrorism' in Yemen, King Salman spared no effort in constructing Iran as 'moderate Islam's' enemy (al-Saud and *SPA* 2017). This construction cemented MBS's 'common Other' and 'common Self' with the US. Considering the common Other, the fight against terrorism was represented as a partnership, whereby the fifty-five Arab and Islamic countries viewed Trump as an 'important partner in fighting the forces of extremism and terrorism and achieving world peace, security, and stability' (al-Saud and *SPA* 2017). With regards to the common Self, the speech focused on sharing the 'same noble feelings in terms of constructive cooperation to renounce extremism and work on countering terrorism in all its forms [and being] in compliance with the orders of our true Islamic religion'.

Constructing a dichotomy, the Saudi monarch's comments appropriated the Iranian narrative of 'true Mohammedan Islam' ('Islam-i Nab-i Mohammadi'). King Salman's narrative questioned Iran's Islamic credentials; the discourse employed against the Iranian state painted Iran's leadership as a group 'who considered themselves as Muslims' and 'seek to link Islam with violence ... and present a distorted image of our religion' (al-Saud and *SPA* 2017) . King Salman – in line with his son's earlier comments – opined that the 'Iranian regime spearheads global terrorism since the Khomeini revolution until today', disrupting '300 years' of tranquillity in Saudi Arabia. He also alluded that the kingdom 'did not witness terrorism or extremism until Khomeini's revolution emerged in 1979' (al-Saud and *SPA* 2017). The crucial aspect of his speech, however, was his bundling together of the 'Iranian regime and its affiliated groups ... and organizations such as Hezbollah and the Houthis' together with 'ISIS (Daesh) and Al-Qaeda and others' (al-Saud and *SPA* 2017). To the world, King Salman represented Iran as employing armed groups, including ones that harboured animosity towards and targeted the Shi'a, such as ISIS and Al-Qaeda, while pursuing its 'expansionist ambitions, criminal practices, and interference in the internal affairs of other countries'. The discourse represented Saudi Arabia as a victim of Iranian ambitions, with the former having 'suffered from and been a target of terrorism because it is the focus of Islam and Qibla of Muslims', while the latter was harbouring 'terrorist thought' that sought to 'achieve its fake legitimacy' by targeting Saudi Arabia, which is Islam's 'centre of gravity' (al-Saud and *SPA* 2017).

Ascending to the podium afterwards, Trump marked the occasion as a renewal of an 'enduring partnership' that began between 'King Abdulaziz, the founder ... working alongside American President Franklin Roosevelt'. Whereas the forefathers 'opened the first chapter', Trump and Salman 'would begin a new chapter that will bring lasting benefits to our citizens' (Trump 2017a). On terrorism and Iran, Trump echoed Salman's narratives and grouped Iran with ISIS and Al-Qaeda, while expressing solidarity with Saudi Arabia and the Islamic world. Constructing his discourse in terms of a 'battle between good and evil' (Trump 2017a), he told the world leaders that 'we must be united in pursuing one goal ... to conquer extremism and vanquish the forces of terrorism' (Trump 2017a). Encouraging his audience that a 'better future' would only be possible if 'nations drive out the terrorists and extremists' (Trump 2017a), the latter included 'ISIS, Al-Qaeda, Hezbollah, Hamas', and their leader, according to Trump, was Iran. In targeting Tehran, Trump echoed the Saudi trope of Iranian expansionism and leadership of terrorism, arguing that 'from Lebanon to Iraq to Yemen, Iran funds, arms, and trains terrorists, militias, and other extremist groups that spread destruction and chaos across the region'. Moreover, Trump represented Iran in a sectarian light, arguing that the regime 'has fuelled the fires of sectarian conflict and terror', accusing Tehran of its 'most tragic and destabilizing interventions' in Syria (Trump 2017a). Through this speech, it was clear that Saudi Arabia in general and the monarch, and his son in particular, had an ally in their rivalry against Iran.

Iran Responds to Trump

The Iranian response to Salman and Trump's speeches was two-fold. First, there was a discourse directed at the international community manufactured by the foreign ministry, and second, there was a discourse aimed at the domestic populace and the Islamic world communicated via the press and Friday sermons. The domestic discourse can be summarized by Khamenei's sermon on the first day of Ramadan during a Quran reading session. As for the message directed at the international community, three main themes were employed: Iranian democracy, elections, regional influence, and calls for peace; Saudi subservience to the US and a Saudi–Israeli conspiracy against Islam; and Trump's extortion of Saudi Arabia and 9/11.

In a series of op-eds and tweets, an immediate response followed from Jawad Zarif, who criticized Trump directly with an implicit reference to the Saudis. Zarif criticized Trump's comment as he thanked 'King Salman ... for the creation of this great moment in history and ... massive investment in America', Zarif accused the president of 'milking KSA of $480 billion' (Zarif 2017e), while mocking Riyadh by comparing it to a 'cash cow'. The Iranian foreign minister in turn employed the trope of democracy in his construction of the Iranian Self and the Saudi Other. Zarif sarcastically referred to the kingdom as a 'bastion of democracy and moderation' (Zarif 2017e), while highlighting Iran as a democracy and its 'people, who – unlike many – do vote' (Zarif 2017e) and were just coming out 'fresh from real elections'. With the democracy trope, Zarif's narrative gave rise to a dichotomy and constructed two images of the Saudi Other. The first featured an emphasis on Saudi monarchical and autocratic rule, while the second, as mentioned, undermined the Saudi Other as the US's 'cash cow', while emphasizing Iran's democratic self-image and it not being subservient to foreign interests.

The Iranian discourse also responded to Trump's speech on his first foreign tour as president, especially in relation to framing Iran as spearheading terrorism, Iranian hegemony, and expansionism, and Tehran as a destabilizing force. Zarif's op-ed in the New Arab defined Iran's role in the region by representing its image as a responsible actor and a force for peace, holding the door ajar and being 'ready to gift peace' to the region, especially to Riyadh (Zarif 2017b). To the Arab world, the Saudi summit was framed in a negative light, after a suggestion of an attempted destabilization of the region. Drawing on the cases of Afghanistan, Yemen, Bahrain, and Syria, Zarif reminded the international audience that 'foreign interventions ... without [an] end in sight' had caused unrest in these countries. In a veiled reference to Saudi Arabia and the GCC, Zarif mentioned 'governments in our region [that] sought to destabilize it, by escalating policies and measures', leading to the promotion of 'extremism and a distorted version of Islam' (Zarif 2017b). Furthermore, the foreign minister employed the theme of sedition and collusion with Israel – an implicit reference to Wahhabism – arguing that it was these regional governments and their policies that allowed for 'deepening bloodletting and infighting among brethren'. One such policy, as Zarif remarked, was 'Iranophobia' that was 'created and promoted by Israel' (Zarif 2017b). Consequently, the gathering in Saudi Arabia was characterized as a conspiracy to continue regional sedition and Wahhabi extremism through a GCC–Israeli collaboration with Iranophobia as its centrepiece. This discourse on collusion with Israel to destabilize the region has been a hallmark of Iranian portrayals of the Saudi Other since 1979, and a trope that was utilized when both states were party to regional turbulence and conflicts, including during the Iran–Iraq war, the Hezbollah–Israel war of 2006, and the Gaza war of 2009. More recently, the wars in Syria had been characterized by Iran as a 'Zionist conspiracy' that ran alongside Saudi Arabia's collaboration and Wahhabism.

In an op-ed in *The New York Times*, Zarif reprimanded the US and Saudi Arabia for the latter's US investments and arms deal, and he presented the arrangement as blackmail, extortion, and blood-money. Zarif rebuked the US state department's elaboration of the deal and argued that 'another $110 billion worth of weapons' will not reduce 'the burden [of the] American military on the long-term security of Saudi Arabia' (Zarif 2017a). By comparing the arms deal with Saudi funding for Saddam Hussein in the Iran–Iraq War of the 1980s, Zarif projected an image of how Washington and Riyadh were gearing up for aggression against Tehran. Framing the Saudi–Trump relationship as one based on extortion, Zarif argued that Trump was 'extorting our Saudi neighbours [and] milking them for money they do not have' (Zarif 2017a), while remarking that the Saudis may have hired the Trump administration to work for the Al Saud. Zarif argued that Trump 'at worst ... could be turning the United States into Saudi Arabia's mercenary in the Middle East' (Zarif 2017a). Correlating the image of the mercenary with the events of 9/11, Zarif described Trump as a hired mercenary for the 'same kingdom that fifteen of the hijackers came from'. The Iranian president Rouhani made a similar argument in his first press conference after his re-election, arguing that Trump was 'willing to trade the blood they gave in 9/11 with billions of dollars in arms sales, [therefore] surrendering to terrorists in the region' (Rouhani 2017b), which was a veiled reference to Saudi Arabia and Al Saud. The Saudi image that the Iranian officials sought to project was that its enemy was weak, the Al Saud were the region's terrorists, Trump was now a hired mercenary, and the Trump and MBS relationship was a terrorist, mercenary one with Iran as their main target. Just as Trump and Saudi Arabia had constructed an image of a 'terrorist, destabilizing, war-mongering Iran', Tehran, through its foreign minister, shaped a counter-image criticizing both the Trump administration and Trump's new-found collaborator, bin Salman. The tropes of the 'cash cow', for example, and the 'hiring of the mercenary' fall under the supra-discourse of Saudi subservience to the US and the latter's exploitation of the Saudi people's wealth. Furthermore, these tropes also sought to denigrate the US, downsizing it from a 'superpower' to a 'gun-for-hire'. This op-ed by Zarif in a prominent US news outlet underlined that the Iranian discourse was aimed at an international audience in general and the US domestic populace in particular. While Zarif was targeting Western and international audiences, Khamenei's discourse was aimed at the domestic audience and the Islamic world.

Khamenei Responds to Trump and Saudi Arabia

The Iranian construction of its Saudi Other, especially in relation to the Trump–Arab summit, was evident in the Supreme Leader's sermon marking the first day of Ramadan on 27 May 2017. Using the Quran as the subject and topic of his sermon, Khamenei had three aims: first, the sermon defined Saudi Arabia as Iran's Other, showing how the reference to Riyadh had evolved over time, exhibiting a directness and increased intensity; second, it offered a certain view of the Islamic world and its leadership; and third, it defined the Iranian Self. This was accomplished by a focus on four main themes: Islamic leadership and the decadence of the Islamic world; Saudi subservience to the West and 'infidels'; the fall and collapse of Saudi Arabia; and the definition of the Iranian Self and Iran as the true representative of Islam. In his speech to Quran reciters on the first day of

Ramadan, Khamenei defined the world of Islam as in turmoil, which he blamed on corrupt leaders. In a reference to Arab leaders in general and Saudi Arabia in particular, Khamenei drew a comparison between 'the demise and fate of Islamic societies' and a 'number of worthless, unworthy, and lowly people' in reference to the leaders who had 'hijacked the world of Islam' (Khamenei 2017b). By employing the trope of hypocrisy – a prominent characterization used since the advent of the Islamic Revolution in 1979 – Khamenei criticized the kingdom's leadership and the monarchy's Islamic identity. The jurist branded Saudi Arabia's leadership as 'distant from the Quran', 'lacking faith', and referring to the yearly 'printing and distribution of millions of copies of the Quran' in Saudi Arabia as a 'show' marked by a lack of real 'belief in the content of the Qur'an' and adherence to its principles (Khamenei 2017b). Khamenei's argument was an attempt to create a counter-image to the Saudi narrative criticizing the Iranian leadership. Just as MBS had previously described the Iranian leadership as radical and apocalyptic with references to occultation and Mahdism, Khamenei defined the Saudi monarchy as hypocritical and as false leaders of the world of Islam, thereby undermining the legitimacy of Islamic authority.

After his representation of Saudi Arabia as lacking Islamic values, Khamenei employed the recurring trope of Saudi subservience to the West. Arguing that the Saudi leadership was cosying up to and 'acting cordially with the infidels' (a reference to the Western powers in general and the US in particular), Khamenei accused the Saudi leadership of 'spending the wealth of their nation' to satisfy the US and Trump (Khamenei 2017b). The image of the monarchy was constructed as corrupt, looting Muslims' wealth, which had 'accumulated in their bank accounts'. It had derived from 'oil, the money of underground mines, [and] the money of national treasures', which was spent on 'infidels' and 'enemies of the people' rather than 'on improving people's lives' (Khamenei 2017b). The trope of Western subservience intertwined with the looting of the Muslims' wealth recalls the discourse of debauchery and mismanagement of the bayt-al-māl, a recurrent trope in the early post-revolutionary era.

To the Iranian people and the Islamic world, Khamenei argued that the fall and collapse of Saudi Arabia was near. In referring to the treatment of the Shi'i populations in Bahrain and Yemen, Khamenei argued that the Saudis treated the 'enemies of Islam cordially' and behaved in an 'anti-religious manner towards the Muslim people of Bahrain and Yemen' (Khamenei 2017b). This cordial behaviour towards the 'enemies of Islam', i.e. the US and the West, was represented in an image of ignorance and the naïveté of the Al Saud as 'fools giving money' and acting like 'lactating cows', that Trump will 'milk … and slaughter when they [Saudi Arabia] no longer have milk' to offer (Khamenei 2017b). This relationship between Saudi Arabia and the US would cause the rise of Muslim nations and the Saudi kingdom would 'perish, be torn down and destroyed' (Khamenei 2017b). As for when this would happen, Khamenei argued that 'it will happen sooner or … later', but Saudi Arabia's fall was imminent (Khamenei 2017b). To the domestic audience and the Islamic world, Khamenei utilized the tropes of sectarianism and Western subservience, alongside using denigrating and demonizing images such as the 'cash cow' to criticize Saudi Arabia's regional and Islamic legitimacy and leadership. While using these images and tropes to construct the Saudi Other, the Iranian Self was naturally presented as the true leader and representative of the world of Islam.

As Khamenei reprimanded Arab leaders in general and Saudi Arabia in particular as weak and exploited by the Western powers and by Trump specifically, the Iranian Self was portrayed as the true representation of an Islamic state and nation. By employing Islamic and Quranic narratives such as the story of Abraham and his belief in God and his request to God to prove to him 'the resurrection of the dead' (Khamenei 2017b), Khamenei interpreted the Islamic Republic and its inception in 1979 as living proof of that solemn and pure belief in God, reminding Iranians of how 'a nation won the imposed war empty-handed' (Khamenei 2017b) in a reference to the Iran–Iraq War of the 1980s, a trope that had its origins in the discourse of early post-revolutionary Iran. In Khamenei's view, it was due to true Islamic belief and his being able to 'communicate with the Qur'an' that Iran has been on the 'path to strong, powerful, dignified, and successful progress' (Khamenei 2017b). The overt message communicated to Iranians was that contemporary Iran was powerful by the grace of God, the Quran, and by following 'pure Mohammedan Islam' (*'Islam-i Nab-i Mohammadi'*), while there was also a covert message suggesting that a young, revolutionary Iran had survived Saddam's assault, while the newly founded coalition of fifty-five states was no match for a more experienced and stronger Islamic Republic. However, in later weeks the region would witness Trump's continued support for Saudi Arabia and his bellicose narrative towards Iran, which gave bin Salman the impetus to push forward with his regional ambitions.

Severing Tehran's Regional Relations: the Qatar Blockade

Two weeks after the summit in Riyadh, three Arab Gulf states – including the UAE and Bahrain, and spearheaded by Saudi Arabia and Egypt – called for the severing of ties with their GCC neighbour Qatar, citing allegations of the latter's financing of terrorist groups, chiefly the Muslim Brotherhood. The four Arab states took the unprecedented step of imposing a blockade on Qatar on 5 June, which included closing all borders with the state, restricting its airspace, maritime lanes, and blocking Qatari citizens from travelling to the countries that had imposed the blockade. There were thirteen conditions set for ending the blockade, which included the shutting down of the Al-Jazeera media outlets, ending support to the Muslim Brotherhood, and, most importantly, curbing 'diplomatic ties with Iran and clos[ing] its diplomatic missions' (Ulrichsen 2020: 257; Zweiri, Rahman, and Kamal 2020: 279). The move was intended to sever any relations that Qatar had with Iran and to bring Doha into the Saudi fold. This was easier said than done since Qatar and Iran share a vast maritime border that includes one of the world's largest gas fields, the North Dome/South Pars gas field, a third of which lies in Iran's territory. Furthermore, the output provided Doha with an income that was equivalent of three-fifths of its GDP (Zweiri and Qawasmi 2021: 96; Hiro 2019:

323). Given this, it would prove very difficult for Qatar to end relations with Tehran, never mind enter a state of enmity with the Islamic Republic.

To understand the Saudi motivation behind the Qatar blockade, it is imperative to understand the events following Trump's support in Saudi Arabia that led to bin Salman's adventurous campaign. In a speech on 23 May during a graduation ceremony at the military academy in Doha, the Qatar emir, Tamim bin Hamad, allegedly made remarks that elucidated his position on Israel, Iran, and the Trump administration. The emir described his relationship with Trump as 'tense' after a meeting together. The media also quoted Tamim as saying 'Trump would not last long in office' (Al-Bawaba 2017). As concerns Israel, the report alleged that Tamim had hoped that Qatar would play a role in brokering a peace deal between the Palestinians and Israel, describing Doha's relationship in a positive light. On Iran, the young leader framed Tehran in terms of neighbourly relations, arguing 'there is no wisdom in harbouring hostility towards Iran'. On the issue of Hezbollah and the Muslim Brotherhood, the media – quoting the Qatar's emir via the Qatar News Agency (QNA) – highlighted Doha's positive relationship with both groups. As a result, the positive framing of Iran, Hezbollah, and the Muslim Brotherhood by Qatar triggered aggressive positions from Riyadh and its allies. These began with the blocking of all Qatari-affiliated media outlets, which had long been seen as a threat to Saudi Arabia and its associates, especially during the events of the Arab Spring. The Qatar blockade was used by both Iran and Saudi Arabia to highlight their selves and others to both regional and domestic audiences, thereby playing a part in exacerbating their rivalry as Iran aided Qatar in dampening the physical and political effects of the blockade, while undermining Saudi regional-power projections and leadership of the GCC in the process. This blockade increased Iran's stake and involvement in GCC affairs and in projecting its discourse on the Persian Gulf, as we will see later in this chapter.

The Qatari officials immediately defended their positions and claimed that the QNA website had been hacked. They argued that these remarks could never have been made because while the emir had indeed attended the graduation ceremony, he had not delivered a speech (Al-Rawi 2021). However, Saudi Arabia and its allies were not convinced. Their media ran the story as it was and used the Qatari arguments to their favour. Saudi newspapers such as *al-Riyadh* framed the Qatar blockade with Iran in mind. The 'so-called hacking of the Qatar News Agency website … was nothing but indications of premeditated intentions' by Doha to cover up the exposing of an alliance with an 'Iranian regime … that expresses greed and hatred against our Arab region' (*Al-Riyadh* 2017d). The alleged Qatari quotes made by the emir were represented as reflecting the collusion between Doha and Tehran against the Arab world. To the Saudi audience, their neighbour Qatar was seen as having 'chosen to replace the Gulf countries as its ally' with an 'artificial guardian', namely Iran (*Al-Riyadh* 2017d) . This 'rapprochement', the Saudi editorials argued, was to 'be exploited to serve Iran's interests', which included 'global terrorism' (*Al-Riyadh* 2017d) . To give the narrative of a sinister Qatari–Iranian collaboration legitimacy, the Saudi press used quotes by the monarch. The editorial sought to remind its readers that Saudi Arabia was 'the Custodian of the

Two Holy Mosques', while the king remarked at the Arab–Islamic summit that 'the Iranian regime has been the spearhead of global terrorism', arguing that 'this country had not known terrorism or extremism for 300 years until the revolution that Khomeini headed in 1979' (*Al-Riyadh* 2017d) . To the Saudi audience, the message was that, like Iran, Qatar also promoted and supported terrorism and extremism, and hence they were in an alliance. This construction of an Iranian–Qatari Other was also used to justify the Saudi-led blockade to the domestic populace as well as the people of the GCC, given that it would seem unusual that one of the Gulf countries would block another, especially in light of their shared history, culture, and tribal kin.

Iran's immediate response was to call for negotiations and talks, as Zarif argued in his tweet that 'Neighbours are permanent; geography can't be changed. Coercion is never the solution. Dialogue is imperative, especially during blessed Ramadan' (Zarif 2017c). This framing by the Iranian foreign minister conveyed three images of the Saudis and their Arab allies: first, a representation of Saudi Arabia as a bully; second, Riyadh as resorting to force rather than talks, making it a regional aggressor; and third, an image of hypocrisy. By mentioning Ramadan in his tweet, Zarif generated an image of non-Islamic acts since Ramadan is known as the 'month of mercy' in Islam. This framing resonated in the statements of the foreign-ministry spokesman, Baharam Ghasemi. The Iranian diplomat expressed concern over the Qatar blockade, and asked for the 'exercise of maximum restraint and [the] avoid[ance of] tension', stating that neighbours 'in the south of the Persian Gulf' needed to settle the 'current dispute … through political and peaceful methods, reminding 'Qatar's three neighbouring governments [that] instrumental use of sanctions in the current interconnected world, while inefficient, is reprehensible, rejected and unacceptable' (Ghasemi 2017b). While Tehran argued for 'frank and transparent talks' (Ghasemi 2017b) between the disputing states, the talks were implicitly tilted in Doha's favour, especially as Iran understood the meaning and weight of sanctions. The Iranian right-wing press laid out the 'real reasons' behind the Qatar blockade by Saudi Arabia and its allies.

The conservative Iranian media outlets represented the Qatar blockade through the lens of the Iranian Self. This was achieved through tropes of regional rivalry, sedition among the GCC states, and the downfall of Saudi Arabia and the rise of Iran. The newspaper *Resalat* characterized it as a 'fire in the reactionary tent' (*Resalat* 2017) and represented the blockade of Qatar as a collapse in the GCC regional order, constructing an image of a Saudi Arabia with hegemonic ambitions that was seeking to control the region through 'Iranophobia' (*Resalat* 2017). The blockade was also framed by Iranian editorials as retribution for Qatar's recognition of 'Iran as an Islamic and regional power' and the Qatari emir's recognition of Iran's military superiority when he called for Riyadh to be restrained in their dealings with Iran, remarking that it was 'not wise to stand against' the Islamic Republic (*Kayhan* 2017b). Qatar's recognition of Iran being a regional power was argued in the Iranian press discourse as being one of the reasons behind the Saudi aggression against Qatar, since Riyadh was viewed as 'losing absolute control over' the GCC states with Qatar becoming more independent in its foreign policy. The

Iranian press interpreted this trope of independence as reflecting a Qatari migration towards the Iranian camp (*Kayhan* 2017b).

The Saudi-led blockade of Qatar was also interpreted from the perspective of Trump's visit to Saudi Arabia and the call to create an Arab–Islamic NATO with Saudi Arabia at the helm, thus projecting an image of Saudi regional hegemony and expansion. The newspaper *Kayhan* argued that this was due to Doha's dissatisfaction with Salman and MBS and their attempt to legitimize their control over the Arab world by 'announcing an end to the era of passive Arab politics' that had led to the creation of the 'coalition of Islamic countries' (*Kayhan* 2017b) . The Iranian editorial discourse also argued that the Trump visit was a ploy by Riyadh to 'reinforce Saudi regional control through Trump's support [by] issuing hot and greasy contracts . . . worth up to $400 billion. However, as Riyadh had thought that it had fulfilled its objectives, 'two days after the summit, voices of dissent were heard' (*Kayhan* 2017b). It was the Qatari opposition to 'the absurdity of bin Salman's views of Saudi power' that, the editorial discourse argued, led to Riyadh's aggression towards Qatar. This image of Saudi hegemony was compounded by allegations in the Iranian press of Saudi plans to 'attempt a coup d'état [or a] military occupation' of Qatar. In the case of a coup attempt, it was argued that Saudi Arabia had no supporters in Qatar while an invasion would lead to the loss of Saudi Arabia's Arab and Islamic leadership since it would be difficult for Riyadh to convince the Arab and Islamic world of a second war with an Arab and Islamic country given its ongoing war in Yemen (*Kayhan* 2017b). These tropes and discourses by the Iranian press highlighted and criticized the leadership and legitimacy of Saudi Arabia as Iran's Other. This legitimacy was portrayed as diminishing since Riyadh had moved to blockading Qatar, restricting its trade, and impeding on Doha's sovereignty. The Saudi Other's legitimacy was also typified by their redeploying the arms deal with Trump so as to project an image of Riyadh's regional hegemony. This regional domination was depicted to the Iranian audience as reflecting Saudi Arabia's plans to invade or instigate regime change in Qatar. In addition, the editorials constructed an image of Saudi treachery towards its Gulf neighbour, including its tribal and Islamic brethren.

Saudi-led actions against Qatar were also framed by Iranian media as an attempt to project Saudi regional losses amid Iranian gains. One such loss was that the newly formed 'Saudi–US alliance' was about to lose a member, highlighting that 'Qatar may be a future Iranian ally' (*Kayhan* 2017b). It is this dynamic as well as the losses in Iraq and Syria, *Kayhan* argued, that had frustrated Riyadh. Drawing on discourses of Islamic terrorism and the war on terror, Saudi Arabia was represented as losing the war since 'ISIS and al-Nusrah and dozens of other terrorist groups that have emerged with the money of Saudi Arabia . . . are disappearing' and are now being replaced by 'all kinds of Revolutionary Guards' (*Kayhan* 2017b). The mention of newly formed Revolutionary Guards was a reference to Ansarullah in Yemen and the Popular Mobilization Units (*Hashd al-Sha 'bi*) in Iraq, both supported by Tehran. The loss of Qatar to Iran was thereby argued in the Iranian media as being a 'matter of great concern to the Saudis' because Riyadh was in a 'battle to try and hold on to their former comrade', Qatar, and was attempting to 'sustain their strongholds against the Islamic Revolution' at a time when Saudi Arabia's 'walls have been severely weakened' (*Kayhan* 2017b). By employing the tropes of Islamic terrorism, the war on terror, and Iran's backing of groups in Iraq and Yemen, Iranian media discourse constructed a Saudi Other as a sponsor of terrorism and a waning regional power, while projecting an image of Saudi weakness and desperation. In these tropes, the Iranian Self was innately represented as a regional leader, with its allies victorious in Yemen and Iraq, and it being the winner of the Syrian war. The Iranian Self, therefore, was portrayed as a regional power increasing its sphere of influence. Nevertheless, Tehran's walls would be breached as ISIS hit too close to home in Tehran.

'Firecrackers' or Terrorist Attacks? ISIS Attacks Tehran

On 7 June, Tehran came under surprising and synchronized terrorist attacks from ISIS. Six ISIS terrorists had infiltrated Iran dressed as women and attacked the Iranian Majles and the mausoleum of Imam Khomeini. The attacks resulted in over fifty injured and twenty-three deaths, including the five ISIS terrorists; it can be argued that this mission was symbolically aimed at the heart of the Islamic Republic because attacking the mausoleum targeted the founder of the revolutionary state, while the parliamentary building was a symbol of the century-old Iranian struggle for public representation and accountability of the executive branches of governance. Iran has had experience with terrorism, namely with the *Haft-e Tir* (7th Tir) attacks against the Islamic Republican Party headquarters and the assassination attempt on Khamenei by MEK/MKO in 1981. More contemporary attacks have included terrorist episodes between 2003 and 2012 by Jundallah, a terrorist militant group based in the Sistan Balochistan region of Iran.

Iran had boasted as late as 2016 of foiling ISIS attacks on its soil, while airing confessions of ISIS members admitting to preparing for terrorist attacks in Tehran and other major Iranian cities (*Press TV* 2016). However, the terrorist attacks in Tehran tarnished the image of stability that the Iranian state and its discourse had promulgated for years. Scholars have gone as far as arguing that by attacking the two symbolic targets, the terrorists 'exposed glaring vulnerabilities in Iran's internal security' (Maloney 2017). This is also compounded by the fact that while the terrorists were from the Sunni sect, they were all Iranian citizens recruited by ISIS. The attacks shook Iran and more implicitly Iran's image of strength, stability, and domestic security both regionally and internationally. This led the Iranian discourse manufacturers to weave in tropes and themes to manage the crisis and the resultant image distortion of the Iranian Self. These tropes included downplaying the weight of the attacks and ascribing the blame to an external actor, while emphasizing Iranian patriotism and unity.

The initial reaction came from Ayatollah Khamenei at a meeting of university students during the month of Ramadan. The attacks were framed as part of Iran's resistance and war against oppression and corruption. The students discussed scientific and academic topics as well as political, cultural, and economic issues, and Khamenei's statements drew on Iran's 'revolutionary path' and the Islamic

Republic's 'development and struggle in different fields', and how 'dominant countries have made increasing progress at an ever-increasing rate', while seeking to hinder Iran and slow its development (Khamenei 2017a). Khamenei downplayed the incidents by referring to them as 'actions' and 'firecrackers' rather than as terrorist attacks; however, the Supreme Leader implicitly attributed the attacks to a conspiracy by 'dominant powers' that 'will have no effect on the will of the Iranian people [as the] Iranian nation is advancing and moving forward' (Khamenei 2017a). The terrorist attacks were framed as an attack on Iran's prestige of 'independence' and cultural and scientific progress on the world stage. Khamenei argued that the attacks were 'too small to influence the will of the Iranian people and the country's officials' (Khamenei 2017a).

Khamenei also defended Iran's security and stability by making a veiled reference to their presence in Syria and Iraq and their war on terror. The Ayatollah maintained that matters would have been much worse had Iran not 'stood at the centre of these seditions' in reference to Syria and Iraq, and it would 'have faced a lot more of these troubles' otherwise, in a reference to the ISIS attacks (Khamenei 2017a). Similarly, the Majles speaker, Ali Larijani, echoed the Supreme Leader's discourse on the ISIS attacks. First, he characterized the incident as a 'minor issue'. At the opening of the parliamentary session after the terrorist attack that occurred in the Islamic Consultative Assembly, the speaker remarked that 'terrorists seek to create problems [and] harm Iran', because the country was 'an active and effective hub in the fight against terrorism', while highlighting the Iranian security forces' role in 'dealing with the terrorists seriously' (Larijani 2017). Nevertheless, the image of Iran's security prowess, stability, and experience at fighting terrorism had been tainted. One way of remedying this image was by laying the blame on adversaries, including the US, Israel and, most notably of all, Saudi Arabia, principally because Khamenei had previously stated that the ideology of ISIS was rooted in Wahhabism and preached by the Saudi ulama and supported by its monarchy (Khamenei 2017d).

The decision to blame Riyadh for the attacks was part of a two-tiered discourse, both explicit and implicit. The indirect blame was apportioned by Zarif, who argued that 'terror-sponsoring despots threaten to bring the fight to our homeland. Proxies attack what their masters despise most: the seat of democracy' (Zarif 2017d). This suggestion of the Saudi sponsorship of terror seemed to arise from bin Salman's comments in his May interview in Al-Arabiya, when he stressed that any conflict between the two states would take place 'inside Iran, not in Saudi Arabia' (al-Saud and *Al-Arabiya* 2017). On the other hand, explicit accusations of Riyadh's hand in the attacks came from the IRGC and Khamenei's advisers. In his statement, the IRGC commander-in-chief, Major General Jafari, stated that Tehran had 'accurate information that . . . in addition to supporting the terrorists, Saudi Arabia has demanded that they carry out operations in Iran'. Furthermore, the IRGC chief argued that the 'US and the Zionist regime have supported' Riyadh and ISIS in conducting these operations in Iran (Jafari 2017). On a similar note, another IRGC general, Hossein Nejat, went further and linked the attacks to Trump's visit to Riyadh. He added that it was proof that Trump and the Al Saud 'regime ordered their proxies to embark on that act' (*Financial Times* 2017). The military discourse on the ISIS attacks on Tehran represented the attacks as a conspiracy and collaboration between the US, Israel, and Saudi Arabia. Furthermore, this discourse was an attempt to project the Saudi Other as a perpetrator of terrorism and subservient to US–Israeli orders against the Islamic Republic. Also, it is interesting how the Iranian discourse constructors drew on MBS's statements, notably his interview that explicitly mentioned taking the war to Iran. Therefore, MBS's narrative highlighted Saudi Arabia's innate enmity towards Iran while the Iranian Self was a victim of regional animosity, a counter-image to the one set out by Trump and King Salman at the Riyadh summit. The Iranian discourse of victimization was also intended to negate the association made by the Saudi foreign minister, al-Jubeir, at Davos, where he hinted that there might be a link or collaboration between Iran and ISIS.

The IRGC's accusatory tone was echoed by other Iranian officials, most notably by Ali Velayati, Rahbar's adviser for foreign affairs. In an interview with the Swedish Parliamentary Research Center, Velayati constructed the attacks as 'Saudi arson [that] Iran will certainly not tolerate' (Velayati 2017). The former diplomat linked the Saudi prince's statements regarding bringing the war to Iran, Trump's visit to Riyadh, and the recent Saudi-led blockade of Qatar as contrasting with Saudi immaturity, inexperience, and insecurity. Velayati characterized the Saudi monarchy as facing a problem of 'immaturity and [the] inexperience of people who act and sometimes speak … which indicates inexperience and indicates a lack of knowledge about Iran and the region' (Velayati 2017). Furthermore, the image of Saudi naïveté was compounded with notions of weakness, sedition, and diplomatic incompetence. First, there was an image of weakness in 'their security that they cannot maintain' (Velayati 2017). Second, the trope of sedition was used by observing that Riyadh was 'taking a lot of money from the Muslim treasury and carrying out medieval actions [by] claiming to make an alliance between Islamic countries by inviting Trump, [thus] creat[ing] a rift and … a dispute between them and Qatar, which is unprecedented in the history of the region' (Velayati 2017). This led to the trope of ineptitude as the regional rift showed 'the incompetence of Saudi diplomacy, which cannot live peacefully with its closest neighbours'(Velayati 2017). By accusing Riyadh and underlining a negative image of the Saudi Arabian Other, Tehran sought to alleviate the effects of the attacks on the image of the Iranian Self. Velayati's discourse on Saudi involvement in the ISIS attacks brought together a plethora of tropes, images, and constructions aimed at domestic, regional, and international audiences. These weaved together the different strands of Iranian discourse genres and amalgamated them into a single discourse aimed at international audiences. The aim of this amalgamation was to refute and counter the images and the tropes set out by Trump and Saudi Arabia since the ascension of King Salman to the throne. Iran had been accused of sponsoring terror, causing regional turmoil, and promoting radical Shi'ism in the Islamic world. By bringing in tropes based on the Qatar blockade and regional rifts, in an implicit reference to Syria and Yemen, as well as Wahhabism's sectarianism, Velayati constructed the Saudi Other as an immature leadership that had resulted in sedition and regional destabilization. However, it would take Tehran more than words to repair its self-image both domestically and internationally.

'Slapping the Enemy': Repairing the Image of the Iranian Self

On 18 June, Iran fired six medium-range surface-to-surface Zolfaghar ballistic missiles from the Kermanshah and Kurdistan provinces in the west of Iran towards ISIS targets, namely a command centre and a suicide-bomb manufacturing facility in Deir-e-Zor, Syria. In a bid to repair the state's image, the Iranian discourse framed the attacks as 'a move to punish the terrorists for the twin attacks on the Iranian parliament and the holy shrine of the late founder of the Islamic Republic, Imam Khomeini, on 7 June' as described in the IRGC statement (IRGC 2017b). The statement also boasted that the missiles 'struck the terrorists with lethal and crushing blows' resulting in 'large numbers of terrorists killed and their equipment, system and weapons destroyed'. The Iranian government had argued that since they sent their advisers to Syria and later Iraq, their mission was to fight terrorism and protect Iran's borders with Syria and Iraq. However, the attacks on 7 June put that narrative in question. It would principally be Khamenei's discourse that sought to reinforce that argument and repair Iran's self-image. By drawing on Shi'i tropes and the Ahl-al-Bayt narrative, the Supreme Leader reminded the domestic populace that had it not been for the 'martyrs defending the holy shrine, we would have to fight the evil seditionists, enemies of Ahl-al-Bayt and the Shi'a people in the cities of Iran' (Khamenei 2017d). The message to Iranians was that matters could have been a lot worse than the attacks that had taken place, had it not been for the Iranian presence in Syria and Iraq along with the 'blood of the martyrs' that had been sacrificed; otherwise, 'the enemy would have brought the battle to our streets by now' (Khamenei 2017d).

The Supreme Leader's discourse on the war on terror also wove in the discourse and themes of a conspiracy against the Islamic Republic. In a bid to alleviate domestic pressure and repair its image, Khamenei portrayed the ISIS attacks as an extension of US enmity towards Iran. Images of Iranian resistance and prestige, the enemy's ignorance, naïveté, and crime, were drawn on. Trump and his administration were represented as 'amateur shivers' *('Chāqū Kishāy-i Tāza Kār')* that had 'just entered the world of crime [and who] stab themselves wherever they go and do not know what they are doing', however 'they do not know the Islamic Republic, the Iranian nation, nor its officials' (Khamenei 2017d). The ISIS attacks were woven into a larger discourse of Iranian resistance and conspiracy against the Islamic Republic. The attack on ISIS targets were allegorically symbolized as a 'slap' (*sīlī*): 'They wanted to slap the Iranian nation ... They wanted to overthrow the regime ... they were buried one by one in longing for this wish' (Khamenei 2017d). Khamenei argued that 'it will be the same after this', i.e. the ISIS attacks; he said, 'Let everyone know – the enemy knows ... that the Islamic Republic stands strong ... they cannot slap us, we will slap them' (Khamenei 2017d). As such, Khamenei was attempting to reinforce and repair the image of a strong Iran that had resisted 'four decades of conspiracies' and, while ascribing these attacks to the US and its regional allies, Khamenei framed the response as one that would hit not only ISIS targets, but its alleged supporters, including the Trump administration, Israel, and Saudi Arabia. This 'slap' would come in the form of the Iranian missile attacks on ISIS targets in Syria.

The IRGC promulgated the trope of the 'slap' and also projected an image of Iranian military power and prestige. The IRGC spokesman, Ramadan Sharif, commented that 'it took eleven days to determine the exact location' of ISIS in Syria. The attacks were framed as an implicit message to Saudi Arabia and its allies wherein the 'terrorists and their regional and international supporters' and any group 'thinking of threatening the national security of Iran' should 'look back at the message'. The attacks were also constructed as a warning to regional states, arguing that 'whether this action will be repeated or not depends on the behaviour of our enemies in different areas' (IRGC 2017a). The Iranian reaction, according to General Rahim-Safavi, the Supreme Leader's adviser for military affairs, 'sends a clear message to American enemies and some countries in the region', principally Saudi Arabia, 'who think that if they think they attack Iran, their aggression will go unanswered' (Rahim-Safavi 2017). Therefore, the missile attacks on ISIS targets were framed as a message and response to the 'terrorists and their masters' (Rouhani 2017a), as Rouhani stated in reference to the US, Israel, and Saudi Arabia. This was compounded by bolstering Iran's image of power and military strength, including its ability to determine targets in a short period of time and launch long-distance attacks over foreign airspace, while reaching those targets accurately.

On a similar note, Iranian editorials framed the IRGC missile attacks on ISIS as a response to Saudi–US enmity. Besides the emphasis on the image of the Iranian Self as a strong regional power, Saudi Arabia as its Other was portrayed as inept, naïve, weak, and dependent on US protection. The newspaper *Kayhan* framed the ISIS attacks on Tehran as part of a conspiracy that began with Trump's invitation to Riyadh. The Saudi capital was argued to have 'invited the US president in order to boost its security and military power [with] fat promises', i.e. military contracts and investments, in exchange for 'full US protection at the slightest infringement of Saudi security' *(Kayhan* 2017a). The editorial contended that 'in a clumsy move [Riyadh had] introduced Iran as its first enemy [and] made every effort to enhance an anti-Iranian front', which included members from 'the Arab region, the Islamic world, and the Western world' *(Kayhan* 2017a). The editorial argued that the Saudi idea of an anti-Iran coalition had failed since the US 'cannot impose its will and foreign policy on two war-torn Arab countries', namely Syria and Iraq *(Kayhan* 2017a). As such, 'it cannot guarantee the security and regional influence of Saudi Arabia'. Here the editorial was underlining the image of Iran's regional power by implicitly arguing that it was due to the Iranian presence in Iraq and Syria that the US could not impose its will on those governments, and therefore the US could not help Riyadh in any confrontation with Tehran *(Kayhan* 2017a).

The image of Iranian power was also enhanced by emphasizing the Iranian missile capability, describing it as not only being able to strike ISIS targets hundreds of miles away, but as also being marked by 'the passage of Iranian short-range missiles through the territory of the two Arab countries behind the Saudi and

Zionist regimes', namely Iraq and Syria *(Kayhan* 2017a*).* The editorial discourse projected an image of the weakness of Iran's adversaries as the IRGC exposed and 'proved the serious vulnerability' of Tel-Aviv and Riyadh. It also argued that this explained the 'strategic importance of firing Iranian missiles at Deir-e-Zor' *(Kayhan* 2017a*).* Another goal of the IRGC-led mission was to make the 'Saudi regime inevitably rethink its affairs' regarding Iran, as the IRGC response had 'severed the relationship between the dollar and security', i.e. Riyadh and Trump's security agreement, along with putting an end to the 'Saudi regime's ... anti-Iranian front', that is the Islamic–Arab coalition *(Kayhan* 2017a*).* The Zolfaghar missiles were argued to have 'broken the barriers and imaginary boundaries', thus showing 'Iran's revolutionary position' *(Kayhan* 2017a*).* In other words, by engaging in the discourse of resistance and the ongoing revolution, the editorial narratives highlighted the prestige and power of the Iranian Self. The discourse of resistance also emphasized the relationship between the ISIS attacks and the Trump–Saudi relationship, that is to say, the Saudi Other subservient to the US had failed to counter Iran, even when it had acquired weapons and security and established an anti-Iranian coalition. The Iranian Self was, therefore, represented as a powerful force unmatched by Saudi Arabia and its allies, and unperturbed by the ISIS attacks. The missile strikes were framed as 'proving Iran's capability, authority, credibility and chronology, and the Islamic Republic's ability to simultaneously avert the threat of Western occupiers and Takfiri terrorists' *(Kayhan* 2017a*).*

This image of Iranian power was also projected by the ulama. The conservative cleric, Ayatollah Ahmad Khatami, used tropes of Islam, leadership, and Western subservience to claim that the 'move sends a message to reactionaries in the region', and that in trusting the United States they have placed trust in a 'spider's web' and spiders have 'the weakest homes' (Khatami 2017). In other words, the Arab states and Saudi Arabia in particular were weak, and Iran was strong because it 'has trusted in Almighty God' (Khatami 2017). This image of Islamic divinity and protection was employed to brand the Iranian Self as possessing a leadership status; it was a state that had achieved 'its lofty divine goals, which is the exaltation of the word of Islam' at the hands of the IRGC who were the 'powerful arms of the Muslim Ummah' (Khatami 2017). Consequently, by labelling the IRGC as the protectors of the Islamic Ummah, the implicit image of the Saudi-led coalition was marked by weakness because it was allied with the United States, which may have looked strong, but was actually feeble. It was this image of the 'spider's web' versus the strength of its military that Iran was attempting to employ to repair the image of the Iranian Self. This happened as Saudi Arabia was getting ready for another reshuffle of its monarchy as Mohammad bin Salman inched closer to the throne.

Inching towards the Throne: Mohammad bin Salman Rises Once More

While grappling with a war in Yemen and ambitions of economic transformation through Vision 2030, King Salman appointed his son, Mohammad bin Salman, as the crown prince by decree while removing Prince bin Nayef from the line of succession, with the support of thirty-one out of the thirty-four members of the Allegiance Council (Ramady 2017: 64). The Saudi media quickly dispelled any rumours of discord, while announcing bin Nayef's 'pledged allegiance to Prince Mohammed bin Salman bin Abdulaziz on the occasion of his selection as the crown prince'*(Al-Arabiya* 2017). Media outlets including newspapers covered their front pages with images of the ceremony *(al-Riyadh* 2017: *Asharq Al-Awsat* 2017; *al-Jazira* 2017). In the ceremony, the first person to pledge allegiance was the Grand Mufti Sheikh Abdulaziz al-Sheikh, who, while holding the Quran, stated that everyone 'must stand hand in hand ... behind our leadership', as he recited the allegiance script, 'By God's book [the Koran] and the laws of His Messenger, I pledge allegiance' *(Al-Arabiya* 2017). Saudi editorial discourses focused primarily on stability and utilized two main themes: the constancy of the Saudi monarchy and bin Salman's image as a leader. These themes were aimed at dispelling the discussion of a coup within the royal family as bin Nayef was removed from his position. Abdulrahman al-Rashed of *Asharq Al-Awsat* argued that 'the resilience of any political system is tested by its ability to organize its governance when positions of power change', implying that MBS's promotion and MBN's replacement took place with 'ease and cooperation' *(Asharq-Al-Awsat* and *Al-Rashed* 2017a). This was an attempt by the Saudi media discourse aimed at domestic and Arab audiences to discourage rumours of a coup and turbulence. The rumours were replaced by constructing an image of the prestige and maturity of the Al Saud's lineage as a responsible actor. By drawing parallels with other regional states, the *Asharq Al-Awsat* article emphasized how, contrary to 'events in the Middle East where change is a difficult occurrence', the Al Saud monarchy 'has been stable for 80 years and able to achieve transition under the leadership of a king who has total allegiance' from the nation *(Asharq-Al-Awsat* and *Al-Rashed* 2017a).

The Saudi editorials also focused on constructing MBS's image as a leader, arguably due to criticism given his lack of experience and seniority when contrasted with both his cousin bin Nayef and other relatives, especially the king's siblings. The Saudi editorials argued that a young leader was imperative for the kingdom's longevity and survival as it would appeal to the largely young demographic dynamic. *Asharq Al-Awsat* argued that since 'sixty per cent of the kingdom's population are under thirty years old, [they have] expectations that the government should feel the plight of the youth' and their needs should be 'reflected in the state's plans'*(Asharq-Al-Awsat* and Al-Rashed 2017a). Consequently, the press discourse argued that the only person who could fulfil these expectations was a 'king injecting youth in the state', i.e. MBS. A similar argument was proposed by *al-Riyadh*, in which it argued that the task belonged to a 'new generation of leadership within the monarchy' *(al-Riyadh* 2017g). To Arab and domestic audiences, the Saudi press discourse constructed four main images: the stability and maturity of the monarchy; the dynamism of the Saudi system reflected in its smooth transition from one generation to the next; the historical prestige of the kingdom; and, above all, the image of a young, crown prince as a 'saviour' leading Saudi Arabia into the future.

The discourse on MBS's leadership was bolstered by constructing an image of him based on his supposed invincibility and him being a prodigy. The newspaper *al-Riyadh* argued that MBS was the man for the job since he acted as a 'minister of defence, his appointment as crown prince was a crowning of his great accomplishments and continual successes' in the short 'period that he has spent serving the state [and] achieving great accomplishments and proved his ability despite the great obstacles he has faced' *(al-Riyadh* 2017g*)*. These accomplishments included 'drawing the roadmap to Vision 2030 ... leading the Islamic coalition fighting terrorism', and the establishment of a 'centre to eradicate extremist thought [to ensure the] political and security stability of the region and the world' *(al-Riyadh* 2017g*)*. This argument gave rise to the construction of MBS's image as a man who understood the world, in a move aimed at allaying any criticism of his inexperience. Ultimately, this image of regional leadership, the *Asharq Al-Awsat* editor-in-chief, Ghassan Charbel opined, was characteristic of a worldly man, a crown prince who was a 'man who knew the world, understood its power play, and the machinations of international relations and economic might' *(Asharq-Al-Awsat* and Charbel 2017b*)*. Saudi editorials, therefore, painted an image of MBS's pragmatism and his sense of realpolitik as well as his economic savviness. As *Asharq Al-Awsat* argued, these characteristics 'were inherently present in the prince' through his upbringing and 'since the establishment of the House of Saud and its monarchy', emphasizing that these traits were 'moulded in him' as he 'was raised in the shadow of King Salman'. The editorials were informing the domestic audience of the identity of not only their newly appointed crown prince, but implicitly their de facto ruler and future monarch and the region's upcoming leader.

The image of MBS's Islamic and regional leadership was also promulgated by the editorial discourse genre with Iran in mind. Saudi editorials targeted not only the domestic audience, but also the Arab world at large as the region supposedly needed a young leader, MBS, to fight extremism and terrorism and defend the Arab and Islamic world. The Saudi discourse represented the Saudi Self as a kingdom with MBS at its helm as a source and guarantor of its stability. Saudi Arabia was argued to be 'residing in an inflamed region ... and it is in jeopardy because it is the safety net of the Gulf, Arab, and Islamic world' *(Asharq-Al-Awsat* and Charbel 2017b*)*. Therefore, MBS had 'played a major role in confronting these dangers', in an implicit referral to Iran and extremism. He had 'built bridges' with regional and world powers, including Trump, through 'three consecutive conferences' held in Riyadh *(Asharq-Al-Awsat* and Charbel 2017b*)*. The discourse of the Saudi Self in the editorials attempted to unify the image of MBS and the kingdom, whereby the image of the crown prince was synonymous with prosperity, stability and security, and leadership of the Arab and Islamic world. This was in response to the Iranian discourse's construction of its Saudi Other, namely of MBS as immature, and as a proponent of sedition and regional instability, while leading a subservient kingdom. Meanwhile, the Saudi discourse highlighted the ascension of the crown prince, bin Salman, and the generational transfer of power was an implicit response to the Iranian discourse that criticized Riyadh's political system and 'lack of democracy' as exemplified by official discourse producers such as Jawad Zarif in relation to the Islamic Republic's recent presidential elections.

The View from Iran

Except for a Friday prayer sermon by the conservative cleric Ayatollah Ahmad Khatami, the Iranian reaction to the promotion of Mohammad bin Salman came predominantly from semi-official news agencies linked with the different Iranian spheres of power. The supra-discourse on bin Salman's promotion had two strands: it promulgated the discourse of a coup within the Al Saud monarchy, and it underlined MBS's lack of experience. The conservative online news agency Mehr argued that there were 'whispers of a power struggle in the House of Saud' between Mohammad bin Salman and his cousin Mohammad bin Nayef. This image of a feuding 'power struggle' brought with it a trope of a 'Saudi King Salman ... who is ageing and suffers from ... Alzheimer's', making the monarchy 'a fertile ground for power-thirsty Saudi princes to ... take over the kingdom's throne after King Salman' dies *(Mehr* and Abadian 2017*)*. The discourse of a coup in the House of Saud was also echoed by the Tasnim News Agency, as were the tropes of the inexperience and immaturity of the newly appointed crown prince and the feuds and disagreements within the monarchy. Tasnim argued that the coup had been 'slow in the making' to avoid any 'backlash and opposition in the Saudi royal court' *(Tasnim* 2017*)*. The trope of a slow-cooked coup was linked to bin Salman's inexperience in running the country. Furthermore, the editorial argued that to ensure the transfer of power took place smoothly, MBS needed time to draw on the extensive power and authority granted to him since 2015 and present himself as a formidable power domestically, regionally, and internationally. Furthermore, the trope of a monarchical feud was also projected in this discourse and intertwined with regional developments, most notably the Qatar crisis. The ousting of Mohammad bin Nayef was projected as marking the rivalry between two princes and 'disagreements inside the ruling dynasty', where bin Nayef's removal was framed as due to his collaboration with Doha and his having 'strong personal relations with Qatar's monarch', and therefore bin Nayef 'chose to remain silent about the recent events' in the GCC. The Iranian discourse constructed the Saudi Other with MBS at its centre to project an image of a monarch who, in addition to being immature and inexperienced, was also a source of domestic and regional instability. The former was symbolized by the trope of a domestic coup and the latter by personalizing the Qatar blockade as a by-product of internal rivalry.

The reformist-leaning media also echoed the narrative of a planned coup to cast a shadow over the ascension of Mohammad bin Salman. The Iranian Students News Agency (ISNA) argued that MBS had enjoyed an external hand helping him to rise to the rank of crown prince, framing Donald Trump as this ally. ISNA argued that there was a 'leaked document that divulged an agreement that was reached between bin Salman and Donald Trump' during the latter's presidential campaign, wherein Trump would 'support bin Salman's ascension to the throne' if he were to win the elections *(ISNA* 2017b*)*. As a result, ISNA argued that 'King

Salman's decision … was Trump's green light' to MBS's promotion. It was this 'green light' that the moderate Entekhab news website argued would allow 'Saudi Arabia to try and provoke Iran' and push it 'to carry out pre-emptive action' under the command of Mohammad bin Salman *(Entekhab* 2017b). This argument also reverberated across the conservative media – in other words, the discourse on MBS was unified across the Iranian political spectrum. MBS's denigration of the Supreme Leader and criticism of Vilāyat-i Faqīh and the concept of the hidden imam, the Mahdi, unified the Iranian voice on Saudi Arabia. Even when the moderate discourse used less polarized narratives and tropes, after MBS's media interviews and by explicitly employing demonizing discourse, the moderates aligned their discourse with that of the conservatives. Representing Mohammad bin Salman as an 'extremist, arrogant, adventurous, and hawkish prince', Mehr argued that the newly appointed crown prince would 'take a new path to fulfil regional expansionist goals' *(Mehr* and Abadian 2017). This Iranian discourse of Saudi regional expansionism along with images and tropes of MBS's naivety and immaturity would become more apparent as the young prince moved to express his presence domestically, regionally, and internationally. This began with news of the alleged kidnapping of an Arab prime minister, the incarceration of Saudi princes, and a harsher Saudi tone towards Iran in interviews with international media outlets.

MBS Goes on the Offensive: MBS Versus 'Hitler'

November 2017 witnessed a series of concurrent events that further pushed Iranian–Saudi rivalry to new heights. On 4 November, Houthi forces launched a missile against Riyadh in retaliation to the Saudi-led bombing of a market in Saada, Yemen, that resulted in the deaths of twenty-five people (Human Rights Watch 2017). On the same day, Saad Hariri, the Lebanese prime minister, visited Riyadh at the invitation of Mohammad bin Salman. Much to the surprise of the international community, the Lebanese prime minister resigned from Riyadh on the Saudi-funded news channel Al-Arabiya. The reason for his resignation was ascribed to Iran's meddling in Lebanon's political affairs and his fear of suffering the same fate as his father (Hiro 2019: 337). On the domestic front, the king ordered the establishment of a committee to investigate public corruption involving senior royals. The committee, which was chaired by the crown prince, would be charged with 'investigations, issuing arrest warrants, travel bans, disclosing and freezing bank accounts and tracking funds' (The National 2017). To the shock of many regional states, the arrests included numerous high-ranking princes, businessmen, and government officials. As Riyadh prepared to host the first Muslim anti-terror summit after the formation of the Islamic Military Counter-Terrorism Coalition, Iran announced its defeat of ISIS.

When considering these events, it is imperative to discuss the nature of the discourse construction in both states. First, Riyadh was on the offensive while the Iranian discourse was on the defensive. This could be explained in terms of Iran experiencing a difficult period domestically as Tehran was grappling with Trump's reversal of the Obama-era policies towards Iran, principally the JCPOA and the return of sanctions. Simultaneously, in both states the discourse of the political elite sought to highlight the Self and the Other. For instance, in Saudi Arabia, as Mohammad bin Salman became more comfortable with his new position, his actions, rhetoric, and self-image narratives also developed, particularly towards Iran. Moreover, as bin Salman promulgated anti-Iran discourses, Tehran sought to deflect and counter these discourses while bolstering a negative image of Saudi Arabia and, by default, reinforcing the image of the Iranian Self. It is also noteworthy that the images constructed by both states were projected with domestic, regional, and international audiences in mind. The discourse emanating from the kingdom was one of MBS's Saudi 'hyper-nationalism' (Al-Rasheed 2017) fighting corruption in contrast to Iran's hegemonic ambitions and expansionism. In Iran, the discourse revolved mainly around Saudi funding of ISIS, sedition in the Islamic world, subservience to the West, and tropes focusing on Mohammad bin Salman's naivety, youth, and adventurism.

Images of Saudi Hyper-Nationalism

The rise of MBS coincided with a growth in nationalistic narratives. However, as Madawi Al-Rasheed argues, the Saudi national narrative has undergone three phases, ranging from 'religious nationalism' after the creation of the Saudi state in 1932, followed by a 'pan-Islamic transnational identity' in the 1960s during the Cold War, and finally the rise of Mohammad bin Salman defined by a 'retreat towards Saudi nationalism' (Al-Rasheed 2017). This nationalism is characterized by an emphasis on developing a stronger national identity, i.e. a rebranding of Saudi identity and a nationalistic revival labelled as 'hyper-nationalism' (Alhussein 2019) with the crown prince at the centre of the new wave of nationalist narratives based on a return to Saudi 'greatness' while moving away from the 'ultra-conservative state'. This ultra-conservative state, according to bin Salman, arose because of the Iranian revolution (al-Saud and *Guardian* 2017).

In an interview with *The Guardian* on 24 October, Mohammad bin Salman defined Riyadh's era of ultra-conservativeness through an Iranian lens: 'What happened in the last 30 years is not Saudi Arabia . . . is not the Middle East' but a result of the revolution that saw the end of Iran's monarchical rule (al-Saud and *Guardian* 2017). The Saudi prince attempted to represent the religious zeal of the Wahhabi clergy as a reaction to Khomeini's 1979 revolution. MBS framed Saudi religious radicalism as an attempt 'to copy this model in different countries, one of them is Saudi Arabia' (al-Saud and *Guardian* 2017). The prince argued that since 'We didn't know how to deal with it', the 'problem' as he defined it, meaning the 'ultra-conservative Islamism' fathered by Khomeini in 1979, had 'spread all over the world' (al-Saud and *Guardian* 2017). This discourse based on blaming the Iranian revolution for Saudi Arabia's ultra-conservative system was a watershed moment in terms of constructing Saudi Arabia's Iranian Other. It was a pretext for transforming the kingdom and replacing Islam as the central image with Saudi hyper-nationalism. This shift from its ultra-conservative image to a more liberal and moderate kingdom was accomplished by beginning to break free from the Islamic and cultural restrictions imposed for decades in Saudi Arabia. The crown prince would promote gender mixing, bring in Western artists, open cinemas, and host boxing matches, activities once prohibited in Saudi Arabia by the Islamist ulama.

MBS was communicating to an international audience that Saudi Arabia was about to change and 'now is the time to get rid of' ultra-conservativism. To the international community, the new image of the Saudi Self would be one based on 'moderate Islam open to the world and all religions'. It would aim to construct an image of a moderate nation and show it as the 'true nature' of Saudi Arabia. MBS argued that '70% of the Saudis are younger than 30 . . . we won't waste 30 years of our life combating extremist thoughts, we will destroy them now and immediately' (al-Saud and *Guardian* 2017). The crown prince propagated three main messages and images. The first was that Saudi Arabia was not innately radical, but moderate and accepting of all faiths. The second was an image of pragmatism and openness to change, especially by putting the youth at the centre of his plans. The third message, based on his interview, was that these plans of opening up the Saudi state to change include an eradication of extremist elements. MBS's statement regarding the eradication of extremist thought had two messages, one implicit and another explicit: the explicit message referred to the Saudi Wahhabi ulama, and the implicit message referred to Iran. Furthermore, the reform that MBS had mentioned did not only focus on the religious elements of the state. In the first week of November, arrest warrants were issued and Mohammad bin Salman's fight against corruption began.

Hegemony, Intervention, and an 'Act of War'

Two events on 4 November 2017 resulted in the intensification of discourses between Iran and Saudi Arabia: first, a missile attack by the Houthis, targeting King Khaled airport in Riyadh, and second, the resignation of the Lebanese prime minister during his Riyadh visit. Both events triggered a new set of Othering discourses directed at Iran by Saudis. The former was considered as an 'act of war' in Saudi eyes (*CNN* 2017), while the latter was labelled as an Iranian intervention in Lebanon's domestic affairs through Hezbollah.

The initial response – and therefore the themes and tropes in relation to the Houthi attack – were constructed by the Saudi foreign minister, Adel al-Jubeir. Speaking to an international audience, al-Jubeir labelled the missile attacks an Iranian 'act of war' (al-Jubeir and *CNN* 2017). In his strategized responses to the CNN anchor, al-Jubeir suggested that the 'real perpetrators' were Iranian nationals from the Shi'i sect. This explicit blaming of Iran and the highlighting of the Shi'i was an attempt to dilute the Houthi identity of the attacks, thereby framing them as an assault 'target[ing] civilians' rather than the airport. Based on this, al-Jubeir reaffirmed Saudi strength and military deterrence by evoking Saudi Arabia's right to respond to Tehran.

He argued that the Islamic Republic 'cannot lob missiles' at the kingdom and 'expect us not to take steps vis-à-vis Iran'. When questioned regarding how Riyadh was certain of the missile's Iranian origins, al-Jubeir stated that it 'was manufactured in Iran ... smuggled in parts into Yemen ... assembled in Yemen by operatives from the Revolutionary Guards and from Hezbollah, [and then] launched against Saudi Arabia' (al-Jubeir and *CNN* 2017). The evidence, he suggested, was based on 'cables [that] have Iranian letters on them [and] suicide boats that ... are Iranian [and] have computers [with] Iranian letters on the keyboards' and are operated by Houthis. He then constructed an image of a hegemonic and expansionist Iran: a state that employed 'proxies' and conducted 'suicide missions'. Moreover, Iran was depicted as an international delinquent who was defying international norms by committing a 'hostile act' and 'defy[ing]; article 51 of the UN charter' by 'interfere[ing] in the affairs of countries ... whether Lebanon ... Yemen ... Syria ... Iraq ... Bahrain' (al-Jubeir and *CNN* 2017). The following day, Saudi media outlets used al-Jubeir's interview on CNN to promulgate specific tropes, accusing Iran of the missile attacks.

Picking up on themes from al-Jubeir's interview, Saudi news outlets opened their editorials with the allegations that 'Iran was the number one sponsor of terrorism' *(al-Riyadh* 2017h) and the 'number one security and peace-destabilizing nuisance in the region' *(al-Riyadh)*; however, Saudi newspapers printed in the kingdom, such as *al-Riyadh*, refrained from mentioning, discussing, or referring to the attacks. Saudi newspapers based in London, such as *Asharq Al-Awsat*, did, however, discuss the incident, labelling it a 'Houthi ballistic missile attack' *(Asharq-Al-Awsat* and Al-Rashed 2017c), possibly attributable to the kingdom's wishes to construct an image of the Self domestically, rather than projecting a certain image to the Arab and Islamic world. Newspapers printed in Saudi Arabia sustained an image of strength, stability, and military supremacy. The attacks by the Houthis after four years of war may have cast doubt in Saudi minds, especially since the Houthis were initially depicted by the Saudi leadership – and in particular by MBS – as a weak militia that would be defeated within weeks. Therefore, by referring to Iran rather than the Houthis, the Saudi editorial discourse represented the war with the Houthis as a 'proxy war' with an 'expansionist Iran' rather than with a small militia in Sanaa. It was also constructed as a war that Riyadh was pursuing on behalf of the international community.

To sustain the discourse of a proxy war with Iran, four themes were employed. First, 'Iran was the number one leading sponsor of instability and terror' *(al-Riyadh* 2017h). Second, there was a return to the 1980s trope of Khomeini's 'export of the revolution', a revival of the Persian empire, and the ethnic subjugation of Arabs. Tehran's war with Riyadh was argued as 'not being based on realpolitik [or] religious and sectarian fundamentals', nor was the war about 'economic competition and gain' *(al-Riyadh* 2017h). Rather, the missile attack was framed as part of a larger war that 'Iran based on Machiavellian principles' with the goal of 'export[ing] Khomeini's revolution [and] create[ing] a Middle Eastern region with colonies loyal to the Persian empire' that will rise on the 'skulls of the non-Persian populations' *(al-Riyadh* 2017h*).* Third, Iran was an irresponsible member of the international community. The newspaper *al-Riyadh* (2017e) echoed and built on al-Jubeir's argument that Iran had broken international norms and law, projecting an image of Iranian hegemony and alleging that Tehran had done so as it 'attempts to find a position of power on the regional map' while allowing it to 'attain an advanced role in the international community' *(al-Riyadh* 2017e*).* Moreover, Saudi editorials called for the 'international community to confront Iran', i.e. they called for a military solution. Using the trope of 'sedition' *(fitna*), Saudi editorial discourse argued that the world should come together and 'stand as a unified dam [against] Iran's plans and their agents in Yemen, Syria, and Lebanon [as] Tehran seeks to create wars and sedition [through a] divide-and-rule policy' *(al-Riyadh* 2017b*).* Therefore, the Saudi editorials assured their domestic audience that 'we' – i.e. the Saudi leadership – 'shall not sit with our hands tied' *(al-Riyadh* 2017b*),* because what Iran 'is doing cannot be tolerated or else it shall continue with its belligerence' *(al-Riyadh* 2017e*).* It was this Saudi-constructed image of Iranian interference in Arab affairs and proxy wars that was also used to justify Hariri's resignation and alleged detention in Riyadh.

On the same day as the attacks, after a meeting with MBS, the Lebanese prime minister, Saad Hariri, addressed the Arab-speaking world from Riyadh and announced his resignation. The reasons behind such an unexpected move were that both Iran and Hezbollah were interfering in Lebanese Arab affairs, echoing Saudi narratives of Tehran spreading chaos and strife throughout the region. Furthermore, Hariri highlighted that his life was also in danger, and he might suffer the same fate as his father in 2005 (Hiro 2019: 337). Beirut characterized Hariri's actions as reflecting his duress and his stay in Riyadh as a kidnapping. The Lebanese president, Michel Aoun, issued a statement affirming that Beirut 'will not accept [Hariri] remaining hostage' in Saudi Arabia, arguing that they 'do not know the reason for his detention' *(Reuters* 2017b*).* Additionally, responses from Iran's ally, Hezbollah, mirrored Saudi accusations against Iran. In a speech on 10 November, the Hezbollah general secretary, Hassan Nasrallah, accused Riyadh of an 'unprecedented Saudi intervention' in the affairs of Lebanon, alleging that 'Saudi Arabia and Saudi officials have declared war on Lebanon and on Hezbollah' (Nasrallah 2017).

As international media outlets reported on the reasons behind Hariri's resignation and, later, on the rumours and allegations surrounding his detention, the Saudi discourse framed the incident as a consequence of Iranian regional intervention, echoing the images, tropes and themes employed when discussing the Houthi attacks on Riyadh. When al-Jubeir addressed an international audience on CNN, he weaved the Iranian intervention in Yemen into Tehran's role in Lebanon (al-Jubeir and *CNN* 2017). When asked about Hariri's resignation, al-Jubeir argued that it was due to 'Hezbollah undercutting him', based on how the Shi'i group was 'doing Iran's bidding', and therefore the 'Lebanese political system became paralyzed' (al-Jubeir and *CNN* 2017) . Then, al-Jubeir accused Hezbollah of 'calling the shots', which eventually led to Hariri saying 'enough is enough' and resigning. When queried on the issue of his alleged detention and kidnapping, al-Jubeir highlighted Hariri's Saudi citizenship and stated that he was 'able to leave the kingdom if he so chooses' (al-Jubeir and *CNN* 2017). The official discourse emanating from al-Jubeir sought to construct two main images in the mind of the audience. First, Hariri's resignation from the kingdom sent a clear message to Iran and the Arab world that Lebanon and its decision-making was controlled from Riyadh, especially since Hariri was a Saudi citizen. The second message was that Iran was the source of the turmoil in the Arab world, and its proxies were its tools of coercion. It is this second image that the Saudi editorial discourse sought to emphasize to both local and external audiences. These Saudi tropes of Iranian intervention and the latter's use of Shi'i proxies, such as Hezbollah and the Houthis, fit into a wider narrative of Iranian expansionism and intervention in the Arab world, particularly after the events of the Arab Spring and the subsequent wars in Syria and Yemen.

As the Hariri story unfolded, Saudi editorial discourse used his resignation speech to construct an image of Iran as Saudi Arabia's Other. The editor-in-chief of *Asharq Al-Awsat* (*Asharq-Al-Awsat* and Charbel 2017a) had parallels in Khomeini's 'drinking from the chalice of poison' when agreeing to a ceasefire with Iraq in 1988. Indeed, the *Asharq Al-Awsat* framed Hariri's decisions during his tenure and his later resignation as 'drinking doses of poison', beginning with 'carrying his father's coffin after the assassination of February 2005, [then a] larger dose of poison in 2009 [when he was] informed that Hezbollah was involved in the assassination of his father' (*Asharq-Al-Awsat* and Charbel 2017a). The final dose was when Hariri agreed to leading a government in collabortion with Hezbollah in order to 'save what was left of the Lebanese state' (*Asharq-Al-Awsat* and Charbel 2017a). However, 'Hariri got tired of drinking poison' and resigned because Lebanon was 'undergoing a shift [away] from its Arab identity [as] Hezbollah utilized Lebanese domestic politics to carry Iran's widespread revolution in the region' (*Asharq-Al-Awsat* and Charbel 2017a). The Saudi discourse sought to project an image of Lebanon as hijacked by Iran through a Hezbollah proxy, with the only solution being for Hariri to 'drink poison', an implicit allegory and parallel to Khomeini, and therefore Hariri had to leave Lebanon and seek protection in the kingdom.

Furthermore, as voices of criticism from Lebanon and the international community were raised against Hariri's alleged detention, Saudi editorial discourse responded to the criticism by emphasizing Saudi–Lebanese relations and Iran as a means of fending off any criticism. Regarding accusations of Saudi interference in Lebanon's domestic affairs, al-Riyadh (2017c) highlighted the 'historic relationship' between Riyadh and Beirut as opposed to Iran's role in 'creating Hezbollah to be a thorn in the side of the Arabs' (al-Riyadh 2017c). This was compounded by Saudi editorials contrasting the image of the Saudi Self with Iran as its Other in relation to Lebanon. Saudi Arabia was a 'historic force of stability, security, and progression' in Lebanon (al-Riyadh 2017f), while Iran's role was framed negatively given Hezbollah's activities, particularly in Syria. Moreover, Saudi editorial discourse also responded to the allegations made in Hezbollah's statements and speeches on Riyadh's kidnapping of Hariri (Nasrallah 2017). Deploying the 'kidnapping' theme,

Saudi editorials *(al-Riyadh* 2017f) argued that it was 'Hezbollah that kidnapped Lebanon' and who had 'held the Lebanese people hostage [so that] Iran can utilize Lebanon as a base to carry out its expansionist regional agendas'. This trope of Iranian expansionism would later be used by Mohammad bin Salman when constructing his image of Iran as Saudi Arabia's main rival, particularly as Iraq and Iran had announced the defeat of ISIS while bin Salman was hosting his own conference in Riyadh to fight extremism. The construction of Iran's image as an expansionist hegemon in the Arab world may have been an attempt by the Saudi discourse constructors to justify MBS's actions with regard to Hariri, his war in Yemen, and the hosting of a conference to fight extremism. This extremism trope as employed by Riyadh was a strategy used to construct Iran as a sponsor of terror with Hezbollah and the Houthis as its tools, while equating Iran's proxies with ISIS and Al-Qaeda.

The Middle East's Hitler and Extremism

In a first meeting of the Arab coalition set up and headed by Riyadh, MBS vowed to pursue extremists and terrorists until they were 'wiped off the face of the earth' (al-Saud 2017). The summit held on 26 November was hosted by Saudi Arabia and included forty members of the Saudi-led coalition, which was set up in 2015 and came a week after Iran announced its defeat of ISIS (Soleimani 2017). General Qassem Soleimani, the Iranian commander tasked with leading the war against ISIS, sent a congratulatory message to the Supreme Leader announcing that the 'Islamic State has been defeated' (Soleimani 2017). In response, Ayatollah Khamenei congratulated Soleimani's efforts, stating that the defeat of ISIS was a 'blow against the past and current governments of America and the regimes linked to it in the region', while framing it as a victory against Saudi Arabia and its allies 'who created this group ... so they could expand their malevolent power in west Asia' (Khamenei 2017e). This image of an Iranian Shi'i victory over 'US–Saudi-sponsored Wahhabi terrorism' came at a time when Riyadh was under serious threat from Houthi missile attacks, particularly since the war against Yemen was approaching its fourth year with no sign of an end. The counter-narrative from Riyadh came primarily from MBS and was further disseminated and expanded on by Saudi newspaper outlets.

In the opening speech at the summit, MBS argued for a collective role with a military coalition fighting terrorism. The speech, given in the presence of defence ministers, framed a leading role for Riyadh and reinforced the image of Saudi Arabia as a protector of Islam. It also underlined its regional and Islamic leadership and legitimacy, while not allowing terrorists 'to distort our peaceful religion' (al-Saud 2017) . MBS was implying that Islam had been hijacked by extremism and terrorism, but that thanks to the Saudi leadership and with him at the helm, 'this ends today, with this alliance'. Despite including forty regional states, this alliance excluded countries that had either fallen victim to ISIS or had fought against the terrorist group, including Iran, Syria, and Iraq. Therefore, since MBS failed to define which groups were terrorists and extremists, it was a veiled accusation against Hezbollah and Iran as promulgated in the editorial and elite discourse, particularly during MBS's media appearances.

Mohammad bin Salman's allegations against Iran did not remain implicit for long. In an interview with *The New York Times* (Friedman and al-Saud 2017), he defined his notion of extremism and terrorism in relation to the image of Saudi Arabia and its Other, Iran. In his discussions with the journalist Thomas Friedman, MBS defined his vision of Saudi Arabia and constructed an image of himself as a saviour, not only of the kingdom, but also of the Arab and Islamic world, which included protecting Saudi Arabia and the world from Iran and its 'extremist thought'. Building on his previous interview with *The Guardian* a month before, MBS doubled down on his drive to modernize the kingdom, and his intention to 'bring Saudi Islam to its more open and modern orientation' that he alleged was 'diverted in 1979' as a result of the Islamic Revolution in Iran (Friedman and al-Saud 2017) . MBS added that he wanted to bring Saudi Arabia back to its natural Self, defined by a 'moderate, balanced Islam that is open to the word and to all religions and all traditions and peoples' (Friedman and al-Saud 2017) .

This mission, MBS argued, would not be 'reinterpreting Islam', but rather 'restoring Islam to its origins' (Friedman and al-Saud 2017). In other words, the image that the world had seen of the kingdom since 1979, represented by ultra-conservative clerics, with its ban on mixed gatherings and theatres – an image that deemed non-Muslims such as Christians and Jews to be infidels – was incompatible with the kingdom; however, it had been caused by an external impetus, namely 'Khomeini's revolution'. This supposed external impetus of the Islamic Revolution as the source of Saudi ultra-conservativism had never been discussed or promulgated before MBS's tenure. According to the crown prince, he sought to use the 'biggest tools' at his disposal, that is the 'Prophet's practices and [daily life in] Saudi Arabia before 1979' (Friedman and al-Saud 2017). MBS projected an image of the Prophet as a moderate Muslim with leanings towards the arts, music, and liberal politics. The prince commented that, 'At the time of the Prophet Muhammad ... there were musical theatres, there was mixing between men and women, there was respect for Christians and Jews in Arabia' (Friedman and al-Saud 2017). He went as far as claiming that the Prophet had set a precedent in terms of gender equality, arguing that 'the first commercial judge in Medina was a woman!' What is evident here is that MBS was representing himself as the restorer of 'true Mohammedan Islam', a leader tasked with bringing the kingdom out of the darkness and back into the light. MBS's interpretation of Islam and the teachings of the Prophet Mohammad was an innovative discourse construction, redefining Islam and its purity based on gender admixture and social liberalization as opposed to the Iranian definition of *Islam-i Nab* (pure Islam) that had its roots in piety, resistance to oppression, and the ways of Ahl-al-Bayt. There were now two conflicting images of Islam: an Iranian definition with its roots in the 1979 Revolution, and a conflicting one that arose with MBS's ascension to power.

This image of Islamic leadership also appeared in his discussion of Riyadh's foreign policy, although this time it used a sectarian framing. Hariri's detention and later resignation were as a 'Sunni Muslim' under pressure from the 'Lebanese

Shiite Hezbollah militia, which is essentially controlled by Tehran' (Friedman and al-Saud 2017). Iran was once again brought into MBS's discourse on Riyadh's regional policies. Like Lebanon, MBS defined Yemen through an Iranian lens, arguing that although there was a 'pro-Saudi legitimate government there, [and the coalition] is now in control of 85% of the country', the remainder of the land had nevertheless fallen under the influence of 'pro-Iranian Houthi rebels [who] launched a missile at Riyadh airport' (Friedman and al-Saud 2017). What MBS was suggesting was that his war was one of 'Saudi-backed legitimacy [against] pro-Iranian Houthi belligerence'. Consequently, the Saudi-led war that was supposed to take weeks would continue until 'no less than one hundred per cent' of Yemen was under its control. This proxy war with Iran now had no end date, particularly since MBS prided himself on having Trump's support, a president who was 'the right person at the right time' (Friedman and al-Saud 2017).

Trump was the 'right person' because he would support Riyadh and its allies in general and MBS in particular in 'building a coalition to stand up to Iran' (Friedman and al-Saud 2017). The 'right time' was because Iran was now a nuclear power, given that Trump had sought to reverse the Obama policies towards Iran, most significantly the JCPOA. According to Friedman, bin Salman represented the Middle East as riddled with 'dysfunction and rivalries within the Sunni Arab world' (Friedman and al-Saud 2017) . These rivalries impeded the formation of 'a unified front' to confront Iran as the state 'indirectly controls four Arab capitals today — Damascus, Sana, Baghdad and Beirut' (Friedman and al-Saud 2017) . It was this alleged Iranian control that MBS lambasted Khamenei for, representing him as 'the new Hitler of the Middle East' (Friedman and al-Saud 2017) , while he also used the image and trope of 'Hitler' and 'Nazism' to justify the war in Yemen, the coalition, and support from Trump, while projecting an image of Saudi power and leadership. The rivalry with Iran now took a Churchillian turn. Like the US-led coalition that fought fascism during World War II, MBS contended that 'we learned from Europe that appeasement doesn't work' (Friedman and al-Saud 2017). Saudi Arabia and its allies 'don't want the new Hitler in Iran to repeat what happened in Europe in the Middle East' (Friedman and al-Saud 2017) . To MBS, Iran was Germany, Khamenei was a Middle Eastern Hitler, and the four Arab countries were the European countries that Nazi Germany invaded. On the other hand, MBS was implicitly represented as the Middle East's Churchill or Eisenhower, leading a coalition of forty countries to liberate the Sunni Arab world from Iran. It was this watershed trope that the Saudi domestic discourse disseminated, particularly in their newspapers.

Brandishing titles such as 'Nazi Iran' *(al-Riyadh* 2017a*)* and 'The Supreme Leader and Hitler' *(Asharq-Al-Awsat* and Al-Rashed 2017b*)*, Saudi editorials built on MBS's comments in *The New York Times*, introducing additional images and tropes emphasizing the prince's denigration of Iran and its Supreme Leader. Building on the tropes of 'Hitler' and 'Nazism', Khamenei was labelled a 'megalomaniac' who had 'followed in the footsteps of Hitler in the 1930s' in an attempt to 'revive an empire that was lost during the First World War' *(al-Riyadh* 2017a*)*. In a direct juxtaposition to Hitler, Khamenei was represented as a power-hungry leader with ambitions to resurrect the Persian empire (*al-Riyadh* 2017a). In contrast, Saudi Arabia was compared to the Allied forces of World War II. However, unlike the Western coalition against Hitler, the kingdom, led by MBS, was 'alerted early to the Guardian Jurist's regional project ... confronted Iran [and] intervened to save Bahrain and Yemen from falling into the Iranian trap' (*al-Riyadh* 2017a). Iran's regional actions and its alleged 'Shi'i Crescent' were juxtaposed with the ambitions of Hitler's Third Reich. However, the Saudi editorial discourse argued that, unlike the allies, Saudi Arabia confronted Iran, 'which would have put the region under the control of the mullahs' who sought to 'revive a bloody project, [namely] exporting the Khomeini revolution' (*al-Riyadh* 2017a).

The device of Hitler and Nazism also saw the use of images of the Holocaust, a trope never used before to construct Iran and the Supreme Leader in Saudi discourse. The newspaper Asharq Al-Awsat (*Asharq-Al-Awsat* and Al-Rashed 2017b) characterized Tehran's 'bloody project' as recalling the Holocaust. However, rather than Jews, Saudi editorial discourse was hinting at a genocide against Sunni Arabs, particularly in the Persian Gulf region. In an editorial discussing MBS's reference to Khamenei and Hitler, Abdulrahman al-Rashed of Asharq Al-Awsat argued that what MBS meant in his opinion was 'clear, [it was] about a leading figure who runs an expansionist regime on the basis of an ideological party that did not bat an eyelid towards the hundreds of thousands of people he exposed to death or helped kill' (*Asharq-Al-Awsat* and Al-Rashed 2017b). It became apparent that this was a veiled reference to a forthcoming Arab Holocaust led by Khamenei and Iran and, like Hitler after the invasion of Poland, Khamenei had 'refused reconciliation and openness with its Arab neighbours and with the West' (*Asharq-Al-Awsat* and Al-Rashed 2017b). Therefore, Khamenei was characterized as following the Nazi strategy of 'building a superior, aggressive military state' (*Asharq-Al-Awsat* and Al-Rashed 2017b). The difference is that where Hitler collaborated with fascists in Italy and Japan, Iran was utilizing a 'network of proxies from terrorist organizations from Indonesia to Central Africa' (*Asharq-Al-Awsat* and Al-Rashed 2017b). However, the tropes of fascism, Nazism, and expansionism did not go unanswered: Tehran also had its own images that it projected to represent itself and Saudi Arabia as its Other, especially in relation to Mohammad bin Salman.

Conclusion

There are two main features characteristic of the construction of the Self and Other in Saudi Arabia and Iran during this period. The first was that Iran reacted to Saudi impetus and discourse constructions. The second was that the discourse construction was multi-layered, i.e. it had an initial first element that grew with the pace and polarization of the events and the discourses employed. Further, the discourse was directly proportional to events, be they international, regional, or domestic. The advent of Trump resulted in a Saudi discourse construction that represented its relationship with Washington as a unified Self and Other, that is to say, both Riyadh and Washington had a common enemy, Iran, and a common goal, namely to fight extremism and reverse Obama-era policies towards Tehran, particularly the JCPOA.

This Saudi representation of a 'common Self' with Trump, and a 'common Other', i.e. Iran, generated reactionary discourses from Tehran. These Iranian discourses pointed at Saudi immaturity, diplomatic incompetence, and irresponsibility, thus producing a multi-layered Othering. Regarding the first layer, the Iranian Self directly responded to its Saudi Other. For instance, when Saudi Arabia represented Iran as the leading sponsor of terror, Iran responded by representing Riyadh as sponsoring ISIS and collaborating with the US and Israel in ISIS attacks in Tehran, while citing MBS's line on 'taking the war to Tehran'. In terms of the second layer, there was a promotion of the Self, which produced the image of the Other. This was exemplified by competing images of regional and Islamic leadership through a redefinition of 'pure Islam' wherein MBS constructed representations of a 'true image' of Saudi Arabia as a naturally moderate state in juxtaposition to an Iran that believed in occultation, Mahdism, and apocalyptic thoughts. In response, the Iranian counter-image was of a hypocritical and false leadership that sought to undermine the legitimacy and authority of Islam, thereby shaping the image of the Iranian Self as the natural and legitimate leader of the world of Islam.

However, in a deeper sense, the construction of the Saudi Other was a form of Iranian mirroring of its own pre-revolutionary monarchical past, from which Iran had tried to distance itself. In other words, by producing a discourse targeting the Saudi monarchy as the Other, Iran was subtly employing its revolutionary discourse to critique the monarchy just as it had criticized the Pahlavi era in its domestic discourse. The discourse of subservience was built into the Iranian psyche from the pre-revolutionary days and in some ways the Saudi monarchy and its relationship with the US reflected the Iranian Shah's relationship with the latter. For Saudi Arabia, this image of ultra-radical Islamism was rejected and built into the discourse of the Iranian revolution as an imposed radicalism that forced the kingdom to deviate from the 'true teachings of the Prophet' that, according to MBS, accepted gender mixing, musical performances and a 'liberal society'. In essence, MBS laid the blame for the Saudi Self's radicalism on the Iranian Other for the latter's revolutionary stance since 1979. This narrative of blaming Iran for Saudi characteristics was used as a vehicle to reconstruct an image of the Saudi Self and the related tropes and images of hyper-nationalism. Under MBS's tenure, Iran was no longer just a rival and an enemy, it was also labelled as the source of Saudi Arabia's radicalism and conservatism. Since the 1980s, Saudi Arabia had depicted itself as the custodian and protector of Islam through the image of the title of its monarch, the Custodian of the Two Holy Mosques. However, under MBS, Saudi Arabia was now protecting Islam from what the state termed 'Iranian radicalism', 'fascism', and the region's 'modern day Hitler'.

Chapter 15

MAXIMUM PRESSURE: TERRORIST ORGANIZATIONS, TANKER WARS, AND ASSASSINATIONS

Introduction

The year 2018 was a turbulent one for both Iran and Saudi Arabia. Trump unilaterally withdrew from the JCPOA, and economic sanctions were re-imposed on Iran. For Saudi Arabia, the war in Yemen and military efforts against the Houthis continued unabated. However, Saudi Arabia's situation became more drastic after Jamal Khashoggi's murder in the Saudi consulate in Istanbul in October 2018. This proved to be a setback for MBS and his efforts to rebrand the kingdom's image and attract foreign investment, while transforming and diversifying his economy, particularly through the privatization of Aramco. While Riyadh encouraged Trump to sustain 'maximum pressure' on Tehran, Iran experienced a sharp decline in Iranian oil exports and revenue. To compound matters, as MBS encouraged Trump to apply more pressure on Iran, the region became embroiled in further turmoil. The designation of the IRGC as a Foreign Terrorist Organization (FTO) in May 2019 and the subsequent tanker disputes that summer led to a 'tit-for-tat' response between Iran and the international community, predominantly Britain and the US, amid the rise of a military voice in Iranian foreign policy.

For Saudi Arabia, its war with the Houthis took a dramatic turn when a missile attack on 14 September 2019 struck the Aramco oil installations in Abqaiq and Khurais, resulting in a 40 per cent decrease in oil output. As for Iran, Trump's 'maximum pressure' campaign was met with Iran's 'maximum resistance'. Both Tehran and Washington became more confrontational towards each other as Tehran called for the departure of US forces from the region, all while Iran was assuming a more effective role in the Syrian war and the affairs of post-ISIS Iraq. On 3 January 2020, after a series of protests outside the US embassy in Baghdad, the Trump administration assassinated the commander of the Quds Force, General Qassem Soleimani, and the leader of the Iraqi Popular Mobilization Units (PMU), Abu Mahdi al-Mohandis, in Baghdad airport. The assassinations shifted Iran's strategy from one of 'maximum resistance' to 'severe revenge'.

In this chapter I argue that the elites in both states prioritized the Self over the Other and therefore took the lead in discourse construction. In Saudi Arabia, this was due to MBS's plans to rebrand the kingdom and fulfil Vision 2030, whereas for Iran, the focus was on alleviating the pressure on its economy and domestic politics after Trump's withdrawal from the JCPOA. I also argue that Trump's 'maximum pressure' and MBS's calls for increased pressure on Iran led to rising regional turbulence as exemplified by the IRGC being designated as an FTO, the sanctions on Iranian oil sales, and a new Tanker War recalling the Iran–Iraq War of the 1980s. These events elevated the IRGC's voice in the Iranian discourse of the Self, uniting Iran's political and religious groups and creating a unified front against a Saudi Other. Furthermore, the designation of the IRGC as an FTO necessitated an attempt to rebrand Iran's image while giving the IRGC a greater voice in Iranian foreign policy. By the same token, the murder of Khashoggi coincided with the Aramco initial public offering (IPO), which led Saudi Arabia to also attempt to rebrand its image both regionally and internationally. I therefore argue that, overall, the discourses between 2018 and 2020 were more about the Self rather than the Other, a dynamic in which the elite shaped the discourses of both states, resulting in the media and religious languages towing the line of the state. Furthermore, I suggest that the Aramco incident of 2019 was a watershed moment in Riyadh's official discourse towards Iran, one where MBS shifted his rhetoric from a confrontational and aggressive discourse towards the Islamic Republic and the Supreme Leader to a less reactionary stance towards Tehran. This shift was also evident in the Saudi elite discourse remaining silent in the aftermath of the Soleimani assassination, while Iran attempted to bolster its self-image. By employing the discourse of 'severe revenge' and equating Soleimani with the image of the Iranian Self, Tehran was trying to shore up its legitimacy and its domestic, regional, and international leadership. By the same token, Riyadh countered Tehran's representation of the Self by redirecting its discourse and demonizing the Iranian Other in its media genres.

Hitler vs. Hitler: Calls for 'Maximum Pressure' on Iran

Trump's withdrawal from the JCPOA in May 2018 signalled the beginning of his 'maximum pressure' campaign to subdue Iran into coming back to the negotiating table for a 'better deal'(Trump 2018). The response from Tehran was a campaign of 'maximum resistance'. Trump's decision was met with rejoicing in capitals such as Tel Aviv and Riyadh since Saudi Arabia had been critical of the JCPOA and welcomed the crippling sanctions on Iranian oil exports. A statement from the Saudi foreign ministry accused Tehran of exploiting the JCPOA to destabilize and target the kingdom while supporting Trump's campaign by framing Iran as an irresponsible international actor and regional menace, accusing it of jeopardizing international trade and its neighbours' security and stability. In a statement, the Saudi foreign ministry argued that

> The Iranian regime, however, took advantage of the economic benefits afforded
> by the lifting of sanctions and used them to continue its destabilizing activities

in the region, especially by developing its ballistic missiles and supporting terrorist organizations in the region, including Hezbollah and the Houthi militias, which used the capabilities provided by Iran to target civilians in the Kingdom of Saudi Arabia and Yemen, as well as repeatedly targeting international shipping lanes in a blatant violation of UN Security Council resolutions.

(*SPA* 2018a)

Weeks before the US withdrawal, MBS argued that Iran was seeking a nuclear weapon. In an interview with CBS news in March 2018, the crown prince openly contended that Riyadh would seek a nuclear weapon if Tehran built one. Doubling down on the 'Hitler of the Middle East' trope, MBS argued that while 'Saudi Arabia does not want to acquire any nuclear bomb … without a doubt if Iran developed a nuclear bomb, we will follow suit as soon as possible' (al-Saud and CBS 2018). In a later interview with the *Wall Street Journal*, MBS called for additional pressure on Iran as the only way to avoid a regional military confrontation with the state, arguing that 'if we do not succeed' in applying economic and political pressure, then there would likely be a 'war with Iran in 10–15 years' (al-Saud 2018). Days later from Paris, the prince accused Iran of supporting terrorism in the Middle East while he employed tropes of terrorism, regional instability, hegemony, and modern-day Nazism to describe Khamenei. It was evident that Riyadh was building a campaign to rally support for more pressure on Iran. Within a few weeks, bin Salman's efforts succeeded when Trump withdrew from the JCPOA and increased pressure on Iran.

The Iranian response to the Saudi rhetoric supporting tougher measures against Tehran can be seen as a continuation of the imagery employed in their representation of MBS in the Iranian discourse. In other words, the Iranian discourse utilized tropes that represented Saudi Arabia as fascist, militarily weak, a primary cause of regional instability, and a sponsor of terrorism. Although tropes relating to regional instability and terrorism were previously utilized during the Iran–Iraq War of the 1980s, the advent of the Taliban in the 1990s, the sectarian wars of Iraq, and later in the conflicts in Syria and Yemen related to the effects of the Arab Spring, the mention of fascism was a counter-response to MBS's narrative of Iranian fascism and the deployment of Hitler and Nazism as symbols of Iranian expansionism and hegemony. Additionally, and echoing MBS referring to Khamenei as Hitler, Iranian discourse focused on the image of the crown prince as a young, inexperienced, and immature politician. The foreign-ministry spokesman, Bahram Qassemi, branded him 'delusional and naïve', with his remarks emanating from 'bitterness' towards Iran (Ghasemi 2018c). As for the prince's remarks regarding Iran seeking a nuclear bomb, Qassemi argued that MBS 'has no idea of politics [and] lacks foresight' (Ghasemi 2018c).

Moreover, the Iranian response to bin Salman's accusation of Iranian sponsorship of regional terrorism during his trip to France was similar to the Saudi narrative. While MBS accused Iran of funding Hezbollah and the Houthis, Iranian discourse accused the Saudi monarchy of being as 'notorious as Zionist regime's officials in epitomis[ing] crime and aggression in the region' (Ghasemi

2018b), thus comparing the Al Saud to Israel in an implicit reference drawing on the wars in Gaza and strikes in Syria. On 14 April the US, France, and the UK carried out a series of military strikes in reprisal for the Douma chemical attacks that the Assad government was alleged to have carried out against civilians on 8 April. Iranian discourse took advantage of the incident to respond to MBS's anti-Iran rhetoric. In a series of tweets on the day of the US-led attacks, Khamenei described the assault as a 'crime' and said that the chemical attacks were carried out by ISIS, which the US had 'played a major role in creating . . . with Saudi money [then] turning them loose on [the] Iraqi and Syrian nations' (Khamenei 2018). The significance of this is that Iran, after being largely silent for five months in reaction to MBS's references to Khamenei as Hitler, accusing Khamenei of wanting to emulate Nazism and engulf the region in turmoil, it was now Iran's turn to respond by employing discourses on terrorism and regional instability. By using the attacks on Syria as a context to respond to MBS – and by extension, to Riyadh – Khamenei intertwined the US, Saudi Arabia and ISIS, framing them as terrorist actors wherein Washington and Riyadh were seen as collaborators in the creation and funding of ISIS while also using terrorism to destabilize the region.

In reaction to MBS's talk of 'military conflict', the Iranian military responded by focusing on the tropes of megalomania, delusion, and military inferiority. The Iranian defence minister, Amir Hatami, not only criticized MBS's 'lack of experience in state affairs', but also suggested the inferiority and weakness of the Saudi armed forces compared with the Iranian military. Employing the identical trope of Nazism and constructing an image of MBS's 'megalomania', Hatami referred to him and his regional war as 'Hitler acting under an illusion of power' with a delusionary and exaggerated self-confidence. This image of deluded Saudi power was compared to Saddam during the 1980s and the US invasion of Iraq in 2003, with the Iranian minister reminding his Saudi counterpart that 'Saddam Hussein . . . as well as the Americans when they attacked Iraq had this delusion of power and strength . . . they failed miserably and plunged the country into the deepest hell' (Hatami 2018). Using the image of Saudi military inferiority to highlight that state's role in the Yemen war, the former head of the IRGC and Khamenei's adviser for military affairs, Yahya Rahim Safavi, argued that if Riyadh's 'military might was superior they could have defeated the Houthis in Yemen, but they have been defeated in three years of unequal war in Yemen' (Rahim Safavi 2018). In referring to naïveté and military inferiority, the Iranian military discourse was constructing two images to communicate to both international and domestic audiences. The first was that Saudi Arabia, Iran's Other, was militarily inferior and weak, and so the Iranian Self was characterized as superior. By using the trope of the war with Saddam, Iranian discourse purposefully sought to remind both Saudi Arabia and the international audience that the United States and Saudi Arabia could not defeat Iran. The second image was an attempt to represent Riyadh as a belligerent, hegemonic force that bullied a powerless Yemeni population while still managing to fail, even though they were supported militarily and politically by the United States. The representation of Saudi Arabia – and particularly MBS – as weak and naïve in military and political affairs was adopted across the spectrum of Iranian discourse genres.

This trope of Saudi military inferiority and MBS's political naïveté was even used by the Iranian foreign minister, Zarif. In a speech at an Iranian university, Zarif referred to MBS as 'simple-minded' and 'young' when it came to military confrontation with Iran. In mimicking Iranian military discourse, Zarif argued that Saudi Arabia'spent $67 billion, and this amount of arms purchases indicates how worried they are', highlighting that Riyadh and its allies 'are acknowledging that they aren't able to resist Iran' (Zarif 2018a). Comparing Tehran and Riyadh, the foreign minister argued that even 'Qatar has brought Saudi Arabia to its knees' stressing that Riyadh and its allies 'aren't even able to overcome Qatar' (Zarif 2018a). To the Iranians, Zarif, much like other Iranian officials, cast doubt on Saudi Arabia's ability to confront or even go to war with Iran, since Riyadh could not even defeat Doha, which was a fraction of the size of Iran. To the international audience, the Iranian official discourse through Zarif built on the military discourse of a weak Saudi Arabia that could not defeat states much smaller and weaker than the kingdom, thus highlighting the Iranian Self as far superior to the kingdom and Riyadh as no match for Tehran. Furthermore, by mentioning Yemen and Qatar, Iranian discourse represented its Saudi Other as a country that acted as a bully, preying on weak and defenceless states. This was a response to MBS's 'Hitler and Nazism' narrative, in which MBS and Saudi Arabia were framed as asserting their power aggressively over neighbouring states, with the implicit recollection of Hitler and his expansion towards Austria and Poland. Furthermore, the joint Saudi–US discourse on Iran and MBS's rhetoric against Khamenei and the Islamic Republic along with his calls for the Trump administration to increase the pressure on Iran pushed the entire spectrum of Iranian discourses to follow the same line and position on Saudi Arabia. Iranian discourse on Saudi Arabia was no longer divided between a pragmatic official discourse and a more polarized non-official discourse. Across the Gulf, MBS's programme of Islamic moderation was kicking in, allowing women to drive, limiting the power of the religious police, and permitting a relatively open society. However, this bid for image transformation and moderation would come crashing down with the news of a Saudi journalist's murder in the Saudi consulate in Istanbul.

Murder at the Consulate

The murder of the Saudi journalist Jamal Khashoggi on 2 October 2018 in Istanbul by a team of Saudi nationals who served in the Saudi security and defence services, erased all the gains MBS had made in his efforts to rebrand the kingdom's image (Al-Rasheed 2021: 94-95). For eighteen days Saudi authorities denied that Khashoggi had died in the consulate. On 19 October, the Saudi government acknowledged in a statement that Khashoggi's death was the result of a brawl in the Saudi consulate *(SPA 2018b)*. Although Khashoggi was a Saudi national once known for his pro-Riyadh positions, since 2017 he had been in self-exile, working as a journalist for *The Washington Post*. It was there that Khashoggi began being critical of the kingdom, and especially of the young crown prince (Riedel 2020). The international ramifications of this incident were so severe that it affected plans outlined by MBS for an investment conference, dubbed 'Davos in the Desert', and other ambitious endeavours such as Neom and international investment proliferation. This murder and its ramifications meant that many prominent participants backed out, hurting Saudi Arabia and MBS's image. This included a number of political leaders such as the US Treasury secretary, the heads of the World Bank and IMF, and the CEOs of major investment banks, among them HSBC, Credit Suisse, and JP Morgan Chase *(CNN* 2018; Gause III 2018*)*.

While the Khashoggi incident was primarily an international crisis, the murder erased the domestic achievements that the crown prince had used to rebrand his and the kingdom's image in international eyes. Indeed, the degrading of MBS's positive image began in the summer with a campaign of arrests that targeted Islamists and liberals (Roussos 2020: 122-123). In June 2018, the kingdom witnessed the lifting of the decades-old ban on women driving. Fulfilling promises he had made previously in his interviews with the international media, MBS relaxed the rules on gender segregation in public and supported measures for more public entertainment (Roussos 2020:124). The religious (morality) police, locally known as al-Hay'ah, had their powers restricted, and a general entertainment authority was set up to encourage more entertainment and tourism in the kingdom *(Reuters* 2019a*)*. While the steps that MBS took to implement these changes went ahead at a rapid rate, there were minor voices of opposition within the kingdom. However, these were not significant enough and did not materialize in the form of any domestic opposition. These voices included Islamists who opposed the rapid liberalization of society and liberal voices that campaigned for more freedoms, including the lifting of the driving ban (Roussos 2020:124). The carpet arrests of the members of both of these groups blemished the praise that MBS had amassed in the West. The Khashoggi murder in Istanbul only compounded these international criticisms and the negative image the crown prince had gained.

Although Trump continued to support MBS, the crown prince had become a polarizing figure in the US. The US Senate took a bipartisan stance and unanimously passed a resolution blaming the crown prince for the murder. The Republican senator Lindsey Graham argued that MBS 'has got to go' *(CNBC* and Higgins 2018*)*. The expert on Saudi affairs, Bruce Riedel, argued that 'to divert attention from the assassination the administration began to support modestly the United Nations mediation effort in Yemen for the first time' (Riedel 2020: 129). The European states equally condemned Saudi Arabia for the murder. British officials argued that relations between the kingdom and the UK were in jeopardy as they were built on 'shared values' (Stephens and Phillips 2021: 63). Germany questioned arms sales to Saudi Arabia, calling for more transparency and accountability on behalf of the kingdom and rejecting the Saudi statement on the murder *(DW* and Merkel 2018*)*. The Arab world overall expressed solidarity with Riyadh. The Arab League criticized the international call for sanctions against Saudi Arabia, accusing these states of 'achieving political goals [by] waving economic sanctions [about] as a policy or tool' (Arab League 2018). In addition, the GCC states accused the international community of 'slander' *(KUNA* 2018*)*, highlighting the position of the kingdom as an 'essential foundation for the security and stability of the Arab and Islamic worlds [and a] strong pillar of stability in the region' *(Dawn MENA 2018)*. While the West criticized and reprimanded Saudi Arabia for its actions, thereby alluding to MBS's irresponsibility as a domestic and international actor, the Arab world, on the other hand, sustained a discourse that protected the image of Saudi Arabia – and particularly MBS – as a legitimate Arab and regional leader in the'War on Terror'. While the Arabs towed the line of a Saudi discourse on the Self, the Western discourse on the kingdom resembled previous Iranian discourses on the Saudi Other's immaturity and irresponsibility.

Initially adopting a wait-and-see approach, Iran employed a pragmatic response to the Khashoggi incident, given Riyadh and the murdered journalist's polarized positions on the Islamic Republic. The foreign-ministry spokesman, Bahram Qassemi, remarked that Tehran would 'prefer to wait until more details and facts are revealed' (Ghasemi 2018a). However, Iran's neutral position shifted as the Trump administration announced sanctions targeting Iran for 'providing material and financial support' to the Taliban and what the US Treasury secretary viewed as Iran's 'distractive role in Afghanistan'. Saudi Arabia had welcomed the sanctions calling on the US to put the IRGC on its FTO list. The official Iranian discourse utilized the Khashoggi incident to respond to the sanctions on Saudi Arabia. The foreign minister, Zarif, argued that the sanctions were imposed 'to deflect from headlines on Saudi brutality in Istanbul [and] Yemen' (Zarif 2018b). Although Iran had initially made an overture towards Saudi Arabia by sticking to a neutral response and refraining from chiming in on the Western narrative regarding Riyadh and MBS, Saudi Arabia still maintained its polarized position towards Iran. It was only when Saudi Arabia had acknowledged and encouraged sanctions on Iran and placed the IRGC on the FTO list that the Iranian discourse shifted back to the Othering of the kingdom. Zarif's comments were aimed at the international community; they attached an image of brutality to Riyadh and MBS given the minister's comments on the war in Yemen and the latest incident in Turkey.

Similarly, Riyadh's support for sanctions against Iranian entities provided an impetus for other Iranian officials to exploit the Khashoggi incident in response to the US sanctions and to criticize Saudi Arabia, albeit without explicitly mentioning MBS. President Rouhani framed the Khashoggi murder as an act perpetrated with the blessing of the US, representing Riyadh and Washington as collaborators and partners in the crime. While chairing a cabinet session, Rouhani referred to it as an 'organized murder' and said that Saudi Arabia, 'without getting support from the US, would not dare to commit such a crime' (Rouhani 2018a). The relationship between Trump and Al Saud was also represented as resembling that of a crime syndicate. Furthermore, the Iranian representation of Saudi Arabia also drew on sectarian and historic narratives. Saudi Arabia was depicted as a kingdom of primitive nomads, a 'tribe ruling a country' that relied on 'a superpower to support them and commit such a crime', while Washington would 'not let any court take action' against Riyadh (Rouhani 2018a). In addition, this image of superpower-sponsored tribalism was followed by highlighting the Wahhabi nature of the Saudi state and its relationship to terrorist groups such as ISIS. Rouhani reacted to

Riyadh's support for US sanctions against Iran by the Iranian authorities supporting the Taliban. Reaffirming Tehran's accusations that Riyadh had created ISIS, the president argued that the act of 'committing such a crime', i.e. the murder and dismemberment of Khashoggi, reflected Saudi Arabia's 'misguided belief system'. The president was alluding to Wahhabism, which had 'created terrorist groups like ISIS in the region' (Rouhani 2018a) . Due to these 'crimes', the head of the Majles' foreign-relations committee, Alaeddin Boroujerdi, argued that the 'Saudi leadership should be tried [of] before an international tribunal', arguing that 'Saudi Arabia has shown its true face [in a] scandal of historic proportions' (Boroujerdi 2018).

A UN report dated 19 June 2019 called for investigations into the Saudi leadership, and most prominently into MBS. The UN special rapporteur, Agnes Callamard, issued a report holding the crown prince responsible for what was described as the 'deliberate, premeditated execution, an extrajudicial killing', in relation to Jamal Khashoggi (OHCHR and Calamard 2019). Adel al-Jubeir, now in his demoted role as minister of state for foreign affairs *(BBC 2018)*, argued that the report 'contains clear contradictions and baseless allegations' (Al-Jubeir 2019b). Although the kingdom confessed to a murder taking place at their Istanbul consulate, with suspects arrested and facing trial, the damage to Saudi Arabia's image in general and MBS in particular was grave. In late 2018, a Saudi public-relations campaign was underway to repair the damage in a bid to improve relations between the US and the kingdom. This included replacing its top diplomat in Washington with its first-ever female ambassador, a young princess named Reema Al Saud, in February 2019 *(News* and Gabrell 2019*)*. However, this relationship would be tested again as the US re-imposed all sanctions on Tehran in November 2018, which saw Iranian oil exports fall to near zero, further exacerbating tensions and pushing the region back to the dark days of the 1980s.

Tit-for-Tat: Tanker Wars 2.0

Since May 2019, Iran's tensions with the international community – and mainly with the US – reached their highest point since the 1980s Iran–Iraq War. The Trump administration's 'maximum pressure' campaign, launched in May 2018, not only strangled the Iranian economy; it also destabilized the Persian Gulf region. The US campaign against Iran witnessed some unprecedented moves, including the IRGC's designation as an FTO. It was the 'first time that the United States has ever named part of another government as [an] FTO'(Trump 2019b). As a result, the Gulf region witnessed a rapid escalation of events, including the deployment of US troops in the Strait of Hormuz, attacks on tankers in the UAE port of Fujairah, the shooting down of US and Iranian drones, the seizure of the tanker *Grace 1* with the help of British forces in Gibraltar, and the reciprocal Iranian seizure of internationally owned tankers, especially the British-flagged ship the Stena Impero (Stephens and Phillips 2021: 89) in a show of behavioural reciprocity. The incidents in the Persian Gulf involving Iranian and foreign tankers were reminiscent of a grave period in Iran's history, as they recalled memories of the 1984–1987 Tanker War during Iran's war with Saddam. Its 2019 equivalent was a near mimicry of the events that had taken place almost three decades before; these had included US support for Saddam and the protection of GCC oil tankers. It was also during this period that Iran suffered huge losses, and so Iranian officials, and particularly the IRGC, took the opportunity to highlight a positive image of the Iranian Self to bolster its power and military supremacy in the Persian Gulf in a bid to remind domestic, regional, and international audiences that the contemporary IRGC was not the IRGC of the 1980s. In other words, Iran was now a more experienced, self-sufficient, and advanced military and regional power, not one based on inexperienced young soldiers fighting a war of attrition. In addition, it was this Iranian Self that wanted to demonstrate to its Saudi Other that Riyadh was no match for Tehran since Iran was now able to confront the US face-to-face. This also allowed the Iranian official discourse to alleviate any domestic pressures and anxieties resulting from Trump's recent sanctions.

With another crisis brewing in the region, the Arab states moved to defuse tensions. Omani and Iraqi delegations visited Iran while trying to mediate between it and the US (Mousavian 2020: 73). However, an Emirati overture to the Iranians stands out. This included two secret visits by a UAE delegation to Iran, a joint UAE–Iran maritime meeting, and the partial withdrawal of UAE forces from Yemen. The Saudis also signalled a request for dialogue. All these measures came as Iran began employing a multitude of strategies to engage the international community in general and the US in particular, while trying to show that the Iranian negotiations with the US were not a result of subordination but an engagement between equals.

Designating the IRGC as a Foreign Terrorist Organization: Labelling Iran as a Terrorist State

In light of Trump's 'maximum pressure' campaign and the hawkish voices resonating from the US administration – namely Bolton's pledges to see Iranian regime change 'by the end of 2018' and more recent calls for a 'change in Iranian behaviour' – Iran's main strategy was of regime survival (Bolton 2018b, 2018a). The Iranian government adopted a position enhancing its ethos of 'resistance', which can be observed in four main discourses: a show of unity within the administration and between the different state and regime organs; the defence of Iranian borders at all costs; the sale and export of Iranian oil irrespective of the political situation; the need to treat Iran with dignity and respect, without humiliation; and the full removal of US sanctions.

These positions, which were apparent in Iran's state narratives, united all the organs of the Islamic Republic and were aimed at international and regional as well as domestic audiences. Iran's strategy of regime survival reflected a certain pragmatism and 'shape shifting' in areas ranging from the effective use of diplomacy to the active use of military intervention. The Iranians, according to Zarif, were applying 'strategic patience'. However, as the US maximized the pressure, Iran shifted positions and adapted to the evolving status quo (Zarif 2019c).The IRGC's designation as an FTO had wounded the Iranian Self and it was, in some sense, equal to branding the Islamic Republic and its government a terrorist state. The IRGC was now the embodiment of that Iranian Self, and so Iranian discourse set out to counter this image of terrorism, while bolstering the image of Iran's power, supremacy, legitimacy, and leadership of the Islamic world and wider region. This designation also had a significant impact on both the Iranian Self and its construction of the Saudi Other.

On 8 April 2019, US President Trump announced that the IRGC would be designated as an FTO because Iran's behaviour and actions were 'fundamentally different from those of other governments' (Trump 2019b). For the first time in history, the US officially applied such a hostile measure on a foreign state institution. The IRGC, a branch of the Iranian armed forces, was now simply labelled a terrorist organization in keeping with groups such as the Taliban and Al-Qaeda. The IRGC threatened 'reciprocal measures' if the US went forward with its designation, while warning that the region would 'lose its peace and quiet' (Jafari 2019). The Iranian response was swift; the Iranian Supreme National Security Council designated the US a 'state sponsor of terrorism' with the military operating under US Central Command (Centcom) in the Middle East and 'its affiliates' being designated a 'terrorist group' *(SNSC* and *Tasnim* 2019*)*. By default, any country associated with the US would be recognized as a terrorist-supporting state in the eyes of the Iranian government. This, therefore, made all the GCC countries supporters of and collaborators with a terrorist state. While the US sanctions were raising obstacles, impeding foreign investment in Iran, and pressuring the Islamic Republic's government to distance itself from the IRGC, the Iranian response was more of a show of unity and support for the military group. Even moderate voices in Iran – those that had supported the 2009 Green Movement and had been alienated since – expressed solidarity with the IRGC. Reformist members of the Majles and their reformist newspapers, critical of the hardliners, expressed their 'unity with the IRGC', going as far as labelling a reformist and moderate as 'also a [revolutionary] guard' *(Etemaad* 2019a; Sadeqi 2019*)*. Iranian lawmakers attended their parliamentary session at the IRGC fatigued. This reflected the fact that the Trump administration's stance had dissolved the divide between the moderate and hard-line camps, assimilating them into a unified front and effectively ending any domestic opposition since all groups and parties perceived the same threat to the state. This had put all Iranian parties in survival mode, a position last seen during the eight-year Iran–Iraq War and more recently since the MBS's rhetoric labelling Khamenei and the Islamic Republic as fascist and Nazi-like.

Khamenei quickly initiated precautionary measures and changed the posture of the IRGC. The probability of military confrontation increased. The former IRGC commander, Mohsen Rezaee, who had served at its helm during the Iran–Iraq War and was afterwards general secretary of the Expediency Council, threatened the US president: 'Mr. Trump, don't let your aircraft carriers come near IRGC vessels' (Rezaee 2019). A reorganization of the IRGC top cadres was ordered, ushering in a more hawkish group to lead it and its forces, in a sign of military readiness for war. General Hossein Salami, then the newly appointed commander of the IRGC, who was known for his vociferous rhetoric calling for the destruction of the USA and Israel, argued that he 'welcomed a war with the US' (Salami 2019b). Salami's threats of a regional war were not limited to the US. In 2018, Salami promulgated a threatening discourse towards Saudi Arabia and the UAE, warning that 'if you cross our red lines, we will surely cross yours', while underlining the 'storm the Iranian nation can create'. The IRGC top commander previously maintained that Saudi Arabia and the UAE had sought to foment 'plots and tensions', warning them of the 'revenge of the Iranian nation' (Salami 2019a). As a result, the threats of war against the US in 2019 sought to indirectly remind Saudi Arabia and the UAE that a war with the US – and especially if the GCC states collaborated with the US – could result in them also being in the line of fire. What was different in 2019 and the discourse of war at this point was the unity evident between the domestic political camps and popular support, particularly after the continual threats made by Trump and MBS, the designation of the IRGC as an FTO, and now the threat to Iran's oil tankers and economy. In addition, Iran's 2019 designation of the US Centcom as a terrorist organization and – by extension – its supporters, not only increased the threat of a regional war but also validated and justified it. The rising voice of the IRGC and a military discourse signalled a gradual shift to a more offensive position, especially with the US announcement of an increase in the number of its troops in the Persian Gulf and the end of the oil waivers, which effectively imposed a global ban on the importation of Iranian oil (*NPR* 2019; *Reuters* 2019b).

By employing the discourse of war, resistance, and a confrontation with the US, the Iranian state aimed to bolster its image to both the region and the Islamic world as the legitimate defender of Islam against the oppressor. This is reminiscent of the Khomeini-era war discourse where the posturing of the Iranian Self and its resisting of the 'Great Satan' represented Saudi Arabia as weak and subservient to the US, bringing into question the latter's legitimacy and leadership of the Arab and Islamic worlds. Since the IRGC was now being targeted, the result was a strengthening of its voice and the rise of military discourse. This also represented a shift within Iran, where in the past the military voice in the state's foreign policy played a largely supporting role. Targeting the IRGC meant that the Revolutionary Guards played a dominant and explicit role in Iranian foreign policy; this was a shift since the Ahmadinejad days, when the former president had introduced the IRGC into mainstream domestic politics.

Given the end of oil waivers, analysts remarked that no past sanction regime by the US administration or any other international actor had ever been this severe (Saikal 2021: 252). These punitive measures resulted in Iranian threats to close the Strait of Hormuz, with Iran edging away from its 'strategic patience' narrative. The US threats of Iranian regime survival pushed the Iranian administration across all branches towards a unified narrative. The Iranian foreign minister's diplomatic discourse reflected a shift from diplomacy to threats of retaliation that recalled Iran's hardliners, namely the IRGC. The Iranian strategy of regime survival had depended on oil sales, while its warning to the international community through its foreign minister was clear. Echoing the IRGC discourse of war, Zarif observed that Iran 'will continue to use the Strait of Hormuz as a safe transit passage for the sale of our oil' and if the US intended to prevent it from doing so, 'it should be prepared for the consequences' (Zarif 2019b). Warnings to Israel, Saudi Arabia, and the UAE were now part of a unified and dominant state narrative bringing together all the branches of the Islamic Republic. Zarif blamed the 'B-Team' – a reference to the US national security adviser, John Bolton, the Israeli prime minister, Benjamin Netanyahu, the Saudi crown prince, Mohammed bin Salman, and the UAE crown prince, Mohammed bin Zayed, as pushing for war between Iran and the US. Zarif's comments included the assumption that Trump did not want war, but the B-team may be 'plotting an accident anywhere in the region, particularly as we get closer to the [2020 US] election' (Zarif 2019b). Zarif's discourse constructed two frames: first, that there was a split within the Trump administration regarding a war with Iran; and second, that the administration was under the influence of Saudi Arabia, the UAE, and Israel.

Two weeks later, four ships were sabotaged in Fujairah port off the coast of the UAE. Two of the tankers were Saudi-owned and one was loaded with oil bound for the US (Torbat 2020: 303; Seliktar and Rezaei 2019: 238). Who had sabotaged the four tankers off the coast of Fujairah remained unclear. While the US blamed Iran or Iranian elements such as the Houthis, Hezbollah, or Hamas for the attacks, the UAE was more reserved (CBS 2019). The Iranian response was to remind the relevant players that an increase in foreign troops and pressure on Iran could lead to unforeseen circumstances and accidents. Zarif opined from New Delhi that Iran 'had previously predicted these sorts of activities aimed at escalating tension in the region' (Zarif 2019a). In addition, Zarif's warnings to the region aligned with the IRGC narrative. This therefore demonstrated that the IRGC had begun to communicate its discourse to the international community through Iran's chief diplomat, underlining the growing IRGC role in Iranian foreign policy. The next day marked a distinct escalation in events. A rocket launched by the Houthis struck a power station in Saudi Arabia's city of Jizan, while an explosive-laden drone attacked the major East–West oil pipeline spanning from Aramco in the Eastern Province to the western oil terminal of Yanbu.

On the same day as the attacks on the UAE port, the Iranian parliament had a closed session with the IRGC commander and his deputies to discuss the 'serious' chances of war with the US. Taking a pragmatic two-track strategy, the Iranian stance was that although the IRGC's 'strategic analysis is that there is not going to be a war', in the event of one, 'Iran will not be defeated and it can end the war in the region victoriously' (Falahatpisheh 2019). Khamenei stressed that 'there will not be any war', and he commented pragmatically that Iran would choose 'the path of resistance' (Khamenei 2019b). The Iranian actors adopted a holistic narrative, suggesting that the UAE, Saudi Arabia, and Israel, along with John Bolton, were aiming to 'drag Trump into a war' (Jamali 2019), which echoed the statement by Zarif in April (Zarif 2019b).

Overlapping with the tanker-sabotage incident and attacks on Saudi oil installations, on 20 June the IRGC shot down a US drone, marking a watershed moment in Iran–US tensions since the Iran–Iraq War, although days prior to the drone incident US officials had explicitly mentioned that 'the United States does not seek conflict with Iran' (Centcom and Shanahan 2019). The discourses emanating from the regional tensions were sending four main messages to the domestic audience, to the international community and, predominantly, to Saudi Arabia and its regional allies. The first was an image of strength projected in the fact that Iran had the military power to defend its borders and confront a superpower – and by default, regional states such as Saudi Arabia, who were militarily inferior to the Islamic Republic. Second, that Iran was a pragmatic, responsible, regional, and international actor that looked for peace before war, thus countering the image of an expansionist warmonger as propagated in the Saudi discourse. Third, that Iran was the protector of the region and stood up to the oppressor, thereby maintaining an image of the Self that was initially constructed in the post-revolutionary discourse of the war between the oppressor and the oppressed. Iran's discourse, therefore, aimed to remind the Islamic world of its central contention, namely its protection of the *mustaza ʿafān* (the oppressed). And fourth, to its people, that Iran could no longer restrain itself given that Trump's 'maximum pressure' campaign was taking a toll on Iran's economy.

As Ray Takeyh has argued, Iran now had 'a narrative of success' that allowed it to posture domestically and make an excuse for negotiating with the US from a position of strength and not weakness (Tekeyh 2019). As Trump backed away from striking Iran, thus avoiding an all-out war, Iranian actors strengthened their posture regarding territorial defence and sovereignty. The attack on the most advanced US drone by an Iranian-manufactured missile defence system was used to bolster regime legitimacy, while underlining Iran's regional strength and prestige. Iranian actors promulgated a central narrative: 'if they start a war, they will not end it' (Akbari 2019). The IRGC claimed that it could have shot down a plane behind the drone that carried thirty-eight military passengers, but it decided not to. The US president made a case for cancelling a retaliatory strike ten minutes before giving the order (Mason and Heavey 2019). The attack, Trump argued, could have resulted in the death of 150 lives, and it would have been an unbalanced response. He went as far as to thank Iran for not shooting down the spy plane with thirty-eight personnel in it *(Washington Post* 2019*)*. The US state department stressed that they would do 'everything to de-escalate tensions with Iran'(Hook and *Reuters* 2019b*)*. On a visit to Saudi Arabia a day after the incident, Brian Hook, of the US state department envoy on Iran, stressed that 'Iran needs to meet diplomacy with diplomacy', and that 'Trump is very willing to sit down with the [Iranian] regime' (Hook and *Reuters* 2019a*)*. Iran's gradual shift away from 'strategic patience' had begun to take effect. This strategic shift was not independent of American rhetoric; however, it was not limited to it either.

Two weeks later, the British Royal Marines – on the US's request – detained the Iranian vessel *Grace-1* on suspicion of carrying oil to Syria, which would have violated EU sanctions. Iran vehemently denied this and the narrative from all Iranian actors was unified in labelling Britain's act one of 'piracy' and calling for 'retaliation' (Hatami 2018; Khamenei 2019a). Iran's Supreme Leader vowed that since the 'British snatched our ship, like pirates ... this act will not be left unanswered', and there would be a response 'at the appropriate time and place' (Khamenei 2019a). The military response came in a form of warning to the British that, before any reciprocal action would be taken, Iran was attempting to 'persuade the British to accept that they have made a transgression and to rectify it' (Yazdi 2019), i.e. to release the Gibraltar-held vessel. John Bolton congratulated the British move as 'excellent news' (Bolton 2019). While Rouhani and Zarif took a diplomatic route to ending the tension, the IRGC adopted a confrontational stance. Zarif and the British foreign secretary, Jeremy Hunt, attempted to negotiate the release of the *Grace-1*, with the latter seeking Tehran's guarantee that the tanker would not supply oil to Syria *(Guardian* 2019*)*. The Iranians declined, as this might set a precedent and give an impression of weakness that would lead to a decline in their support for Bashar al-Assad.

In a tit-for-tat response, on 19 July the IRGC seized a British tanker, the *Stena Impero*, shrouding the events in a discourse of sovereignty and legality. Zarif informed the British that the seizure 'was due to maritime violations and [was] requested by the relevant port authorities' (Bolton 2019). Like the Grace-1, the British vessel had to undergo a legal process in Iran for its release. Iran was attempting to send a clear message to regional and international audiences, and especially to the US; one highlighting the image of the Iranian Self, namely that the Islamic Republic controlled the Strait of Hormuz and the waters of the Persian Gulf, and that it was the region's legitimate leader and security guarantor. To the Arab states of the Persian Gulf, specifically Saudi Arabia and the UAE, the intention was to warn them that their tankers could also face the same consequences. The Iranian line leading up to the tanker seizure was clear: 'If we cannot export our oil, no one else will'1 (Rouhani 2018b). To the rest of the world, and specifically to the remaining signatories of the JCPOA, it served as a reminder that if they did not move fast enough to alleviate the US 'maximum pressure' campaign and the zero-oil policy strangling Iran, then matters could take a more dangerous turn. The Iranian discourses resulting from the tanker seizure included an explicit discursive construction of Iranian leadership and legitimacy. On the other hand, these discourses also sent an implicit message to Saudi Arabia, namely that only Iran could guarantee the security of the region and Saudi Arabia's oil exports, and Riyadh's livelihood was being held hostage by Iranian regional power. This stress by the Iranian leadership and the state's regional power innately constructed Saudi Arabia as dependent on foreign and external powers, whereas Iran could see to its own safety and security needs.

The IRGC-led seizures had strong domestic connotations; both the hard-line and moderate-leaning press celebrated them. A headline in the hard-line newspaper *Kayhan* read 'A tanker for a tanker' *(Kayhan* 2019*)*, while *Etemaad*, a newspaper known for its support of moderates, ridiculed the UK, with a headline

1. First announced by Ali Akbar Velayati, the Supreme Leader's adviser for international affairs, Valdai Talks, 13 July 2018

labelling it 'Little Britain'*(Etemaad* 2019b*)*. This came as the IRGC attempted to win hearts and minds in Iran. The effects of the economic strangulation caused by the US sanctions and natural disasters in the south of Iran (Lemon 2019), threatened the image of the IRGC and its promises to rebuild flood-stricken areas. With the seizure of the *Stena Impero* and Iran's tactic of behavioural reciprocity, the Islamic Republic was trying to implement its strategy of regime survival on all levels, while maintaining its domestic image of strength and stability.

US–Iranian Tensions and Their Implications for the Middle East

The Iranian narrative towards the Saudis shifted as Trump's 'maximum pressure' campaign paralysed the Iranian economy. The IRGC's designation as an FTO, the strangulation of Iran's oil exports, and the increase in military pressure on Iran led even the most pragmatic voice in Iran, Javad Zarif, to argue that, in reference to Saudi Arabia and the UAE, if there is 'hostility in the region I don't think anybody will be immune from it' *(*Zarif and *Lobelog* 2019*)*. Iranian rhetoric cautioned the GCC states that Trump's presence at the helm was temporary and that assisting him in offsetting the shortage in Iranian oil could have ramifications. Rouhani had previously criticized the GCC states, warning them that they did not 'realize that it means clear enmity with the Iranian people' (Rouhani 2019b). Faced with this rhetoric, the UAE and Saudi Arabia shifted their narrative towards Iran. Given the recent events in the Persian Gulf and the Strait of Hormuz, along with the alleged Iranian-backed attacks by the Houthis on UAE and on Saudi oil installations and airports (Rand and Miller 2020: 59), both states came out against a war with Iran, with more evident signs of rapprochement coming from the UAE.

In a shift, the Arab media aligned to Iran featured articles suggesting that the UAE had sent a secret delegation to the Islamic Republic to discuss a possible way out of the impasse in the Gulf and Yemen. Contrary to previous information strategies, the press leak was first sent to an Arab source with links to groups funded by or allied with Iran. The leak was then quoted by the Iranian newspapers, and it was later confirmed by an Iranian ex-official with close links to the administration. On 11 July, the newspaper *Al-Akhbar* stated that diplomatic sources close to the Iranian administration had revealed that days after the Fujairah incident, a high-level Emirati security delegation visited Iran twice with an 'irresistible offer' *(Al-Akhbar* 2019*)*. The proposal had three components: the normalization of relations between both states, a joint maritime-security framework to ensure the secure flow of oil from all the GCC countries and Iran, and a readiness to immediately withdraw from Yemen. The offer, according to the newspaper, was rejected, with Iran arguing that they had nothing to negotiate because the UAE had 'crossed a red line'. Not long after the press release, the news was promulgated to a primarily Arab audience through widely watched Arabic news networks *(*Al-Mayadeen and Mousavi 2019*;* Al-Jazeera and *Dehghan* 2019*)*. A former Iranian diplomat, Amir Mousawi and the former defence minister and current adviser to Khamenei, Hossein Dehghan, alleged that the UAE had sent an official coastguard delegation to Iran to discuss maritime security. This development coincided with news of UAE forces withdrawing from Yemen, abandoning the Saudis to fight the Houthis alone (Barany 2021: 287). The Islamic Republic strategized its response and discourse construction. By using the Arab media outlets, Iran sought to communicate its message directly to Arab audiences in general and the GCC in particular. In addition, it constructed the Iranian Self as a powerful entity with a regional upper hand, exploiting the narrative that the UAE had now sought to negotiate with Iran and break away from both its GCC ally, Saudi Arabia, and from the US. Furthermore, Iran also constructed an implicit image of the Saudi Other as isolated and left alone to tend to its predicaments. This was evident as the Iranian actors highlighted the alleged UAE–Iran talks and their relationship with the war in Yemen. To the Arab audience, Iran constructed its Saudi Other as weak and isolated, as it was losing both a war and its grip on regional power.

In response to the Iranian narratives, both Emirati and Saudi officials emphasized their wish to reach a political solution to avoid hostilities with Iran. The UAE's minister of state for foreign affairs, Anwar Gargash, argued that both Saudi Arabia and the UAE did not seek confrontation with Iran (Gargash 2019). Similarly, the Saudi ambassador to the UN, Abdullah Al-Moualimi, claimed that they did not want a war with the Islamic Republic and signalled that the Yemen war should be ended (Gargash 2019). One of Riyadh's most hostile critics of Iran, the minister of state for foreign affairs, Adel al-Jubeir, stated that 'Saudi Arabia does not want a war with Iran' *(BBC* 2019). This Saudi discourse was a departure from the confrontational discourse represented by MBS in 2017, which called for 'taking the war to Iran' amid joint comments with the US administration that Iranian extremism should be fought. The official Saudi discourse was now presenting a more pragmatic Self, one that sought regional peace and stability. Furthermore, the official Saudi and UAE discourses constructed a counter-image to Iran's implicit representation of an isolated Saudi Arabia and a fragmented GCC. Also, while the GCC states were unanimous in that they did not wish for any military confrontation with Iran, they differed in their relationship with the state and the maritime security of the Persian Gulf. This caused a schism within the GCC. On the one hand, officials from Oman, Qatar, and the UAE met with the Iranians to discuss maritime-security cooperation, while on the other hand Bahrain and Saudi Arabia supported a US initiative to create an international naval force to guarantee shipping-lane security in the Gulf. The results of Trump's 'maximum pressure' campaign thus far had had adverse effects on the region. However, instead of Iran being further isolated from the GCC, the results of the Iranian discourses conveyed a pragmatism and willingness to resolve matters through dialogue. This appeared to have influenced its relations with some of the GCC states as they put their security and economic interests before war and aggression. For Saudi Arabia, these signs of pragmatism would not be displayed by its diplomatic officials, as would become evident in September 2019 when the Houthis attacked the heart of the Saudi oil industry, Aramco. This resulted in a shift in MBS's position on and discourse towards the Islamic Republic.

The Aramco Attacks: Saudi Arabia's 'Black September'

On 14 September 2019, the Aramco oil installations were attacked with a barrage of missiles and drones, in what the Israeli analyst Uzi Rubin labelled Saudi Arabia's 'Black September' (Rubin 2019). The Yemeni Houthis took responsibility for the attack. The international response was mixed, ranging from accusations that the missiles and drones were Iranian-made to allegations that Iran was directly behind the attacks. The latter view was epitomized by the remarks of the US secretary of state, Mike Pompeo (Pompeo 2019). At first, Trump stopped short of blaming Iran. However, by 18 September, the US president had stated that 'it was "looking like" Iran was behind the attack' (Brown and Trump 2019). In a telephone conversation with MBS, Trump offered to support 'Saudi Arabia's self-defence'(Axelrod and Trump 2019; *SPA* 2019c).

The Saudi response was marked by pragmatic silence at first. Both the king (al-Saud 2019c) and crown prince (*SPA* 2019a) did not blame Iran or the Houthis until 16 September, but they represented the attack as a 'dangerous escalation, not only towards the kingdom, but the entire world' (al-Saud 2019c). The Iranian reply was an outright rejection of the US and Riyadh's claims. Zarif argued that because the US had 'failed at maximum pressure', it was 'turning to maximum deceit' by blaming Iran (Zarif 2019d). Rouhani shifted the blame to the US and its regional allies. In an initial response to Press TV, the Iranian president argued that the US and Israel were involved in the war in Yemen by 'supporting the UAE and Saudi Arabia, transferring weapons, and providing intelligence' (Rouhani 2019a), without mentioning the attacks on the Saudi oil facilities. However, in a later press conference with his Turkish counterpart, Rouhani framed the attacks as a reciprocal measure, emphasizing that the 'Yemeni people are exercising their legitimate right of defence [while these] attacks were a reciprocal response to aggression against Yemen' by Saudi Arabia and its allies (Rouhani and *Reuters* 2019). The Iranian discourse in response to the Aramco attacks had two main strands. The first entailed a distancing of the state from the Houthi missile attacks by countering the US narrative of Iranian involvement and constructing the war in Yemen as a collaboration between Saudi Arabia, the US, and Israel, implicitly drawing on the discourse of Saudi subservience. Second, the attacks were legitimized in the official Iranian discourse by highlighting the Houthis' right to self-defence, thereby representing Saudi Arabia as a belligerent force attacking a defenceless Yemen.

The monarchy's silence may have been due to ongoing investigations. However, even after the initial investigations, MBS's response clearly backtracked from his generally aggressive tone towards Iran. Indeed, the Aramco attack saw a clear reversal of his 2017 rhetoric of 'not wait[ing] for the battle to take place in Saudi Arabia ... we are working to take the battle to them in Iran' (*Asharq-Al-Awsat* 2019). While keeping in step with the US 'maximum pressure' discourses, supporting Pompeo's allegations that Iran had carried out an 'act of war', the crown prince now argued that a 'political and peaceful solution is much better than the military one' (al-Saud and *CBS* 2019). The shift in monarchical discourse could be attributed to a fear that a war with Iran would not only have a severe impact on global energy prices, but it would also jeopardize and possibly end MBS's 2030 Vision, with the Aramco initial public offering being the jewel in his crown. Moreover, Trump's position after the attacks changed in that he stopped short of being willing to go to war in defence of Riyadh, arguing that 'I don't want war with anybody', signalling his willingness to meet the Iranian president, even after alleging that the evidence was pointing towards Iran's involvement (Trump 2019c). Consequently, the monarchy took a 'back seat' role in discourse production, giving the cue for both state actors and the media to promulgate the discourse towards Iran, the former being led by Adel al-Jubeir and the latter by the Saudi press.

One could argue that the role of both the media and al-Jubeir in representing Iran in the public sphere worked in synergy, whereby both drew on the image of Saudi Arabia and Iran with the media focused on the domestic and Arab audience, while al-Jubeir concentrated on the international community. The main discourses concentrated on representing an image of Saudi legitimacy, strength, and stability, while projecting Iran as an international pariah. In the period immediately following the Aramco attacks, al-Jubeir used the trope of the'maximum pressure' campaign to construct an image of Iran as an international outlaw that was calling for tougher actions and criticizing the EU's position on negotiation with the Islamic Republic given that 'appeasement with Iran does not work' (Al-Jubeir 2019a). A narrative calling for a more forceful approach to dealing with Iran was evident in al-Jubeir's reflection on Iran, where he characterized it as a 'deceivingly hegemonic and bipolar state'; one that 'projects an image of wanting to talk to the world', while seeking 'to expand the revolution and take over the region', in an implicit reference to the IRGC (*CNN* and Al-Jubeir 2019).

Building on al-Jubeir's narrative, the domestic press remarked that the Saudi public 'was not surprised at the Iranian attacks' but was surprised at 'the softness, flexibility, and tolerance of the crimes of this hateful regime' *(al-Jazirah 2019b)*. The newspaper *al-Jazirah* represented the attacks as the 'expansionist policies of the Persian State', alluding to Iran's ambition to recreate a hegemonic Persian Empire that would 'target the stability of the kingdom ... and disrupt the superpower status of Saudi Arabia and its development plans' *(al-Jazirah 2019b)*. Even as MBS softened his rhetoric and tone, calling for a political resolution to matters, the media discourse drew on an image of Saudi pragmatism rather than fear of war with Iran. The newspaper *al-Riyadh (al-Riyadh* 2019d*)* constructed the monarchy's stance using an image of a pragmatic Self and the kingdom as a responsible international actor. The Saudi audience were asked to view the monarchy's calls for dialogue as reflecting the 'wisdom of leadership' emanating from a kingdom that was in a state of law, and that strives for peace on the basis of strength, not on weakness *(al-Riyadh* 2019d*)*.

The advent of the protests in Iraq and Lebanon in October coincided with the period immediately after the Aramco attacks and marked by preparation for the Aramco IPO. The protests were used by the Saudi press to further shape the rhetoric and polarized representation of Iran. While the Saudi state remained silent overall, the media led the discourse construction, with *al-Riyadh* hoping *(al-Riyadh* 2019c*)* 'for an end to Iranian interference in the Arab' world. In so doing, the media brought back the 1980s Saddam era's anti-Iranian rhetoric. In addition to the usual 'Persian hegemony' language, the Saudi media discourse divided the Shi'i population into Arab Shi'i and Persian Shi'i groupings, representing the Shi'a in Iraq and Lebanon as now seeking liberation from 'Tehran's penetration into Iraqi politics ... [the] exploitation of shrines in Iraq [and attempts] to infiltrate the Iraqi street, by spreading sectarian [and] divisive rhetoric' *(al-Riyadh* 2019b). The picture of Iran portrayed by Saudi Arabia to the Arab masses was one of plight and suffering *(al-Jazirah* 2019a; *Asharq-Al-Awsat* 2019) of the Arabs caused by a 'hegemonic sectarian Iran that seeks to export its revolution and infiltrate the Arab masses by hijacking the Arab Spring' *(al-Jazirah* 2019a). As the Arab protests increased and gained momentum, on 14 November the Iranian masses protested across one hundred cities, emboldening the Saudi discourse further in the use of the Saudi Self and other narratives. The editorials in *al-Riyadh* and *al-Jazirah* represented *(al-Jazirah* 2019c) the Iranian people as victims of a regime that was oil rich but kept its people poor *(al-Riyadh* 2019a). By employing superior–inferior dichotomies, Saudi editorials represented Iran as inferior vis-à-vis a wealthy Saudi Arabia that, courtesy of MBS's vision, was being propelled towards great prosperity.

The Aramco IPO emerged as a cornerstone for both Saudi economic liberalization and Vision 2030, therefore holding a crucial position in the Saudi self-image. The Saudi discourse construction once again shifted to the control of the state as evidenced by the monarchical discourse. The king's message to the Saudi public reflected an image of legitimacy, stability, and the resistance of the Saudi Self versus an Iranian enemy as its other *(al-Saud* 2019b). A narrative of piety and Islamic leadership was deployed and Islamic credentials were promulgated, reflecting a monarchy 'implementing the law of God and adhering to the Islamic faith' *(al-Saud* 2019b). The Saudi leadership was defined as 'preserving security and stability', while the kingdom's status as a responsible international state was highlighted as 'abiding by the United Nations Charter'. To the Arab and Islamic world, the discourse of the Saudi Self highlighted its image of leadership, namely one that enjoyed the 'firm support of the joint Arab and Islamic world' *(al-Saud* 2019b) .

Saudi Arabia's message on Iran was two-tiered. Domestically, oil production and revenues were stable, and the kingdom was working with the international community to 'immediately halt blatant Iranian interference in the internal affairs of other countries'*(al-Saud* 2019a). After the IPO price had finally been announced, a more explicit discourse was propagated by Saudi Arabia at the GCC summit *(al-Saud 2019a)*. Press rhetoric was synonymous with the state: the 'Iranian regime continues its hostile actions to undermine security, stability, and support for terrorism', being matched by a call for an end to Iran's aspirations by working 'with the international community to stop the interference of this regime ... secure energy sources, safety of waterways and freedom of marine navigation'*(al-Saud* 2019a). As the Aramco IPO went forward and Saudi Arabia attained one of its goals, its discourse towards Iran began to shift once again back towards a polarized rhetoric. Domestic developments within the kingdom in addition to the continuing protests in Iraq and Lebanon created a political vacuum that opened up new fronts in the rivalry between Iran and Saudi Arabia, along with opportunities for dialogue in order to thaw relations. This would become evident as the year was ending and Trump began the final year of his presidency.

'Severe Revenge': Iran's 9/11

The year 2020 began with a watershed event that shook not only the Middle East, but the world at large. On 3 January 2020, the commander of the Iranian IRGC Quds Force, General Qassem Soleimani, and the head of the Iran-aligned Iraqi armed group Kata'ib Hezbollah and member of the PMU, Abu Mahdi al-Mohandis, were assassinated in a drone strike at Baghdad airport after disembarking from a flight from Damascus. The Iraqi prime minister, Adel Abdulmahdi, stated that Soleimani was in Iraq on a diplomatic mission, delivering an Iranian response to an Iraqi initiative to establish détente and rapprochement between Tehran and Riyadh *(Al-Monitor* and Rozen 2020*)*. The days that followed put the whole world on edge, as narratives of a possible *World War III* surged across popular media platforms (NY Times 2020).

Trump's reaction was to justify the attacks as a 'defensive action' designed to 'stop a war' *(Washington Post* and Trump 2020*)*. In addition, Trump demonized the deceased Soleimani, defining him as 'a monster' and arguing that he was 'planning a big attack and bad attack for us', based on alleged intelligence that Soleimani and his local allies 'were looking to blow up our embassy'. Reasoning further, Trump argued that 'somebody died, one of our military people died. People were badly wounded just a week before' *(Politico* and Trump 2020*)*, referring to an attack on the K-1 Air Base in the Kirkuk province of Iraq on 27 December 2019. The US accused the Iranian-aligned Kata'ib Hezbollah, a subgroup of the Hashd Al-Sha'bi (Iraq's PMU) of being behind the attack *(Times* 2019*)*. The casualties included the death of an Arab-American civilian contractor and the injuring of four members of the US military and two Iraqi security personnel (Garland 2019). A later attempt to storm the US embassy compound in Baghdad on 31 December further agitated the US. The slogans 'Death to America' and the sight of rocks and Molotov cocktails (Cafiero 2021: 133) recalled for Iran's adversaries the early days of the revolution and the storming of the US embassy in Tehran. On the same evening, Trump stated 'Iran will be held fully responsible for lives lost, or damage incurred, at any of our facilities. They will pay a very BIG PRICE! This is not a Warning, it is a Threat' (Trump 2019a). The 'price' came less than three days later. The response from Iran, however, was on a different scale and magnitude as, according to the Islamic Republic, the US also had a 'price' to pay.

The assassination of Soleimani came as a severe blow not only in terms of removing the architect of Iran's security apparatus in the MENA region, but also to the image of the Iranian Self. Domestically, Soleimani was the image of the model Iranian; he had been decorated with titles such as maktabī (one who follows Islam in its totality), *inghilabī* (revolutionary), a soldier of Ahl-al-Bayt and the

'Hidden Imam' (*'sarbāz-i Imam'*). Khamenei had bestowed on him the title 'living martyr' (*'Shahīd-i Zinda'*). Regionally, the commander reflected Iran's military prowess and leadership, and he was known as the liberator of Iraq and Syria from ISIS besides being the US and Israel's arch-enemy. As a result, the Iranians instantaneously vowed to take revenge and this was visible across all the different Iranian discourse genres.

In the first response, Khamenei immediately pledged 'severe revenge' (*'intiqām-i sakht'*), arguing that Soleimani's 'efforts and path won't be stopped by his martyrdom' (Khamenei 2020b). The message served three purposes. First, Khamenei was managing the blow to Iran's image given that his main confidant and military commander had been assassinated by Trump. Two days prior, Khamenei had mocked Trump's 'threat' by charging that 'You can't do anything,' and that the US president was not 'logical' since Washington's 'crimes in Iraq, Afghanistan … have made nations hate you' (Khamenei 2020a). Second, in domestic terms, Iran had been challenged and its image of Islamic leadership and resistance to US hegemony and forty years of revolutionary anti-imperialist slogans were now brought into question. Third, Iran's image among its regional allies was also compromised. The assassination of Soleimani and the Iraqi PMU deputy commander, al-Mohandis, had to be avenged, as any failure to retaliate would risk Iran losing its status and image of leadership, not only in Iraq, but also in the different countries in which it had strongholds and regional allies, such as Lebanon, Syria, and Yemen. In addition, Iran's rivals and adversaries, such as Israel and Saudi Arabia, were also waiting for an Iranian response and failure to act would construct an image of Iranian weakness and hollow propaganda. In a television statement, Khamenei stressed that 'the jihad of resistance will continue with a doubled motivation' and that what was about to come would be nothing short of the 'definite victory [that] awaits the fighters in the holy war'(Khamenei 2020a). The Guardian Jurist assured Iran's domestic audience, as well the country's allies and rivals, that 'Soleimani's martyrdom will make Iran more decisive [in its resolve] to resist America's expansionism and to defend our Islamic values'(Khamenei 2020a). Therefore, Iran immediately began managing the image of the Iranian Self through official, media, and religious discourses and narratives, all of which played to one tune composed by Khamenei, namely the supra-discourse of 'severe revenge'. At the beginning, this was only concerned with the Iranian Self; the Saudi response came later and was ushered in by Trump's response.

Zarif labelled the act 'an extremely dangerous and foolish escalation'. While pointing the finger at Washington, the Iranian foreign minister claimed that, 'The US bears responsibility for all consequences of its rogue adventurism' (Zarif 2020a). Moreover, he said this while highlighting the image of Soleimani as an 'effective force fighting Daesh [ISIS], al-Nusrah, Al-Qaeda et al' (Zarif 2020a). In so doing, Zarif implied a juxtaposition whereby in assassinating Soleimani, the US was aiding terrorism. The Iranian narrative was that the commander was responsible for the defeat of terrorism and his death was tacitly framed as a sigh of relief for ISIS and other terrorist groups. Drawing on the discourse of resistance and terrorism, Zarif labelled the incident as having been carried out by 'American terrorist forces' sanctioning their 'brutality and stupidity' (Zarif 2020a). He echoed the Supreme Leader's resistance and anti-American imperialism discourse in saying that 'assassinating Commander Soleimani ... will undoubtedly make the tree of resistance in the region and the world more prosperous' (Khamenei 2020a).

Iran's military apparatus vowed a 'crushing revenge'. The defence minister, Amir Hatami, remarked that the 'unjust assassination [would result in] revenge from all those involved and responsible for his assassination' (Hatami 2020). The IRGC discourse was more explicit. General Gholamali Abuhamzeh, the commander of the IRGC in Iran's southern province of Kerman, threatened both the wider region and the West. In relation to the latter, the general argued that the 'Strait of Hormuz is a vital [maritime] thoroughfare for the West [with] a large number of American destroyers and warships cross[ing] the Strait of Hormuz, the Sea of Oman and the Persian Gulf' (Abuhamzeh 2020). Regionally, 'thirty-five vital American targets in the Middle East have been identified and are within the reach of the Islamic Republic'(Abuhamzeh 2020). While implicitly threatening regional states such as Saudi Arabia, the IRGC discourse explicitly warned that 'Tel Aviv – the US's heart and life – is also within our reach'(Abuhamzeh 2020). Iran's military discourse attracted familiar threats from Washington. Trump argued that if Tehran were to strike US interests and assets, then '52 Iranian sites ... very high level & important to Iran and the Iranian culture [that] represent the fifty-two American hostages taken by Iran many years ago' (Trump 2020). The US was warning Iran not to attack and to de-escalate. Such threats were increasing the likelihood of regional armed conflict. Although Iran's warning was aimed at the US and Israel, it was also a challenge to the GCC states, particularly since they host numerous American bases and were within easy reach of Iran. Furthermore, the targets would not only be attacked from Iran.

Iran's regional allies could also have joined any counterstrike, especially since the war in Yemen was ongoing, Hezbollah was in Syria and South Lebanon, and the Iranian-aligned armed groups in Iraq also sought revenge for their commander. Initially, Iran's discourse concentrated primarily on the crisis management of its image after such a symbolic and central figure was assassinated. By drawing on tropes of martyrdom and severe revenge, the Iranian domestic discourse sought to assuage its domestic image before the Iranian people. Another message was directed at Iran's regional allies. By employing tropes and narratives relating to both Israel and regional targets while vowing for revenge, Iran attempted to assure its allies that it would also seek revenge if one of them was attacked, in tropes aimed at reinforcing Iran's image of legitimacy, leadership, and strength. To its regional adversaries, particularly Saudi Arabia, the Iranian discourse of the Self and tropes based on attacking regional targets were all perceived as a veiled threat in case they thought Iran was weak, and so they decided to launch an attack against the Islamic Republic.

The events that followed led to a chain reaction. In a blow to the US, the Iraqi parliament that convened on 5 January voted in favour of 'work[ing] towards ending the presence of all foreign troops on Iraqi soil'(*Al-Jazeera 2020*). Much to Washington's dismay, it was Iran's first win as one of the aspects of its 'severe revenge' was to push the US out of the region. The vote – although boycotted by the Kurdish and Sunni political parties – was a rebuke of the airstrike on Iraqi soil and the breaching of its sovereignty. The US and its allies moved to convince the Iraqi prime minister to rethink his decision, citing the harm it would bring Iraq in its war against ISIS. However, Iraqi officials were said to be preparing the necessary paperwork for the withdrawal of all foreign forces from Iraqi soil *(CNN 2020)*. Another act of 'severe revenge' was largely also a bid to recalibrate its image, in that Iran resiled itself from the JCPOA restrictions it had agreed to in 2015. Zarif announced that that 'there will no longer be any restriction on [the] number of centrifuges'(Zarif 2020b). Iran had now decided to drastically increase the number of its centrifuges, thus allowing it to enrich larger quantities of uranium, at higher concentrations, and in a shorter timeframe. Furthermore, Iran used Soleimani's assassination to alleviate the mounting pressure inflicted by Trump's withdrawal from the JCPOA. Moreover, Iran's response also had domestic, regional, and international messages. First, to the Iranian people, Iran wanted to show that its response to the assassination would not go unanswered and that Tehran was not intimidated by the United States. In addition, Iran represented the incident and the image of Soleimani as being larger than just revenge for a commander's assassination. For Iran, Soleimani represented a beloved commander, a fallen hero, but implicitly there was more at stake; he was the embodiment of the Islamic Republic and its achievements in the region, particularly after the fall of Saddam in 2003. As such, Soleimani's assassination was woven into the discourses of the Iranian Self regionally. This was evident in the actions the Iranian allied groups in Iraq undertook to hasten the departure of the US forces from there, particularly since an Iraqi commander, Abu Mahdi al-Mohandis, had also been assassinated and because Soleimani was on an official visit to Iraq and was an adviser to the Iraqi government. Therefore, Iran attempted to project its regional power and represent its revenge for this incident as not just revenge for Soleimani's assassination but also for the transgression committed against the Iranian Self and the whole region by promising to push the US out. To the international audience, Iran aimed to show that it was a mature actor that respected international treaties and laws; however, once a treaty was broken, Iran would respond in equal measure. In this case, Trump had not only reneged on the JCPOA but also, in Iran's eyes, breached the sovereignty of Iraq and assassinated a governmental representative. Therefore, the Iranian response aimed to represent itself as patient and pragmatic only until its sovereignty was infringed upon. In this case, the assassination of Soleimani was an infringement on the Iranian Self. Against the backdrop of these chaotic events, Iran's GCC neighbours – and particularly Saudi Arabia – were silent, observing the reaction and discourse of the Iranian Self.

The View from Riyadh: Distancing and De-escalation

The Saudi response to the Soleimani assassination could be defined as bifurcated. Saudi officials distanced themselves from the attack and called for calm and de-escalation *(Asharq-Al-Awsat 2020a)*. Non-state actors appeared on foreign news networks to discuss the Saudi position in relation to Iran, taking over the role of the official Saudi discourse on Iran and its slain commander. Media outlets, represented by editorials, once again took front seat in projecting the Saudi discourse on Iran while promulgating familiar anti-Iran narratives and tropes. Riyadh's official public response was cautious and calculated; the statement from the ministry of foreign affairs framed the attacks as a consequence of the 'escalation of tensions and terrorist acts [in] fraternal Iraq' *(SPA 2020c)*. Without mentioning Iran in the statement, Riyadh framed the assassination as a result of 'terrorist acts [carried out by] terrorist militias' *(SPA 2020c)*, in an allusion to the pro-Iran PMU groups. However, Riyadh had one main issue in sight – 'the importance of self-restraint'. This was a message echoed by Adel al-Jubeir who reflected on the need to 'ward off all acts that may lead to aggravating the situation, with unbearable consequences' (Al-Jubeir 2020). Indeed, the Saudi discourse after the assassination of Soleimani can be divided into two aspects. First, there was an official discourse that focused on restraint and regional stability, thereby promoting an image of the Saudi Self as a responsible regional actor. Second, there was a domestic discourse highlighted by media editorials that focused on the Iranian Other, drawing on tropes of terrorism, regional expansion, hegemony, and sectarianism.

It should be noted that al-Jubeir's message was not a customary act, and it came as part of a crisis-management strategy following a call between the US secretary of state, Mike Pompeo, and MBS. Pompeo 'thanked the crown prince for Saudi Arabia's steadfast support [and] for recognizing the aggressive threats posed by the ... Quds Force' (Pompeo 2020). The Saudis feared that Pompeo's message would aggravate the Iranians and lead them to believe that Riyadh was complicit in the operation. The Saudi reaction was swift. The foreign ministry issued their own official summary of the call in which they emphasized the 'efforts being exerted to defuse tensions in the region', while calling for the maintenance of 'peace and stability' *(Arab News 2020)*. At the ministerial level, the official Saudi narrative was marked by calls for de-escalation and regional stability. However, the Saudi calls for restraint did not suffice. Speaking on condition of anonymity, a Saudi official stressed that Riyadh 'was not consulted regarding the US strike'*(Arab News 2020)*. In hope of averting another attack such as the one that targeted Aramco in 2019, both the king and the crown prince made calls to Tehran's friends in Iraq. The king contacted the Iraqi president, Barham Saleh, while the crown prince contacted the prime minister, Adel Abdulmahdi. Both had one message, namely 'the need for measures to defuse tensions'*(SPA 2020b)* and to 'calm the situation and de-escalate tensions' *(SPA 2020b)*. A few days later, at a press conference held after a summit involving Arab and African foreign ministers from states that border the Red Sea and the Gulf of Aden, the Saudi foreign minister, Faisal bin Farhan al-Saud, assured the region in general and especially his guests that the kingdom was 'very keen that the situation ... doesn't escalate any further' *(SPA 2020a)*. However, Saudi Arabia's domestically manufactured discourse featured a different narrative.

The Saudi domestic media outlets celebrated the assassination of Soleimani with jubilation. A few hours after the assassination, the locally printed newspaper, *al-Riyadh*, published an article titled 'The General of Blood'*(al-Riyadh 2020)*. The article had three main themes. The first was to define the identity and role of Soleimani; the second theme was to represent the attack as an end to Iranian regional power and ambitions; and the third, to construct an image of an Iranian regime agent and aggressor in a bid to denigrate and vilify both Soleimani and the state. Reminding the reader of 'Iranian regional policies', Soleimani was described as having a 'black history' that was 'full of conspiracies [and the] killing of innocents'*(al-Riyadh 2020)*. Borrowing from themes of Iranian hegemony, the editorial discourse framed the slain general as the state's 'beating stick' and the enforcer of 'Iranian policies to impose control' over the region. Furthermore, the Saudi discourse assured its readers that 'with the death of General Soleimani' the Islamic Republic has 'lost its most important pillar', arguing that his death was 'a shock for the regime', which would now encounter difficulties in 'implementing its expansionist policies' *(al-Riyadh 2020)*. This vilification was not limited to Iran's regional activities, with al-Riyadh responding to Iranian discourse highlighting Soleimani as a 'man of the people'. The editorial argued that Soleimani's 'iron and fire' was used against his own people *(al-Riyadh 2020)* . The Saudi domestic discourse framed Soleimani as a hitman for the state, i.e. as someone who 'suppress[ed] the demonstrations in Iran . . . dealing harshly with demonstrators . . . who were his own people' *(al-Riyadh 2020)*. Consequently, the image of the Iranian government as a tyrannical dictatorship was projected through the image of Soleimani as its 'beating stick', as he was accused of being responsible for carrying out operations against 'his own kind'*(al-Riyadh 2020)*. The editorials took on the role of denigrating Iran on behalf of the Saudi state. Where Riyadh may have attempted to distance itself from any Iranian repercussions or reprisals, the editorials constructed the narratives on Soleimani and Iran's regional role. These editorials not only constructed an image of the Iranian Self through the image of Soleimani, but they also attempted to create a counter-image to the Iranian Self that was constructed by Tehran's international and domestic discourses, including tropes focusing on demonizing the Iranian Other as they employed tropes representing the people of the Arab region as victims of 'Iranian interference'.

The London-based *Asharq-Al-Awsat* (2020b), with a readership that spans the Arab-speaking world, promulgated an editorial discourse that was more explicit in constructing an image of Iranian hegemony by employing tropes of the 'Persian Empire' and 'sectarian war' (*Asharq-Al-Awsat* 2020b). Labelled as a 'mistake invented by the Iranian regime', Asharq-Al-Awsat argued that while the Islamic Republic wanted Soleimani as a 'symbol of its empire', after the US strike the assassination had become a 'symbol of Iran's defeat' (*Asharq-Al-Awsat* 2020b). To the Arab reader, Iran was represented as a chaotic destroyer of the Arab world. Its 'four-star general' who was once a 'mysterious ghost for years [had] appeared in battle zones' and become a 'public figure [through] destruction' (*Asharq-Al-Awsat* 2020b). Stopping short of explicitly employing sectarian terms, the editorial discourse drew parallels between the stardom that Soleimani had acquired, and his camaraderie and command of 'armed young men and bearded sheikhs in the Hashd, Hezbollah and 'Asa'ib, with photos of him published from the 'destroyed streets of Aleppo, at the gates of Iraqi Mosul, and in the Lebanese district of Baalbek' (*Asharq-Al-Awsat* 2020b). This demonization strategy was also employed to construct an image of Iranian hypocrisy. *Asharq-Al-Awsat* argued that while Soleimani tried to 'paint a benign image of himself in public', he was 'the most dangerous Iranian man the world has known'. Furthermore, juxtaposing 'the images of Soleimani with children' with the events in the Arab Spring, the Saudi editorials emphasized the trope of carnage and death. *Asharq-Al-Awsat* argued that Soleimani was responsible for 'mass killings in Syria', 'burying thousands of families alive in their homes', and 'founding militias that sowed terror' in Arab cities(*Asharq-Al-Awsat* 2020b). Through their editorials, Saudi Arabia aimed to highlight, promulgate, and remind the Arab-speaking world that while Iran sought to commemorate a hero and project an image of a heroic general internationally, to Saudi Arabia and the Arab and Sunni world, Soleimani was an enemy and a 'war criminal' (*Asharq-Al-Awsat* 2020b). In a possible bid to prepare the remedy before the ailment, Saudi editorial discourse had begun its propagation and defamation of the image of Soleimani before Iran held its million-man funeral proceedings that spanned multiple Iraqi and Iranian cities. It was now Iran's turn to construct and represent the image of Qassem Soleimani and what he meant to Iran, its self-image, and the world. These tropes would construct and frame Iran through discourses of sectarianism, hegemony, expansionism, and the thirst of Arab blood. First implemented during the post-revolutionary Khomeini era, particularly during the Iran–Iraq War, these discourses were then recycled and promulgated during both states' subsequent rivalry, including the Lebanon–Israel War of 2006, the Gaza War of 2009, the events following the Arab Spring, and Iran's increasing regional influence in Lebanon, Syria, and Yemen.

Mourning a Hero: Iran's Million-Person Funeral

In a scene that shook the region, a million-person march turned out across Iran to mark the funeral. The processions began in the Iranian cities of Ahvaz and Mashhad followed by Qom and Tehran. The mourners observed the funeral as if it were the Ashura holiday, wearing black and beating their chest to recitations of *nawha* and *ta'ziya* (mourning poetry). The chief slogan, however, was 'Death to America'. Iranian officials were not bashful in shedding their tears. Khamenei wept as he said his last prayers standing over the coffin. Soleimani's successor, Esmail Gha'ani, emphasized Tehran's message to Iran's domestic audience and the world at large, namely that 'Iran would seek revenge . . . God the Almighty has promised to get his revenge, and God is the main avenger', promising that 'certainly, actions will be taken' (Ghaani 2020).

A mythical status had been bestowed on Soleimani even before his death. Iranian discourse, especially its conservative-leaning variants, labelled the commander the 'protector of the shrine' of Sayeda Zainab ('*Mudāfi'-i Haram*'). This image was intertwined with his war with ISIS in defence of Shi'ism and the role he took with Hezbollah and Hamas in fighting Israel. To the Iranians, Soleimani was a man who defended their borders from ISIS and kept Iran safe as the Iranians compared their country's stability with their regional neighbours such as Iraq, Afghanistan, Libya, and Syria. This image was imperative in projecting

Iran's power and strength domestically, regionally, and internationally. Soleimani's assassination unified the Iranian domestic discourse and, by default, the image of the Iranian Self. Regardless of their political direction or religious leanings, the Iranian people created a common front in their commemoration of and reaction to the incident. Indeed, the reaction to the US strike against Soleimani recalled the ISIS strike in Tehran in 2017 and the designation of the IRGC as an FTO in that all political and religious groups were unified in their stance. This incident was another part of the chain of events that helped to fill and mend the gaps and schisms left after the 2009 Green Movement. For the youth, Soleimani was either compared with Imam Hussein if they were religious, or with Rustam from the Shahnameh, the Book of Kings *(IRNA 2020)*, if they were more secular. The assassination of Soleimani recharged these images of Persian and Islamic mythology. Iranian domestic discourse, particularly the editorials and Friday sermons, drew mainly on tropes of Ahl-al-Bayt and Ashura. These discourses, ranging across all Iranian editorials and clerical sermons, drew parallels between the assassination of Soleimani and the martyrdom of Imam Hussein in Karbala in his revolt against Yazid, in a battle that is framed as a war between good and evil, Islam versus infidelity *(Kufr)*, and the oppressor versus the oppressed *(IRNA 2020)*. This juxtaposition and allegory helped to construct the image of the Iranian Self, where Soleimani was Imam Hussein and Trump and his regional allies were Yazid and his army, in an implicit reference to the GCC states, particularly Saudi Arabia. Domestically, the images from the Ahl-al-Bayt narrative focused on the Supreme Leader and his significant and prominent relationship with Soleimani. This imagology included Imam Ali and his confidant and general, Malik al-Ashtar. – the former was positioned alongside the Supreme Leader, Ali Khamenei, and the latter alongside Qassem Soleimani *(ISNA 2020)*. These images and tropes were predominant in constructing and representing the image of Iran in its domestic discourse, eternalizing the image of the hero, legitimizing the state's regional activities, restoring Iran's image of power and its projection, and recharging its ongoing revolution. In addition, these images formed the focus of speeches by the elite, especially by the Supreme Leader, which were made after Iran decided to begin its acts of 'severe revenge' on the US.

Slapping the Enemy: Operation Martyr Soleimani

On 8 January Operation Martyr Soleimani was executed at the same time of the day that he had been killed. Missiles were fired at the US bases in Iraq. According to Pentagon officials, an estimated dozen missiles were launched from Iran targeting the Ayn al-Asad airbase in western Iraq and an airbase in Erbil, in the Kurdish region in the north. The Iraqi military, however, claimed that a total of thirty-nine missiles were launched *(Independent 2020)*, and they branded the mission a success. However, conflicting reports emerged with the US downplaying the attack, while Iran emphasized the operation's success. Branding them 'American terrorists', Iranian state television claimed that eighty members of the US armed forces had been killed and equipment and helicopters destroyed. The immediate comment from Iran's officials conveyed both deterrence and a warning. Zarif's message to the US was two-tiered. In a bid to demonstrate Iran's image as a law-abiding and responsible international actor as opposed to the US and Trump, the attacks were framed as 'proportionate measures in self-defence', with an emphasis on Iran's legal right 'under Article 51 of [the] UN Charter' (Zarif 2020c). Furthermore, Iran highlighted that it 'does not seek escalation or war' and it drew attention to Tehran's right to 'defend ourselves against any aggression' (Zarif 2020c). The military apparatus also warned the US against any retaliation. The IRGC stated that, if the US retaliated, then the war would become regional as Iran would strike Israel *(Guardian* 2020*)*. Here, Iran aimed to incorporate an image of a powerful military, while underlining an image of pragmatism and restraint. These images of power, restraint, and pragmatism can also be observed in other Iranian discourse genres.

On 9 January Khamenei gave his first public speech since the assassination of Soleimani and the subsequent missile launch at US targets in Iraq, with both the date and the place being of great significance. He addressed citizens in the holy city of Qom, marking the anniversary of the city's 1978 protests against the Shah. Khamenei's sermon was an opportunity to reemphasize the identity and image of Iranian Self by representing Soleimani as the model revolutionary (*Inqilābī*). The speech was also a chance to remind the Iranian people that Soleimani was a symbol of Iran's continued struggle and commitment to Khomeini's revolution that had emerged from the seminaries of Qom. The main intention of the speech was to project an image of an active revolutionary state, while emphasizing popular support for this revolution both domestically and regionally. Perhaps the most interesting part of the speech was that Khamenei did not name, criticize, or demonize Iran's regional rivals, including Saudi Arabia. The focus instead was on a unified Islamic enemy, namely the US and Israel.

In his speech Khamenei described Soleimani using superlatives, constructing the image of a courageous and wise martyr. Labelling him as an 'honourable commander of Islam and Iran', Khamenei sought to embody an image of Iranian leadership in Soleimani with an appeal that resonated throughout the Islamic world (Khamenei 2020c), implying that Soleimani's death was a loss not just to Iran but to the Islamic world as a whole. The Supreme Leader emphasized that the qualities that this 'Islamic Commander' possessed were not only evident on the battlefield but also in politics, stating that 'Hajj Qassem would bravely enter the middle of danger' at times of war, where 'he acted wisely, with thought, and logically'. Soleimani was also epitomized as a political tactician as, 'In the area of politics, he enjoyed courage and wisdom at the same time' (Khamenei 2020c). Iran's focus on the image of Qassem Soleimani, framed from a mythical and religious perspective, was an attempt to underline the significance of Soleimani's persona not only to Iran but also to the Islamic world. Iran, since its revolution in 1979, had represented itself in its discourse as a continuation of Imam Ali's caliphate. Therefore, the assassination of Soleimani was equated to the martyrdom of an infallible. In other words, he was a modern-day Imam Hussein while to Khamenei – the modern-day Imam Ali – he was a modern-day Malik al-Ashtar.

Such religious imagery and comparisons were not a form of hyperbole or emotional constructions, instead, they reflected the psyche of the Islamic Republic and the centrality of Shi'i narratives of Imam Hussein's martyrdom and Soleimani's assassination to Iran's self-image and ideology.

This image of religious zeal, courage, and political prowess was used to highlight Iran's regional power, leadership, and defence of the Islamic world. The Supreme Leader's speech conveyed these images, while also defining the centrality of the image of Soleimani domestically, regionally, and internationally. Also, by underlining the centrality of Soleimani's assassination, the official Iranian discourse emphasized the Iranian Self and its regional status by focusing on tropes of 'US–Zionist hegemony', Palestine, the fighting of oppression, as well as its others, such as Israel, the US, and Saudi Arabia (Khamenei 2020c). Khamenei contended that 'Martyr Soleimani's wisdom and courage neutralized all the illegitimate plots of the US in West Asia [and all] the enemies of Hajj Qassem are well aware of this fact'(Khamenei 2020c). Soleimani's 'impact' on Israel, Palestine, and Lebanon was also used to highlight Iran's image of Islamic leadership and 'resistance to Zionism' (Khamenei 2020c). Through the discourse of the 'oppressed versus the oppressor', the Supreme Leader drew on events such as Operation Cast Lead in 2009, arguing that 'the great man empowered' the Palestinians and 'enabled a small region like Gaza to stand up to . . . Zionists [such] that the Zionist regime was forced to request a ceasefire after just forty-eight hours'(Khamenei 2020c). On the matter of Iraq, the ayatollah framed Iran's role as a protector of Iraqi democracy and rights as well as exploitation by the US. Khamenei argued that 'Soleimani defeated US plans' in Iraq, since the 'Americans wanted Iraq to be either like the Tāghūt (tyrannical Pahlavi) regime, or some other such regime as the Saudis, whom they say are like milking cows'(Khamenei 2020c). This defeat was due to the 'help' Iran gave Iraq through Qassem Soleimani, as he encouraged and prepared 'devout Iraqi agents, brave Iraqi youth and the religious authorities in Iraq to stand up to this plot' (Khamenei 2020c).

Iran's role in Lebanon was also underlined. Tehran's image as a liberator and defender was projected through the image of Soleimani. According to Khamenei, the commander was the person who had stood up to the 'Americans [that] wanted to deprive Lebanon of . . . independence' and stopped them by creating Hezbollah, which is now the 'hand and the eye of Lebanon'(Khamenei 2020c). Khamenei was implicitly saying that had it not been for Iran, Hezbollah would not have been created, and Iran then sent Soleimani to 'make them more powerful day after day'. Without Iran, Lebanon would have ended up like Palestine and the Golan Heights in Syria (Khamenei 2020c). Khamenei was explicitly attributing responsibility to the Iranian leadership for keeping states such as Lebanon free from foreign invasion, while implicitly representing other regional states, such as Saudi Arabia, as weak, as being 'milked' for their wealth, and thus as subservient to 'Americans and the Zionists'. These discourses were foregrounded in earlier incidents going as far back as the Iran–Iraq War in the 1980s, which initiated the first construction of the Saudi Other as subservient to the US and Israel. The discourses were later utilized during the Ahmadinejad era, particularly during the civil war in Iraq in

2005, the Hezbollah–Israel War in 2006, and more recently in reaction to MBS taking the war to Tehran and labelling Khamenei as Hitler and Iran as a Nazi state.

Focusing on the domestic populace, Khamenei sought to restore the image of the revolution and the identity of the state, arguing that 'certain people have portrayed the revolution as dead in Iran' and stressing that the 'martyrdom proved that the revolution is alive' by pointing out the marches and public turnout (Khamenei 2020c). Indeed, the identity of the revolutionary state that, according to Khomeini's ideals, was based on fighting oppression and defending the oppressed, and fighting the 'Great Satan' and 'Zionism' was also brought into the discourse. In his speech Khamenei argued that it was the US that 'portrayed this great Mujahid, Commander … as a terrorist', in reference to the US designating the IRGC as an FTO, thus resulting in his assassination. Iran's response was framed as 'severe revenge' whereas the US was 'slapped', and Khamenei argued that military actions were not enough (Khamenei 2020c). Khamenei was alluding to the fact that avenging Soleimani would not be restricted to armed conflict, while Iran's ultimate goal was to 'end the presence of the US in the West Asian region'.

By drawing on tropes of sedition and US hegemony, Khamenei framed the US presence as an enemy that 'brought war to this region, disputes, seditions, destructions' (Khamenei 2020c). Refraining from threatening any regional state or government, Khamenei defined what constituted an enemy in Tehran's mindset while presenting Iran – and by default, the Iranian Self – as a pragmatic and peaceful regional state and actor. Khamenei pushed the bellicose rhetoric aside and stated that 'We should know the enemy … I should explicitly say the enemy means America [and] the Zionist regime' (Khamenei 2020c). In an implied reference to regional rivals such as Saudi Arabia, Khamenei argued, 'Some of the governments, inside or outside the region, should not be regarded as a part of the enemy as long as they haven't made a move in favour of the enemy [while] those regional or outside powers who have sometimes made remarks against us as our enemy are not regarded as our enemy' (Khamenei 2020c). Khamenei was tacitly extending an olive branch, implying a chance for regional détente. The image of Iran as standing up to the US and fighting a superpower with the intention of pushing the US out of the region was accompanied by an image of benevolence and an attempt to reassure the region that Tehran had no intention of regional destabilization, nor had it planned similar military operations against other countries, namely the GCC states, such as Saudi Arabia. Khamenei's olive branch may have been a response to Saudi Arabia's silence in its official discourse and Riyadh's call for calm. Khamenei's discourse towards Saudi Arabia was more concerned with highlighting the Iranian Self rather than with attacking the Saudi Other. By constructing the Iranian Self as a stabilizing regional factor and a neighbour, the Supreme Leader's discourse emphasized Soleimani's role in combating the US regional presence and the role of Iran's 'severe revenge' in pushing the US out of the region. By focusing on the image of the Self and the US as its Other, Iran was implicitly representing itself as a more powerful and capable nation than Saudi Arabia, thereby constructing Iran as the true leader and defender of the Islamic world, while degrading Saudi Arabia's status as a legitimate leader of the Arab and Islamic world.

Conclusion

The promotion of Mohammad bin Salman to the position of crown prince brought with it a plethora of events and incidents that impacted both Iran and Saudi Arabia. On the domestic level, the murder of Jamal Khashoggi was a setback for MBS and his endeavours to rebrand the image of Saudi Arabia, attract foreign investments, and fulfil his Vision 2030. For Iran, Trump's aggressive stance was compounded by Riyadh's encouragement to withdraw from the JCPOA and apply Trump's 'maximum pressure' regime on Tehran. With MBS's rise to power, many events occurred and a barrage of discourses, narratives, repertoires, and motifs were employed in the representation of the Self and the Other in Iranian and Saudi discourse. Furthermore, with different events came different shifts in the discourses representing the Self and the Other. For instance, as MBS characterized the Islamic Republic and its Supreme Leader as Nazis and Hitler, respectively, the Iranian discourse in response to these tropes was limited to representing MBS as a naïve, immature actor who is not familiar with world politics and international relations. However, as Saudi Arabia became more proactive in promoting US sanctions on Iran, particularly the IRGC as an FTO, Iranian discourse was unified across all genres in their explicit denigration of Saudi Arabia. These tropes of denigration included the highlighting of the issue of Khashoggi and its association with images of Saudi tribalism, Wahhabism, and discourses of terrorist support (e.g. for ISIS), and a vocal shift from a position of silence before Trump's 'maximum pressure' campaign.

For Iran, a second shift came about as Tehran applied 'behavioural reciprocity' in reaction to its oil exports dropping to near zero levels, the deployment of US troops to the Persian Gulf and the Strait of Hormuz, the shooting down of a US drone, along with the seizure of tankers that led to a second Tanker War reminiscent of the 1980s war with Iraq. Since the IRGC was targeted, its voice within Iranian foreign policy was strengthened, as was its discourse manufacture and representation of the Self. Tropes of war, resistance, and confrontation with the US and Iran's regional image of leadership was represented in the IRGC discourse. These discourses found their origins in the Khomeini-era war, posturing the Self as combating the 'Great Satan' and representing the Saudi Other as subservient to the US. Saudi Arabia's shift, on the other hand, came as the Aramco oil installations were attacked by the Houthis. As Trump threatened Iran with military action, his threats did not materialize, much to the disappointment of Riyadh. Hence, it is here that MBS began backtracking from his bellicose discourse towards Iran, calling for dialogue and mentioning amicable regional relations.

Iran's watershed moment was the assassination of the commander of the Quds Force, Qassem Soleimani, which had a severe impact on the image of the Iranian Self. Through the supra-discourse of 'severe revenge', the retaliatory attacks on the

US base in Iraq, and a million-person march across Iran, Tehran sought to manage its image of the Iranian Self. This crisis management included using tropes of martyrdom and narratives of an Israeli conspiracy, while vowing for revenge. Therefore, the Iranian discourse aimed to reaffirm and assure its allies and its domestic populace of the Islamic Republic's legitimacy, leadership, and strength. In response to the Iranian discourses of the Self came a cautious silence from Saudi officials and a distancing from the events. However, the task of discussing this incident was left to the editorials. The Iranian domestic discourse projected images of religious zeal, courage, and political prowess, to highlight Iran's regional power and leadership and emphasize Soleimani's value to Iran and the Islamic world. The Saudi editorial discourse attempted to counter these images. While Iranian discourse used the tropes of Ahl-al-Bayt, comparing the assassination of Soleimani to that of Malik al-Ashtar, Imam Ali's general – and by default, representing Ayatollah Khamenei as the 'Imam Ali of our times' – the Saudi editorial discourse negated Soleimani's heroic image. By employing a sectarian narrative, Saudi domestic discourse reminded the Arab-speaking world that Soleimani was an 'enemy' and a 'war criminal' who had targeted 'Arab-Sunni' states. These demonizing tropes and narratives and the mutual representation of the Other would not cease with the assassination of Soleimani. Trump's departure from the White House would bring with it another assassination, this time of 'Iran's Oppenheimer', that is, the 'father of its nuclear programme', Mohsen Fakhrizadeh, and a new round of mutual Othering.

Chapter 16

CONCLUSION

This book has explored the 'representation of the Other' in Saudi–Iranian relations between 1979 and 2020, analysing discourse in three main genres: elite political speech, religious discourse in the form of Friday prayer sermons, and media discourse as represented by newspaper editorials. The approach taken to examining Saudi–Iranian confrontation and Shi'i–Wahhabi strife is diachronic. The multiple epochs in focus covered the tenures of six Iranian presidents and two supreme leaders, and the reign of four Saudi kings. These periods allowed me to examine discourses of Othering during periods of significant change in relation to the internal political situation in the two states and their bilateral relations. The periods examined included the turbulent years immediately after the revolution, including the hajj of 1987 and the death of Khomeini in 1989, the post-war period of détente and rapprochement in the Rafsanjani and Khatami presidencies (1988–2005), the gradual return of rivalry as witnessed in the Ahmadinejad presidency (2005–2013) after the fall of Saddam, and the Rouhani tenure (2013–2021), which witnessed the tumultuous period of the Arab Spring and its consequent regional wars.

This book makes several important arguments. The first is that Saudi–Iranian Othering was overwhelmingly responsive to changes in political relations between the two states, and the images each side (or Self) had of the Other drew on different historical backgrounds, cultures, religious structures, and beliefs. This in turn formed a vocabulary that each state mobilized in different ways in national, regional, and international contexts. Second, there is a relationship between political, economic, and international events and the changes in the discourses used, which reflects shifts in Iranian–Saudi relations. While differences in political and religious opinions may possibly construct negative representations of the Other, they may not necessarily inhibit the construction of a positive discourse. Furthermore, the discourse in both states across all three genres, demonstrated a close intertextual relationship managed by political elites. Mutual Othering discourse also drew on deeply rooted religious and political symbolic repertoires, utilized for given state agendas and for both internal and external consumption. Finally, in this book, I argued that Othering discourses operating on a domestic level were intended to bolster regime legitimacy and public loyalty to the ruling system through the creation of 'the necessary enemy', while externally aimed discourses operate in a similar way to enlist support for the strategic claims of the Saudi and Iranian states.

Overall, this work makes a novel contribution to the existing scholarship on the Saudi and Iranian relationship on different levels. First, it marks a theoretical and methodological shift away from realist and neorealist, security-orientated, geopolitical perspectives. In so doing, it moves towards a deeper analysis of national-level institutions in both Iran and Saudi Arabia, including of their roles and agency. Knowledge of these nuances helps understand the mutual 'Othering' that took place and how political decisions unfolded. Crucially, this approach is possible as primary sources from both Arabic and Persian have been extensively used. Second, it contests the popular and generalized perception of the Saudi–Iranian relationship as religious or sectarian in origin and intention, arguing instead that it is based on political motives, and that religious and sectarian identities are employed as tools for 'Othering'. Finally, an interdependency emerges in the narratives: the Self–Other articulations are relational, and the positions promoted by official institutions on both sides emerge as a reaction to earlier comments and positions taken.

However, no study is without limitations. Access to data was the most problematic issue. Both states apply restrictions and stringent laws regarding the dissemination of data. The data analysed during the post-revolutionary period lacked many of the Saudi Friday prayer sermons. This made a more extensive analysis of religious discourse in Saudi Arabia for some periods difficult to complete. Similarly, archival problems, mainly related to the absence of some issues of the newspaper *al-Madina* between 2006 and 2008, may have had a slight impact on the Saudi editorial discourse analysis. Third, an analysis of further data from Iran and Saudi Arabia would result in an improved overview of the extent of the rivalry and discourse construction in both countries. This further data would include local Friday sermons from different cities. These sermons were not broadcast on television, satellite, or radio, but they have been archived locally or online on the websites of the Friday imams.

What is the importance of this book's findings? First, they identify a paradigm shift away from conventional geopolitical and sectarian paradigms, which have been dominant to date. These conventional notions contend that the relations between the two states are governed primarily by a competition over regional control and the spreading of Shi'ism or Wahhabism in the Islamic world. The framework of Othering suggests that religious and sectarian identities remained a propaganda tool, yet the nature of the agenda promoted by both sides was political in nature. This points to the need to go beyond the conventional geopolitical paradigm of religious rivalry. The Othering framework also marks a shift in the longstanding understanding of 'rivalry' in the Saudi–Iranian setting, where the relations between these two sides were dependent on each side's perceptions of the other, rather than embodying any innate or deeply grounded ideological fervour.

The findings have policy implications too. First, they inform us of complexities and of a need to observe the triad of political, religious, and media institutions in both countries, which reflect elite policymaking perspectives and preferences due to the intertwined nature of the three respective institutions. Equally, the approach taken here allows us to understand how information circulates in political and public spheres, while also identifying how the Self and the Other are not only constructed in discursive spheres but also influence shifts in policies and regional politics. To finish, let us take a broader look at some of the theoretical insights and patterns that were manifest over the forty-year period considered here. We begin with the function and nature of Othering, before considering themes and repertoires, and finally actors, audience, and discourse generation.

The Function and Nature of Othering

In Iranian and Saudi discourse, Othering is a phenomenon related to political rivalry and religious conflict. This Othering was based on the Iranian and Saudi leaderships' respective discourses of legitimacy. It relates to political rivalry as during this period the two states competed for the leadership of the Arab world, mainly through the discourse of the Palestinian–Israeli conflict and the Arab–Israeli peace process. Furthermore, religious rivalry was evident in competition over the leadership of the Islamic world. Therefore, when contention and rivalry is visible in Iranian–Saudi discourses, the image of the Self is defined through a comparison with the Other. The Self is defined along ontological and existential lines: the former deals with identity and the nature of being, while the latter is concerned with the survival of the Self. In 1979, the Islamic Revolution as well as the siege of Mecca exaggerated these ontological and existential notions in both states.

When the Other's legitimacy and leadership is negatively constructed, the legitimacy and leadership of the Self is inherently emphasized in a positive light. Again, this works on both ontological and existential levels. Ontological constructions concern the identity of the political propaganda, whereas existential constructions use religious narratives and polemics to define and bolster the image of the Self and the Other. In this case, the issue of religion and sectarianism developed as the relationship between the two states shifted, namely, religion – and sect to be more precise – was not an area of contention in the early days of the post-revolutionary period. What began as a narrative of acceptance and mutual respect later shifted to discourses characterized by animosity and denigration.

The themes set by the leadership also interrelate in an interesting way. In Iran, the main themes and narratives are set by the valī-yi faqīh. In Saudi Arabia, the king sets the themes, although this responsibility shifted when the king was incapacitated due to poor health. More recently, under King Salman, the crown prince has taken a proactive role given the number of positions he holds within the leadership.[1] In both states, the themes and narratives directed towards the Other

---

1. The positions that MBS holds include the deputy prime minister, minister of defense, chairman of the Council of Economic and Development Affairs and chairman of the Council of Political and Security Affairs.

were constructed and disseminated in a top-down fashion. The representation of the Other was developed by the elite and disseminated to different layers of society as state propaganda through religious and media discourses. One key difference is that in Iran, the media maintained some level of independence from the elite narrative and showed considerable differentiation among media outlets, whereas Saudi editorial lines maintained the elite discourse. Moreover, in Iran, with the rise of semi-official news networks and social and online media platforms, a more diverse set of voices appeared with various political leanings and affiliations, catering to reformists, conservatives, and the military.

The structure of both states also played a major role in the relationship between their respective political, religious, and media discourses. Iranian discourses were inseparable from one another, mainly due to the structure of the state and authority. The valī-yi faqīh set the main discourses and the other genres referenced or built on this by using different Islamic and political narratives. The Self has an inseparable legitimacy of political and religious authority because the position of the Supreme Leader – the Guardian Jurist – combines religious and political leadership. The discourse in Saudi Arabia was interrelated. The state structure resulted in the ulama giving the king legitimacy. This was a dominant characteristic in Saudi Arabia until the ascension of King Salman to the throne and the rise of MBS, when the latter moved to rebrand the image of the kingdom, shifting from ultra-conservatism to hyper-nationalism, thus sidelining the role of the ulama. The king mainly set the tone of the discourse, and this was continued by other elite elements. The religious discourse did not directly promulgate the discourse of the elite or build on it; however, it sought to sustain and support it through discourses of legitimacy and leadership. The role of the media, in contrast, promulgated the discourse of the elite.

The Discursive Practice of Othering: Themes and Repertoires

Iranian–Saudi Othering exhibits two main supra-themes that have recurred throughout all the epochs analysed.[2] These include subservience to Western and 'Zionist' powers, and sub-themes based on Arab-Islamic hegemony, such as the revival of the Persian empire through Iranian expansion in the Middle East. Consequently, these two supra-themes gave rise to different sub-themes, tropes, and repertoires, which were political and religious in nature. Between 1979 and 1983, the sub-themes of Saudi Arabia as a puppet of the US and Zionism were first constructed. The Al Saud were described as a 'neo-Shah regime', one submissive to their 'American masters'. Such explicit denigration, at least at this intensity, was not observed in the post-Khomeini era until 2010, when neo-Khomeini discourses

---

2. Seven epochs – six Iranian presidencies and in 2015, Saudi Arabia started setting watershed events and this came with Salman's reign i.e., the Yemen War, while the seventh epoch is the Trump presidency.

gradually returned during the Ahmadinejad presidency, becoming more prevalent as the Arab Spring took place and becoming stronger during the Syrian and Yemeni wars under the Rouhani leadership. An Iranian discourse of Saudi subservience to the US and Israel was observed in the Ahmadinejad era. The 34-Day War in 2006 and the Gaza War in 2008 brought back the sub-themes of the Arab and Sunni clergy's silence alongside subservience to the West and 'Zionism'. Meanwhile, the Saudi Othering of Iran framed Iran in a similar light. During the Iran–Iraq War, themes of Iranian collusion with Israel were introduced. These themes were revisited once again during the Rouhani tenure. As the cold war between Iran and Saudi Arabia became hot in Syria and Yemen, the sub-themes of Takfiri-Wahhabism and sedition along with a Western-Zionist conspiracy to destroy the Islamic world through the promotion of Saudi-led sectarianism came to dominate.

The discourses of Othering manifested themselves in two ways as these repertoires surfaced in the form of 'building blocks' or 'interpretative repertoires'. In this analysis, four 'supra-themes' of Othering emerged in post-revolutionary period, namely: (i) subservience to imperialism and Zionism, (ii) regional expansion through hegemony and sedition, (iii) deception and hidden agendas, and (iv) domestic and social inequalities. Different metaphors, stereotypes, and predication strategies were employed under each of these themes, facilitating the discursive construction of the Iranian and Saudi Other.

Predicational strategies and themes were applied to the discursive construction and demonization of the Other, thereby further typifying the political and religious repertoires. The religious repertoires, such as the one of fitna, were employed in the Saudi discourse to paint the Iranian Other as a source of sedition and a force dividing the Ummah. This was superimposed with political propaganda that built a narrative of covert collaboration and treachery against the Arab world. Furthermore, the notion circulated that a Khomeini-led Iran was trying to pursue a programme of Shi'i expansion, while attempting to resurrect the Persian empire's advances during the Iran–Iraq war. These tropes of Persian expansionism made a return as the events of the Arab Spring gained momentum, as Iran believed that the protests were based on an Islamic awakening with its origins in the Islamic Revolution. This view contrasted with Saudi fears that viewed Iran's aid to Assad and Tehran's later support for the Houthis as Persian and Shi'i regional expansionism.

Geopolitical concerns emerge in this book as a crucial trope shared between the Saudi and Iranian construction of the Self and Other. To construct Iran's Other, the geopolitical trope functioned at two levels. First, given the US's active intervention in the region, the idea of the 'Ominous Triangle' was devised, whereby Iranian editorials used a carefully crafted discourse to point to the US and its regional ally Pakistan. Instead of explicitly mentioning the Saudi regime, Wahhabism was underlined as the major driving force. The importance of this implicit reference, which separated Saudi Arabia from Wahhabism, could relate to the sustainability of détente and rapprochement with Saudi Arabia, especially since the Khatami era was marked as an era of collaboration and joint regional leadership as both states shared a common enemy (Saddam) and an economic recession. The geopolitical trope and the explicit mention of Saudi Arabia and US intervention in the affairs of the Middle East became prominent after the Arab Spring and peaked as MBS ascended to the position of crown prince, becoming the central figure in the manufacture and promulgation of Saudi discourses on the Self and Other. During this period, the Iranian discourse promulgators did not separate out or differentiate between Wahhabism and the monarchy, particularly in the case of the Takfiris in Syria. Iranian discourse employed a geopolitical trope that intertwined Saudi Arabia, Wahhabism, and the US, where the kingdom was framed as having 'groomed the Wahhabi Takfiris' taking their direction and orders from the US.

The Production of Iranian–Saudi Discourses: Actors and Audiences

The nature of inter-state relations and the constructions of the Other in both Iran and Saudi Arabia were formulated by the upper-level elites. In the case of Iran, this was represented by Khomeini (1979–89) and Khamenei (1989–) as they led the decision-making after the revolution. In Saudi Arabia, the king and crown prince were the two key powerholders. The discourse of *valī-yi faqīh* was mainly targeted towards both the domestic and broader Islamic audience with the aim of highlighting the image of the Iranian Self while underlining its leadership of the Islamic community. In a similar fashion, the discourses in the case of the Saudi monarchy were disseminated to both domestic and international audiences, woven around the Saudi monarch and the crown prince. For example, these discourses are evident in the speeches made on the anniversaries of the hajj and Ramadan. The discourse propagated by Khomeini and Khamenei represented – albeit implicitly – the Saudi Other, which appeared explicitly in other genres, such as in the editorials and political speeches in the *majles* and other ministries, which were aimed at the domestic audience. In contrast, the discourse propagated by the monarchs and crown princes – namely by Khalid, Fahd, Abdullah, Salman, and MBS – reflected the notion of an Islamic brotherly community and the unity of people with faith. The Saudi editorials and ministerial discourses concerned with domestic issues – especially, those of the ministry of the interior – explicitly reflected and connected the incidents between both countries. A negative discursive projection and representation became explicitly visible, especially during the hajj incidents of 1987 and 2015, alongside allegations of who was behind the Kuwaiti refinery and Khobar bombings of 1981 and 1996 respectively.

The discourses emanating from the ulama were also aimed at both domestic and international audiences. One example of this is evident in the Friday sermons in Iran prior to satellite television and the internet era. They were recited in Persian for the domestic masses before a separate segment in Arabic for the broader Islamic world. With the gradual introduction of new technology over the following decades, this shifted to translated and dubbed sermons, such as those made by the online news network al-Alam in Arabic and Press TV in English in the case of Iran and media outlets, or al-Arabiya and the more recent English versions of the Saudi newspapers such as *Asharq Al-Awsat*. Meanwhile, Saudi sermons were targeted at the domestic Saudi masses and the broader Islamic world, and they were disseminated via television with subtitles followed by live coverage of the Mecca prayers from the mid-1980s onwards.

By the détente and rapprochement era of the mid-1990s, there were shifts in how information was disseminated, targeted, and communicated in both Iran and Saudi Arabia. These shifts had two key aspects. First, there was a change in approach towards the Other. In the case of Iran, this came with an effort to balance ending isolation and keeping hold of the revolutionary spirit, whereas in the case of Saudi Arabia, it was evidenced by a recognition of Iran's détente and rapprochement alongside a shift in the Other at internal and external levels. Second, the shift paralleled the change in polity, i.e. in the case of Iran with the election of the presidents Khatami and Rafsanjani, and in Saudi Arabia, the ascension of Abdullah after Fahd and a move to a more Islamist and pan-Arab ideology. In this period, institutions in both Iran and Saudi Arabia adopted a very cautious approach, marking a departure from the direct name-calling of the 1980s. Remarkably, in this period, both the Iranian and Saudi governments refrained from explicitly framing each other.

The third period saw a remarkable change in how discourses were generated and propagated as well as how the audiences were targeted. In the early phase, both Saudi Arabia and Iran maintained détente and rapprochement. The key propagators of the discourse in this period were the elites. In the case of Iran, Khamenei persisted with implicit references to Saudi Arabia. Meanwhile, in Saudi Arabia, the monarch and the crown prince remained the major manufacturers of the discourses of the Saudi Self and the Iranian Other. The fourth period, marked by King Salman and MBS being at the helm of Saudi Arabia, witnessed an explicit Othering across all genres in both countries, including the *valy-i faqih* in Iran and the monarchy in Saudi Arabia. The discursive struggle was explicit and promulgated by both Khamenei and his discursive counterparts, Salman and MBS.

The primary goal in this discursive struggle remained that of the leadership. Up to the events of the Arab Spring, both discourse manufacturers sought to validate their leadership by claiming the struggle of Palestine through constructed themes. The discourses of the Iranian Self on the Saudi Other came with implicit references, both in the Friday sermons and the Iranian dailies' editorials. The former targeted both domestic and international audiences as in previous cases, whereas the rise of digital media made the editorials widely accessible to both domestic and international audiences. Nevertheless, they were aimed primarily at the domestic audience. The discourses of the Saudi Self surfaced mainly through the editorials, and these had a wider domestic subscription level and readership because they were published in Arabic. In both states, the media were strictly regulated and therefore editorials – despite their being more explicit than the elite actors – were still published along state ideological lines. The editorials consequently acted as disseminators of government propaganda to a wider audience, both domestically and internationally. In addition, these discourses tried to generate support among the public to legitimize their Self by denigrating (implicitly or explicitly) the Other.

With the events of the Arab Spring – primarily the Bahrain protests – the discourse on Palestine was only used by Iran to validate the leadership vis-à-vis the Saudi Other. The Iranian discourse focused on the struggle of Palestine and Saudi subservience to Zionism as a dominant supra-theme used to validate Iranian leadership of the Islamic world. Saudi Arabia, in contrast, did not employ the tropes of Israel and Palestine but focused on Iranian expansionism and interference in Arab affairs instead. By 2015 and the ascension of MBS to crown prince, the international media scene became an open space in which both countries took the discursive struggle. The discursive construction of Iranian expansion was manufactured by MBS, and it was highlighted to the international community through tropes of Hitler and fascism to validate and legitimize Saudi Arabia's leadership of the Arab and Islamic world, while also justifying the war in Yemen and rebranding the image of the Kingdom. These tropes of Hitler and Nazism emanated from a supra-discourse of Iranian expansion and hegemony and were disseminated to Arab and Saudi audiences through the press discourse.

Concluding Remarks: How Othering Defines the Self As a State Propaganda Tool

The Saudi and Iranian discourses emerged in an action-reaction dynamic, wherein the Othering process was important for asserting and actualizing the Self. There is a clear and direct correlation that emerges in this research between the Iranian and Saudi discourses, their character and genealogy. This was the norm until MBS rose to power and began a discourse of warmongering (directed at Iran), fascism, and Nazism, in which he branded Saudi Arabia's ultra-conservative identity as a symptom of Iran's 1979 Islamic Revolution. Up to 2015, the relationship was based on a reaction to the discourse of Othering rather than any causality or reaction to regional and international events or incidents. This Othering discourse was produced, propagated, and rationalized in a specific context to actualize the meaning of the discourse while developing another discourse to attach meaning to the relationship.

Like the Iranian discourse, the Saudi elite discourse and sermons were implicit in their engagement with Iran. The discursive struggle between the Iranian and the Saudi Self proved to define broader events in the region. With this, we see that the discourses of Saudi and Iranian Othering was of a similar character, i.e. both discourses asserted state dominance and leadership over the region and the subject of Islamic leadership resided in the ontology of these states more than any realpolitik or hegemonic struggle. The discursive struggle shows the genealogical shifts in Iranian–Saudi relations that were specific to certain discourses produced and initiated only through the Other in the Self.

The primary significance of Othering is embedded in the ontology of the states and signifies their assertions of legitimacy. In the case of both Saudi and Iran, the

Othering was implicit and explicit, depending on the political situation in the region and their domestic issues. However, there was a complete volte-face and shift in this relationship of discourse construction and Othering, wherein Saudi Arabia's discourses became explicit at the monarchical level. This was evident with the onset of the war in Yemen and MBS's rise to power. MBS brought about a shift in an 'unspoken protocol' of discourse construction between the two countries, wherein general the Supreme Leader and the monarch would not explicitly target each other, leaving the denigration and explicit Othering to the domestic discourses for their domestic audiences.

As I have noted throughout this book, both countries were susceptible to domestic, regional, and international events. The election of every US president, for example, brought with it incidents and events that affected the construction of the Self and the Other in Iranian and Saudi discourse. Since the 1979 Islamic Revolution, there had been a direct confrontation between the US and Iran. This included events such as the US Hostage Crisis, US support for Iraq during the eight-year-long war, the placing of Iran on the 'axis of evil', and the barrage of sanctions over the four decades. However, nothing compares to the confrontation and ramifications that resulted from the Trump presidency. The Saudi–US 'common Othering' of Iran, amid MBS's encouragement of the US to withdraw from the nuclear deal and apply a strategy of 'maximum pressure' on the Islamic Republic were staples of a Trump–MBS collaboration that generated explicit discourses of Iranian Othering, and nearly led to a full military confrontation between Tehran and Washington. Nevertheless, the end of the Trump administration and the ushering in of a Democrat to the White House, Joe Biden, with strong views on MBS has not stopped Saudi Arabia's activities in the Middle East. The war in Yemen along with the Iranian–Saudi mutual rhetoric and Othering continue. However, what has changed is an increased call for dialogue and negotiations between Islam's two main powers and rivals.

EPILOGUE

A scholarly discussion of Iran and Saudi Arabia, covering a region as turbulent as the Middle East, is an ever-dynamic topic. Between the time of writing (spring 2022) and this monograph's date of publication, many events will have likely occurred in the Middle East that are yet to be covered and analysed. Presently, just over two years have passed since the watershed event of the assassination of Qassem Soleimani, but this would not be the last assassination of a senior Iranian figure. In November 2020, Iran's father of the nuclear programme, Mohsin Fakhrizadeh was assassinated on the outskirts of Tehran in Absard by what was alleged to be an Israeli-led mission in collaboration with the United States (Motamedi 2020) who gave their blessing. Fakhrizadeh's assassination within the borders of Iran dealt a major blow to the image of the Iranian Self. This incident came as Trump had lost his re-election to the Democrat candidate Joe Biden just over three weeks earlier. Iranian accusations were not limited to Israel's involvement in the assassination. Iranian figures, such as Zarif, accused Saudi Arabia of colluding with Israel in a 'conspiracy' to assassinate one of Iran's most senior nuclear scientists (*Reuters* 2020). This accusation arrived a few days before the incident, with rumours of a secret meeting between Netanyahu and MBS in Neom (*Al-Jazeera* 2020). Furthermore, this alleged Israeli–Saudi collaboration was rumoured to have come to fruition as Tel Aviv normalized relations with Abu Dhabi and Bahrain in what became known as the Abraham Accords, in September 2020.

This major blow to the image of the Iranian Self due to the consecutive assassinations of two of its major leaders added to the detrimental effects of Trump's maximum pressure campaign, which were also sustained by the Biden administration. In turn, this led Iran to take actions to bolster its image of power and leadership regionally and internationally. This was accomplished in two ways. Iran defied the sanctions imposed by the US on its oil sales first of all to project its status as a regional and international power, and second, to sustain its economy through 'maximum resistance'. In May 2020 – after Soleimani's assassination – Iran sent fuel to Venezuela in five tankers under the Iranian flag, aiding the Maduro-led government against the US sanctions imposed on Caracas (O'Brien 2020). Similarly, in September 2021 – after Fakhrizadeh's assassination – Iran sent oil to Lebanon via Syria amid the power shortages and economic meltdown in Lebanon, to demonstrate its ability to break the economic sanctions and the siege on Iran and its regional allies (*Reuters* 2021b).

Joe Biden's election as president raised the alarm in the Middle East, particularly in Saudi Arabia, as the president-elect had labelled Saudi Arabia a pariah state during his campaign. Biden's stance towards MBS in particular, and MBS's alleged role in the murder of Jamal Khashoggi as well as the Qatar blockade was a case in point (Emmons, Chávez, and Lacy 2019). This prompted not only Saudi Arabia but also the United Arab Emirates to end their blockade of Qatar to alleviate any pressure that may ensue from the newly elected US administration. The Al-Ula declaration was signed as a result of efforts by the late emir of Kuwait, Sabah al-Ahmed al-Sabah, and his successor, Nawaf al-Sabah, along with the late Sultan Qaboos of Oman, therefore ending a three-year blockade of Qatar (Khedr 2021). The normalization of relations with Qatar was not only imperative because of the arrival of a US president who was critical of MBS's moves, but also because of the negatively impacted economies due to low oil prices and a pandemic that had ravaged the world economies, including Saudi Arabia and its allies. Furthermore, the recalibration of GCC relations would see the opening of Saudi and UAE airspace to Qatar, and this therefore deprived Iran of much-needed revenue linked to Qatar's use of Iranian airspace.

The swearing-in of Biden in January 2021 would attempt to re-introduce the US's Obama-era foreign policy in world politics. One of the main files that the Biden administration had mentioned as they campaigned was Washington's return to the Joint Comprehensive Plan of Action (JCPOA) (Biden 2022). Furthermore, as the newly elected US president attempted to recalibrate US foreign policy, the Biden administration and the EU attempted to encourage Iran to return to the negotiation table and enter direct talks with the United States. At the same time, Iran was also in the middle of a presidential race that saw the election of a conservative cleric, Ebrahim Raisi, as Iran's eighth president since the 1979 Islamic Revolution. Similarly, the newly elected Iranian administration also sought to recalibrate Iran's foreign policy with its neighbours. By continuing Rouhani's calls for détente and rapprochement with Tehran's neighbours, Raisi also highlighted that Iran sought warmer relations with its neighbours, particularly with Saudi Arabia (*Tehran Times* 2021). However, while Saudi Arabia had agreed to work towards a calmer region, Riyadh's chief diplomat repeated the famous mantra that 'Iran should prove its intentions through actions and not mere words' and that 'foreign policy in Iran is controlled by Khamenei and not the president' (*Arab News* 2021). Nevertheless, Tehran and Riyadh had already held four rounds of private talks at the security and intelligence levels hosted by Iraq and Oman, including a 'track two like' meeting at the academic and think-tank level in Jordan. According to Saudi analysts (Alghannam 2022), the talks in Iraq, hosted and mediated by the Iraqi prime minister, Mustafa Al-Kadhimi, were positive, signalling a slight thaw in the relations. On 17 January 2022 three Iranian diplomats resumed their posts at the OIC in Saudi Arabia after six years (*IRNA* 2022). However, there is no decrease in rivalry in sight. Tensions in Syria and Yemen are still ongoing, Bashar al-Assad is still in Syria with full support from Iran, and the Houthi war with Saudi Arabia is still ongoing and approaching its seventh year at the time of writing. Furthermore, the US withdrawal from Afghanistan and the ascension of the Taliban to power in Kabul was also a major regional shift for both states.

In August 2021, the US and its allies made their final withdrawal from Afghanistan, fulfilling the terms and conditions of two years of negotiations—initiated by the Trump administration in 2018—with the Taliban in Doha. The

Taliban were Iran's enemy, especially after the beheading of the Iranian diplomats in Mazar-i-Sharif in 1998 and allies of Saudi Arabia up to the 9/11 events in New York, but now the table has somewhat turned. Given the spillover and the turbulent relationship between Doha and Riyadh, Saudi Arabia and UAE were not active in the Taliban talks held in Qatar. Analysts have argued that the Arab states of the Persian Gulf, particularly the UAE and Saudi Arabia, have been competing with Qatar over influence in Afghanistan – albeit with no major success. Both Riyadh and Abu Dhabi have reopened their diplomatic missions in Kabul, but it seems that Doha has been victorious as it now represents the US diplomatically in Kabul, and it has aided the international community in hosting and transporting people out of Afghanistan.

Similarly, Iran has also made some gains over Saudi Arabia in this arena. Besides positive relations with Doha, Iran's border with Afghanistan and shared core issues have allowed the state to take a proactive role in Iranian–Afghan relations in general, while mending inter-Afghan rivalry in particular. These issues include: increased drug trafficking, cross-border trade, water shortages, discrimination against the Afghan Shi'i minorities, and the rising threat of ISIS-Khorasan (ISIS-K) (Nada 2021). Furthermore, a clear sign of the result of Iran's proactive role and the thaw in the relations between Iran and the Taliban came as the latter condemned Qassem Soleimani's assassination. The Taliban expressed 'deep regret over his martyrdom', going as far as describing IRGC commander as a 'great warrior' (*Al-Arabiya* and Fazeli 2020). Two rounds of meetings were held in Tehran between the Taliban and various Afghanistan factions hosted by the Iranian foreign ministry in July 2021 and later in January 2022 (*Al-Monitor* and Siddiqui 2022; Karimi and Rahim 2021). This is not surprising. Iran's hosting of Afghani refugees since the Soviet invasion in 1979, and the shared history, religion, and culture with the Shi'i ethnic minorities, the Hazara in particular and Afghanistan in general, gives Iran an upper hand and larger stake in Afghanistan than Saudi Arabia. Furthermore, Iran had supported Afghani political factions such as the Northern Alliance led by Ahmad Shah Masood since the days of the Afghan civil war. IRGC commanders such as Soleimani and his successor Esmail Qaani had strong relations with various Afghan leaders. The IRGC under the leadership of Soleimani trained and sent the Afghan 'Fatimiyoun Brigades' to support other Iran-aligned groups in Syria. For Saudi Arabia, the shift in identity has altered its relationship with the Taliban. MBS's move towards hypernationalism and departure from Islamic identity, especially Wahabbism, may have also hindered Riyadh's relations with the Taliban. The once Islamic clergy in Saudi Arabia are no longer as active, and the bridge between the Saudi ulama and the Taliban may have been diluted if not severed.

Amid these regional changes, it is imperative to mention that as Iran was seen to be returning to its revolutionary ideological roots, through the election of a conservative cleric like Raisi and the disqualification of Iran's moderate and reformist candidates from the Guardian Council, Riyadh came to be perceived as eschewing its religious roots for hypernationalism. MBS's ambition to open up and diversify the economy, such as following steps devised to attract tourists to Saudi

Arabia, not only led to Riyadh hosting sports competitions and musical concerts, but also went as far as considering the legalization of alcohol in certain parts of the kingdom, such as Neom (*AFP* 2021). It can therefore be argued that Saudi Arabia's image is metamorphosing from one of Islamic and regional leadership to one of a more international, economic, and tourism-oriented hub. However, in the meantime Iran has doubled down on its Islamic and regional image while showing that it can also remain pragmatic and fluid in its relations with the international community. This image can be defined as a hybrid approach combining Ahmadinejad- and Khatami-style presidencies. In other words, while the Raisi foreign policy team – led by conservative members such as the foreign minister, Abdollahian – is calling for détente and rapprochement with Saudi Arabia, the IRGC is posturing with an image of strength and regional military power. This is what I term a 'velvet glove versus an iron fist' policy, where Iran may be ready to build bridges with its neighbours and negotiate with the international community, yet it will stand firm and respond militarily to any threat it perceives to itself or its allies. This bifurcated policy is also based on what experts argue is the saturation of IRGC's posturing (Tabatabai 2022). That is to say, Iran has militarily projected an image of strength, formidability, and the power of the Iranian Self regionally and internationally, i.e. through the 'Iron fist', and it is now focused on thawing relations, and mending and building bridges with its neighbours, particularly with Saudi Arabia and the UAE, through détente and rapprochement, the 'velvet glove'.

In the aftermath of the Aramco attacks in September 2019, the war in Yemen has witnessed clashes with the Houthis approaching the Yemeni city of Marib and taking back control of swaths of land occupied by Saudi-aligned Yemeni forces. By the end of 2021, with the support of the UAE, the Giants Forces (*'alwiyat al-'amāliqah*) regained lost territory in north Yemen (Sa'da) prompting the Houthis to direct their missiles and drones towards a new front, the UAE. In January 2022, Houthi drones and missiles struck Abu Dhabi, the capital of the UAE (*Reuters* 2022b). The situation was reminiscent of scenes that Riyadh had witnessed since its war began in 2015. Although the Houthis are known to be allied with Iran, Iranian foreign ministry officials crafted a carefully worded statement, arguing that military attacks would not solve the regional crisis (Ghantous and Hafezi 2022). This comes at a time where Iran had pursued regional détente and rapprochement with its neighbours, particularly since the UAE's head of intelligence, Tahnoon bin Zayed, had visited Tehran in December 2021 (Narallah 2021) and had invited the Iranian president to visit Abu Dhabi (Hafezi 2021). Furthermore, bin Zayed's visit was an attempt to alleviate Iran's worries about the growing relationship between Tel Aviv and Abu Dhabi as the two countries signed security, tourism, and manufacturing treaties. Also, the détente between Iran and the UAE is crucial to Iran's nuclear programme, particularly since Iran has sought to harness support from the GCC states that were once against the JCPOA signed in 2015.

The Raisi administration brought with it a complete revamp of the Iranian administration, including the nuclear negotiating team. The once moderate and reformist members of the Iranian administration that negotiated a JCPOA in 2015 have departed and been replaced with a team led by a member of the Supreme Leader's immediate circle, Ali Bagheri Kani (*Reuters* 2021a). The P5+1 was now negotiating directly with the office of the Supreme Leader and not with the Western-educated Zarif and his team. While Iran and the US are still not talking directly to each other, at the time of writing this monograph, the Wall Street Journal announced that the US may soon return to the JCPOA (Norman 2022). This comes as Iran has demanded that the United States provide guarantees that it will never leave the JCPOA again and if it does, it shall not resume any sanctions on Iran. Furthermore, Iranian demands have included the removal of all Trump-era sanctions imposed on Iran. According to Reuters, these number 700 sanctions, and they most likely include the removal of the IRGC and its Quds Force from being designated a Foreign Terrorist Organization (FTO), a move that would be extremely difficult for the Biden administration to apply and would certainly upset Iran's regional foes, such as Israel and Saudi Arabia (Psaledakis and Mohammed 2021). Nevertheless, in early 2022 talks have taken place on the renewal of waivers (Hansler, Atwood, and *CNN* 2022) and unfreezing of assets of Iranian funds in foreign banks, such as South Korea (*Reuters* 2022a), thus allowing Iran to buy much-needed food and medicine. Iran's regional adversaries – particularly Saudi Arabia and Israel – fear that the removal of sanctions and the return of revenue to Tehran would renourish Iran's regional allies, allowing Tehran to further expand and tighten its grip on countries such as Syria, Lebanon, and Iraq.

The recent elections in Iraq resulted in major losses for pro-Iran political parties and resulted in Muqtada al-Sadr's party – once allied with Iran – winning majority seats in parliament. The post-Soleimani Iranian influence in Iraq has seemingly waned and the new commander of the Quds Force, Esmail Qaani, has not managed to replicate the successes of his much-missed predecessor. The turbulence in Iraq and the splintering of the Shi'i alliance, once allied with Iran, have not only caused problems for Tehran but also for the United States. The departure of US forces from Iraq continues to be a contentious issue and a demand made by the PMU forces that were once under the command of the late Abu Mahdi al-Muhandis and Qassem Soleimani. Also, it is important to mention that Iran's revenge for Soleimani's assassination entailed an end to the US presence in the Middle East, particularly in Iraq. Moreover, Iran's losses in Iraq have given rise to a nationalist narrative. The fiery cleric Muqtada al-Sadr has adopted a pro-Arab position and called for national unity, going as far as citing Ayatollah Khomeini's 1979 slogan 'Neither East nor West', in an implicit reference to neither wanting Iran nor the United States to have any influence on Iraq (Al-Sadr 2022). In parallel, this has opened up a space for the GCC states, particularly the UAE and Saudi Arabia, to become proactive in normalizing relations with Baghdad – a position that they had left vacant for Tehran since the fall of Saddam in 2003. Reciprocal visits by Iraqi and Saudi officials, including a recent delegation sent by MBS to visit Baghdad, sought to bring Iraq back to the Arab forefront and distance it from any Iranian influence (*Arab News* 2020). More recently, trade and economic treaties have been signed between Baghdad and other Arab capitals (Mahmoud 2021). These include energy deals to supply Iraq with electricity via countries such as

Egypt and Saudi Arabia, as well as foreign direct investment (FDI) into the Iraqi economy and infrastructure by Riyadh and Abu Dhabi (Gnana 2022). These trade deals arguably seek to dilute Iranian influence in Baghdad and Iraqi reliance on Tehran. Consequently, any significant re-energizing of the Iranian economy, and of the revenue that may result upon resuming the JCPOA, may worry Iraq's GCC neighbours. While currently supported by the GCC countries, including Saudi Arabia, the removal of sanctions and freedom of trade that Iran would gain after a US return to the JCPOA would be a source of worry. One major concern is Iran regaining its influence and its financial lifeline, thus allowing it to revitalize and support its regional allies, from Bashar al-Assad in Syria to Hezbollah in Lebanon, and the different PMU groups in Iraq, not to mention the Houthi allies in Yemen.

While the GCC states, particularly Saudi Arabia, have changed their position with regards to the JCPOA, another main concern is Iran's ballistic missile programme. Since the Biden administration has come to power, there have been calls – particularly by Riyadh – to discuss Iran's missile defence programme alongside its nuclear file (Borck 2021), a demand strongly rejected by Tehran. However, the Raisi administration, through its foreign minister, Abdolahian, has continued along the Rouhani path of dialogue with Iran's regional neighbours (*Tehran Times* 2022). In January 2021, after the inauguration of the Biden administration, the GCC states called for a seat at the JCPOA negotiating table out of fear that Washington and Tehran may strike a deal over the region at the expense of Iran's Persian Gulf neighbours (*Al-Arabiya* and Taha 2021). Since then, Iranian officials have continued the discourse of friendship and fraternity. They have called for direct talks and cooperation between Iran and its neighbours without 'foreign intervention', stating that 'the US was a problem' (Zarif 2021). This call for talks was extended to include the resumption of relations between Tehran and Riyadh in January 2022 when Iran's foreign minister Abdolahian described the dialogue with Saudi Arabia as 'positive and constructive' in reference to the four rounds of talks held in Baghdad since 2019 (*Al-Jazeera* and Abdolahian 2022). The Saudi position has included a repetition of mantras, stating that 'Arab hands are extended' to Tehran, on the condition that the Islamic Republic allays concerns over 'the security and stability of the region', accusing Iran of having a destabilizing role in the region, after the most recent Houthi attacks on Riyadh and Abu Dhabi (*Saudi Gazette* 2022).

As Iran and the international community seek a return to the JCPOA and the alleviation of regional tensions, Saudi Arabia is seemingly having difficulties in putting the past behind it. These difficulties do not only include the discourses, narratives, demonization, and rivalry between both states, but also how Riyadh and its young de facto ruler can accept a middle ground and negotiate an end to an endless, bloody war that was only supposed to take three weeks. This comes at a time when the world is trying to grapple with a post-COVID-19 crisis, decarbonization, and the waning of fossil fuels, alongside an international geopolitical shift where the US has signalled a toning down of its interference and presence in the Persian Gulf region. This winding down of a regional presence is also visible in the US having signalled an end to its wars and a departure from

Afghanistan in August 2021, shifting its focus towards a larger, more crucial adversary, China. A move signalled once by Obama as he called for an American pivot or 'rebalance' towards East Asia (White House 2015). Moreover, the Russian-Ukrainian war that erupted on 24 February 2022 took the world by surprise and storm. The international community, mainly the West, took a rapid and sharp approach towards Moscow by applying sanctions on the Russian economy, particularly its energy sector. The GCC states, on the other hand, were split in their reaction. Riyadh and Abu Dhabi took on a more neutral approach due to these Arab Gulf states' partnership with Russia as members of the OPEC+ group of countries which secures much needed oil revenue to revitalise their economies post-COVID-19. Furthermore, attempts by the hydrocarbon-rich GCC states to diversify their economies and create jobs for their very young populations, through mega-projects such as Neom and tourism in Al-Ula, would require foreign investments to succeed. These investments depend on regional stability and an end to wars. This can only happen when the region's two largest centres of Islamic power shift their discourses and narratives towards fraternity, cooperation, peace, and mutual benefits, as reflected 'in the words of Kings and Clerics'.

GLOSSARY

Ahl al-Bayt People of the House, or family. It refers to the household of Prophet Mohammad.

Ajam (**sing.** *ajamī*) Arabic phrase meaning non-Arab; is also utilized in the Arabian Peninsula to refer to those of Iranian origin.

Alawite An offshoot of Shi'i Islam and a syncretic sect of Twelver Shi'ism who revere Imam Ali, the Prophet Mohammad's cousin. They are mainly centred in Syria.

Alwaʿd al-Sādiq (Fulfilled Promise) A Hezbollah operation launched in July 2006 to kidnap two Israeli soldiers in northern Israel.

Ashura A day of mourning the martyrdom of Imam Hussein, the grandson of the Prophet Mohammed, in 680 AD at Karbala in modern-day Iraq.

Ayatollah Translated as a 'Sign of God', is a high-ranking title given to Twelver Shī'i clerics. Shi'i clerics attain this title after completing the *bahth al-kharij* (external research), the final stage of their seminary education, and attain the level of *'mujtahid'*.

Basīj Translated as 'The Mobilisation', are a voluntary paramilitary force established in 1979 by Ayatollah Khomeini. They are one of the five forces of the Iranian Revolutionary Guard Corps. They were instrumental in fighting during the Iran–Iraq war.

Difāʿ-i Muqadas The Iranian title referring to the Iran–Iraq war. It is translated to *Holy Defence* or *Sacred Defence*.

Hajj Is an Islamic pilgrimage to Mecca. It is compulsory for all physically and financially able Muslims to perform this pilgrimage once in their lifetime.

Hamas Is an acronym of the Palestinian Islamic Resistance Movement (*Ḥarakat al-Muqāwamah al-ʾIslāmiyyah*). It was founded in 1987 after the first intifadah and since 2007 the de facto governing authority of the Gaza Strip.

Imam A cleric that leads prayers in a mosque. In Shi'i thought, an Imam is a divinely selected, infallible Islamic leader of the line of Imam Ali and Prophet Mohammad. The term can also be employed to mean an Islamic leader that claims descent from the Prophet Mohammad, such as Imam Khomeini in Iran or Imam Musa al-Sadr in Iraq.

Intifadah Palestinian uprisings in the West Bank and Gaza Strip in 1987 and 2000. They aimed at ending Israel's occupation of both Palestinian territories and create an independent Palestinian state.

Islām-i Nāb-i Muhamadī Pure or Pristine Mohammadian Islam.

Istikbār/Istikbār-i Jahānī A term that referred to Imperialism, Global Oppression and Arrogance.

Jāhiliyah The 'age of ignorance' signifying the era prior to the advent of Islam. It is an Islamic concept of the period of the time before Islam that is defined by 'ignorance'.

Karbala A city in Iraq and the place of the martyrdom of Imam Hussein and his mausoleum.

Kharijites/Khawārij (sing. Kharijī) Translated as 'The Revolters'. An Islamic sect with a belief that any man can be Caliph regardless of belonging to the tribe of Quraish and through election (*shūrah*), provided he is pious. The first group revolted and assassinated Imam Ali after they fought under his command in the Battle of Sifin.

Khat-i Imām Translated as 'The Imam Khomeini's line'. Students and clerics who followed, supported, and advocated the political thoughts of Imam Khomeini on the establishment of the Islamic Republic after the revolution of 1979.

Mahdi Translated literally as 'The Directed One', 'Guide' or 'Leader' and one that is 'fit to direct other'. According to Shi'i thought, the Mahdi is the twelfth infallible Imam. The Mahdi is in a period of occultation and will appear again at the end of the world. The Sunnis believe that he has not appeared.

Majlis-i Khubrigān Translated as the 'Assembly of Experts'. It was first established in 1983 and is empowered to appoint, dismiss, and question the Supreme Leader.

Majūsī (pl. *Majūs*) A term meaning 'Magi' or 'Zoroastrians'. During the Iran–Iraq war, the term was employed with pejorative intentions to refer to Iranians in general. Iraqi propaganda employed the term to frame Iranians as non-sincere Muslims and still hold pre-Islamic beliefs.

Maktabī A person that follows Islam comprehensively.

Miḥrāb An area or niche in the mosque which marks the direction of Mecca (Qiblah). It is the position which the Imam takes in leading prayer.

Muftī An cleric that expounds the law, by issuing edicts (fatwā).

Muharram Is the first month of the Islamic calendar, and literally means 'that which is forbidden'. The first ten days of the month is observed as a period of commemoration by the Shi'a for the martyrdom of Imam Hussain.

Munāfiq (pl. *Munafiqīn*) Hypocrites.

Mustaz'af (pl. *Mustaz'afān* (farsi)/*Mustaz'afīn*) The oppressed.

Mustakbir (pl. *Mustakbirīn*) The oppressor.

Nasibī (pl. *Nawāsib*) Is a Shi'i term that literally means 'to propose' or 'to have' (*nasaba*) hatred for the Ahl al-lbayt. Contemporarily, it has been employed to refer to Salafis and Wahhabis.

Rafiḍī (pl. *Rawāfiḍ/Rāfiḍah*) Translated as 'rejecters' or 'rejectionists'. Utilized in contemporary times by Sunnis to refer to the Shi'a since they 'reject' the caliph succession of the first three caliphs as Prophet Mohammad's successors.

Safawī Literally meaning 'Safavid' and used by Wahhabi and Salafi clerics to refer to Iranians and their desires to resurrect a Persian Saffavid empire and convert the region to Shi'ism.

Taqiya Literally meaning to 'guard oneself'. It is a Shi'i principle that allows for 'pious fraud'. To protect and save oneself from persecution, the Shi'i may conceal his identity and pass himself as a Sunni to escape death or imprisonment. In contemporary times, the term has been employed to negatively refer to Shi'a as liars and hypocrites.

Tawhīd Literally means 'oneness'. It is the central part of the monotheistic principle of Islam.

'**ālim** (pl. **ulama**) A cleric of the Islamic faith.

Ummah An Islamic community.

Umayyads Are the second of the four major caliphates after the Rashidun caliphate following the death of the Prophet Mohammad. The dynasty began with Mu'awiya I.

Vali-yi Faqīh Translated as 'Guardian of the Faith' and is an Islamic Jurist. In Iran the title is held by the Supreme Leader of the Revolution.

Wahhābī A member of the Wahhabi group of the Sunni sect founded by Mohammad bin Abdul-Wahhab (1703-1792). They are known for their strict and puritanical observance of Islamic teachings, known as Salafi teachings. Wahhabism strongly condemns the Shi'i practices of visiting shrines and revering the saints as heresy. Contemporarily, the term has been employed to refer to Saudi clerics and those that adhere and follow the Saudi Islamic seminaries in Mecca and Medina.

Yazīd The second caliph of the Ummayad dynasty. He was known to order the killing the Imam Hussain at the battle of Karbala in 680AD.

REFERENCES

Aal Taleb, S. 2006. 'Mecca Friday Sermon 24/02/2006.' In *Sermons- Khutab*, edited by Ministry of Islamic Affairs. Mecca, Saudi Arabia: Ministry of Islamic Affairs, Dawah and Guidance.

Aal Taleb, S. 2006. 'Mecca Friday Sermon 11/08/2006.' In *Sermons-Khutab*, edited by Ministry of Islamic Affairs. Mecca, Saudi Arabia: Ministry of Islamic Affairs, Dawah and Guidance.

Aarts, Paul, and Joris Van Duijne. 2009. 'Saudi Arabia After US-Iranian Détente: Left in the Lurch', *Middle East Policy*, 16: 64–78.

Abbas, H. 2021. *The Prophet's Heir: The Life of Ali ibn Abi Talib* (Yale University Press: New Haven, CT).

Abdolahian, A.H. 2012. 'Abdolahian Deputy Foreign Minister Interview with Fars News', *ISNA*, 17/11/2011 [26/08/1390], p. 2.

Abdolahian, A.H. 2014. 'Interview with Fars News', *Fars*, 17/06/2014.

Abdolahian, A.H. 2014. 'Interview with ISNA', *ISNA*, 15/10/2014 [23/07/1393].

Abdolahian, A.H., Dina Esfandiary, and Ariane Tabatabai. 2015. 'Iran's ISIS Policy', *International Affairs*, 91: 1–15.

Abdolahian, A.H. and Shargh. 2015. 'Hussain amīr ʿabd al-lahīān, muʿāvin-i ʿarabī va āfrīqāyī-yi vizārat-i khārija az nāguftah hāyi raftan-i safīr-i ʿarabistān mīgūyad', *Shargh*, 14/01/2015 [24/10/1393], p. 1.

Abdolahian, A.H. 2011. 'Deputy Foreign Minister Abdolahian Statement on Saudi involvement in Bahrain', *IRNA*, 16/03/2011 [25/12/1389], p. 2.

Abidi, A.H.H., and K.R. Singh. 1991. *The Gulf Crisis* (Lancer Books: New York).

Abuhamzeh, G. 2020. 'Vital American Targets in Region Within Reach: Iranian Commander', *Tasnim*, 04/01/2020.

Abu-Nasr, D. 2002. 'Saudi-owned paper said censored after critical editorial', Associated Press, Accessed 10/03/2014. http://staugustine.com/stories/032402/wor_595374.shtml.

Adib-Moghaddam, A. 2006. *The International Politics of the Persian Gulf: A Cultural Genealogy* (Taylor & Francis: Oxford).

Afkham, M. 2015. 'Foreign Ministry Spokeswoman Statement on the Death of King Abdullah of Saudi Arabia', *Kayhan*, 25/01/2015 [04/11/1393].

Afkham, M., and Fars. 2014. 'Foreign Ministry Spokeswoman: Improvement of Iran-Saudi Arabia Relations on Right Path', *Fars News*, 20/08/2014.

Afkham, M., and Fars. 2015. 'Foreign Ministry Spokeswoman Statement on Saudi Attacks on Yemen', *Jahan News*, 26/03/2015 [06/01/1394].

Afkham, M., and Mehr. 2015. 'Saudi attacks on Yemen will spread insecurity to all region: Afkham', *Mehr News*, 26/03/2015.

AFP. 1993. 'Iran's Parliament Condemns Saudi "Insult" to Islam 30 May 1993.' In *Press Release*, edited by *AFP*. Tehran, IR Iran: *AFP*.

AFP. 2021. 'Saudi Arabia megacity project flirts with major taboo: alcohol', France24, Accessed 01/02/2022. https://www.france24.com/en/live-news/20211027-saudi-arabia-megacity-project-flirts-with-major-taboo-alcohol.

Afrasiabi, K., and A. Maleki. 2003. 'Iran's Foreign Policy After 11 September', *The Brown Journal of World Affairs*, 9: 255–65.

Aftab-e Yazd. 2005. 'Playing with Open Eyes (Bāzī Bā Chishm-i Bāz)', *Aftab-e Yazd*, 16/10/2005 [24/07/1384].

Aftab-e Yazd. 2005. 'The Smell of Recovery (Bū-yi Bihbūd)', *Aftab-e Yazd*, 15/10/2005 [23/07/1384].

Aftab-e Yazd. 2006. 'Lessons from Samiraa ('ibratī Az Sāmirā')', *Aftab-e Yazd*, 25/02/2006 [06/12/1384].

Aftab-e Yazd. 2013. 'Hashemi's Special Role in the Relations with Saudi Arabia', *Aftab-e Yazd*, 22/12/2013, p. 1.

Ahakhavan-Kazemi, B. 2000. 'Vāgirāyī hā wa hamgirāyī hā dar ravābiṭ-i īrān wa 'arabistān, 'muṭāli'āt-i khāvarmiyānih', *Muṭāli'āt-i Khāvarmiyānih*, 22: 115–46.

Ahmadinejad, M. 2005. 'Ahmadinejad Presidential Candidacy Statement'. In *Speeches*, edited by IRNA. Tehran, IR Iran: IRNA.

Ahmadinejad, M. 2005. 'Ahmadinejad Presidential Victory Speech'. In *Speeches*, edited by IRNA. Tehran, IR Iran: IRNA.

Ahmadinejad, M. 2005. 'Ahmadinejad Press Conference', *Jomhouri Eslami*, 27/06/2005 [06/04/1384].

Ahmadinejad, M. 2005. 'Ahmadinejad Press Conference at OIC-Saudi Arabia.' In *International Speeches*, edited by IRNA. Tehran, IR Iran: IRNA.

Ahmadinejad, M. 2005. 'Ahmadinejad Speech at OIC-Saudi Arabia.' In *International Speeches*, edited by IRNA. Tehran, IR Iran: IRNA.

Ahmadinejad, M. 2005. 'Ahmadinejad Speech at the UN General Assembly.' In *International Speeches*, edited by IRNA. Tehran, IR Iran: IRNA.

Ahmadinejad, M. 2005. 'Ahmadinejad Speech During the Visit of Syrian President Bashar Al-Assad.' In *International Visitors*, edited by IRNA. Tehran, IR Iran: IRNA.

Ahmadinejad, M. 2005. 'Ahmadinejad Speech – Ferdowsi University Mashhad.' In *Speeches*, edited by IRNA. Tehran, IR Iran: IRNA.

Ahmadinejad, M. 2005. 'Ahmadinejad Speech to Majles Members', *Kayhan*, 21/06/2005 [31/03/1384].

Ahmadinejad, M. 2005. 'Conference Opening Speech.' In *A World Without Zionism Conference*. Tehran: IRNA.

Ahmadinejad, M. 2006. 'Speech at the Opening Session.' In *International Quds Conference*. Tehran: IRNA.

Ahmadinejad, M. 2006. 'Statement on Hezbollah-Israel War.' In *President Statements*, edited by IRNA. Tehran, IR Iran: IRNA.

Ahmadinejad, M. 2006. 'Statement on the Bombing of the Askari Shrine.' In *President Statements*, edited by IRNA. Tehran, IR Iran: IRNA.

Ahmadinejad, M. 2009. 'Statement on 9th Dey March.' In IRNA. Tehran: IRNA.

Ahmadinejad, M. 2011. 'In response to Fars News Agency.' In *Statements*, edited by Fars News. Tehran: Fars News Agency.

Ahmadinejad, M. 2011. 'President Ahmadinejad Speech in Yazd.' In *President Speeches*, edited by IRNA. Tehran, IR Iran: IRNA.

Ahmadinejad, M. 2011. 'President Speech to Iranian Ambassadors', *IRNA*, 28/12/2011 [07/10/1390].

Ahmadinejad, M. 2011. 'President: Serving the community through self-sacrifice is the most valuable work in the Islamic Republic', *Dolat.ir*, 16/03/2011 [24/12/1389].

Ahmadinejad, M. 2011. 'President's Press Conference 18/03/1390', *Kayhan*, 08/06/2011 [18/03/1390].

Ahmadinejad, M. 2012. 'Ahmadinejad France 24 Interview 31/05/2012', France 24.

Ahmadinejad, M. 2012. 'Ahmadinejad OIC Speech at the Emergency Meeting Mecca August 2012', *bpsp.ir*, 16/08/2012 [26/05/1391].

Ahmadinejad, M. 2013. 'Ahmadinejad Statement on General Hassan Shateri Assassasination in Syria', *Kayhan*, 16/02/2013 [28/11/1391].

Akbari, A. 2019. 'Friday Sermon 21/06/2019.' In *Friday Sermons – Dar Maktab-i Jom'ih*, edited by Centre for Cultural Documents of the Islamic Revolution. Tehran: Ministry of Islamic Guidance.

Akhavan-Kazemi, B. 2000. 'Divergences and Convergences in Iran Saudi Arabia Relations', *Quarterly Journal of Middle East Studies*, Summer: 115–46.

Al Ash-Sheikh, A. 2011. 'Kingdom's Mufti Friday Sermon – Riyadh', Aseer Foundation for Press and Publishing, Accessed 10/09/2021. https://www.alwatan.com.sa/article/78946.

Al Ash-Sheikh, A. 2016. 'Al-muftī ya'udd tahajjum Khāmina'i 'adā'an majūsiyyan', Mecca Newspaper, Accessed 14/02/2021. https://makkahnewspaper.com/article/194059/%D8%A7%D9%84%D8%A8%D9%84%D8%AF/%D8%A7%D9%84%D9%85%D9%81%D8%AA%D9%8A-%D9%8A%D8%B9%D8%AF-%D8%AA%D9%87%D8%AC%D9%85-%D8%AE%D8%A7%D9%85%D9%86%D8%A6%D9%8A-%D8%B9%D8%AF%D8%A7%D1-%D9%85%D8%AC%D9%88%D8%B3%D9%8A%D8%A7.

Al Ash-Sheikh, A., and A. Qa'idi. 2011. 'Abdulaziz Al ash-Sheikh Friday Sermon in Riyadh', YouTube, Accessed 01/12/2021. https://youtu.be/bK2XWIeoh74.

Al-Ahram. 1980. 'Khalid informs Saddam of Saudi Arabia's Support for Iraq.' In *Al-Ahram*. Cairo: King Khalid bin Abdul Aziz Database.

Al-Akhbar. 2019. 'The "Exit Strategy" from Yemen: the UAE seeks help from Iran', *Al-Akhbar*, 11/07/2019.

Al-Alam. 2012. 'The Satellite "Atlantic Bird 2" Cuts Off the Broadcast of Al-Alam Channel.' In, edited by Al-Alam Broadcasting. Tehran, I.R. Iran: IRIB.

Alam Al-Hoda, A. 2009. 'Speech on Tehran March 30/12/2009', 31/12/2009 [10/10/1388].

Al-Arabiya. 2014. 'Saudi FM: "Iran must withdraw 'occupying' forces from Syria", alarabiya.net, Accessed 10/01/2020. https://english.alarabiya.net/News/middle-east/2014/10/13/Saudi-FM-Iran-must-withdraw-occupying-forces-from-Syria.

Al-Arabiya. 2017. 'Al-Su'ūdiyyūn yubāyi'ūn Muḥammad ibn Salmān waliyyan li-l-'ahd', alarabiya.net, Accessed 15/02/2021. https://ara.tv/gvcfh.

Al-Arabiya, and A. Al-Askar. 2014. 'Iran deputy foreign minister to visit Saudi Arabia', alarabiya.net, Accessed 10/01/2020. https://english.alarabiya.net/News/middle-east/2014/08/25/Iran-deputy-foreign-minister-to-visit-Saudi-Arabia.

Al-Arabiya, and Y. Fazeli. 2020. 'Taliban condemn killing of Iran's Qassem Soleimani', alarabiya.net, Accessed 01/02/2022. https://english.alarabiya.net/News/middle-east/2020/01/05/Taliban-condemn-killing-of-Iran-s-Qassem-Soleimani-.

Al-Arabiya, and R. Taha. 2021. 'Gulf states, Israel demand seat at Iran nuclear deal negotiations: UAE Diplomat', alarabiya.net, Accessed 01/02/2022. https://english.alarabiya.net/News/gulf/2021/01/20/Gulf-states-Israel-demand-seat-at-Iran-nuclear-deal-negotiations-UAE-Diplomat.

Alarabiya.net. 2012. 'Iran's Military Units Jamming the Syrian Opposition Communications.' In Dubai, UAE: Alarabiya.net.

Albaharna, Husain M. 1968. *The Legal Status of the Arabian Gulf States: A Study of Their Treaty Relations and Their International Problems* (Manchester U.P.; Oceana Publications: Manchester; Dobbs Ferry, N.Y.).

Al-Bawaba. 2009. 'Ishtibāk fī sāḥat al-masjid al-nabawī ba'd muwājahāt al-Baqī'', Al-Bawaba, Accessed 01/02/2021. https://www.albawaba.com/ar/%D8%A3%D8%AE%D8%A8%D8%A7%D8%B1/%D8%A7%D8%B4%D8%AA%D8%A8%D8%A7%D9%83-%D9%81%D9%8A-%D8%B3%D8%A7%D8%AD%D8%A9-%D8%A7%D9%84%D9%85%D8%B3

%D8%AC%D8%AF-%D8%A7%D9%84%D9%86%D8%A8%D9%88%D9%8A-%D8%
A8%D8%B9%D8%AF-%D9%85%D9%88%D8%A7%D8%AC%D9%87%D8%A7%D8%
AA-%D8%A7%D9%84%D8%A8%D9%82%D9%8A%D8%B9?fbclid=IwAR2u5hteI8KU
4NGwtJ_KFLPs9kxf0Gc4y_V3qf_Ddl6KJGGt2vjXuGE8x84.

Al-Bawaba. 2017. 'Qatar Just Seemed to Rip into its Allies and Social Media is in Meltdown', *Al-Bawaba*, 24/05/2017.

Al-Dakhil, T. 2017. 'Wu'ūd Rūḥānī.. hal tuṣaddaq?', *Al-Riyadh*, 20/06/2013, p. 1.

Alexander, Michele G., Marilynn B. Brewer, and Richard K. Hermann. 1999. 'Images and Affect: A Functional Analysis of Out-Group Stereotypes', *Journal of Personality and Social Psychology*, 77: 78–93.

Al-Faisal, S. 1997. 'Prince Saud Al-Faisal bin Abdul Aziz Foreign Ministry Press Conference on Velayati Visit', *SPA*, 10/11/1997.

Al-Faisal, S. 1999. 'Saudi Foreign Minister Prince Saudi Al-Faisal Ibn Abdulaziz Statement on President Khatami's Visit to Riyadh', *SPA*, 17/05/1999.

Alfoneh, Ali. 2009. 'Iran's Presidential Election: A Predictable Victory for Khamenei', *Middle Eastern Outlook*, May 2009.

Algar, H. 2011. 'Imām-i Jom'a'. In *Encyclopædia Iranica*, 386–91. New York.

Alghannam, H. 2022. 'Saudi-Iran Relations', Youtube, Accessed 26/02/2022. https://www.youtube.com/watch?v=MneDNhEKUxA.

Al-Hayat. 1996. 'al-Harb 'alā al-'irhāb: Tafjīr Zahrān Yusari' Min Tabalwur al-Qarār al-Duwalī', *Al-Hayat*, 01/07/1996, p. 9.

Al-Hayat. 2006. 'Al-Fitna Wa Mas'ūliyat Ahli-l-'irāq', *Al-Hayat*, 23/02/2006.

Al-Hazimi, N. 2011. '*Ayām ma'a Juhaymān* (Arab Network for Research and Publishing: Riyadh).

Alhussein, Eman. 2019. *Saudi First: How Hyper-nationalism is Transforming Saudi Arabia* (European Council on Foreign Relations.).

Al-Jazeera. 2009. 'Clerics Reject Saudi fatwa on pro-Gaza demonstrations 13 February 2009.' In *BBC Monitoring*, edited by Al-Jazeera.net. London: BBC Monitoring International Reports.

Al-Jazeera. 2011. 'Bahrain king speaks of "foiled foreign plot"', Al Jazeera Media Network, Accessed 10/01/2020. https://www.aljazeera.com/news/2011/3/21/bahrain-king-speaks-of-foiled-foreign-plot.

Al-Jazeera. 2012. 'Syrian rebels say hostages "Iranian soldiers"', aljazeera.net, Accessed 13/03/2020. https://www.aljazeera.com/news/2012/8/5/syrian-rebels-say-hostages-iranian-soldiers.

Al-Jazeera. 2012. 'US recognises Syrian opposition coalition', aljazeera.com, Accessed 11/03/2020. https://www.aljazeera.com/news/2012/12/12/us-recognises-syrian-opposition-coalition.

Al-Jazeera. 2013. 'Qaradawi attacks Nasrallah', al-jazeera.net, Accessed 11/03/2020. https://aja.me/3w3j9.

Al-Jazeera. 2015. 'Itifāq Hūthī Ma'a Irān litwasee3 Meenā Al-Hudaydah', aljazeera.net, Accessed 09/03/2020. https://www.aljazeera.net/news/arabic/2015/3/14/%D8%A7%D8
%AA%D9%81%D8%A7%D9%82-%D8%AD%D9%88%D8%AB%D9%8A-%D8%
A5%D9%8A%D8%B1%D8%A7%D9%86%D9%8A-%D8%A8%D9%85%D8%
AC%D8%A7%D9%84-%D8%A7%D9%84%D8%B7%D8%A7%D9%82%D8%A9.

Al-Jazeera. 2020. 'Iraqi parliament calls for expulsion of foreign troops', aljazeera.com, Accessed 01/12/2021. https://www.aljazeera.com/news/2020/1/5/iraqi-parliament-calls-for-expulsion-of-foreign-troops.

Al-Jazeera. 2020. 'Netanyahu met MBS, Pompeo in Saudi Arabia: Israeli media', aljazeera. com, Accessed 01/02/2022. https://www.aljazeera.com/news/2020/11/23/netanyahu-met-with-mbs-pompeo-in-saudi-arabia-israeli-sources.

Al-Jazeera, and A.H. Abdolahian. 2022. 'Interview with Iranian Foreign Minister A.H. Abdolahian', aljazeera.net, Accessed 01/02/2022. https://www.aljazeera.net/news/2022/1/9/%D9%86%D9%88%D9%88%D9%8A-%D8%A5%D9%8A%D8%B1%D8%A7%D9%86-%D9%85%D8%A8%D8%A7%D8%AD%D8%AB%D8%A7%D8%AA-%D9%81%D9%8A%D9%8A%D9%86%D8%A7.

Al-Jazeera, and H. Dehghan. 2019. 'Interview with the Military Adviser to the Supreme Leader, 26 July 2019', Al-Jazeera Media, Accessed 10/01/2020. https://www.youtube.com/watch?v=Idqtl8EeoD0.

Al-Jazira. 1980. 'Telephone Conversation Between King Khalid and Saddam Hussein.' In *Al-Jazira*. Riyadh: King Khalid bin Abdul Aziz Database.

al-Jazirah. 2011. 'GCC Summit Final Statement Mecca', *Al-Jazirah*, 11/03/2011.

al-Jazirah. 2013. 'Taʿlīqan ʿalā taʾyīd al-Shaykh al-Qaraḍāwī li-ʿulamāʾ al-Mamlaka tujāh Ḥizb Allāh', *Al-Jazirah*, 07/06/2013, p. 9.

al-Jazirah. 2015. 'Al-ʿahd huwa al-ʿahd', *Al-Jazirah*, Accessed 15/02/2021. https://www.al-jazirah.com/2015/20150430/ria1.htm.

al-Jazirah. 2015. 'ʿĀṣifat al-ḥazm bidāya li-istiqrār al-Yaman', *al-Jazirah*, 27/03/2015, p. 9.

al-Jazirah. 2015. 'Ḥīn lā yanfaʿ al-bukāʾ, *al-Jazirah*, 29/03/2015, p. 9.

al-Jazirah. 2015. 'Li-kay lā tabkī Īrān marra ukhrā', *al-Jazirah*, 30/03/2015, p. 9.

al-Jazirah. 2015. 'Mā baʿd al-ṣabr.. mā baʿd al-ḥulm', *al-Jazirah*, 28/03/2015], p. 9.

al-Jazirah. 2015. 'Min qaṣr al-ḥukm ilā qaṣr Muqrin', *al-Jazirah*, 01/05/2015], p. 9.

al-Jazirah. 2015. 'Tawaqqafat al-ʿāṣifa.. wa-baqiya al-ḥazm', *al-Jazirah*, 26/04/2015, p. 1.

al-Jazirah. 2019. 'Fatīl al-ḥarb min Īrān', *al-Jazirah*, 19/09/2019, p. 1.

al-Jazirah. 2019. 'Īrān bayn al-ʿIrāq wa-Lubnan', *al-Jazirah*, 04/11/2019, p. 1.

al-Jazirah. 2019. 'Layl Īrān al-ṭawīl', *al-Jazirah*, 17/11/2019, p. 9.

al-Jubeir, A. 2015. 'Saudi Arabia Rejects Iran's Criticism of Hajj Tragedy', *Saudi Embassy, Washington DC*, 27/09/2015.

al-Jubeir, A. 2015. 'Statement on Beginning of Operation Decisive Force', 26/03/2015.

al-Jubeir, A. 2016. 'Foreign Minister Announces the Kingdom's Cutting its Diplomatic Relations with Iran, withdrawing its personnel within 48 hrs', *SPA*, 04/01/2016.

al-Jubeir, A. 2017. 'Speech Davos World Economic Forum', 19/01/2017.

al-Jubeir, A. 2019. 'A Conversation With Minister Adel al-Jubeir of Saudi Arabia', *CFR*, 24/09/2019.

al-Jubeir, A. 2019. 'Saudi Minister of State for Foreign Affairs Statement in Response to Khashoggi Calamard Report', *Arab News*, 19/06/2019.

al-Jubeir, A. 2020. 'Adel Al-Jubeir Twitter 03 January 2020', Accessed 15/01/2021. https://twitter.com/AdelAljubeir/status/1213232867377123329.

al-Jubeir, A., and W. Blitzer. 2017. 'The Situation Room–Transcript of Interview with Adel Al-Jubeir', cnn.com, Accessed 15/01/2020. http://transcripts.cnn.com/TRANSCRIPTS/1607/16/se.03.html.

al-Jubeir, A., and CNN. 2017. 'Interview with Saudi Foreign Minister', Accessed 15/01/2020. https://edition.cnn.com/2017/11/06/middleeast/saudi-foreign-minister-interview/index.html.

Al-Kawaz, M. 2014. *Al-ʿilāqāt al-Suʿuwwdiya Al-ʾīrāniya 1979–2011* (Al Manhal: Amman).

Al-Khaleej. 2015. 'ʿĀṣifat al-ḥazm.. ḥikmat muʾassis al-Suʿūdiyya al-latī ṣārat ʿamaliyya ʿaskariyya', Al-Khaleej Online, Accessed 09/03/2021. https://alkhaleejonline.net/%D8%

B3%D9%8A%D8%A7%D8%B3%D8%A9/%D8%B9%D8%A7%D8%B5%D9%81%D8
%A9-%D8%A7%D9%84%D8%AD%D8%B2%D9%85-%D8%AD%D9%83%D9%85%
D8%A9-%D9%85%D8%A4%D8%B3%D8%B3-%D8%A7%D9%84%D8%B3%D8%B9
%D9%88%D8%AF%D9%8A%D8%A9-%D8%A7%D9%84%D8%AA%D9%8A-%
D8%B5%D8%A7%D8%B1%D8%AA-%D8%B9%D9%85%D9%84%D9%8A%D8%A9-
%D8%B9%D8%B3%D9%83%D8%B1%D9%8A%D8%A9.

Al-Madina. 1980. 'Sultān: Rudūd Tukhrisu al-ʾalsina', *Al-Madina*, 26/12/1980 [18/02/1401],
p. 2.

Al-Madina. 1981. 'Al-dars al-Suʿūdī ... Min Safqat al-ʾāwāks', *Al-Madina*, 02/11/1981
[04/01/1402], p. 2.

Al-Madina. 1981. 'al-Madāmīn al-Khayirah Fī Hadīth al-Fahd', *Al-Madina*, 10/08/1981
[09/10/1401], p. 2.

Al-Madina. 1981. 'Lā Khayār ʾamām al-ʿArab Afzal Min al-Mashrūʿ al-Suʿūdī', *Al-Madina*,
27/11/1981 [29/01/1402], p. 2.

Al-Madina. 1981. 'Man Yalūmunā', *Al-Madina*, 29/09/1981 [30/11/1401], p. 2.

Al-Madina. 1981. 'Mathā Yurīdūn al-Munāfiqūn Fī Irān Min al-Mamlaka wa Mashrūʿahā',
Al-Madina, 23/11/1981 [25/01/1402], p. 2.

Al-Madina. 1981. 'Najāhātunā al-Siyāsiya', *Al-Madina*, 13/09/1981 [14/11/1401], p. 2.

Al-Madina. 1981. 'Quwāt Al-Mamlaka..Quwah lil-Islām Wa lil-Muslimīn', *Al-Madina*,
04/11/1981 [06/01/1402], p. 2.

Al-Madina. 1982. 'al-Tahāluf al-ʾīrānī a-Lībī al-ʾisrāʾīlī', *Al-Madina*, 29/05/1982
[05/08/1402], p. 2.

Al-Madina. 1982. 'Kalima Mukhlisah Min ʾajl Hadaf Nabīl', *Al-Madina*, 01/01/1982
[05/03/1402], p. 2.

Al-Madina. 1997. 'al-Quds ʿinwān al-Hal Wa-l-ʿaqd', *Al-Madina*, 06/03/1997 [26/10/1417],
p. 2.

Al-Madina. 1997. 'Irān Maʿa Khatami al-Mumarasa Wal-Khitāb', *Al-Madina*, 13/08/1997
[10/04/1418], p. 2.

Al-Madina. 1997. 'Ithā Ghāba al-Salām Falaysa lilʿarab Ma Yakhsarūnah', *Al-Madina*,
04/03/1997 [24/10/1417], p. 2.

Al-Madina. 1997. 'Mafhūm al-Mamlaka Lil-salām al-Shāmil', *Al-Madina*, 26/03/1997
[17/11/1417], p. 2.

Al-Madina. 1997. 'Talat Abu-Ghnaym Tabhath ʿan Jarafāt ʿarabiya', *Al-Madina*, 19/03/1997
[10/11/1417], p. 2.

Al-Madina. 1998. 'Nitinyāhu li-Washington: Ana il-tabākh al-Wahīd', *Al-Madina*,
25/03/1997 [26/11/1418], p. 2.

Al-Maeena, K. 2001. 'Kingdom, Iran sign historic agreement', Saudi Research and
Publishing Company, Accessed 24/02/2022. https://www.arabnews.com/node/211187.

Al-Mayadeen, and A. Mousavi. 2019. 'Game of Nations, 24 July 2019', Al-Mayadeen
Channel, Accessed 10/01/2020. https://www.almayadeen.net/episodes/965670/%D9%8
4%D8%B9%D8%A8%D8%A9-%D8%A7%D9%84%D8%A3%D9%85%D9%85_%D9%
87%D9%84-%D8%B5%D8%A7%D8%B1%D8%AA-%D8%A3%D9%85%D9%8A%D8
%B1%D9%83%D8%A7-%D8%A3%D9%82%D8%B1%D8%A8-%D8%A5%D9%84%
D9%89-%D8%A7%D9%84%D8%AD%D8%B1%D8%A8-%D9%85%D9%86-%D8%A
7%D9%84%D8%AA%D9%81%D8%A7%D9%88%D8%B6.

Al-Monitor, and A. Hashem. 2014. 'Rafsanjani offers road map for Iran-Saudi ties',
Al-Monitor, Accessed 10/01/2020. https://www.al-monitor.com/originals/2014/05/
iran-saudi-arabia-relations-road-map-rafsanjani-regional.html.

Al-Monitor, and L. Rozen. 2020. 'Pompeo mocks claim Soleimani was part of Iraq-
brokered Iran-Saudi indirect talks', *Al-Monitor*, 07/01/2020.

Al-Monitor, and S. Siddiqui. 2022. 'Will Iran recognize Taliban government in Afghanistan?', Al-Monitor, Accessed 01/02/2022. https://www.al-monitor.com/ originals/2022/01/will-iran-recognize-taliban-government-afghanistan.

Al-Nadwa. 1982. 'Completion of Three Housing Projects in Jeddah, Riyadh and Dammam.' In *Al-Nadwa*. King Khalid bin Abdul Aziz Online Database.

al-Nimr, N.B. 2009. 'Khuṭba- mawqifunā min intifāḍat al-Baqīʿ', YouTube.com, Accessed 01/12/2021. https://youtu.be/ZfhPIgFJ9pA.

Al-Rasheed, M. 1996. 'God, the king and the nation: Political rhetoric in Saudi Arabia in the 1990s', *The Middle East Journal*: 359–71.

Al-Rasheed, M. 1998. 'The Shi'a of Saudi Arabia: A Minority in Search of Cultural Authenticity', *British Journal of Middle Eastern Studies*, 25: 121–38.

Al-Rasheed, M. 2010. *A History of Saudi Arabia* (Cambridge University Press: Cambridge).

Al-Rasheed, M. 2017. 'The New Populist Nationalism in Saudi Arabia: Imagined Utopia by Royal Decree', Accessed 05/05/2020. https://blogs.lse.ac.uk/mec/2020/05/05/the-new-populist-nationalism-in-saudi-arabia-imagined-utopia-by-royal-decree/.

Al-Rasheed, M. 2021. *The Son King: Reform and Repression in Saudi Arabia* (Oxford University Press: Oxford).

Al-Rawi, A. 2021. *Cyberwars in the Middle East* (Rutgers University Press: New Brunswick, NJ).

Al-Riyadh. 1979. 'al-Muqātilūn Bihibr al-Maʿlūmāt', *Al-Riyadh*, 03/12/1979 [13/01/1400].

Al-Riyadh. 1979. 'al-Yaqazah al-Dāʾima', *Al-Riyadh*, 28/11/1979 [08/01/1400], p. 1.

Al-Riyadh. 1979. 'Muntahā al-Hikmah', *Al-Riyadh*, 22/11/1979 [03/01/1400], p. 1.

Al-Riyadh. 1979. 'Official Statement on the Siege of the Grand Mosque', *Al-Riyadh*, 22/11/1979 [03/01/1400], p. 1.

Al-Riyadh. 1979. 'Rijāl al-Dīn Wa al-Dawlah Wa Muwājahat al-Khawārij', *Al-Riyadh*, 02/12/1979 [12/01/1400].

Al-Riyadh. 1980. 'al-Sabr al-Dduwalī', *Al-Riyadh*, 09/10/1980, p. 1.

Al-Riyadh. 1980. 'Fahd Interview with Al-Safir Newspaper', *Al-Riyadh*, 13–14/01/1980, p. 1.

Al-Riyadh. 1981. 'ʾamn al-Khalīj … Taʿāmul maʿa al-Haqīqa', *Al-Riyadh*, 28/12/1981, pp. 1, 17.

Al-Riyadh. 1981. 'ʾayāt al-Hiqd Wa al-Takhrīb', *Al-Riyadh*, 15/12/1981, p. 1.

Al-Riyadh. 1981. 'ʾindamā Taltaqī Tahrān wa Talʾabīb', *Al-Riyadh*, 02/10/1981, p. 1.

Al-Riyadh. 1981. 'ʾindamā Yakūn al-Tarīkh Shāhidan', *Al-Riyadh*, 28/11/1981, p. 1.

Al-Riyadh. 1981. 'Tasdīr al-ʾazamāt', *Al-Riyadh*, 28/09/1981, p. 1.

Al-Riyadh. 1982. 'al-ʾahdāf al-Haqīqiya Lil-harb al-ʿirāqiya al-ʾirāniya', *Al-Riyadh*, 22/05/1982, p. 1.

Al-Riyadh. 1982. 'al-Khalīj..al-Bināʾ..Wa al-ʾistiqrār', *Al-Riyadh*, 26/05/1982, p. 1.

Al-Riyadh. 1982. 'al-Tahadī Wa al-Muwājaha', *Al-Riyadh*, 24/01/1982, p. 1.

Al-Riyadh. 1982. 'al-Waqiʿ … Wa ʾawhām al-ʾayāt', *Al-Riyadh*, 02/01/1982, pp. 1, 17.

Al-Riyadh. 1997. 'Afkār al-ʾarānib Wa Afʿāl al-ʾusūd', *Al-Riyadh*, 22/02/1997, p. 1.

Al-Riyadh. 1997. 'al-ʾamīr Nāyif ..Wa Rasānat al-Masʾūliya', *Al-Riyadh*, 11/04/1997, p. 1.

Al-Riyadh. 1997. 'al-Jawlāt al-Siyāsia al-Nājiha', *Al-Riyadh*, 14/03/1997, p. 1.

Al-Riyadh. 1997. 'Al-Mamlaka..Haraka ʿalā al-Jabha al-ʿarabiya..Wal-ʾislāmiya', *Al-Riyadh*, 03/07/1997, p. 1.

Al-Riyadh. 1997. 'Al-Mamlaka..Wa Dibumāsiyat-l-ʿamal al-Qawmī', *Al-Riyadh*, 27/02/1997, p. 1.

Al-Riyadh. 1997. 'Al-Mamlaka..Wa Iran Fī Siyaghat Mustaqbal Baʿīd', *Al-Riyadh*, 17/03/1997, p. 1.

Al-Riyadh. 1997. 'Asharq Al-Awsat Bayna Qimatayn', *Al-Riyadh*, 14/12/1997, p. 1.

Al-Riyadh. 1997. 'Hal Badaʾa ʿahd Islāmī Jadīd', *Al-Riyadh*, 10/12/1997, p. 1.

Al-Riyadh. 1997. 'Isrāʾil..Wa-l-liʿb al-ʿarabī al-Mur', *Al-Riyadh*, 11/03/1997, p. 1.

Al-Riyadh. 1997. 'Khātamī . . . wa ʾāmāl Biʾilāqāt Tayiba Maʿa al-ʿarab', *Al-Riyadh*, 04/08/1997, p. 1.

Al-Riyadh. 1997. 'Qimat Tahrān..Hal Takūn Bidaya Li-takatul Islāmī Jadīd', *Al-Riyadh*, 08/12/1997, p. 1.

Al-Riyadh. 1997. 'Qimat Tahrān..Hal Tatakhid Mawqifan Min Isrāʾīl', *Al-Riyadh*, 05/12/1997, p. 1.

Al-Riyadh. 1997. 'Rūsiyā.. Bayna al-Hawiya al-ʿurubiya..Wal-Tatalu' al-ʾāsiyawī', *Al-Riyadh*, 26/03/1997, p. 1.

Al-Riyadh. 1997. 'Tabal al-ʿarab Faraqasat Isrāʾīl', *Al-Riyadh*, 10/03/1997, p. 1.

Al-Riyadh. 1997. 'Wa Kayf Nastaʾīd Baʿd Quwaitinā al-Siyāsiya', *Al-Riyadh*, 03/04/1997, p. 1.

Al-Riyadh. 1997. 'Wa Ladaynā Mantiqinā Fī Kafaʾatinā al-ʿamniya', *Al-Riyadh*, 10/04/1997, p. 1.

Al-Riyadh. 1997. 'Wa Limādhā al-ʿilāqa Maʿa Amrīkā!?_2', *Al-Riyadh*, 26/02/1997, p. 1.

Al-Riyadh. 1997. 'Ziyārat Tadhāmun wa Taʿmīq al-Rawābit', *Al-Riyadh*, 27/06/1997, p. 1.

Al-Riyadh. 2005. 'al-Malik ʿabdallah . . . Wa Qiyādat Qimat al-Taʾsīs lil-ʿamal al-ʾIsāmī', *Al-Riyadh*, 08/12/2005.

Al-Riyadh. 2005. 'Qimat al-Turuq al-Maftūha . . . Am al-Mughlaqa?!', *Al-Riyadh*, 06/12/2005.

Al-Riyadh. 2006. 'al-ʿirāq Fī Mahab il-ʾawāsif', *Al-Riyadh*, 26/02/2006.

Al-Riyadh. 2006. 'Muqadimat Hurūb Tawīla Bayna al-ʿarab Wa Isrāʾīl', *Al-Riyadh*, 13/07/2006.

Al-Riyadh. 2006. 'Salām Muʿatal Fī ʾāfāq Harb Mustamira', *Al-Riyadh*, 20/07/2006.

Al-Riyadh. 2006. 'Wa Ahlām Al-Walīd', *Al-Riyadh*, 17/07/2006.

Al-Riyadh. 2009. 'Iran al-Dawlah ʾam al-Thawra', *Al-Riyadh*, 20/02/2009, p. 1.

Al-Riyadh. 2009. 'Īrān.. ḍaḥiyyat al-taghyīr.. wa-l-taghayyur', *Al-Riyadh*, 24/06/2009, p. 1.

Al-Riyadh. 2009. 'Īrān.. hāmish al-ḥurriyya lā yaqtul', *Al-Riyadh*, 21/08/2009, p. 1.

Al-Riyadh. 2009. 'Īrān.. makhāḍ al-intikhābāt', *Al-Riyadh*, 11/06/2009, p. 1.

Al-Riyadh. 2009. 'Manābi' al-khilāf ʿalā taʾsīs al-dawla al-ḥadītha', *Al-Riyadh*, 03/08/2009, p. 1.

Al-Riyadh. 2009. 'Referral of those accused of causing chaos near the Prophet's Mosque to the Public Prosecution', *Al-Riyadh*, 22/02/2009, p. 1.

Al-Riyadh. 2010. 'Al-dīmūqrāṭiyya lā taṣluḥ li-l-ʿArab', *Al-Riyadh*, 25/12/2010, p. 1.

Al-Riyadh. 2010. 'Wa-naḥnu ma' ʿalāqāt mumayyaza ma' Īrān', *Al-Riyadh*, 20/12/2010, p. 1.

Al-Riyadh. 2011. 'Al-ab al-akbar li-kull al-ʿArab', *Al-Riyadh*, 20/12/2011, p. 1.

Al-Riyadh. 2011. 'Al-baṭāla amām al-ḥulūl al-mustaḥīla', *Al-Riyadh*, 06/01/2011, p. 1.

Al-Riyadh. 2011. 'Al-ḥilf al-Fārisī al-Shīʿī yatafakkak', *Al-Riyadh*, 20/08/2011, p. 1.

Al-Riyadh. 2011. 'Al-ʿIrāq wa-Sūriyya.. wa-mustaqbaluhumā ma' Īrān', *Al-Riyadh*, 18/12/2011, p. 1.

Al-Riyadh. 2011. 'Al-ittiḥād al-Khalījī.. min al-fikra ilā al-taṭbīq', *Al-Riyadh*, 21/12/2011, p. 1.

Al-Riyadh. 2011. 'Al-rajul al-shujāʿ fī zaman al-takhādhul al-ʿArabī', *Al-Riyadh*, 08/08/2011, p. 1.

Al-Riyadh. 2011. 'Al-rajul al-shujāʿ fī zaman al-takhādhul al-ʿArabī', *Al-Riyadh*, 09/08/2011, p. 1.

Al-Riyadh. 2011. 'Al-ṭarīq li-l-ḥurriyya.. wa-l-taḥarrur', *Al-Riyadh*, 07/02/2011, p. 1.

Al-Riyadh. 2011. 'Al-thawrāt.. wa-l-dawr al-iqlīmī al-murīb', *Al-Riyadh*, 13/03/2011, p. 1.

Al-Riyadh. 2011. 'Al-thawrāt wa-muḥīṭuhā.. man yuʾaththar fī l-ākhir?', *Al-Riyadh*, 27/04/2011, p. 1.

Al-Riyadh. 2011. 'Al-Yaman ṣāra sa 'īdan', *Al-Riyadh*, 25/11/2011, p. 1.

Al-Riyadh. 2011. 'Da 'ūhum biṣamtihim yas 'adūn', *Al-Riyadh*, 06/08/2011, p. 1.

Al-Riyadh. 2011. 'Hal bu 'itha Hūlākū min jadīd?', *Al-Riyadh*, 06/04/2011, p. 1.

Al-Riyadh. 2011. 'Īrān dawla irhābiyya!!', *Al-Riyadh*, 14/11/2011, p. 1.

Al-Riyadh. 2011. 'Īrān dawla taḥtarif al-irhāb', *Al-Riyadh*, 13/10/2011, p. 1.

Al-Riyadh. 2011. 'Īrān fī muwājahat al-idāna al-duwaliyya', *Al-Riyadh*, 20/11/2011, p. 1.

Al-Riyadh. 2011. 'Īrān.. 'uqdat al-madhhab.. wa-l-wahm al-imbiraṭūrī', *Al-Riyadh*, 03/04/2011, p. 1.

Al-Riyadh. 2011. 'Lā.. li-ayy wiṣāya khārijiyya', *Al-Riyadh*, 10/03/2011, p. 1.

Al-Riyadh. 2011. 'Ma 'āziq Īrān.. al-waḍ ' fī Sūriyya.. wa- 'uqdat al-marja 'iyya', *Al-Riyadh*, 11/08/2011, p. 1.

Al-Riyadh. 2011. 'Mādhā ta 'nī al-khiyārāt al-ukhrā li-Amrīka tujāh Īrān?', *Al-Riyadh*, 15/10/2011, p. 1.

Al-Riyadh. 2011. 'Mā jarā fī Miṣr laysa thawra khumayyniyya', *Al-Riyadh*, 09/02/2011, p. 1.

Al-Riyadh. 2011. 'Makhāṭir mā ba 'd al-thawrāt', *Al-Riyadh*, 11/03/2011, p. 1.

Al-Riyadh. 2011. 'Mashrū ' inqādh Khalījī li-l-Baḥrayn', *Al-Riyadh*, 19/02/2011, p. 1.

Al-Riyadh. 2011. 'Qimmat al-ḥisābāt al-mu 'aqqada', *Al-Riyadh*, 19/12/2011, p. 1.

Al-Riyadh. 2011. 'Siyāsat al-taḍlīl.. wa-l-khidā ', *Al-Riyadh*, 12/03/2011, p. 1.

Al-Riyadh. 2011. 'Sūriyā.. bi-ayy ittijāh tasīr?', *Al-Riyadh*, 19/04/2011, p. 1.

Al-Riyadh. 2011. 'Sūriyā.. wa-hawājis al-jīrān', *Al-Riyadh*, 11/06/2011, p. 1.

Al-Riyadh. 2011. 'Sūriyā.. irhāb al-sulṭa.. wa-ṣumūd al-sha 'b', *Al-Riyadh*, 27/08/2011, p. 1.

Al-Riyadh. 2011. 'Thawrat muhammashīn.. am fawḍāhum?', *Al-Riyadh*, 31/01/2011, p. 1.

Al-Riyadh. 2011. 'Turkiyā.. Īrān.. hal min 'awda li-ṣirā ' jadīd?', *Al-Riyadh*, 10/10/2011, p. 1.

Al-Riyadh. 2011. 'Wa-ayna shujā 'at al-Jāmi 'a al- 'Arabiyya?', *Al-Riyadh*, 11/12/2011, p. 1.

Al-Riyadh. 2011. 'Wa-lam taduqq ajrās al-fawḍā', *Al-Riyadh*, 14/03/2011, p. 1.

Al-Riyadh. 2011. 'Wa-saqaṭat jumhūriyyāt al-tawrīth', *Al-Riyadh*, 06/02/2011, p. 1.

Al-Riyadh. 2012. 'Al-balad al-mufakhkhakh!', *Al-Riyadh*, 18/10/2012, p. 1.

Al-Riyadh. 2012. 'Al-farḍiyya al-mustaḥīla', *Al-Riyadh*, 16/01/2012, p. 1.

Al-Riyadh. 2012. 'Al-ḥiwār al-mamnū ' ma ' Rūsiyā', *Al-Riyadh*, 23/02/2012, p. 1.

Al-Riyadh. 2012. 'Al-mutalā 'ibūn fī Lubnān!!', *Al-Riyadh*, 24/05/2012, p. 1.

Al-Riyadh. 2012. 'Al-taqṣīr al- 'Arabī fī Sūriyā', *Al-Riyadh*, 22/02/2012, p. 1.

Al-Riyadh. 2012. 'Hal taḥālafat al-Qā 'ida ma ' niẓām Dimashq?', *Al-Riyadh*, 24/10/2012, p. 1.

Al-Riyadh. 2012. 'Hal taḥsim Dimashq nihāyat al-Asad?', *Al-Riyadh*, 19/07/2012, p. 1.

Al-Riyadh. 2012. 'Ḥarb iqlīmiyya 'alā l-arḍ al-Sūriyya', *Al-Riyadh*, 09/08/2012, p. 1.

Al-Riyadh. 2012. 'Irhāb mufta 'al.. am ḥaqīqī?', *Al-Riyadh*, 06/08/2012, p. 1.

Al-Riyadh. 2012. 'Mā hiya dawāfi ' al-munāwarāt al- 'askariyya fī l-Khalīj?', *Al-Riyadh*, 18/09/2012, p. 1.

Al-Riyadh. 2012. 'Nuḥāwir aṣḥāb al-adyān.. fa-limādhā lā nuḥāwir anfusanā?', *Al-Riyadh*, 16/08/2012, p. 1.

Al-Riyadh. 2012. 'Sūriyā.. dawlat al-mukhāda 'a', *Al-Riyadh*, 19/05/2012, p. 1.

Al-Riyadh. 2012. 'Sūriyā.. ḥalaqat al-ṣirā ' al-duwalī', *Al-Riyadh*, 20/02/2012, p. 1.

Al-Riyadh. 2012. 'Sūriyya amām al-tadwīl', *Al-Riyadh*, 29/01/2012, p. 1.

Al-Riyadh. 2012. 'Tha 'ālib Sūriyā sayufshilūn al-mubādara', *Al-Riyadh*, 24/12/2012, p. 1.

Al-Riyadh. 2012. 'Wa-bada 'at al-masāḥāt taḍīq 'alā l-Asad', *Al-Riyadh*, 20/07/2012, p. 1.

Al-Riyadh. 2013. 'Al-intiṣār al-ilāhī fī l-Quṣayr', *Al-Riyadh*, 22/05/2013, p. 1.

Al-Riyadh. 2013. 'Al- 'Irāq.. siyādat al-fawḍā', *Al-Riyadh*, 27/02/2013, p. 1.

Al-Riyadh. 2013. 'Dākhil Sūriyya.. ḥarb 'ālamiyya muṣaghghara', *Al-Riyadh*, 11/06/2013, p. 1.

Al-Riyadh. 2013. 'Hal nu 'akkid annanā lasnā al-ḥā 'iṭ al-qaṣīr?', *Al-Riyadh*, 23/02/2013, p. 1.

Al-Riyadh. 2013. 'Ḥizb Allāh.. munaẓẓama irhābiyya', *Al-Riyadh*, 01/06/2013, p. 1.

Al-Riyadh. 2013. 'Īrān wa-Isrā'īl.. wa-baynahumā Sūriyā', *Al-Riyadh*, 05/02/2013, p. 1.

Al-Riyadh. 2013. 'Mā hiya nawāyā Isrā'īl ma' al-ḥāla al-Sūriyya?', *Al-Riyadh*, 01/02/2013, p. 1.

Al-Riyadh. 2013. 'Naṣr Allāh.. Lubnānī am Fārisī?', *Al-Riyadh*, 27/05/2013, p. 1.

Al-Riyadh. 2013. 'Sūriyā.. hal takūn qā'idat ḥarb Sunniyya.. Shī'iyya?', *Al-Riyadh*, 24/04/2013, p. 1.

Al-Riyadh. 2013. ''Ulamā' al-Islām.. al-taḍāmun wa-mas'ūliyyat mā yajrī li-Sūriyā', *Al-Riyadh*, 08/06/2013, p. 1.

Al-Riyadh. 2017. 'Al-siyāda al-Lubnāniyya', *Al-Riyadh*, 12/11/2017, p. 1.

Al-Riyadh. 2017. 'Ikhtilāf al-ḥāl', *Al-Riyadh*, 11/11/2017, p. 1.

Al-Riyadh. 2017. 'Īrān al-Nāziyya', *Al-Riyadh*, 26/11/2017, p. 1.

Al-Riyadh. 2017. 'Lubnān yadfa' al-thaman', *Al-Riyadh*, 13/11/2017, p. 1.

Al-Riyadh. 2017. 'Muḥammad bin Salmān.. waliyyan li-l-'ahd', *Al-Riyadh*, 22/06/2017, p. 1.

Al-Riyadh. 2017. 'Ta'āmul mukhtalif', *Al-Riyadh*, 09/11/2017, p. 1.

Al-Riyadh. 2017. 'Taḥāluf al-maṣāliḥ al-'ābira', *Al-Riyadh*, 29/05/2017, p. 1.

Al-Riyadh. 2017. 'Wāqi' jadīd', *Al-Riyadh*, 08/11/2017, p. 1.

Al-Riyadh. 2019. 'Al-aḥlām al-ḍā'i'a', *Al-Riyadh*, 23/11/2019, p. 1.

Al-Riyadh. 2019. 'Al-inkishāf al-Īrānī', *Al-Riyadh*, 18/10/2019, p. 1.

Al-Riyadh. 2019. 'Al-'Irāq wa-maḥādhīr al-fawḍā', *Al-Riyadh*, 04/10/2019, p. 1.

Al-Riyadh. 2019. 'Risāla ilā l-'ālam', *Al-Riyadh*, 01/10/2019, p. 1.

Al-Riyadh. 2020. 'Jinirāl al-dam', *Al-Riyadh*, 04/01/2020, p. 1.

Al-Sadr, M. 2022. 'Sayyid Muqtada Al-Sadr Twitter 08 February 2022', twitter.com, Accessed 15/02/2022. https://twitter.com/Mu_AlSadr/status/1491099678708240384?cx t=HHwWgMDUob7QubEpAAAA.

al-Saud, A. 1988. 'Crown Prince Abdullah bin Abdulaziz Press Interview with Asharq Al-Awsat', *Asharq Al-Awsat*, 18/06/1988, p. 1.

al-Saud, A. 1996. 'Crown Prince Abdullah bin Abdulaziz Press Statement.' In *Royal Statements*, edited by SPA. Riyadh, KSA: SPA.

al-Saud, A. 1996. 'Crown Prince Abdullah bin Abdulaziz Speech at the 17th Annual GCC Summit.' In *Royal Statements*, edited by SPA. Riyadh, KSA: SPA.

al-Saud, A. 1997. 'Crown Prince Abdullah bin Abdulaziz Press Interview at the OIC Summit Tehran.' In *Royal Statements*, edited by SPA. Riyadh, KSA: SPA.

al-Saud, A. 1997. 'Crown Prince Abdullah bin Abdulaziz Press Statement on Arrival to Tehran for the OIC Summit.' In *Royal Statements*, edited by SPA. Riyadh, KSA: SPA.

al-Saud, A. 1997. 'Crown Prince Abdullah bin Abdulaziz Speech at Extraordinary OIC Conference in Islamabad.' In *Royal Statements*, edited by SPA. Riyadh, KSA: SPA.

al-Saud, A. 1997. 'Crown Prince Abdullah bin Abdulaziz Speech at OIC Summit in Tehran.' In *Royal Statements*, edited by SPA. Riyadh, KSA: SPA.

al-Saud, A. 2005. 'Crown Prince Abdullah bin Abdulaziz Al-Saud Annual Hajj Speech 21 May 2005.' In *Royal Statements*, edited by SPA. Riyadh: SPA.

al-Saud, A. 2005. 'Crown Prince Abdullah bin Abdulaziz Al-Saud Interview with Le Monde.' In *Royal Statements*, edited by SPA. Riyadh, KSA: KSA.

al-Saud, A. 2005. 'Crown Prince Abdullah bin Abdulaziz Al-Saud Speech to the Hajj Pilgrims.' In *Royal Statements*, edited by SPA. Riyadh: SPA.

al-Saud, A. 2005. 'Crown Prince Abdullah bin Abadulaziz Speech at the International Terrorism Conference in Riyadh.' In *Royal Statements*, edited by SPA. Riyadh, KSA: King Abdulazizi Publishers.

al-Saud, A. 2005. 'King's Speech at the OIC Opening Session 8 December 2005.' In *Royal Statements*, edited by SPA. Riyadh, KSA: SPA.

al-Saud, A. 2005. 'King's Speech on Rafsanjani Visit 18 September 2005.' In *Royal Statements*, edited by SPA. Riyadh, KSA: SPA.

al-Saud, A. 2005. 'Telegram on Ahmadinejad Victory 26 June 2005.' In *Royal Statements*, edited by SPA. Riyadh, KSA: SPA.

al-Saud, A. 2006. 'King's Statement Arab League Meeting in Kuwait 27 February 2006.' In *Royal Statements*, edited by SPA. Riyadh, KSA: SPA.

al-Saud, A. 2011. 'Custodian of the Two Holy Mosques and Egyptian President – Phone call 29 January 2011.' In *Royal Statements*, edited by SPA. Riyadh, KSA: SPA.

al-Saud, A. 2011. 'Custodian of the Two Holy Mosques Speech on Syria', alarabiya.net, Accessed 24/08/2021. https://www.alarabiya.net/articles/2011%2F08%2F08%2F161279.

al-Saud, A. 2011. 'King Abdullah bin Abdulaziz Al-Saud Receives a Telephone Call from President Obama 30 January 2011.' In *Royal Statements*, edited by SPA. Riyadh, KSA: SPA.

al-Saud, A. 2011. 'King's Statement at the Opening of the Thirty Second Round of the Supreme Council of the GCC 20 December 2011.' In *Royal Statements*, edited by SPA. Riyadh, KSA: SPA.

al-Saud, A. 2012. 'The Custodian of the Two Holy Mosques receives a phone call from the Russian President 22 February 2012.' In *Royal Statements*, edited by SPA. Riyadh, KSA: SPA.

al-Saud, A. 2012. 'Custodian of the Two Holy Mosques receives National Guard guests participating in the National Festival for Heritage and Culture 10 February 2012.' In *Royal Statements*, edited by SPA. Riyadh, KSA: SPA.

al-Saud, A. 2012. 'The Custodian of the Two Holy Mosques Sends a Telegram to the President of the Lebanese Republic.' In *Royal Statements*, edited by SPA. Riyadh, KSA: SPA.

al-Saud, A. 2012. 'King Abdullah Speech in Response to the Chinese and Russian Veto on Syria.' In *Royal Statements*, edited by SPA. Riyadh, KSA: Al-Watan.

al-Saud, F. 1980. 'Prince Fahd Press Statement 09/01/1980.' In *Royal Statements*, edited by SPA. Riyadh, KSA: SPA.

al-Saud, A. 1981. 'Crown Prince Fahd Statement on Bahrain Coup Attempt', *Al-Riyadh*, 15/12/1981, pp. 1, 2.

al-Saud, A. 1981. 'Crown Prince Fahd Statement on Middle East Peace Plan.' In *Saudi Press Agency Archive*. Riyadh: King Khalid bin Abdul Aziz Database.

al-Saud, A. 1987. 'Statement at the Islamic conference of the Muslim World League.' In *Royal Statements*, edited by SPA. Riyadh, KSA: SPA.

al-Saud, A. 1988. 'Custodian of the Two Holy Mosques Statement on Iran-Iraq Ceasefire.' In *Royal Statements*, edited by SPA. Riyadh, KSA: SPA.

al-Saud, A. 1989. 'Custodian of the Two Holy Mosques Hajj Speech 1989.' In *Royal Statements*, edited by SPA. Riyadh, KSA: SPA.

al-Saud, F. 1991. 'Custodian of the Two Holy Mosques Statement in Meeting with Kuwait's Crown Prince February 1991.' In *Royal Statements*, edited by SPA. Riyadh, KSA: SPA.

al-Saud, F. 1991. 'Custodian of the Two Holy Mosques Statement on the Liberation of Kuwait March 1991.' In *Royal Statements*, edited by SPA. Riyadh, KSA: SPA.

al-Saud, F. 1996. 'King Fahd ibn Abdulaziz Telephone Conversation with the President of Yemen Ali Abdullah Saleh 27 June 1996.' In *Royal Statements*, edited by SPA. Riyadh, KSA: SPA.

al-Saud, F. 1997. 'King Fahd ibn Abdulaziz Speech on the Hajj April 1997.' In *Royal Statements*, edited by SPA. Riyadh, KSA: SPA.

al-Saud, F. 1997. 'King Fahd ibn Abdulaziz Speech to Ministerial Cabinet 18 March 1997.' In *Royal Statements*, edited by SPA. Riyadh, KSA: SPA.

al-Saud, F. 1997. 'King Fahd ibn Abdulaziz Speech to the Shurah Council 22 January 1997.' In *Royal Statements*, edited by SPA. Riyadh, KSA: SPA.

al-Saud, F. 1997. 'King Fahd ibn Abdulaziz Telegram to President Khatami on Presidential Election 24 May 1997.' In *Royal Statements*, edited by SPA. Riyadh, KSA: SPA.

al-Saud, F. 1998. 'King Fahd Ibn Abdulaziz meeting with Rafsanjani 23 February 1998.' In *Royal Statements*, edited by SPA, 2. Riyadh, KSA: SPA.

al-Saud, F. 1999. 'King Fahd Speech on Meeting Khatami in Riyadh 17 May 1999.' In *Royal Statements*, edited by SPA, 2. Riyadh, KSA: SPA.

al-Saud, F. 2005. 'Custodian of the Two Holy Mosques Telegram on Ahmadinejad Victory 26 June 2005.' In *Royal Statements*, edited by SPA. Riyadh, KSA: SPA.

Al-Saud, F.S. 2003. *Iran, Saudi Arabia and the Gulf: Power Politics in Transition 1968–1971* (I.B. Tauris: London).

al-Saud, K. 1979. 'King Khalid ibn Abdul Aziz Speech After Cleansing the Grand Mosque.' In *Saudi Press Agency Archive*. King Khalid Online Database.

al-Saud, K. 1979. 'King Khalid Telegram to Khomeini.' In *Saudi Press Agency Archive*. King Khalid ibn Abdul Aziz Online Database.

al-Saud, K. 1981. 'King Khalid letter to Khomeini on Iranian Hajj Pilgrims 9 October 1981.' In *King's Statements*. Riyadh: King Khalid bin Abdul Aziz Database.

al-Saud, M.B.S. 2017. 'MBS Statement Islamic Coalition Terrorism Summit Transcript 26 November 2017', YouTube.com, Accessed 13/01/2021. https://www.youtube.com/watch?v=BsUMuUoGguc.

al-Saud, M.B.S. 2017. 'Mohammad bin Salman Speech Trascript 22 May 2017.' In *Royal Speeches*, edited by Government Unified Platform. Riyadh, KSA: SPA.

al-Saud, M.B.S. 2018. 'Saudi Prince Calls for Stepped-Up Pressure on Iran', Dow Jones & Company, Inc., Accessed 01/04/2020. https://www.wsj.com/articles/saudi-prince-calls-for-stepped-up-pressure-on-iran-1522365518?mod=e2tw.

al-Saud, M.B.S. 2019. '60 Minutes: Mohammad bin Salman denies ordering Khashoggi murder, but says he takes responsibility for it', CBS Interactive, Accessed 01/04/2020. https://www.cbsnews.com/news/mohammad-bin-salman-denies-ordering-khashoggi-murder-but-says-he-takes-responsibility-for-it-60-minutes-2019-09-29/.

al-Saud, M.B.S., and Al-Arabiya. 2017. 'Mohammad bin Salman Al-Arabiya Interview Transcript 03 May 2017', alarabiya.net, Accessed 14/01/2021. https://english.alarabiya.net/features/2017/05/03/Read-the-full-transcript-of-Mohammed-Bin-Salman-s-interview.

al-Saud, M.B.S., and CBS. 2018. 'Saudi Arabia's heir to the throne talks to 60 Minutes', CBS Interactive, Accessed 01/04/2020. https://www.cbsnews.com/news/saudi-crown-prince-talks-to-60-minutes/.

al-Saud, M.B.S., and *Economist*. 2016. 'Transcript of the Interview with Mohammad bin Salman', *The Economist*, Accessed 01/04/2020. https://www.economist.com/middle-east-and-africa/2016/01/06/transcript-interview-with-muhammad-bin-salman.

al-Saud, M.B.S., and *The Guardian*. 2017. 'Mohammad bin Salman Interview with The Guardian Transcript 24 October 2017', *The Guardian*, Accessed 14/01/2021. https://www.theguardian.com/world/2017/oct/24/i-will-return-saudi-arabia-moderate-islam-crown-prince.

al-Saud, N. 1979. 'Prince Nayef ibn Abdul Aziz Ministry of Interior Press Conference after the Seige of the Grand Mosque', *Asharq Al-Awsat*, 8/12/1979 [18/1/1400], p. 1.

al-Saud, N. 1979. 'Prince Nayif bin Abdul Aziz Ministry Press Conference 5 December 1979.' In *Ministry of Interior Statements*, edited by SPA. Riyadh: Saudi Press Agency.

al-Saud, N. 1980. 'Prince Nayif bin Abdul Aziz Ministry of Interior Press Release 8 June 1980.' In *SPA*, edited by Ministry of Interior. Riyadh, KSA: SPA.

al-Saud, N. 1981. 'Prince Nayef ibn Abdul Aziz Ministry of Interior Statement on Hajj Demonstrations', *Asharq Al-Awsat*, 27/09/1981, p. 1.

al-Saud, N. 1981. 'Prince Nayef ibn Abdul Aziz Ministry of Interior Statement on Bahrain Coup Attempt.' In Riyadh: Asharq Al-Awsat (ASAA).

al-Saud, N. 1987. 'Prince Nayef bin Abdulaziz Press Conference Statement in Light of Hajj Incident 25 August 1987.' In *SPA*, edited by Ministry of Interior. Riyadh, KSA: SPA.

al-Saud, N. 1988. 'Press Conference with Asharq Al-Awsat May 1988', *Asharq Al-Awsat*, 25/05/1988, p. 1.

al-Saud, N. 1996. 'Prince Nayif bin Abdul Aziz Press Interview with Asharq Al-Awsat', *Asharq Al-Awsat*, 17/12/1996, p. 1.

al-Saud, N. 1996. 'Prince Nayif bin Abdul Aziz Press Interview with Reuters', *Reuters*, 10/11/1996.

al-Saud, N. 1997. 'Prince Nayif bin Abdul Aziz Ministry Press Conference on Khobar Bombings in Mecca April 1997.' In *Statements of the Ministry of Interior*, edited by Ministry of Interior. Riyadh, KSA: SPA.

al-Saud, N. 2005. 'Press Conference of Saudi Minister of the Interior 5 February 2005.' In *Royal Statements*, edited by SPA. Riyadh, KSA: SPA.

al-Saud, N. 2006. 'Saudi Minister of the Interior on the Closing Session of the Annual Conference of the Committees of Promotion of Virtue and Prevention of Vice 21 September 2006.' In *Royal Statements*, edited by SPA. Riyadh, KSA: SPA.

al-Saud, N. 2007. 'Saudi Minister of the Interior to a Congregation of Islamic Scholars and Imams 20 June 2007.' In *Royal Statements*, edited by SPA. Riyadh, KSA: SPA.

al-Saud, N. 2009. 'Saudi Interior Minister, Prince Nayef bin Abdulaziz Interview with the Saudi Newspaper Okaz 14 March 2009.' In *Royal Statements*, edited by SPA. Riyadh, KSA: SPA.

al-Saud, N. 2011. 'His Highness the Second Deputy Prime Minister and Minister of Interior makes contact with the King of the Kingdom of Bahrain 20 February 2011.' In *Royal Statements*, edited by SPA. Riyadh, KSA: SPA.

al-Saud, S. 1997. 'Prince Sultan bin Abdul Aziz Ministry of Defence Interview with Asharq Al-Awsat', *Asharq Al-Awsat*, 17/03/1997, p. 1.

al-Saud, S. 1997. 'Prince Sultan bin Abdul Aziz Ministry of Defence Interview with Saudi Press Agency 9 June 1997.' In *Interviews*, edited by SPA. Riyadh, KSA: SPA.

al-Saud, S. 1997. 'Prince Sultan bin Abdul Aziz Ministry of Defence Press Conference on Visit to Washington DC. 26 February 1997.' In *Statements of the Ministry of Defence*, edited by Ministry of Defence. Riyadh, KSA: SPA.

al-Saud, S. 1999. 'Prince Sultan bin Abdul Aziz Ministry of Defence Statement on Iran Visit 2 May 1999.' In *Interviews*, edited by Saudi TV Channel 1. Riyadh, KSA: Saudi TV.

al-Saud, S. 1999. 'SPA Press Conference with Saudi Defence Minister Prince Sultan ibn Abdulaziz Al-Saud 05 May 1999.' In *Royal Statements*, edited by SPA. Riyadh, KSA: SPA.

al-Saud, S. 2015. 'Kalimat khādim al-ḥaramayn al-sharīfayn al-Malik Salmān ibn ʿAbd al-ʿAzīz Āl Suʿūd fī iftitāḥ al-qimma al-ʿArabiyya al-ʿādiyya al-26 bi-madīnat Sharm al-Shaykh 28 March 2015.' In *Royal Statements*, edited by SPA. Riyadh, KSA: SPA.

al-Saud, S. 2015. 'King Salman Decree Relieving Muqrin bin Abdulaziz al-Saud of Duties 29 March 2015.' In *Royal Statements*, edited by SPA. Riyadh, KSA: SPA.

al-Saud, S. 2015. 'King Salman Speech GCC Summit', Unified National Platform, Saudi Arabia, Accessed 10/06/2021. https://www.my.gov.sa/wps/portal/snp/content/news/newsDetails/CONT-news-060520151/!ut/p/z1/jZFbT4NAEIX_ii88ws5wk_iGUC9EWEkBcV8MGAoklCULuum_d1ONSb20nbeZfOdk5gxhpCRsrN77tlp6PlaD6p-Z-xI9ejb6gNSDdAVpEOKDZWYA1CVPeyDBFdyhjRRs8wbSMPQTJ8MIC5e

wc_TfALWcawXEl9RfFwjgnKeHf8qHU_p1JUh0ClIpmCIO4pawqVo6vR83nJQBTTJ
9bOSsgwuOCehcoNqHHbrR28hWbpib TlQABPYXcCyyHw6_M9kDR45
WF7UDrz8f6I-15anVRbNpRCOMN6HG3bJM85UGGkgpjZbzdmiMV77V4C9
Jx-eFlIckmbZ5XsqdBf29zuqd_AA6N6q0/dz/d5/L2dBISEvZ0FBIS9nQSEh/.

al-Saud, S. 2019. 'King Salman affirms the Kingdom's ability to deal with cowardly attacks', *Al-Riyadh*, 17/09/2019, p. 1.

al-Saud, S. 2019. 'King's Speech at the GCC Summit', *al-Medina*, 10/12/2019, p. 1.

al-Saud, S. 2019. 'King's Speech at the Shura Council', al-Eqtesadiya, Accessed 02/07/2021. https://www.aleqt.com/2019/11/20/article_1716681.html.

al-Saud, S., and SPA. 2013. 'Custodian of the Two Holy Mosques congratulates President Hassan Rouhani on his victory in the Iranian presidential elections', SPA, Accessed 14/01/2021. https://www.spa.gov.sa/1120803.

al-Saud, S., and SPA. 2017. 'Custodian of the Two Holy Mosques Speech Transcript 22 May 2017', SPA, Accessed 14/01/2021. https://www.my.gov.sa/wps/portal/snp/content/news/newsDetails/CONT-news-222052017.

al-Saud, S.F. 1987. 'Saudi Foreign Minister Statement at the OIC Summit in Amman 25 March 1988.' In *Royal Statements*, edited by SPA. Riyadh, KSA: SPA.

al-Saud, S.F. 1990. 'Saudi Foreign Minister's Statement During Meeting with Iranian Counterpart 30 September 1990.' In *Royal Statements*, edited by Foreign Ministry. Riyadh, KSA: SPA.

al-Saud, S.F. 1991. 'Foreign Minister's Statement During Visit to Tehran.' In *Foreign State Visits*, edited by *IRIB*. Tehran, IR Iran: *IRIB*.

al-Saud, S.F. 2005. 'Saudi Foreign Minister Press Conference on the Sidelines of the International Conference to Combatting Terrorism 6 February 2005.' In *Royal Statements*, edited by Foreign Ministry. Riyadh, KSA: SPA.

al-Saud, S.F. 2005. 'Saudi Foreign Minister Speech at the US Council for Foreign Relations 23 September 2005.' In *Royal Statements*, edited by Foreign Ministry. Riyadh, KSA: Saudi Ministry of Foreign Affairs.

al-Saud, S.F. 2005. 'Saudi Foreign Minister Speech to the Saudi-British Chamber of Commerce on 23 February 2005.' In *Royal Statements*, edited by Foreign Ministry. Riyadh, KSA: SPA.

al-Saud, S.F. 2006. 'Saudi Foreign Minister Press Conference After Meeting Prime Minister Tony Blair on 25 July 2006.' In *Royal Statements*, edited by SPA. Riyadh, KSA: SPA.

al-Saud, S.F. 2006. 'Saudi Foreign Minister Press Conference After Meeting Secretary Condoleezza Rice 22 February 2006.' In *Royal Statements*, edited by SPA. Riyadh, KSA: SPA.

al-Saud, S.F. 2006. 'Saudi Foreign Minister Press Conference in Jeddah on 19 July 2006.' In *Royal Statements*, edited by SPA. Riyadh, KSA: SPA.

al-Saud, S.F. 2006. 'Saudi Foreign Minister Weekly Press Conference on 3 August 2006.' In *Royal Statements*, edited by SPA. Riyadh, KSA: SPA.

al-Saud, S.F. 2009. 'Saudi Foreign Minister, Prince Saud Al-Faisal Meeting with Iranian Foreign Minister.' In *Royal Statements*, edited by Foreign Ministry. Riyadh, KSA: SPA.

al-Saud, S.F. 2009. 'Saudi Foreign Minister, Prince Saud Al-Faisal Statement Arab League 3 March 2009.' In *Royal Statements*, edited by Foreign Ministry. Riyadh, KSA: SPA.

al-Saud, S.F. 2011. 'Statement at the Press Conference, Mecca 9 March 2011.' In *Royal Statements*, edited by Foreign Ministry. Riyadh, KSA: SPA.

al-Saud, S.F. 2012. 'His Highness the Foreign Minister calls on the Arab League to reconsider its initiatives 12 February 2012.' In *Royal Statements*, edited by Foreign Ministry. Riyadh, KSA: SPA.

al-Saud, S.F. 2012. 'Saudi Foreign Minister, Prince Saud Al-Faisal Statement Arab League 22 January 2012.' In *Royal Statements*, edited by Foreign Ministry. Riyadh, KSA: SPA.

al-Saud, T.F. 2005. 'Saudi Ambassador Speech at the Annual Conference of the Middle East Institute 7 November 2005.' In *Royal Statements*, edited by Foreign Ministry. Riyadh, KSA: Ministry of Foreign Affairs.

al-Saud, T.F. 2006. 'Saudi Ambassador's Speech at the New America Foundation 31 July 2007.' In *Royal Statements*, edited by Foreign Ministry. Riyadh, KSA: Saudi Ministry of Foreign Affairs.

al-Saud, T.F. 2016. 'Turki al-Faisal al-Saud Speech at the MKO/MEK Conference 9 July 2016', Youtube, Accessed 05/05/2020. https://youtu.be/sJq1y3iV6go.

AlSharif, A. 2011. 'Saudi activists eye protests, wait for new cabinet', *Reuters*, 28/02/2011.

Al-Shehri, A. 2014. 'Iran Determined to Develop Ties with Saudi Arabia', Kuwait News Agency. https://www.kuna.net.kw/ArticleDetails.aspx?id=2364282&Language=en.

Al-Sudairi, Turki. 2011. 'Let Us Understand the Risks of the Existing Evidence', *Al-Riyadh*, 15/10/2011.

Alsultan, F.M., and P. Saeid. 2016. *The Development of Saudi-Iranian Relations since the 1990s: Between Conflict and Accommodation* (Taylor & Francis: Abingdon, UK).

Al-Tamimi, N.M. 2013. *China-Saudi Arabia Relations, 1990–2012: Marriage of Convenience Or Strategic Alliance?* (Routledge: Abingdon).

AlToraifi, A. 2012. 'Understanding the role of state identity in foreign policy decision-making: the rise of Saudi-Iranian rapprochement (1997–2009)', PhD Thesis, The London School of Economics and Political Science (LSE).

Al-Yassini, A. 1985. *Religion and State in the Kingdom of Saudi Arabia* (Westview Press: Boulder, CO).

Amineh, M.P. 2007. *The Greater Middle East in Global Politics: Social Science Perspectives on the Changing Geography of the World Politics* (Brill).

Amirahmadi, Hooshang. 1993. 'Iranian-Saudi Arabian Relations since the Revolution.' In Hooshang Amirahmadi and Nader Entessar (eds.), *Iran and the Arab World* (Macmillan Press Ltd.: London).

Amirahmadi, H., and N. Entessar. 1993. *Iran and the Arab world* (Macmillan Press Ltd.: London).

Amnesty International. 2011. 'Bahrain report must lead to action over protest abuses', *Amnesty International Report*, 21/11/2011.

Amnesty International. 2014. 'Saudi Arabia: Appalling death sentence against Shi'a cleric must be quashed', 15/10/2014.

Antonopoulos, P., and D. Cottle. 2017. *Syria: The Hegemonic Flashpoint between Iran and Saudi Arabia?* (Vij Books India Private Limited).

AP. 1998. 'Ayatollah Rejects U.S.-Iran Ties.' In *Press Release*, edited by AP. New York: AP.

AP News. 2014. 'Iran FM says he's ready to meet Saudi counterpart', Associated Press, Accessed 10/01/2020. https://www.timesofisrael.com/iran-fm-says-hes-ready-to-meet-saudi-counterpart/.

Arab League. 2018. 'Arab League Statement Rejecting Sanctions on Saudi Arabia', *WAFA*, 20/10/2018.

Arab News. 2014. 'Thaw in Saudi-Iran ties as FMs meet in US', *Arab News*, Accessed 02/03/2020. https://www.arabnews.com/node/634386/amp.

Arab News. 2020. 'Saudi Arabia calls for restraint after Soleimani killing', *Arab News*, 03/01/2020.

Arab News. 2020. 'Saudi delegation visits Iraq', *Arab News*, Accessed 01/02/2022. https://arab.news/zx3dn.

Arab News. 2021. 'Saudi Arabia will judge new Iran president Raisi by "reality on the ground": FM', *Arab News*, Accessed 01/02/2022. https://www.arabnews.com/node/1881271/saudi-arabia.

Arkin, W.M. 2011. *Divining Victory: Airpower in the 2006 Israel-Hezbollah War* (Lulu.com).

Asafari, M.H. 2014. 'Saudi Invitation to Zarif Not Enough, Riyadh Should Change', *Fars*, 19/05/2014.

Asefi, H.R. 2005. 'Government Spokesman Press Conference', *IRNA*, 26/06/2005 [05/04/1384].

Asharq Al-Awsat. 1980. 'Interview with Prince Saud Al-Faisal.' In *Saudi Press Agency Archive*. Riyadh: King Khalid bin Abdul Aziz Database.

Asharq Al-Awsat. 1990. 'Al-ra'y', *Asharq Al-Awsat*, 03/10/1990, p. 1.

Asharq-Al-Awsat. 1979. 'al-'ihtimāmāt al-thalāth', *Asharq Al-Awsat*, 27/11/1979 [08/01/1400], p. 5.

Asharq-Al-Awsat. 1979. 'al-Kābūs', *Asharq Al-Awsat*, 24/11/1979, p. 5.

Asharq-Al-Awsat. 1979. 'Yawm al-'ikhtibār', *Asharq Al-Awsat*, 23/11/1979, p. 5.

Asharq-Al-Awsat. 1980. 'Wa Māzā fa'alta Yā Saddm Hussain?', *Asharq Al-Awsat*, 10/12/1980, p. 9.

Asharq-Al-Awsat. 1981. 'al-'arabī Wa-l-'ajnabī', *Asharq Al-Awsat*, 28/09/1981, p. 9.

Asharq-Al-Awsat. 1981. ''Āwāks lil Su'ūdiyya', *Asharq Al-Awsat*, 05/05/1981, p. 9.

Asharq-Al-Awsat. 1981. 'Hal Yarham al-Tarīkh', *Asharq Al-Awsat*, 26/11/1981, p. 9.

Asharq-Al-Awsat. 1981. 'Muhimat al-'amīr 'Abdalah', *Asharq Al-Awsat*, 29/09/1981, p. 9.

Asharq-Al-Awsat. 1981. 'Natījat Ashawt al-'awal', *Asharq Al-Awsat*, 27/11/1981, p. 9.

Asharq-Al-Awsat. 1982. 'Interview with Foreign Minister Prince Saud Al-Faisal', *Asharq Al-Awsat*, 15/05/1982.

Asharq-Al-Awsat. 1996. 'al-Irhāb Wa Uslūb al-'isābāt', *Asharq Al-Awsat*, 27/06/1996, p. 9.

Asharq-Al-Awsat. 1997. 'al-Hiwār Lughat al-Mustaqbal...Wa al-Maslaha', *Asharq Al-Awsat*, 11/12/1997, p. 9.

Asharq-Al-Awsat. 1997. 'Crown Prince Abdullah To Attend the OIC Summit in Tehran', *Asharq Al-Awsat*, 28/03/1997, p. 1.

Asharq-Al-Awsat. 1997. 'Fashal Netenyahu..Wa 'udwāniyatihi', *Asharq Al-Awsat*, 03/07/1997, p. 9.

Asharq-Al-Awsat. 1997. 'Haq al-Naghdh al-Amrīkī', *Asharq Al-Awsat*, 09/03/1997, p. 9.

Asharq-Al-Awsat. 1997. 'Hiwār Duwal al-Jiwār', *Asharq Al-Awsat*, 10/06/1997, p. 9.

Asharq-Al-Awsat. 1997. ''indamā Lā Yakūn al-Hal al-'amnī..Halan', *Asharq Al-Awsat*, 10/04/1997, p. 9.

Asharq-Al-Awsat. 1997. 'Interview with the Iranian Ambassador to Saudi Arabia-Mohammad Reza Nouri', *Asharq Al-Awsat*, 28/03/1997.

Asharq-Al-Awsat. 1997. 'Iran Khatami', *Asharq Al-Awsat*, 03/08/1997, p. 9.

Asharq-Al-Awsat. 1997. 'Isrā'īl Tatahadā al-'ālam', *Asharq Al-Awsat*, 23/03/1997, p. 9.

Asharq-Al-Awsat. 1997. 'Safha Jadīda wa Lugha Mushtaraka', *Asharq Al-Awsat*, 12/12/1997, p. 9.

Asharq-Al-Awsat. 1997. 'Tahadiyāt Islāmiya Fī Tahrān', *Asharq Al-Awsat*, 08/12/1997, p. 9.

Asharq-Al-Awsat. 1997. 'Tawsī' Anātū', *Asharq Al-Awsat*, 28/05/1997, p. 9.

Asharq-Al-Awsat. 1999. 'Saudi Defence Minister to Visit the Islamic Republic of Iran', *Asharq Al-Awsat*, 02/05/1999, p. 1.

Asharq-Al-Awsat. 2006. 'Hākathā Yajib 'an Takūn al-Qimah', *Asharq Al-Awsat*, 16/07/2006, p. 9.

Asharq-Al-Awsat. 2006. 'Mā Hāthā-l-tabsīt Yā Sayid', *Asharq Al-Awsat*, 27/07/2006, p. 9.

Asharq-Al-Awsat. 2006. 'Mithla Mā 'aqidtumūhā Hilūhā', *Asharq Al-Awsat*, 15/07/2006, p. 9.

Asharq-Al-Awsat. 2006. 'Wa 'ahlām al-Walīd', *Asharq Al-Awsat*, 17/07/2006, p. 9.

Asharq-Al-Awsat. 2008. 'Dimā' Ghazah Mashrū' Tijārī', *Asharq Al-Awsat*, 28/12/2008, p. 9.

Asharq-Al-Awsat. 2008. 'Ma'sāt Ghazah: 'asābi' Iran al-Khafiyah', *Asharq Al-Awsat*, 31/12/2008, p. 9.

Asharq-Al-Awsat. 2008. 'Nasrallah Hiyya al-Harb 'alā Miṣr', *Asharq-Al-Awsat*, 30/12/2008.

Asharq-Al-Awsat. 2009. 'Hamās: 'imā Iran 'aw al-'arab', *Asharq Al-Awsat*, 19/01/2009, p. 9.

Asharq-Al-Awsat. 2009. 'Hamās Taqūd 'akbar 'amaliya 'intihāriya', *Asharq Al-Awsat*, 02/02/2009, p. 9.

Asharq-Al-Awsat. 2009. 'Īrān.. al-ma'raka bada'at wa-lam tantahi', *Asharq Al-Awsat*, 17/06/2009, p. 9.

Asharq-Al-Awsat. 2009. 'Iran Tastaghil al-Fazā'i' Fī Ghazah Lilnayl Min Misr', *Asharq Al-Awsat*, 01/01/2009, p. 9.

Asharq-Al-Awsat. 2009. 'Min Taqsīm Falastīn 'ilā Tahdīd al-Bahrain', *Asharq-Al-Awsat*, 14/02/2009, p. 9.

Asharq-Al-Awsat. 2009. 'Nijād.. li-l-Lāh darruhu', *Asharq Al-Awsat*, 14/06/2009, p. 9.

Asharq-Al-Awsat. 2010. 'Idhan.. man yaḍi' siyāsat Īrān al-khārijiyya?', *Asharq Al-Awsat*, 20/12/2010, p. 9.

Asharq-Al-Awsat. 2010. 'I'tidhār.. wa-da'wa li-l-ightisāl', *Asharq Al-Awsat*, 21/12/2010, p. 9.

Asharq-Al-Awsat. 2010. 'Khuṣūmat al-Islāmiyyīn al-'ālamiyyīn li-Tūnis', *Asharq Al-Awsat*, 29/12/2010, p. 9.

Asharq-Al-Awsat. 2010. 'Tūnis laysat al-aswa' bal risāla li-l-ghayr', *Asharq Al-Awsat*, 28/12/2010, p. 9.

Asharq-Al-Awsat. 2011. 'Al-Baḥrayn: man yataḥaddath.. Ṭahrān am Wāshinṭun?', *Asharq Al-Awsat*, 17/03/2011, p. 9.

Asharq-Al-Awsat. 2011. 'Bayn Hīlārī wa-l-murshid al-Īrānī!', *Asharq Al-Awsat*, 05/03/2011, p. 9.

Asharq-Al-Awsat. 2011. 'Hal hiya al-sharāra al-Sūriyya?', *Asharq Al-Awsat*, 20/03/2011, p. 9.

Asharq-Al-Awsat. 2011. 'Intifāḍāt al-baṭāla wa-l-zayt wa-l-sukkar', *Asharq Al-Awsat*, 11/01/2011, p. 9.

Asharq-Al-Awsat. 2013. 'Ḥattā law kāna Rūḥānī', *Asharq Al-Awsat*, 16/06/2013, p. 9.

Asharq-Al-Awsat. 2013. 'Ūbāmā yunqidh Ḥizb Allāh', *Asharq Al-Awsat*, 21/10/2013, p. 9.

Asharq-Al-Awsat. 2014. 'Īrān turīd al-Ḥūthiyyīn mithl Ḥizb Allāh', *Asharq Al-Awsat*, 21/10/2014, p. 9.

Asharq-Al-Awsat. 2015. 'Al-Su'ūdiyya anqadhat al-manṭiqa', *Asharq Al-Awsat*, 28/03/2015, p. 9.

Asharq-Al-Awsat. 2015. ''Aṣifat al-ḥazm.. mā al-lādhī taḥaqqaqa?', *Asharq Al-Awsat*, 23/04/2015, p. 9.

Asharq-Al-Awsat. 2017. 'Infirājāt muhimma li-l-Riyāḍ', *Asharq Al-Awsat*, 16/03/2017, p. 9.

Asharq-Al-Awsat. 2019. 'Judrān al-'Irāq wa-Lubnān wa-l-khayṭ al-Īrānī', *Asharq Al-Awsat*, 11/11/2019, p. 9.

Asharq-Al-Awsat. 2020. 'Maqtal Sulaymānī.. tarāju' am intiqām?', *Asharq Al-Awsat*, 05/01/2020, p. 9.

Asharq-Al-Awsat. 2020. 'Saudi Arabia Calls for Restraint after Soleimani's Killing', *Asharq Al-Awsat*, 03/01/2020, p. 9.

Asharq-Al-Awsat, and A. Al-Rashed. 2017. 'Al-Amīr Muḥammad ibn Salmān wa-l-ḥukm al-Su'ūdī', *Asharq Al-Awsat*, 22/06/2017, p. 9.

Asharq-Al-Awsat, and A. Al-Rashed. 2017. 'Al-Murshid wa-Hitlar', *Asharq Al-Awsat*, 30/11/2017, p. 9.

Asharq-Al-Awsat, and A. Al-Rashed. 2017. 'Khiyārāt al-ḥarb ma' Īrān', *Asharq Al-Awsat*, 07/11/2017, p. 9.

Asharq-Al-Awsat, and A. Al-Rashid. 2013. 'Marḥaban bi-l-ṣadīq al-qadīm Rūḥānī', *Asharq Al-Awsat*, 17/06/2013, p. 9.

Asharq-Al-Awsat, and G. Charbel. 2017. 'Al-Ḥarīrī wa-jurʿāt al-samm', *Asharq Al-Awsat*, 06/11/2017, p. 9.

Asharq-Al-Awsat, and G. Charbel. 2017. 'Rajul wa-jīl wa-marḥala', *Asharq Al-Awsat*, 22/06/2017, p. 9.

Assakina.com. 2010. 'Documents: Cleansing the Grand Mosque of the Deviant Group in 1400H', The Ministry of Islamic Affairs, Endowments, Dawa and Guidance, Accessed 01/03/2015. http://www.assakina.com/center/files/5421.html#ixzz3h7UuaVeD.

Axelrod, T, and D.J. Trump. 2019. 'Trump speaks with Saudi crown prince after Houthi attacks on oil refineries', The Hill, Accessed 13/11/2021. https://thehill.com/homenews/administration/461428-trump-speaks-with-saudi-crown-prince-after-houthi-attacks-on-oil.

Ayalon, A. 1992. *Middle East Contemporary Survey 1990* (Westview Press: Boulder, CO).

Badeeb, S.B. 1993. *Saudi-Iranian Relations, 1932–82* (Echoes: Centre for Arab and Iranian Studies, London).

Bar, S. 2005. 'Sunnis and Shiites: Between Rapprochement and Conflict', *Current Trends in Islamist Ideology*, 2: 87–96.

Barany, Z. 2021. *Armies of Arabia: Military Politics and Effectiveness in the Gulf* (Oxford University Press: Oxford).

Bastani, H. 2007. 'A Major False Interpretation.' In *Rooz Online*. Iran Gooya media group.

BBC. 2011. 'Syria says twin suicide bombings in Damascus kill 44', British Broadcasting Corporation, Accessed 05/03/2020. https://www.bbc.co.uk/news/world-middle-east-16313879.

BBC. 2013. 'Hezbollah linked to Burgas bus bombing in Bulgaria', British Broadcasting Corporation, Accessed 05/03/2020. https://www.bbc.co.uk/news/world-europe-21342192.

BBC. 2013. 'Israeli 'air strike on convoy on Syria-Lebanon border', British Broadcasting Corporation, Accessed 05/03/2020. https://www.bbc.co.uk/news/world-middle-east-21264632.

BBC. 2013. 'John Kerry praises US-Saudi ties as "enduring"', British Broadcasting Corporation, Accessed 05/03/2020. https://www.bbc.co.uk/news/world-middle-east-24799662.

BBC. 2014. 'Iraq conflict: Militants "seize" city of Tal Afar', British Broadcasting Corporation, Accessed 05/03/2020. https://www.bbc.co.uk/news/world-middle-east-27865759.

BBC. 2018. 'Saudi Arabia demotes foreign minister in wake of Khashoggi case', British Broadcasting Corporation, Accessed 10/10/2021. https://www.bbc.co.uk/news/world-middle-east-46695216.

BBC. 2019. 'Adel al-Jubeir: "Saudi Arabia does not want a war with Iran"', British Broadcasting Corporation, Accessed 14/11/2021. https://www.bbc.co.uk/news/av/world-middle-east-48460860.

BBC Monitoring. 2009. 'Media Environment Guide: Iran.' In *BBC Monitoring*. London, UK: BBC.

Beeman, William O. 1976. 'What is (Iranian) national character? A sociolinguistic approach', *Iranian Studies*, 9: 22–48.

Beeman, W.O. 2005. *The 'Great Satan' Vs. The 'Mad Mullahs': How the United States and Iran Demonize Each Other* (Praeger Publishers: London).

Beheshti, M. 1980. 'Sukhanrānī-yi Ayatollah Beheshti dar majmaʿ-i Ḥizb', *Jomhouri Eslami*, 29/01/1980 [09/11/1358], p. 3.

Benjamin, D., and S. Simon. 2002. *The Age of Sacred Terror* (Random House Publishing Group: London).

Bergen, P.L. 2001. *Holy War, Inc.: Inside the Secret World of Osama bin Laden* (Simon & Schuster).

Berger, L. 2009. 'Iran and the Arab World: A view from Riyadh', *Middle East Review of International Affairs*, 13: 24–33.

Biden, J. 2022. 'Remarks by President Biden in Press Conference', The White House, Accessed 01/02/2022. https://www.whitehouse.gov/briefing-room/speeches-remarks/2022/01/19/remarks-by-president-biden-in-press-conference-6/.

Bin Humaid, S. 2005. 'Friday Sermon 08/12/2005.' In *Sermons-Khutab*, edited by Ministry of Islamic Affairs. Mecca, Saudi Arabia: Ministry of Islamic Affairs, Dawah and Guidance.

Bin Jabreen, S. 2006. 'Fatwa on Supporting Hezbollah.' In *Religious Statements*, edited by SPA. Mecca, Saudi Arabia: SPA.

Bin Laden, O. 2004. 'Full Transcript of Audio Tape 16/12/2004', https://sources.marefa.org/, Accessed 03/01/2018. https://sources.marefa.org/%D9%86%D8%B5_%D8%AE%D8%B7%D8%A7%D8%A8_%D8%A3%D8%B3%D8%A7%D9%85%D8%A9_%D8%A8%D9%86_%D9%84%D8%A7%D8%AF%D9%86_4_%D8%B0%D9%88_%D8%A7%D9%84%D9%82%D8%B9%D8%AF%D8%A9_1425_%D9%87%D9%80_%E2%80%93_16_%D8%AF%D9%8A%D8%B3%D9%85%D8%A8%D8%B1/%D9%83%D8%A7%D9%86%D9%88%D9%86_%D8%A7%D9%84%D8%A3%D9%88%D9%84_2004_%D9%85.

Binder, L., and Rand Corporation. 1969. *Factors influencing Iran's international role* (Rand Corp. Santa Monica).

Blanchard, C.M. 2010. *Saudi Arabia: Background and U. S. Relations* (Diane Publishing Company: Washington DC).

Blank, L.R., and G.P. Noone. 2018. *International Law and Armed Conflict: Fundamental Principles and Contemporary Challenges in the Law of War* (Wolters Kluwer).

Bolton, J. 2018. 'John Bolton PM Netenyahu Press Conference in Tel Aviv, Israel', YouTube, Accessed 02/10/2021. https://youtu.be/YaPNAU2mAgA.

Bolton, J. 2018. 'John Bolton speech MKO Conference 2019', YouTube, Accessed 02/10/2021. https://youtu.be/hTMh24qlyQA.

Bolton, J. 2019. 'BoltonTwitter 04 July 2019', twitter.com, Accessed 02/12/2021. https://twitter.com/AmbJohnBolton/status/1146877026751647756?s=20.

Borck, T. 2021. 'The Gulf States and the Iran Nuclear Deal: Between a Rock and a Hard Place', Royal United Services Institute (RUSI), Accessed 12/02/2022. https://rusi.org/explore-our-research/publications/commentary/gulf-states-and-iran-nuclear-deal-between-rock-and-hard-place.

Boroujerdi, A. 2011. 'Boroujerdi in a letter to her German counterpart: Why have European parliaments been silenced in the face of Saudi crimes in Bahrain?', *Kayhan*, 17/03/2011 [26/12/1389], p. 2.

Boroujerdi, A. 2015. 'Head of Parliamentary Commission Reaction to Yemen War', *IRNA*, 26/03/2015, p. 1.

Boroujerdi, A. 2018. 'Boroujerdi on Khashoggi Murder', *ISNA*, 26/10/2018.

Boroujerdi, A., and Vatan Emrooz. 2014. 'Declaration of Al-Saud War', Vatan Emrouz, Accessed 13/04/2020. http://www.vatanemrooz.ir/newspaper/page/1440/1/126921/0.

Boutros-Ghali, B., and United Nations. 1996. *The United Nations and the Iraq-Kuwait Conflict, 1990–1996* (Department of Public Information, United Nations).

Bradley, J.R. 2015. *Saudi Arabia Exposed: Inside a Kingdom in Crisis* (St. Martin's Press).

Bregman, A. 2016. *Israel's Wars: A History Since 1947* (Taylor & Francis).

Bronson, R. 2006. *Thicker than Oil: America's Uneasy Partnership with Saudi Arabia* (Oxford University Press: New York).

Brown, D., and D.J. Trump. 2019. 'Trump stops short of blaming Iran for Saudi attack.' In Washington DC: Politico.

Brunner, Rainer. 2011. 'Interesting Times: Egypt and Shi'ism at the begining of the Twenty-First Century.' In O. Bengio and M. Litvak (eds.), *The Sunna and Shi'a in History: Division and Ecumenism in the Muslim Middle East* (Palgrave Macmillan: London).

Bruno, G, and J. Afridi. 2009. 'Presidential Power in Iran', CFR, Accessed 15/03/2022.

Bunzel, C. 2018. 'The Kingdom and the Caliphate: Saudi Arabia and the Islamic State.' In F. Wehrey (ed.), *Beyond Sunni and Shia: The Roots of Sectarianism in a Changing Middle East* (Oxford University Press: New York).

Burns, J. 1997. 'In Afghanistan, a Triumph of Fundamentalism', *New York Times*, 26/05/1997.

Cafiero, G. 2021. 'The Changing Role of Political Islam in Iraq.' In K. Al-Jaber and K.C. Ulrichsen (eds.), *Political Islam in the Gulf* (Gulf International Forum).

Calabrese, J. 2020. 'The Saudi-Iran Strategic Rivalry', *Shocks and Rivalries in the Middle East and North Africa*: 59.

Campagna, J. 2006. 'Saudi Arabia report: Princes, Clerics, and Censors', Committee to Protect Journalists, Accessed 15/06/2013. http://cpj.org/reports/2006/05/saudi-06.php.

CBC. 2017. 'Hezbollah leader blasts "unprecedented Saudi intervention" in Lebanon', *CBC*, 10/11/2017.

CBS. 2019. 'Iran news: Details of tanker "sabotage" murky as Trump warns Iran and U.S. casts first blame', *CBS News*, 14/05/2019.

Centcom, and P. Shanahan. 2019. 'Statement Acting Secretary of Defence', *Centcom*, 20/06/2019.

Chalk, P. 2013. *Encyclopedia of Terrorism* (ABC-CLIO: Santa Barbara, CA).

Christian Science Monitor, and M. Houk. 1990. 'Interview with Iranian Foreign Minister', *Christian Science Monitor*, 28/09/1990, p. 1.

Chubin, S. 1979. 'Repercussions of the crisis in Iran', *Survival*, 21: 98–106.

Chubin, S. 2006. *Iran's Nuclear Ambitions* (Carnegie Endowment for International Peace: Washington DC).

Chubin, S. 2009. 'Iran's Power in Context', *Survival*, 51: 165–90.

Chubin, S. 2012. 'Iran and the Arab Spring: Ascendancy Frustrated', *GRC Gulf Papers*: 21–27.

Chubin, S., and C. Tripp. 1996. *Iran-Saudi Arabia Relations and Regional Order: Iran and Saudi Arabia in the Balance of Power in the Gulf* (Oxford University Press for the International Institute for Strategic Studies: Oxford).

Chubin, S., and C. Tripp. 2011. 'Secretary Clinton on Middle East Political Unrest', National Cable Satellite Corporation, Accessed 01/12/2021. https://www.c-span.org/video/?298075-2/secretary-clinton-middle-east-political-unrest.

Chubin, S., and C. Tripp. 2014. *Iran-Saudi Arabia Relations and Regional Order* (Taylor & Francis: Abingdon).

Churkin, V., and UN. 2011. 'Vitaly Churkin UN Statement on Resolution to Adopt Draft Resolution SC/10403 Condemning Syria's Crackdown', *United Nations*, 04/10/2011.

Clawson, P. 1998. *Iran Under Khatami: A Political, Economic, and Military Assessment* (Washington Institute for Near East Policy).

Clinton, H. 2011. 'Remarks With Egyptian Foreign Minister Nabil Al-Araby', US Department of State, Accessed 01/12/2021. https://2009-2017.state.gov/secretary/20092013clinton/rm/2011/03/158404.htm.

CNBC, and T. Higgins. 2018. 'Lindsey Graham says Saudi Crown Prince Mohammed bin Salman "has got to go," calls for royal power shuffle', CNBC, Accessed 14/10/2021. https://www.cnbc.com/2018/10/16/lindsey-graham-says-saudi-crown-prince-bin-salman-has-got-to-go.html.

CNN. 2011. 'Clinton calls intervention in Bahrain "alarming"', Cable News Network (Warner Media Company), Accessed 10/01/2020. https://www.aljazeera.com/news/2011/3/21/bahrain-king-speaks-of-foiled-foreign-plot.

CNN. 2011. 'Iḥtijāj Kuwaytī 'shadīd' 'alā 'shabakat tajassus' Īrāniyya', Cable News Network (Warner Media Company), Accessed 10/01/2020 http://archive.arabic.cnn.com/2011/middle_east/3/31/kuwait.iran/index.html.

CNN. 2011. 'Iranian plot to kill Saudi ambassador thwarted, U.S. officials say', Cable News Network (Warner Media Company), Accessed 10/01/2020. https://edition.cnn.com/2011/10/11/justice/iran-saudi-plot/index.html.

CNN. 2012. 'Obama authorized covert support for Syrian rebels, sources say', Cable News Network (Warner Media Company), Accessed 10/01/2020. https://edition.cnn.com/2012/08/01/us/syria-rebels-us-aid/index.html.

CNN. 2018. 'Saudi investment conference opens in the shadow of Khashoggi's death', Cable News Network (Warner Media Company), Accessed 10/01/2020. https://edition.cnn.com/2018/10/23/business/saudi-arabia-investment-conference/index.html.

CNN. 2020. 'Iraqi Parliament votes for plan to end US troop presence in Iraq after Soleimani killing', Cable News Network (Warner Media Company), Accessed 10/01/2020. https://edition.cnn.com/2020/01/05/world/soleimani-us-iran-attack/index.html.

CNN, and A. Al-Jubeir. 2019. 'Connect the World – Adel Al-Jubeir', CNN, Accessed 10/01/2020. http://edition.cnn.com/TRANSCRIPTS/1909/22/ctw.01.html.

Cordesman, A.H. 2003. *Saudi Arabia Enters the Twenty-first Century: The military and international security dimensions* (Praeger: Westport: Boulder, CO).

Cordesman, A.H. 2003. *Saudi Arabia Enters the Twenty-first Century: The Political, Foreign Policy, Economic, and Energy Dimensions* (Praeger: Westport, CO).

Cordesman, A.H. 2009. *The 'Gaza War': A Strategic Analysis* (CSIS: Washington DC).

Cordesman, A.H., and N.E. Obaid. 2005. *National Security in Saudi Arabia: Threats, Responses, and Challenges* (Praeger Security International: Westport, CO).

Daily Star. 2012. 'Lebanese Army Imposes Rule of Law in Tripoli', *Daily Star*, 16/05/2012, p. 1.

Darwich, May. 2020. 'Escalation in Failed Military Interventions: Saudi and Emirati Quagmires in Yemen', *Global Policy*, 11: 103–12.

Davis, J. 2016. *The Arab Spring and Arab Thaw: Unfinished Revolutions and the Quest for Democracy* (Taylor & Francis).

DAWN MENA. 2018. 'Bahrain Statement on Khashoggi Murder', *DAWN MENA*, 2018.

de Buitrago, Sybille Reinke. 2015. 'Self-Other Constructions, Difference and Threat: US and Arab "Othering" of Iran.' In Elizabeth Monier (ed.), *Regional Insecurity After the Arab Uprisings* (Palgrave-Macmillan: London).

de Buitrago, Sybille Reinke. 2016. 'The role of emotions in US security policy towards Iran', *Global Affairs*, 2: 155–64.

Dehghan, H., and Al-Manar. 2017. 'Wazīr al-difāʿ al-Īrānī li-l-Manār: idhā irtakabat al-Riyāḍ ayy ḥamāqa fa-lan yabqā min al-Suʿūdiyya makān āmin ghayr Makka wa-Madīna', Accessed 01/02/2020. https://www.almanar.com.lb/1994540.

Dodge, Toby. 2012. 'From the "Arab awakening" to the Arab Spring: the post-colonial State in the Middle East', *After the Arab Spring: Power Shift in the Middle East*: 5–11.

Donya-yi-Iqtisad, and Majles. 2011. 'Statement by MPs in support of the people of the region', *Kayhan*, 07/04/2011 [18/01/1390], p. 2.

Doran, M.S. 2011. 'The Heirs of Nasser: Who Will Benefit From the Second Arab Revolution?', *Foreign Affairs*, 90: 17–25.

Dougherty, B.K. 2019. *Historical Dictionary of Iraq* (Rowman & Littlefield Publishers: UK).

Downs, K. 2012. 'A theoretical analysis of the Saudi-Iranian rivalry in Bahrain', *Journal of Politics & International Studies*, 8: 13.

DW. 2012. 'EU begins boycott of Iranian oil', Deutsche Welle, Accessed 15/11/2021. https://www.dw.com/en/eu-begins-boycott-of-iranian-oil/a-16064179.

DW, and A. Merkel. 2018. 'Merkel Statement on Khashaoggi Murder', *DW*, 20/10/2018.

Ebel, F. 2011. 'Self-immolation persists as grim form of protest in Tunisia', Associated Press, Accessed 11/10/2021. https://apnews.com/article/international-news-tunisia-coronavirus-pandemic-fires-tunis-a995219697e8085918bfa54a63880a3b.

Ehteshami, A. 2002. 'The Foreign Policy of Iran.' In Raymond A. Hinnebusch and Anoushiravan Ehteshami (eds.), *Syria and Iran* (Routledge: London).

Ehteshami, A. 2013. *Dynamics of change in the Persian Gulf: Political Economy, War and Revolution* (Routledge: Abingdon, UK.).

Ehteshami, A. 2017. *Iran: Stuck in Transition* (Taylor & Francis: Abingdon).

Ehteshami, A., and N. Horesh. 2019. *How China's Rise is Changing the Middle East* (Taylor & Francis: Abingdon).

Ehteshami, A., and M. Zweiri. 2007. *Iran and the Rise of Its Neoconservatives: The Politics of Tehran's Silent Revolution* (I.B. Tauris: London, UK).

Elaph. 2011. 'Saudi Arabia reassures Bahrain and its people: "Our army is at your disposal".' Elaph Publishing Limited, Accessed 01/02/2021. https://elaph.com/Web/news/2011/2/633421.html.

Elaph. 2011. 'Saudi Arabia reassures Bahrain and its people: "Our army is at your disposal".' 'Updated', Elaph Publishing Limited, Accessed 01/02/2021. https://elaph.com/Web/news/2011/2/633421.html.

El-Shazly, N.E.S. 2016. *The Gulf Tanker War: Iran and Iraq's Maritime Swordplay* (Palgrave Macmillan: London).

Emami-Kashani, M. 1982. 'Friday Sermon', *Jomhouri Eslami*, 16/10/1982 [24/07/1361], p. 7.

Emami-Kashani, M. 1990. 'Friday Sermon', *Jomhouri Eslami*, 31/08/1990 [09/06/1369], p. 7.

Emami-Kashani, M. 1998. 'Friday Sermon 13/03/1998.' In *Friday Sermons – Dar Maktab-i Jom' ih*, edited by Centre for Cultural Documents of the Islamic Revolution. Tehran, IR Iran: Ministry of Islamic Guidance.

Emami-Kashani, M. 2005. 'Friday Sermon 14/10/2005.' In Tehran.

Emami-Kashani, M. 2006. 'Friday Sermon 10/03/2006.' In *Friday Sermons – Dar Maktab-i Jom' ih*, edited by Centre for Cultural Documents of the Islamic Revolution. Tehran, IR Iran: Ministry of Islamic Guidance.

Emami-Kashani, M. 2011. 'Friday Sermon 12/03/2011.' In *Friday Sermons – Dar Maktab-i Jom' ih*, edited by Centre for Cultural Documents of the Islamic Revolution. Tehran, IR Iran: Ministry of Islamic Guidance.

Emami-Kashani, M. 2012. 'Friday Sermon 26/11/2012.' In *Friday Sermons*, edited by Center for Cultural Documents of the Islamic Revolution. Tehran: Ministry of Islamic Guidance.

Emami-Kashani, M. 2014. 'Friday Sermon 13/06/2014.' In *Friday Sermons – Dar Maktab-i Jom'ih*, edited by Centre for Cultural Documents of the Islamic Revolution. Tehran, IR Iran: Ministry of Islamic Guidance.

Emami-Kashani, M. 2015. 'Friday Sermon 25/09/2015.' In *Friday Sermons – Dar Maktab-i Jom'ih*, edited by Centre for Cultural Documents of the Islamic Revolution. Tehran, IR Iran: Ministry of Islamic Guidance.

Emmons, A., A. Chávez, and A. Lacy. 2019. 'Joe Biden, in Departure From Obama Policy, Says He Would Make Saudi Arabia a "Pariah"', The Intercept, Accessed 01/02/2022. https://theintercept.com/2019/11/21/democratic-debate-joe-biden-saudi-arabia/.

Ende, Werner. 2010. 'Baqī' al-Gharqad.' In *Encyclopaedia of Islam*, edited by K Fleet, G Krämer, D Matringe, Nawas and J.E. Rowson. London, UK: Brill.

Entekhab. 2017. 'Paāsukh bi chand pursish-i kilīdī darbārih-yi taghyīr-i valī'ahd-i su'ūdī/ bā intikhāb-i bin salmān, bā chih nuskha-yi az 'arabistān muvājih khvāhīm shud?', Entekhab, Accessed 10/10/2020. http://entekhab.ir/fa/news/350823.

Entekhab. 2017. 'Piyām-i tasliyat-i pādshāh-i 'arabistān va dū maqām-i arshad-i dūlatī bih khānivādih-yi āyatullah hāshmī', Accessed 10/10/2020. Entekhab.ir/001L07.

Esfandiary, D., and A. Tabatabai. 2015. 'Iran's ISIS policy', *International Affairs*, 91: 1–15.

Esposito, J.L., and J.O. Voll. 1996. *Islam and Democracy* (Oxford University Press: Oxford).

Etemaad. 2006. ''īn Hamih Fitnih! Tadbīr Chīst?', *Etemaad*, 25/02/2006 [06/12/1384].

Etemaad. 2014. 'Zakhm-i dā'sh bar pay', *Etemaad*, 12/06/2014 [22/03/1393], p. 1.

Etemaad. 2015. 'Bā raft va āmad hā yī chand shāhzadih mushkil Arabistān hal nami shavad', *Etemaad*, 30/04/2015 [10/02/1394], p. 1.

Etemaad. 2017. 'Nigāh-i dīplamāsī- tihrān va riyāż: qadam-i avval, nigāh-i ākhar', *Etemaad*, 25/01/2017 [06/11/1395].

Etemaad. 2019. 'Brītāniyā-yi ṣaghīr', *Etemaad*, 21/07/2019 [30/04/1398], p. 1.

Etemaad. 2019. 'Vākunush-i ra'īs-i kumīti-yi siyāsiyūn ummīd bih talāsh-i amīrī tirūrist-i khwāndan sipāh: niyāzmand-i insijām-i dākhilī va vahṣdat miyān-i nīrū-hā-yi khūdī hastīm', *Etemaad* 08/04/2019 [19/01/1398], p. 1.

Ettela'at. 2009. 'Gustarish-i Jang-i Ghazah', *Ettela'at*, 09/01/2009 [20/10/1387], p. 1.

Ettela'at. 2009. 'Hasbunā Allah wa Ni'm-a al-wakīl', *Ettela'at*, 21/01/2009 [02/11/1387], p. 1.

Ettela'at. 1979. 'Khomeini meets with Clerics in Qom', *Ettela'at*, 03/07/1979 [12/04/1358], p. 1.

Ettela'at. 1979. 'Results of the Assembly of Experts Elections', *Ettela'at*, 19/08/1979 [27/05/1358].

Ettela'at. 1980. 'Maktaby, Inqilāby, Jawān', *Ettela'at*, 22/07/1980 [31/04/1359], pp. 1, 2.

Ettela'at. 1980. 'Nang-i 'abadī Bar Carter Wa Ham Pālagīhāyash-2', *Ettela'at*, 26/04/1980 [06/02/1359], p. 1.

Ettela'at. 1981. 'Bā Diplomāsī-yi Tahājomī-yi Tawti'ahā-yi Shaytān-i Buzurg Rā Dar Ham Bishkunīm', *Ettela'at*, 19/12/1981 [28/09/1360], p. 16.

Ettela'at. 1981. 'Barāyih Nābūdī-yi 'Isrā'īl ''amal' Bāyad Kard', *Ettela'at*, 21/12/1981 [30/09/1360], p. 16.

Ettela'at. 1981. 'Qahramān-i Jang Kīst', *Ettela'at*, 07/01/1981 [17/10/1359], pp. 1, 2.

Ettela'at. 1981. 'Su'ūdī: 'īn Hamih 'aslihah Barā-yi Chih Mikhāhad', *Ettela'at*, 26/02/1981 [07/12/1359], p. 16.

Ettela'at. 1981. 'Tawti'ah-yi Ṭa'if bih 'Ijrā Darmi'āyad?!', *Ettela'at*, 18/04/1981 [27/01/1360], pp. 1, 2.

Ettela'at. 1982. ''Az Riyāz Tā Qulhak: Wa Amā... Su'ūdīhā', *Ettela'at*, 03/05/1982 [13/02/1361], pp. 1, 2.

Ettela'at. 1982. 'Khamenei Press, Radia and Television Conference', *Ettela'at*, 09/01/1982 [19/10/1360], p. 1.

Ettela'at. 2006. ''āghāzī Bar Payān-i Hayāt-i Rijīm-i Sihyonistī', *Ettela'at*, 15/07/2006 [24/04/1385], p. 1.

Ettela'at. 2006. 'Bun Bast-i Hal-i Siyāsī-yi Jang-i Lubnān', *Ettela'at*, 24/07/2006 [02/05/1385], p. 1.

Ettela'at. 2006. 'Fitni-yi Buzurg 'alayh-i Shī'ayān', *Ettela'at*, 23/02/2006 [04/12/1384], p. 2.

Ettela'at. 2006. 'Jang-i Āmrīkā Dar Lubnān', *Ettela'at*, 05/08/2006 [14/05/1385], p. 1.

Ettela'at. 2006. 'Khush Būd Gar Mahak-i Tajrubih 'āyad bih Mayān', *Ettela'at*, 23/07/2006 [01/05/1385], p. 1.

Ettela'at. 2006. 'Pīrūzī-yi Hizbollah; Tawaludih Khawarmiyānih-yi Jadīd', *Ettela'at*, 15/08/2006 [24/05/1385].

Falahatpisheh, H. 2019. 'Chairman of the Majles National Security and Foreign Policy Committee', *ISNA 12 May /05/2019*. 12/05/2019 [22/02/1398].

Farhi, Farideh. 2010. 'The Parliament'. In R.B. Wright (ed.), *The Iran Primer: Power, Politics, and U.S. Policy* (United States Institute of Peace: Washington DC).

Fars. 2015. 'Mina Tragedy Death Toll Exceeds 4,000', *Fars*, 29/09/2015.

Fattah, Hassan. 2005. 'Spreading the Word: Who's Who in the Arab Media', *New York Times*, Accessed 10/03/2022. http://www.nytimes.com/2005/02/06/weekinreview/06fatt.html?st=cse&sq=%22al+hayat%22+%22Al+Sharq+Al+Awsat%22&scp=2.

Felter, J., and B. Fishman. 2008. 'Iranian Strategy in Iraq'. In *Combatting Terrorism at West Point: Occasional Paper Series*. West Point Military Academy: New York.

Financial Times. 2017. 'Revolutionary Guards blame Saudi Arabia for Tehran terror attack', *FT*, 07/06/2017, p. 1.

Finlay, D.J., O.R. Holsti, and R.R. Fagen. 1967. *Enemies in Politics* (Rand McNally: Chicago).

Firouzabadi, H. 2012. 'Chief of Staff General Firouzabadi Press Statement', *Kayhan*, 30/05/2012 [10/03/1391].

Firouzabadi, H. 2012. 'Chief of Staff of the Armed Forces Major General Firouzabadi Statement on Events in Syria', *Kayhan*, 24/12/2012 [04/10/1391].

Fischer, Michael M.J. 2010. 'The rhythmic beat of the revolution in Iran', *Cultural Anthropology*, 25: 497–543.

Fisk, R. 1996. 'Interview With Saudi Dissident Bin Ladin', *The Independent*, 10/07/1996.

Fleischer, A. 2003. 'Press Briefing with Ari Fleischer May 14, 2003', Gerhard Peters. John T. Woolley, Accessed 09/04/2018. http://www.presidency.ucsb.edu/ws/?pid=61092.

Foreign Ministry. 1990. 'Foreign Ministry Second Statement on Iraqi Invasion of Kuwait', *IRIB Television Service*, 03/08/1980.

Foreign Ministry. 1990. 'Foreign Ministry Statement on Iraqi Invasion of Kuwait', *IRIB Television Service*, 02/08/1980.

Foucault, M. 2002. *Archaeology of Knowledge* (Routledge: Abingdon).

Foucault, M. 2002. *The Essential Works of Foucault, 1954–1984* (Penguin: London).

Foucault, M. 2012. *Discipline & Punish: The Birth of the Prison* (Knopf Doubleday Publishing Group).

Foucault, M., G. Burchell, C. Gordon, and P. Miller. 1991. *The Foucault Effect: Studies in Governmentality* (University of Chicago Press: Chicago).

Fraihat, F.I. 2020. *Iran and Saudi Arabia: Taming a Chaotic Conflict* (Edinburgh University Press).

Freeh, L.J. 2007. *My FBI: Bringing Down the Mafia, Investigating Bill Clinton, and Fighting the War on Terror* (St. Martin's Press).

Friedman, T., and M.B.S. al-Saud. 2017. 'Opinion: Saudi Arabia's Arab Spring, at Last', *NY Times*, Accessed 24/08/2020. https://www.nytimes.com/2017/11/23/opinion/saudi-prince-mbs-arab-spring.html.

Furtig, H. 2002. *Iran's Rivalry with Saudi Arabia Between the Gulf Wars* (Ithaca Press: Reading).

Galindo-Marines, A. 2001. 'The Relationship Between the Ulama and the Government in the Contemporary Saudi Arabian Kingdom: An Interdependent Relationship?', University of Durham.

Gargash, A. 2019. 'Anwar GargashTwitter 02 August 2019', twitter.com, Accessed 02/12/2021. https://twitter.com/AnwarGargash/status/1213035692592422912.

Garland, C. 2019. 'American defense contractor killed, troops wounded in rocket attack on base in Kirkuk' In New York: Stars & Stripes.

Garrett, M. 2018. *Mr. Trump's Wild Ride: The Thrills, Chills, Screams, and Occasional Blackouts of an Extraordinary Presidency* (St. Martin's Publishing Group).

Gause III, F.G. 2002. 'The Foreign Policy of Saudi Arabia.' In Raymond Hinnebusch and Anoushiravan Ehteshami (eds.), *The foreign policies of Middle East states* (Routledge: London).

Gause III, F.G. 2010. *The International Relations of the Persian Gulf* (Cambridge University Press: Cambridge).

Gause III, F.G. 2011. 'The Gulf Regional System and the Arab Spring.' In *The Montreal Review*. Montreal: The Montreal Review.

Gause III, F.G. 2013. 'Why the Iran Deal Scares Saudi Arabia', *The New Yorker*, 26.

Gause III, F.G. 2014. 'Beyond sectarianism: The new Middle East cold war', *Brookings Doha Center Analysis Paper*, 11: 1–27.

Gause III, F.G. 2018. *After the Killing of Jamal Khashoggi: Muhammad bin Salman and the Future of Saudi-US Relations* (Center for Strategic & International Studies).

GCC. 2011. ' Final Statement GCC 18th Summit Mecca 2011', *Secratariat General of the GCC*, 11/03/2011.

Ghaani, E. 2020. 'Commander of Quds Force Speech 05 June 2020.' In *IRGC Statements*, edited by IRNA. Tehran, IR Iran: IRNA.

Ghalibaf, M. 2005. 'Ghalibaf Interview with Shargh News.' In *Shargh News*, edited by Shargh News. Shargh News.

Ghantous, G., and P. Hafezi. 2022. 'UAE raid raises Yemen stakes, draws closer scrutiny of Iran allies', *Thomson Reuters*, Accessed 01/02/2022. https://www.reuters.com/world/middle-east/uae-raid-raises-yemen-stakes-draws-closer-scrutiny-iran-allies-2022-01-18/.

Ghasemi, Bahram. 2017. 'Foreign Ministry Spokesman Statements 03 May 2017', *MNA*, 03/05/2017 [13/02/1396].

Ghasemi, Bahram. 2017. 'Foreign Ministry Spokesman Statements 07 June 2017', *MNA*, 07/06/2017 [17/03/1396].

Ghasemi, B. 2018. 'Foreign Ministry Spokesman News Conference', *IRNA*, 15/10/2018 [23/07/1397].

Ghasemi, B. 2018. 'Iranian Foreign Ministry Spokesman Statement in Response to Saudi Crown Prince', *MNA*, 11/04/2018 [22/01/1397], p. 2.

Ghasemi, B. 2018. 'Iranian Foreign Ministry Spokesman Statement in Response to Saudi Crown Prince CBS Interview', *MNA*, 15/03/2018 [24/12/1396], p. 2.

Gheissari, A. 2009. *Contemporary Iran: Economy, Society, Politics* (Oxford University Press: Oxford).

Ghobadzdeh, N., and S. Akbarzadeh. 2015. 'Sectarianism and the Prevalence of "Othering" in Islamic Thought', *Third World Quarterly*, 36: 691–704.

Gladstone, R. 2015. 'Death Toll From Hajj Stampede Reaches 2,411 in New Estimate', *NY Times*, 03/01/2016.

Gnana, J. 2022. 'Saudi Arabia, Iraq sign agreement to link electrical power grids', S&P Global, Accessed 15/02/2022. https://www.spglobal.com/commodity-insights/en/market-insights/latest-news/electric-power/012522-saudi-arabia-iraq-sign-agreement-to-link-electrical-power-grids.

Gold, D. 2013. 'The Arab World Fears the "Safavid"', Israel Hayom, Accessed 15/03/2022.

Guardian, The. 1996. 'Saudis hold 40 Suspects in Dhahran Bombing', *The Guardian*, 02/11/1996, p. 1.

Guardian, The. 2011. 'Bahrain says terror suspects linked to Iran's Revolutionary Guard', *The Guardian*, 14/11/2011, p. 1.

Guardian, The. 2012. 'Syrian rebels retreat from Baba Amr district of Homs', *The Guardian*, 02/03/2012, p. 1.

Guardian, The. 2013. 'Elite Iranian general assassinated near Syria-Lebanon border', *The Guardian*, 14/02/2013, p. 1.

Guardian, The. 2014. 'Iran sends troops into Iraq to aid fight against Isis militants', *The Guardian*, 14/06/2014, p. 1.

Guardian, The. 2014. 'Iraq crisis: US willing to work with Iran but officials play down military talk', *The Guardian*, 16/06/2014, p. 1.

Guardian, The. 2014. 'Qassem Suleimani photo makeover reveals Iran's new publicity strategy', *The Guardian*, 14/10/2014, p. 1.

Guardian, The. 2017. 'Trump Approved Yemen Raid', *The Guardian*, 02/02/2017, p. 1.

Guardian, The. 2019. 'UK may help release Iranian oil tanker if it gets Syria guarantee', *The Guardian*, 13/07/2019, p. 1.

Guardian, The. 2020. 'Iran launches missiles at Iraq airbases hosting US and coalition troops', *The Guardian*, 08/01/2020, p. 1.

Gulf News Agency. 1979. 'Interview with Prince Abdullah bin Abdul Aziz.' In *Saudi Press Association Archives*. Riyadh: King Khalid bin Abdul Aziz Database.

Habeeb, W.M. 2012. *The Middle East in Turmoil: Conflict, Revolution, and Change: Conflict, Revolution, and Change* (ABC-CLIO: Santa Barbara, CA).

Hadad-Adel, G.A. 2006. 'Majles Speaker Statement on Askari Shrine Bombing.' In *Majles Statements*, edited by IRNA. Tehran: IRNA.

Haeri, Safa. 2007. 'A Shi'a-Sunni War of International Dimension Looms Ahead', Iran Press Service, Accessed 01/04/2014. http://www.iran-press-service.com/ips/articles-2007/august-2007/saudi_fatwa_1807.shtml.

Hafezi, P. 2021. 'UAE security official pays rare visit to Iran to discuss ties, regional issues', *Thomson Reuters*, Accessed 01/02/2022. https://www.reuters.com/article/us-iran-emirates-idAFKBN2IL0ME.

Hajizadeh, A.A. 2011. 'IRGC Aerospace Commander warns US officials', *Fars News*, 09/11/2011 [18/18/1390].

Hammond, A. 2008. 'Maintaining Saudi Arabia's Cordon Sanitaire in the Arab Media.' In M. Al-Rasheed (ed.), *Kingdom Without Borders: Saudi Political, Religious and Media Frontiers* (Columbia University Press: India).

Hammond, A. 2009. 'Arab states gloat at Iran strife, but wary of result', *Reuters*, 22/06/2009.

Han, J., and H. Hakimian. 2019. 'The Regional Security Complex in the Persian Gulf: The Contours of Iran's GCC Policy', *Asian Journal of Middle Eastern and Islamic Studies*, 13: 493–508.

Hansler, J., K. Atwood, and CNN. 2022. 'Biden administration restores Iran sanctions waiver as time runs out to salvage nuclear deal', CNN, Accessed 20/02/2022. https://edition.cnn.com/2022/02/04/politics/iran-civil-nuclear-waiver-restored/index.html.

Harre, R., and L. van Langenhove. 1999. *Positioning Theory: Moral Contexts of International Action* (Blackwell: Oxford).

Hasan, H. 2011. 'Syrian Ambassador Statement on Events in Syria', *Kayhan*, 27/12/2011[06/10/1390], p. 2.

Hassan, M. 2017. 'Donald Trump Said Saudi Arabia Was Behind 9/11. Now He's Going There on His First Foreign Trip', *The Intercept*, 18/05/2017.

Hatami, A. 2018. 'Hatami: Saudi crown prince trapped in illusion of power', *MNA*, 09/04/2018 [20/01/1397], p. 2.

Hatami, A. 2020. 'Minister of Defence Statement on Assassination of Qassem Soleimani', *MNA*, 04/01/2020, p. 2.

Helms, C.M. 1981. *The Cohesion of Saudi Arabia: Evolution of Political Identity* (Johns Hopkins University Press: Baltimore, MD).

Henderson, S. 2007. 'Saudi Arabia: The Nightmare of Iraq.' In *Policy Focus 70*: 33–40. Washington Institute for Near East Policy: Washington DC.

Herrmann, R.K. 1985. 'Analyzing Soviet Images of the United States: A Psychological Theory and Empirical Study', *Journal of Conflict Resolution*, 29: 665–97.

Herrmann, R.K., and M.P. Fischerkeller. 1995. 'Beyond the enemy image and spiral model: cognitive strategic research after the cold war', *International Organization*, 49: 415–50.

Hertog, S. 2011. *Princes, Brokers, and Bureaucrats: Oil and the State in Saudi Arabia* (Cornell University Press: New York).

Herzig, E. 2004. 'Regionalism, Iran and Central Asia', *International Affairs*, 80: 503–17.

Hinnebusch, R.A. 2003. *The International Politics of the Middle East* (Palgrave: Manchester).

Hiro, D. 2001. *Neighbors, Not Friends: Iraq and Iran after the Gulf Wars* (Taylor & Francis: New York).

Hiro, D. 2013. *Iran Under the Ayatollahs* (Taylor & Francis: New York).

Hiro, D. 2019. *Cold War in the Islamic World: Saudi Arabia, Iran and the Struggle for Supremacy* (Oxford University Press: New York).

Hook, B., and Reuters. 2019. 'Trump is willing to talk to Iran, top U.S. adviser says', *Reuters*, Accessed 15/11/2021. https://www.reuters.com/article/uk-mideast-iran-usa-diplomacy-idAFKCN1TP1DD.

Hook, B., and Reuters. 2019. 'U.S. envoy says important to de-escalate tension with Iran', *Reuters*, Accessed 20/05/2020. https://www.reuters.com/article/us-mideast-iran-usa-saudi-idUSKCN1TM195.

Howard, P.N., and M.M. Hussain. 2013. *Democracy's Fourth Wave?: Digital Media and the Arab Spring* (Oxford University Press: New York).

Hujailan, J. 1997. 'GCC General Secretary Press Interview with Al-Etihad Newspaper (UAE)', *SPA*, 04/09/1997.

Hujailan, J. 1997. 'GCC General Secretary Press Statement', *SPA*, 05/08/1997.

Human Rights Watch. 2011. 'Bahrain's Human Rights Crisis', *Human Rights Watch Report*, 05/07/2011.

Human Rights Council. 2011. 'Interim report of the Secretary-General on the situation of human rights in Iran', 14/03/2011.

Human Rights Watch. 2011. 'Saudi Arabia: Free Political Activists', *Human Rights Watch Report*, 19/02/2011.

Human Rights Watch. 2017. 'Yemen: Houthi Strike on Saudi Airport Likely War Crime', 07/11/2017.

Hunter, S. 2010. *Iran's Foreign Policy in the Post-Soviet Era: Resisting the New International Order* (Praeger).

Hunter, S.T. 1990. *Iran and the World : Continuity in a Revolutionary Decade* (Indiana University Press: Bloomington).

Huthayfi, A.A. 1998. 'Friday Sermon 27/02/1998.' In *Sermons–Khutab*, edited by Ministry of Islamic Affairs. Madina, Saudi Arabia: Ministry of Islamic Affairs, Dawah and Guidance.

Ibrahim, Yousef. 1997. 'Al Hayat: A Journalistic Noah's Ark', *New York Times*, Accessed 10/03/2022. http://www.nytimes.com/1997/01/15/world/al-hayat-a-journalistic-noah-s-ark.html.

Ikonomou, P.F. 2020. *Global Nuclear Developments: Insights from a Former IAEA Nuclear Inspector* (Springer International Publishing).

Illahi, M. 2020. *Citadel of Shia Imams: Persecution & Resistance* (Friesen Press).

IMP, and Monroe Price. 2012. 'Iran Media Programme-Etemaad', Center for Global Communication Studies, University of Pennsylvania, Accessed 20/03/2014.

Independent, The. 2020. 'Iran missile strike: Two US-Iraq bases hit by 22 rockets in revenge attacks as crisis escalates', *The Independent*, 07/01/2020, p. 1.

Iran, and J. Zarif. 2014. 'Zarif meets with former French Foreign Minister: The other side should show their willingness to reach an agreement', *Iran*, 08/10/2014 [16/07/1393].

Iran Diplomacy. 2011. 'Interview with Ayatollah Hashemi Rafsanjani.' In *Iran Diplomacy*, edited by Mohammad Sadeq Kharrazi. Tehran.

Iranian Foreign Ministry. 1981. 'Foreign Ministry Statement on Fahd Peace Plan', *Jomhouri Eslami*, 14/08/1981 [23/05/1360], p. 2.

Iranian Foreign Ministry. 1997. 'Foreign Ministry Spokesman on Afghanistan', *Jomhouri Eslami*, 26/05/1997 [05/03/1376], p. 2.

IRGC. 2013. 'IRGC Statement on the Death of General Hassan Shateri in Syria', *IRNA*, 17/02/2013 [29/11/1391].

IRGC. 2017. 'Intiqām-i khūn-i shuhdā-yi hṣādisa-yi tirūristī rā mīgīrīm', Youth Journalists Club, Accessed 01/10/2020. https://www.yjc.news/00Pfzx.

IRGC. 2017. 'IRGC Spokesman Statement', 22/06/2017 [01/04/1396].

IRIB. 2009. 'Presidential Debate, Ahmadinejad and Mousavi, 03/06/2009', *IRIB*.

IRNA. 1990. 'Statement', *IRNA*, 19/09/1990 [28/06/1369].

IRNA. 1997. 'Iranian Foreign Minister Statement Visit to Saudi Arabia', *IRNA*, 16/03/1997.

IRNA. 1997. 'Minister of State Abdulaziz Khoweiter Visit to Iran', *IRNA*, 01/07/1997.

IRNA. 1997. 'Rafsanjani Statement on Extraordinary OIC Summit in Islamabad', *IRNA*, 24/03/1997.

IRNA. 1998. 'Iranian Government Spokesman on Rafsanjani's Visit to Saudi Arabia', *IRNA*, 18/02/1998.

IRNA. 1998. 'Saudi Shurah Council Speaker Visit to the Islamic Republic of Iran', *IRNA*, 21/11/1998 [30/08/1377].

IRNA. 2020. 'Ustād-i dānishgāh-i shīrāz: marg andīshī dar vujūd-i sardār sulaimānī tabalvūrī khāsṣṣ dāsht', IRNA, Accessed 10/09/2022. irna.ir/xjCtgr.

IRNA. 2022. 'OIC can play key role in Riyadh-Tehran de-escalation', IRNA, Accessed 01/02/2022. https://en.irna.ir/news/84619097/OIC-can-play-key-role-in-Riyadh-Tehran-de-escalation.

IRNA, and Majles. 2011. '257 members of the Iranian parliament announced their support for the uprising of the nations of Bahrain, Libya and Yemen', *IRNA*, 15/03/2011 [24/12/1389], p. 2.

IRNA, and A.A. Salehi. 2011. 'Salehi Letter to UN Secretary General', *IRNA*, 15/04/2011 [26/01/1390], p. 2.

Ismael, T.Y., and J.S. Ismael. 1994. *The Gulf War and the New World Order: International Relations of the Middle East* (University Press of Florida).

ISNA. 2013. 'The Supreme Leader agrees with "heroic flexibility" from the perspective of foreign media'.

ISNA. 2017. 'āchmaz shudan-i valī ʿahd-i sābiq dar bāzī', Accessed 01/09/2021. https://www.isna.ir/news/96033118127/.

ISNA. 2017. 'Tashrīh ahdāf-i safar-i vazīr-i khārijih-yi Kuwait bih Tehran', *ISNA*, Accessed 01/09/2020. https://www.isna.ir/news/95110503733/.

ISNA. 2020. 'Raʾīs-i sāzmān-i ʿaqīdatī siyāsī-yi vizārat-i difāʿ: qāsim sulaimānī amīr-i muslimīn-i jahān būd', *ISNA*, Accessed 01/09/2021. https://www.isna.ir/news/98101511790/.

Jaberi Ansari, H. 2016. 'Iran strongly condemns Nimr execution', *Press TV*, 02/01/2016.

Jafari, M.A. 2015. 'Farmāndih-yi sipāh: hilāl-i shiʿī dar hāl-i gīrī ast', Dolat Bahar, Accessed 02/02/2019. http://www.ghatreh.com/news/nn25763498/%D9%81%D8%B1%D9%85%D8%A7%D9%86%D8%AF%D9%87-%D8%B3%D9%BE%D8%A7%D9%87-%D9%87%D9%84%D8%A7%D9%84-%D8%B4%DB%8C%D8%B9%DB%8C-%D8%AD%D8%A7%D9%84-%D8%B4%DA%A9%D9%84-%DA%AF%DB%8C%D8%B1%DB%8C-%D8%A7%D8%B3%D8%AA.

Jafari, M.A. 2017. 'IRGC Commander Reaction to ISIS Terrorist Attacks', *Kayhan*, 14/06/2017 [24/03/1396], p. 2.

Jafari, M.A. 2019. 'IRGC Commander Reaction to IRGC on FTO', *SNN*, Accessed 10/03/2020. https://snn.ir/003AZo.

Jahan News. 2014. 'Jurists and Scholars Warning to Riyadh about the execution of Sheikh Nimr', *Jahan News*, Accessed 01/04/2019. https://www.jahannews.com/analysis/386287/%D8%A2%D9%86%D9%87%D8%A7%DB%8C%DB%8C-%D8%AD%DA%A9%D9%85-%D8%A7%D8%B9%D8%AF%D8%A7%D9%85-%D8%B4%DB%8C%D8%AE-%D9%86%D9%85%D8%B1-%D8%B5%D8%A7%D8%AF%D8%B1-%DA%A9%D8%B1%D8%AF%D9%86%D8%AF-%D8%A8%D8%AF%D8%A7%D9%86%D9%86%D8%AF-%D8%AC%D9%87%D8%A7%D9%86-%D8%A7%D8%B3%D9%84%D8%A7%D9%85-%D9%BE%D8%A7%D8%B3%D8%AE-%D8%A2%D9%86%D8%A7%D9%86-%D8%AE%D9%88%D8%A7%D9%87%D8%AF.

Jahner, Ariel. 2012. 'Saudi Arabia and Iran: The struggle for power and influence in the Gulf', *International Affairs Review*, 20: 37–50.

Jalili, S. 2013. 'Secretary General of the Supreme National Security Council, Saeed Jalili Meets Syrian President Bashar Assad', *IRIB*, 02/02/2013 [14/11/1391].

Jamali, M.J. 2019. 'The Fujairah explosion was a predetermined scenario for John Bolton', *Majles.ir*, 14/05/2019 [24/02/1398].

Jannati, A. 1998. 'Friday Sermon 06/03/1998' In *Friday Sermons – Dar Maktab-i Jomʿih*, edited by Centre for Cultural Documents of the Islamic Revolution. Tehran, IR Iran: Ministry of Islamic Guidance.

Jannati, A. 1998. 'Friday Sermon 18/09/1998.' In *Friday Sermons – Dar Maktab-i Jomʿih*, edited by Centre for Cultural Documents of the Islamic Revolution. Tehran, IR Iran: Ministry of Islamic Guidance.

Jannati, A. 2005. 'Friday Sermon 16/09/2005.' In *Friday Sermons – Dar Maktab-i Jomʿih*, edited by Centre for Cultural Documents of the Islamic Revolution. Tehran, IR Iran: Ministry of Islamic Guidance.

Jannati, A. 2006. 'Friday Sermon 17/02/2006.' In *Friday Sermons – Dar Maktab-i Jomʿih*, edited by Centre for Cultural Documents of the Islamic Revolution. Tehran, IR Iran: Ministry of Islamic Guidance.

Jannati, A. 2011. 'Friday Sermon 18/03/2011.' In *Friday Sermons – Dar Maktab-i Jomʿih*, edited by Centre for Cultural Documents of the Islamic Revolution. Tehran, IR Iran: Ministry of Islamic Guidance.

Jannati, A. 2011. 'Friday Sermon 26/11/2011.' In *Friday Sermons – Dar Maktab-i Jom'ih*, edited by Centre for Cultural Documents of the Islamic Revolution. Tehran, IR Iran: Ministry of Islamic Guidance.

Jannati, A. 2012. 'Friday Sermon 04/08/2012.' In *Friday Sermons – Dar Maktab-i Jom'ih*, edited by Centre for Cultural Documents of the Islamic Revolution. Tehran, IR Iran: Ministry of Islamic Guidance.

Jannati, A. 2015. 'Friday Sermon 30/01/2015.' In *Friday Sermons – Dar Maktab-i Jom'ih*, edited by Centre for Cultural Documents of the Islamic Revolution. Tehran, IR Iran: Ministry of Islamic Guidance.

Javani, Y., and ABNA. 2014. 'General Javani in explaining the photo of Sardar Soleimani with the Peshmerga', *ABNA*, 12/10/2014 [20/07/1393].

Javani, Y., and ABNA. 2014. 'The presence of General Soleimani in the region creates a united front / we will not allow insecurity to be drawn to our borders', *ABNA*, 17/11/2014 [26/08/1393].

Jazayeri, M. 2012. 'Deputy Chief of Staff of the Armed Forces: The arrival of Syria's friends will deal a decisive blows to the enemies and the reactionary Arabs', *Fars News Agency*, 25/07/2012 [04/05/1391].

Jazayeri, M. 2012. 'General Jazayeri Statement on Syria to the Young Journalists Club 06/10/1391', *YJC*, 26/12/2012 [06/10/1391].

Jett, D.C. 2017. *The Iran Nuclear Deal: Bombs, Bureaucrats, and Billionaires* (Springer International Publishing).

Johnston, D. 1996. 'F.B.I. Pulls Out of Joint Inquiry On Fatal Blast in Saudi Arabia', *New York Times*, 02/11/1996.

Jomhouri Eslami. 1979. 'Makah: Mī'ād Gāh-i Muqadas-i Islām Wa Bāzār Kālahāy-i Pūsīdih-yi Gharb', *Jomhouri Eslami*, 08/12/1979 [17/09/1358], p. 6.

Jomhouri Eslami. 1979. 'Payām-i Tārīkhī-yi Imām Khomainī. Khitāb Bih Hamih Khāharān Wa Barādarān-i Musalmān', *Jomhouri Eslami*, 30/09/1979 [08/07/1358], pp. 1, 4.

Jomhouri Eslami. 1980. ''ab'ād-i Gustarda-yi Jang-i Iran wa Amrikā', *Jomhouri Eslami*, 23/09/1980 [01/07/1359], p. 1.

Jomhouri Eslami. 1980. ''āli Su'ūd Bā Ghulāmān-i Khānih Zādih-yi Gharb', *Jomhouri Eslami*, 23/12/1980 [02/10/1359].

Jomhouri Eslami. 1980. ''āli Su'ūd Nawkarān-i Wāqi'ī-yi Impīryalism', *Jomhouri Eslami*, 23/09/1980 [12/08/1359].

Jomhouri Eslami. 1980. ''āyandi-yi 'inqilāb', *Jomhouri Eslami*, 27/01/1980 [07/11/1358], pp. 1, 2.

Jomhouri Eslami. 1980. ''az 'bbraha Tā Carter', *Jomhouri Eslami*, 26/04/1980 [06/02/1359], pp. 1, 2.

Jomhouri Eslami. 1980. 'Khat-i Sāzish. Khat-i Imam', *Jomhouri Eslami*, 19/02/1980 [30/11/1358], pp. 1, 2.

Jomhouri Eslami. 1980. 'Mawzi'-i Kishwarhā-yi Mantiqih Nisbat Bih Jang-i 'arāq Bā Iran', *Jomhouri Eslami*, 11/11/1980 [20/08/1359].

Jomhouri Eslami. 1980. 'Mujahideen Khalgh Press Interview', *Jomhouri Eslami*, 05/09/1980 [14/06/1359], p. 2.

Jomhouri Eslami. 1980. 'Sadhā Nafar Dar 'arabistān Majrūh Wa Bāzdāsht Shudan', *Jomhouri Eslami*, 06/02/1980 [17/11/1358], pp. 1, 2.

Jomhouri Eslami. 1980. 'Sukhanī Bā Namāyandagān-i Majlis', *Jomhouri Eslami*, 23/07/1980 [01/05/1359], pp. 1, 2.

Jomhouri Eslami. 1980. 'Sukhanrānī-yi Ayatollah Beheshti Dar Majma'-i Hizb', *Jomhouri Eslami*, 29/01/1980 [09/11/1358], p. 3.

Jomhouri Eslami. 1980. 'Wihdat Wa Marz Bandīhā', *Jomhouri Eslami*, 04/09/1980 [13/06/1359], pp. 1–2.

Jomhouri Eslami. 1981. ''abrhā-yi Fitnih 'az Rāh Mirasand', *Jomhouri Eslami*, 10/11/1981 [19/08/1360], pp. 1, 4.

Jomhouri Eslami. 1981. ''abrhā-yi Fitnih 'az Rāh Mirasand-2', *Jomhouri Eslami*, 11/11/1981 [20/08/1360], pp. 1, 4.

Jomhouri Eslami. 1981. ''āl-i Su'ūd: Ghulāmān-i Khānih Zādi-yi Gharb', *Jomhouri Eslami*, 11/01/1981 [21/10/1359], p. 3.

Jomhouri Eslami. 1981. ''Āncheh Dar Bahrayn Guzasht', *Jomhouri Eslami*, 20/12/1981 [29/09/1360], pp. 1, 15.

Jomhouri Eslami. 1981. ''arabistān-i Su'ūdī: Talāsh Barā-yi Tashdīd-i 'ikhtināq', *Jomhouri Eslami*, 02/03/1981 [11/12/1359], p. 3.

Jomhouri Eslami. 1981. 'Barāy-i Hifz-i Kalimih-yi 'ulyā', *Jomhouri Eslami*, 19/12/1981 [28/08/1360], pp. 1, 4.

Jomhouri Eslami. 1981. 'Haj Wa 'inqilāb', *Jomhouri Eslami*, 28/10/1981 [06/08/1360], pp. 1, 10.

Jomhouri Eslami. 1981. 'Irān Pur 'az Bihishtī-yi', *Jomhouri Eslami*, 01/07/1981 [10/04/1360], pp. 1, 3.

Jomhouri Eslami. 1981. 'Khat-i Tā'if', *Jomhouri Eslami*, 20/04/1981 [31/01/1360], pp. 1, 3.

Jomhouri Eslami. 1981. 'Khāwarmiyānih-yi Bīhūsh', *Jomhouri Eslami*, 15/08/1981 [24/05/1360], pp. 1, 9.

Jomhouri Eslami. 1981. 'Khomeini Speech on Presidential Innauguration, Eid Adha and Dead of Sadat', *Jomhouri Eslami*, 10/10/1981 [18/07/1360], pp. 12, 11.

Jomhouri Eslami. 1981. 'Khomeini Speech to Sunni Clerics from Kurdistan Province 09/03/1360', *Jomhouri Eslami*, 31/05/1981 [10/03/1360], p. 12.

Jomhouri Eslami. 1981. 'Kunfirāns-i Islāmī', *Jomhouri Eslami*, 04/01/1981 [14/10/1359], p. 3.

Jomhouri Eslami. 1981. 'Qiyām-i Ka'bah', *Jomhouri Eslami*, 30/04/1981 [10/02/1360], p. 2.

Jomhouri Eslami. 1981. 'Rafsanjani Speech in Majles 15/07/1360', *Jomhouri Eslami*, 08/10/1981 [16/07/1360], p. 12.

Jomhouri Eslami. 1981. 'Risālat Rādio Tilwiziyūn Dar Gustarish-i Inqilāb', *Jomhouri Eslami*, 10/08/1981 [19/05/1360], pp. 1, 2.

Jomhouri Eslami. 1981. 'Tafriqih-yi Shī'ih Sunī Tawti'ih-yi Amrīkā', *Jomhouri Eslami*, 15/04/1981 [26/01/1360], pp. 1, 3.

Jomhouri Eslami. 1981. 'Talāsh-i Bīhūdih-yi 'imarāt Mutahida-yi 'arabī', *Jomhouri Eslami*, 14/07/1981 [23/04/1360], pp. 1, 4.

Jomhouri Eslami. 1982. ''ahdāf-i Nīrūhā-yi Chand Milatī Dar Bayrūt', *Jomhouri Eslami*, 13/10/1982 [21/07/1361], p. 11.

Jomhouri Eslami. 1982. 'Amniyat-i Dast-i Jam'ī', *Jomhouri Eslami*, 27/02/1982 [08/12/1360], pp. 1, 4.

Jomhouri Eslami. 1982. 'Dar Chazābah', *Jomhouri Eslami*, 22/02/1982 [03/12/1360], pp. 1, 11.

Jomhouri Eslami. 1982. 'Hubūt-i Farzand-i 'ādam', *Jomhouri Eslami*, 22/04/1982 [02/02/1361], pp. 1, 24.

Jomhouri Eslami. 1982. ''Irtijā'-i Mantaqih 'intihār Mīkunad', *Jomhouri Eslami*, 10/06/1982 [20/03/1361], pp. 1, 2.

Jomhouri Eslami. 1982. 'Khamenei Press, Radio and Television Conference', *Jomhouri Eslami*, 09/01/1982 [19/10/1360], pp. 9, 12.

Jomhouri Eslami. 1982. 'Prime Minister Mousavi Press Interview with Jomhouri Eslami', *Jomhouri Eslami*, 26/08/1982 [04/06/1361], pp. 12, 11.

Jomhouri Eslami. 1982. 'Tā Dīr Nashudih', *Jomhouri Eslami*, 15/05/1982 [25/02/1361], pp. 1, 11.

Jomhouri Eslami. 1982. 'Tā Siyāh Ruwwy Shavad', *Jomhouri Eslami*, 28/04/1982 [08/02/1361], pp. 1, 10.

Jomhouri Eslami. 1997. 'ʿāghāz-i Dū Maʾmūriyat', *Jomhouri Eslami*, 13/12/1997 [22/09/1376], p. 1.

Jomhouri Eslami. 1997. ' Bī Tawāfutī Dar Barābar-i Tahawulāti Afghanistān Bi Maslihat-i Mā Nīst', *Jomhouri Eslami*, 26/05/1997 [05/03/1376], p. 16.

Jomhouri Eslami. 1997. 'Interview with the Iranian Ambassador to Saudi Arabia-Mohammad Reza Nouri', *Jomhouri Eslami*, 08/07/1997 [17/04/1376].

Jomhouri Eslami. 1997. 'Khamenei, Payvand-i Wihdat-i Islāmī', *Jomhouri Eslami*, 10/12/1997 [18/09/1376], pp. 1, 2.

Jomhouri Eslami. 1997. 'Khurūsh ʾalaiha Istikbār: Fasl-i Mushtarak-i Hamih-yi Nīrūhā-yi Inqilāb', *Jomhouri Eslami*, 05/11/1997 [14/08/1376], pp. 1, 2.

Jomhouri Eslami. 1997. 'Sāl-i Muwafaghiyathā-yi Buzurg', *Jomhouri Eslami*, 18/03/1997 [28/12/1375], pp. 1, 4.

Jomhouri Eslami. 1997. 'Ṭālibān, ʿāmil-i Nāʾamnī Dar Mantiqih', *Jomhouri Eslami*, 27/05/1997 [06/03/1376], pp. 1, 11.

Jomhouri Eslami. 1998. 'Crown Prince Abdullah Apology to Rafsanjani on Madina Incident', *Jomhouri Eslami*, 08/03/1998 [17/12/1376], p. 2.

Jomhouri Eslami. 1998. 'Diplumāsī-yi Munfaʿil-i Mā!', *Jumhouri Eslami*, 10/08/1998 [19/05/1377], pp. 1, 2.

Jomhouri Eslami. 1998. 'Masʾalih-yi Afghanistān Wa ʾamniyat-i Milī-yi Mā', *Jomhouri Eslami*, 11/08/1998 [20/05/1377], pp. 1, 2.

Jomhouri Eslami. 1998. 'Pākistān Bayad Tajāwuz-i Nizāmī Bih Afghānisān Rā Pāyān Dahad', *Jomhouri Eslami*, 09/08/1998 [18/05/1377], p. 14.

Jomhouri Eslami. 1998. 'Past-i Tar Az Tālibān', *Jomhouri Eslami*, 05/09/1998 [14/06/1377], pp. 1, 2.

Jomhouri Eslami. 1998. 'Tahlīl Siyāsī-yi Haftih', *Jomhouri Eslami*, 17/09/1998 [26/06/1377], p. 16.

Jomhouri Eslami. 2005. 'Zarūrat-i ʾistādigī dar barābar-i siyāsathā-yi dugānani-yi gharb', *Jomhouri Eslami*, 06/08/2005 [15/05/1384].

Jomhouri Eslami. 2006. 'Nawbat-i Gām-i ʾākhar ʾast', *Jomhouri Eslami*, 15/08/2006 [24/05/1385].

Jomhouri Eslami. 2006. 'Sukūt Khiyānat ʾast', *Jomhouri Eslami*, 15/07/2006 [24/04/1385].

Jomhouri Eslami. 2006. 'Wuʿāz-i Mutakabirīn', *Jomhouri Eslami*, 25/07/2006 [03/05/1385].

Jomhouri Eslami. 2008. 'Darbārhā-yi ʿarab Masʾūl-i Jināyāt-i Sahyunīst Hā Dar Ghazah', *Jomhouri Eslami*, 30/12/2008 [10/10/1387].

Jomhouri Eslami. 2008. 'Hamdastī Kufār-i Harbī Wa Munāfiqān-i ʾumat', *Jomhouri Eslami*, 31/12/2008 [11/10/1387].

Jomhouri Eslami. 2008. 'Jināyāt-i Ghazah Wa Bī ʿamalī-yi Musalmānān', *Jomhouri Eslami*, 28/12/2008 [08/10/1387], p. 1.

Jomhouri Eslami. 2009. 'Kul-i Yawm ʿāshūrā', *Jomhouri Eslami*, 05/01/2009 [16/10/1387].

Jomhouri Eslami. 2009. 'Naburd-i Ghazah Shikast-i Sahyunīsm va ʾirtijāʿ-i ʿarab', *Jomhouri Eslami*, 12/01/2009 [23/10/1387].

Jomhouri Eslami. 2009. 'Pardahā-yī Kih Bālā Raftand', *Jomhouri Eslami*, 14/01/2009 [25/10/1387].

Jomhouri Eslami. 1989. 'Sar Maqalah', *Jomhouri Eslami*, 24/09/1989 [02/07/1368].

Jomhouri Eslami. 1990. 'Sar Maqalah', *Jomhouri Eslami*, 13/08/1990 [22/05/1369].

Jomhouri Eslami. 1990. 'Sar Maqalah', *Jomhouri Eslami*, 20/08/1990 [29/05/1369].

Jomhouri Eslami. 1990. 'Sar Maqalah', *Jomhouri Eslami*, 26/08/1990 [04/06/1369].

Jomhouri Eslami. 1990. 'Sar Maqalah', *Jomhouri Eslami*, 10/09/1990 [19/06/1369].

Jomhouri Eslami. 1990. 'Sar Maqalah', *Jomhouri Eslami*, 13/09/1990 [22/06/1369].

Jones, T.C. 2010. *Desert Kingdom* (Harvard University Press: Cambridge, MA).

Kaldor, M. 1990. *The Imaginary War: Understanding the East-West Conflict* (Blackwell: London).

Kamalipour, Y.R. 2010. *Media, Power, and Politics in the Digital Age: The 2009 Presidential Election Uprising in Iran* (Rowman & Littlefield Publishers: London).

Kamrava, M. 2011. *The International Politics of the Persian Gulf* (Syracuse University Press).

Kamrava, M. 2014. *Beyond the Arab Spring: The Evolving Ruling Bargain in the Middle East* (Oxford University Press).

Kamrava, M. 2020. *Routledge Handbook of Persian Gulf Politics* (Taylor & Francis).

Kamrava, M., and H. Hassan-Yari. 2004. 'Suspended Equilibrium in Iran's Political System', *The Muslim World*, 94: 495–524.

Karimi, N., and F. Rahim. 2021. 'Iran hosts high-level Afghan peace talks as fighting surges', *AFP*, Accessed 01/02/2022. https://apnews.com/article/joe-biden-middle-east-iran-c92c36feaaf1b0a84d5e08963fa9673b.

Karsh, E. 2009. *The Iran-Iraq War* (Rosen Publishers: New York).

Kayālī, A. 2009. *Dirāsāt fī al-ʾidwān al-ʾisrāeylī ʾalā qitāʿ Ghazah* (Al-Zaytouna Centre for Studies and Consultations: Beirut, Lebanon).

Kayhan. 1980. 'Zabūn-i Khudumūnī', *Kayhan*, 23/07/1980 [01/05/1359], p. 3.

Kayhan. 1981. 'Talīʿih-yi Pīrūzī', *Kayhan*, 06/01/1981 [16/10/1359], pp. 1, 10.

Kayhan. 1988. 'Yadasht-i Ruz', *Kayhan*, 30/04/1988 [10/02/1367], p. 1.

Kayhan. 1989. 'Yadasht-i Ruz', *Kayhan*, 23/09/1989 [01/07/1368], p. 1.

Kayhan. 1990. 'Yadasht-i Ruz', *Kayhan*, 16/08/1990 [25/05/1369], p. 1.

Kayhan. 1997. 'Hunar ʾān ʾast Kih. .', *Kayhan*, 30/11/1997 [09/09/1376], p. 2.

Kayhan. 1997. 'ʾijlās-i Tihrān Wa ʾānchih Bāyad. .', *Kayhan*, 16/03/1997 [26/12/1375], p. 1.

Kayhan. 1997. 'Jahān-i Islām: ʾufuqhā-yi ʾāyandeh', *Kayhan*, 10/12/1997 [19/09/1376], p. 2.

Kayhan. 1997. 'Kunfirāns-i Islāmī Az Wāqiʿiyat Bih Haqīqat', *Kayhan*, 13/12/1997 [22/09/1376], p. 2.

Kayhan. 1997. 'Payām-i ʾaslī', *Kayhan*, 27/05/1997 [06/03/1376], p. 2.

Kayhan. 1998. 'Bāzī-yi Khatarnāk', *Kayhan*, 16/09/1998 [24/06/1377], p. 2.

Kayhan. 1998. 'Du Payam', *Kayhan*, 19/09/1998 [27/06/1377], p. 2.

Kayhan. 1998. 'Dūstān-i Pākistānī! Rā Az Tawahum Barhānīd', *Kayhan*, 10/08/1998 [19/05/1377], p. 2.

Kayhan. 1998. 'Nawbat-i Pākistān?', *Kayhan*, 06/08/1998 [15/05/1377], p. 2.

Kayhan. 2006. 'ʾān Chih 'Muqāwamat' Rā Zībātar Nishān Mīdahad', *Kayhan*, 15/07/2006 [24/04/1385], p. 1.

Kayhan. 2006. 'Digargūnī Dar Sih Jughrāfiyā', *Kayhan*, 24/07/2006 [02/05/1385], p. 1.

Kayhan. 2006. 'Furmūl-i Qudrat', *Kayhan*, 07/01/2006 [17/10/1384], p. 1.

Kayhan. 2006. 'Guftih Mīshawad. .', *Kayhan*, 15/01/2006 [25/10/1384], p. 1.

Kayhan. 2006. 'Musalas-i Tanhā', *Kayhan*, 09/08/2006 [18/05/1385], p. 1.

Kayhan. 2006. 'Partū-yi ʾaz Rukh-i ʾū', *Kayhan*, 29/07/2006 [07/05/1385], p. 1.

Kayhan. 2006. 'Wa Khaybar Dar Pīsh ʾast', *Kayhan*, 17/08/2006 [26/05/1385], p. 1.

Kayhan. 2008. 'Ghazah Nabāyad Tanhā Bimānad', *Kayhan*, 29/12/2008 [09/10/1387], p. 1.

Kayhan. 2008. 'Jahan-i Islam Dar Intizār-i Intiqām-i Rūz-i Atash wa Khūn dar Ghazah Sarān-i Arab Murdih-and', *Kayhan*, 28/12/2008 [08/10/1387], p. 1.

Kayhan. 2008. 'Subh Nazdīk Ast', *Kayhan*, 30/12/2008 [10/10/1387], p. 1.

Kayhan. 2009. 'Az ʿaqab Nishīnī Pūlikānī Tā Gidā-yī', *Kayhan*, 18/01/2009 [29/10/1387], p. 1.

Kayhan. 2009. 'Az ʿāshūrā-yi sāl-i 61 tā-lilāh', *Kayhan*, 24/12/2009 [03/10/1388], p. 1.

Kayhan. 2009. 'Jūshish-i Ghairathā-yi Insānī', *Kayhan*, 15/01/2009 [26/10/1387], p. 1.

Kayhan. 2009. 'Karbalā-yi Ghazah', *Kayhan*, 10/01/2009 [21/10/1387], p. 1.

Kayhan. 2009. 'Rūzih Hazrat-i Qāsim', *Kayhan*, 05/01/2009 [16/10/1387], p. 1.

Kayhan. 2011. ''Amaliyāt-i khūnīn-i vāshingtan-riyāż ʿalaihi baghdād! chirā?', *Kayhan*, 24/12/2011 [03/10/1390], p. 1.

Kayhan. 2011. ''Amaliyāt-i tāzih kārhā', *Kayhan*, 26/05/2011 [05/03/1390], p. 1.

Kayhan. 2011. 'Bunbast-i America dar Suriyih', *Kayhan*, 05/05/2011 [15/02/1390], p. 1.

Kayhan. 2011. 'Diktātūr-I Tunis ki Az Khodatān Būd', *Kayhan*, 16/01/2011 [26/10/1389], p. 1.

Kayhan. 2011. 'Fāz-i sivvum-i jang-i 33 rūzih', *Kayhan*, 10/04/2011 [21/01/1390] p. 1.

Kayhan. 2011. 'Jahsh-i taqvīm bih sāl-i 2025', *Kayhan*, 04/04/2011 [15/01/1390], p. 1.

Kayhan. 2011. 'naqsh-i bar āb', *Kayhan*, 16/03/2011 [25/12/1389], p. 1.

Kayhan. 2011. 'Partāb bar miyānih-yi dahih-yi chehel', *Kayhan*, 08/08/2011 [17/05/1390], p. 1.

Kayhan. 2011. 'Rāz-i ʿasabāniyat', *Kayhan*, 22/02/2011 [03/12/1389], p. 1.

Kayhan. 2011. 'Sahṣīfih-yi bīdārī', *Kayhan*, 16/04/2011 [27/01/1390] p. 1.

Kayhan. 2011. 'Sipāh-i quds ism-i ramz-i chīst?', *Kayhan*, 19/10/2011 [27/07/1390], p. 1.

Kayhan. 2011. 'Suqūthā-yi zanjīra-yi', *Kayhan*, 19/01/2011 [29/10/1389], p. 1.

Kayhan. 2012. 'America dar Suriyih chirā bākht?'', *Kayhan*, 24/07/2012 [03/05/1391], p. 1.

Kayhan. 2012. ''āmil-i hṣawlā-yi sūriyih hamān ʿāmil-i qānā-yi lubnān', *Kayhan*, 31/05/2012 [11/03/1391], p. 1.

Kayhan. 2012. 'Girih hāyi amniyatī-yi suriyih', *Kayhan*, 06/12/2012 [16/09/1391], p. 1.

Kayhan. 2012. 'Halab, hamsāyigī-yi bait al-muqaddas yā ūrshalīm', *Kayhan*, 31/07/2012 [10/05/1391], p. 1.

Kayhan. 2012. 'Khaṭṭ-i mughālaṭih dar tahṣlīl-i ravand-i inqilāb hā', *Kayhan*, 19/07/2012 [29/04/1391], p. 1.

Kayhan. 2012. 'Khaṭṭ-i muqāvimat va khaṭā-yi muhṣāsabāt', *Kayhan*, 11/07/2012 [21/04/1391], p. 1.

Kayhan. 2012. 'Mahṣbūbiyat-i Irān va buhṣrān-i Suriyih', *Kayhan*, 19/12/2012 [29/09/1391], p. 1.

Kayhan. 2012. 'Muqāvimat-i sarnavisht sāz', *Kayhan*, 07/08/2012 [17/05/1391], p. 1.

Kayhan. 2012. 'Nustālzhī-yi tārīkhī yā harās az qudrat-i muqāvimat', *Kayhan*, 22/07/2012 [01/05/1391], p. 1.

Kayhan. 2012. 'Pīrūzī-yi darakhshān-i muqāvimat dar sūriyih'', *Kayhan*, 08/03/2012 [18/12/1390], p. 1.

Kayhan. 2012. 'Sūrīyih chālīsh-i imparātūrī', *Kayhan*, 09/07/2012 [19/04/1391], p. 1.

Kayhan. 2012. ''Yadāsht-i Rūz- Bāz sāzī-yi kamp daivīd dar Tūnis', *Kayhan*, 26/02/2012 [07/12/1390], p. 1.

Kayhan. 2013. 'Hijr bin ʿaddī yak bār-i digih qiyām kard', *Kayhan*, 06/05/2013 [16/02/1392], p. 1.

Kayhan. 2013. 'Khalīfih garī dar dast pūkht-i jadīd-i gharb', *Kayhan*, 24/01/2013 [05/11/1391], p. 1.

Kayhan. 2014. 'With 300 armored vehicles, the Iraqi army cleared Samarra with the death of 100 ISIS terrorists', *Kayhan*, p. 12.

Kayhan. 2014. 'Yadāsht-i Rūz – The Lock and Key of Western Iraq's Security Crisis قفل و کلید بحران امنیتی غرب عراق', *Kayhan*, 10/06/2014 [24/03/1393], p. 1.

Kayhan. 2014. 'Yadāsht-i Rūz – The Caricatures In Samarra have come to life! کاریکاتورهایی اکه در سامرا جان گرفتند!', *Kayhan*, p. 2.

Kayhan. 2015.'ʿarabistān paz az malik Abdullah', *Kayhan,* 23/01/2015 [03/11/1393], p. 1.

Kayhan. 2015.'Dastāvard hā yā az dast dādih hā?', *Kayhan,* 04/04/2015 [15/01/1394], p. 1.

Kayhan. 2015.'Kaʿba dar masīr-i utūbān', *Kayhan,* 03/05/2015 [13/02/1394], p. 1.

Kayhan. 2015.'Yaman; viyatnām-i ʿarabistān', *Kayhan,* 09/04/2015 [20/01/1394], p. 1.

Kayhan. 2017.'ādris hāyi ishtibāh-i riyāż', *Kayhan,* 07/06/2017 [17/03/1396], p. 1.

Kayhan. 2017.'Baʿd az shalīʾk-i mushak hā', *Kayhan,* 21/06/2017 [31/03/1396] p. 1.

Kayhan. 2019.'Yadāsht-i Rūz – Tanker for a Tanker', *Kayhan,* 21/07/2019 [30/04/1398], p. 1.

Kazimi, Nibras. 2006.'Zarqawi's Anti-Shia Legacy: Original or Borrowed?', *Current Trends in Islamist Ideology,* 4: 53–72.

Kechichian, J.A. 2003.'Testing the Saudi "Will to Power": Challenges Confronting Prince Abdallah', *Middle East Policy,* 10: 100–15.

Kechichian, J. A. 2013. *Legal and Political Reforms in Saudi Arabia* (Routledge: Abingdon).

Keddie, N.R., and R. P. Matthee. 2002. *Iran and the Surrounding World Since 1501: Interactions in Culture and Cultural Politics* (University of Washington Press: Seattle, WA).

Kepel, G., and H. Randolph. 2020. *Away from Chaos: The Middle East and the Challenge to the West* (Columbia University Press: Colombia, OH).

Kerry, J., and S. al-Saud. 2013.'Remarks with Saudi Arabian Foreign Minister Saud al-Faisal', US State Department, Accessed 24/08/2020. https://2009-2017.state.gov/secretary/remarks/2013/11/216236.htm.

Keynoush, B. 2016. *Saudi Arabia and Iran: Friends or Foes?* (Palgrave Macmillan: New York).

Khalkhali, S. 1990.'Majles Statement'. In *IRNA,* 1. Tehran, IR Iran: IRNA.

Khamenei, A. 1980.'Friday Sermon', *Jomhouri Eslami,* 05/04/1980 [16/01/1959], p. 1.

Khamenei, A. 1980.'Friday Sermon', *Jomhouri Eslami,* 12/04/1980 [23/01/1959], p. 1.

Khamenei, A. 1980.'Friday Sermon', *Jomhouri Eslami,* 03/05/1980 [13/02/1359], p. 1.

Khamenei, A. 1980.'Friday Sermon', *Jomhouri Eslami,* 19/07/1980 [28/04/1359], p. 3.

Khamenei, A. 1980.'Friday Sermon', *Jomhouri Eslami,* 30/08/1980 [08/06/1359], p. 1.

Khamenei, A. 1980.'Friday Sermon', *Jomhouri Eslami,* 04/10/1980 [12/07/1359], p. 12.

Khamenei, A. 1980.'Friday Sermon', *Jomhouri Eslami,* 25/01/1981 [05/11/1359], p. 3.

Khamenei, A. 1980.'Friday Sermon', *Jomhouri Eslami,* 06/02/1981 [17/11/1359], p. 1.

Khamenei, A. 1981.'Friday Prayer Sermon', *Jomhouri Eslami,* 30/05/1981 [09/03/1360], pp. 8, 5.

Khamenei, A. 1981.'Friday Sermon', *Jomhouri Eslami,* 23/01/1981 [03/11/1359], p. 1.

Khamenei, A. 1981.'Friday Sermon', *Jomhouri Eslami,* 05/02/1981 [16/11/1359], p. 1.

Khamenei, A. 1983.'Khamenei Speech- Graduation of the Army College', *Jomhouri Eslami,* 05/10/1983 [13/07/1362], p. 10.

Khamenei, A. 1989.'Sermon on Hajj 1989'. In *IRNA,* 1. Tehran, IR Iran: IRNA.

Khamenei, A. 1990.'Bayānāt dar dīdār-i jamʿī az farzandān-i mumtāz shāhid wa jānbāzān-i Mashhad wa Tehran wa ustāni-i Kurdisātan'. In *IRNA,* 1. Tehran, IR Iran: IRNA.

Khamenei, A. 1990.'Statement on American Troops in Saudi Arabia'. In *IRNA,* 1. Tehran, IR Iran: IRNA.

Khamenei, A. 1997.'Khamenei Speech – OIC Summit Tehran', *Jomhouri Eslami,* 10/12/1997 [19/09/1376], pp. 1, 3.

Khamenei, A. 1997.'Khamenei Speech on Meeting Crown Prince Abdullah Ibn Abdulaziz', *Jomhouri Eslami,* 10/12/1997 [19/09/1376], p. 2.

Khamenei, A. 1997.'Khamenei Speech on Prophet's Birth', *Jomhouri Eslami,* 24/07/1997 [02/05/1376], pp. 1, 3.

Khamenei, A. 1998. 'Khamenei Statement on Taliban Crimes Towards the Afghan People', *Jomhouri Eslami,* 15/09/1998 [24/06/1377], pp. 1, 3.

Khamenei, A. 1999. 'Khamenei Speech on Prince Sultan Ibn Abdulaziz Visit to the Islamic Republic of Iran.' In *IRNA,* 1. Tehran, IR Iran: IRNA.

Khamenei, A. 2005. 'Quds Day Sermon 21 October 2005.' In *Statements,* edited by IRNA. Tehran, IR Iran: IRNA.

Khamenei, A. 2006. 'Speech on the Birth of Imam Ali', *IRNA,* 08/08/2006 [17/05/1385], p. 1.

Khamenei, A. 2006. 'Speech on the Bombing of Askari Shrine 23 February 2006.' In *Statements,* edited by IRNA. Tehran, IR Iran: IRNA.

Khamenei, A. 2006. 'Speech on the Visit of President of Venezuela Hugo Chavez', *IRNA,* 29/07/2006 [07/05/1385], p. 1.

Khamenei, A. 2006. 'Speech to Members of the Expediency Council', *IRNA,* 31/08/2006 [09/06/1385], p. 1.

Khamenei, A. 2006. 'Speech to Poets of Ahlulbayt', *IRNA,* 15/07/2006 [24/04/1385], p. 1.

Khamenei, A. 2006. 'Speech-Islamic Unity Conference', *IRNA,* 21/08/2006 [30/05/1385], p. 1.

Khamenei, A. 2008. 'Statement on Israeli Attacks on Gaza', *IRNA,* 28/12/2008 [08/10/1387], p. 1.

Khamenei, A. 2009. 'Statement in Meeting with Members of the Union of Islamic Students' Associations in Europe', *Office for the Preservation and Publication of the Works of the Grand Ayatollah Seyyed Ali Khamenei* 31/10/2009 [10/10/1388].

Khamenei, A. 2009. 'Statement on the 10th Elections 1388', *IRNA,* 04/06/2009 [14/03/1388].

Khamenei, A. 2011. 'Friday Sermon on Anniversary of Martyrdom of Imam Ali ibn Musa Al-Redha', Cultural Research Institute of the Islamic Revolution, Accessed 20/09/2020. https://khl.ink/f/10955.

Khamenei, A. 2011. 'Nowruz message on the occasion of the beginning of 1390, 'Year of Economic Jihad'', *Office for the Preservation and Publication of the Works of the Grand Ayatollah Seyyed Ali Khamenei* 21/03/2011 [01/01/1390].

Khamenei, A. 2011. 'Speech on the Anniversary of Prophet's First Revelation', *Office for the Preservation and Publication of the Works of the Grand Ayatollah Seyyed Ali Khamenei* 02/07/2011 [11/04/1390].

Khamenei, A. 2012. 'Supreme Leader Friday Prayer Sermon on the Anniversary of 22 Bahman, 10th Fajr', Cultural Research Institute of the Islamic Revolution, Accessed 20/09/2020. https://farsi.khamenei.ir/speech-content?id=18923.

Khamenei, A. 2012. 'Supreme Leader Meeting with Leader of Islamic Jihad Movement', *Office for the Preservation and Publication of the Works of the Grand Ayatollah Seyyed Ali Khamenei* 01/02/2012 [12/11/1390].

Khamenei, A. 2013. 'Qadrdānī-yi maqām-i mu'azzam-i rahbarī az tīm-i hastih-yi īrān; rahbar-i inqilāb- pushtabānī-yi millat 'āmil-i muvvafaqiyat-i hastih būd', Khamenei.ir, Accessed 10/11/2019. https://www.magiran.com/article/2855119.

Khamenei, A. 2013. 'Supreme Leader's Statement on the Dessecration of the Tomb of Hujr ibn Ady during a meeting with officials involved in presidential elections and town and village councils', *Office for the Preservation and Publication of the Works of the Grand Ayatollah Seyyed Ali Khamenei* 06/05/2013 [16/02/1392].

Khamenei, A. 2014. 'Bayānāt dar maḥfil-i uns bā qur'ān', Khamenei.ir, Accessed 10/11/2019. https://farsi.khamenei.ir/speech-content?id=26828.

Khamenei, A. 2014. 'Dī dar amī r-i Kuwait bā rahbar-i inghilāb', Khamenei.ir, Accessed 19/03/2020. https://farsi.khamenei.ir/news-content?id=26581.

Khamenei, A. 2014. 'Dīdār-i raʾīs wa masʾūlān-i quvvih-yi qażāʾīh bā rahbar-i inqilāb', Khamenei.ir, Accessed 15/01/2020. https://farsi.khamenei.ir/news-content?id=26754.

Khamenei, A. 2014. 'Rahbar-i inqilāb dar dīdār-i amīr-i Kuwait: takfiri hā dar āyandih balā yi jān-i ḥamāyān-i khūd mīshavand', *Kayhan,* 03/06/2014 [13/03/1393], p. 1.

Khamenei, A. 2014. 'Supreme Leader meeting with the families of the martyrs of the 7th of Tir and a group of the families of the martyrs of Tehran', *Khamenei.ir,* 29/06/2014 [10/04/1393].

Khamenei, A. 2015. 'Bayānāt dar dīdār-i maddāḥān-i ahl-i bait ʾalihim al-salām', Khamenei.ir, Accessed 10/02/2020. https://khl.ink/f/29415.

Khamenei, A. 2015. 'Statements at the beginning of the session the post-jurisprudence course regarding the Mena tragedy', *Khamenei.ir,* 27/09/2015 [05/07/1394].

Khamenei, A. 2016. 'Statement at a Meeting with the families of martyrs of the 2015 Mina and Grand Mosque Incident', *Khamenei.ir,* 07/09/2016.

Khamenei, A. 2016. 'Statement Made During Course to Clerics at the Post-Jurisprudence Level', *Khamenei.ir,* 03/01/2016.

Khamenei, A. 2017. 'Ayatollah Khamenei Sermon on Tehran ISIS Attacks 07 June 2017', The Office of the Supreme Leader, Accessed 27/11/2021. https://farsi.khamenei.ir/speech-content?id=36775.

Khamenei, A. 2017. 'Ayatollah Khamenei speech during an assembly with commanders and personnel of the Islamic Republic of Iran's Army Air Force 07/02/2017', The Office of the Supreme Leader, Accessed 02/10/2021. https://english.khamenei.ir/news/4625/The-new-U-S-President-reveals-the-true-nature-of-the-United.

Khamenei, A. 2017. 'Khamenei Sermon 27/05/2017', The Office of the Supreme Leader, Accessed 02/10/2021. https://www.leader.ir/fa/speech/18355/%D9%85%D8%AD%D9%81%D9%84-%D8%A7%D9%86%D8%B3-%D8%A8%D8%A7-%D9%82%D8%B1%D8%A2%D9%86-%DA%A9%D8%B1%DB%8C%D9%85-%D8%AF%D8%B1-%D8%AD%D8%B6%D9%88%D8%B1-%D8%B1%D9%87%D8%A8%D8%B1-%D9%85%D8%B9%D8%B8%D9%85-%D8%A7%D9%86%D9%82%D9%84%D8%A7%D8%A8-%D8%A7%D8%B3%D9%84%D8%A7%D9%85%DB%8C.

Khamenei, A. 2017. 'Khamenei Speech at the meeting with Reciters of the Holy Quran 27 May 2017', The Office of the Supreme Leader, Accessed 05/12/2021. https://farsi.khamenei.ir/speech-content?id=36663.

Khamenei, A. 2017. 'Statements in the meeting of the families of the border guards and the defender of the shrine 18 June 2017', The Office of the Supreme Leader, Accessed 02/10/2021. https://www.leader.ir/fa/speech/18551/%D8%AF%DB%8C%D8%AF%D8%A7%D8%B1-%D8%AC%D9%85%D8%B9%DB%8C-%D8%A7%D8%B2-%D8%AE%D8%A7%D9%86%D9%88%D8%A7%D8%AF%D9%87E2%80%8C%D9%87%D8%A7%DB%8C-%D8%B4%D9%87%D8%AF%D8%A7%DB%8C-%D9%85%D8%B1%D8%B2%D8%A8%D8%A7%D9%86-%D9%88-%D9%85%D8%AF%D8%A7%D9%81%D8%B9-%D8%AD%D8%B1%D9%85.

Khamenei, A. 2017. 'The Supreme Leader's response to General Qassem Soleimani's letter about the end of ISIL/ISIS Domination', The Office of the Supreme Leader, Accessed 13/10/2021. https://farsi.khamenei.ir/message-content?id=38249.

Khamenei, A. 2018. 'Ayatollah Khamenei Twitter 14 April 2018', twittter.com, Accessed 02/10/2021. https://twitter.com/khamenei_ir/status/985076544849801216.

Khamenei, A. 2019. 'Speech to the Nation's Friday Imams', Cultural Research Institute of the Islamic Revolution, Accessed 20/09/2020. https://farsi.khamenei.ir/speech-content?id=43057.

Khamenei, A. 2019. 'Statements in the meeting with State officials', The Office of the Supreme Leader, Accessed 12/10/2021. https://khl.ink/f/42512.

Khamenei, A. 2020. 'Ayatollah Khamenei Twitter 1 January 2020', twitter.com, Accessed
    02/10/2021. https://twitter.com/khamenei_ir/status/1212301034871279616?lang=en.
Khamenei, A. 2020. 'Ayatollah Khamenei Twitter 3 January 2020', twitter.com, Accessed
    02/10/2021. https://twitter.com/khamenei_ir/status/985076544849801216.
Khamenei, A. 2020. 'Speech in Qom: Iran recent strikes merely a slap, US must leave
    region', The Office of the Supreme Leader, Accessed 02/10/2021. https://www.leader.ir/
    en/content/24025/www.leader.ir.
Khan, S.B. 2013. 'The western media and Iran's presidential election 2009: The visual
    framing of a Green Revolution', *International Journal of Liberal Arts and Social Science*,
    4: 11–30.
Kharrazi, K. 1997. 'Statement on Statement on Arrival to Saudi Arabia', *IRNA*, 09/11/1997.
Kharrazi, K. 1998. 'Statement on Iranian Diplomats in Afghanistan', *Jomhouri Eslami*,
    08/09/1998 [17/06/1377], p. 2.
Khatami, A. 2006. 'Friday Sermon 28/07/2006.' In *Friday Sermons – Dar Maktab-i Jom'ih*,
    edited by Centre for Cultural Documents of the Islamic Revolution. Tehran, IR Iran:
    Ministry of Islamic Guidance.
Khatami, A. 2009. 'Friday Sermon 06/03/2009.' In *Friday Sermons – Dar Maktab-i Jom'ih*,
    edited by Centre for Cultural Documents of the Islamic Revolution. Tehran, IR Iran:
    Ministry of Islamic Guidance.
Khatami, A. 2009. 'Friday Sermon 09/01/2009.' In *Friday Sermons – Dar Maktab-i Jom'ih*,
    edited by Centre for Cultural Documents of the Islamic Revolution. Tehran, IR Iran:
    Ministry of Islamic Guidance.
Khatami, A. 2012. 'Ayatollah Ahmad Khatami Quds Day Speech on Quds Day.' In *Friday
    Sermons – Dar Maktab-i Jom'ih*, edited by Centre for Cultural Documents of the
    Islamic Revolution. Tehran, IR Iran: Ministry of Islamic Guidance.
Khatami, A. 2015. 'Friday Sermon 11/04/2015.' In *Friday Sermons – Dar Maktab-i Jom'ih*,
    edited by Centre for Cultural Documents of the Islamic Revolution. Tehran, IR Iran:
    Ministry of Islamic Guidance.
Khatami, A. 2017. 'Member of the Assembly of Experts Statement', *Resalat*, 21/06/2017
    [31/03/1396], p. 2.
Khatami, M. 1997. 'Khatami Inauguration Speech', *Johouri Eslami*, 04/08/1997
    [13/05/1376].
Khatami, M. 1997. 'Khatami Press Conference', *Jomhouri Eslami*, 28/05/1997 [07/03/1376].
Khatami, M. 1997. 'Khatami Speech- OIC Summit Tehran', *Jomhouri Eslami*, 10/12/1997
    [19/09/1376], pp. 2, 15.
Khatami, M. 1997. 'Khatami Speech on Meeting Crown Prince Abdullah Ibn Abdulaziz',
    Jomhouri Eslami, 10/12/1997 [19/09/1376], p. 2.
Khatami, M. 1997. 'Khatami Speech to Majles', *Johouri Eslami*, 05/08/1997 [14/05/1376].
Khatami, M. 1998. 'Khatami Speech on Eighth International Conference on Praying',
    Jomhouri Eslami, 13/09/1998 [22/06/1377].
Khatami, M. 1999. 'Khatami Press Conference', *Jomhouri Eslami*, 03/05/1999 [12/02/1378].
Khatami, M. 1999. 'Khatami Speech on Meeting Crown Prince Abdullah Ibn Abdulaziz in
    Riyadh', *Jomhouri Eslami*, 18/05/1999 [28/02/1378], p. 2.
Khatami, M. 1999. 'Khatami Speech on Meeting Defence Minister Prince Sultan Ibn
    Abdulaziz', *Jomhouri Eslami*, 04/05/1999 [14/02/1378], p. 2.
Khatami, M. 1999. 'Khatami Speech on Meeting King Fahd Ibn Abdulaziz in Riyadh',
    Jomhouri Eslami, 17/05/1999 [27/02/1378], p. 2.
Khatami, M. 1999. 'Khatami Speech on Meeting the Saudi Foreign Minister Prince Saudi
    Al-Faisal Ibn Abdulaziz in Riyadh', *Jomhouri Eslami*, 17/05/1999 [27/02/1378], p. 2.

Khatib, D.K., and M. Maziad. 2018. *The Arab Gulf States and the West: Perceptions and Realities – Opportunities and Perils* (Taylor & Francis: Abingdon).

Khatib, L., and E. Lust. 2014. *Taking to the Streets: The Transformation of Arab Activism* (Johns Hopkins University Press: Baltimore, MD).

Khedr, H. 2021. 'Gulf Reconciliation Will Bring Positive Regional Impact: No Development in Arab Countries Without Diplomatic Dialogue', Al-Majalla, Accessed 01/02/2022. https://eng.majalla.com/node/123171/politicsgulf-reconciliation-will-bring-positive-regional-impact.

Khiabany, G. 2009. *Iranian Media: The Paradox of Modernity* (Taylor & Francis: Abingdon).

Khomeini, R. 1979. 'Payām-e tāriyykhī-e Imām Khomainī. Khiṭāb bih hameh khāharān wa baradarān-e mosalmān (Imam Khomeini's Historic Message: Sermon to all the muslim sisters and brothers on the eve of Hajj).' In 1, 4. Tehran: Jomhouri Eslami.

Khomeini, R. 1979. 'The Resolving of Hardships and Deprivations, the Objectives of the Enemies and the United States; Foreign Policies Towards Other Nations', *Sahifeh-ye Imam*, 11.

Khomeini, R. 1979. 'Speech on Siege of Mecca', 21/11/1979 [30/08/1358].

Khomeini, R. 1980. 'A call to the Iraqi people to overthrow the Ba'athist government in Iraq', *Sahifeh-ye Imam*, 13.

Khomeini, R. 1980. 'The Duty of the Guardian Council', *Sahifeh-ye Imam*, 13.

Khomeini, R. 1980. 'Khomeini Speech Regarding Opening of Schools, (Political) Groups and Recent Events – 31/06/1359', *Jomhouri Eslami*, 23/09/1980 [01/07/1359], p. 12.

Khomeini, R. 1980. 'Khomenin Speech to the Iraqi Nation – 2/07/1359', *Jomhouri Eslami*, 04/10/1980 [13/07/1359], p. 12.

Khomeini, R. 1980. 'Speech on Operation Eagle Claw', *Sahifeh-ye Imam*, 12: 234–45.

Khomeini, R. 1980. 'Telegram to Crown Prince Fahd', *Sahifeh-ye Imam*, 12.

Khomeini, R. 1980. 'Telegram to King Khaled', *Sahifeh-ye Imam*, 12.

Khomeini, R. 1981. 'Disregard of the Muslim States toward the Problems of the Islamic World – False Claims of the Advocates of Human Rights', *Sahifeh-ye Imam*, 14.

Khomeini, R. 1981. 'Honouring Beheshti and the Martyrs of Seventh Tir', *Sahifeh-ye Imam*, 15.

Khomeini, R. 1981. 'Khomeini Speech on Inaugaration of Khamenei Presidency – 17/07/1360', *Jomhour Eslami*, 08/07/1981 [18/07/1360], p. 12.

Khomeini, R. 1981. 'Khomeini Speech on Seventh Tir Bombings – 08/04/1360', *Jomhour Eslami*, 30/06/1981 [09/04/1360], p. 8.

Khomeini, R. 1981. 'Khomeini Speech on the visit of the Minister and Heads of Departments of the Ministry of Education – 25/07/1360', *Jomhour Eslami*, 18/10/1981 [26/07/1360], p. 12.

Khomeini, R. 1981. 'Khomeini Speech to Friday Prayer Imams of Ilam and Bakhtaran', *Jomhouri Eslami*, 30/12/1981 [09/10/1360], p. 12.

Khomeini, R. 1981. 'Letter: Response to King Khalid – Criticism of the Actions of Saudi Officials', *Sahifeh-ye Imam*, 15: 5.

Khomeini, R. 1981. 'Speech to Ayatullah Hakim, the Combatant Clerics of Iraq, and the Expelled Muslims of Iraq', *Sahifeh-ye Imam*, 14: 237–41.

Khomeini, R. 1981. 'Speech to the Mine Workers of the Steel Industry', *Sahifeh-ye Imam*, 14.

Khomeini, R. 1981. 'Speech to the Officials of Martyrs Foundation', *Sahifeh-ye Imam*, 15.

Khomeini, R. 1983. 'Khomeini Norouz Sermon', *Jomhouri Eslami*, 29/03/1983 [29/12/1361], p. 12.

Khomeini, R. 1984. 'Khomeini Speech on Sixth Anniversary of the Islamic Revolution – 22/11/1362', *Jomhouri Eslami*, 12/02/1984 [23/11/1362], pp. 15,16.

Khomeini, R. 1987. 'Annual Hajj Sermon', *IRNA*, 10/04/1387 [01/07/1366].

Khomeini, R. 1987. 'Statement in Protest to Hajj Pilgrim Deaths', *IRNA*, 04/08/1987 [13/05/1366].

Khomeini, R. 1988. 'Statement on Hajj and Resolution 598', *IRNA*, 20/07/1988 [29/04/1367].

Khomeini, R. 1988. 'Statement on New Year', *IRNA*, 19/03/1988 [29/12/1366].

Khomeini, R. 1989. 'Matn-i kāmil vasiyatnāmih-yi ilāhī siyāsī-yi haẓrat-i imām khumainī raḥimahu allāh', Khamenei.ir, Accessed 15/10/2021. https://farsi.khamenei.ir/imam-content?id=9447.

Khoshroo, G. 2017. 'Iran UN Ambassador Khoshroo's letter to UN.' In *Speeches*, edited by IRNA. Tehran, IR Iran: IRNA.

KhosraviNik, M. 2015. *Discourse, Identity and Legitimacy: Self and Other in Representations of Iran's Nuclear Programme* (John Benjamins Publishing Company: Philadelphia, PA).

Khosrokhavar, F., and D. Macey. 2005. *Suicide Bombers: Allah's New Martyrs* (Pluto Press: Michigan).

Khoury, L., and S. Dana. 2009. 'Hezbollah's War of Position: The Arab-Islamic Revolutionary Praxis', *The Arab World Geographer*, 12: 136–49.

Knickmeyer, E. 2013. 'Spy Chief Distances Saudis From U.S.', Dow Jones & Company Inc., Accessed 10/01/2020. https://www.wsj.com/articles/SB10001424052702303902404579150011732240016.

Korany, B. 1991. 'The Foreign Policy of Saudi Arabia.' In B. Korany and A.H. Dessouki (eds.), *The Foreign Policies of Arab States: The Challenge of Change* (Westview Press: Boulder, CO).

Korany, B., and M.A. Fattah. 2010. 'Irreconcilable Role-Partners?: Saudi Foreign Policy between the Ulama and the US.' In Bahgat Korany and Ali E. Hillal Dessouki (eds.), *The Foreign Policies of Arab States: The Challenge of Globalization* (The American University in Cairo Press: Cairo, Egypt).

Kowsari, E. 2014. 'Kowsari: The Westerners are After the Division of Iraq', *Resalat*, 12/06/2014 [22/03/1393], p. 1.

Kozhanov, N. 2021. *Russia's Relations with the GCC and Iran* (Springer Singapore).

Kramer, M. 2009. *Arab Awakening and Islamic Revival: The Politics of Ideas in the Middle East* (Routledge: Abingdon).

KUNA. 2017. 'Kuwait to deliver message to Iran – Deputy FM', *KUNA*, Accessed 13/09/2020. https://www.kuna.net.kw/ArticleDetails.aspx?id=2585757&language=en.

KUNA. 2018. 'Kuwait Reiterates Support for Saudi Measures on Khashoggi Affair', *KUNA*, 25/10/2018.

Lacroix, S. 2014. 'Saudi Islamists and the Arab Spring', *LSE Kuwait Programme on Development, Governance and Globalisation in the Gulf States*, 36.

Lagonikos, I.T. 2005. 'Ideology in Editorials: A Comparison of Selected Editorials in English-medium Newspapers After September 11', Rhodes University.

Lambeth, Benjamin S. 2012. 'Israel's War in Gaza: A Paradigm of Effective Military Learning and Adaptation', *International Security*, 37: 81–118.

Larijani, A. 2011. 'Majles Speaker Statement on Bahrain', *Kayhan*, 16/03/2011 [25/12/1389], p. 2.

Larijani, A. 2012. 'Ali Larijani Interview with Al-Alam News Network', *Kayhan*, 24/07/2012 [03/05/1391], p. 2.

Larijani, A. 2013. 'Speech at the Ayatollah Taskhiri International Conference', *Ettela'at*, 28/01/2013 [09/11/1391], p. 2.

Larijani, A. 2017. 'Ali Larijani Statement During Majles Session in the Aftermath of the ISIS Attacks.' In *Majles Statements*, edited by IRNA. Tehran, IR Iran: IRNA.

Larijani, A., and CNN. 2014. 'Transcript of Ali Larijani Interview with Christian Amanpur', *CNN,* 14/10/2014.

Lawzi, S. 1980. 'Prince Fahd Interview'. In *Al-Hawadeth* Beirut: al-Hawadeth, UK.

Lea, D. 2001. *A Political Chronology of the Middle East* (Routledge: Abingdon).

Lemon, J. 2019. 'Iran's Foreign Minister Blasts Trump's Sanctions As "Economic Terrorism," Accusing U.S. of Blocking Humanitarian Aid', *Time,* 02/04/2019.

Leonard, T.M. 2013. *Encyclopedia of the Developing World* (Taylor & Francis: Abingdon).

Lindstrom, R. 1979. 'Tensions Rise Among Saudi Shi'as in Eastern Province'. In *Siege of Mecca Unclassified Documents,* edited by American Consulate Dhahran. Washington DC: US State Department.

Lindstrom, R. 1979. 'Update on Mood of Saudi Shi'as and Current Security Situation.' In *Siege of Mecca Unclassified Documents,* edited by American Consulate Dhahran. Washington DC: US State Department.

Mabon, S. 2013. *Saudi Arabia and Iran: Soft Power Rivalry in the Middle East* (I.B. Tauris: London).

Maddy-weitzman, B. 1997. *Middle East Contemporary Survey: Volume XIX, 1995* (Avalon Publishing: Portland, OR).

Mahmoud, S. 2021. 'Iraq and Saudi Arabia to sign deals worth billions of dollars', The National, Accessed 01/02/2022. https://www.thenationalnews.com/business/energy/2021/11/01/iraq-and-saudi-arabia-to-sign-deals-worth-billions-of-dollars/.

Mahtafar, Ara. 2010. 'Mojtaba Vahedi: Ahmadinejad-Khamenei Rift Widening', *PBS,* Accessed 17/03/2014. http://www.pbs.org/wgbh/pages/frontline/tehranbureau/2010/03/karroubi-aide-ahmadinejad-khamenei-rift-widening.html.

Majles. 2012. 'Majles statement in support of the Syrian government and people', *YJC,* 30/07/2012 [09/05/1391]), p. 2.

Majles. 2014. 'Majles Statement Regarding the Death Penalty Against Ayatollah Nimr Baqer Al-Nimr', *Official Newspaper of the Islamic Consultative Assembly,* 21/10/2014 [29/07/1393].

Majles. 2015. 'Majles Statement Condemning Yemen War', *IRNA,* 06/04/2015 [17/01/1394].

Makarem Shirazi, N. 2009. 'Statement condemning the insult of the extremist Wahhabis of Saudi Arabia to the Shiites', *Dolat.ir,* 25/02/2009 [07/12/1387].

Makarem Shirazi, N. 2012. 'Statement on Syria and Saudi-US Support for the Opposition', *Dolat.ir,* 04/08/2012 [14/05/1391].

Malik, H. 1990. *Domestic Determinants of Soviet Foreign Policy Towards South Asia and the Middle East* (Macmillan: Basingstoke).

Maloney, S. 2017. 'ISIS attacks Iran and accusations fly', *Markaz, Brookings,* 09/06/2017.

Marschall, Christin. 2003. *Iran's Persian Gulf Policy: From Khomeini to Khatami* (Taylor & Francis: London).

Mason, J., and S. Heavey. 2019. 'Trump says he aborted retaliatory strike to spare Iranian lives', *Thomson Reuters,* Accessed 02/05/2021. https://www.reuters.com/article/us-mideast-iran-usa/trump-says-he-aborted-retaliatory-strike-to-spare-iranian-lives-idUSKCN1TL07P.

Mason, R. 2014. *Foreign Policy in Iran and Saudi Arabia: Economics and Diplomacy in the Middle East* (Bloomsbury Publishing: London).

Matthiesen, Toby. 2009. 'The Shi'a of Saudi Arabia at a crossroads', *Middle East Report Online,* 6.

Matthiesen, T. 2010. *The Other Saudis* (Cambridge University Press: Cambridge).

Mehmanparast, R. 2011. 'Foreign Ministry Spokesman on Recent Developments in Lebanon and Tunisia', *ISNA,* 15/01/2011 [25/10/1389], p. 2.

Mehmanparast, R. 2011. 'The Iranian Foreign Ministry condemned the bloody events in Bahrain', *IRNA,* 18/02/2011 [30/11/1389], p. 2.

Mehmanparast, R. 2012. 'Iranian Foreign Ministry Spokesman Statement on Events in Syria', *ISNA,* 29/05/2012 [09/03/1391], p. 2.

Mehr, and R.H. Abadian. 2017. 'Kuditay-i narm dar Arabistan', Mehr News Agency, Accessed 01/10/2020. https://www.mehrnews.com/news/4010687/%da%a9%d9%88%d8%af%d8%aa%d8%a7%db%8c-%d9%86%d8%b1%d9%85-%d8%af%d8%b1-%d8%b9%d8%b1%d8%a8%d8%b3%d8%aa%d8%a7%d9%86-%d8%b3%d8%b9%d9%88%d8%af%db%8c-%d8%a8%d9%86-%d8%b3%d9%84%d9%85%d8%a7%d9%86-%d8%a8d9%87-%d8%a2%d8%b1%d8%b2%d9%88%db%8c%d8%b4-%d8%b1%d8%b3%db%8c%d8%af.

Menashri, D. 2012. *Post-Revolutionary Politics in Iran: Religion, Society and Power* (Taylor & Francis: Abingdon).

Meshkini, A. 1991. 'Ayatollah Meshkini Chairman of Expediency Council Statement', *IRNA,* 01/02/1991 [12/11/1369].

Meyerhoff, M. 2006. *Introducing Sociolinguistics* (Routledge: Abingdon).

Milani, M.M. 1992. 'Iran's active neutrality during the Kuwaiti crisis: Reasons and ramifications', *New Political Science,* 11: 41–60.

Milani, M.M. 1994. *The Making of Iran's Islamic Revolution: From Monarchy to Islamic Republic* (Westview Press: Oxford).

Mirzaee, Meisam, and Sajjad Gharibeh. 2015. 'A Critical Discourse Analysis of Selected Iranian and Saudi Arabian Print Media on Civil War in Syria', *International Journal of Foreign Language Teaching and Research,* 3: 67–78.

Mohammad, T. 2011. 'Transformation in Iran's Foreign Policy Decision Making on Iraq: 1989–2009', City, University of London.

Mohtashemi, A.A. 1990. 'Majles Statement on Iraq Invasion of Kuwait 27 September 1990.' In *Majles Statements,* edited by IRNA. Tehran, IR Iran: IRNA.

Mohtashemi, A.A. 1991. 'Majles Statement- Annihilation of the USA 24 January 1991.' In *Majles Statements,* edited by IRNA. Tehran, IR Iran: IRNA.

Mohtashemi, A.A. 1991. 'Majles Statement on Kuwait and Iraq 20 January 1991.' In *Majles Statements,* edited by IRNA. Tehran, IR Iran: IRNA.

Molavi, A. 2006. 'The Saudi ship is quietly, firmly shifting course', *Daily Star,* 30/01/2006.

Monshipouri, M. 2016. *Inside the Islamic Republic: Social Change in Post-Khomeini Iran* (Oxford University Press: Oxford).

Montazeri, H. 1987. 'Statement in the Congress on the Sanctity and Security of the Holy Mosques', *IRNA,* 27/11/1987 [11/09/1366].

Moore-Gilbert, B. 1997. *Postcolonial Theory: Contexts, Practices, Politics* (Verso: London).

Motamedi, M. 2020. 'Iran buries slain nuclear scientist, promises retaliation', aljazeera.com, Accessed 01/02/2022. https://www.aljazeera.com/news/2020/11/30/iran-buries-assassinated-scientist-amid-promises-of-retaliation.

Mottaki, M. 2009. 'Speech at Tehran Friday Sermon.' In *Speeches of Government Officials,* edited by IRNA. Tehran, IR Iran: IRNA.

Mousavi Ardabili, A. 1990. 'Friday Sermon', *Jomhouri Eslami,* 24/08/1990 [26/05/1369], p. 1.

Mousavi Ardabili, A. 1990. 'Friday Sermon', *Jomhouri Eslami,* 14/09/1990 [23/06/1369].

Mousavi, M.H. 1983. 'Prime Minister Friday Sermon Speech', *Ettela'at,* 25/08/1984 [03/06/1363], p. 1.

Mousavian, H. 2012. 'Five Reasons the US Should Stay Out Of Syria', Al-Monitor, Accessed 10/01/2020. https://www.al-monitor.com/originals/2013/05/role-iran-and-regional-parties-syria-conflict.html#ixzz7CcvcxeyA.

Mousavian, S.H. 2020. *A New Structure for Security, Peace, and Cooperation in the Persian Gulf* (Rowman & Littlefield Publishers: Lanham, MD).

Mousavian, S.H., and S. Shahidsaless. 2014. *Iran and the United States: An Insider's View on the Failed Past and the Road to Peace* (Bloomsbury Publishing: London).

Mousavi-Khoeiniha, M. 1987. 'Statement in Response to Kuwait Invitation of Foreign Navies.' In *Speeches*, edited by IRNA. Tehran, IR Iran: IRNA.

Moussavi, M.H. 1982. 'Prime Minister Speech – 13/01/1361', *Jomhouri Eslami*, 03/04/1982 [14/01/1361], p. 9.

Movahedi-Kermani, M. 2005. 'Speech to IRGC and Basij.' In *IRGC Speeches*, edited by IRNA. Tehran, IR Iran: Sobh-i Sadeq.

Mubarak, H., and C. Rose. 2009. 'Charlie Rose Interview with President of Egypt, Hosni Mubarak', *PBS*, Accessed 01/12/2021. https://youtu.be/3BYtqr53Q_U.

Murden, S. 1995. *Emergent Regional Powers and International Relations in the Gulf, 1988–1991* (Ithaca Press: New York).

Murray, S.K., and J. Meyers. 1999. 'Do People Need Foreign Enemies?: American Leaders' Beliefs after the Soviet Demise', *Journal of Conflict Resolution*, 43: 555–69.

Nabavi, E. 2005. 'Ahmadinejad, The Asphalt Genius', *Gooya News*, 01/06/2005 [11/03/1384].

Nada, G. 2021. 'Iran, Afghanistan and the Taliban', USIP.org, Accessed 01/02/2022. https://iranprimer.usip.org/blog/2021/jul/28/iran-afghanistan-and-taliban.

Naff, T. 1985. *Gulf security and the Iran-Iraq war* (National Defense University Press; Middle East Research Institute: Washington DC).

Nagraj, A. 2013. 'Revealed: 10 Oldest Newspapers In The GCC', *Gulf Business*, Accessed 10/03/. http://gulfbusiness.com/2013/03/revealed-10-oldest-newspapers-in-the-gcc/#.UtWFDmRdWi8.

Narallah, T. 2021. 'Sheikh Tahnoon bin Zayed Al Nahyan received by Ebrahim Raisi, President of Iran', *Gulf News*, Accessed 01/02/2022. https://gulfnews.com/uae/government/sheikh-tahnoon-bin-zayed-al-nahyan-received-by-ebrahim-raisi-president-of-iran-1.1638780578715.

Nasr, Vali. 2006. 'When the Shiites Rise', *Foreign Affairs*, 85: 58–74.

Nasr, Vali. 2007. *The Shia Revival : How Conflicts Within Islam Will Shape the Future* (W.W. Norton: London).

Nasrallah, H. 2013. 'S. Hassan Nasrallah Speech on on the Commemoration of Araba'een', Lebanon Communication Group, Accessed 01/12/2021. https://video.moqawama.org/details.php?cid=1&linkid=1114.

Nasrallah, H. 2013. 'S. Hassan Nasrallah Speech on on the latest developments – April 30, 2013', Lebanon Communication Group, Accessed 01/12/2021. https://video.moqawama.org/details.php?cid=1&linkid=1164.

Nasrallah, H. 2017. 'S. Hassan Nasrallah Statement on Hariri Resignation', *Al-Jazeera*, Accessed 01/12/2021. https://www.youtube.com/watch?v=uCSo-mbHqFc.

Nevo, J. 1998. 'Religion and national identity in Saudi Arabia', *Middle Eastern Studies*, 34: 34–53.

News, AP, and J. Gabrell. 2019. 'First Saudi female ambassador replaces king's son in US', Associated Press, Accessed 02/05/2021. https://apnews.com/article/north-america-international-news-jamal-khashoggi-saudi-arabia-united-states-50590fb09236414e833b91c02ee51263.

News, AP, and H. Hendawi. 2014. 'Iran's general in Iraq, militants seize key city', Associated Press, Accessed 02/05/2021. https://apnews.com/article/30cd7542949541fbb984d083f2e311a6.

Niblock, T. 2004. *Saudi Arabia: Power, Legitimacy and Survival* (Taylor & Francis: Abingdon).

Nobakht, M.B., and IRIB. 2015. 'Iran official: Saudi FM remarks hollow 30 September 2015.' In *Speeches*, edited by IRIB. Tehran, IR Iran: IRIB.

Nohlen, D., F. Grotz, and C. Hartmann. 2001. *Elections in Asia and the Pacific A Data Handbook* (Oxford University Press: Oxford).

Noori-Hamadani, H. 2011. 'Statement in a Meeting with Members of Agricultural Jihad', *Resalat*, 18/01/2011 [28/10/1389], p. 2.

Norman, L. 2022. 'U.S. Nears Return to Iran Nuclear Deal: Agreement could be completed as early as the next couple of days, officials say, but some differences remain', Dow Jones & Company, Inc., Accessed 01/03/2022. https://www.wsj.com/articles/u-s-nears-return-to-iran-nuclear-deal-11645458466.

Northam, J. 2015. 'Lifting Sanctions Will Release $100 Billion To Iran. Then What?', *NPR*, Accessed 01/09/2020. https://www.npr.org/sections/parallels/2015/07/16/423562391/lifting-sanctions-will-release-100-billion-to-iran-then-what?t=1637804041282.

NPR. 1996. 'U.S. Defence Secretary William Perry Interview with National Public Radio', *National Public Radio*, 02/08/1996.

NPR. 2015. 'Trump Calls For "Total And Complete Shutdown Of Muslims Entering U.S."', *NPR*, Accessed 01/09/2020. https://text.npr.org/458836388.

NPR. 2019. 'Trump Additional Troops Gulf', *NPR*, Accessed 21/01/2020. https://www.npr.org/2019/05/24/726680414/trump-orders-an-additional-1-500-troops-to-the-middle-east.

Nuruzzaman, M. 2012. 'Conflicts between Iran and the Gulf Arab States: An Economic Evaluation', *Strategic Analysis*, 36: 1–13.

NY Times. 2009. 'Iran Council Certifies Ahmadinejad Victory', The New York Times Company, Accessed 01/04/2021. https://www.nytimes.com/2009/06/30/world/middleeast/30iran.html.

NY Times. 2011. 'Gates Tells Bahrain's King that "Baby Steps" to Reform Aren't Enough', The New York Times Company, Accessed 10/01/2020. https://www.nytimes.com/2011/03/13/world/middleeast/13military.html.

NY Times. 2011. 'Saudi Troops Enter Bahrain to Help Put Down Unrest', The New York Times Company, Accessed 07/03/2020. https://www.nytimes.com/2011/03/15/world/middleeast/15bahrain.html.

NY Times. 2016. 'Iranian Protesters Ransack Saudi Embassy After Execution of Shiite Cleric', *NY Times*, Accessed 02/11/2020. https://www.nytimes.com/2016/01/03/world/middleeast/saudi-arabia-executes-47-sheikh-nimr-shiite-cleric.html.

NY Times. 2020. 'What to Know About the Death of Iranian General Suleimani', *NY Times*, Accessed 17/03/2021. https://www.nytimes.com/2020/01/03/world/middleeast/suleimani-dead.html.

NY Times, and D.J. Trump. 2016. 'Transcript: Donald Trump Expounds on His Foreign Policy', *NY Times*, Accessed 12/08/2021. https://www.nytimes.com/2016/03/27/us/politics/donald-trump-transcript.html.

Obama, B. 2011. 'Statement by the President on violence in Bahrain, Libya and Yemen', The White House-Office of the Press Secretary, Accessed 02/05/2021. https://obamawhitehouse.archives.gov/the-press-office/2011/02/18/statement-president-violence-bahrain-libya-and-yemen-0.

Obama, B. 2015. 'Remarks by President Obama in Press Conference after GCC Summit', The White House, Accessed 23/09/2021. https://obamawhitehouse.archives.gov/the-press-office/2015/05/14/remarks-president-obama-press-conference-after-gcc-summit.

Obama, B. 2016. 'The Obama Doctrine', *The Atlantic*, Accessed 03/05/2021. https://www. theatlantic.com/magazine/archive/2016/04/the-obama-doctrine/471525/.

O'Brien, A. 2020. 'Iran oil shipment: Venezuelan military to escort fuel tankers', aljazeera. com, Accessed 01/02/2022. https://www.aljazeera.com/videos/2020/5/21/iran-oil-shipment-venezuelan-military-to-escort-fuel-tankers.

Ochsenwald, W. 1981. 'Saudi Arabia and the Islamic Revival', *International Journal of Middle East Studies*, 13: 271–86.

OHCHR, and A. Calamard. 2019. 'Annex to the Report of the Special Rapporteur on extrajudicial, summary or arbitrary executions: Investigation into the unlawful death of Mr. Jamal Khashoggi', *United Nations*, 19/06/2019.

Okaz. 1998. 'Interview with Ayatollah Hashemi Rafsanjani', *Okaz*, 23/02/1998.

Okruhlik, G. 2003. 'Saudi Arabian-Iranian Relations: External Rapprochement and Internal Consolidation', *Middle East Policy*, 10: 113–25.

Ostovar, A. 2018. 'Sectarianism and Iranian Foreign Policy.' In F. Wehrey (ed.), *Beyond Sunni and Shia: The Roots of Sectarianism in a Changing Middle East* (Oxford University Press: New York).

Palmer, M. 2018. *The Future of the Middle East: Faith, Force, and Finance* (Rowman & Littlefield Publishers: Lanham, MD).

Pargoo, M., and S. Akbarzadeh. 2021. *Presidential Elections in Iran: Islamic Idealism since the Revolution* (Cambridge University Press: Cambridge).

Parker, I. 1999. *Critical Textwork: An Introduction to Varieties of Discourse and Analysis* (Open University Press: Buckingham).

Partrick, N. 2016. *Saudi Arabian Foreign Policy: Conflict and Cooperation* (Bloomsbury Publishing: London).

Pedersen, J. 2012. 'Khaṭīb.' In *Encyclopaedia of Islam*, edited by P. Bearman, Th. Bianquis, C.E. Bosworth, E. van Donzel, and W.P. Heinrichs, Brill Online.

Peterson, S. 2010. *Let the Swords Encircle Me: Iran – A Journey Behind the Headlines* (Simon & Schuster: New York).

Phillips, C. 2020. *The Battle for Syria: International Rivalry in the New Middle East* (Yale University Press: New Haven, CT).

Piscatori, James. 1985. 'Islamic Values and National Interest: The Foreign Policy of Saudi Arabia.' In Adeed Dawisha (ed.), *Islam in Foreign Policy* (Cambridge University Press: Cambridge).

Pittard, D.J.H., W.J. Bryant, and G.D. Petraeus. 2019. *Hunting the Caliphate: America's War on ISIS and the Dawn of the Strike Cell* (Post Hill Press: Franklin, TN).

Politico, and D.J. Trump. 2020. 'Trump claims Soleimani was planning to blow up U.S. embassy', *Politico*, Accessed 13/04/2021. https://www.politico.com/news/2020/01/09/trump-soleimani-embassy-plot-096717.

Pompeo, M. 2019. 'Pompeo Twitter 14 September 2019', twitter.com, Accessed 01/20/2021. https://twitter.com/secpompeo/status/1172963090746548225.

Pompeo, M. 2020. 'Secretary Michael R. Pompeo's Call with Saudi Crown Prince Mohammed bin Salman Al Saud.' Washington DC: US Department of State.

Potter, L.G., and G.G. Sick. 2002. *Security in the Persian Gulf: Origins, Obstacles, and the Search for Consensus* (Palgrave Macmillan: London).

Press TV. 2013. 'Ali Akbar Velayati Interview', velayati.ir, Accessed 13/10/2021. https://velayati.ir/fa/news/930/%D8%A7%D9%86%D8%AA%D8%AE%D8%A7%D8%A8%D8%A7%D8%AA-%D8%A2%D8%B2%D8%A7%D8%AF-%D8%AF%D8%B1-%D8%B3%D9%88%D8%B1%DB%8C%D9%87-%D8%A8%D8%A7-%D8%AD%D8%B6%D9%88%D8%B1-%DA%A9%D8%B4%D9%88%D8%B1%D9%87%D8%A7%DB%

8C-%D8%A7%D8%B3%D9%84%D8%A7%D9%85%DB%8C-%D8%A8%D8%B1%DA
%AF%D8%B2%D8%A7%D8%B1-%D8%B4%D9%88%D8%AF.

Psaledakis, D., and A. Mohammed. 2021. 'U.S. tiptoes through sanctions minefield toward Iran nuclear deal', *Thomson Reuters*, Accessed 01/02/2022. https://www.reuters.com/world/middle-east/us-tiptoes-through-sanctions-minefield-toward-iran-nuclear-deal-2021-05-17/.

Quandt, W.B. 1981. *Saudi Arabia in the 1980s: Foreign Policy, Security, and Oil* (Brookings Institution: Washington DC).

Rafizadeh, S., and M. Alimardani. 2013. 'The Political Affiliations of Iranian Newspapers.' In *The Iran Media Program* edited by Monroe Price. Pennsylvania, PA: University of Pennsylvania.

Rafsanjani, A.H. 1981. 'Friday Sermon', *Jomhouri Eslami*, 04/09/981 [13/06/1360], p. 3.

Rafsanjani, A.H. 1987. 'Statement in Protest to Hajj Pilgrim Deaths 2 August 1987.' In *Speeches*, edited by IRNA. Tehran, IR Iran: IRNA.

Rafsanjani, A.H. 1988. 'Statement 20 December 1988.' In *Speeches*, edited by IRNA. Tehran, IR Iran: IRNA.

Rafsanjani, A.H. 1989. 'Majles Statement 12 July 1989.' In *Speeches*, edited by IRNA. Tehran, IR Iran: IRNA.

Rafsanjani, A.H. 1990. 'Friday Sermon 24/08/1990.' In *Speeches*, edited by IRNA. Tehran, IR Iran: IRNA.

Rafsanjani, A.H. 1991. 'Statement During Saudi Foreign Minister's Visit to Tehran', *IRIB*, 06/06/1991 [16/03/1370].

Rafsanjani, A.H. 2005. 'Friday Sermon 12/08/2005.' In *Speeches*, edited by IRNA. Tehran, IR Iran: IRNA.

Rafsanjani, A.H. 2005. 'Rafsanjani Interview with Okaz', *Okaz*, 25/09/2005.

Rafsanjani, A.H. 2005. 'Rafsanjani Speech on Visit to Riyadh 18/09/2005' In. Tehran.

Rafsanjani, A.H. 2005. 'Rafsanjani Speech on Visit to Riyadh 21/09/2005.' In. Tehran: IRNA.

Rafsanjani, A.H. 2005. 'Rafsanjani Speech on Visit to Saudi Arabia 24/09/2005.' In. Tehran: IRNA.

Rafsanjani, A.H. 2006. 'Friday Sermon 24/02/2006.' In *Speeches*, edited by IRNA. Tehran, IR Iran: IRNA.

Rafsanjani, A.H. 2006. 'Friday Sermon 03/03/2006.' In *Speeches*, edited by IRNA. Tehran, IR Iran: IRNA.

Rafsanjani, A.H. 2006. 'Friday Sermon 03/03/2006.' In *Speeches*, edited by IRNA. Tehran, IR Iran: IRNA.

Rafsanjani, A.H. 2006. 'Friday Sermon 21/07/2006' In *Speeches*, edited by IRNA. Tehran, IR Iran: IRNA.

Rafsanjani, A.H. 2009. 'Friday Sermon 02/01/2009.' In *Speeches*, edited by IRNA. Tehran, IR Iran: IRNA.

Rafsanjani, A.H. 2012. *Balance sheet and memories of Hashemi Rafsanjani* (Daftare Nashre Maarefe Enghelab: Tehran, IR Iran).

Rafsanjani, A.H. 2014. 'Ayatollah Hashemi dar guft-i gu-yi ikhtisasi ba intikhab', Entekhab.ir ketabenaab.com, Accessed 03/08/2021. http://www.ketabenaab.com/1392/10/22/%D8%A2%DB%8C%D8%AA-%D8%A7%D9%84%D9%84%D9%87-%D9%87%D8%A7%D8%B4%D9%85%DB%8C-%D8%AF%D8%B1-%DA%AF%D9%81%D8%AA-%D9%88-%DA%AF%D9%88%DB%8C-%D8%A7%D8%AE%D8%AA%D8%B5%D8%A7%D8%B5%DB%8C-%D8%A8%D8%A7-%C2%AB%D8%A7%D9%86%D8%AA%D8%AE%D8%A7%D8%A8%C2%BB--%D8%B1%D9%88%D8%AD%D8%A7%D9%86

D9%8A-%D8%A7%D8%B2-%D9%85%D9%88%D8%A7%D8%B6%D8%B9%D8
%B4-%D8%B9%D9%82%D8%A8-%D9%86%D8%B4%DB%8C%D9%86%DB%8C-
%D9%86%DA%A9%D8%B1%D8%AF%D9%87.html.

Rafsanjani, A.H. 2014. 'Details of Hashemi's letter to the King of Saudi Arabia', *Tabnak*, 26/10/2014 [04/08/1393].

Rafsanjani, A.H. 2015. 'Rafsanjani Statement on Death of King Abdullah of Saudi Arabia', 24/01/2014 [03/11/1393].

Rafsanjani, A.H., and R.K. Ramazani. 1990. 'Address by Ali Akbar Hashemi-Rafsanjani, President of the Islamic Republic of Iran', *Middle East Journal*, 44: 458–66.

Rafsanjani, A.H. 1981. 'Friday Sermon', *Jomhouri Eslami*, 21/08/1981 [30/05/1360], p. 3.

Rafsanjani, A.H. 1981. 'Friday Sermon', *Jomhouri Eslami*, 20/11/1981 [29/08/1360], p. 3.

Rafsanjani, A.H. 1981. 'Friday Sermon', *Jomhouri Eslami*, 18/12/1981 [27/09/1360], p. 3.

Rafsanjani, A.H. 1981. 'Rafsanjani Majles Speech – 18/06/1359', *Ettelaat* 10/09/1980 [19/06/1359], p. 1.

Rafsanjani, A.H. 1981. 'Rafsanjani Majles Speech – 13/11/1359.' In *Majles*. Tehran: Jomhouri Eslami.

Rafsanjani, A.H. 1982. 'Friday Sermon', *Jomhouri Eslami*, 30/01/1982 [10/11/1360], p. 3.

Rafsanjani, A.H. 1982. 'Friday Sermon', *Jomhouri Eslami*, 26/06/1982 [05/04/1361], p. 3.

Rafsanjani, A.H. 1997. 'Rafsanjani Press Conference', *Jomhouri Eslami*, 26/05/1997 [05/03/1376], pp. 1, 2, 4.

Rafsanjani, A.H. 1997. 'Rafsanjani Press Interview', *Jomhouri Eslami*, 19/07/1997 [28/04/1376], pp. 14, 15, 2.

Rafsanjani, A.H. 1997. 'Rafsanjani Speech in the Conference on Islamic Unity', *Jomhouri Eslami*, 22/07/1997 [31/04/1376], pp. 1, 3, 13.

Rafsanjani, A.H. 1997. 'Rafsanjani Speech on Meeting Crown Prince Abdullah Ibn Abdulaziz', *Jomhouri Eslami*, 09/12/1997 [18/09/1376], p. 2.

Rafsanjani, A.H. 1998. 'Rafsanjani Speech on the Visit of Sheikh Ahmad Yaseen', *Jomhouri Eslami*, 03/05/1998 [13/02/1377], p. 2.

Rafsanjani, A.H. 1998. 'Rafsanjani Speech to the Saudi Shurah Council', *IRNA*, 23/02/1998 [04/12/1376].

Rafsanjani, A.H. 1999. 'Rafsanjani Speech on Visit of Saudi Defence Minister', *Jomhouri Eslami*, 06/05/1999 [15/02/1378], p. 2.

Rahim-Safavi, Y. 2017. 'Statement on the Missile Attack on ISIS Bases in Syria', *Kayhan*, 22/06/2017 [01/04/1396], p. 3.

Rahim Safavi, Y. 2018. 'Advisor to Supreme Leader General Yahya Rahim Safavi Statement on Saudi Crown Prince', 02/05/2018 [12/02/1397], p. 2.

Rahmani-Fazli, A., and Entekhab. 2014. 'Karbalā wa Najaf Khat-i qirmiz-i māst', Entekhab. ir, Accessed 15/10/2021. entekhab.ir/000kKg.

Raja'i, M. 1980. 'Prime Minister Speech', *Jomhouri Eslami*, 09/09/1980 [18/06/1359], pp. 1, 3.

Raja'i, M. 1981. 'Prime Minister Speech in Mazandaran', *Jomhouri Eslami*, 14/02/1981 [2511/1359], pp. 1, 3.

Rakel, Eva. 2004. 'Paradigms of Iranian Policy in Central Eurasia and Beyond.' In M.P. Amineh and H. Houweling (eds.), *Central Eurasia in Global Politics: Conflict, Security, and Development* (Brill: Leiden).

Rakel, E.P. 2008. 'The Iranian Political Elite, State and Society Relations, and Foreign Relations Since the Islamic Revolution', University of Amsterdam.

Ram, H. 1994. *Myth and Mobilization in Revolutionary Iran: The Use of the Friday Congregational Sermon* (American University Press: Washington DC).

Ramady, M.A. 2017. *Saudi Aramco 2030: Post IPO challenges* (Springer International Publishing: Germany).

Ramazani, R.K. 1985. 'Iran's Islamic Revolution and the Persian Gulf', *Current History (pre-1986)*, 84: 5.

Ramazani, R.K. 1986. *Revolutionary Iran: Challenge and Response in the Middle East* (Johns Hopkins University Press: Baltimore, MD).

Ramazani, Rouhoullah K. 1988. 'The Iran-Iraq War and the Persian Gulf Crisis', *Current History*, 87: 61.

Ramazani, R. K. 1992. 'Iran's Foreign Policy: Both North and South', *Middle East Journal*, 46: 393–412.

Rand, D.H., and A.P. Miller. 2020. *Re-Engaging the Middle East: A New Vision for U.S. Policy* (Brookings Institution Press: Washington DC).

Rasid. 2009. 'Iʿtisām al-Baqīʾ', Rasid News Network – Shabakat Rasid al-Ikhbariya, Accessed 01/02/2021. https://web.archive.org/web/20090225084710/http://rasid12.myvnc.com/artc.php?id=27063.

Razwy, S.A.A. 2014. *A Restatement of the History of Islam and Muslims* (Lulu.com: Morrisville, NC).

Reah, D. 2002. *The Language of Newspapers* (Routledge: Abingdon).

Resalat. 1997. 'Afghanistān: Rāhi Dushwāri-yi Istiqrār', *Resalat*, 28/05/1997 [07/03/1376], pp. 1, 16.

Resalat. 1997. 'Faghat Rīsmān-i Khodā Chang Bizanīd)', *Resalat*, 09/12/1997 [18/09/1376], pp. 1, 16.

Resalat. 1997. 'Musalmān Zīstan', *Resalat*, 06/12/1997 [15/09/1376], pp. 1, 16.

Resalat. 1998. 'Haq-i Mujazāt-i Jināyatgarān', *Resalat*, 12/09/1998 [21/06/1377], pp. 1, 16.

Resalat. 1998. 'Mawj-i Tarīkī Dar Afghanistān', *Resalat*, 10/08/1998 [19/05/1377], pp. 1, 16.

Resalat. 1998. 'Tālibān: Taswīr-i Zisht-i ʾaz Yik Hukūmat', *Resalat*, 16/08/1998 [25/05/1377], pp. 1, 16.

Resalat. 2006. 'ʿArtish-i Nā Marʿī)', *Resalat*, 19/07/2006 [28/04/1385].

Resalat. 2006. 'Dū Padīdih-yi Talkh', *Resalat*, 09/08/2006 [18/05/1385].

Resalat. 2006. 'Jināyāt-i Harāmiyān Dar Haram', *Resalat*, 23/02/2006 [04/12/1384].

Resalat. 2006. 'Sharārat-i Tarurism Wa Khardūrizī-yi Musalmānān', *Resalat*, 25/02/2006 [06/12/1384].

Resalat. 2006. 'Suʾālāt-i Matrah dar Jahān-i ʿarab', *Resalat*, 25/07/2006 [03/05/1385].

Resalat. 2009. 'Rūnumāyī dar ʿāshūrāyī 88', *Resalat*, 30/12/2009 [09/10/1388], p. 1.

Resalat. 2011. 'Kābūshā-yi shāhānih va rūyā-hā-yi istiʿamārī', *Resalat*, 18/01/2011 [28/10/1389].

Resalat. 2012. 'Amaliyat-i teruristi-yi mushtarak-i al-qaʾidih wa amrika dar dimashq', *Resalat*, 19/07/2012 [29/04/1391].

Resalat. 2014. 'Artish-i Araq mawaziʾ-i terorist ha dar musil ra bumbaran kard', *Resalat*.

Resalat. 2014. 'Iraqi Army and ISIS battle in Mosul; Neutralizing new tribal sedition in Iraq', *Resalat*.

Resalat. 2017. 'ātash dar khīmih-yi irtijāʾ', *Resalat*, 07/06/2017 [17/03/1396], p. 1.

Reuters. 2011. 'Iran says five of its citizens kidnapped in Syria', *Thomson Reuters*, Accessed 10/01/2020. https://www.reuters.com/article/us-iran-syria-kidnap-idUSTRE7BK0UE20111221.

Reuters. 2012. ' "Friends of Syria" condemn Assad but see more killing', *Thomson Reuters*, Accessed 10/01/2020. https://www.reuters.com/article/us-syria-meeting-tunis-idUSTRE81N16820120224.

Reuters. 2013. 'Arab summit may struggle to paper over Syria opposition rifts', *Thomson Reuters*, Accessed 10/01/2020. https://www.reuters.com/article/uk-syria-crisis-arab-summit-idUKBRE92O0MG20130325.

Reuters. 2013. 'Iran says seeks better cooperation with Saudi Arabia', *Thomson Reuters*, Accessed 22/02/2020. https://www.reuters.com/article/iran-nuclear-gulf-idUSL5N0JG08H20131201.

Reuters. 2013. 'Iran to avenge killing of Guard commander in Syria: official', *Thomson Reuters*, Accessed 10/01/2020. https://www.reuters.com/article/us-syria-crisis-iran-idUSBRE91F03C20130216.

Reuters. 2013. 'Iranian Guards commander killed in Syria', *Thomson Reuters*, Accessed 10/01/2020. https://www.reuters.com/article/us-syria-crisis-iran-idUSBRE91D0EY20130214.

Reuters. 2013. 'Israel hits Syria arms convoy to Lebanon: sources', *Thomson Reuters*, Accessed 10/01/2020. https://www.reuters.com/article/us-syria-israel-attack-idUSBRE90T0K120130131.

Reuters. 2013. 'Obama, Iran's Rouhani Hold Historic Phone Call', *Thomson Reuters*, Accessed 10/01/2020. https://www.reuters.com/article/us-un-assembly-iran-idUSBRE98Q16S20130928.

Reuters. 2014. 'Iranian foreign minister says he cannot visit Saudi Arabia', *Thomson Reuters*, Accessed 22/02/2020. https://www.reuters.com/article/uk-iran-saudi-zarif-idUKKBN0EC1ML20140601.

Reuters. 2014. 'Iranians play role in breaking IS siege of Iraqi town', *Thomson Reuters*, Accessed 18/01/2020. https://www.reuters.com/article/us-iraq-security-miltias-iran-idUSKBN0GW2Y420140901.

Reuters. 2017. 'Iran's missile test "not a message" to Trump', *Reuters*, Accessed 15/11/2021. https://www.reuters.com/article/us-usa-iran-trump-idUSKBN15L19X?feedType=RSS&feedName=Iran&virtualBrandChannel=10209&utm_source=dlvr.it&utm_medium=twitter.

Reuters. 2017. 'Lebanon accuses Saudi Arabia of holding its PM hostage', *Reuters*, Accessed 02/08/2020. https://www.reuters.com/article/us-lebanon-politics-idUSKBN1DF18A.

Reuters. 2017. 'Saudi deputy crown prince, Trump meeting a "turning point": Saudi adviser', *Reuters*, Accessed 18/03/2020. https://www.reuters.com/article/us-saudi-usa-idUSKBN16L2CT.

Reuters. 2019. 'Saudi Arabia eyes billions of dollars in entertainment investments', *Thomson Reuters*, Accessed 13/06/2020. https://www.reuters.com/article/us-saudi-entertainment-idUSKCN1PG2NY.

Reuters. 2019. 'USA Iran Oil', *Thomson Reuters*, Accessed 17/06/2020. https://www.reuters.com/article/us-usa-iran-oil-idUSKCN1RX0R1.

Reuters. 2020. 'Saudi minister rejects Iranian accusation on scientist's killing', *Thomson Reuters*, Accessed 01/02/2022. https://www.reuters.com/article/uk-iran-nuclear-scientist-saudi-idUKKBN28B61A.

Reuters. 2021. 'Iran replaces deputy foreign minister Araqchi who led nuclear talks', *Thomson Reuters*, Accessed 01/02/2022. https://www.reuters.com/world/middle-east/iran-replaces-deputy-foreign-minister-araqchi-who-led-nuclear-talks-2021-09-14/.

Reuters. 2021. 'Iranian fuel will be delivered by truck to Lebanon via Syria – sources', *Thomson Reuters*, Accessed 01/02/2022. https://www.reuters.com/world/middle-east/iranian-fuel-will-be-delivered-by-truck-lebanon-via-syria-sources-2021-09-02/.

Reuters. 2022. 'South Korea, Iran discuss resuming oil trade, unfreezing funds', *Thomson Reuters*, Accessed 25/02/2022. https://www.reuters.com/business/energy/skorea-iran-hold-talks-resuming-iranian-oil-imports-unfreezing-iranian-fund-2022-02-16/.

Reuters. 2022. 'Yemen's Houthis say attacked UAE with drones, missiles', *Thomson Reuters*, Accessed 01/02/2022. https://www.reuters.com/world/yemens-houthis-say-attacked-uae-with-drones-missiles-2022-01-31/.

Reuters, and A. Al-Askar. 2013. 'Region will lose sleep over Iran deal – Saudi adviser', *Thomson Reuters*, Accessed 14/10/2021. https://www.reuters.com/article/uk-iran-nuclear-saudi-fears/region-will-lose-sleep-over-iran-deal-saudi-adviser-idUKBRE9AN07920131124.

Reuters, and S. al-Saud. 2014. 'Saudi foreign minister says has invited Iran's Zarif to visit', *Thomson Reuters*, Accessed 14/10/2021. https://www.reuters.com/article/us-saudi-iran-idUSBREA4C0GU20140513.

Reuters, and A. Asseri. 2015. 'Saudi-led coalition announces end to Yemen operation', *Thomson Reuters*, Accessed 10/12/2021. https://www.reuters.com/article/us-yemen-security-saudi-idUSKBN0NC24T20150421.

Rezaee, M. 2019. 'Mohsen Rezaee Twitter 08 April 2019', twitter.com, Accessed 07/01/2021. https://twitter.com/ir_rezaee/status/1115467176926941184?ref_src=twsrc%5Etfw.

Ricks, T.E. 2002. 'Briefing Depicted Saudis as Enemies: Ultimatum Urged To Pentagon Board', *The Washington Post*, 06/08/2002, p. A1.

Riedel, B. 2015. 'Yemen's war shakes up the Saudi palace.' In *Markaz*. Brookings Institute: Washington DC.

Riedel, B. 2020. 'Saudi Arabia's Role in the Yemen Crisis.' In S.W Day and N. Brehony (eds.), *Global, Regional, and Local Dynamics in the Yemen Crisis* (Springer: Germany).

Rieger, R. 2014. 'In search of stability: Saudi Arabia and the Arab Spring.' In *Gulf Research Meeting (GRM) 2013*, edited by GRM Papers. Cambridge, UK: Gulf Research Center.

Rouhani, H. 1990. 'Roundtable Discussion Iran TV Channel 1', *IRIB*, 30/08/1990 [08/06/1369].

Rouhani, H. 2013. 'Rouhani Press Conference', *Dolat.ir*, 23/09/2013 [01/07/1392].

Rouhani, H. 2013. 'Rouhani Statement at the 68th Session UN General Assembly', *UN*, 24/09/2013 [02/07/1392].

Rouhani, H. 2013. 'Rouhani Statement Before Departure to UN', *Dolat.ir*, 23/09/2013 [01/07/1392].

Rouhani, H. 2013. 'Rouhani: Americans are [the world's] Chief and it is easier to deal with the chief', *Iran Diplomacy*, 14/05/2013 [24/02/1392].

Rouhani, H. 2013. 'The first press conference of the president-elect', *President.ir*, 17/06/2013 [27/03/1392].

Rouhani, H. 2014. 'Rouhani Statement on Events in Iraq', *President.ir*, 14/06/2014 [24/03/1393].

Rouhani, H. 2014. 'Transcript of Rouhani Interview with Iran TV Channel 1', *Kayhan*, 29/04/2014 [09/02/1393].

Rouhani, H. 2015. 'Duktur Rouhani dar ijlās majmaʿ-yi jahānī-yi ahl-i bait', *President.ir*, Accessed 10/10/2020. https://president.ir/fa/88711.

Rouhani, H. 2015. 'Payām-i tasliyat-i raʾīs-i jumhūr bih munāsibat-i dargozasht malik Abdullah bin Abdulaziz āl-i suʿūd-i pādshāh-i ʿarabistān', *President.ir*, I Accessed 10/10/2020. https://www.president.ir/fa/84023.

Rouhani, H. 2015. 'Rouhani Speech on Visit to City of Gilan', *ISNA*, 16/04/2015 [27/01/1394].

Rouhani, H. 2016. 'Statement made in a meeting with the Danish FM', *President.ir*, 05/01/2016.

Rouhani, H. 2017. 'President Statement at the Cabinet Meeting 22 June 2017', *ISNA*, 22/06/2017 [01/04/1396].

Rouhani, H. 2017. 'Rouhani Press conf ISNA 22 May 2017', *ISNA,* 22/05/2017 [01/03/1396].

Rouhani, H. 2018. 'President at cabinet session', *President.ir,* 24/10/2018 [02/08/1397].

Rouhani, H. 2018. 'President Statement on US Oil Sanctions', *President.ir,* 04/12/2018 [13/09/1397].

Rouhani, H. 2019. 'President Rouhani: US plots, wrong plans behind regional crises', *Press TV,* 15/09/2019, p. 2.

Rouhani, H. 2019. 'President Speech 22 April 2019', *IRINN,* 22/04/2019 [02/02/1398], p. 2.

Rouhani, H., and Al-Majalla. 2013. 'Rouhani Interview with Saudi Asharq Al-Awsat Newspaper', *Al-Majalla,* June 2013.

Rouhani, H., and ISNA. 2014. 'Rouhani Interview with ISNA: We will not allow terrorists to disrupt the security and stability of Iraq', *ISNA,* 13/06/2014 [23/03/1393].

Rouhani, H., and Reuters. 2019. 'Iran's Rouhani says Aramco attacks were a reciprocal response by Yemen', *Thomson Reuters,* Accessed 20/09/2020. https://www.reuters.com/article/us-saudi-aramco-iran-rouhani-idUSKBN1W12AE.

Roussos, S. 2020. *Religion and International Relations in the Middle East* (MDPI AG: Switzerland).

Rubin, U. 2019. 'Saudi Arabia's Black September', *The Jerusalem Institute for Strategy and Security,* 15/10/2019.

Rugh, W.A. 2004. *Arab Mass Media: Newspapers, Radio, and Television in Arab Politics* (Praeger: Westport, CO).

S., Michael. 2006. 'Hostage-Taker, Reformer, Pessimist: An Iranian Life', *New York Times,* Accessed 17/03/2014. http://www.nytimes.com/2006/04/29/world/middleeast/29abdi.html?pagewanted=all&_r=0.

Sabahi, Farian. 2013. 'Iran, Iranian Media and Sunnite Islam.' In Brigitte Maréchal, Sami Zemni and Sabrina Mervin (eds.), *The Dynamics of Sunni-Shia Relationships: Doctrine, Transnationalism, Intellectuals and the Media* (Hurst: London).

Sabet-Saidi, Shahriar. 2011. 'Iranian-European Relations: A Strategic Partnership?' In A. Ehteshami and M. Zweiri (eds.), *Iran's Foreign Policy: From Khatami to Ahmadinejad* (Ithaca Press: Lebanon).

Sadeghi-Boroujerdi, E. 2019. *Revolution and its Discontents: Political Thought and Reform in Iran* (Cambridge University Press: Cambridge).

Sadeqi, M. 2019. 'Mahmud Sadeqi MP Statement', *YJC,* 08/04/2019.

Sadjadpour, K. 2008. *Reading Khamenei: The World View of Iran's Most Powerful Leader* (Carnegie Endowment for International Peace: Washington DC).

Safavi, Y.R. 2006. 'IRGC Commander Speech on Martyrdom of Fatema Zahraa.' In *Speeches IRGC,* edited by IRNA. Tehran, IR Iran: IRNA.

Safran, N. 1985. *Saudi Arabia: The Ceaseless Quest for Security* (Belknap Press of Harvard University Press: Cambridge MA).

Safran, Nadav. 1988. *Saudi Arabia: The Ceaseless Quest for Security* (Cornell University Press: Ithaca, NY).

Said, Edward. 1978. *Orientalism* (Pantheon Books: New York).

Saikal, A. 2021. *Iran Rising: The Survival and Future of the Islamic Republic* (Princeton University Press: New York).

Salami, H. 2011. 'Deputy Head of IRGC, General Salami Response to White House Officials', *Kayhan,* 09/11/2011 [18/18/1390].

Salami, H. 2019. 'IRGC Commander Friday Sermon Speech', *Kayhan,* 28/09/2019 [19/07/1398], p. 3.

Salami, H. 2019. 'IRGC Commander Hossein speech Salami 13 April 2019)'.

Salehi, A.A. 2011. 'Foreign Minister, Iran warns Al Saud about military occupation and killing of Bahrainis', *Kayhan*, 16/03/2011 [25/12/1389], p. 2.

Samar, Reza Ghafar, and Babak Mahdavy. 2009. 'Identities in the Headlines of Iranian National Newspapers', *Linguistics Journal*, 4.

Samir, A., and E. Solomon. 2012. 'Arab League suspends Syria mission as violence rages', *Thomson Reuters*, Accessed 31/07/2021. https://www.reuters.com/article/syria-idINDEE80Q0B520120128.

Saudi Cabinet. 1997. 'Saudi Ministerial Cabinet Statement', 04/03/1997, p. 2.

Saudi Cabinet. 2013. 'Saudi Arabia Official Statement on Iran's Nuclear Agreement', *al-Riyadh*, 26/11/2013.

Saudi Foreign Ministry. 1996. 'Saudi Ambassador Ghazi Algosaibi Statement on the Khobar Bombings', 26/06/1996, p. 2.

Saudi Foreign Ministry. 2013. 'Statement by Saudi Foreign Ministry on UN Security Council Membership', 18/10/2013.

Saudi Gazette. 2022. 'Arab hands extended to Iran if they stop threatening region's security': Prince Faisal discusses Tehran destabilizing behavior with his Jordanian counterpart', *Saudi Gazette*, Accessed 01/02/2022. https://saudigazette.com.sa/article/615437.

Saunders, Harold. 1985. 'The Iran-Iraq War: Implications for US Policy.' In Thomas Naff (ed.), *Gulf Security and the Iran-Iraq War* (National Defense University Press: Washington DC).

Schaffer, Mark. 2011. 'Individual and Group Decision Making.' In S.W. Hook and C.M. Jones (eds.), *Routledge Handbook of American Foreign Policy* (Taylor & Francis: Oxford).

Seliktar, O., and F. Rezaei. 2019. *Iran, Revolution, and Proxy Wars* (Springer International Publishing: Germany).

Shafaqna. 2013. 'Alī Shamkhānī, dabīr-i shūrā-yi ʿālī-yi amniyat-yi millī-yi īrān shud', International Shia News Association, Accessed 15/10/2020. https://web.archive.org/web/20130912231802/http:/www.shafaqna.com/persian/other-services/countries/iran/item/51228-%D8%B9%D9%84%DB%8C-%D8%B4%D9%85%D8%AE%D8%A7%D9%86%DB%8C%D8%8C-%D8%AF%D8%A8%DB%8C%D8%B1-%D8%B4%D9%88%D8%B1%D8%A7%DB%8C-%D8%B9%D8%A7%D9%84%DB%8C-%D8%A7%D9%85%D9%86%DB%8C%D8%AA-%D9%85%D9%84%DB%8C-%D8%A7%DB%8C%D8%B1%D8%A7%D9%86-%D8%B4%D8%AF.html.

Shahab Ahmed, Zahid. 2019. 'Understanding Saudi Arabia's Influence on Pakistan: The Case of the Islamic Military Alliance to Fight Terrorism', *The Muslim World*, 109: 308–26.

Shahi, A. 2013. *The Politics of Truth Management in Saudi Arabia* (Routledge: Abingdon).

Shahidi, H. 2007. *Journalism in Iran: From Mission to Profession* (Routledge: Abdingdon).

Shamkhani, A. 1999. 'Interview Iranian Minister of Defence Ali Shamkhani', *Ra'ay Al-Aam*, 06/05/1999.

Shamkhani, A. 2014. 'The presence of ISIS terrorists in Iraq is a warning signal for the region', *Resalat*, 12/06/2014 [22/03/1393].

Shamkhani, A. 2015. 'Secretary of the Supreme National Security Council Statement on Hajj Mina Incident', *Fars*, 29/09/2015 [08/03/1394].

Shamkhani, A. 2017. 'SNSC General Secretary Statement', *IRNA* 25/01/2017 [06/11/1395].

Shariati, Ali. 1981. 'Martyrdom: Arise and Bear Witness', *Trans. AA Ghassemy. Tehran: Ministry of Islamic Guidance*.

Sharif, R., and IRGC. 2012. 'IRGC Head of Public Relations: The words of General Jafari have been distorted', *IRNA*, 16/09/2012 [29/06/1391].

Shayegan, Ahmad. 2013. 'Rafsanjani Comeback, Family Planning, World Cup Fever', World Crunch, Accessed 28/03/2014. http://www.worldcrunch.com/world-affairs/iran-files-rafsanjani-comeback-family-planning-world-cup-fever/world-cup-islam-ahmadinejad-rafsanjani-geneva/c1s14560/#.UzgPIc7vE4d.

Sheibani, M.R. 2011. 'Iranian Ambassador in Damascus Statement on US interference in Syria', *Kayhan*, 11/07/2011 [20/04/1390], p. 2.

Sheibani, M.R. 2012. 'Iranian Ambassador in Damascus Speech on Anniversary of Iranian Revolution', *Kayhan*, 13/02/2012 [24/11/1390], p. 2.

Sherrill, C.W. 2018. *Losing Legitimacy: The End of Khomeini's Charismatic Shadow and Regional Security* (Lexington Books: London).

Sidiqqi, K. 2012. 'Friday Sermon 28/10/2012.' In *Friday Sermons – Dar Maktab-i Jom'ih*, edited by Centre for Cultural Documents of the Islamic Revolution. Tehran, IR Iran: Ministry of Islamic Guidance.

Sidiqqi, K. 2012. 'Friday Sermon 03/11/2012.' In *Friday Sermons – Dar Maktab-i Jom'ih*, edited by Centre for Cultural Documents of the Islamic Revolution. Tehran, IR Iran: Ministry of Islamic Guidance.

Simons, G. 2016. *Iraq: From Sumer to Saddam* (Palgrave Macmillan: London).

SNSC, and Tasnim. 2019. 'Supreme National Security Council Declared Centcom and its Affliates "Terrorists"', *Tasnim*, 08/04/2019 [19/01/1398].

Soleimani, Q. 2011. 'Commander of the Quds Force Speech at the Imam Ali Mosque in Kerman', *Kayhan*, 26/11/2011 [05/09/1390], p. 1.

Soleimani, Q. 2017. 'Commander of the Quds Force Letter to Supreme Leader', Khamenei. ir, Accessed 17/05/2020. https://farsi.khamenei.ir/message-content?id=38249.

SPA. 1987. 'Statement Emergency Meeting Council of Ministers', *SPA*, 01/08/1987.

SPA. 1990. 'Minister of Pilgrimage and Religious Trusts Statement on Meeting with Iranian Pilgrimage Delegation', *SPA*, 04/04/1991.

SPA. 1997. 'Iran Saudi Sign Trade Agreements', *SPA*, 01/07/1997.

SPA. 1997. 'Statement on Velayati Visit to Saudi Arabia', *SPA*, 23/03/1997.

SPA. 1998. 'Saudi Shurah Council Speaker Visit to the Islamic Republic of Iran', *SPA*, 21/11/1998.

SPA. 1999. 'Joint Press Conference with Iranian Vice President and Saudi Defence Minister, Prince Sultan ibn Abdulaziz', *SPA*, 05/05/1999.

SPA. 2006. 'Saudi Royal Court Statement on the Israel Attacks on Lebanon.' In *Royal Statements*, edited by SPA. Riyadh, KSA: SPA.

SPA. 2015. 'Statement on the Conclusion of the Riyadh Summit on Yemen', *SPA*, 19/05/2015.

SPA. 2016. 'Ministry of Interior Statement', *SPA*, 02/01/2016.

SPA. 2018. 'Kingdom of Saudi Arabia's Statement on the United States Withdrawal from the JCPOA', *SPA*, 09/05/2018.

SPA. 2018. 'Saudi Public Prosecutor: Preliminary Investigations into Case of Citizen Jamal Khashoggi Showed his Death', *SPA*, 20/10/2018.

SPA. 2019. 'HRH Crown Prince Receives Phone Call from British Premier', *SPA*, 14/09/2019.

SPA. 2019. 'HRH Crown Prince Receives Phone Call from Iraqi President', *SPA*, 04/01/2020.

SPA. 2019. 'HRH Crown Prince Receives Phone Call from US President', *SPA*, 14/09/2019.

SPA. 2020. 'Foreign Minister: The Council of Arab and African Coastal States of the Red Sea and the Gulf of Aden is a Joint Action System for Coordination and Cooperation', *SPA*, 06/01/2020.

SPA. 2020. 'King Calls Iraqi President', *SPA*, 04/01/2020.

SPA. 2020. 'KSA Follows Events in fraternal Iraq, Resulting from Escalation of Tensions, Terrorist Acts, It previously Denounced, Warned of their Repercussions – An Official Source Announces', *SPA*, 03/01/2020.

SPA/WAS. 1997. 'Statement on Velayati Visit to Saudi Arabia', *SPA*, 24/03/1997.

Sreberny, A., and G. Khiabany. 2010. *Blogistan: The Internet and Politics in Iran* (Bloomsbury Publishing: London).

Steavenson, W. 2011. 'A Debate in Cairo', *The New Yorker*, Accessed 11/06/2020. https:// www.newyorker.com/news/news-desk/a-debate-in-cairo.

Stein, E. 2012. 'Egypt.' In *After the Arab Spring: Power Shift in the Middle East*, edited by N. Kitchen, 23–27.

Stein, H.F. 1985. 'Psychological Complementarity in Soviet-American Relations', *Political Psychology*, 6: 249–61.

Stenslie, S. 2010. *Regime Stability in Saudi Arabia: The Challenge of Succession* (Routledge: Abingdon).

Stephens, M. 2015. 'Yemen campaign key test for Saudi Arabia', British Broadcasting Corporation, Accessed 10/01/2020. https://www.bbc.co.uk/news/world-middle-east-32091835.

Stephens, M., and C. Phillips. 2021. *What Next for Britain in the Middle East?: Security, Trade and Foreign Policy after Brexit* (Bloomsbury Publishing: London).

Sterner, M. 1985. 'The Gulf Cooperation Council and Persian Gulf Security.' In T. Naff (ed.), *Gulf Security and the Iran-Iraq War* (National Defense University Press: Washington DC).

Stutser, D. 2016. 'Iran Claims Saudi Airstrike Hit Embassy in Yemen.' In *Foreign Policy*.

Sudais, A. 2006. 'Friday Sermon 22/07/2006.' In *Sermons – Khutab*, edited by Ministry of Islamic Affairs. Mecca, Saudi Arabia: Ministry of Islamic Affairs, Dawah and Guidance.

Sudais, A. 2006. 'Friday Sermon 05/08/2006.' In *Sermons – Khutab*, edited by Ministry of Islamic Affairs. Mecca, Saudi Arabia: Ministry of Islamic Affairs, Dawah and Guidance.

Tabatabai, A. 2022. 'Saudi-Iran Relations', Youtube, Accessed 26/02/2022. https://www. youtube.com/watch?v—neDNhEKUxA.

Taheri, A. 2006. 'Imperialist Iran: Revolutionaries Imitate Ambitions of Ancient Persia', *New York Post*, 17/12/2006, p. 11.

Takeyh, R. 2009. *Guardians of the Revolution: Iran and the World in the Age of the Ayatollahs* (Oxford University Press: Oxford).

Taskhiri, M.A. 1987. 'Statement at the OIC Summit in Amman 25 March 1988.' In *Statements*, edited by IRNA. Tehran, IR Iran: IRNA.

Tasnim. 2017. 'Tasnim News Agency 21/06/2017 [31/03/1396]', Tasnim News Agency, Accessed 27/03/2021. https://tn.ai/1442874.

Tazmini, G. 2009. *Khatami's Iran: The Islamic Republic and the Turbulent Path to Reform* (I.B. Tauris: London, UK).

Tehran Times. 2016. 'Iran marks 2009 rallies', *Tehran Times*, Accessed 01/06/2021. https:// www.tehrantimes.com/news/409614/Iran-marks-2009-rallies.

Tehran Times. 2021. 'Ayatollah Raisi breaks the ice of Iran-Saudi relations', *Tehran Times*, Accessed 01/02/2022. https://www.tehrantimes.com/news/463398/Ayatollah-Raisi-breaks-the-ice-of-Iran-Saudi-relations.

Tehran Times. 2022. 'Iran FM visits Oman, says Tehran prioritizes strong ties with Muscat', *Tehran Times*, Accessed 12/02/2022. https://www.tehrantimes.com/news/468951/ Iran-FM-visits-Oman-says-Tehran-prioritizes-strong-ties-with.

Tekeyh, R. 2019. 'The Real Reason Iran Has Been Provoking Trump', Politico.com, Accessed 21/03/2021. https://www.politico.com/magazine/story/2019/06/22/trump-iran-policy-227207/.

Telegraph, The. 2012. 'Iran sends elite troops to aid Bashar al-Assad regime in Syria', *The Telegraph*, Accessed 09/03/2021. https://www.telegraph.co.uk/news/worldnews/middleeast/iran/9526858/Iran-sends-elite-troops-to-aid-Bashar-al-Assad-regime-in-Syria.html.

Terrill, W.A. 2011. *The Saudi-Iranian Rivalry and the Future of Middle East Security* (Strategic Studies Institute, U.S. Army War College: Carlisle, PA).

The National. 2017. 'Saudi Arabia arrests princes, ministers and business figures in anti-corruption crackdown', *The National*, Accessed 09/03/2021. https://www.thenationalnews.com/world/gcc/saudi-arabia-arrests-princes-ministers-and-business-figures-in-anti-corruption-crackdown-1.673073?src=ilaw&videoId=5644227740001.

The Times, and D.J. Trump. 2017. 'Full transcript of interview with Donald Trump', *The Times*, Accessed 09/03/2021. https://www.thetimes.co.uk/article/full-transcript-of-interview-with-donald-trump-5d39sr09d.

Time. 1990. 'Saudi Arabia A Tragic Ascension to Paradise', *Time Magazine*, 16/07/1990.

Times, N.Y. 2011. 'Arab League Delegates Arrive in Syria', The New York Times Company, Accessed 08/03/2020. https://www.nytimes.com/2011/12/23/world/middleeast/arab-league-delegates-arrive-in-syria.html.

Times, N.Y. 2012. 'Syrian Rebels Land Deadly Blow to Assad's Inner Circle', The New York Times Company, Accessed 01/04/2021. https://www.nytimes.com/2012/07/19/world/middleeast/suicide-attack-reported-in-damascus-as-more-generals-flee.html.

Times, New York. 2019. 'American Airstrikes Rally Iraqis Against U.S.' New York Times.

Torbat, A.E. 2020. *Politics of Oil and Nuclear Technology in Iran* (Springer International Publishing: Germany).

Trifiletti, Elena, Rossella Falvo, Carla Dazzi, and Dora Capozza. 2012. 'Political Orientation and Images of the United States in Italy', *Social Behavior and Personality: an International Journal*, 40: 85–91.

Trofimov, Y. 2008. *The Siege of Mecca: The Forgotten Uprising in Islam's Holiest Shrine* (Penguin Books: London).

Trump, D.J. 2015. 'Donald Trump Tweet 29 June 2015', twitter.com, Accessed 01/10/2021. https://www.presidency.ucsb.edu/documents/tweets-june-29-2015.

Trump, D.J. 2017. 'Donald Trump Riyadh Visit Transcript', *CNN*, 21/05/2017.

Trump, D.J. 2017. 'Donald Trump Suggested Saudi Arabia Was Behind 9/11 Multiple Times Wednesday', *Intelligencer*, 17/02/2016.

Trump, D.J. 2017. 'Donald Trump Twitter 03 February 2017', twitter.com, Accessed 01/10/2021.

Trump, D.J. 2018. 'Full Transcript of Trump's Speech on the Iran Deal.' *New York Times.*

Trump, D.J. 2019. 'Donald Trump Twitter 31 December 2019', twitter.com, Accessed 01/10/2021. https://twitter.com/realDonaldTrump/status/1212121026072592384?ref_src=twsrc%5Etfw.

Trump, D.J. 2019. 'President Donald J. Trump Is Holding the Iranian Regime Accountable for Its Global Campaign of Terrorism', The White House, Accessed 23/09/2021. https://trumpwhitehouse.archives.gov/briefings-statements/president-donald-j-trump-holding-iranian-regime-accountable-global-campaign-terrorism/?utm_source=link.

Trump, D.J. 2019. 'Remarks by President Trump and Crown Prince Salman of Bahrain Before Bilateral Meeting', The White House, Accessed 01/12/2020. https://trumpwhitehouse.archives.gov/briefings-statements/remarks-president-trump-crown-prince-salman-bahrain-bilateral-meeting/.

Trump, D.J. 2020. 'Donald Trump Twitter 4 January 2020', twitter.com, Accessed 01/10/2021. https://twitter.com/realDonaldTrump/status/1213593975732527112?ref_src=twsrc%5Etfw.

Trump, D.J. 2020. *The Tweets of President Donald J. Trump: The Most Liked and Retweeted Tweets from the Inauguration through the Impeachment Trial* (Forefront Books: USA).

Tschannen, R.A. 2013. 'Syria militants exhume grave of Prophet's companion', *Muslim Times*, Accessed 10/07/2020. https://themuslimtimes.info/2013/05/02/syria-militants-exhume-grave-of-prophets-companion/.

Press TV. 2016. 'Iran airs footage of Daesh confessions on foiled attacks in Tehran'.

Ulrichsen, K.C. 2020. *Qatar and the Gulf Crisis* (Oxford University Press: Oxford, UK).

UN. 2009. 'UN humanitarian chief continues assessing needs in post-conflict Gaza', UN News Center, Accessed 15/06/2013. http://www.un.org/apps/news/story.asp?NewsID=29657&Cr=gaza&Cr1#.UfFsyqzhdyh.

UN. 2011. 'General Assembly Adopts Text Deploring Plot to Assassinate Saudi Arabian Envoy to United States; Calls on Iran to Help Bring Perpetrators to Justice', *United Nations*, 18/11/2011.

UN. 2011. 'Security Council Fails to Adopt Draft Resolution Condemning Syria's Crackdown on Anti-Government Protestors, Owing to Veto by Russian Federation, China', *United Nations*, 04/10/2011.

UN. 2012. 'Security Council Fails to Adopt Draft Resolution on Syria as Russian Federation, China Veto Text Supporting Arab League's Proposed Peace Plan', *United Nations*, 04/02/2012.

Uskowi, N. 2018. *Temperature Rising: Iran's Revolutionary Guards and Wars in the Middle East* (Rowman & Littlefield Publishers: Lanham, MD).

Vahidi, A. 2011. 'Minister of Defence General Ahmad Vahidi Press Statement', Holy Defense Science and Education Research Institute, Accessed 09/02/2021. http://dsrc.ir/news/view.aspx?nid=6585.

Vahidi, A. 2012. 'Statement on the 48 Iranian hostages in Syria', *Shargh*, 05/08/2012 [15/05/1391].

van Dijk, Teun. 2005. *Ideology and Discourse: A Multidisciplinary Introduction* (Pompeu Fabra University: Barcelona, Spain).

Velayati, A.A. 1981. '68th Inter-Parliamentary Conference.' In *Jomhouri Eslami*, 3. Havana, Cuba: Jomhouri Eslami.

Velayati, A.A. 1990. 'Roundtable Discussion Iran TV Channel 1', *IRIB*, 30/08/1990 [08/06/1369].

Velayati, A.A. 1990. 'Statement During Meeting with Saudi Counterpart', *IRIB*, 30/09/1990 [08/07/1369].

Velayati, A.A. 1990. 'UN General Assembly Statement', *IRIB*, 28/09/1990.

Velayati, A.A. 1991. 'Statement During Visit to Saudi Arabia', *IRIB*, 25/04/1991 [05/02/1370].

Velayati, A.A. 1997. 'Iranian Foreign Minister Statement to IRNA', *IRNA*, 16/03/1997.

Velayati, A.A. 1997. 'Iranian Foreign Minister Statement to IRNA on Trip to Saudi Arabia', *IRNA*, 15/03/1997.

Velayati, A.A. 2011. 'Velayati Press Conference with Fars News Agency 04/09/2011', *IRNA*, 04/09/2011 [13/06/1390].

Velayati, A.A. 2012. 'International Youth Conference on Islamic Awakening 09/11/1390', *IRNA*, 29/01/2012 [09/11/1390].

Velayati, A.A. 2012. 'Velayati Interview with Arab Press 21/01/2012', *Kayhan*, 21/01/2012 [01/11/1390].

Velayati, A.A. 2012. 'Velayati Speech During IRGC Ceremony 25/02/2012', *IRNA,* 25/02/2012 [06/12/1390].

Velayati, A.A. 2014. 'Velayati meets with former French Foreign Minister', *Iran,* 08/10/2014 [16/07/1393].

Velayati, A.A. 2014. 'Vilāyatī dar nishastī bā ʿulemā va buzurgān-i zaydī-yi yaman', Velayati. ir, Accessed 09/01/2021. https://velayati.ir/fa/news/1217/%D8%A7%DB%8C%D8%B1 %D8%A7%D9%86-%D8%A7%D8%B2-%D8%A7%D9%86%D8%B5%D8%A7%D8%B 1%D8%A7%D9%84%D9%84%D9%87-%D8%AF%D8%B1- %DB%8C%D9%85%D9%86-%D8%AD%D9%85%D8%A7%DB%8C%D8%AA- %D9%85%DB%8C-%DA%A9%D9%86%D8%AF.

Velayati, A.A. 2015. 'Velayati Statement on Hajj Incident', *Velayati.ir,* 29/05/2015 [08/03/1394].

Velayati, A.A. 2017. 'Velayati Interview with Head of Swedish Parliament Research Centre 15/07/2017', *Kayhan,* 15/07/2017 [24/04/1396].

Walsh, James. 2017. 'Iran and Iraq.' in Ehteshami A., Quilliam N. and Bahgat G. (eds.), *Security and Bilateral Issues between Iran and its Arab Neighbours.* (Palgrave Macmillan: London).

WAN-IFRA. 2008. 'Saudi Arabia: Media Market Description.' In *World Press Trends 2008,* edited by World Association of Newspapers and News Publishers, 743–47. Darmstadt, Germany.

Wareing, S. 2004. 'What is Language and What Does it Do?' in L. Thomas, I. Singh and J.S. Peccei (eds.), *Language, Society and Power: An Introduction* (Routledge: Abingdon).

Washington Post. 2019. 'After a tense week, Trump strikes an unusually friendly tone toward Iran', *Washington Post,* Accessed 01/04/2021. https://www.washingtonpost.com/ world/irans-foreign-minister-tweets-images-he-saysleaves-no-doubt-us-drone-was- over-iranian-airspace/2019/06/22/38f8ee08-94f8-11e9-956a-88c291ab5c38_story.html.

Washington Post, and D.J. Trump. 2020. 'Trump says Iranian military leader was killed by drone strike "to stop a war," warns Iran not to retaliate', *Washington Post,* 03/01/2020.

Wastnidge, Edward. 2011. 'Detente and Dialogue: Iran and the OIC during the Khatami Era (1997–2005)', *Politics, Religion & Ideology,* 12: 413–31.

Watt, W.M. 1974. *Muhammad: Prophet and Statesman* (Oxford University Press: Oxford).

Wehrey, F. 2013. *Sectarian Politics in the Gulf: From the Iraq War to the Arab Uprisings* (Columbia University Press: New York).

Wehrey, F. 2018. *Beyond Sunni and Shia: The Roots of Sectarianism in a Changing Middle East* (Oxford University Press: New York).

Wehrey, F., T.W. Karasik, Rand Corporation, L. Hansell, A. Nader, and J. Ghez. 2009. *Saudi-Iranian Relations Since the Fall of Saddam: Rivalry, Cooperation, and Implications for U.S. Policy* (Rand Corporation: Santa Monica, CA).

Wehrey, F.M. 2013. *The Forgotten Uprising in Eastern Saudi Arabia* (Carnegie Endowment for International Peace: Washington DC).

Wetherell, M., and J. Potter. 1988. 'Discourse Analysis and the Identification of Interpretative Repertoires.' In C. Antaki (ed.), *Analysing Everyday Explanation* (Sage: London).

White House. 2015. 'FACT SHEET: Advancing the Rebalance to Asia and the Pacific', The White House, Office of the Private Secretary. https://obamawhitehouse.archives.gov/ the-press-office/2015/11/16/fact-sheet-advancing-rebalance-asia-and-pacific.

Willig, C. 2008. *Introducing Qualitative Research in Psychology* (McGraw-Hill Education: Maidenhead).

Willig, C., and W. Stainton-Rogers. 2007. *The SAGE Handbook of Qualitative Research in Psychology* (SAGE Publications: London).

Wilson, P.W., and D. Graham. 1994. *Saudi Arabia : The Coming Storm* (M.E. Sharpe: Armonk, NY).

Witkowska, Joanna. 2008. 'Creating false enemies: John Bull and Uncle Sam as food for anti-Western propaganda in Poland', *Journal of Transatlantic Studies*, 6: 123–30.

Yarbakhsh, Elisabeth Jane. 2014. 'Green martyrdom and the Iranian state', *Continuum*, 28: 77–87.

Yazdi, M. 1997. 'Friday Sermon 07/06/1997.' In *Friday Sermons – Dar Maktab-i Jom'ih*, edited by Centre for Cultural Documents of the Islamic Revolution. Tehran: Ministry of Islamic Guidance.

Yazdi, M.R. 2019. 'General Mohammad Reza Yazdi, commander of the IRGC's Mohammad Rasoul Allah Division Speech', *Fars*, 17/07/2019 [26/04/1398].

Young, W., D. Stebbins, B. Frederick, and O. Al-Shahery. 2014. *Spillover from the Conflict in Syria: An Assessment of the Factors that Aid and Impede the Spread of Violence* (R and Corporation: Santa Monica, CA).

Zaccara, Luciano. 2016. 'Iran 2016: From the Saudi Embassy Attack to the Demise of Rafsanjani'.

Zanganeh, B. 1998. 'Majles Session Inquiry.' In *Majles Energy Committee*. Tehran: Jomhouri Eslami.

Zarif, J. 2013. 'Zarif Facebook 03 December 2013', facebook.com, Accessed 01/10/2021. https://www.facebook.com/jzarif/posts/716219425056175.

Zarif, J. 2015. 'Wākunush-i Zarif bih ḥamlah-yi 'arabistān bih yaman', irdiplomacy.ir, Accessed 09/01/2021. http://irdiplomacy.ir/fa/news/1945721/%D9%88%D8%A7%DA%A9%D9%86%D8%B4-%D8%B8%D8%B1%DB%8C%D9%81-%D8%A8%D9%87-%D8%AD%D9%85%D9%84%D9%87-%D8%B9%D8%B1%D8%A8%D8%B3%D8%AA%D8%A7%D9%86-%D8%A8%D9%87-%DB%8C%D9%85%D9%86.

Zarif, J. 2017. 'Beautiful Military Can't Buy Peace', *NY Times*, 26/05/2016.

Zarif, J. 2017. 'Iran is ready to gift peace to Middle East', *The New Arab*, 22/05/2017.

Zarif, J. 2017. 'Zarif, Davos World Economic Forum', Youtube.com, Accessed 01/10/2021. https://youtu.be/vUW78n7f3tc.

Zarif, J. 2017. 'Zarif Twitter 20 March 2017', twitter.com, Accessed 01/10/2021. https://twitter.com/JZarif/status/865815474726211584?ref_src=twsrc%5Etfw%7Ctwcamp%5Etweetembed%7Ctwterm%5E865815474726211584%7Ctwgr%5E%7Ctwcon%5Es1_&ref_url=https%3A%2F%2Firanprimer.usip.org%2Fblog%2F2017%2Fmay%2F23%2Firan-reacts-trump-remarks.

Zarif, J. 2017. 'Zarif Twitter 21 March 2017', twitter.com, Accessed 01/10/2021. https://twitter.com/JZarif/status/866360950345125889?ref_src=twsrc%5Etfw%7Ctwcamp%5Etweetembed%7Ctwterm%5E866360950345125889%7Ctwgr%5E%7Ctwcon%5Es1_&ref_url=https%3A%2F%2Firanprimer.usip.org%2Fblog%2F2017%2Fmay%2F23%2Firan-reacts-trump-remarks.

Zarif, J. 2017. 'Zarif Twitter 21 May 2017', twitter.com, Accessed 01/10/2021. https://twitter.com/JZarif/status/866360950345125889?ref_src=twsrc%5Etfw%7Ctwcamp%5Etweetembed%7Ctwterm%5E866360950345125889%7Ctwgr%5E%7Ctwcon%5Es1_&ref_url=https%3A%2F%2Firanprimer.usip.org%2Fblog%2F2017%2Fmay%2F23%2Firan-reacts-trump-remarks.

Zarif, J. 2017. 'Zarif Twitter 05 June 2017', twitter.com, Accessed 01/10/2021. https://twitter.com/jzarif/status/871706969962315776?lang=en.

Zarif, J. 2017. 'Zarif Twitter 07 June 2017', twitter.com, Accessed 01/10/2021. https://twitter.com/jzarif/status/872543822525464577?lang=fi.

Zarif, J. 2018. 'Iranian Foreign Minister Speech at Amir Kabir University on Teacher's Day', *Donya-e Eghtessad,* 01/05/2018 [11/02/1397], p. 2.

Zarif, J. 2018. 'Zarif Twitter 24 October 2018', twitter.com, Accessed 01/10/2021. https://twitter.com/JZarif/status/1055115575364673536.

Zarif, J. 2019. 'Iranian Foreign Minister Press Conference New Delhi 13 May 2019', *IRNA,* 13/05/2019, p. 2.

Zarif, J. 2019. 'Iranian Foreign Minister Speech Asian Society 28/04/2019', Youtube, Accessed 21/09/2020. https://www.youtube.com/watch?v=EXbkKaJ1wvk.

Zarif, J. 2019. 'Iranian Foreign Minister Speech in Meeting with Japanese Premier Shinzo Abe', *MNA,* 16/05/2019 [26/02/1398], p. 2.

Zarif, J. 2019. 'Zarif Twitter 15 September 2019', twitter.com, Accessed 01/10/2021. https://twitter.com/JZarif/status/1173162202926333952?ref_src=twsrc%5Etfw%7Ctwcamp%5Etweetembed%7Ctwterm%5E1173162202926333952%7Ctwgr%5E%7Ctwcon%5Es1_&ref_url=https%3A%2F%2Firanprimer.usip.org%2Fblog%2F2019%2Fsep%2F18%2Ftimeline-saudi-oil-attacks.

Zarif, J. 2020. 'Zarif Twitter 03 January 2020', twitter.com, Accessed 01/10/2021. https://twitter.com/jzarif/status/1212946202280579073?lang=en.

Zarif, J. 2020. 'Zarif Twitter 05 January 2020', twitter.com, Accessed 01/102/2021. https://twitter.com/JZarif/status/1213900666164432900?ref_src=twsrc%5Etfw%7Ctwcamp%5Etweetembed%7Ctwterm%5E1213900666164432900%7Ctwgr%5E%7Ctwcon%5Es1_c10&ref_url=https%3A%2F%2Fwww.cnn.com%2F2020%2F01%2F05%2Fworld%2Fsoleimani-us-iran-attack%2Findex.html.

Zarif, J. 2020. 'Zarif Twitter 08 January 2020', twitter.com, Accessed 01/10/2021. https://twitter.com/JZarif/status/1214736614217469953?ref_src=twsrc%5Etfw%7Ctwcamp%5Etweetembed%7Ctwterm%5E1214736614217469953%7Ctwgr%5E%7Ctwcon%5Es1_&ref_url=https%3A%2F%2Firanprimer.usip.org%2Findex.php%2Fblog%2F2020%2Fjan%2F06%2Fpart-1-us-assassinates-soleimani.

Zarif, J. 2021. 'Zarif Twitter 19 January 2021', twitter.com, Accessed 01/02/2022. https://twitter.com/JZarif/status/1351617822930173955?s=20&t=Fnb6usQmSbWl4I8bVuIChw.

Zarif, J., and Lobelog. 2019. 'Iranian Foreign Minister Interview with Lobelog 30/04/2019', *Lobelog,* 30/04/2019, p. 2.

Zarras, Konstantinos. 2018. 'Assessing the Regional Influence and Relations of Turkey and Saudi Arabia After the Arab Spring.' In Hüseyin Işıksal and Oğuzhan Göksel (eds.), *Turkey's Relations with the Middle East: Political Encounters after the Arab Spring.*

Zeino-Mahmalat, E. 2012. 'Saudi Arabia's and Iran's Iraq Policies in the Post-Gulf War Era: Re-Thinking Foreign Policy Analysis in the Gulf at the Intersection of Power, Interests, and Ideas', University of Hamburg.

Ziadé, Nassib G. 1988. 'League of Arab States: Communiques from Summit Meetings in Amman and Algiers', *International Legal Materials,* 27: 1646–59.

Zibakalam, S. 2015. 'Letter to Ayatollah Jannati in Response to Friday Prayer Sermon', boyernews.com, Accessed 14/11/2021. https://boyernews.com/?p=138352.

Zolghadr, M.B. 2005. 'Speech at the Anniversary of Martrydom of Fatima Zahra.' In *Speeches,* edited by ISNA. Tehran, IR Iran: ISNA.

Zweiri, M., and F.A. Qawasmi. 2021. *Contemporary Qatar: Examining State and Society* (Springer Singapore: Singapore).

Zweiri, M., M.M. Rahman, and A. Kamal. 2020. *The 2017 Gulf Crisis: An Interdisciplinary Approach* (Springer Singapore: Singapore).